Displays the window you use to reconcile, or balance, the current account

Displays the Create Report dialog box, which you can use to produce reports on the financial information you collect with Quicken

Starts the Financial Address Book program, a computerized names and addresses database

Displays a list of the special features available in Quicken Deluxe

Starts the Mutual Fund Finder, a program you can use to select a mutual fund that meets your criteria

Starts the Windows Help application and loads the Quicken Help file

Mastering Quicken 6

Mastering™ Quicken® 6

Stephen L. Nelson

SYBEX®

San Francisco · Paris · Düsseldorf · Soest

Acquisitions Manager: Kristine Plachy
Acquisitions & Developmental Editor: Richard Mills
Editors: Brenda Frink and Alison Moncrieff
Project Editor: Linda Good
Technical Editor: Maryann Brown
Book Designer: Suzanne Albertson
Graphic Illustrator: Dan Schiff
Desktop Publisher: Franz Baumhackl
Production Coordinator: Anton Reut
Proofreaders: Grey Magauran and Michael Tom
Indexer: Matthew Spence
Cover Designer: Design Site
Cover Photographer: Mark Johann

Screen reproductions produced with Collage Complete.

Collage Complete is a trademark of Inner Media Inc.

SYBEX is a registered trademark of SYBEX Inc.
Mastering is a trademark of SYBEX Inc.

Library of Congress Card Number: 96-70664
ISBN: 0-7821-1998-0

Manufactured in the United States of America

10 9 8 7 6 5 4 3 2

Acknowledgments

A lot of people at Sybex worked very hard to see that this book provides you with maximum value. They spent weeks and, in some cases, months of their time thinking about you and how to make one part of your life—using Quicken 6 for Windows—easier.

Many thanks to acquisitions editor Kristine Plachy, developmental editor Richard Mills, editors Brenda Frink and Alison Moncrieff, project editor Linda Good, technical editor Maryann Brown, desktop publisher Franz Baumhackl, production coordinator Anton Reut, proofreaders Grey Magauran and Michael Tom, and indexer Matthew Spence.

Thanks also to Vincent Abella, Pat Coleman, Kaarin Dolliver, and Saul Candib, who helped with various pieces and parts of the book, including rewriting chapters and reshooting figures for the newest version of Quicken.

Contents at a Glance

Table of Contents

Introduction

Mastering Quicken 6 for Windows is not like other Quicken books you have seen. Other books are organized by product feature or menu command or simply repeat information from the Quicken user guide, but this book is *task-oriented*. It describes how you accomplish key personal, investment, and business financial tasks using Quicken.

How to Use This Book

If you haven't yet installed Quicken for Windows, start with Appendix A to find out how to do it. Appendix A also explains how to set up your initial bank account. If you're just starting with Quicken, turn to Part One, *The ABCs of Quicken*. Part One covers the mechanics of using Quicken—information you need before you can truly unleash the power of this simple-yet-sophisticated product.

If you use Quicken at home, turn to Part Two, *Quicken and Your Personal Finances*. It describes how Quicken can help you with credit cards, loans, mortgages, insurance, taxes, and even saving for retirement.

If you're an active investor, turn to Part Three, *Quicken for Investors*, for information and advice about using Quicken to track investments in mutual funds, stocks, bonds, and real estate.

If you're an entrepreneur, professional, or bookkeeper using Quicken in a business setting, turn to Part Four, *Quicken in a Small Business*. It covers topics important to anyone who uses Quicken as a business-accounting system.

At the end of many of the chapters in Parts Two, Three, and Four is a *Road to Riches* section. Each *Road to Riches* section is a discussion of financial-management concepts and techniques related to the material covered in the chapter. You'll get tips and tricks on achieving financial independence, investing wisely, simplifying your financial affairs, succeeding as a business owner, and more. You can skip this material if you're interested only in the mechanics of using Quicken. But if you have time even to skim one or two of these sections, you'll find them well worth your while.

At the end of this book, I've provided four appendixes: Appendix A describes how to install the Quicken 6 program. Appendix B describes how to use QuickPay, an add-on program designed to prepare payroll for a small business. Appendix C explains how to search for financial advice on the Internet. Appendix D describes how to use Quicken in Canada.

Finally, a glossary at the end of the book provides a handy financial dictionary of almost one thousand terms. In this glossary, you can look up just about any financial term or phrase you read in this book or in a newspaper.

You Don't Need Windows 95

In this book, the Quicken windows and dialog boxes show Quicken 6 for Windows 95. Does that mean you can't use this book if you're running Windows NT or Windows 3.1? Of course not. Quicken 6 for Windows works with Windows 3.1, Windows 95, and Windows NT. Quicken 6 looks a little different if your PC runs Windows 3.1, but it works the same. (You won't be able to take advantage of long file names and a few other features specific to Windows 95.)

I do make one assumption about you if you're running Windows 3.1. I assume that you know how to start Windows 3.1 and that you know how to use it to start programs like Quicken. By the time you read this, personal computers will no longer be sold with Windows 3.1. They will only be sold with Windows 95, Windows NT or with other operating systems such as OS/2. So, if your personal computer is running Windows 3.1, you probably aren't a new user and probably do know how to start Windows 3.1 and Windows 3.1 programs.

Conventions Used in This Book

The early chapters of this book give explicit directions for making menu selections and filling out dialog boxes with both the mouse and keyboard. In later chapters I simply tell you to select, click, or enter, and I leave it to you to choose the method that works best for you.

To indicate that you choose a menu command, this book uses the symbol ➤. For example, if you're asked to select Close from the Report menu, the text says, "choose Report ➤ Close."

Material that you need to type is shown in boldface, and optional steps in the procedures are italic.

To highlight important aspects of Quicken operations, you'll see short Notes, Tips, and Warnings throughout the book:

Notes give you a little more information about a topic.

Tips tell you a technique for getting something done more efficiently.

Warnings alert you to problems you may encounter in carrying out a function discussed in the text.

You will find sidebars—short essays about using the program—throughout this book. Sidebars provide useful advice and tell you how to make important decisions. Each sidebar has a title and appears in a box with a dark background.

The ABCs of Quicken

Quicken is a powerful tool, but before you can unleash its power, you'll need to familarize yourself with how it works. The first 11 chapters of *Mastering Quicken 6* help you to do just this.

Chapter 1, *Getting Started,* talks mostly about mechanics, including how to work within the Windows operating environment. Chapter 2, *Using the Quicken Register,* describes how you record payments and deposits in the Quicken register. Chapter 3, *Printing Checks,* shows you how to produce checks with Quicken. In Chapter 4, *Tracking Your Finances with Reports,* you learn how to use Quicken's reports to extract the financial information you collect in the Quicken register, review the reports in each of Quicken's three report families, and create custom reports. Chapter 5, *Balancing Bank Accounts,* describes how to quickly balance your bank account with Quicken—and what to do when you can't get an account to balance. In Chapter 6, *Customizing the Way Quicken Works,* you'll see how to change the way Quicken works by adjusting preferences and customizing the icon bar. Chapter 7, *Protecting Your Financial Records,* gives details on using passwords and backup files. Chapter 8, *Charting Your Finances,* discusses how to chart the financial information you collect in the Quicken registers. Chapter 9, *Paying Bills Electronically,* explains how to use Pay On-Line and CheckFree, the two electronic bill-paying services available to Quicken users. Chapter 10, *Banking Online,* describes how to sign up for and begin using Quicken's online-banking capabilities. Finally, Chapter 11, *Exploring Quicken Deluxe,* discusses and reviews the extra capabilities and programs that Quicken Deluxe—a supercharged version of Quicken—provides.

CHAPTER 1
Getting Started

FEATURING

You'll find it helpful to learn a few things about Microsoft Windows 95 and the Quicken for Windows product before you start using Quicken. In this chapter, you'll learn the basics: how to start Quicken, how to find your way around the Quicken Application Window, and how to get online help as you use Quicken. If you've already worked with Quicken for Windows a bit or if you're comfortable using another Windows 95 application, you can skim this chapter.

Before You Start

In this chapter, I assume you've already done the following two things:

▶ Installed the Quicken software.

▶ Set up at least one bank account.

If you haven't done either of these things, refer to Appendix A. It tells you how to install the Quicken software and how to set up your first account.

 NOTE This chapter refers to Windows 95 in several places. If you're a Windows NT version 4.0 user, you should know that everything I say here about Windows 95 also applies to Windows NT version 4.0.

Starting Quicken for Windows

Once you (or someone else) has installed the Quicken for Windows application, starting Quicken is easy. Here's what you do:

1. Turn on your personal computer.

   Windows starts and then displays the Windows 95 desktop, as shown in Figure 1.1.

2. Double-click on the Quicken shortcut.

   The Quicken application window appears, as shown in Figure 1.2. When you first start Quicken, you'll see the Quicken Tips dialog box in the foreground of this window. You can choose to see this dialog box every time you start Quicken, or you can uncheck the Show Tips at Startup check box so that it does not appear. (The Show Tips at Startup check box is in the lower left-hand corner of the Quicken Tips dialog box.) To close the Quicken Tips dialog box now, click on the Done button or the Close button.

Figure 1.1.   *The Windows 95 Desktop*

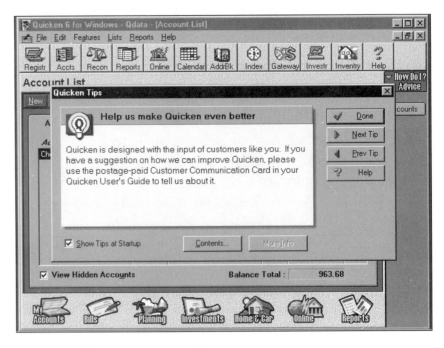

Figure 1.2.   *The Quicken application window*

The Quicken application window now looks like that in Figure 1.3. It shows the Account List document window, the Iconbar, and the HomeBase icons. If you don't see the Iconbar on your Quicken window, right-click in the space just to the right of the Activity Bar icons at the bottom of the screen and click on Show Top Iconbar.

The Account List document window   *The Iconbar*

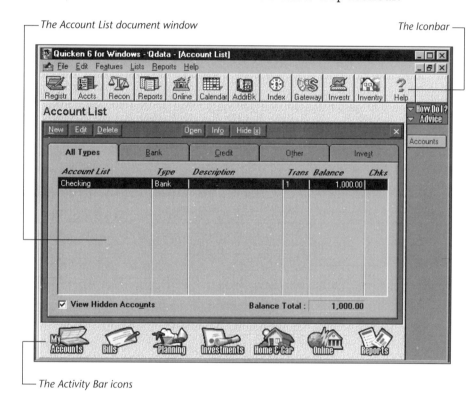

The Activity Bar icons

Figure 1.3.   **The Account List document window, the Iconbar, and the Activity Bar icons in the Quicken application window**

A Quick Geography Lesson in Quicken

If you haven't worked with a Windows 95 application before, you need to learn about three things in the Windows 95 interface: windows, menu commands, and dialog boxes. This knowledge will make using Quicken for Windows—and any other Windows 95 application—easy and straightforward.

The Quicken Application Window

All the information Quicken displays for you appears in an application window. The layout of the Quicken application is very simple: The Quicken title bar and menu bar are at the top of the application window. The *Iconbar,* located just below the menu bar, is a series of icons, or buttons, that allow for fast selection of frequently used menu commands. (You can customize the Iconbar so that clicking on a particular icon does whatever you want it to do. For details, see Chapter 6, *Customizing the Way Quicken Works.*)

 NOTE In the pages that follow, I'll name some of the various icons and describe what the different icons do. For a complete list of icons along with their descriptions, see the inside front cover of this book.

Working with Menus and Commands

To tell Quicken what you want it to do, you issue *commands.* For example, if you want Quicken to print something, you choose the File ➤ Print command. If you want Quicken to delete a check, you choose the Edit ➤ Transaction ➤ Delete command. A *menu* is simply a list of commands.

Much of this book talks about how you use commands to accomplish specific personal finance, investment, and business-management tasks with Quicken. To use the commands, you'll need to know how to choose commands in Quicken for Windows.

It is worth noting that in the Windows 95 operating environment there are usually three ways to choose most commands. Let's look at these methods now. In subsequent chapters, I'll assume you've already selected the method you want to use; so I won't describe keystroke or mouse-clicking mechanics.

 NOTE Although Quicken's windows and dialog boxes look slightly different in Windows 3.1, the Quicken program works the same way in Windows 3.1 as it does in Windows 95 or Windows NT version 4.0. If you're a Windows 3.1 user, what you read here still applies to Quicken version 6.

Using the Keyboard to Select and Deselect Commands

You can select any command using the keyboard. To do so, you do three things: activate the menu bar, display a menu, and then choose a command. Let's suppose you want to choose the File ➤ Print List command. (Go ahead and follow along with the discussion here—you can't hurt anything or foul up your data.)

1. Press Alt and the underlined letter in the menu you want to display. For example, to activate the File menu, press Alt and then F.

    This activates the selected menu. To show you've selected the menu, Quicken drops down the menu, or activates it, as shown in Figure 1.4.

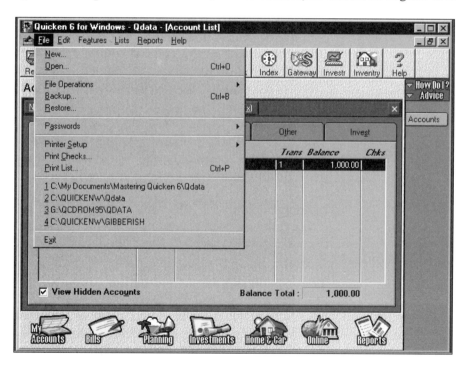

Figure 1.4.   **The activated Quicken File menu**

2. Select the command you want. You can use the ↑ and ↓ keys to high-
    light the command and then press Enter, or you can press the under-
    lined letter of the command name. To select the Print List command
    once the File menu is displayed, you can press P.

> NOTE Some menu commands, when selected, display menus of additional
> commands. If a command name is followed by a triangle, it displays a menu
> of additional commands. For example, the File Operations command is fol-
> lowed by a triangle. This tells you that choosing the File Operations com-
> mand actually displays another menu of commands.

Not every command makes sense in every situation. Quicken disables
commands that you shouldn't or can't choose. To identify these disabled commands, Quicken displays their names in gray letters.
(Quicken displays the names of enabled commands in black letters.)

Using Shortcuts to Choose Commands

Take another look at Figure 1.4, the Quicken File menu. To the right
of some of the commands, the File menu shows key combinations. To
the right of the File ➤ Open command, you see the key combination
Ctrl+O. To the right of the File ➤ Print List command, you see the
key combination Ctrl+P. This means you can select this command in
a way that bypasses the menu: Press Ctrl and hold it down, and then
press P. Quicken displays the Print Register dialog box.

In Windows applications, these key combinations represent *shortcuts*:
You can press a key combination to choose a command. In effect,
pressing a command's shortcut key combination does two things at
once: it activates the menu and it chooses a command. The menus must
be closed and the menu bar deselected for the Shortcut keys to work.

> TIP Learn the shortcuts for those commands you choose over and over. You
> can do this just by paying attention to the menus you display. Key combina-
> tions appear to the right of many menu commands.

Using the Mouse to Select and Deselect Commands

If you have a mouse, you'll want to use it to choose commands. Once you get used to the pointing, clicking, and dragging, using a mouse is a fast, easy way to tell Quicken what you want it to do.

To choose a command with a mouse, point to the menu you want to display and click the mouse's left button. (This action is called *clicking on* the object.)

Once you click on the menu, Quicken displays it. Next, you simply click on the command you want to use. For example, choosing the File ➤ Print List command requires two clicks: First, you click on the File menu name. Second, you click on the Print List command. Quicken displays the Print dialog box, as shown in Figure 1.5.

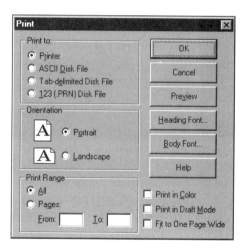

Figure 1.5. **The Print dialog box**

To deselect a command you've selected with the mouse, you can press Esc or click in an empty area of the screen. If choosing a command caused Quicken to display a dialog box, you can remove the dialog box by clicking on the dialog box's Close button. The Close button is the small square with an *x* in the upper right corner of the application window. (I'll talk more about the Close button and the other Windows command buttons later on in the chapter.)

NOTE You don't have to stick to one command selection method. You can mix and match the keyboard, shortcut, and mouse methods. For example, you can display a menu using the mouse and then use the keyboard to select a command.

The Quicken Document Windows

In the area beneath the menu bar, Quicken displays document windows. It is in these document windows that you can find things such as the check form you fill out to record a check and the register you use to track account balances. Click on the Register icon in the Iconbar, and Quicken displays the Account Register document window, as shown in Figure 1.6. Quicken can display many other kinds of information in document windows.

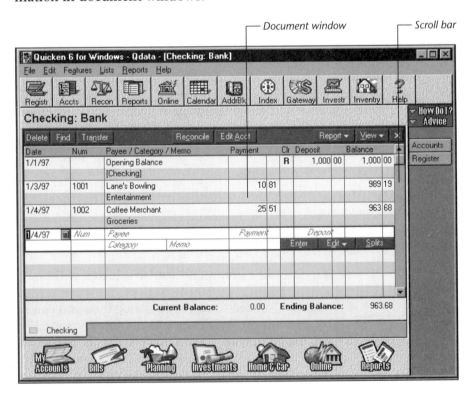

Figure 1.6. The Quicken application window contains the Quicken document window.

NOTE Document windows are part of the Windows 95 interface. Like Quicken for Windows, other Windows 95 applications use document windows to display things inside the application window. A Windows-based word processor, for example, uses document windows to display letters, reports, and whatever else you write. A Windows-based spreadsheet application uses document windows to display your spreadsheets.

Moving Around in a Document Window

If a document window isn't big enough to display everything that's supposed to fit in it, Windows 95 puts a *scroll bar* along the right and bottom edges of the window. Figure 1.6 shows a vertical scroll bar along the window's right edge.

One way to you can move up and down in a document window that has a vertical scroll bar is by pressing the PgDn and PgUp keys. In a window with a horizontal scroll bar along the bottom edge, you can use the Tab key to move right and the Shift+Tab key combination to move left. (To use a key combination such as Shift+Tab, you press both keys simultaneously.)

If you're comfortable pointing, clicking, and dragging the mouse, you can use your mouse to move up, down, left, and right in a document window. You can move up one *page* (screenful of information) by clicking on the up arrow at the top of the vertical scroll bar. You can move down one page by clicking on the down arrow at the bottom of the vertical scroll bar. As you move up and down, Quicken moves the scroll bar marker—it's just a square—up or down the scroll bar. This marker shows you your position relative to the entire document.

To use your mouse to move left and right, use the horizontal scroll bar. Mechanically, it works the same way as a vertical scroll bar. You can click on the arrows at either end of the horizontal scroll bar to move one row (transaction in register) or column to either the left or the right.

You can also *drag* the scroll bar marker in the direction you want to go. To do this, point to the scroll bar marker, hold down the left mouse button, and then move the mouse up or down (or right or left). As you drag the mouse, Quicken scrolls the contents of the document window.

There's still another way to scroll through a document window with a mouse. You can click on the scroll bar itself. For example, clicking above the vertical scroll bar's marker does the same thing as pressing the PgUp key. Clicking below the vertical scroll bar's marker does the same thing as pressing the PgDn key. Clicking to the right of this marker on the horizontal scroll bar is the same thing as pressing Tab, and clicking to the left is the same as pressing Shift+Tab.

Working with More Than One Document Window

Quicken lets you display more than one document window inside its application window. Initially, Quicken displays the Account List document window. But if you click, for example, on the Register icon on the Iconbar, Quicken displays the Register window on top of any other document windows already displayed, as shown in Figure 1.7.

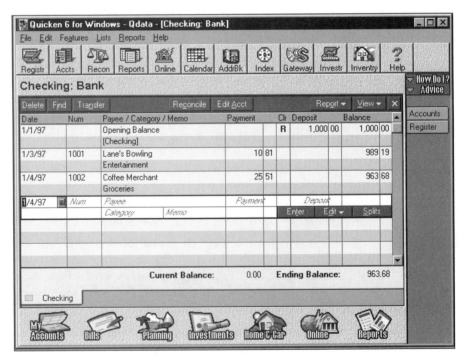

Figure 1.7. **The Quicken application window with both the Account List and Register document windows open**

The ABCs of Quicken

 NOTE You can click on the other icons to move to different document windows. You can also click on the Activity Bar icons at the bottom of the screen to display a menu that lists other document windows.

To show you that more than one document window is open, Quicken displays buttons, called QuickTabs, along the right edge of the application window. To move to another open document window, you simply click on its QuickTab. For example, if you want to schedule a payment, you can click on the Bills Activity Bar icon and choose Schedule a Future Payment. As shown in Figure 1.8, Quicken then displays the Calendar document window as well as the Account List document window and the Register document window.

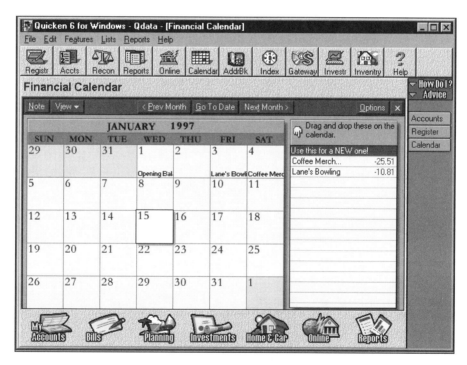

Figure 1.8. *The Quicken application with three document windows open: the Account List document window, the Register document window, and the Calendar document window*

NOTE Because it will become tiresome if I always use the phrase "document window," I'll only use it the first few times I refer to a particular document window in a chapter. For example, since I've now referred to the Account List document window several times, I'll simply refer to this window as the Account List for the rest of the chapter.

Here's a key concept to remember: one of the document windows shown in an application window is *active*, and all the other document windows are *inactive*. This concept is important to remember because the commands you choose affect only the active document window. What's more, you can enter information into only the active document window.

The active window is always the window at the top of a stack of windows. Another way to tell which window is active is to look at the QuickTab buttons. The active document window's tab button is a lighter color than the other, inactive, document windows' tabs. To activate a window, you can click on its tab button.

RESIZING AND MOVING WINDOWS

In some applications, you get to resize and move the document windows. This isn't the case in Quicken because Quicken wants to treat document windows like the pages of a book. For this reason, the usual Window menu is not available, and some Control-menu commands aren't available. They're disabled.

You can, however, resize and relocate the Quicken application window. To do this, you use the application window's Control-menu commands or the window buttons in the top right corner of the application window. The window buttons are the easiest to use. The button that looks like a bar or hyphen minimizes the application window so it only appears as a button on the Windows taskbar. (To "unminimize" the application, simply click on its task bar button.) The button that looks like either a box with a dark top edge or a couple of boxes with dark top edges alternatively maximizes the application window to fill the entire screen or restores a window to its previous, unminimized size. The button with the *x* closes the application window (which is the same thing as closing the application). To move a window, drag its title bar. If you want more information about how all this works or about how to use the control menu commands, refer to a good book on Windows, such as Robert Cowart's *Mastering Windows 95* (Sybex 1995).

Working with Dialog Boxes

Quicken often needs additional information from you when you tell it to execute a particular command. To get that information, the program displays a *dialog box*. Figure 1.9 shows the parts of the Print Register dialog box, which Quicken displays whenever you choose the Print Register command from the File menu. (For the Print Register command to be displayed, the active document window must show an account register. Click on the Register icon and then select the File ➤ Print Register command.) Dialog boxes contain boxes, lists, and buttons that allow you to provide additional information.

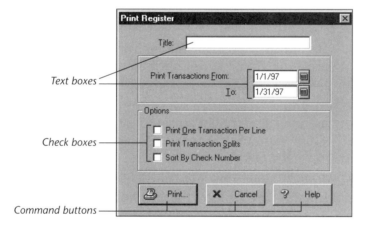

Figure 1.9. **Elements of a dialog box**

 NOTE You can tell which commands display dialog boxes. Whenever a command name is followed by three periods (...), choosing the command displays a dialog box.

Text Boxes

A *text box* is simply a blank you fill in. In the Print Register dialog box, shown in Figure 1.9, the blanks next to Title, Print Transactions From, and To are text boxes. You use them to add a title or label to a register and to tell Quicken the range of dates you want a register to include. (I'll talk about this dialog box more in Chapter 2. For now, just focus on the mechanics.)

To enter information into a text box, you first need to activate the text box. You can do this either by clicking on the text box with the mouse or by pressing Tab or Shift+Tab until the text box is highlighted.

Once you've clicked on the text box, you're ready to enter data. If the text box already holds data, Quicken selects and highlights the current contents. When this is the case, you can replace the selected contents of the text box contents by typing.

If you don't want to replace text box contents but instead want to insert or add to the current contents, you position the insertion bar—a flashing vertical I-beam—at the position where you want to add new text:

▶ **Beginning.** To place the insertion bar at the beginning of a text box, press the Home key or click on the very first character position in the text box.

▶ **Middle.** To insert characters into the middle of the text box, you can use the left and right arrow keys to move the insertion bar to the point where you want to insert characters, or you can click the mouse to move the insertion bar there.

▶ **End.** To place the insertion bar at the end of the text box, press the End key or click after the very last character in the current text box.

Once you've positioned the insertion bar, begin typing.

NOTE If a text box is empty (like the Title text box in Figure 1.9), selecting the text box simply causes Quicken to put the insertion bar at the start of the text box.

Command Buttons

Command buttons tell Quicken what you want it to do with the information you've entered into the dialog box. Most dialog boxes have an OK command button, which tells Quicken to proceed to the next step. If a dialog box is displayed to collect information for a command, selecting OK initiates the command.

In some cases, the OK command button is replaced by an equivalent command button that names the action that occurs when the command is executed. For example, the Print Register dialog box doesn't provide an OK command button. But it does provide a Print command button. In this case, the Print command button is equivalent to an OK command button.

Most dialog boxes have a Cancel command button, which tells Quicken not to accept any information you've entered and to return to what you were doing before. Dialog boxes commonly provide other command buttons too.

You can select command buttons in several ways. You can click on the command button, or you can highlight the command button using the Tab and Shift+Tab keys and then press Enter. If a command button shows a thick dark border—and one of the commands usually does— you can select it by pressing Enter. (The command button with the thick dark border is the *default* command button.) If a command button's name has an underlined letter in it, you can press the Alt key and the underlined letter to select the command button.

Option Buttons

Earlier in the chapter, I mentioned that you can move between the open document windows by clicking on the QuickTab buttons. You can choose to display these buttons either on the right of the document window or on the left.

When you have a mutually exclusive set of choices such as this, Quicken uses *option buttons* to present your choices. In the General Options dialog box shown in Figure 1.10, the QuickTabs option buttons let you choose the Quick Tabs' position on your screen.

NOTE To see the General Options dialog box, select the Edit ➤ Options command and then choose Quicken Program. Quicken displays the General Options dialog box shown in Figure 1.10.

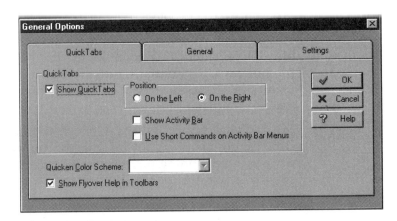

Figure 1.10. **The General Options dialog box**

To mark an option button with the mouse, you click on it. To indicate your choice, Quicken inserts a black dot, or bullet, in the button you choose. Figure 1.10 shows the On the Right option button marked with the bullet.

To mark an option button with the keyboard, highlight the selected option button by using the Tab or Shift+Tab keys. Then use the ↑ and ↓ keys to move the bullet to one of the other option buttons. Quicken then moves the bullet to mark your choice.

Check Boxes

Check boxes amount to on/off switches. Figure 1.10 shows four check boxes: Show Quick Tabs, Show Activity Bar, Provide Alt-key Access to Quick Tabs, and Show Flyover Help in Toolbars. (Don't worry what these check boxes do for right now. I'll talk about them in later chapters.)

The easiest way to turn on (or turn off) a check box is to click the mouse. If you click a check box that's turned on—indicated by a check mark in the box—Quicken turns off the check box and removes the check mark. If you click a check box that's turned off—one that is empty—Quicken turns on the check box and adds a check mark to it.

You can also turn check boxes on and off using the keyboard. For example, you can highlight the check box using the Tab and Shift+Tab keys; then you can use the spacebar to alternately turn the check box on and off. Or you can press the Alt key and then the underlined letter in the check box name to alternately turn the check box on and off. Pressing Alt+Q, for example, toggles the Show Quick Tabs check box on and off.

List Boxes

If you want to choose from a series of items, Quicken uses a *list box* to display your choices. In Figure 1.10, for example, the Quicken Color Scheme box is really a list box. Quicken doesn't display the Quicken Color Scheme list until you tell it to. If you want to change the Quicken Color Scheme option, you display, or *drop down*, the list box's list and then you select one of the list entries by clicking on it.

To drop down a list box, you can click on the down arrow at the end of the list box, or you can select it using the Tab or Shift+Tab keys and then pressing Alt+↓.

To select an entry in a drop-down list, you click on the entry with the mouse, or you highlight the entry with the arrow keys and press Enter.

TIP   When a list box is active, pressing a letter key—such as *S*—selects the first entry that starts with the letter. If a list box's entries don't fit within the list box, Quicken adds a vertical scroll bar to it. You can use it to scroll through the list box's entries. A list box's scroll bar works just like a document window's scroll bar.

Combo Boxes

One other element of the Windows 95 user interface bears mentioning: *combo boxes*. Combo boxes are a hybrid. A combo box looks like a text box but works like both a text box and a list box. Everything I've said about text boxes and list boxes is true for combo boxes. For example, you can enter information into a combo box by typing, or you can activate a list box for the combo box and select a list entry that then goes into the combo box. Many of the fields you fill in Quicken for Windows 95 are combo boxes, as you'll see in the pages that follow.

Finding Help When You Need It

Quicken uses the standard Windows 95 Help application. This application is really a separate program that opens a heavily indexed text file of information about the active application.

Using the Help Icon

You can start the Help application in several ways. The easiest—and most common—way is to click on the Help icon on the Iconbar. Quicken starts the Help application and displays the first page of help file information about whatever you're doing. If, for example, you click on the Help icon when the Register window is displayed, Quicken displays the Help application window with information about the Register and how to use it, as shown in Figure 1.11.

Figure 1.11.   **The Help application window with the first page of Quicken help information**

Some help windows, such as the Register help window, include a cross-reference to a video demonstration. (You'll need a sound card and speakers to take advantage of this feature. If you have them, I encourage you to follow along at your computer.) To play the video demonstration, insert your Quicken CD-ROM and click on Show Me.

Quicken displays a VCR-like screen (see Figure 1.12) that has a Start button (the one with the greater than symbol), a Pause button (the one with the vertical bar), and a slider that moves across the screen as the video plays. (The button with the *X* closes the dialog box.) The length of the video (in seconds) is shown in the lower-right corner. To get a list of other video demonstrations in Quicken, choose Help Topics. You'll see the titles under Show Me.

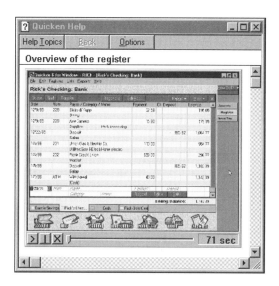

Figure 1.12.   **The Show Me video of the Overview of the Register**

In Figure 1.11, the word *transactions* is underlined. Click on it to see a definition. For more information about a Register help topic that is listed at the bottom of this help window, click on its button. (Whenever you point to a help topic, Help changes the mouse pointer to a pointing hand.) For example, if you click on the button beside An Overview of Account Registers, Quicken displays the appropriate page from the User's Guide, as shown in Figure 1.13. If you click on one of these subtopics, Help displays information about that subtopic. For example, if you click on Entering a basic transaction, as shown in Figure 1.13, Help displays its first page of information on entering a transaction into the register, as shown in Figure 1.14.

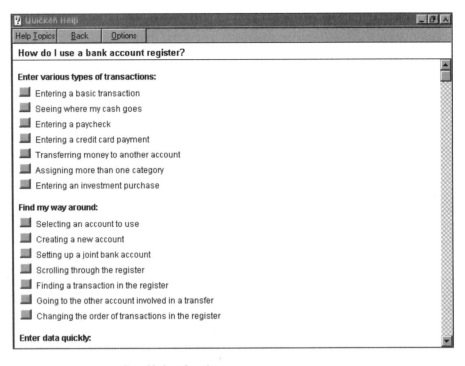

Figure 1.13.　A pop-up list of help subtopics

To page through the help information displayed about a particular topic, use either the PgDn and PgUp keys or the vertical scroll bar.

If there are other help topics referenced in a screenful of help information, Help displays these topic names in underlined green letters. You can access help information about one of these other topics by clicking on the topic name. In Figure 1.14, for example, the "Category" topic is underlined and displayed in green; so you can click on it to display its help information.

When you click on the What's Important in This Window? button, Help displays a list of all the buttons and fields in the Register window. Clicking on any one of these buttons displays an explanation of what the button does and how to use it. When you click on the Troubleshooting button, Help displays a list of problems common to the active window. Click on the button next to the problem to display solutions.

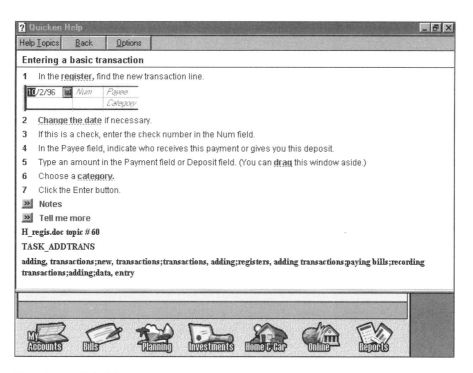

Figure 1.14. **Help information**

Using the Help Menu Commands

If you start the Help application using the Help menu, you will see several Help menu commands.

The Contents command displays the Help Topics: Quicken Help window, which lists "books" that provide information on Quicken procedures, examples of how to set up Quicken to suit your financial needs, and expert financial advice. In this window, you can also select the Index or the Find tab to search for a particular help topic. Choosing the Index command on the Help menu also allows you to search for a particular topic.

Pressing F1 or choosing Help on This Window from the Help menu displays the help topic for the active window.

The Introduction command displays a description of new features in Quicken 6 Deluxe. (I discuss Quicken 6 Deluxe in Chapter 11, *Exploring Quicken Deluxe.*)

The QuickTours command lets you start nine different online tutorials about using Quicken in your day-to-day record keeping and in your long-term financial planning. Each tour takes five to ten minutes, depending on how fast you read. To view a QuickTour tutorial, click on one of the command buttons that appears in the QuickTour window shown in Figure 1.15.

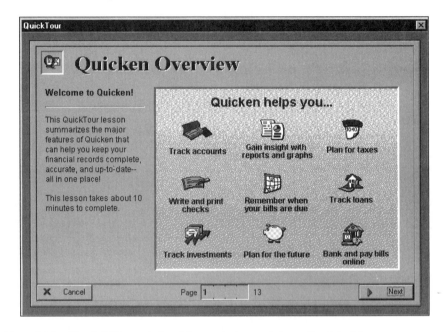

Figure 1.15. **The QuickTour window lets you start any of nine online tutorials.**

The Quicken Tips command displays the Quicken Tips window. This is the same window you may see when you start Quicken:

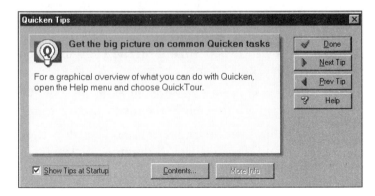

The Show Qcards command turns on and off Quicken's Qcards feature. Qcards are textual or audio messages that contain information about the selected box or button.

For example, if you've turned Quicken's Qcards on and you've selected a text box that's supposed to hold the name of the bank where your checking account is, the Qcard will provide you with hints and tips about filling in the box.

> **TIP** Qcards are great the first few times you use a window, but they become a little bit annoying after you've learned the basics.

The About Quicken command displays the Quicken copyright notice in a dialog box. To close the dialog box, you just press Esc.

> **NOTE** Quicken Deluxe has different Help menu commands. I describe how you use these commands in Chapter 11, *Exploring Quicken Deluxe*.

Additional Help

By now you've probably noticed a couple of buttons on the right side of your screen, just above the QuickTabs: How Do I? and Advice. Click on the How Do I? button to display help for a task related to the active window. For example, if Register is the active window, clicking on How Do I? displays help for entering information in the Register. Click on the Advice button to display a list of topics for which you can get financial information, for example, tracking automobile expenses for two cars.

CHAPTER 2

Using the Quicken Register

FEATURING

FIRST things first: you'll probably want to start using Quicken by tracking the money that flows into and out of the bank account you use most frequently. You'll be able to summarize your financial affairs in a way you've never done before, and you'll learn the basics of working with the Quicken program.

Before You Start

Before you can use the Quicken register to track the money that flows into and out of your bank account, you need to do the following:

▶ Install and set up Quicken—which really means you need to copy the Quicken application onto your hard disk and set up your first bank account. If you haven't already done these two things, refer to Appendix A, *Installing Quicken 6 and Setting Up Your First Accounts*.

▶ Learn how to work with the Windows 95 operating environment. If you don't already know how to do this, take the time to review Chapter 1, *Getting Started*.

Recording Checks, Other Payments, and Deposits

With Quicken running, you'll need to display the Register document window for the bank account you want to work with. If you have only one bank account, Quicken automatically displays that account in the Register document window whenever you open the register.

TIP If you don't see the account that you want to work with in the Register document window, display the Account List window by clicking on the Accounts icon on the Iconbar or by clicking on the Accounts QuickTab. Select the account you want and then choose the Open button.

Figure 2.1 shows the Quicken Register document window. Quicken highlights the first empty row in the register. (If the next empty row of the register isn't highlighted, you can use the ↑ and ↓ keys to highlight it. Or, you can choose Edit ▶ Transaction ▶ New.)

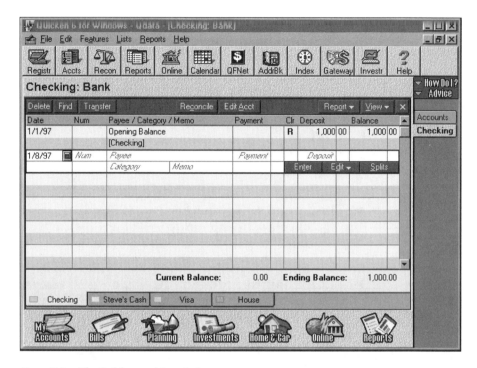

Figure 2.1.   The Quicken register window

To record a payment from an account into the empty register row, follow these steps:

1. Enter the payment date into the Date field (text box). You may need to highlight the Date text box if it isn't already selected.

    Quicken automatically enters the present date based on your computer's internal clock. If the date is not correct, consult your Windows 95 documentation for information on resetting the clock and calendar. If the date shown isn't the transaction date, enter the date in **_MM/DD/YY_** fashion. (You don't have to enter the year number if the one Quicken already shows is correct.)

    When the Date text box is selected, Quicken provides several shortcuts for quickly changing the display date:

    *   Press + and − to adjust the date ahead or back one day at a time. (If you press the key that shows the = and the + symbol, you don't have to hold the Shift key: if you press =, Quicken assumes you really mean +.)

The ABCs of Quicken

- Press **T** to set the date to today's date. Press **M** to adjust the date to the first day in the month and **H** to adjust the date to the last day in the month. (Quicken uses *M* and *H* because *M* is the first letter in the word "month" and *H* is the last letter.) Press **Y** to adjust the date to the first day in the year and **R** to adjust the date to the last date in the year. (*Y* is the first letter in the word "year" and *R* is the last letter.)

- Click on the button at the right end of the active date field to open a small calendar. The calendar highlights the current month and day; you can change months by clicking on the arrows at the top of the calendar and change dates by clicking the mouse directly on the date.

2. Once the date is correct, press Tab or click on the Num field, which is a combo box. Quicken activates a list box that contains abbreviations for the different bank-account transactions. If you're recording a handwritten check, type the check number, or select the Next Check Num entry to calculate the handwritten check's number by adding one to the previous check number. If you're recording a cash-machine withdrawal, select the ATM entry from the list box. If you're recording a electronic-funds transfer, select the EFT entry from the list box.

NOTE You use the Deposit entry in the Num list box for deposits, as I'll discuss later in the chapter. You use the Print Check entry to identify checks you want to print, as described in Chapter 3. You use the Send and Transfer entries for online banking and bill-paying transactions, as Chapter 10 describes.

3. Move to the Payee field by clicking on it or pressing Tab until you reach it. Enter the name of the payee. If this is the first time you've recorded a payment to this payee, type the payee's name. If you've paid this payee before, you can select the payee's name from the Payee drop-down list.

TIP Use the same exact payee name every time you record a transaction from any given payee. You can easily do so, using the Payee drop-down list. If you do so, you'll find it easy to summarize your spending by payee.

4. Move to the Payment field and enter the amount of the payment. You don't have to enter dollar signs or commas. You must use a period, though, to identify any cents.

 NOTE When you enter the Payment or Deposit text box, a small calculator icon appears at the right end of the field. Clicking on the calculator icon with the mouse opens a small calculator. You can enter numbers by clicking on the calculator with the mouse or by using the number keys on your keyboard. The result of the calculation appears in the Payment or Deposit field. If you use the numeric keypad on your keyboard, be sure the NumLock button is on.

5. *If you want to mark cleared transactions and the transaction you're entering into the register has already cleared or been recorded by the bank,* click in the Clr text box, and a *C* will appear. The *C* indicates that you have manually cleared the transaction. When Quicken reconciles a transaction, an *R* appears.

   Normally, you mark checks as cleared as part of reconciling a bank account. If you're entering old transactions—say you're following my advice to start your Quicken record keeping as of the start of the current year and so you have some old, cleared transactions to enter—you can mark these transactions with a *C* in the Clr column to make your reconciliation easier.

6. Categorize the transaction by moving the cursor to the Category combo box. From the list of existing categories that appears, select the category that best describes the payment.

   Creating a Category A check to your landlord for rent, for example, might be categorized as Rent. If you can't find an expense category that describes the payment, you can enter a short category description directly into the Category text box. If you want to create a category named, for example, Software, type **Software**. Press Enter twice, and Quicken displays the Set Up Category dialog box, as shown in Figure 2.2. The new category name you entered shows in the Name text box. If you want, enter a description of the category in the Description text box. Verify that the Expense or Subcategory Of option button is marked so Quicken knows this is a category used to track spending. Finally, mark the Tax-related check box if this expense category is tax deductible.

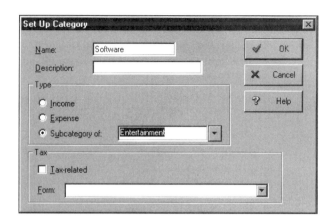

Figure 2.2. **The Set Up Category dialog box**

The Subcategory Of text box allows you to create more detailed categorization. In Figure 2.2, Software is a subcategory of the category Entertainment. (Entertainment is an expense category.) When you enter software in the register, Quicken lists the category as Entertainment: Softw. When you create reports, the expense accumulates in the Entertainment category. In other words, the definition of the parent category as either expense or income sets the definition for subcategories.

 NOTE I'll talk more about categories in later chapters. See Chapter 14, *Estimating and Preparing Income Taxes,* for help setting up category lists that easily support your income-tax planning and preparation. See Chapter 15, *Planning Your Personal Finances,* for a discussion of how to use categories and subcategories as budgeting tools.

7. *If you want to add a memo description of the transaction,* highlight the Memo text box by clicking on it or by pressing Tab. Then, enter a brief description.

You can enter anything you want in the Memo text box. Note, though, that there's no reason to duplicate information you've entered or will enter some place else.

8. Click on the Enter button (it appears just below the Deposit text box) to enter the transaction data into the register.

Quicken updates the bank-account balance and highlights the next empty row in the register.

NOTE Quicken also records transactions into the register if you press Enter when the Memo box is highlighted or if you press Ctrl+Enter when any of the text or combo boxes are highlighted.

Figure 2.3 shows a register with two checks: a check for $51.20 to Bob's Place for software and another for $200, written to Armstrong Commons to pay January's rent. Quicken categorizes the check as Rent. The box at the bottom of the screen is the *memorized transactions box*. Quicken has memorized the transactions, and now they appear in the memorized transactions box.

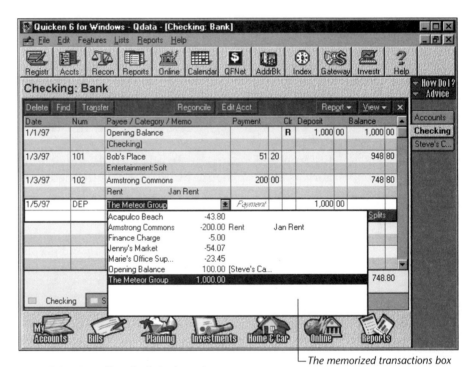

└─ *The memorized transactions box*

Figure 2.3.   **Recording checks in the register**

Using QuickFill to Speed Up Data Entry

Quicken provides QuickFill, a data-entry aid that you run into as soon as you start recording transactions. QuickFill keeps lists of the entries you make in the Payee and Category combo boxes. (In fact, it's Quick-Fill's list that Quicken displays in the Payee and Category drop-down–list boxes.) When you make a new entry in a text box, QuickFill matches your new entry against the first entry in its list that looks similar. Then it fills the text box with this similar-looking entry.

This sounds unwieldy, but it works wonderfully well. If, for example, you enter the Payee name Armstrong Commons, then the next time you begin typing something into the Payee combo box that starts out with the letters *ARM*, QuickFill completes the combo box so it shows Armstrong Commons. You can then move to the next field.

> **TIP** If it turns out you're typing something completely different from what QuickFill guesses that you're typing, it's not a problem. Just keep typing. What you type replaces whatever QuickFill supplies.

In the case of a payee name, QuickFill does even more than fill the Payee field. If you accept the payee name supplied by QuickFill and move to the next field, QuickFill fills in the rest of the transaction's fields using the previous transaction's information. For example, if you let QuickFill fill in the payee name Armstrong Commons, and then you press Tab to move to the Payment text box, then QuickFill uses the amount, memo, and category information from the previous Armstrong Commons transaction. Because checks you write to the same payee usually have similar features, QuickFill's automatic completion saves lots of data-entry time.

Recording Deposits

To record the money that flows into an account, you record a deposit transaction into the next empty row of the register. Follow these steps:

1. Enter the deposit date: Highlight the Date text box, if necessary, then enter the date in *MM/DD/YY* fashion. Again, you don't have to enter the year number if it's already correct.

2. Identify the transaction as a deposit. Highlight the Num combo box. If you're making a regular deposit into the account, select the Deposit entry from the list box shown below. If you're recording a wire transfer deposit, select the EFT entry.

3. Enter the person or company from whom you received the money you're depositing: Move to the Paid By combo box. If this is the first time you've recorded a payment from this person or business, type the person's or firm's name. If you've previously recorded a check from the person or business, activate the Paid By drop-down list and select the person's or business's name from it.

4. Enter the deposit amount: Highlight the Deposit text box and enter the amount. Don't enter dollar signs or commas. Do enter a period to identify the cents.

5. *If the deposit you're entering into the register has already been recorded by the bank,* click in the Clr (Clear) text box. You would probably do this only if you're entering old transactions or if the transaction is an automatic deposit, such as an automatic payroll deposit.

6. Categorize the deposit using the Category drop-down list.

   A check from your employer, for example, might best be categorized as Salary. A check from a customer might best be categorized as Sales. If you can't find an income category that describes the deposit, enter a short category name directly into the Category combo box and press Enter. Quicken asks if you want to create a new category. If you do, click on the Yes button; Quicken displays the Set Up Category dialog box, shown in Figure 2.2. Enter the category name you want to use in the Name text box. If you want, enter a description of the category in the Description text box. Verify that the Income option button is marked so that Quicken knows this is a category used to track income. Finally, mark the Tax-related check box if this income category is taxable. (It probably is.)

7. *If you want to add a memo description,* click in the Memo text box. Then enter a brief description. If you're depositing a payroll check, you might want to record the payroll check date or payment period. Or if you're depositing a customer or client check, you might want to record the invoice being paid.

8. Click on the Enter button to record the deposit into the register. Quicken updates the bank account balance and highlights the next empty row in the register.

TIP   Quicken also records transactions into the register if you press Enter when the selection cursor is on the Memo box or if you press Ctrl+Enter when the selection cursor is in any of the text or combo boxes.

Figure 2.4 shows a $1000 payroll deposit from your fictitious employer, The Meteor Group. Note that the check is categorized as Salary.

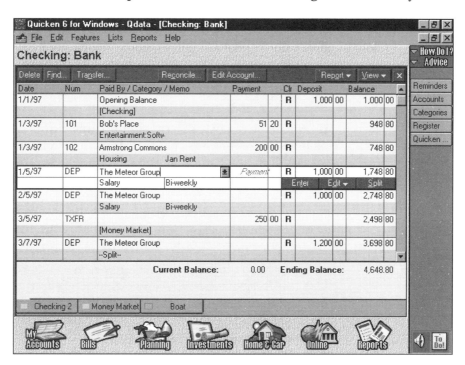

Figure 2.4.   **The register after you've categorized a deposit as Salary**

ENTERING SPECIAL CHARACTERS

Sometimes the text you'll want to enter includes characters that aren't on the keyboard. You can't, for example, enter a Japanese Yen symbol (¥) or a British Pound symbol (£) by using a key on your keyboard. You can, however, still use these sorts of special characters. All you do is hold down the Alt key and then type the character set code—usually the ANSI code—for the special character you want. For example, to enter the Japanese Yen symbol, you hold down Alt and type **0165** on the numeric keypad. When you release the Alt key, Quicken displays the ¥ symbol. If you have questions about which character set codes represent which characters, refer to the Windows User's Guide.

What to Do If You Make a Mistake

Your typing skills aren't perfect, of course. What's more, you will sometimes enter transactions into your registers using bad source documents (an erroneous deposit slip, for example). These little problems don't have to cause you much concern because Quicken provides a rich set of tools for fixing data-entry mistakes.

Fix-It Basics

If you make a mistake entering a transaction, all you need to do is change the erroneous piece of data. If you haven't yet recorded the transaction, you can move the selection cursor to the incorrect field. If you have recorded the transaction, you need to find the transaction and then highlight it either by clicking the mouse on it or by using the ↑ and ↓ keys. Then, you highlight the incorrect field by clicking on it or by using the Tab and Shift+Tab keys. At this point you can replace the incorrect entry by typing over it.

You can also edit the incorrect entry rather than replacing it altogether. Use the Backspace key to erase characters to the left of the insertion bar and then type the correct data. You can also reposition the insertion bar with the arrow keys, erase characters to the right with the Delete key, and then type the correct data.

Once you make your fix, record the transaction with the new, updated information—for example, by selecting the Enter button, which appears near the bottom of the Register document window.

Three Fix-It Tools Everyone Should Use

Three of the fix-it tools Quicken provides are so easy and so handy that everyone—even new users—should learn to use them. The following descriptions are intentionally brief, by the way. Your best bet for learning these tools is to just start using them as soon as possible.

Tool	When You Use It
Edit ➤ Transaction ➤ Restore	To reverse the more recent editing changes made in the selected text or combo box. (This works only as long as the text or combo box is still selected, though. You can't undo edits made to the previously-selected text or combo box.)
Edit ➤ Transaction ➤ Void	To void a transaction already entered into the register. (Quicken marks the transaction as void so it isn't included in account balances or category titles but leaves the transaction in the register so you have a record of the transaction's existence.)
Edit ➤ Transaction ➤ Delete	To permanently remove a transaction from the register. (Quicken asks you to confirm the deletion with a message box.) Delete appears as a command button at the top of the Register window and as an Edit menu command, and Delete Transaction appears as a command on the shortcut menu that see when you click on the Edit command button.

 NOTE Alongside the Enter and Edit command buttons, the Register window contains a Splits button. I'll talk about how to use this button in the *Split Transactions* section later in this chapter.

More Editing Tools

Once you're comfortable with the three fix-it tools just described, you may want to use the more powerful fix-it commands Quicken provides: Copy, Cut, Paste, Find, Find/Replace, and Recategorize.

Cutting, Copying, and Pasting Data

With the Copy, Cut, and Paste commands, you can copy or cut the contents of one text or combo box and paste them into another text or combo box. This means you can move text easily if you've stuck something into the wrong text box. It also means you can type something once and then copy it (or a portion of it) as many times as you need.

To copy and cut text box contents, you follow the same basic process. First, select the text box containing the text. Next, position the insertion bar at the start of the chunk of text you want to copy. Then, highlight the rest of the chunk of text by dragging the mouse or by holding down the Shift key and then using the ← and → keys.

Once you've selected the text, choose the Edit ➤ Copy or Edit ➤ Cut command. (Copying duplicates the selected text and stores the duplicate copy in the Windows 95 Clipboard, a temporary storage area. Cutting moves the selected text to the Windows 95 Clipboard.)

Next, indicate where you want to place the copied or cut item. To do this, first identify the text or combo box by selecting it. Then use the mouse or the arrow keys to move the insertion bar within the text or combo box to the location where you want to place the text. Once you've indicated the destination location, choose Edit ➤ Paste.

COPYING DATA TO AND FROM WINDOWS 95 APPLICATIONS

The Cut, Copy, and Paste commands are supported by the Windows 95 operating environment, and they appear in most Windows 95 applications. This means you can copy and cut chunks of text among different Windows applications. For example, you can select a chunk of text in Quicken, copy or cut the text so that it gets stored in the Clipboard, switch to another application, and then use this application's Paste command to move the text stored in the Clipboard to a text box in this other application. (To switch between open Windows applications, press Alt+Tab until the desired application is selected.)

Finding a Transaction

If you know you made a mistake but don't know where, you can use the Find and Find/Replace commands. Let's look at the Find command first.

Find locates transactions within a register. To choose this command, select Edit ➤ Find & Replace ➤ Find or click on the Find command button at the top of the register. Quicken displays the Quicken Find dialog box, as shown in Figure 2.5. Enter whatever it is you're looking for in the Find text box. In the case of an error, for example, this might be a name you misspelled.

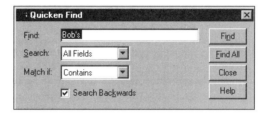

Figure 2.5. **Use the Quicken Find dialog box to describe transactions you're looking for.**

Use the Search drop-down–list box to specify which fields you want to search. The default, or suggested, setting is All Fields. But if you activate the drop-down list, you can choose to search only the fields you fill in as part of recording a transaction into your register.

Use the Match if drop-down–list box to specify what constitutes a match:

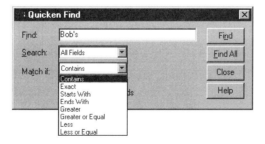

You can specify, for example, that the match be exact—in other words, that the bit of text or the number you entered in the Find text box must exactly match a field's contents in order for Quicken to consider the pair as matched. Or, you can specify that the text you entered in the Find box only match what starts or ends a field's contents. The Match if drop-down list also provides a complete set of mathematical operators such as greater than, less than, greater than or equal to, less than or equal to, and so on, just in case you want to search for an amount.

SEARCHING WITH WILDCARDS

Quicken provides three wildcard characters you can use in the Find text box. A question mark (?) can stand for any single character. If you specify **?at**, for example, Quicken will find bat, cat, hat and so on—any three letter word that ends with the letters *AT*. Two periods (..) stand for any group of characters. You can use the two periods at the beginning, in the middle, or at the end of the word or text. If you specify **..ville**, for example, Quicken will find Marysville, Seville, Coupe de ville, and so on. The tilde character (~) indicates you want to find a field that doesn't contain an entry. If you want to find a transaction that doesn't use the category Household, you enter ~**Household.** You can combine wildcard characters. For example, the Find text entry ~**?at** will find fields that don't contain three letter words ending with the letters *AT*.

Once you've described the search criteria, you select the Find command button. Quicken searches from the selected transaction backward. (You can unmark the Search Backwards check box if you want to search from the selected transaction forward.) If Quicken finds a transaction that matches your search criteria, it activates the register but leaves the Find document window active in case you want to use it again. You can click on the transaction to make a change to it. You can continue your search by clicking in the Find document window and selecting the Find command button again. When you finish with the Find document window, click on its Close button.

If you want to build a list of all the transactions that match the search criteria, select the Find document window's Find All command button. In this situation, Quicken displays a list of matching transactions, as shown in Figure 2.6.

To edit a transaction or see it in complete detail, double-click on it in the list or select it with the arrow keys and then press Enter. (This tells Quicken to select the transaction in the register.) When you're done, select the Close command button to remove the matching transactions list and the Find document window.

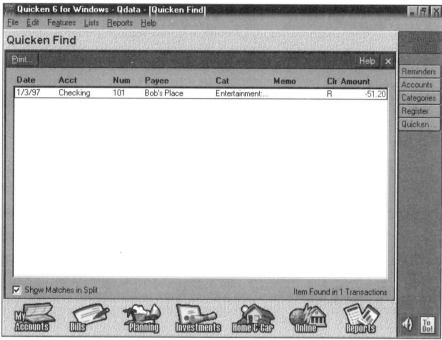

Figure 2.6.   When you choose the Find All command button in the Find document window, Quicken builds a list of transactions that match your search criteria.

TIP If you use the Find All command button, Quicken expands the Find document window so that it looks like a regular, page-sized window. (Until you do this, the Find document window looks more like a dialog box than it does a window even though the Find box really is and works like a document window.)

The Replace Command for Making Many Transaction Changes

The Edit ➤ Find & Replace ➤ Find/Replace command is a more powerful version of Edit ➤ Find & Replace ➤ Find. It lets you change a field in all the transactions that match your search criteria. When you choose the Edit ➤ Find & Replace ➤ Find/Replace command, Quicken displays the Find and Replace dialog box, as shown in Figure 2.7.

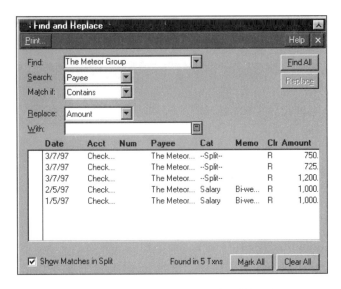

Figure 2.7. **The Find and Replace dialog box lets you make editing changes to a set of trans-actions that match your search criteria.**

In the Find and Replace dialog box, you use the Find, Search, and Match if boxes the same way you use their counterparts on the Find document window. Once you've entered the search criteria using these boxes, you select the Find All command button to locate all the trans-actions that match your search criteria. Quicken then displays these matching transactions in a list box at the bottom of the screen. You use the Replace drop-down–list box to specify what field in the match-ing transactions you want to change. If you want to change the amount, for example, you activate the Replace drop-down–list box and select Amount. You use the With text box to specify the replacement text or value.

 TIP If you enter a value in the Find text box, Quicken assumes that you are trying to find an amount and makes Amount the default selection in the Replace drop-down list. Once you enter the value in the Find text box, press Enter or click on Find All to locate all the Amount transactions.

To specify which matching transactions you actually want to replace with the contents of the With box, click on each transaction to mark it with a check mark. Use the Mark All button to add a check mark to all the matching transactions. Use the Clear All button to remove check marks from all the matching transactions.

When only the transactions you want to change are marked with check marks, select the Replace button. Quicken displays a message box asking you to confirm your change. Select OK. Quicken then makes the replacements and displays a message box that tells you the number of replacements made.

Using the Quicken Calculator

Quicken includes a simple pop-up calculator. You can start the calculator by choosing the Edit ➤ Use Calculator command. Quicken starts the calculator and displays it on top of the Quicken application window, as shown in Figure 2.8.

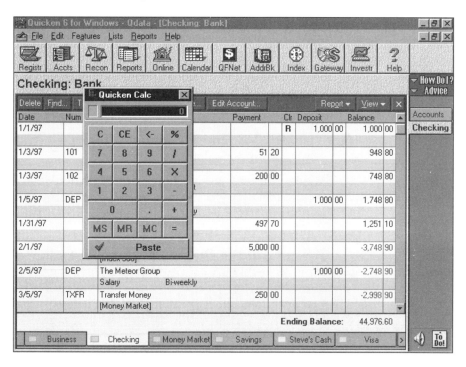

Figure 2.8. The Quicken calculator

To add two numbers—such as 24 and 93—type the first number, the plus symbol, the second number, and then click on the equals sign or press Enter:

24+93=

If you want to use the mouse, you can click on the calculator's keys because these are really command buttons. For example, to enter the value 24, you can click on the 2 and then on the 4. (The calculator displays 24 if you do this.)

To subtract one number from another—5 from 25, say—enter the first number, the minus symbol, the second number, and then the equals sign:

25–5=

To multiply or divide numbers with the calculator, simply use the asterisk symbol as the multiplication operator and the slash symbol as the division operator. For example, to multiply 25 by 1250, enter the following:

25*1250=

And to divide 32000 by 4, enter the following:

32000/4=

The MR, MS, and MC buttons, respectively, recall, save, and clear entries from the calculator memory.

When you're done working with the calculator, you can double-click on the calculator's Control-menu icon and choose Close to close the application. Or you can click anywhere on the Quicken application window to make it the active window.

If you make the Quicken application window active, the calculator remains visible on your screen. To place the value shown on the calculator display into a text box on the application window, select the text box and then select the calculator's Paste command button.

Setting Up Additional Bank Accounts

As part of installing Quicken, you set up at least one bank account. (In fact, the preceding discussion assumes you've done so.) You'll want to set up additional accounts in Quicken for each of your other bank accounts, so that you can track the account balances and the money flowing into and out of all of them.

Adding a New Bank Account

To set up another bank account, follow these steps:

1. Click on the Account icon button, or choose Lists ➤ Account to display the Account List document window, as shown in Figure 2.9.

    This window is just a big list box of the accounts you are using Quicken to track.

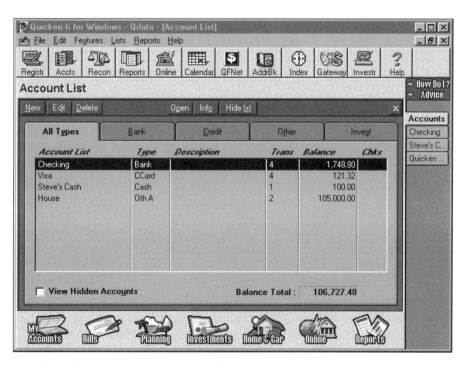

*Figure 2.9.   **The Account List document window***

2. Click on the New button at the top of the Account List document window or point to the My Accounts HomeBase icon and select Create a New Account to display the Account Setup window, as shown in Figure 2.10. (If a Qcard appears, double-click on its Control-menu box to close it.)

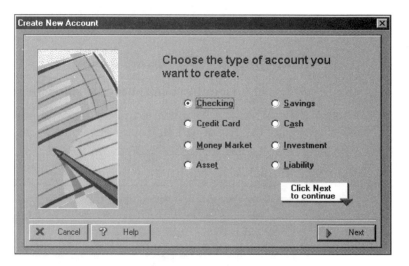

Figure 2.10.   **The Account Setup window**

3. Click on the Checking, Savings, or Money Market option button to tell Quicken you want to set up another bank account. Then, click on Next. No matter which button you choose, the process works the same: Quicken next displays the Checking Account Setup dialog box, Savings Account Setup dialog box, or Money Market Setup dialog box.

    Later chapters describe how you set up and why you use the other account types shown in Figure 2.10. For now, let's concentrate on setting up a checking, savings, or money market account.

4. Click on the Summary tab so that Quicken displays in just one place text boxes and buttons for all the information you need to collect, as shown in Figure 2.11.

5. In the Account Name text box, enter a bank account name and, optionally, a description.

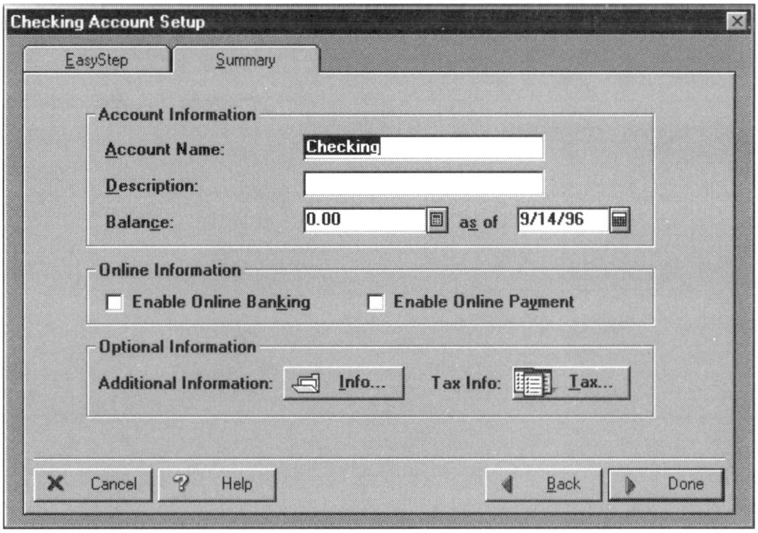

*Figure 2.11. **The Summary tab of the Account Setup dialog boxes lets you enter in one place all the information needed to set up the typical account.***

6. In the Description text box, you have the option of describing the account in more detail, such as by providing the bank name or account number.

7. Enter the bank-account balance and bank-statement date in the text boxes provided. As noted in Appendix A, unless you have meticulous records, the best approach is usually to use the balance from your bank statement and then adjust this balance (so it's correct) by recording any uncleared transactions.

8. Indicate whether this account is one you'll use for online banking or bill paying. (If you do this, Quicken will ask you for some additional information about the bank. I talk more about online banking and bill paying in Chapter 9, *Paying Bills Electronically*, and in Chapter 10, *Banking Online*.)

9. Optionally, click on the Info button to display a dialog box (as shown below) that lets you collect and store more information about the account, including the bank name, the account number, the name of the person you deal with at the bank (such as a personal banker, private banker, or loan officer), and the telephone number. You can typically get all of this information from your last bank statement. When you finish entering this information—if you do enter it—click on OK.

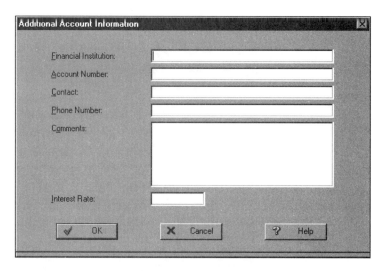

10. Optionally, click on the Tax button in the Account Setup dialog box to display a dialog box that lets you tell Quicken that moving money into and out of this checking account has an impact on your income taxes:

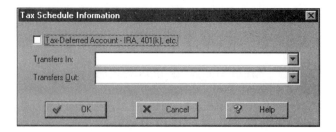

NOTE Most people won't have to worry about the Tax button, but if you're keeping, for example, Individual Retirement Account (IRA) money in a checking account or money market account and then writing checks on this account as a way to withdraw money from the IRA account, you probably want to click on the Tax button. When Quicken displays the Tax Schedule Information dialog box, mark the Tax Deferred Account check box. Then use the Transfers In drop-down–list box to specify which tax form and line transfers into this account should be reported. Use the Transfers Out drop-down–list box to specify which tax form and line transfers (or withdrawals) from the this account should be reported. When you finish entering this information, click on OK.

11. Click on Next if you indicated that you will use Online Banking or Online Bill Payment. (Quicken only provides a Next button if you indicated you will do this.) Quicken prompts you for the information it needs to connect to your bank electronically. If you're banking online or paying bills online, you'll have received a welcome letter from your bank. This welcome letter provides the information you need to answer the questions that Quicken asks.

12. Click on Done. Quicken redisplays the Account List window.

Telling Quicken Which Account You Want to Work With

To record payments and deposits for an account, you need to be able to see the account in the register. To see the register for the account you want to work with, double-click on its name in the Account List.

Transferring Money between Accounts

Once you start working with multiple accounts, you'll need to know how to record *account transfers*—movements of money from one account to another account.

Recording account transfers in the Register window is very easy. Enter the date in the date field and then tab to the Num field. Click on the arrow button and select Transfer Funds and then enter the amount in the Payment field. Tab to the Category field and select the account to which you wish to transfer the funds from the bottom of drop-down list. Figure 2.12 shows an account transfer: $250 deposited into the Money Market account from the checking account. To identify the transaction as an account transfer, Quicken places brackets around the account name.

You can also use the Transfer dialog box shown in Figure 2.13 to record account transfers. To use the Transfer dialog box, select the Transfer button that appears at the top of the register. Then, use the text and combo boxes it provides to give the transfer date and amount as well as the names of the accounts the money moves between. Using the Transfer dialog box to record transfers has a couple of advantages over Using the Register window to record transfers. One advantage is that the Transfer dialog box visually shows you that only four pieces of information are necessary to record a transfer. Another advantage is that you aren't limited to recording a transfer transaction from or to the account shown in the active register. You can specify any source or destination account.

Quicken is clever about how it records account transfers. If you enter a transfer transaction into, say, the checking account, and the transaction shows the money as coming from the Money Market account,

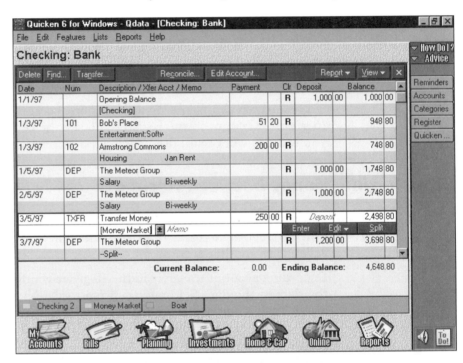

Figure 2.12.   **An account transfer transaction, showing money transferred from the checking account to the Money Market account**

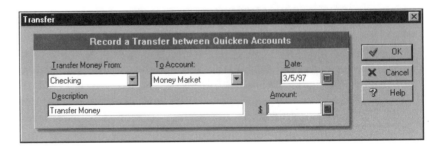

Figure 2.13.   **The Transfer dialog box**

Quicken also enters the transfer transaction into the Money Market account. For example, if you did enter the transfer transaction shown in Figure 2.13, Quicken would record the related transfer transaction into the Money Market account register, as shown in Figure 2.14.

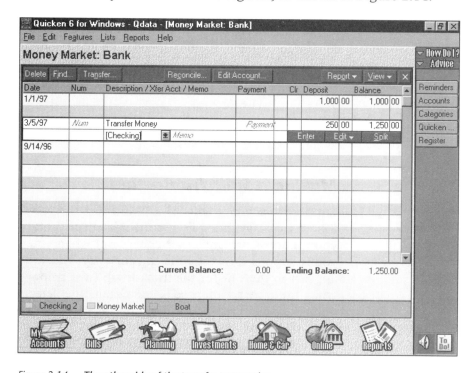

Figure 2.14.   The other side of the transfer transaction

If you edit a transfer transaction in one register, Quicken may even update the matching transfer transaction in the other register. Changes to a transfer transaction's date or amount get made to the matching transfer transaction too. (However, changes to a transfer transaction's other fields—such as its check number, memo description, and cleared status—don't get made to the matching transfer transaction.)

TIP   You can flip between the two sides of a transfer with a couple of mouse clicks or a shortcut-key combination. If the highlighted transaction in a register is a transfer, the Edit ➤ Go to Transfer command moves you to the other side of the transfer. You can select this command with the keyboard or mouse, or you can use its command shortcut, Ctrl+X.

Split Transactions

Not every check you write can fairly be categorized using a single category. For example, a check written to a particular supermarket covering both groceries and automobile supplies can't be described using a single category.

Similarly, not every deposit you make can be fairly categorized using a single category. A check that includes your regular wages and a reimbursement for travel expenses can't entirely be described as wages (or as expense reimbursement).

Fortunately, Quicken provides a handy way to deal with this record-keeping reality: split transactions.

Making a Split Transaction

Suppose you want to record a $100 check that pays $75 of groceries and $25 of birthday gifts. To record this check, you follow the same steps you use to record any other check. But when you get to the step where you're supposed to enter the category, you select the Splits button which appears in the row for the transaction (just below the Balance column) when the transaction is selected. When you select Splits, Quicken displays the Split Transaction Window, as shown in Figure 2.15.

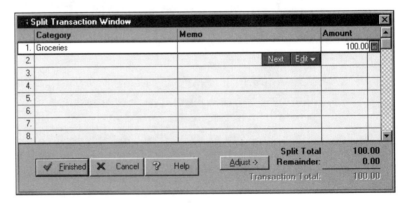

Figure 2.15. **The Split Transaction Window**

Here's what you do to use the Split Transaction Window:

1. Categorize the first expense paid with the check: Place the cursor in the first Category combo box. Activate the drop-down list. Then, choose the first spending category—in this case, it's Groceries—paid with the check.

2. *If you want a memo description of the expenditure,* place the cursor in the first Memo text box. Then, enter a description of the expenditure.

3. Enter the first expense category amount: Place the cursor in the first Amount text box and enter the amount. (Because the first spending category is Groceries and you spent $75 on groceries, type 75.)

> TIP   You don't have to enter split amounts in dollars. If you enter a percentage, such as 75 percent, Quicken calculates the split amount by multiplying the split percentage by the transaction total. If the transaction total is $100 and you enter a split transaction amount as **75%**, Quicken calculates 75 percent of 100 and enters $75 as the split transaction amount. Clicking on the Calculator icon that appears when you move to an Amount field opens a small calculator keyboard you can use to calculate the split amount directly into the field.

4. Repeat steps 1 through 3 for the other spending category, Gifts Given.

> NOTE To record a transaction with more than two spending categories, repeat steps one through three as many times as necessary. If you need more than eight categories to split the transaction, use the vertical scroll bar in the Splits dialog box to page down to more split-transaction lines. You can split a transaction into as many as thirty categories.

5. Verify that the split-transaction lines agree with the register.

   When you finish describing each of the spending categories for a check, the total of the individual split-transaction lines you've entered should agree with the payment you entered. If it doesn't agree, you can click on the Adjust button in the Splits dialog box to adjust the Payment amount shown in the register to whatever the split-transaction lines total. In addition, you can either enter additional split-transaction lines or adjust one of the split-transaction lines already entered.

TIP   You can easily tell whether the total of the split-transaction lines equals the payment amount entered in the register. Quicken uses the empty split-transaction line beneath the last split-transaction you entered to show the difference between the payment amount and the total of the individual split-transaction lines.

Figure 2.16 shows the Splits dialog box, filled out to record a $100 check that pays $75 for groceries and $25 for gifts.

	Category	Memo	Amount	
1.	Groceries		75 00	
2.	Gifts Given	Birthday gift for Sarah	25 00	
3.		Next Edit ▾		
4.				
5.				
6.				
7.				
8.				

Split Total   100.00
Remainder: 0.00
Transaction Total: 100.00

Figure 2.16.   *A completed Split Transaction Window, recording $75 of groceries expense and $25 of gift expense*

Removing a Split Transaction

To remove a split transaction—a split category and amount shows in the Splits dialog box—select Splits in the Category field and click on the X button next to it. You might use this technique, for example, to delete an erroneous split transaction line. You can click on the checkmark button to go back to the Splits dialog box.

Splitting Deposit Transactions

Splitting a deposit transaction works the same way as splitting a payment transaction. You enter the deposit in the usual way, including the deposit amount. Then, when you get to the Category combo box, you click on the Splits command button. Quicken displays the Splits dialog box, and you describe each of the income categories in a deposit using different split transaction lines. Figure 2.17 shows how you might record a $1,200 deposit that represents $1,000 of salary and $200 of bonus.

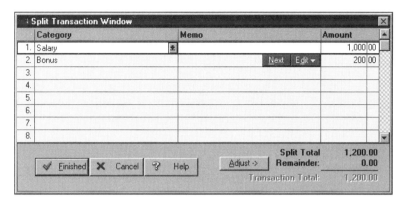

Figure 2.17. *A completed Split Transaction Window, recording $1,000 of salary and $200 of bonus*

Splitting Combined Transactions

You now know how to use more than one expense category to describe a payment and how to use more than one income category to describe a deposit. But you aren't limited to using just expense or just income categories on a split transaction. You can mix and match your categories.

For example, if you go to the bank and deposit your $750 payroll check but keep $25 of cash for Friday-night fun, you fill out the Splits dialog box, as shown in Figure 2.18. Your net deposit is really $725. You would record the deposit amount as $725, and you would complete the Splits dialog box as shown in Figure 2.18.

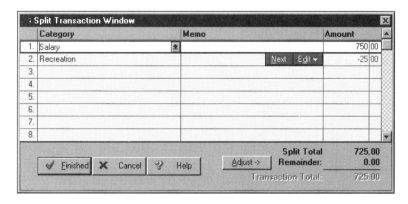

Figure 2.18. *A completed Split Transaction Window, recording $750 of salary income and $25 of recreation expense*

One thing that's initially tricky about splitting combined income and expense transactions is the sign of the split transaction line amounts. In Figure 2.18, the $750 of salary shows as positive, and the $25 of recreation shows as negative. (On a color monitor, the negative $25 also shows in red to further identify the value as a negative number.) This isn't, however, because salary income increases the account balance or because recreation expense decreases the account balance.

Quicken just adds up the amount of the split-transaction lines. So you use negative split-transaction amounts—such as the $25 of recreation expense—to reduce the total split-transaction lines.

Say, for example, you want to record the purchase of an item your employer manufactures—a new $1,500 hot tub. If you'll pay $750 by writing a check and also forfeit a $750 payroll check, you would record this split transaction as shown in Figure 2.19.

 NOTE You can also use the Splits dialog box to describe account transfers. Chapter 20, *Payroll*, shows how you split transactions between expense categories and account transfers as part of preparing employee payroll.

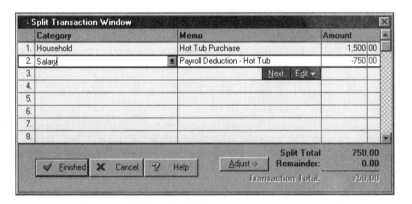

Figure 2.19.   A completed Split Transaction Window, recording $750 of salary income and $1,500 of household expense

Changing a Split Transaction

Editing the details of a split transaction works very much like you might expect—with one minor exception.

To display the Split Transaction Window so that you can make changes, click on the Splits button or click on the button that has a check mark. Quicken opens the Split Transaction Window. From there, you can make whatever changes you want by replacing categories, memo descriptions, or amounts. You make these changes, of course, by clicking on the text box you want to change and then typing the new information.

You can also remove the splits from a transaction. In other words, you can tell Quicken you want to "unsplit" a transaction. To do this, click on the Cancel button—it looks like a small *X*—that appears next to the Category drop-down list (see Figure 2.20).

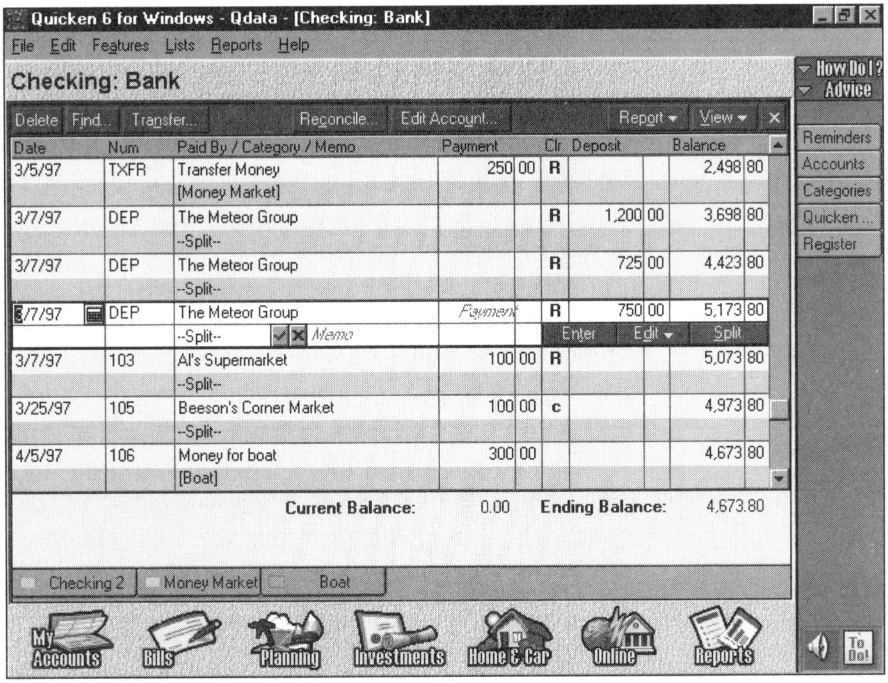

Figure 2.20. **Quicken adds buttons next to a split transaction.**

By the way, the most common reason that you want to "unsplit" a transaction is that QuickFill has filled out the Split Transaction Window for you even though it shouldn't have. For example, if you write a $100 check to Beeson's Corner Market and split the check as $75 groceries and $25 gifts, Quicken's QuickFill feature memorizes this information.

The next time you write a check to Beeson's Corner Market, It copies all the information you used to describe the last check. This includes, of course, the split-transaction information. If the current check to Beeson's is only for groceries, you'll want to unsplit the transaction.

 NOTE There's nothing wrong with having only a single split-transaction line. Everything still works right within Quicken. The only disadvantage of this single split-transaction line is that you need to select the transaction and open the Splits dialog box to see how a check or a deposit was categorized.

Record-Keeping Tricks

If you're just getting started with a checkbook program like Quicken, incorporating the program into your record-keeping routine can be a little awkward. To smooth this process, here is a handful of helpful ideas:

► Batch your payment and deposits together so that you can enter them as a group. Starting Quicken and displaying an account register isn't difficult, but doing it several times a day for every transaction is time-consuming. You'll find it works best to sit down about once a week and enter the previous week's transactions. (This should also work fine for businesses. Even large businesses don't pay bills every day. They batch them and then process them together once or twice a week.)

► Keep documentation of the checks you write by hand so that you can remember, for example, what you paid with check 1245. (Those checks that come with noncarbon copies are handy because you always create a record of the checks you write by hand.)

► Be sure to keep the documentation—deposit slips, ATM receipts, and so forth—that describes the other transactions you'll want to enter into your register. Because you won't be carrying your computer around with you everywhere you go, you'll want some paper documentation you can review whenever you do sit down at your computer to do financial record keeping.

Printing an Account Register

It's a good idea to print an account register at the end of the month. This paper record provides a hard copy of the transactions you've entered and acts as a permanent backup copy of your financial records. You can keep this copy with the bank account statement you receive. (You probably won't need the register unless you someday need to restore your financial records from a backup copy.)

To print an account register, first display the account in the register. You can double-click on its name in the Account List or click on its QuickTab. Then follow these steps:

1. Choose the File ➤ Print Register command to display the Print Register dialog box, as shown in Figure 2.21.

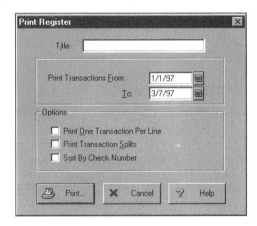

Figure 2.21. **The Print Register dialog box**

2. *If you want to enter a title for the register,* use the Title text box. (If you don't enter a title, Quicken uses Account Register for the title.)

3. Enter the range of dates you want the register to include using the Print Transactions From and To text boxes.

NOTE If you look closely at the Print Transactions From and To text boxes, you'll see something that resembles (sort of) a small calendar. Click on this calendar to display a pop-up calendar you can use to quickly enter a date into the text box. The calendar highlights the date already shown in the text box, but you can change months by clicking on the arrows at the top of the calendar and change dates by clicking the mouse directly on the date.

4. *If you want to pack each transaction onto a single line of the printed check register,* mark the Print One Transaction Per Line check box. (Usually, you won't want to do this as it just makes everything harder to read.)

5. *If you want to print split-transaction information*—and you probably do if you've been splitting transactions—mark the Print Transaction Splits check box.

6. *If you want to print transactions not in order of entry date but in order of check number,* mark the Sort by Check Number check box.

7. Click on the Print command button when you're ready to print. Quicken displays the Print dialog box, as shown in Figure 2.22.

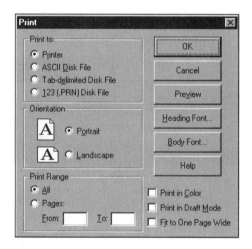

Figure 2.22.   **The Print dialog box**

8. Click on OK. Quicken passes the register information to Windows 95 and it prints your register. Figure 2.23 shows a printed Quicken check register.

 TIP   Chapter 4, *Tracking Your Finances with Reports,* explains how you can use the Print dialog box to control the way Quicken prints reports such as the register.

Check Register

Checking   Page 1
8/20/1997

Date	Num	Transaction	Payment	C	Deposit	Balance
1/1/1997		Opening Balance cat: [Checking]		R	1,000.00	1,000.00
1/3/1997	101	Bob's Place cat: Entertainment:Software	51.20			948.80
1/3/1997	102	Armstrong Commons cat: Rent memo: Jan Rent	200.00			748.80
1/5/1997	DEP	The Meteor Group cat: Salary memo: Bi-weekly			1,000.00	1,748.80
2/5/1997	DEP	The Meteor Group cat: Salary memo: Bi-weekly			1,000.00	2,748.80
3/5/1997	TXFR	Transfer Money cat: [Money Market]	250.00			2,498.80
3/7/1997	DEP	The Meteor Group cat: --SPLIT--			1,200.00	3,698.80
3/7/1997	DEP	The Meteor Group cat: --SPLIT--			725.00	4,423.80
3/7/1997	DEP	The Meteor Group cat: --SPLIT--			750.00	5,173.80
3/7/1997	103	Al's Supermarket cat: --SPLIT--	100.00			5,073.80
3/15/1997	104	James D. Hughes, Attorney cat: Legal memo: opinion in patent case	285.00			4,788.80
3/25/1997	105	Beeson's Corner Market cat: Groceries	125.00			4,663.80

Figure 2.23. **A printed Quicken check register**

CHAPTER 3
Printing Checks

FEATURING

Preparing to print checks

Telling Quicken which checks to print

Sending checks to the printer

Reprinting checks that didn't come out right

O NCE you've worked a bit with a Quicken register and used it to track a bank account balance and the money that flows into and out of an account, you'll want to consider printing checks using Quicken. Doing so will save you time—particularly if you now hand-write a lot of checks. What's more, printing checks with Quicken lets you produce professional-looking, accurate checks.

Before You Start

Before you can print checks in Quicken, you need to:

▶ Install the Quicken program through Windows 95 and set up a bank account (see Appendix A).

▶ Order and receive the check forms you'll print. (The Quicken packaging contains check order form information. You can also print a check supplies order form by choosing the Marketplace from the Online selection on the Features menu.)

 NOTE You'll find it much easier to print checks if you're already familiar with the Quicken register.

Collecting Check Information

Once you've completed the necessary prerequisites, you're ready to begin describing the checks you want to print. If you've been using the Quicken register to track a bank account, you'll notice that many of the steps are mechanically identical; the only difference is that Quicken supplies a different document window for you to use.

Telling Quicken You Want to Write Checks on an Account

To tell Quicken you want to write checks you'll print, first open the register for the account on which you want to write a check, then choose the Features ➤ Paying Bills ➤ Write Checks command. Figure 3.1 shows the Write Checks document window with the Checking account active. You will also have tabs for each of your bank accounts at the bottom of the Write Checks window. To select another account on which you want to write a check, you just click that account's tab.

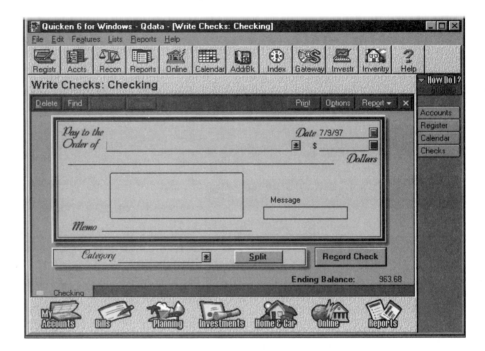

Figure 3.1.   The Write Checks document window

Describing a Check You Want Quicken to Print

Once you've identified the account and displayed the Write Checks
document window, you're ready to begin describing the checks you
want Quicken to print. This process largely mirrors the process you use
for recording a hand-written check into the Quicken Register.

To describe a check you want Quicken to print, follow these steps:

1. In the Date field (which automatically shows the current date), enter
    the check date, which is the date you'll print the check. Highlight the
    Date text box. If the date shown isn't the check date, enter the date in
    MM/DD/YY format. You don't have to enter the year number unless
    the one Quicken already shows is not correct.

NOTE Quicken provides shortcuts you can use to set the date. They are described in Chapter 2.

2. Name the payee in the Pay to the Order of field: Highlight the Payee combo box. If this is the first time you've recorded a payment to the payee, type the payee's name. If you've written a check to the payee before, activate the Payee drop-down list and select the payee name from it.

Bob's Place	-51.20 Entertainm...
Coffee Merchant	-25.51 Groceries
Lane's Bowling	-10.81 Entertainm...
The Meteor Group	-750.00 --Splits--

3. Enter the check amount: Select the Payment text box and enter the payment amount. You don't have to enter dollar signs and commas. Include a period though, to identify any cents. Once you enter the payment amount, Quicken writes out the payment amount in words in the space below the Payee combo box.

4. *If you'll use an envelope with a window* (in this case, the address you enter will show through the envelope window), transfer the payee name to the first line of the address block by placing the cursor in the address box and pressing the ' (apostrophe) character. Enter the street address line and the city and state address lines.

5. *If you want to add a memo description,* move to the Memo text box and enter a brief description. You can enter anything you want into this field. Note, though, that there's no reason to duplicate information you've entered or will enter someplace else. (If a check pays a particular invoice or on a specific account, consider using the Memo text box to record this bit of information.)

6. Categorize the transaction by using the Category drop-down list:

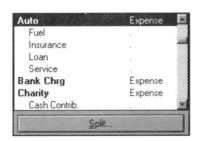

If you can't find an expense category that describes the payment, you can enter a short category description directly into the Category text box and press Enter. In the Set Up Category dialog box, shown in Figure 3.2, enter the category name you want to use. If you want, enter a description of the category in the Description text box. Verify that the Expense option button is marked so Quicken knows this is a category used to track spending. Finally, mark the Tax-related check box if this expense category is tax deductible.

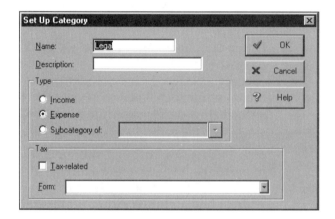

Figure 3.2.   **The Set Up Category dialog box**

7. Select Record Check to record the check.

Quicken updates the bank account balance, scrolls the completed check form off the window, and then displays another blank Write Checks window. Quicken also tells you the total value of the checks you have to print on the Checks to Print line. And if you've set your display properties to a resolution higher than 640 x 480, Quicken even displays a Checks to Print box that lists the important information about each check. You can enter another check in the Write Checks window by repeating the steps described above. Figure 3.3 shows a $285 check written to James D. Hughes, Attorney, to pay a legal bill. The check is categorized as Legal. (A little later in the chapter I'll show what this check looks like when it's printed.)

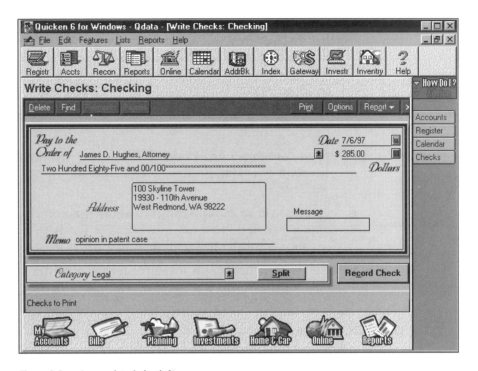

Figure 3.3. **A completed check form**

Some Helpful Hints on Check Writing

Quicken simplifies the process of filling out the Write Checks document window. Here are several tips that make the whole process even easier.

When you click on the Record Check command button or press Enter to signal to Quicken you're finished describing a check, Quicken actually records the check into your register. So don't be concerned if you later flip to the Register window and see the check there.

If you do flip to the register, you'll notice that the Num text box for the check shows Print. This is what identifies the check as one Quicken will later print. In fact, you can enter checks you want to print directly into the register by typing **Print** in the text box. You can't, however, record a payee address into the register, so you probably won't ever want to use the directly into the register approach.

Another thing to note is that Quicken provides almost all of the same helpful features and capabilities for the Write Checks document window that it does for the Register document window, as described in Chapter 2. Here are the most important features of the Write Checks window:

▶ QuickFill is available, and you can use it to help enter payee names and category names.

▶ Split categories are available. You can display the Splits dialog box simply by clicking on the Splits command button in the Write Checks window.

▶ Checks you write for deposit to another account can be recorded as account transfers. Just choose Transfer funds to... and the name of the account from the Category combo box.

▶ Edit menu commands available for the Register window are also available for the Write Checks window. (See Chapter 2.)

Printing Your Checks

Once you've entered the checks you want to print, you're ready to print some or even all of them. Printing checks on an impact printer works in roughly the same way as printing checks on a laser or ink-jet printer. The only difference is that some of the dialog boxes look slightly different. The steps below are written for a laser or ink-jet printer:

1. Load the preprinted check forms into your printer. If you use a laser printer, for example, remove the paper tray and place the appropriate number of check form sheets there. If you use an impact printer with tractor feed, unload the paper you currently have loaded and replace this paper with your check forms.

2. Choose the File ➤ Print Checks command to display the Select Checks to Print dialog box shown in Figure 3.4. (The Print button on the Write Checks window also displays the Select Checks to Print dialog box.)

TIP The Select Checks to Print dialog box title also names the bank account on which the checks will be written. In Figure 3.4, the bank account is checking. It's a good idea to confirm this information.

*Figure 3.4.   **The Select Checks to Print: Checking dialog box***

3. Give the number of the first check form: Move the selection cursor to the First Check Number text box. Then enter the number preprinted on the first check form you'll print. This is important! You want to make sure the way Quicken numbers your checks is the same way the bank numbers them on your bank statement.

4. Use the Print option button set to indicate which checks you want to print:

   • **Print all checks.** Mark the All Checks button to tell Quicken you want to print all the checks you entered.

   • **Print checks through a date.** Mark the Checks Dated Through button to print checks only through a specified date. Specify this date using the text box that appears to the right of the option button.

   • **Print some checks.** Mark the Selected Checks button if you want to print some but not all of the checks you entered. Then click on the Choose command button. Quicken displays the dialog box shown in Figure 3.5, which lists all the checks Quicken can print. Initially, all the checks are marked with a check mark, meaning Quicken thinks it should print them. To indicate you don't want to print a check, highlight the check with the mouse or the arrow keys. Then press the spacebar or single-click on the check. Quicken changes the check's print status. When you've "unmarked" each of the checks you don't want to print, select Done to return to the dialog box shown in Figure 3.4.

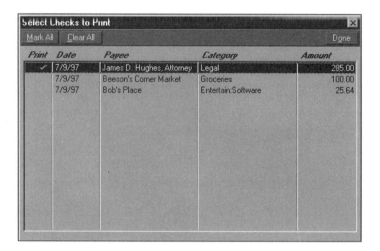

Figure 3.5. **Quicken lists the checks to print.**

 NOTE Pressing the spacebar and double-clicking the mouse both toggle the selected check's status between Print (indicated with a check mark) and Don't Print (indicated with a blank). If you make a mistake and want to start over, click on the Mark All command button to mark the status of all the checks as Print. (If all the print statuses are Print, clicking on the Mark All button changes the print statuses to blank.)

5. Tell Quicken which check form style you'll use: Activate the Check Style drop-down–list box. Then choose the check style—the one you ordered and will print on—from the list Quicken displays. If you ordered regular laser printer checks, for example, choose the Standard check style.

6. Click on the appropriate Checks on First Page button to indicate how many check forms appear on the first page of the laser check forms you loaded into your printer.

   If there's only one check form per page, only the One button will be enabled. It will be the default—and only possible—choice. If you're using tractor forms on your printer, the Checks on First Page buttons in the Print Checks dialog box will be grayed out (unavailable).

7. *If you're printing on a laser printer and want a copy of the check forms you print,* enter the number of copies you want in the Additional Copies text box. (This text box is not available when you're using an impact

printer because on an impact printer you can produce multiple copies using multipart check forms.)

8. Select the OK button, and Quicken prints the checks and displays a message asking if the checks printed correctly, as shown in Figure 3.6.

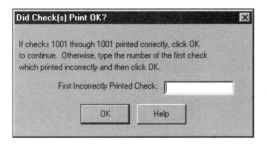

Figure 3.6.   The Did Check(s) Print OK? message box

9. If the checks printed correctly, select OK. If they didn't, enter the check number of the first check that printed incorrectly in the text box provided in the Did Checks Print OK? message box. (This might happen, for instance, if the forms were misaligned or jammed in your printer.) Doing so and clicking on OK causes Quicken to redisplay the Print Checks dialog box. Then you repeat steps 2 through 8 to reprint the checks correctly. Figure 3.7 shows an example check form using the same data shown in Figure 3.3.

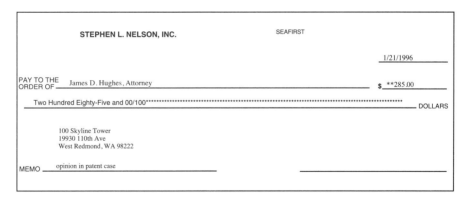

Figure 3.7.   A sample check using the same data shown in Figure 3.3

Check-Printing Problems

One common problem you can have with check printing is misaligned forms. It may be that the printed information appears a character or two too far to the left, too high, or too low.

To correct check alignment problems, choose the File ➤ Printer Setup ➤ For Printing Checks command. When Quicken displays the Check Printer Setup dialog box, shown in Figure 3.8, select the Align command. Quicken displays the Align Checks dialog box, as shown in Figure 3.9. Use the Checks on page buttons—Full Page of Checks, Two Checks on Page, and One Check on Page—to tell Quicken how many checks you're printing per page. This is the first, and most basic, thing you need to check. If Quicken thinks it can print three checks on a page that has only two check forms, it's a sure recipe for printer-alignment troubles.

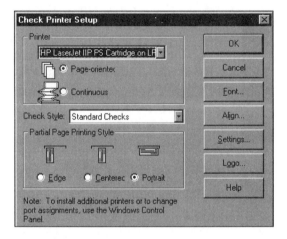

Figure 3.8.   **The Check Printer Setup dialog box**

When you click on one of the Checks on Page buttons on the Check Printer Alignment dialog box, Quicken displays the Fine Alignment dialog box shown in Figure 3.10. To correct the actual forms alignment you can use either the Vertical and Horizontal text boxes or the mouse. I think using a mouse is the easiest way. You simply click on the buttons to the right of the Vertical and Horizontal text boxes to move the check data to its correct position. Is the text printing a bit too high? Click on the button with the down-arrow. Too far to the left? Click on the button with the right-arrow.

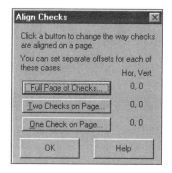

Figure 3.9. **The Align Checks dialog box**

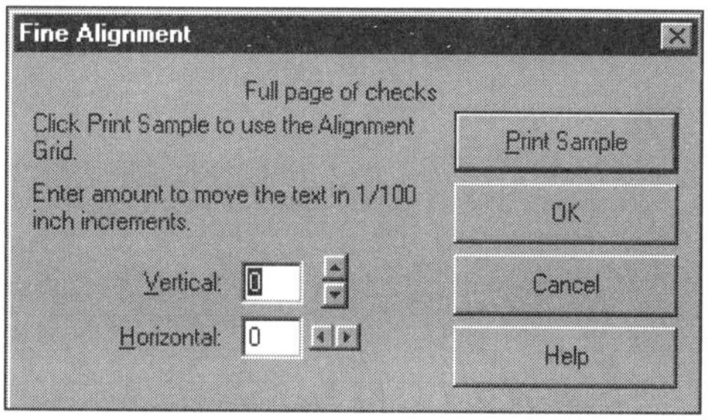

Figure 3.10. **The Fine Alignment dialog box**

If you're really having troubles and don't mind using up a few check forms, you can try printing another sample check form. A cheaper way is to print samples on plain paper, then hold them over the real checks to check the alignment.

You can check the alignment by clicking on the Print Sample button (in the Fine Alignment dialog box). Quicken prints a sample check that fills up each of the fields on a check form. You can use this check to make sure Quicken is printing the right information in the right places.

A more precise (but more cumbersome) way to change the alignment is to enter the correct horizontal and vertical alignment values for your printer in the Horizontal and Vertical text boxes.

Enter values in hundredths of an inch. Positive values move the text right or up. Conversely, preceding the number with a minus sign moves the text down or to the left. When your alignment is satisfactory, click on OK to save the setup.

CHAPTER 4

Tracking Your Finances with Reports

FEATURING

Summarizing data in simple reports

Printing a report

Customizing reports

Memorizing reports and using them again

USING the information you collect using the Quicken Register and Write Checks document windows, Quicken creates a database that describes your personal or business financial affairs. Although you don't ever have to "do anything" with this financial database, Quicken's powerful reporting and charting features let you review, summarize, and organize it in ways that almost surely will provide valuable and interesting insights.

This chapter shows you how to produce and use Quicken reports and how to customize these reports so that they more closely fit your needs. There's only one prerequisite to using Quicken's reporting and charting features: entering transactions into its registers. If you've done this, you're ready to begin producing reports and charts.

 NOTE Chapter 8 explains how you produce charts that can show you things reports never will.

Quicken's Simple Reports

Quicken provides a couple of simple-to-use reports that new users will want to make immediate use of: Snapshots and Easy Answer Reports. I will describe these reports first.

QuickReports for Summarizing Register Information

QuickReports summarize information in a register. The easiest way to illustrate how they work is with an example. Suppose for the sake of illustration that you're reviewing the checks you've received from various merchants. You see a large deposit from The Meteor Group, then another, and then you wonder how much money you've received from The Meteor Group over the year.

To answer this question with a QuickReport, select a transaction where the payee is The Meteor Group, and then select the Report button at the top of the Account Register document window. Quicken displays a menu with commands corresponding to the various QuickReport options available for the selected transaction. (One option will be Payments received from The Meteor Group.) When you select one of the QuickReport options, Quicken produces the report. Quicken displays this report in a separate document window on your screen, as shown in Figure 4.1.

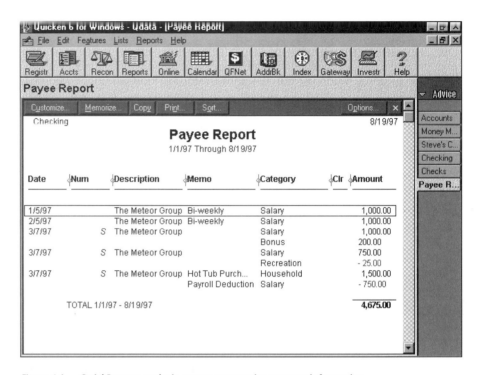

Figure 4.1.   QuickReports make it easy to summarize account information.

You can create QuickReports that summarize by payee or by category and that plot expense category information in a chart. If you want to print a report (but not a chart), you can select the Print command button, which appears at the top of the report document window. (I'll talk more about how you print reports in the next report section.) To remove the QuickReport document window from your screen, select the Close command button.

Snapshot Reports with Summary Graphs and Tables

A great report for new users is the Snapshot report. To produce a Snapshot report, choose the Reports ➤ Snapshots command. When you do, Quicken displays a one-page snapshot of your financial condition. The snapshot provides four reports or charts that summarize various aspects of your financial condition. To more clearly see one of the reports or charts, click on it and then click on the Enlarge command button. Figure 4.2 shows an enlarged snapshot of monthly expenses depicted in a pie chart. To print a snapshot report, select the Print command button.

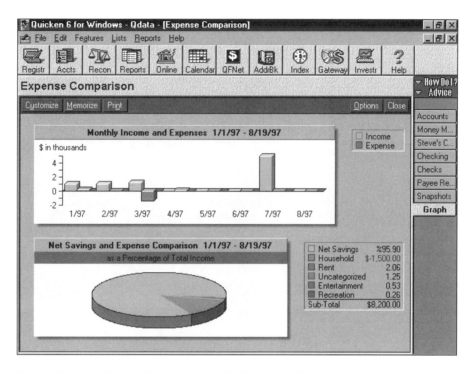

Figure 4.2.   Snapshot reports use graphs and tables to provide information about your financial condition.

If you want to change the appearance of a snapshot report, select the Customize command button. Quicken displays the Customize Snapshots dialog box, as shown in Figure 4.3.

You can use the Choose the Snapshot to Customize option buttons at the top of the dialog box to specify which snapshot component you want to change. Once you've chosen a particular component, use the Snapshot Type list box to select another report or graph by clicking on it. (If you select a graph, you can use the Snapshot Display option buttons to specify whether you want the information displayed in a chart or in a table.)

TIP You can customize the graphs that appear as individual snapshots in a snapshots report. For more information about how to customize graphs, refer to Chapter 8, *Charting Your Finances.*

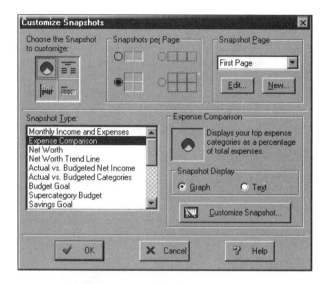

*Figure 4.3.　**Use the Customize Snapshots dialog box to change the appearance of a Snapshot report.***

You can use the Snapshots per Page option buttons to specify how many snapshots appear in a document window at a time. Initially, four snapshots appear in the document window page, but you can choose to view two, three or six snapshots per page.

If you want to add another page of snapshots, select the New command button (you'll find it below the Snapshot Page drop-down–list box). Give the new page a name. Add graphs and reports to the new snapshot page by clicking (in the Choose Snapshot to Customize area) where you want the graphs or reports to go and then clicking in the Snapshot Type list box.

If you want to print a Snapshot report, you can select the Print command button which appears at the top of the report document window. (I'll talk more about how you print reports in the next report section.) To remove the Snapshot report document window from your screen, select the Close command button.

EasyAnswer Reports for Answering Financial Questions

EasyAnswer Reports work by letting you ask a question. Quicken then selects the report that best answers your question.

To use the EasyAnswer Reports, choose the Reports ➤ EasyAnswer Reports command. Quicken displays the EasyAnswer Reports & Graphs window, as shown in Figure 4.4.

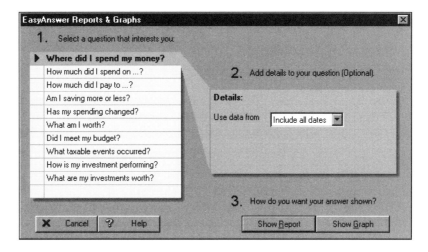

Figure 4.4.   **The EasyAnswer Reports & Graphs window**

To use an EasyAnswer Report, you click on the question you want to ask and then click on the Show Report button. When you do, Quicken produces an onscreen report that answers the question.

You can change the nature of the question by activating the Details drop-down–list box that provides key words or phrases to the question text and selecting a new key word or phrase. For example, if you want to ask the first question, "Where did I spend my money?" you can specify the last part of the question as Last Year, Last Month, and so on.

Quicken's Advanced Reports

In addition to the simple reports such as Snapshots and EasyAnswer Reports, Quicken produces dozens of what I call advanced reports. On the Reports menu, these advanced reports are grouped into four sets:

▶ Home reports, which summarize personal financial information

▶ Investment reports, which summarize investment-account information

▶ Business reports, which summarize business financial information

▶ Other reports, which summarize account information in a way you describe

These reports are summarized in Tables 4.1 through 4.3.

Home, Business, and Investment reports are preformatted to save you time. By comparison, reports categorized under the Other command provide basic unformatted starting points for creating your own customized reports, as discussed later in this chapter.

NOTE Until you start using Quicken to keep track of your investments, it won't make much sense for you to produce investment reports. Chapters 17 and 18 describe how you perform investment record keeping in Quicken.

Table 4.1.   Quicken Home Reports

Report	When You Use It
Cash Flow	To summarize the money that flows into and out of bank accounts. If you've set up cash or credit-card accounts, the money that flows into and out of these accounts is summarized by category too.
Monthly Budget	To compare your actual income and spending by category with the budget you've assigned for each income and expense category. This report summarizes income and expense categories for bank, cash, and credit-card accounts.

Table 4.1. **Quicken Home Reports (cont.)**

Report	When You Use It
Itemized Categories	To summarize all the transactions in all your accounts by income and expense category. The difference between an itemized-category report and a cash-flow report is that cash-flow reports don't include transactions from Quicken's special liability, asset, and investment account types.
Tax Summary	To summarize your taxable income and tax deductions. The difference between an itemized-category report and a tax-summary report is that the tax-summary report includes only those categories you (or Quicken) marked as tax-related.
Net Worth	To show the account balances in all your accounts. A net-worth report is unusual in that it doesn't summarize financial activity for a period of time, but rather your financial condition at a point in time. Therefore, you don't enter a range of dates when you create the report, but rather a specific date for which you want to know account balances.
Tax Schedule	To summarize your tax-related categories by input line on your personal or business federal income tax return. You don't need to be concerned with which tax return line a category gets reported on unless you're exporting data directly to a tax-preparation package.
Missing Checks	To identify checks that have not cleared. This includes transactions from all the accounts you've set up—not just your bank, cash, or credit-card accounts.
Comparison	Compares transaction totals for two time periods. For example, you can use a comparison report to compare your spending by category last month with your spending by category this month.

Table 4.2.   Quicken Business Reports

Report	When You Use It
P&L Statement	To summarize the financial activity by income and expense category. A P&L, or profit and loss, statement, shows transactions from all the accounts you've set up—not just your bank, cash, or credit-card accounts.
P&L Comparison	To summarize the financial activity by income and expense category for two periods so you can compare them
Cash Flow	To summarize the money that flows into and out of bank accounts. If you've set up cash or credit-card accounts, the money that flows into and out of these accounts is summarized by category too.
A/P by Vendor	To see the unprinted checks stored in each of the bank accounts. (A/P stands for accounts payable.)
A/R by Customer	To see the uncleared transactions in each of the asset accounts you've set up. (A/R stands for accounts receivable.)
Job/Project	To summarize your transactions from all your accounts by income and expense categories—and by classes
Payroll	To summarize all payroll-related transactions— such as when you need to prepare quarterly and annual payroll-tax reports and returns.
Balance Sheet	To show the account balances in all your accounts. (Like the nearly identical home net-worth report, a balance sheet doesn't summarize financial activity for a period of time, but rather your financial condition at a point in time. You don't enter a range of dates when you create the report, but rather a specific date for which you want to know account balances.)

Table 4.2.   **Quicken Business Reports (cont.)**

Report	When You Use It
Missing Checks	To identify checks that have not cleared. Transactions are presented in date order, with uncleared checks highlighted in red on your screen.
Comparison	To compare transaction totals for two time periods. For example, you can use a comparison report to compare your sales revenue by category last month with your sales revenue by category this month.

Table 4.3.   **Quicken Investment Reports**

Report	When You Use It
Portfolio Value	To summarize the current market value of each of the securities you hold in your investment portfolio—individual stocks, bonds, shares of mutual funds, and so on
Investment Performance	To calculate the returns on the individual securities you hold in your investment portfolio
Capital Gains	To calculate your realized capital gains and losses
Investment Income	To summarize financial transactions by income for an investment account or multiple investment accounts
Investment Transactions	To list all the transactions you've entered into an investment-account register

Report-Printing Basics

To print any report, follow these steps:

1. Choose the Home, Business, or Investment command from the Reports menu to display a list of the reports in the report group you select. (The reports Quicken displays will match those listed in Tables 4.1, 4.2, and 4.3.)

2. Choose the specific report you want to produce. For example, if you want to print a cash-flow report, choose the Cash Flow command from the Home Reports menu. No matter which report you choose, Quicken displays the Create Report window.

Figure 4.5 shows the Create Report window with the Cash Flow type selected. Other Home, Business, and Investment Report menu commands, however, display the same Create Report window. You choose the report types to view by clicking on the tabs at the top of the Create Report dialog box.

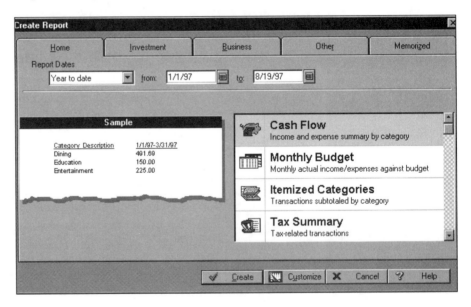

Figure 4.5. **The Create Report window**

3. Quicken assumes that reports you produce should describe financial activity from the start of the year through the current date. *If you want to describe some other period of financial activity,* click on the arrow or calendar icon at the right end of the three Report Dates combo boxes. The left-hand box opens to a series of durations such as Month to Date, Last Month, and so on. Clicking on the arrow or calendar icon on the Date combo boxes opens small calendars you can use to change to any month and select any date.

4. Click on Create to open the report.

   Quicken opens a Report window for the report you request. Figure 4.6 shows a personal cash-flow report in a new document window. This is the report Quicken produces if you choose the Cash Flow command from the Home Reports menu.

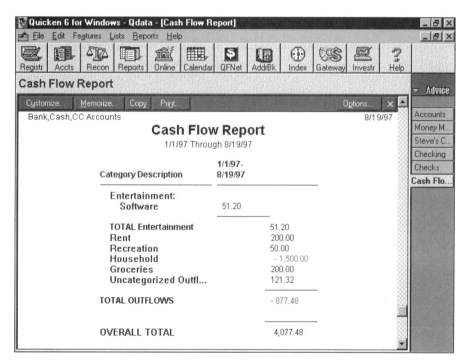

Figure 4.6.   A home Cash Flow report, summarizing data entered in Quicken's registers

5. To print a paper copy of the report displayed in the active document window, click on the Print command button in the row of command buttons at the top of the Report document window to display the Print Report dialog box:

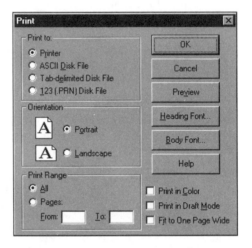

 NOTE To remove the Report document window from the Quicken application window, click on the Close command button (at the top of the Report document window).

6. Use the Print To option buttons to indicate how a report should be printed:

   • To print a report on paper (which means sending it to your printer, the most common choice), click on the Printer option button.

   • To print to exportable file formats such as ASCII and Lotus 1-2-3, choose one of the other Print to option buttons.

 TIP To preview what you are about to print, choose the Preview button, which displays a screen preview of your paper report.

 TIP If you're proficient with a spreadsheet, you can print a Quicken report as a 1-2-3 file and then import it into just about any spreadsheet program, such as 1-2-3, Excel, Quattro Pro, Works, and so on. You might want to do this to tap a spreadsheet's more powerful and more flexible modeling tools.

7. Use the Orientation option buttons to specify how Quicken should print the report on the page: Portrait or Landscape.

8. *If you want to print only a page or range of pages of the report,* mark the Pages option button. Then use the From and To text boxes to specify the page range.

9. *If you are using a color printer,* check the Print in Color box to see your financial red ink in printed red ink or to see other color effects similar to those you see onscreen.

10. *If you want to accelerate printing speed when print quality isn't important,* click on the Print in Draft Mode check box.

11. *If you want Quicken to fit the report's information across the width of a single page,* mark the Fit to One Page Wide check box.

12. Select OK when the Print Report dialog box is complete.

    If you're printing to a printer, Quicken sends the report to Windows 95. It does the actual work of printing the report. If you indicate that you want to print an ASCII file or a 1-2-3 file, Quicken displays the Create Disk File dialog box:

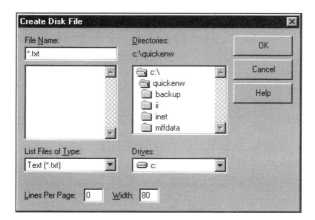

13. *If you're printing to disk,* use the Create Disk File dialog box to indicate the path and filename for the disk file. For example, to create a file named REPORT.TXT in the Quicken directory on your C hard drive, enter the full path name, C:\QUICKENW\REPORT.TXT, in the File Name text box.

ZOOMING IN ON A REPORT

Quicken provides QuickZoom, a handy feature that you can use in any Report window. Here's how it works: Say you've got a question about a figure that appears on a report. You simply point to the figure with the mouse. (Quicken changes the mouse pointer to a magnifying glass with a Z where the magnifying glass lens should be.) Then you double-click the mouse. Quicken prepares a list of the individual transactions that, collectively, make up the figure on which you've clicked. This list gets displayed in its own Report document window. (If you wish to look at a transaction underlying the report, you can double-click again to be taken to that specific transaction in the register.) QuickZoom, then, means you never need to wonder why some expense category is so high or what income transactions go into a sales figure—a double-click of the mouse produces a report that answers the question. Figure 4.7 shows a QuickZoom report created by double-clicking on the Groceries total in Figure 4.6.

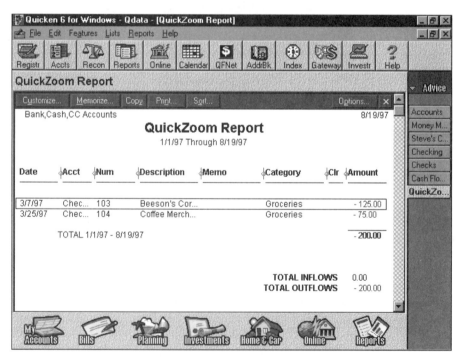

Figure 4.7.   A QuickZoom report shows the individual transactions that go together to explain a summary figure on a report.

NOTE See Chapters 17, 18, and 19 for more information on investment record keeping in Quicken.

Changing the Way Your Reports Are Printed

Quicken lets you have it your way when it comes to printing your reports: you choose the font, font style, and font size. To make this change, you click on the Heading Font or Body Font command buttons on the Print dialog box. When you do, Quicken displays the dialog box shown in Figure 4.8 (if you click on the Heading Font command button) or a similar dialog box (if you click on the Body Font command button).

Figure 4.8. **The Report/List Header Font dialog box**

Use the Font box and list box to select a *font*, or typeface. Use the Font Style box or list box to add boldface or italics to the report header. Use the Size box or list box to select a point size (one point equals 1/72 of an inch). You can see the effect of your font, font style, and point size changes by examining the Sample box.

Describing Your Report Preferences

To customize a report, you change the report preferences settings: Choose the Edit ➤ Options ➤ Reports command. When Quicken displays the Report Options dialog box, shown in Figure 4.9, make the changes you want.

For example, use the Account Display option buttons to indicate whether you want Quicken to display the account name, a description, or both. (This preference setting has no effect when you've chosen to display all accounts or just selected accounts. In this case, Quicken uses the description All Accounts or Selected Accounts.)

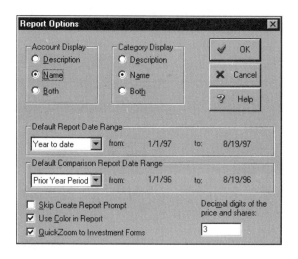

Figure 4.9. **The Report Options dialog box**

Use the Category Display option buttons to indicate whether, when Quicken summarizes by categories, it should use the 15-character category name, the 20-character category description, or both the name and the description. (When a category doesn't have a description, Quicken uses the category name regardless of what the Category Display option buttons show.)

Use the Default Report Date Range and Default Comparison Report Date Range text boxes to tell Quicken what it should suggest as the range of dates covered in the report.

Mark the Skip Create Report Prompt check box if the default settings on the Create Report window are what you want. If you don't mark the check box, Quicken displays the Create Report window, which you can use to customize the report Quicken produces.

Mark the QuickZoom to Investment Forms check box to jump from a specific investment transaction to an investment form for that transaction.

Mark the Use Color in Report check box if you want Quicken to use color in the Report document windows. (Of course, this box setting doesn't affect the color Quicken uses for reports it prints on a black-and-white printer.)

Creating Custom Reports

The standard Home, Business, and Investment reports provided by Quicken almost always provide you with the information you need. But you aren't limited to viewing the information in your financial database—the transactions you've collected in the Quicken registers—using these standard reports. You can customize any of them, or you can use the basic reports stored in the Other category. You can change the contents of your report while creating it or while it is displayed on your screen.

Before you begin customizing a report, it's helpful if you understand that all Quicken reports are derived from one of five basic reports:

Report Type	What It Does
Transaction	Lists register transactions
Summary	Summarizes register transactions
Comparison	Shows two sets of summary numbers, such as last year's category totals and this year's category totals, as well as the difference between the two sets
Budget	Shows actual category totals, budgeted category totals, and the difference between the two
Account Balances	Shows account balance information

These are the types you'll find listed if you select the tab called Other in the Create Report window. As the foundation upon which all the other preformatted reports are built, these reports are useful prototypes for customization. Understanding the five Other report types also gives you a good idea of just what's possible in the way of report customization.

Although customizing reports in Quicken isn't difficult, you may want to postpone it until you're comfortable entering transactions into registers. Most of what you do when you customize a report is simply describe how you want register information organized and summarized. The more familiar you are with the information that goes into a register, the easier it is to customize.

Customization is similar for all types, so I'll describe the general procedures and then comment on the items that vary by report type. The action begins from the Create Report window, which you open by choosing the command for the type of report you want to customize. The Create Report window for any report type includes a Customize button—and, yes, that's a picture of a power drill on it.

Click on the Customize button to open the customization windows. Figure 4.10 shows the window for customizing a summary report; similar to the other report-customization windows. By clicking on the dialog box tabs—Display, Accounts, Include, and Advanced—you get boxes and option buttons for customizing the reports in various ways. In the following sections, I'll explain the customization options (by tab) for each major type of report.

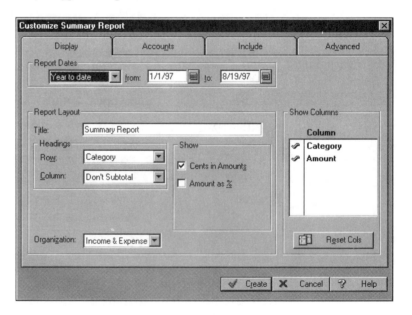

Figure 4.10.   **The Customize Summary Report window**

Customizing a Summary Report

Customizing a Summary report is like customizing any other report type, once you select the Summary report type. To begin customization, choose the Reports ➤ Other ➤ Summary command. Click on the Customize command button to open a Customize Summary Report window.

Changing Summary-Report Display Settings

The Report Dates boxes let you specify the range of dates that the report covers. You can specify a date range either by inputting a starting and ending date in the From and To boxes, or by selecting a report duration from the Report Dates drop-down–list box, as shown below:

The display settings let you change the report name, select headings for rows and columns, and reorganize the summary structure of your report.

You use the Title text box to replace the generic report title with a more specific description by highlighting the text box and entering the desired report title or description.

In the Headings box, the Row drop-down–list box offers choices to create a row for each category, class, payee, or account. The Column drop-down–list box provides a Don't Subtotal entry, a series of time-related subtotaling entries (a week, two weeks, half a month, and so on), and the Category, Class, Payee, and Account column subtotaling options.

The Show box contains two check boxes. The Cents in Amounts box, if checked, displays amounts in dollars and cents. If unchecked, the amounts are shown rounded to the nearest dollar. The Amount as % check box, if checked, also shows amounts as percentages of the total. Leaving the box unchecked shows amounts as dollars and cents.

Use the Organization drop-down–list box to tell Quicken how it should arrange the report's information: by income and expense or on a cash flow basis. Select Income & Expense if you want to organize the report into three parts: income-category summaries, expense-category summaries, and account-transfer summaries. Select Cash Flow Basis if you want to organize the report into two parts, cash inflows and cash outflows. Select Supercategory if you want to group and total report information by supercategories.

Changing Summary-Report Account Settings

Clicking on the Accounts tab displays options for specifying which accounts' transactions should be included in the report. The Accounts tab of the Customize Summary Report dialog box is shown in Figure 4.11. Summary reports preselect the current account. If you want to change the account selection, follow these steps:

1. Click on the Account Type button for the kind of account you want. Add other types if you want by clicking on them.

2. Click on the Mark All button to put a check mark next to all listed accounts, or click on individual account names to deselect or reselect them until you have the selection you want.

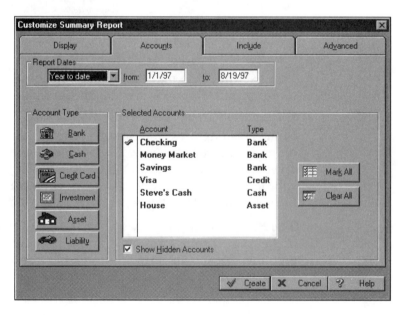

Figure 4.11.   The Account settings let you choose which accounts to include in a report.

Changing Summary-Report Include Settings

The Include settings let you filter the transactions in a register so that only those meeting certain criteria appear in the report. The Include tab of the Customize Summary Report dialog box is shown in Figure 4.12. You filter transactions in this way when, for example, you're looking for a specific transaction (such as grocery checks for more than $50), want to build a report that includes only a subset of the information in a regular summary report (perhaps just your housing and household expenses), or want to slice your data in a way that's slightly different from what your existing categories and classes allow (you want to see what you're spending on groceries at Beeson's Corner Market).

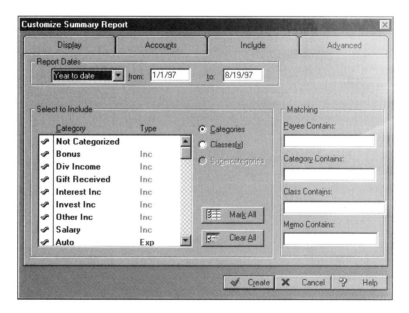

Figure 4.12.   **The Include tab of the Customize Summary Report dialog box**

NOTE If you're confused by this "class" business, don't worry—you haven't missed something. Classes are another tool you can use to summarize financial information. I'll describe how to use classes to track individual real estate investments in Chapter 19.

The list in the Select to Include box initially includes all categories as well as a Not Categorized category. Clicking on a category alternately selects or deselects it. Clicking on the Mark All button selects all categories. Clicking on the Clear All button deselects all categories.

Click on the Classes button to display defined classes in the list. Classes are selected and deselected the same way categories are.

You can also limit, or *filter,* the information included in a summary report. For example, you might want to see a report that includes only checks categorized as Entertainment. To limit the information in a summary report, use the Matching boxes: Payee Contains, Category Contains, Class Contains, and Memo Contains.

To use the Matching boxes, follow these steps:

1. Enter the name of the payee whose transactions you want to show. For example, to include only those transactions with the payee name Armstrong Commons, type **Armstrong Commons** into the Payee Contains text box.

MATCH CHARACTERS FOR INCLUDING OR EXCLUDING PAYEES

To include payee names that start with the word Armstrong, type **Armstrong..** . To include payee names that end with the word Armstrong, type **..Armstrong**. To include payee names that just use the word Armstrong, type **=Armstrong**. To exclude payee names that show or use Armstrong, you use the tilde (~). For example, to exclude payee names that start with Armstrong, type **~Armstrong**. These tricks—using two periods and the tilde, which Quicken calls match characters—work for the Payee Contains, Memo Contains, Category Contains, and Class Contains drop-down boxes.

2. Enter the category you want included transactions to show. For example, to include only those transactions with the category Salary, type **Salary** in the Category Contains text box.

3. Enter the class you want the included transactions to show. For example, to include only those transactions with the class Marlborough, type **Marlborough** into the Class Contains text box or select it from the QuickFill list of classes.

4. Enter the memo description you want the included transactions to show. For example, to include only those transactions with the memo description Payroll, type **Payroll** into the Memo Contains drop-down box.

Changing Summary-Report Advanced Settings

In addition to the Display, Accounts, and Include settings, Quicken also provides an eclectic set of additional customization options. These options allow you to further filter the transactions appearing on the report by choosing transactions by amount or type. The Advanced tab of the Customize Summary Report dialog box is shown in Figure 4.13.

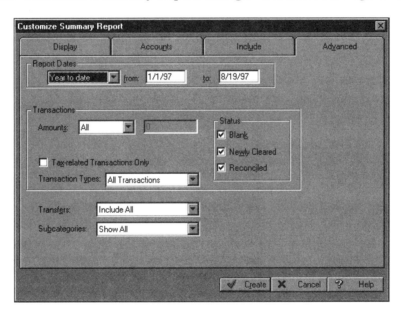

Figure 4.13. **The Advanced tab of the Customize Summary Report dialog box**

The Amounts drop-down list lets you include all transactions or only those less than, equal to, or greater than the number you enter in the adjacent text box.

The Include Unrealized Gains check box, if checked, adds income rows to your report to document the impact of the increase or decrease in security prices. If you leave the box unchecked, unrealized security gains are not shown. (This checkbox only appears if you've set up an investment account.)

The Tax-related Transactions Only check box, if checked, shows only transactions you have assigned to tax-related categories in Quicken's category lists. Leaving it unchecked shows all transactions.

The Transaction Types drop-down–list lets you choose to include all transactions or to show only payments, deposits, or unprinted checks in your report.

The Status check boxes allow you to prepare a summary report that focuses on blank, newly cleared, or reconciled checks. Normally, to show all items in your reports you leave all three boxes checked (their default state). Selectively unchecking the boxes produces specialized reports focusing on only the checked type of item.

The Transfers drop-down–list lets you include all or exclude all transfer transactions from the report. You can also choose Exclude Internal to hide transfers between accounts included in the report.

The Subcategories drop-down–list shows all subcategories when Show All is selected. You can also choose Hide All to not display subcategories or Show Reversed to group categories under subcategories, which has the effect of grouping subcategories that are normally separated under different categories.

Customizing a Transaction Report

Like the Summary report, the Transaction report has a variety of customization options.

To begin customization, choose Reports ➤ Other ➤ Transaction. In the Create Report window, click on the Customize command button to open a Customize Transaction Report window.

Changing Transaction-Report Display Settings

The Transaction Reports Display tab works the same basic way as the Summary Report Display tab. You can change the report name, select headings for rows and columns, and reorganize the summary structure of your report.

In the Title text box, replace the generic report title with a more specific description: highlight the text box and enter the desired report title or description.

In the Headings box, the Subtotal By drop-down–list defines an additional column for a variety of time periods or the Category, Class, Payee, Account, and Tax Schedule categories. A Don't Subtotal entry creates only a single column.

The Sort By drop-down list contains six options:

Option	What It Does
None	Sorts by account type, account name, and date
Date/Acct	Sorts by date and then by account type and account name
Acct/Chk#	Orders entries by account type and then by check number
Amount	Sorts from the smallest to the largest amount
Payee	Sorts alphabetically by payee
Category	Sorts alphabetically by category

In the Organization drop-down–list box, tell Quicken how to arrange the report's information: by income and expense or on a cash-flow basis. Select Income & Expense if you want to organize the report into three parts: income category summaries, expense category summaries, and account transfer summaries. Select Cash Flow Basis if you want to organize the report into two parts: cash inflows and cash outflows.

The Show box contains three check boxes:

Check Box	What It Does
Cents in Amounts	Displays amounts in dollars and cents. If unchecked, the amounts are shown rounded to the nearest dollar.
Totals Only	Shows only the total amount of the transactions meeting the other report criteria
Split Transaction Detail	Includes detail from split transactions

Changing Other Transaction-Report Settings

With the exception of the layout settings noted in the previous section, the procedures and options for customizing a transaction report are similar to the procedures described for customizing a summary report. Refer to the summary report sections earlier in this chapter that discuss the Accounts, Include, and Advanced customization options.

Customizing Other Reports

There are three other types of basic reports whose customization needs to be touched on: Comparison, Budget, and Account Balances. If you've reviewed the options described in the preceding analysis of customizing a summary report, you will have no surprises as you approach these three. They're all somewhat simpler than either the Summary or Transaction report; in many cases, you have fewer options to deal with.

There are one or two wrinkles, though. The Comparison report has Difference As % and Difference In $ check boxes in its Display tab. Checking these boxes generates columns that show the percentage and dollar differences between the categories chosen for the report.

The Account Balances report has a setting called Interval, which creates a column with totals for the time period you select from a drop-down–list. The Account Balances report also has two different choices in the Organization layout area. You can choose Net Worth to print your net worth as the last item on the report. Choose Balance Sheet to print net worth as a liability with total liabilities and equity following.

Memorizing the Custom Reports You Create

You can go to quite a bit of effort to create customized reports that summarize the information you've collected in the Quicken registers. Sometimes, of course, you'll be creating a customized report for one-time use. But when you end up creating a customized report you'll want to repeatedly use, you'll want to *memorize* the customization settings, filters, and options. This means that when you want to produce the report, you can reuse the memorized report.

Memorizing Custom Reports

Memorizing a report is simple. After you've generated the report, select the Memorize command button, which appears in the command button row at the top of every Report document window. Quicken displays the Memorize Report dialog box shown in Figure 4.14.

Figure 4.14. **The Memorize Report dialog box**

Enter a name for the report to be memorized in the Title text box. Then use the Report Dates option buttons to indicate whether you want to use the textual description of the report date range (the Named Range [Year to Date] option button)—in Figure 4.14 from January 1 of the current year to April 13 of the current year—or the actual fixed date (the Custom option button)—in Figure 4.15, from January 1, 1997, to April 13, 1997. Or click on None to use the default report date ranges. (You can specify and change this range using the Edit ➤ Options ➤ Reports command, as described earlier in this chapter.)

Optionally, use the Description box to provide additional information about the report—such as why you've created the memorized report or when it should be used.

The Icon option lets you assign an icon to the memorized report. This icon will appear next to the report name and description on the window from which you select the report. (I talk next about selecting a memorized report.)

Using a Previously Memorized Report

Once you memorize a report, you can produce a new copy of the memorized report any time by selecting it from the Memorized Reports menu. To display this menu, choose the Reports ➤ Other ➤ Memorized Reports command. Figure 4.15 shows what the Memorized Reports tab of the Create Report window looks like if you've created a single memorized report named Special Cash Flow Report.

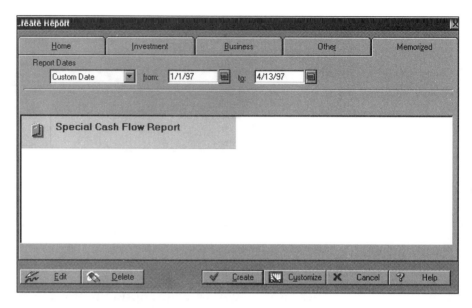

Figure 4.15.   **The Memorized tab of the Create Report window**

Printing a report that appears on the Memorized Reports menu works just like printing a report that appears on the Home, Business, or Investments Report menu.

Rules for Retaining Documents

You've probably wondered how long you should keep your canceled checks and how long it makes sense to hang onto old tax returns. Now that you have Quicken producing all these handy reports, see Table 4.4 for some guidelines useful for determining how long you should hold onto these things. This table summarizes the usual document-retention rules for Quicken reports—and for several other business documents and forms as well. These rules are based on conservative applications of the relevant statutory and regulatory requirements, as well as statutes of limitations.

Table 4.4. **Document Retention Rules and Guidelines**

Document or Form	Years Retained
Asset purchase records (including investment registers)	Seven years after asset is sold or disposed of
Backup Files	One year
Checks, canceled	Permanently
Check registers	Permanently
Monthly home tax summaries and schedules	Three years
Yearly home tax summaries and schedules	Seven years after filing a return based on report
Other home reports (including investment reports)	One year
Monthly business P&L and tax reports	Three years
Yearly business P&L and tax reports	Seven years
Other business reports	One year

CHAPTER 5

Balancing Bank Accounts

FEATURING

Understanding the Reconciliation screen

Balancing an account with a bank statement

Troubleshooting accounts that won't balance

Printing a reconciliation report

FROM time to time you'll need to balance the bank accounts you track with Quicken. Balancing explains the difference between what your records say you have in a bank account and what the bank says you have in a bank account. By regularly balancing bank accounts, you catch both the errors you've made and the errors the bank has made, and you can thereby ensure the accuracy of your financial record keeping.

There's no magic in this, of course. All Quicken does is automate and expedite the balancing you would (or should) normally do by hand. With Quicken, balancing a bank account takes only minutes.

Before You Start

To balance a bank account with Quicken, you need your most recent bank statements. In addition, you must have

▶ Tracked the bank account's activity—your payments and deposits—with Quicken.

▶ Provided an accurate starting balance for the bank account when you originally set it up.

> NOTE If you didn't provide an accurate starting balance when you originally set up the bank account, all is not lost. You can still balance your account. Later in the chapter, I explain how.

Understanding the Reconciliation Process

Balancing a bank account has a very simple premise: the difference between what your records show as an account balance and what the bank's records show as an account balance should equal the sum of your uncleared payments and deposits.

Let's set up a simple example to show how the reconciliation process works. Suppose your records of a bank account show the account balance as $50 and the bank's records show the account balance as $95. Furthermore, suppose your records show a $50 check that you've written but that has not yet cleared the bank, and suppose the bank's records show a $5 monthly service charge that you haven't yet recorded into the Quicken register.

Clearly, the $50 balance in your register doesn't equal the $95 balance shown on the bank account statement. But this will almost always be the case. The real question is whether the difference between the two balances can be explained. If the difference can be explained, the account balances. If the difference can't be explained, the account doesn't balance.

Determining whether an account balances requires four simple steps:

1. Record any transactions shown on the bank statement that should be but aren't shown in your register. For example, if the bank statement shows a $5 monthly service charge, you'll need to record this payment in your register. In the simple example we're using, recording this transaction adjusts the balance shown in your records to $45 because $50 minus $5 equals $45.

> **NOTE** Your bank statement may show other transactions that your records don't: payments for bank services, credit card fees, and deposits for things like monthly interest income. Your bank statement may also show transactions that you initiated but forgot to record, such as cash machine withdrawals.

2. Add up the uncleared transactions. (Subtract the total of the uncleared deposits from the total of the uncleared checks.) In our example, there's just one uncleared transaction—the $50 check—so the sum of the uncleared transactions is $50.

> **NOTE** In a more typical case, you might have recorded numerous checks that the bank hasn't recorded, or there might be deposits that you've recorded but that the bank hasn't.

3. Determine the difference between what your records show as the account balance and what the bank's records show as the account balance. In the example, your records now show $45 as the account balance. The bank's records show $95, so there's a $50 difference between your records and the bank's records.

4. Verify that the uncleared transactions total (calculated in step 2) equals the difference between your records and the bank's records (calculated in step 3). In our example, we know that $50 equals $50; so we've now explained the difference between your record and the bank's records.

WHEN AN ACCOUNT WON'T BALANCE

Sometimes, of course, an account won't balance. Although an account that doesn't balance can be perplexing and even infuriating, the basic reasons for imbalance are always straightforward:

▶ The bank's balance is wrong because its starting balance is wrong or because one or more transactions are wrong or missing.

▶ Your account balance is wrong for one of the same reasons.

▶ The uncleared transaction total is incorrect.

In my experience, it's unlikely that the bank's balance is wrong or that the bank missed or incorrectly recorded a transaction. Whatever else may be true about banks, they generally do a very good job of financial record keeping.

So when there's a problem with a bank account, it usually stems from one of two situations: either you've come up with an incorrect uncleared transaction total, or your records' account balance is wrong. To get the account to balance, you need to find the error in your records or the error in the uncleared transaction total.

A little later in the chapter, I'll describe tricks for finding errors in your record keeping. For now though, let's discuss how to reconcile bank statements using Quicken.

Balancing an Account in Quicken

To balance a bank account in Quicken, display the bank account in the active document window. Usually, the active document window is the Register window (shown in Figure 5.1), but it could also be the Write Checks window.

As discussed earlier, be sure the bank statement doesn't show any payments or deposits that you need to record in the register. The only bank account transactions you don't need to record are the monthly service charge and the interest income—Quicken lets you record these as part of reconciling the account. Any other new transactions the bank account statement shows need to be recorded.

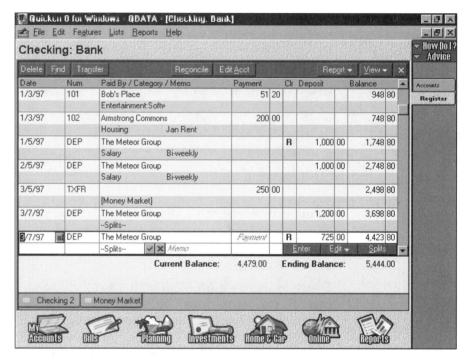

Figure 5.1.   Getting ready to balance a bank account

CRIME-STOPPER'S TEXTBOOK: CATCHING FORGERS

When you reconcile your bank accounts, review the canceled checks to be sure that they haven't been altered and that whoever was supposed to sign the check really did sign. Fraudulently altering or marking a document (such as a check form) to change another person's liability constitues forgery, and reviewing canceled checks may be the only way you'll catch a forger.

As long as you immediately report forgery to the bank, you probably won't suffer any losses. This may not be true, however, if you've been careless (Did you leave a checkbook on the dashboard of your car and leave your car's windows open? Did you hire someone whom you knew to be a convicted check-forging felon?) or if you delay reviewing the canceled checks or reporting forgery to the bank.

Long after I began telling people to review their canceled checks, a new employee of mine stole a sheet of blank checks and wrote himself extra weekly payroll checks. I caught him when I reviewed my canceled checks and realized that he had forged my signature.

Once you've entered the missing transactions shown on the statement, follow these steps:

1. Click on the Recon button to display the Reconcile Bank Statement dialog box. Figure 5.2. shows the Reconcile Bank Statement: Checking dialog box—in my example I'm balancing a checking account.

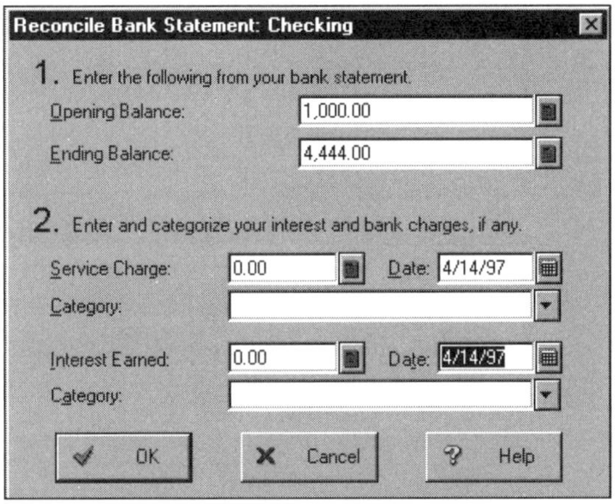

Figure 5.2. **The Reconcile Bank Statement: Checking dialog box, showing an opening balance of $1000**

2. Verify that the amount shown in the Opening Balance text box is the starting bank-account balance on your bank statement. If it isn't, correct it.

   The first time you reconcile an account, Quicken uses your starting account balance. The subsequent times you reconcile an account, Quicken uses the Ending Balance from the previous reconciliation.

3. Enter the ending bank account balance from your bank statement in the Ending Balance text box; simply place the cursor in the text box and type the figure.

4. In the Service Charge box, enter the monthly service charge shown on the bank statement if you haven't done so already.

5. In the Service Charge Date box, tell Quicken when the service charge occurred.

6. In the Category box, categorize the service charge. (If you don't remember which category you want to use, click on the arrow at the

right of the box and then select the category you want from the drop-down list.)

7. In the Interest Earned box, enter the monthly interest income shown on the bank statement if you haven't done so already.

8. In the Interest Earned Date box, enter the date the bank added the interest to your account.

9. In the Category box, enter the appropriate category (or click on the arrow at the right of the box and select the category you want from the drop-down list).

10. Click on OK when you've described the bank statement information using the Reconcile Bank Statement. You'll see a Reconcile Bank Statement window, like the one shown shown in Figure 5.3.

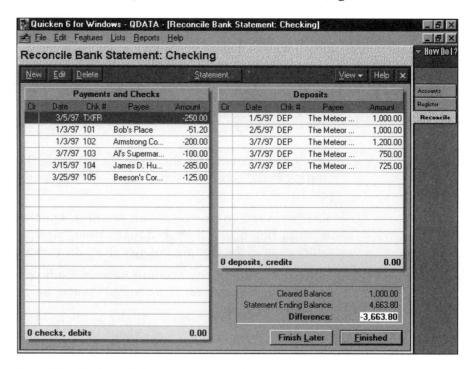

Figure 5.3. **The Reconcile Bank Statement: Checking window**

NOTE If you have a question about a transaction shown in the Reconcile Bank Statement window, select the transaction either by using the arrow keys or by clicking the mouse. Then select the Edit command button. (It's the second button from the left.) Quicken displays the bank account's register in its document window, with the cursor in the transaction. You can examine the transaction in more detail—including the split transaction lines. When you're ready to return to the Reconcile Bank Account dialog box, click on the Reconcile QuickTab.

11. Review the list of transactions shown in the Reconcile Bank Statement window and mark each transaction that has cleared by highlighting it. Quicken places a check mark next to it. (If you accidentally mark a transaction as cleared when it shouldn't be, click on it with the mouse or press the spacebar.)

 TIP To rearrange the entries in the reconciliation lists by date rather than by check number, choose View ➤ Sort by Date. To put them back in check number order, choose View ➤ Sort by Check Number.

12. Select Finished when the difference between the cleared balance and the bank statement balance is zero. Figure 5.4 shows how the Reconciliation window should look when you've successfully reconciled an account.

 TIP If you made a mistake entering your ending bank account balance, you can return to the Reconcile Bank Statement dialog box shown in Figure 5.2 by selecting the Statement button. The Statement button appears in the center at the top of the Reconcile Bank Statement window shown in Figure 5.3.

As you indicate which transactions have cleared, Quicken continually calculates a Cleared Balance figure at the bottom of the screen. The Cleared Balance is just your records' bank account balance minus all the uncleared transactions. When this Cleared Balance equals the bank statement balance, your account balances because the uncleared transactions total explains the difference between your records and the bank's records.

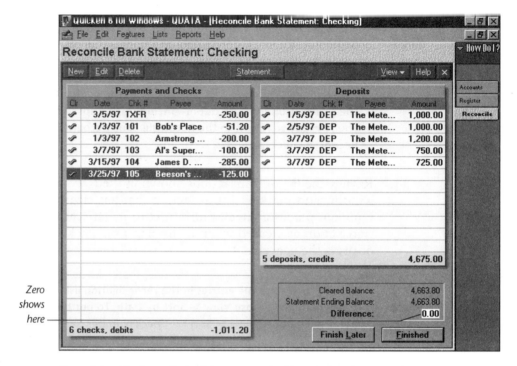

Figure 5.4.   **The Reconcile Bank Statement: Checking window showing a difference of zero**

When you select the Finished button, Quicken updates the status of the transactions you marked as cleared by changing each asterisk to an R. Then it displays a message box congratulating you on finishing the reconciliation and asking you if you want to print a report describing the reconciliation. The message box is shown in Figure 5.5.

13. If you want to produce a report that summarizes the reconciliation, select Yes in the Reconciliation Complete dialog box to display the Reconciliation Report Setup dialog box, shown in Figure 5.6.

14. If you want to record a title or description for the report, enter it in the Report Title text box.

15. In the Show Reconciliation to Bank Balance as of text box, enter the date (in ***MM/DD/YY*** format) through which cleared and uncleared transactions should be reported.

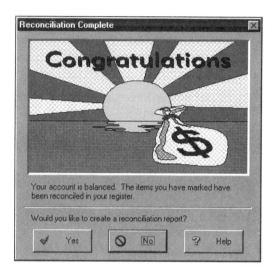

Figure 5.5. **The Congratulations message. This screen asks if you want to create a reconciliation report.**

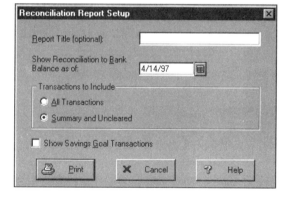

Figure 5.6. **The Reconciliation Report Setup dialog box**

16. Use the Transactions to Include option buttons to indicate what you want to show on the report. Mark the All Transactions option button if you want all the transactions from the last reconciliation through the Show Reconciliation for Bank Balance as of date to show on the report. (You usually won't need to show this level of detail.) Mark the Summary and Uncleared option buttons if you want summary information

and the individual uncleared transactions to show. (If you're printing a reconciliation report, this is the option you'll usually want; it individually lists the uncleared transactions that explain the difference between your records and the bank's.)

17. Either select Print to produce the reconciliation report, or use the Print To option buttons to indicate where Quicken should send the reconciliation report.

   Quicken then either sends the reconciliation report to Windows 95 so that your report can be printed, or (if you click on any of the three "Disk" radio buttons) Quicken prompts you for the complete path name of the reconciliation report disk file.

DO YOU NEED A RECONCILIATION REPORT?

In most cases, you probably don't need a reconciliation report. The report simply documents the fact that you reconciled an account. And after all, you already know that you reconciled the account. The one time it probably does make sense to print a reconciliation report is when you're reconciling an account for someone else. For example, if you're a bookkeeper and you use Quicken in your work, it makes sense for you to document that you've completed a reconciliation so that you can show your employer that you've balanced the account.

What to Do If You Can't Reconcile an Account

If you can't get a bank account to reconcile, either you can tell Quicken to force your records to agree with the bank's (this isn't a very good idea), or you can suspend the reconciliation, attempt to find the error that's causing you problems, and then restart the reconciliation. I'll describe both approaches here, although the former should only be used as a last resort or when you haven't been able to get an account to reconcile for several months in a row.

Postponing a Reconciliation
So You Can Find Your Error

If you diligently entered each of the new transactions your bank statement showed and carefully marked each cleared transaction in the Reconcile Bank Statement dialog box, and your account won't reconcile, here's what you should do:

First, click on Finish Later in the Reconcile Bank Statement dialog box. This tells Quicken not to complete the reconciliation. Quicken closes the dialog box but leaves intact the transactions you've marked as cleared. (It does this by putting an R in the Clr text box in the account register.)

Next, review your records—particularly the transactions you entered since the last reconciliation—for any errors. I've already mentioned two of the things that foul up reconciliations: transactions you haven't yet but still need to enter and transactions you incorrectly marked as cleared or uncleared. If you've double-checked your records for these errors, consider these other potential errors:

Backward numbers. Look for transactions you may have entered backward—deposits you entered as payments or vice versa. These errors can be tricky to spot because every transaction looks right except for one tiny thing: the sign of the amount is wrong. You can often find backward transactions by dividing the unexplained difference by two and then looking for a transaction equal to the result. If the unexplained difference is $101.50, for example, it may be that you entered a $50.75 transaction backward.

Transposed numbers. Look for amounts with transposed numbers. These errors are also tricky to locate because all the digits are correct, but they aren't in the right order: $46.25 entered as $42.65, for example. If the difference is evenly divisible by nine, look for transposed numbers in the amount. For example, if you do enter **$42.65** instead of **$46.25**, the difference in the Reconcile Bank Account dialog box will equal $3.60. The $3.60 amount is evenly divisible by nine, so the difference suggests a transposition error.

Transactions entered twice. Look for transactions you've erroneously entered twice. These are usually pretty easy to spot. A telltale sign is that the difference shown equals the amount of a transaction correctly marked as cleared or left as uncleared.

Once you find and correct the error causing the discrepancy, restart the reconciliation process by choosing the Recon button. Fill out the Reconcile Bank Statement dialog box and the Reconcile Bank Statement window to continue marking transactions as cleared or uncleared. Then, when the difference equals zero, select Finished.

Forcing Your Records to Agree with the Bank's

If you can't get an account to reconcile, you can force your records to agree with the bank's. The one time it is reasonable to do so—at least in my opinion—is when you've attempted to reconcile your account for two or three or (better yet) four months and you find that you always have the same unexplained difference. In this case, you know that the uncleared transactions total explains the difference, so the problem you can't find is either in the bank's records (which is unlikely) or in yours. By forcing your records to agree with the bank's you implicitly admit that the problem is yours and not the bank's.

To make this adjustment, you just click on the Finished command button in the Reconcile Bank Statement window—even though you're not finished and the difference doesn't equal zero. Quicken displays the Adjust Balance dialog box, as shown in Figure 5.7.

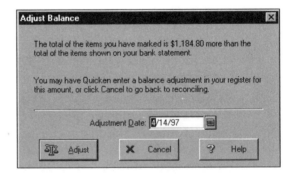

*Figure 5.7.   **The Adjust Balance dialog box***

To make the adjustment, simply enter the date on which the adjustment transaction should be recorded and click on Adjust Balance. Quicken records an adjustment transaction that forces your records to agree with the bank's. For example, if your records show the account balance as three dollars too high, Quicken just adds a payment transaction for three dollars and marks the transaction as cleared.

Quicken doesn't normally categorize adjustment transactions, but you may choose to do so. Because you never found the error, you don't actually know which category should be used. Here are two things you can do:

▶ You can use the category you use for the largest share of your spending. As a practical matter, the adjustment transaction will then have the least effect on this category's totals (because this category will show the largest category totals). What's more, there's a pretty good chance the record-keeping error affects this category.

▶ You can set up a Balance Adjustment category that you can use to summarize your reconciliation balance adjustments. This doesn't actually make your category reporting any better, but it does make it easy to see just what portion of your spending is unknown.

CHAPTER 6

Customizing the Way Quicken Works

FEATURING

QUICKEN lets you have it your way. You can make a whole series of changes to the way Quicken works. Many of the changes are largely cosmetic—they affect only the way Quicken looks. But some of the changes are more structural—they affect either the way Quicken works or the way you work with Quicken. I'll describe each of these sets of possible changes in this chapter.

 NOTE The only prerequisite for this chapter is to know how to work with Windows 95.

Changes to Consider As Soon As You're Comfortable

Three of the changes you can make are so easy you can (and should) consider making them as soon as you're comfortable working with Quicken and entering transactions into a register.

Removing Qcard Message Boxes

I haven't shown them in this book, but you're surely familiar with Quicken's Qcards. As you move from text box to text box or button to button, Quicken displays Qcards.

These Qcards tell you what goes where and what to do next. They also become distracting and—dare I say—annoying once you've seen them a few dozen times.

Fortunately, Quicken lets you remove the Qcards. To do so, choose the Help ➤ Show Qcards command. To show you've turned off all Qcards, Quicken removes the small check mark from in front of the menu command.

 NOTE If you're using the multimedia version of Quicken called Quicken Deluxe, Quicken replaces its textual Qcards with audio Qcards. Audio Qcards basically work the same way that textual Qcards work, except that they include sound. To start and stop the audio clips of an audio Qcard, click on the card's Play and Stop buttons.

You control an individual Qcard with the small button in its upper-right corner. Clicking on this button turns off the Qcard. You can restore the card by turning on all cards using the Help ➤ Show Qcards command.

Getting a One-Line View of the Register

Switching to a one-line view of the register is another change you may want to make. This change lets you pack more information into the Register window. To switch to a one-line view, just click on the View button in the top right of the Register document window, then choose One-Line Display. Quicken condenses all the information normally shown in two lines into one line by using shorter text boxes and omitting the Memo text box. If you click on the View button again, you find that Quicken has placed a check next to One-Line Display to indicate that it is active. Choose One-Line Display again to switch back to the two-line view. Figure 6.1 shows the one-line version of the register.

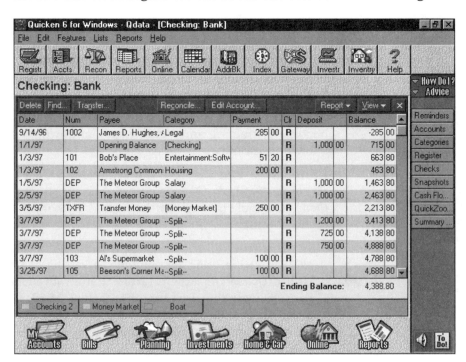

Figure 6.1.   The one-line view of a Quicken register

NOTE The View menu also provides commands for sorting the transactions that appear in the register: Sort by Date, Sort by Amount (Largest First), Sort by Amount (Smallest First), Sort by Check Number, and Sort by Order Entered. If you're reviewing the contents of your register (rather than entering data into it), you can often use these sorting commands to organize your register and to more easily locate specific transactions.

Saving a Desktop

Quicken calls the application window area beneath the menu bar the *desktop*. Whenever you start Quicken, it displays the desktop just the way you left it. Windows will be the same size and in the same location as when you last exited Quicken. You can change this, however and have Quicken use a standard desktop whenever you start.

To do so, first arrange the desktop exactly the way you want it to appear. Select the document windows you want displayed and arrange the windows the way you want. Then choose the Edit ➤ Options ➤ Desktop command. Quicken displays the Save Desktop dialog box:

Selecting the Save Current Desktop button tells Quicken to preserve the arrangement of the desktop as it is. When you select Save Current Desktop, the Save Desktop on Exit button is deactivated, which makes sense because you want to freeze your present configuration, not save whatever you have when you exit.

If you prefer to start with the desktop window looking as you leave it upon exit, click on the Save Desktop on Exit check box. When you quit Quicken, the window arrangement is saved and will be restored when you return.

Changing the Way Quicken Works

You can also make other changes in the way Quicken works. For example, you can fine-tune aspects of check printing; you can control QuickFill's operation; and you can tell Quicken how it should validate the transactions you enter.

Fine-Tuning the Check-Printing Feature

You can control which information Quicken prints on a check and the appearance of that information. To do this, display the Write Checks document window—by choosing the Features ➤ Paying Bills ➤ Write Checks command—and then click on the Options command button. Quicken will display the Check Options dialog box shown in Figure 6.2.

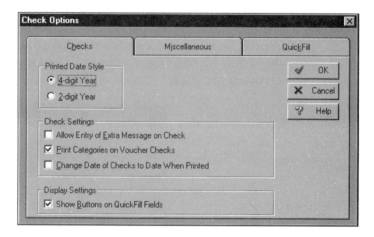

Figure 6.2.   The Checks tab in the Check Options dialog box

TIP At the top of a document window, you will often see a row of buttons. These buttons change according to the active document window. Although they seem to merely duplicate commands that are available by using the menus, you can often save yourself a few steps by using them. That can add up to a lot of saved time after a while, so try to get in the habit of using these toolbar buttons whenever they are available.

Use the Printed Date Style option buttons to specify how you would like Quicken to print the year on your check forms. The two option buttons show how a particular year appears. If the check date is July 4, 1997, for example, you have these choices:

Button	What You See
4-digit Year	7/4/1997
2-digit Year	7/4/97

The Allow Entry of Extra Message on Check check box tells Quicken to add another text box to the Write Checks window so you can include another piece of data on the check form. Figure 6.3 shows the Write Checks: Checking window after the Allow Entry of Extra Message on Check check box has been marked. The extra message will appear on the printed check in roughly the same position as the message box shown in the Write Checks window.

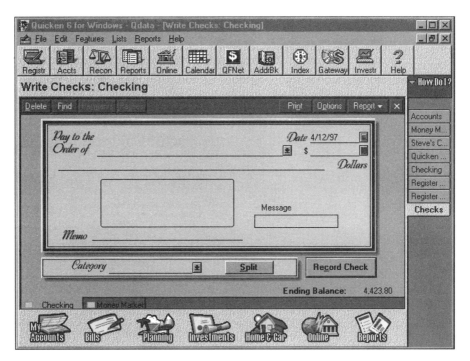

Figure 6.3. **The Write Checks: Checking window with an extra message line added**

The Print Categories on Voucher Checks check box tells Quicken to print what you've entered as a check's category or split category information on the voucher portion of a check. You'll want to mark this box if you use Quicken to prepare employee payroll checks. You can use the split category information to describe an employee's gross wages and payroll deductions.

The Change Date of Checks to Date When Printed check box in the Check Options dialog box lets you exercise control over which date gets printed on a check: the system date at the time you print the check, or the date you (or someone else) entered in the check register. To use the system date as the date printed on the check, mark the check box. To use the date you entered in the check register, leave the check box unmarked.

Controlling How QuickFill Works

QuickFill is an valuable feature, but it's a little overzealous. If you want, you can limit when and how it works.

To change the way QuickFill works, display the Check Options dialog box as described earlier and click on the QuickFill tab. Quicken displays the Check Options dialog box with the QuickFill settings, as shown in Figure 6.4.

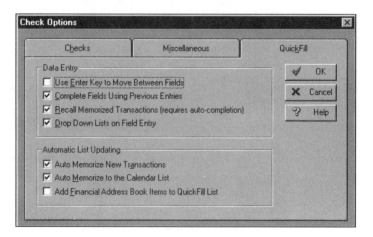

Figure 6.4. **The Check Options dialog box, showing the QuickFill tab**

Memorizing Transactions Automatically

Unless you tell it otherwise, QuickFill copies every new transaction's information to a list called, appropriately enough, the Memorized Transactions list. You can then set up QuickFill to automatically use memorized transactions to enter new transactions. If you don't want QuickFill to automatically memorize transactions—for example, because you want to conserve memory and disk space—unmark the Automatic Memorization of New Transactions check box.

TIP For the average Quicken user, it's easiest to let QuickFill memorize transactions. However, you can also memorize a transaction yourself by choosing the Edit ➤ Transaction ➤ Memorize command.

Turning QuickFill Field Filling On and Off

QuickFill is such a handy feature and time-saver that I can't imagine why you would want to turn it off. But if you do want to turn it off, use the Complete Fields Using Previous Entries check box. When you unmark this box, QuickFill automatically fills in the payee and category if what you're typing looks like it might be the start of a payee or category that you've used before. Unmark the check box if you don't want QuickFill to fill in the payee and category automatically.

Using Memorized Transactions

To tell QuickFill to find a memorized transaction with the same payee name that you entered into the Payee text box and to then use this memorized transaction to fill the rest of the transaction's text boxes, leave the Recall Memorized Transactions check box marked. If you don't want QuickFill to retrieve memorized transactions, remove the check mark from the box.

NOTE To use a memorized transaction's data to enter a new transaction quickly, just display the Memorized Transaction list—by choosing Lists ➤ Memorized Transactions —and select the memorized transaction you want to enter into the next empty row of the register.

Controlling the Num, Payee, and Category Drop-Down Lists

Whenever you highlight the Num, Payee, or Category combo box in either the Register window or the Write Checks window, QuickFill displays a drop-down list. For the Register document window's Num combo box, Quicken displays a drop-down list of transaction codes. For the Payee and Category combo boxes, QuickFill displays drop-down lists of previously-used payee names and of the categories you've set up.

Normally you'll find the display of these drop-down lists very helpful. If you don't, though, you can tell Quicken you don't want to see them. Just unmark the Drop Down Lists on Field Entry check box.

Adding Transactions to the Financial Calendar

If you mark the Auto Memorize to the Calendar List check box, Quicken adds check transactions to the Financial Calendar's list of transactions. (Chapter 20, *Payroll*, describes how you can use the Financial Calendar for monitoring important payroll transactions.)

Retrieving Names and Addresses from the Address Book

If you place a check mark in the Add Financial Address Book Items to QuickFill List check box, Quicken will "QuickFill" both the Payee field and the Pay to the Order Of field using names and addresses you've stored in the Address Book that comes with Quicken Deluxe.

 NOTE Chapter 11, *Exploring Quicken Deluxe*, describes Quicken Deluxe's features and how to use them.

Controlling Data Entry

You can determine how Quicken should error-check the transactions you enter and what other safety measures it should take to minimize the chances that you'll enter erroneous transactions into the Write Checks document window. To address these information-safety issues, display the Check Options dialog box as described earlier and then click on the Miscellaneous tab. Quicken displays the Check Options dialog box with the Miscellaneous settings, as shown in Figure 6.5.

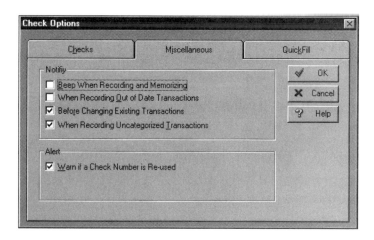

Figure 6.5. **The Miscellaneous tab in the Check Options dialog box**

TIP **The Enter Key Moves Between Fields check box tells Quicken that it should treat the Enter key like the Tab key. When this check box is marked, pressing Enter will highlight the next text box—just as pressing Tab does.**

Normally Quicken tells your computer to beep whenever you record a transaction or you add a transaction to the memorized transaction list. If you don't want Quicken to beep, unmark the Beep When Recording and Memorizing check box.

To make sure you categorize all your transactions, mark the Warn When Recording Uncategorized Transactions check box. If you later try to record a transaction that doesn't show a category, Quicken displays a message box asking you to confirm that you want to record the transaction without a category. (You can still record transactions without categories if you mark this check box, but it'll be more work.)

Mark the Request Confirmation Before Changing Existing Transactions check box if you want Quicken to display a message box that asks you to confirm your action every time you edit a reconciled transaction. (To confirm your edit, just select the message box's Yes command button.) Confirming changes to a reconciled transaction is a good idea—you shouldn't be editing transactions that agree with a previous bank statement.

The Warn If a Check Number is Re-used check box tells Quicken to display a message box that warns you whenever you enter a check number that has already appeared in the register. Because a check number should uniquely identify a check, you should use a given check number only once—so leave this check box on.

More Changes You Can Make

There are several additional preference-setting changes that you can make. To make them, choose the Edit ➤ Options ➤ Quicken Program command. Quicken will display the General Options dialog box, which has three tabs: QuickTabs, General, and Settings. If it is not already showing, click on the Quick Tabs tab to display the options shown in Figure 6.6.

The QuickTabs options let you specify how Quicken will display its document windows. Initially, Quicken provides document windows that fill the Quicken application window. QuickTabs appear to the side of the document window and allow you to page through the open documents quickly.

By unmarking the Show QuickTabs check box, you can instruct Quicken to use normal, Windows 95-style document windows rather than QuickTabs.

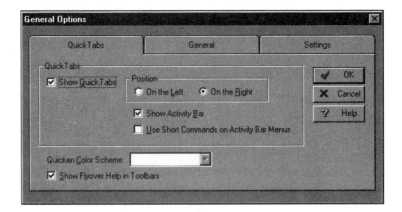

Figure 6.6. **The QuickTabs tab in the General Options dialog box**

If you are using the QuickTabs, you can tell Quicken whether to place them on the left side or the right side of the document window by clicking on the appropriate option button in the Position box.

At the bottom of the document window, the Show Activity Bar Icons check box will display icons which allow you quick access to different functions of Quicken, such as the planners and online services. Be sure there's a check mark in this box if you would like this function to be enabled when you are using Quicken.

The Use Short Commands on Activity Bar menus check box tells Quicken to use short command names when you click on Activity Bar icons, rather than the usual lengthy command names.

The Quicken Color Scheme drop-down list changes the colors of Quicken's screen elements. From this drop-down list, you can change the color scheme to something that you find visually pleasing. For instance, if you don't like the Default 256-Color scheme, you can choose a theme such as Spring or Mesa.

When you check Show Flyover Help in Toolbars, Quicken displays a short description of the button's function whenever you leave the pointer over a Toolbar button. You probably want to leave this check box marked, unless you know Quicken extremely well.

As you can see in Figure 6.7, clicking on the General tab of the General Options dialog box displays even more options for customizing Quicken.

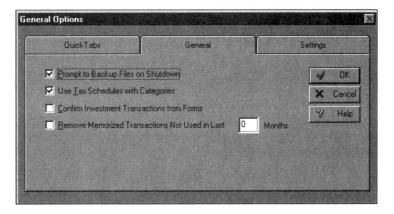

*Figure 6.7.   **The General tab in the General Options dialog box***

Marking the Prompt to Backup Files on Shutdown check box asks Quicken to remind you to make backup copies of your data files every time you quit Quicken.

TIP It's a good idea to back up your data files frequently. The more often you change your data, the more often you should back up your changes.

If you want to export Quicken data directly to a tax-preparation package, mark the Use Tax Schedules with Categories check box. This tells Quicken that it should ask you on which tax schedule and on which line a tax-related category should be placed (see Chapter 14, *Estimating and Preparing Income Taxes*).

If you mark the Confirm Investment Transactions from Forms check box, you'll be required to confirm a transaction entered on an investment form as correct before Quicken will record it.

The Remove Memorized Transactions Not Used In Last [*Number*] Months check box and text box let you clean up and reduce the size of your memorized transactions list. To remove old memorized transactions, mark the check box and then, in the text box, enter the number of months after which an unused memorized transaction should be deleted.

Click on the Settings tab to view the set of options shown in Figure 6.8.

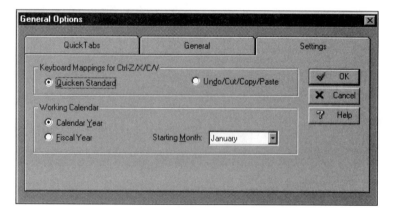

Figure 6.8.   **The Settings tab in the General Options dialog box**

The Keyboard Mappings for Ctrl-Z/X/C/V options tell Quicken whether you want to use the command shortcuts Ctrl+Z, Ctrl+X, Ctrl+C, and Ctrl+V the Quicken way or the Windows 95 way. If you want to adjust this option, you'll know it. If you're someone who uses command short-cuts regularly (either in Quicken or in other Windows 95 applications), you'll want the shortcuts to work the way you expect.

The Working Calendar option buttons let you use a fiscal (or account-ing) year that's different from the calendar year. Individuals who use Quicken probably don't need to worry about this, but some businesses and many nonprofit organizations use a non-calendar fiscal year. If you want to do this, mark the Fiscal Year option button and then use the Starting Month drop-down list to indicate when your fiscal year starts.

Expanding the Power of Quicken

In addition to the minor tweaks described in the preceding paragraphs, you can make changes that expand the power of Quicken. For example, you can tell Quicken it should look at the dates of unprinted checks to see if they should be paid, and you can customize the Iconbar so it provides even more convenience.

Using the Billminder Utility as a Tickler System

Intuit packages two programs in the Quicken box: the Quicken pro-gram, which is what you've been using for your financial record keep-ing, and a program called Billminder. Billminder looks through the unprinted checks in your bank account registers and any reminder messages or scheduled transactions that you've posted on the Financial Calendar (something I talk about in Chapter 20, *Payroll*). If it finds a check that should be paid, a reminder message that should be read, or a scheduled transaction that should be entered, Quicken displays a mes-sage box telling you so. Depending on how you set up the Billminder program, the message box appears when you start Windows, when you start Quicken, or when you start either one.

To use the Billminder program, choose the Edit ➤ Options ➤ Remind-ers command. Quicken displays the Reminder Options dialog box, as shown in Figure 6.9.

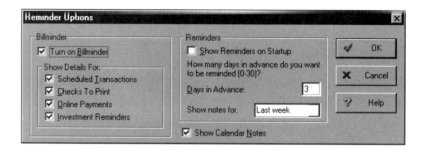

Figure 6.9.   **The Reminder Options dialog box**

To tell Quicken and the Billminder program to display messages when you start Quicken, mark the Turn on Billminder check box.

Next, tell Quicken how many days in advance you want to be reminded of unprinted checks that need to be printed, reminder messages, and scheduled transactions. To do this, enter the number of days in the Days in Advance text box. This setting should probably be the same as the longest number of days you go between your uses of Quicken. For example, if you only use Quicken once a week (perhaps your routine is to record your checking-account activity on Saturday mornings), you'll always want to be reminded of the unprinted checks that should be printed over the next week.

NOTE This reminder makes sense if you think about it. If you're recording payments and deposits on the first Saturday of the month, and the next time you'll work with Quicken will be the second Saturday of the month, you should print any checks on the first Saturday that need to be paid before the second Saturday. By the second Saturday, these unprinted checks will already be overdue.

To tell Quicken and the Billminder to display a message box in Windows 95 when you turn on your computer, mark the Show Reminders on Startup check box. (You might do this, for example, if you regularly use your computer but don't regularly start Quicken.) If you don't want Quicken to display its messages at startup, unmark the check box.

NOTE You can add reminder notes to the Financial Calendar. If you want Billminder to also alert you to these items, mark the Show Calendar Notes check box.

When you finish using the Billminder Preferences dialog box, click on OK to close the dialog box and save your settings.

Adding Buttons to and Customizing the Iconbar

Quicken 6 comes with an Iconbar. It provides clickable buttons that you can use instead of activating menus and then selecting commands. Normally, the Iconbar automatically appears when you first install Quicken. However, if it doesn't appear, you can add it very simply by choosing the Edit ➤ Options ➤ Iconbar command. When you do this, Quicken displays the Customize Iconbar dialog box shown in Figure 6.10.

*Figure 6.10.   **The Customize Iconbar dialog box***

To add the Iconbar to the Quicken application window, mark the Show Icons check box. You'll probably also appreciate it if the buttons are labeled, so mark the Show Text check box, too. Figure 6.11 shows the Quicken application window after the Iconbar is added. (You might want to take a peek back at Figure 6.1; it shows the Quicken application window before the Iconbar is added.)

The icons on the Iconbar can be tremendous time-savers. Instead of opening a menu and choosing a command, you can just click on an icon and go directly to the activity you want. The standard Iconbar contains a selection of the most useful buttons, but as you develop your own style of using Quicken, you may want to tailor the buttons to fit your needs. The Customize Iconbar dialog box, shown in Figure 6.10, contains tools for editing and adding icons.

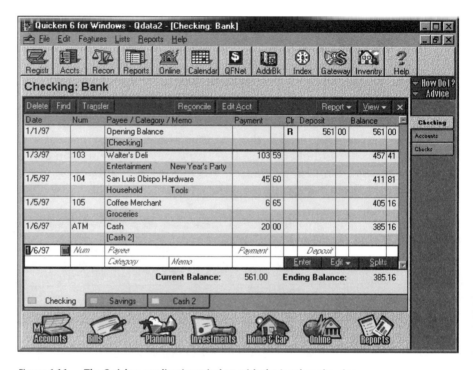

Figure 6.11.   **The Quicken application window with the Iconbar showing**

The simplest change to make is to unmark either of the two check boxes in the dialog box to turn off either the icon images or the icon text. Turning off the text below the images narrows the Iconbar and leaves a bit more space for the application screen, but you need to memorize the meaning of the icons before doing this. Turning off the image but leaving the text narrows the Iconbar even more; although the resulting iconbar isn't very attractive, it's still useful. Check or uncheck the appropriate boxes to adjust the Iconbar's appearance. If you want to turn the Iconbar off completely, simply uncheck both boxes.

To add a new icon, select the New button in the Customize Iconbar dialog box. The Add Action to Iconbar window will open, as shown in Figure 6.12. The scrolling list in the window contains all the Quicken actions to which you can attach an icon. As you highlight various actions, the related icon appears in the middle of the window next to the word Graphic. Click on OK to place the new icon on the Iconbar.

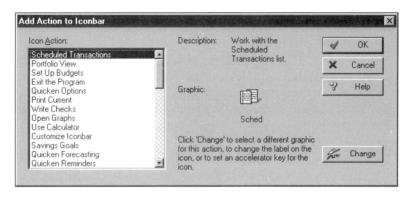

Figure 6.12. **The Add Action to Iconbar window**

If you want to customize further, you can click on the Change button to open a secondary window in which you can choose a different image and change the text on your icon. You can also assign a speed key combination to use with the Alt and Shift keys to activate the icon action. For example, if you designate K as the speed key for activating your new icon, you can hold down the Alt and Shift keys while pressing K to run the action associated with the new icon.

TIP When the Iconbar contains more icons than it can display, Quicken activates arrows at the ends of the Iconbar. You can then scroll the Iconbar by clicking on an arrow. Better yet, Quicken allows you to drag icons into a new position so you can keep important ones visible while less-used ones are scrolled out of view. To reposition an icon, point to it with the mouse, hold down the left mouse button, and drag the button horizontally to a new position. When you release the button, the icon will be repositioned, bumping other icons to the right of its new position.

Once you have clicked on an Iconbar Item, the Edit command button in the Customize Iconbar dialog box opens a window identical to the one shown in Figure 6.12—except it's labeled Edit Action on Iconbar. The button selected in the Customize Iconbar dialog box is automatically displayed, and you can scroll the list to see other buttons. You can change the text or image on the button, but use care—a duplicated image or confusing label could cause problems for you or others using the changed icon.

The Customize Iconbar dialog box's Delete command button removes the selected icon from the Iconbar.

If you get carried away with customization and want to get back to the basics, click on the Reset command button to return the Iconbar to its original configuration.

Setting Modem Preferences

The Online Banking and Online Bill Payment services that work with Quicken use a modem to transfer computer information over your telephone lines. The Set Up Modem dialog box, shown in Figure 6.13, lets you specify the dial type, the dialing prefix (if necessary), and the call waiting disabled prefix (if you have call waiting) after Quicken has tried to configure itself for your modem automatically. (To get to this screen, select Features ➤ Online ➤ Modem Setup.)

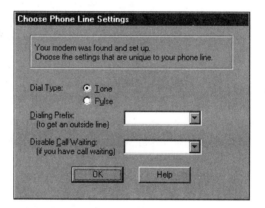

Figure 6.13.   **The Set Up Modem dialog box**

Changing the Way the Register Looks and Works

Quicken lets you change the way the Account Register works and looks, too. Many of the changes you can make are identical to the changes you can make in the Write Checks window.

TIP Quicken lets you make the same kinds of changes to the Account Register that you can make to the Check Register.

Changing the Register Display Options

To make changes to the register preferences, choose Edit ➤ Options ➤ Register. Quicken displays the Register Options dialog box shown in Figure 6.14.

In the Display tab, the Show Date In First Column check box acts as a toggle switch. Mark this check box if you want to see the date field first and the transaction number field second. Unmark this check box if you want to see the transaction number field first and the date field second. The Show Memo before Category check box also acts as a toggle switch, flip-flopping the position of the Memo and Category boxes in the register. The Show Buttons on QuickFill Fields check box turns on and off the drop-down list that appears at the end of all fields that work with QuickFill.

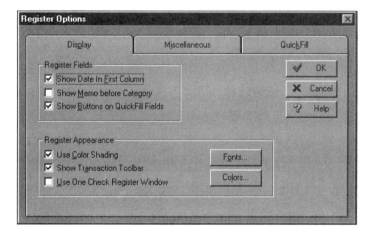

Figure 6.14. **The Register Options dialog box lets you change the way the Account Register looks and works.**

The Use Color Shading check box turns on and off the shading that appears on the second line of each transaction. The Show Transaction Toolbar check box, if marked, tells Quicken to display the Record, Edit, and Splits buttons in the selected transaction's row of the Register. If the Use One Check Register Window check box is left unmarked, Quicken opens a new window for every register you open. If it is marked, only one register window is opened at a time, but it will change to whatever account register you wish to examine.

Changing Font Preferences

Quicken adds the ability to change font and font size for the screen display of registers and lists. Unless used with care, this option can leave you worse off than when you began. The default font is MS Sans Serif, a Windows font created for legibility on the computer screen. Other fonts, which may look elegant on paper, can be hard to read on the screen.

Choose the Edit ➤ Options ➤ Register command, and Quicken displays the Register Options dialog box. Click on the Fonts button. Quicken displays the Choose Register Font dialog box, which lets you preview your choice. This dialog box is shown in Figure 6.15. Choose carefully, with an eye to legibility. Scroll through the font list and highlight a font to select it. Choose a size and, if desired, check the Bold check box. Click on OK to set a new default. If you do not like the new default, you can later return to MS Sans Serif by choosing the Reset button in this dialog box.

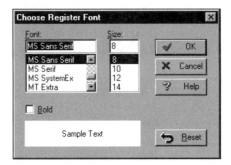

Figure 6.15.   **The Choose Register Font dialog box**

Changing Register Colors

There are six possible account types in Quicken. Assigning colors to registers can help you distinguish them from one another and prevent mistaken entries in the wrong register. To use this feature, choose the Edit ➤ Options ➤ Register command, and Quicken displays the Register Options dialog box. Click on the Colors button. Quicken displays the Choose Register Colors dialog box shown in Figure 6.16. Activate one of the drop-down–list boxes—Bank, Cash, Credit Card, Asset, Liability, or Investment—and click on your color of choice. Click on OK to complete the selection. The Reset button allows you to return to Quicken's preset color scheme.

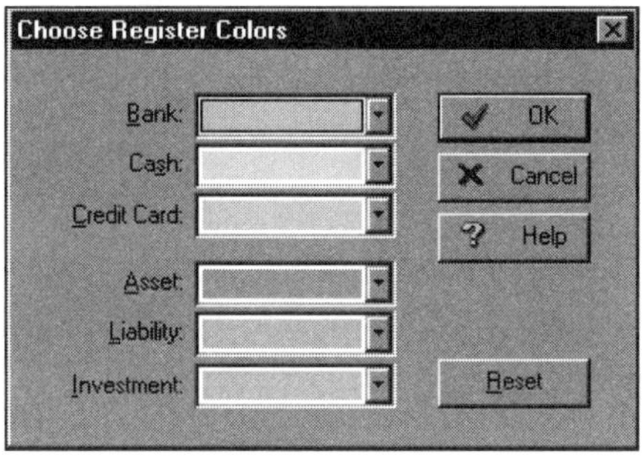

Figure 6.16. **The Choose Register Colors dialog box**

CHAPTER 7

Protecting Your Financial Records

FEATURING

Backing up your Quicken data

Restoring data from a backup file

Protecting data with passwords

Securing your data physically

IF the information you're collecting with Quicken is important—and it almost certainly is—you'll want to take steps to protect the information. After all, if you're using Quicken as a personal financial record-keeping system, the Quicken data files may describe things such as your net worth, the cash you have available for retirement and next week's groceries, and the tax deductions you're entitled to. If you're using Quicken as a business record-keeping tool, the Quicken data files describe the assets you own and the liabilities you owe. They also contain the information necessary to calculate your profits.

Backing Up and Restoring Your Data

You've heard it perhaps a hundred times before, but I'm going to say it again: you need to back up your data files. You don't want to lose your financial records just because your hard disk fails or just because someone accidentally or intentionally deletes or corrupts the data files.

QUICKEN'S "HIDDEN" BACKUP

Quicken has an elegant feature you may never be aware of unless you suffer a data loss disaster or are the type who likes to poke around on your hard disk. When Quicken is installed, it creates a subdirectory named Backup. Periodically, as you leave a session with Quicken, your data is copied to the Backup directory without any notice to you.

This is a fine feature for those of us who forget to make backups. If you lose or damage your main data file, you can use the File ➤ Restore command, as described later in this chapter, to copy the backup data to your Quicken directory. Remember, however, that this data will not survive the loss of your hard disk or computer. Keep on making backups to removable media so the data won't be lost if the computer is damaged or destroyed.

When you look at the Backup directory, you'll notice several different copies of your files there. If you're running low on disk space, you might want to delete all but the most recent copy of your files.

Backing Up Your Files

It's easy to back up the Quicken data files that contain your financial records. All you do is copy the data files to a floppy disk and store the floppy disk in a safe place.

> **TIP** Store the backup floppy disk in another location. You don't want whatever corrupts or destroys your original Quicken data files—a fire, a burglar, a nefarious employee, or whatever—to also corrupt or destroy your backup copy of the data files.

To back up your Quicken data files, follow these steps:

1. Insert a blank, formatted floppy disk into the drive you will use to back up.

2. Choose the File ➤ Backup command to display the Select Backup Drive dialog box, as shown in Figure 7.1.

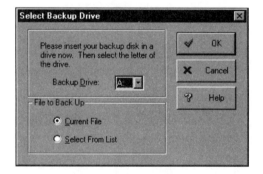

Figure 7.1. Select Backup Drive dialog box, showing drive A as the backup drive

3. Use option buttons in the File to Back Up box to indicate which file you want to back up: the current file or another file, selected from a list.

4. Use the Backup Drive list box to select the floppy drive you'll use to create the backup. Click on OK.

5. *If in step 3 you indicated you want to select the file that should be backed up,* Quicken displays the Back Up Quicken File dialog box shown in Figure 7.2. Use the Drives drop-down–list box to select the drive where the original Quicken data file you want to back up is stored. Use the Directories drop-down–list box to select the path of the original Quicken data file you want to back up. Select the Quicken data file you want to back up from the File Name list box and click on OK.

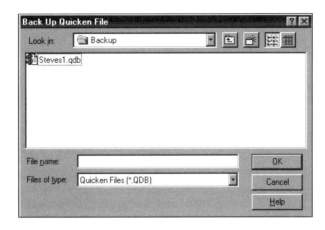

Figure 7.2. **Back Up Quicken File dialog box**

 TIP If you know the complete path name of the file you want to back up—the drive, the directory or directories, and the file name—you can enter this information directly into the File Name text box.

If you've backed up the data on the same disk before, Quicken will display a message box asking you to confirm the backup before Quicken replaces the old file with the newer one.

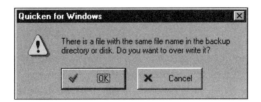

As Quicken backs up the data files, it displays a message box to tell you what it's doing. When it finishes, it displays another message box to tell you it's completed backing up.

Click on OK in this dialog box.

BACKUP BACKUPS

It's a good idea to have "backup backups"—in other words, different copies of files you've backed up. You can do this by using two or three floppy disks for your backups and then alternating your use of these floppy disks. Use one disk for week one, a second disk for week two, and a third disk for week three; and then start the cycle over again by using the first disk for week four.

Why should you do this? Let's say you back up every week and something (perhaps a power surge) happens that damages your Quicken data files. If you try to use the most recent week's backup floppy disk to restore your financial records, you may find that it too has a problem. (Floppy disks are more unreliable than hard disks.) But if you also have a backup copy from the previous week's backup operation, you can try it as a last resort.

Backup Reminder Messages

Quicken will remind you to back up your file if you haven't recently backed up. To do this, Quicken displays a reminder message when you choose the File ➤ Exit command:

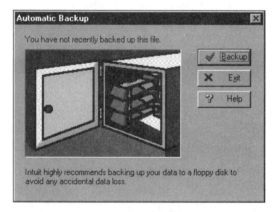

You can choose to start the backup process by selecting the Backup command button, which appears on the message box. Or you can exit without backing up by choosing the Exit command button, which also appears on the message box.

How to Restore from a Backup in Seven Easy Steps

If your Quicken data files are corrupted, your problems are pretty minor as long as you have a recent backup copy of the data files to work with. To restore a damaged file, copy the contents of the backup data files to your hard disk.

> **NOTE** One common data-file problem is corruption of the index file Quicken uses to organize your transaction data. Fortunately, if this index file becomes corrupted Quicken automatically rebuilds the index for you without requiring you to restore the entire set of Quicken data files. You will know if this happens; Quicken displays a message box telling you the index file is damaged and that it is rebuilding the file for you.

To restore Quicken data files from the backup copy of the files, follow these steps:

1. Insert the disk with the backup copy of the Quicken data file into your floppy drive.

2. Choose the File ➤ Restore command to display the Restore Quicken File dialog box, as shown in Figure 7.3.

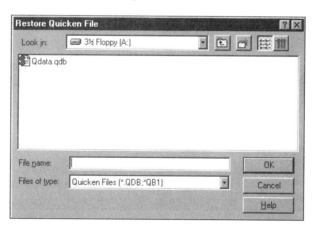

Figure 7.3. **Restore Quicken File dialog box**

3. Activate the Drives drop-down–list box and select the floppy drive containing the backup disk.

4. Click on the data file you want to restore.

5. Click on OK. Quicken displays a message box asking you to confirm that you want to overwrite the current version of the file.

6. To restore the data file by replacing the current, hard-disk version of the data file with the backup copy stored on the floppy disk, click on OK. Quicken displays a message box telling you it's restoring the data file.

7. When the restoration is complete, click on OK in the message box telling you the file has been restored successfully.

Once you've copied the backup data files to your hard disk, you'll need to reenter each transaction that you've recorded since the backup. If you've been printing registers, you can use them to get the information you need to reenter the transactions. If you haven't been printing registers, you'll need to use whatever other source documentation you have—bank statements, invoices, canceled checks, and so on.

TIP Back up your Quicken data files immediately after you finish the restoration. It may be that whatever corrupted or damaged the original data file will again corrupt or damage it. This would be a good time to start that second backup disk I suggested earlier in this chapter.

WARNING If you don't back up your data and you lose your Quicken data files, you'll have to reenter all of your transactions.

USING OTHER BACKUP UTILITIES

You can use other backup utilities, such as PC Tools Deluxe or a tape backup utility, to back up the Quicken data files. Simply follow the specific utility's instructions.

But keep in mind that you don't need to back up any of the Quicken program files (any files with the extension .BAT, .EXE, or .DLL). You need to back up only the Quicken data files—several individual files that make up the complete set of data files Quicken uses to store your financial records. Quicken uses the same file name as it uses for the Quicken program files—such as QDATA—but different extensions, such as .ABD, .NPC, .QDB, .QEL, .QMD, and so on. Therefore, make sure you back up all the files that have either the QDATA file name Quicken supplies or the file name you've supplied.

Using Passwords to Restrict Access to Financial Data

Quicken also lets you assign passwords to files. Once you've done so, a person can neither use a file nor view its contents without first supplying the password. Quicken also lets you create a special type of password called a *transaction password,* which limits the transaction dates a person can use when entering transactions.

Locking Up a File by Assigning a Password

To lock up a file so no person without the password gets access to the file, assign a file-level password to the file. Simply follow these steps:

1. Choose the File ➤ Passwords ➤ File command.

2. In the pop-up menu that opens, choose File to open the Set Up Password dialog box shown in Figure 7.4.

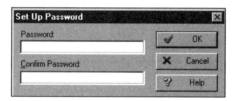

Figure 7.4.   **Set Up Password dialog box**

3. Enter the password you want to use in the Password text box, enter the same password in the Confirm Password text box, and then click on OK.

NOTE You can use any combination of characters, but Quicken won't differentiate between upper- and lowercase characters. From Quicken's perspective, GLADIOLA, Gladiola, and gLADiola are all the same password.

WARNING   As you type the password, Quicken displays asterisks instead of the actual characters you type. This safeguard prevents someone from learning your password by seeing it on the screen. Be careful though: someone can still learn your password by watching which keys you type on your keyboard.

Quicken compares what you entered in the Password text box with what you entered in the Confirm Password text box. As long as the two passwords are identical, Quicken closes the Set Up Password dialog box. You now have a password.

 NOTE If the two entries aren't identical, Quicken displays a message box alerting you to the error, and then Quicken redisplays the Set Up Password dialog box. You'll need to enter the same password in both the Password and Confirm Password text boxes.

 WARNING Don't forget your password! Forgetting a password is the same as losing or corrupting your data files and not having a backup copy of the file; you need to start all over from scratch. Keep a copy of your file password someplace safe. For example, if you use Quicken at work, you might want to keep a record of your password at home.

You won't need to use the password as part of the current session. But the next time you or someone else tries to access the file (probably the next time you start Quicken), Quicken will display a dialog box like the one shown in Figure 7.5. You'll need to enter your password in order to access the file.

Figure 7.5.   Quicken Password dialog box

Using a Transaction Password

Quicken also supplies another type of password, a *transaction password*. This password prevents people who don't have the transaction password from entering transactions that fall before a certain date. Use a transaction password so that, for example, a new user can't accidentally foul up last year's financial records while entering this year's transactions.

To set up a transaction-level password, follow these steps:

1. Choose the File ➤ Passwords command. In the pop-up menu that appears, choose Transaction. Quicken displays the Password to Modify Existing Transactions dialog box, shown in Figure 7.6.

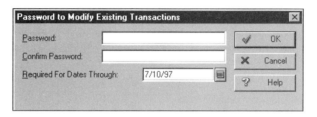

Figure 7.6. **Password to Modify Existing Transactions dialog box**

2. Enter a password into both the Password and Confirm Password text boxes. As with file-level passwords, you can use any combination of characters, and Quicken doesn't differentiate between upper- and lower-case characters.

3. Enter the transaction date for (or before) which the user will have to supply the transaction-level password. Clicking on the arrow at the right end of the text box opens a pop-up calendar you can use to choose a date. Click on OK to display the Confirm Password dialog box.

   Quicken compares what you entered in the Password text box with what you entered in the Confirm Password text box. As long as the two passwords are identical, Quicken closes the Password to Modify Existing Transactions dialog box. You now have a transaction-level password. Now Quicken will require you (and anyone else) to enter the transaction password before recording or editing a transaction dated on or before the specified transaction date.

Changing File-Level and Transaction-Level Passwords

You can change file-level and transaction-level passwords the same way you add them. One change you can make is to replace a password with a blank password, which is the same as telling Quicken you no longer want to use a password.

To change the file-level password, follow these steps:

1. Choose the File ➤ Passwords ➤ File command to display the Change Password dialog box:

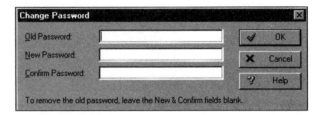

2. Enter the current file-level password in the Old Password text box.

3. Enter the replacement password in the New Password text box and the Confirm Password text box. (If you want to just get rid of the file-level password and not supply a replacement, leave the New Password text box and the Confirm Password text box blank.) Click on OK.

From this point forward, the new replacement password will control access to the file.

If you want to change the transaction-level password, follow a similar sequence of steps:

1. Choose the File ➤ Passwords ➤ Transaction command to display the Change Transaction Password dialog box:

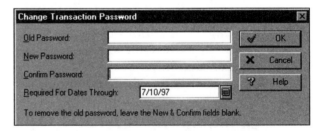

2. Enter the current transaction-level password in the Old Password text box.

3. Enter the replacement transaction-level password in the New Password text box and in the Confirm Password text box. (If you want to just get rid of the transaction-level password and not supply a replacement, leave the New Password text box and the Confirm Password text box blank.)

4. In the Required For Dates Through text box, enter the date that determines when a transaction-level password is required.

5. Click on OK.

From this point forward, Quicken will require the new transaction password whenever anyone attempts to enter a transaction or modify a transaction that falls on or before the cut-off date you specified in step 4.

Physical Security Measures

In terms of computer security, it's easy to focus on things like file backups and passwords. But don't forget about physical security measures.

If you're using Quicken in a business, for example, it's a good idea to restrict access to the computer that runs the Quicken program and on which the Quicken data files are stored. With computers as relatively inexpensive as they are, for example, you might want to dedicate a computer to Quicken and prohibit people from using the computer for other things. (Large businesses routinely restrict access to their computer systems by providing tighter security and controlled access to their management information systems areas.)

You might want to put the computer that runs Quicken and stores the data files in a locked office. This deterrent wouldn't stop a determined criminal, of course. But with every obstacle you put in the path of a thief, you decrease your chances of becoming a victim.

Another physical measure relates to the check forms you use. Be sure to use a signature that's not easily duplicated (forged). Signatures that consist of a wavy line and a couple of i-dots (or are those t-crosses?) aren't going to be easily detected as forgeries by anyone—including yourself.

And while you don't need to worry about the way Quicken fills out a check, be sure to carefully and completely fill out the check forms you write by hand. Figure 7.7 shows a check form that I've purposely filled in sloppily, with blank spaces in the amount box and on the amount line. Figure 7.8 shows the same check form with some minor changes.

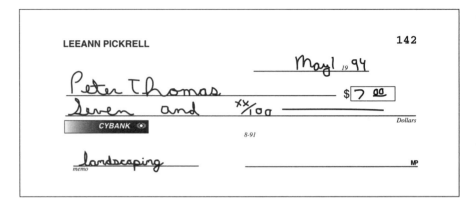

Figure 7.7.   *A check form that's been completed so sloppily it's easily altered*

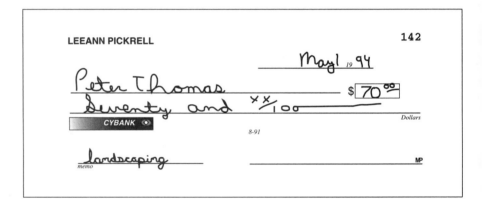

Figure 7.8.   *The same check form as shown in Figure 7.7 after it's been altered*

NOTE It's usually the bank's responsibility, not yours, to detect check forgeries. Forgery is any altering or marking that changes your liability, so filling in the extra words and numbers on the check form shown in **Figure 7.7** constitutes forgery. It might not be you who suffers the loss if you are a victim of check forgery. You may have to absorb some of the loss if you're negligent, however, or if you delay reporting a forgery to the bank.

CHAPTER 8

Charting Your Finances

FEATURING

Creating a chart

QuickZooming on the data in a chart

Creating budget variance,
net worth and investments graphs

Making graphs work your way

TABULAR presentations of quantitative information, like the Quicken reports with their rows and columns of data, work well when you want access to details or when you want to-the-dollar or to-the-penny precision. Sometimes, though, a chart works better. Charts let you summarize your financial data in a picture, often let you see trends you might otherwise miss, and sometimes let you see—or at least detect—relationships in the data being graphed that otherwise would remain hidden.

NOTE You don't need any special skills or knowledge to chart data with Quicken. You do, however, need to have collected the data you want to chart by keeping records of your financial affairs using the Quicken registers.

How to Create Your First Chart in 60 Seconds

To create a chart you simply choose a few commands from menus and tell Quicken which information you need it to chart. To illustrate how this approach works, let's suppose you want to plot a chart that shows your income and expenses over a month.

Drawing an On-Screen Report

To create an on-screen report in a document window, follow these steps:

1. Choose the Reports ➤ Graphs ➤ Income and Expense command to display the Create Graph dialog box, as shown in Figure 8.1.

2. Verify that Income and Expenses is chosen.

3. Tell Quicken which months' data it should graph, using either the drop-down–list box or the From and To text boxes. The drop-down–list box contains descriptions such as Year To Date or Current Quarter. Choosing one of these will automatically change the From and To text boxes appropriately. You can also change the From and To text boxes directly. For example, to plot monthly income and expense data for January through April 1997, type **1/97** in the From text box and **4/97** in the To text box (See Figure 8.1). The drop-down–list box automatically changes to Custom Date.

Figure 8.1.   **The Create Graph dialog box, with beginning and ending dates filled in**

4. Quicken assumes that all the accounts in a file should be included in a graph. *If, instead, you want to select the accounts,* click on the Customize button in the Create Graph window, and the Customize Graph dialog box will open. If it is not already showing, click on the Accounts tab, as shown in Figure 8.2. Select and deselect the accounts to use by clicking on the account or pressing the spacebar. (The spacebar and clicking act as toggle switches: they alternately mark an account to be included and then not to be included.)

5. Quicken assumes that all your categories should be included in a report. *If, instead, you want to designate categories to plot,* click on the Categories tab in the Customize Graph dialog box, as shown in Figure 8.3. Customize the category selection as you did the account selection in step 4.

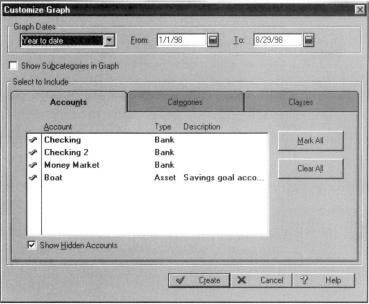

Figure 8.2. The Customize Graph dialog box showing the Accounts tab

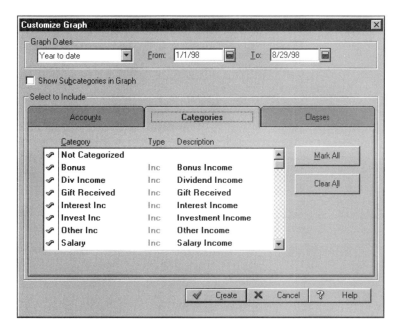

Figure 8.3. The Customize Graph dialog box showing the Categories tab

6. *If you want to have subcategories plotted separately from their parent category,* click on the Show Subcategories in Graph check box in the Customize Graph dialog box.

7. Quicken assumes you want to graph data from all classes. *If, instead, you want to designate classes to graph,* click on the Classes tab in the Customize Graph dialog box. (This tab only appears if you have created any classes.) Customize the class selection as you did in step 4.

8. When your selections are complete, click on OK, and Quicken creates the income and expense graph using just the data you specified. Figure 8.4 shows an Income and Expense Graph.

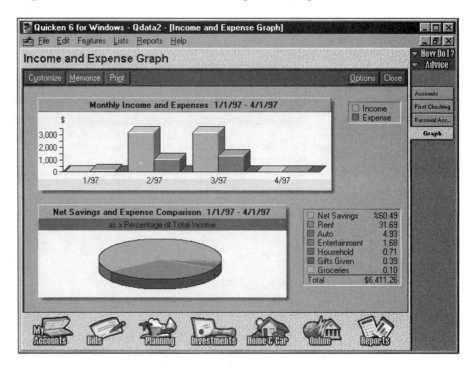

Figure 8.4. **The Income and Expense Graph window**

In the top half of the graph window, Quicken displays a bar graph of total income and total expenses by month. In the bottom half of the graph window, Quicken displays a pie graph of the expense categories as percentages of the total expenses.

NOTE You can use the Customize button in the top-left corner of the Graph document window to change the time period graphed and the filter information.

Memorizing Graphs

Just as you can memorize reports, you can memorize graphs. By doing so, you get to save any special graph creation settings—such as the accounts or categories you want to use. The graph memorization process works identically to the report memorization process. Once you've produced a graph you want to save for future use, click on the Memorize button on the Graph document window. When Quicken displays the Memorize Graph dialog box, as shown below, give the memorized graph a name and select OK.

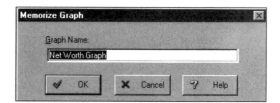

The next time you want to display the graph, choose the Reports ➤ Graphs ➤ Memorized Graphs command and select the memorized graph from the list that Quicken displays. The list in Figure 8.5 shows one graph.

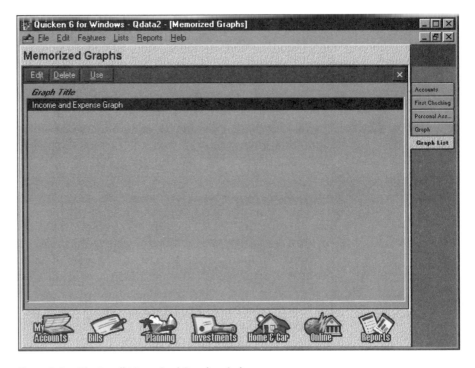

Figure 8.5.   **The Recall Memorized Graphs window**

Printing the Graph in the Active Document Window

To print the graph in the active document window, choose the File ➤ Print Graph command or click on the Print button. Quicken sends the graph to Windows 95 to begin printing.

Graphs are more work to print than text, so a page of graphs will take longer than a page of report information. As Quicken and Windows 95 work to print your graph, you'll see a message box on your screen telling you the graph is being printed.

NOTE Three-dimensional graphs like the one shown in Figure 8.4 may look more interesting than the two-dimensional variety, but they are also less precise visually. If you want to add precision to your graphs by plotting them in 2-D, see the last section of this chapter.

QuickZooming on a Graph's Data Markers

Data markers are the symbols a chart uses to show its information: the bars in a bar chart, the slices in a pie chart, and so on. If you want more information about a particular data marker's data—say, you want to see another graph that further describes a slice of a pie chart—you can use QuickZoom. The cursor changes to a magnifying glass when it points to a data marker. Just double-click on the data marker you want to further explore. Quicken draws another graph, which shows information about the selected data marker. If you use QuickZoom on the slice of a pie to get more information about your net savings, for example, QuickZoom produces a more detailed chart, as shown in Figure 8.6.

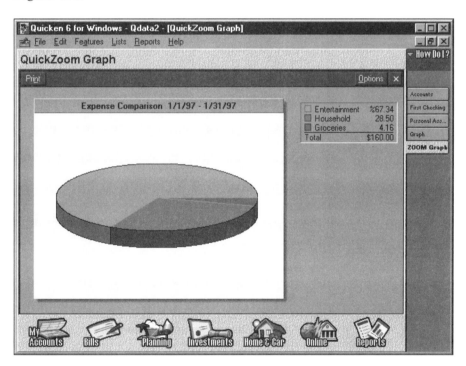

Figure 8.6. A QuickZoom graph lets you see details of the chart date.

Part 1

The ABCs of Quicken

You can even QuickZoom on a QuickZoom graph. In this case, Quick-Zoom produces a QuickZoom Expense Comparison report showing the individual transactions that make up the values plotted in a QuickZoom graph. Figure 8.7 shows the QuickZoom Expense Comparison report that describes the Entertainment category data plotted in the QuickZoom graph in Figure 8.6.

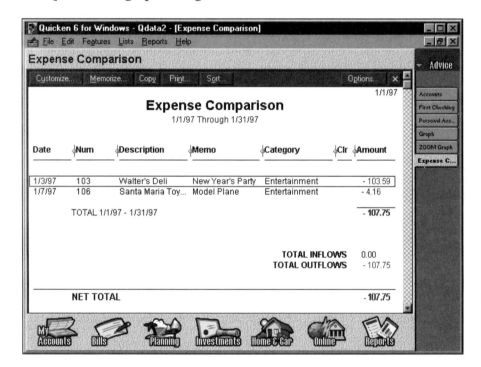

Figure 8.7.   A QuickZoom Expense Comparison report shows you transactions plotted in Figure 8.6's QuickZoom graph.

TIP If you begin using QuickZoom to create QuickZoom reports, you'll very quickly create a collection of graph document windows. Remember that you can individually close windows by clicking on the Close button. Sometimes this button's label says Close and other times the button shows an X.

Looking at the Other Charts

Quicken produces several graphs in addition to the Income and Expense graph just described. When you choose any subset of the Graphs command from the Reports menu or click on the Graphs icon on the Iconbar, Quicken takes you to the Create Graph dialog box (see Figure 8.1). If you choose a Reports ➤ Graphs command, Quicken selects the option button for the type of graph you chose. There are six buttons, each corresponding to a graph: Income and Expenses (which you've already seen), Budget Variance, Net Worth, Investment, Performance, and Asset Allocation.

The Budget Variance Graph

A Budget Variance graph compares your actual income and expense to your budgeted income and expense. To create this graph, you must first have created a budget (see Chapter 15, *Planning Your Personal Finances*). Then you follow a process similar to that used for creating an Income and Expense graph. You choose the Reports ➤ Graphs ➤ Budget Variance command. This selects the Budget Variance Graph option button in the Create Graph dialog box. You then indicate which actual and budget data you want plotted.

Figure 8.8 shows the Budget Variance graph in its own document window. The top half of the window shows a bar graph of the monthly variances (difference) between the total actual income and the total budgeted income and the monthly variances between the total actual spending and the total budgeted spending.

NOTE Setting up a budget is discussed in Chapter 15.

The graph in the bottom half of the window compares actual and budgeted amounts, category by category.

NOTE You print, QuickZoom, and close Budget Variance graphs the same way you print, QuickZoom, and close Income and Expense graphs.

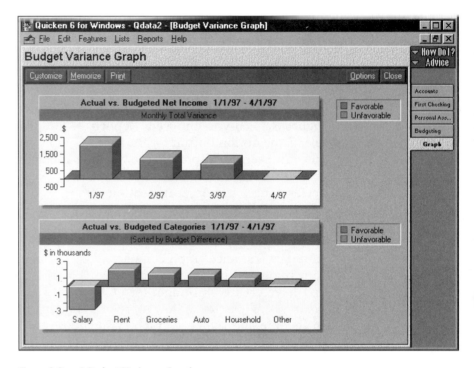

Figure 8.8.   *A Budget Variance Graph*

The Net Worth Graph

A Net Worth graph shows your total assets, total liabilities, and result-ing net worth on a month-to-month basis. To create this graph, follow the same basic process you use to create Income and Expense and Budget Variance graphs. First, choose the Reports ➤ Graph ➤ Net Worth command. When Quicken displays the Create Graph dialog box with the Net Worth option button selected, you can use the same procedures as before to indicate which accounts, categories, and classes you want plotted in the Net Worth graph.

Part
1

The ABCs of Quicken

When you click on the Create command button in the Customize Graph dialog box, Quicken draws the graph. Figure 8.9 shows an example Net Worth graph. Quicken uses the bars to show your total assets and your total liabilities. It uses a small square to represent the net value, or your net worth, within each bar. It then draws a line to plot your net worth. You print, QuickZoom, and close the Net Worth graph document windows the same way you do other graph document windows.

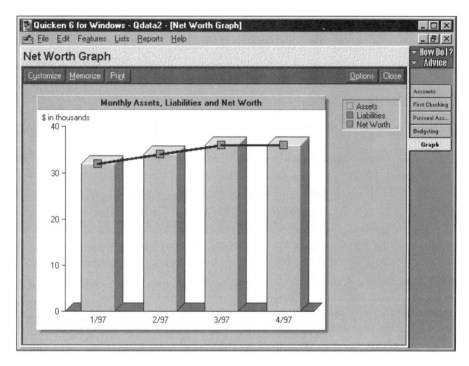

Figure 8.9.   A Net Worth Graph

TIP   In a bar chart, you can click and hold down the mouse button on any area of a bar to display its exact amount.

The Investments Graphs

If you're using Quicken for your investment record keeping, you can produce a bar chart that shows your total investment portfolio values by month, as well as the annualized average return. You can also produce a pie chart that summarizes your holdings by investment class. (You need to have begun using Quicken for investment record keeping to produce these investment graphs. See Chapters 15 and 16 for more information.)

To produce an investment performance graph, follow these steps:

1. Choose the Reports ➤ Graphs ➤ Investment performance command to display the Create Graph dialog box (see Figure 8.1).

2. Tell Quicken which months' investment data it should graph using the From and To text boxes. For example, to plot investment portfolio values and returns from January 1994 through December 1996, type **1/94** in the From text box and **12/96** in the To text box.

3. Quicken assumes that all the accounts in a file should be included in a graph. *If instead you want to select specific investment accounts,* click on the Customize button in the Create Graph window. When the Customize Graph dialog box opens, click on the Accounts tab, then select and de-select the investment accounts to use. Click on OK when all the investment accounts from which data should be graphed are checked.

4. Quicken assumes that all your securities should be included in a report. *If instead you want to select which securities should be plotted,* click on the Securities tab in the Customize Graph dialog box and mark securities in the dialog box, as shown in Figure 8.10. Click on OK, and Quicken creates the graph.

In the top half of the graph window shown in Figure 8.11, Quicken displays a bar graph of the total investment portfolio value by security at the end of each month. In the bottom half of the graph window, Quicken displays another bar chart, this time showing the average annual total return for the portfolio.

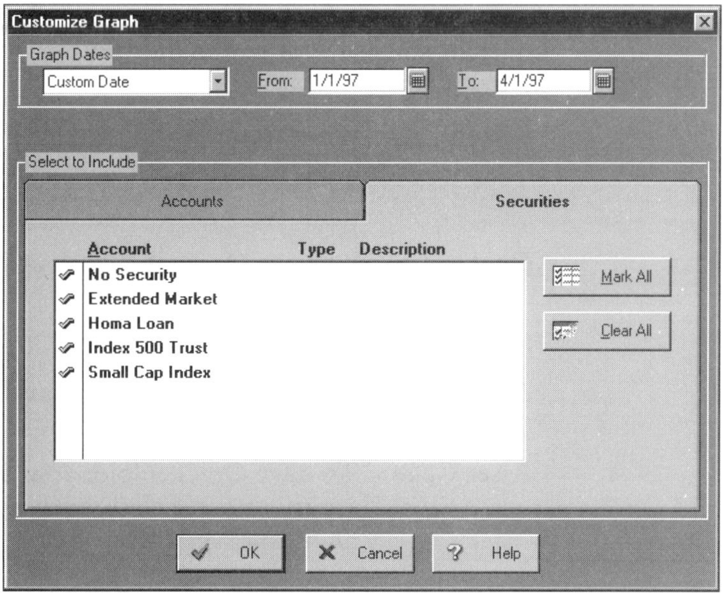

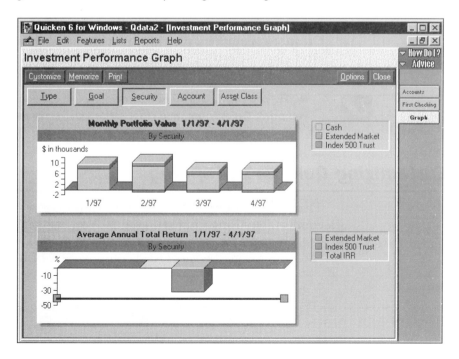

Figure 8.10. **The Customize Graph dialog box showing the Securities tab**

Figure 8.11. **An Investment Performance Graph**

Along the top edge of the Investment Performance Graph window, Quicken adds several command buttons you can use to rearrange the plotted data:

Button	When You Use It
Type	To have Quicken plot your investment data by investment type
Goal	To have Quicken plot your investment data by investment goal
Security	To return to the original, by-security plotting
Account	To have Quicken plot your investment data by investment account
Asset Class	To have Quicken plot your investment data by the security's asset class, such as Money Market or Domestic Small Cap

To produce an investment-allocation graph, you follow the same basic procedure: Choose Reports ➤ Graphs ➤ Investment Asset Allocation. When Quicken displays the Create Graph dialog box, specify the date as of which you reported the allocation information. Then, click on Create to generate a pie chart that shows your investment holdings by asset class.

 NOTE You print, QuickZoom, and close investments graphs the same way you print, QuickZoom, and close other Quicken graphs.

Customizing Quicken's Graphing

There are a couple of customizations you can make once you're comfortable using Quicken graphs. You can get rid of the Qcards that explain and describe how you work in a graph document window, and you can change the way Quicken draws and prints your graphs.

Removing the Graph's Qcards

Qcards are great only as long as you need the information they supply. Once you stop needing them, you'll want to remove them permanently. To remove the Qcards for graph procedures, click on the button in the upper-left corner of the Qcard. That card will not reappear. To turn on or turn off all Qcards, choose the Help ➤ Show Qcards command.

Changing the Graph-Drawing Ground Rules

To change the way Quicken draws many of the graphs you see and the way it prints them, click on the Options button on the Graph document window. Quicken displays the Graph Options dialog box, as shown in Figure 8.12.

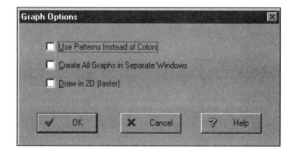

Figure 8.12. **The Graph Options dialog box**

By default, Quicken displays charts on screen with colored segments. When you choose Use Patterns Instead of Colors, Quicken displays all charts using black-and-white patterns on the screen.

The typical Quicken graph has two parts—for example, a bar chart and a pie chart. Checking Create All Graphs in Separate Windows causes Quicken to print each part in its own window, which can be separately moved and sized. By default, both charts print in a single window.

If you want to use more precise, two-dimensional pie and bar graphs, mark the Draw in 2D check box. Figure 8.13 shows a two-dimensional Income and Expense graph with cross-hatching.

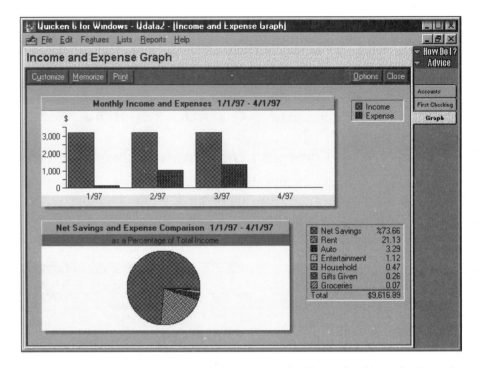

Figure 8.13.   A two-dimensional Income and Expense Graph with cross-hatching rather than color

NOTE Some people feel that pie charts don't do a very good job of summarizing data because they can be used to visually depict only small data sets. Also, making pie charts three-dimensional distorts the slices of the pie—those in the background appear smaller than they are, while those in the foreground appear larger.

CHAPTER 9

Paying Bills Electronically

FEATURING

Deciding whether to pay bills electronically

Signing up for an
electronic bill payment service

Using the new Online Payment service

QUICKEN lets you pay bills electronically using the Online Payment electronic bill payment service. With Online Payment, you use a modem to transmit information to another computer about bills you need to pay. Then the Online Payment service pays your bills for you.

Is Electronic Bill Payment for You?

Why would you use a service like Online Payment? Electronic bill payment delivers a major benefit: For the same work you go through to record payments in a Quicken register, you also get to pay a bill. (If you pay a bill with a check, in comparison, you still have a check to print or handwrite and an envelope to stuff, address, and mail.)

There are only two potential drawbacks to using an electronic bill payment service. One is that it does require you to be a bit more organized in your billpaying. You need to transmit electronic payment information to the Online Payment service a few days early so the service has time to process your payment. If you're always juggling those last few bills, this might not work. (If you pay the mortgage with a handwritten check, for example, you may want the option of paying the mortgage on the last day and personally running the check down to the bank.)

Another potential drawback is that some merchants don't like to deal with electronic payments. Reportedly, some banks with their own electronic bill payment services have balked at accepting electronic bill payments.

Online Payment can be a little confusing to merchants. If I use Online Payment to pay my $50 Puget Power utility bill, for example, Online Payment adds up all the Puget Power utility bills Online Payment users have asked it to pay. Then Online Payment pays Puget Power with one big check—it might be tens of thousands of dollars—and gives Puget Power a list of all the Puget Power customers for whom the check pays utility bills. Some merchants do not like this system.

One other drawback is that, to use Online Payment, you must bank with one of Quicken's financial institution partners. This really isn't so bad, since the list of banks which participate is pretty extensive, and chances are you already bank with one.

AN ONLINE BILL PAYMENT SERVICE CHOICE

As of this writing, Quicken is also including CheckFree, another online bill payment service, with Quicken 6, although they have said that Online Payment is a better value for their customers. Here are a few reasons why Online Payment might be the better choice:

▶ The financial transactions in Online Payment are handled directly by your bank, rather than the CheckFree Corporation. If you are also using Online Banking, this makes one less company to deal with. It also means that you work with a local service.

▶ Online Payment implements several helpful details in their service, such as automatic confirmation of payments and automatic adjustment of lead time, depending on the method of payment.

▶ Most importantly, since Online Payment is an Intuit service, it will be constantly upgraded with Quicken, and the integration of the two programs should remain fairly seamless. (Intuit is the parent company of Quicken.)

Intuit discourages its users from using CheckFree, so I haven't included step-by-step instructions in this book. For your information, however, it operates in a manner very similar to Online Payment.

HOW MUCH DOES IT COST?

The cost of the Online Payment service varies, depending on your bank. My bank, right now, charges $4.95 a month for the first 20 payments in a month, then $.50 for each additional payment..

Does the price of the service seem expensive? If you consider how much it costs to mail in a payment—$.32—it's not so bad. And the check form you use to pay a bill may not be cheap. (For business checks and computer checks, you can easily pay a dime a form.) Services like Online Payments can actually save you money.

Signing Up for Online Payment

You sign up for Online Payment by filling out the Online Services Agreement that comes in the Quicken package or by filling out forms that are available through your bank. You may need to include a voided check with your sign-up paperwork. A few days after you mail in your signed service agreement, you get a welcome letter from either your bank or Intuit Services Corporation. It provides the information you need to set up Quicken for the Online Payment service. Principally, this means you mark the Enable Online Payment check box on the Summary tab of the Checking Account Setup dialog box. After that, you provide a few pieces of information that Quicken asks for. (The welcome letter supplies this information.)

 NOTE You can choose your own personal security code number. Usually, on your first call-in, you use your regular bank PIN number. Then the system will ask you to change the PIN for your new Online Payment account.

Using Online Payment

If you know how Quicken works, you'll have no trouble with Online Payment. Once you've told Quicken that you want to use the Online Payment service with a particular account, the only "extra" tasks you need to complete are building a list of electronic payees (the merchants, banks, and individuals that the Online Payment service pays), and learning to electronically transmit payment instructions to the Online Payment service center.

 NOTE To tell Quicken you want to use Online Payment with an account, display the Account List window by clicking on the Accts button on the icon bar, select the account, and then click on Edit. When Quicken displays the Edit Bank Account dialog box, mark the Enable Online Payment check box. Then click on Next. When Quicken prompts you to do so in the next dialog box, provide the additional information.

Describing Electronic Payees

Your first step in setting up Quicken for the Online Payment service is to create a list of the merchants you pay regularly. To do this, choose the Lists ➤ Online Payees command. Quicken then displays the Online Payee List window shown in Figure 9.1.

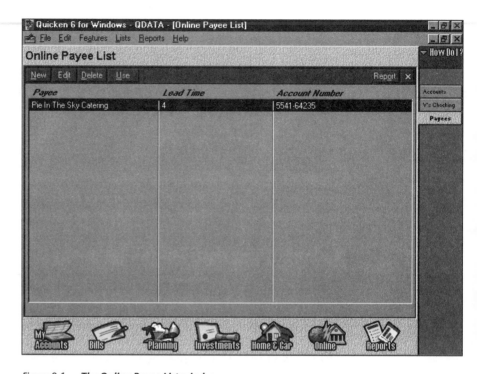

*Figure 9.1.   **The Online Payee List window***

To describe an electronic payee, click on the New button, then describe the merchant, bank, or individual you'll pay by using the Set Up Online Payee dialog box. It is shown in Figure 9.2. Follow these steps to fill in the dialog box:

1. Enter the name of the electronic payee as shown on the last billing statement or invoice.

2. Enter the street address on the first line and the post office box on the second line. You want to enter the exact same address here that you use when you're mailing payments to the payee.

3. Enter the city, state, and zip code into the text boxes provided.

4. Enter the account number the payee uses to identify your account into the Account number text box. You should be able to get this number from your last bill or statement.

5. In the Phone text box, enter the telephone number you're supposed to call if you have a billing question.

6. Click on OK. Quicken adds the payee to the online payee list. If you have additional payees to describe, click on the New command button on the Online Payee List and repeat steps 1 through 6.

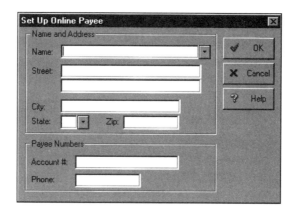

Figure 9.2. The Set Up Online Payee dialog box

Paying a Bill with Online Payment

To pay a bill with the Online Payment service, display the Online Payment window by choosing the Features ➤ Online ➤ Online Payments command. Quicken displays the Online Banking/Investment Centers window with the Payments tab displayed, as shown in Figure 9.3.

Notice that the form is very similar to a check, with a few important differences: There is a drop-down–list box you use to select the account you're using, the Delivery Date is automatically shown as ASAP, and the Pay to the Order Of line is called Payee.

You enter an electronic payment in almost the same way you enter a regular check. There are only two differences in the way you enter an electronic check: You must select which bank account you're using for the payment, and when you get to the Payee line, you must specify an electronic payee.

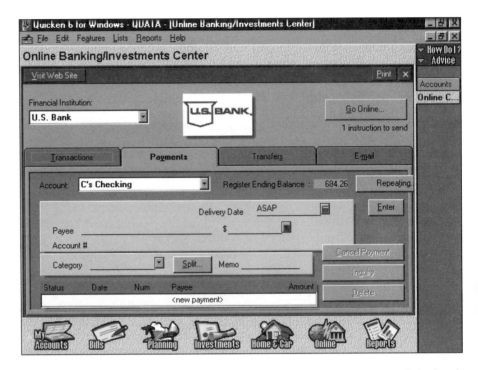

Figure 9.3.   The Online Banking/Investments Center window, with the Payments tab displayed

You can specify an electronic payee by entering a new electronic payee into the Payee text box. As you type, if the Payee is on your Online Payee List, Quicken will attempt automatically to fill in the rest of the name. If not, when you click on Enter, Quicken displays a dialog box. As shown below, Quicken asks if you'd like to set up a new payee or select one from the existing list. If you click on Setup, Quicken displays the Set Up Online Payee dialog box so you can supply the information necessary to make an electronic payment (see Figure 9.2).

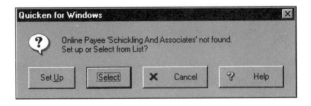

Figure 9.4 shows the Online Banking/Investments Center window describing an electronic payment. Note that you describe electronic payments in the same way that you describe a check you want to print.

After you have filled out the form, press Enter. Quicken adds your payment to the list, and displays its current status in the text box at the bottom of the window. Note that Quicken has not sent the payment to your bank yet. It is stored on your computer until you send your transactions to the bank by clicking on Go Online, which we will do in the next section.

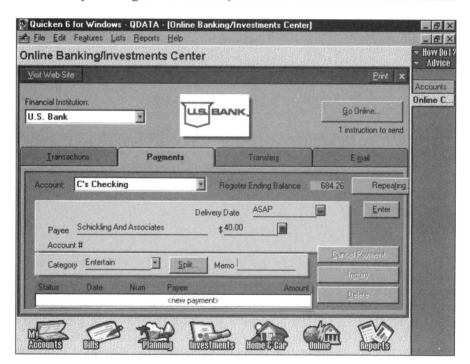

Figure 9.4.   *The Online Banking/Investments Center window describing an electronic payment*

Sending Electronic Payments

Once you've described all of your electronic payments, making the actual payments is a snap. All you do is display the Online Banking/ Investments Center window and then you click on the Go Online command. Quicken displays the Instructions to Send dialog box, shown in Figure 9.5. It shows a list of the online payments you have recorded up to that point, along with any other online transactions waiting to be sent.

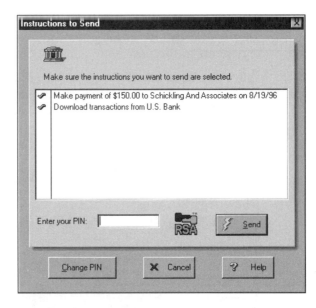

Figure 9.5.   **The Instructions to Send dialog box**

PERSONAL IDENTIFICATION NUMBERS, OR PINS

Online Payment uses a PIN as a way to keep your account information private. When you instruct the Online Payment computer to actually process payments, Quicken supplies your account number and you supply your PIN. The Online Payment computer then verifies the numbers you and Quicken provided and lets you transmit payment instructions. While this process may sound dangerous—after all, someone only needs to know your account number and PIN to start tapping your account—this security system is the same one you now use with your automated teller machine (ATM) card.

By the way, as an extra measure of security, some of the banks that provide the Online Payment service require you to change your PIN every time you transmit payment information. This little gambit means that even if someone discovered the PIN number you were using last week, it wouldn't be any help this week. What's more, if a miscreant did access your Online Payment account, he or she would have to change your PIN. And that change means the next time you try to send payments, you would find someone had accessed your account and changed your PIN. The bottom line is that PINs work very well as long as you keep the number a secret and don't forget it.

NOTE The first time you attempt to use one of Quicken's online services such as Online Payment, Quicken prompts you to set up an Intuit Membership. It also sets up your modem. The Intuit Membership is free and simply identifies you to the computer system that provides Quicken's online services. Setting up your modem isn't anything you need to worry about. Typically, Quicken takes care of everything. Accordingly, you won't have any trouble with either task. Just follow the on-screen instructions that Quicken provides.

If you see an electronic payment in the Instructions to Send window that you don't want to transmit, at least not yet, click on it. This "unmarks" the electronic payment so Quicken won't send it. To later "mark" the electronic payment so Quicken will send it, click on it again.

When everything is ready, click on the Enter your PIN text box, type your PIN, and click on Send.

TIP Before you start using regular electronic payments, experiment with the feature by sending yourself an electronic payment for some nominal amount, such as a $1.00. You'll learn how long Online Payment takes to pay your bills and get payments to the electronic payee. And you'll understand how Online Payment uses the electronic payee information you provide.

Making Regular Payments with Online Payment

Some bills are paid regularly. You might pay them every month, for example. A mortgage payment or rent check. A car loan payment. Medical insurance. To make it easier to pay this type of repeating transaction, Quicken lets you schedule a transaction so that it is paid automatically until you tell the Online Payment service to stop paying it. For example, if you're supposed to make, say, an $800-a-month mortgage payment by the tenth of every month and you've got thirty years of these monthly payments, you can tell Online Payment to send in your $800 every month by the tenth.

To describe such a repeating transaction, follow these steps:

1. Display the Online Banking/Investments window by choosing the Features ➤ Online ➤ Online Payments command. Make sure the Payments tab is showing.

2. Click on the Repeating button oo Quicken displays the Create Repeating Online Payment dialog box shown in Figure 9.6.

Figure 9.6.　The Create Repeating Online Payment dialog box

3. Enter the date of the first repeating payment you'll make using the Online Payment service by using the First Payment text box.

4. Select the account which will be used for the payment with the Account drop-down–list box.

5. Select the electronic payee from the Payee drop-down–list box.

6. Optionally, provide a memo description of the payment using the Memo text box.

7. Use the Category drop-down–list box to describe the payment as falling into some expense category. (If you want to split the payment, click on the Splits button and then fill out the Splits dialog box in the usual way.)

8. Use the Amount text box to provide the payment amount.

9. Use the Schedule buttons and boxes to describe how often and for how long you'll make this payment. Activate the Frequency drop-down list and select a payment frequency—monthly, bi-monthly, semi-monthly, bi-weekly, and so on. Then use the Duration buttons and the Stop After Pmts text box to describe how many payments you'll make. If you have a $500-a-month rent check you'll pay indefinitely, mark the

Unlimited option button. If you have a $750 mortgage payment you'll pay monthly for 30 years, mark the Stop After option button and enter 360 into the Stop After Pmts text box. (As you probably know, thirty years of monthly payments is the same thing as 360 payments.)

10. Use the Prompt to Go Online text box to specify how far in advance Quicken should remind you to transmit this payment. In general, you should transmit payments about five days before they're due.

11. Click on OK. Quicken closes the Create Repeating Online Payment dialog box. To create additional online repeating payments, repeat steps 2 through 11.

If You Have Problems with Electronic Payments

When you have problems with an electronic payment, you do the same things you would do if the payment had been made with a paper check. If you've transmitted an electronic payment by mistake, you can try to stop payment. If you have questions about a particular payment, you can contact the bank—or the Online Payment people.

▶ **Stopping a payment.** To stop payment, open the Online Banking/ Investments Center window by choosing Features ➤ Online ➤ Online Payments. If necessary, use the scroll bar next to the Status text box at the bottom of the screen to check the status of your payment. If it says Unsent under the date, highlight the transaction by clicking on it, then press Delete. When Quicken asks you to confirm the deletion, click on Yes. If it says Sent, click on the transaction to highlight it, then click on the Stop Payment button. Quicken asks you to confirm your stop payment request, then connects to your bank and attempts to stop payment. (This works only if the payment hasn't already been made by your bank, of course.) If the stop payment request works, Quicken voids the electronic payment.

▶ **Seeing electronic payment information.** To see electronic payment information, open the Online Banking/Investments Center window by choosing Features ➤ Online ➤ Online Payments. The scroll box at the bottom of the screen lists any current online transactions.

▶ **Asking about earlier payments.** To ask about an earlier payment, open the Online Banking/Investments Center window by choosing Features ➤ Online ➤ Online Payments, and click on the Payments tab. Use the scroll box at the bottom of the screen to find the payment, then highlight it by clicking on it, then click on the Inquiry button. Quicken displays a dialog box that identifies the payment and provides space for you to type your question or describe your problem. The dialog box also allows you to transmit your inquiry to your bank immediately.

Getting Help from Your Bank

There are two ways you can get help from your bank:

▶ Call them at the number listed on your bank's Welcome Letter

▶ Send them an electronic mail message.

Begin all e-mail functions by opening the Online Banking/Investments Center window. You do this by choosing Features ➤ Online ➤ Online Payments. Then click on the E-mail tab, as shown in Figure 9.7.

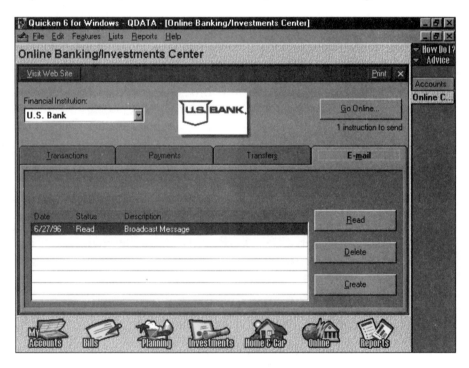

Figure 9.7.   The Online Banking/Investments Center window, with the E-mail tab showing

To send an e-mail message, click on Create, and Quicken opens the Select Message Type dialog box. If you are inquiring about a payment select Inquire about a payment otherwise select Online banking message. As shown below, Quicken opens a form for sending e-mail to your bank. Complete the form, then click on OK.

Message to U.S. Bank	☒
Date:	Wed Jan 01 1997 10 01 19 pm
To:	Cust. Service at U.S. Bank
From:	Stephen L. Nelson
Subject:	Stop Payment
Regarding account:	C's Checking ▾
Message:	

Message:
```
Would it be possible to enlist your help in stopping an
online bill payment? Any help you can give me would be
greatly appreciated.|
```

[⚡ OK] [✗ Cancel] [? Help]

All electronic mail messages from your bank are automatically "mailed" to you whenever you connect to your bank to do your online banking. Incoming messages are listed on the E-mail tab of the Online Banking/Investment Centers window.

To read a mail message, select it in the first list box by clicking on it, then click on the Read button. Quicken displays the message text in the message box.

NOTE If you want to delete a message, select the message and click on the Delete button.

CHAPTER 10
Banking Online

FEATURING

Signing up for Online Banking

Preparing to use Online Banking

Using Online Banking with Quicken

Resolving Online Banking problems

ONLINE Banking is a major feature in Quicken 6 and it's surprisingly easy to use. With Online Banking, you can move money between accounts and even pay a credit card bill if the credit card is issued by the bank with which you do your online banking. You can also receive your bank statement electronically.

There aren't any hard-and-fast prerequisites for using Online Banking. However, you'll find Online Banking easiest if you've been using Quicken for at least a few weeks and have reconciled the accounts you want to use a time or two. You'll also, of course, need to sign up for online banking service with your bank.

NOTE The previous chapter describes and discusses Quicken 6's Online Payment feature. If you're set up for Online Banking, you can probably sign up for the Online Payment feature by simply telephoning your bank.

Signing Up for Online Banking

Signing up for Online Banking isn't difficult, but you do need to telephone your bank and ask whether your bank provides online banking service. If your bank doesn't provide the service, you can find a bank that does by choosing Get Started with Online Banking/Investments. Click on the Online Activity Bar icon. Then, click on the Financial Institutions button at the bottom of the screen to display the logos of numerous major banks that provide online services in cooperation with Quicken. Read through the brochures to learn what services a bank offers and how to contact a bank

Setting Up Quicken for the Online Banking Service

To tell Quicken you want to use Online Banking with an account, display the Account List window by clicking on the Accts button on the Iconbar, selecting the account, and then clicking on Edit. When Quicken displays the Edit Bank Account dialog box, mark the Enable On-Line Banking check box. Click on Next. Quicken prompts you for additional information, as shown in Figure 10.1. Click on Done when you've provided the information.

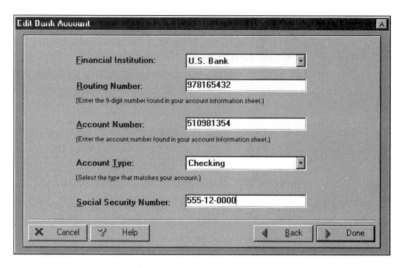

Figure 10.1.   **When you enable the Online Banking feature, Quicken asks you for additional information.**

 NOTE You get the additional information needed to set up an account for Online Banking from the welcome letter that your bank sends once you sign up for online banking service.

Using Online Banking

Using Online Banking is quite simple. When you want to get account balance information or move money between accounts, you choose the Features ➤ Online ➤ Online Banking/Investments command. Quicken displays the Online Banking/Investments Center window, as shown in Figure 10.2.

To retrieve your account balance and cleared transactions for all your online banking accounts, including bank accounts and credit-card accounts, follow these steps:

1. Click on the Go Online button. Quicken opens the Instructions to Send window, shown in Figure 10.3. The Instructions to Send window shows all of the transactions that Online Banking will conduct once it goes online. (Quicken automatically assumes you will want to download any transactions.) If you do not want Quicken to send a particular transaction while online, click on the transaction, and Quicken removes the check mark to indicate that the transaction will not be sent.

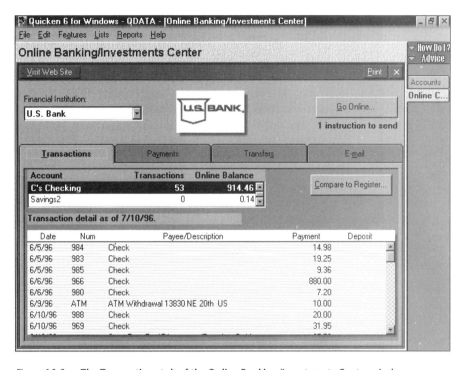

Figure 10.2. **The Transactions tab of the Online Banking/Investments Center window**

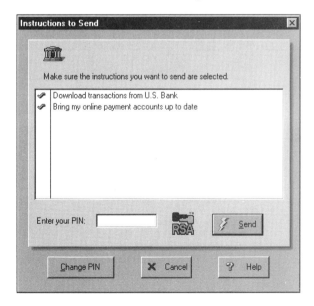

Figure 10.3. **The Instructions to Send window**

2. Click in the Enter your PIN text box and type in your PIN. The bank included your PIN with the information it sent when you activated Online Banking.

3. Click on Send. Quicken connects to the bank and transfers the information from your computer to the bank. Online Banking retrieves transactions from your bank and picks up any new transactions it can't find in your register. Online Banking also marks transactions that have cleared the bank as cleared.

Approving Online Transactions

Quicken holds the transactions it has downloaded so you can approve them before you put them in your account registers. To examine the transactions, click on the Transactions tab in the Online Banking/Investments Center window, shown in Figure 10.4.

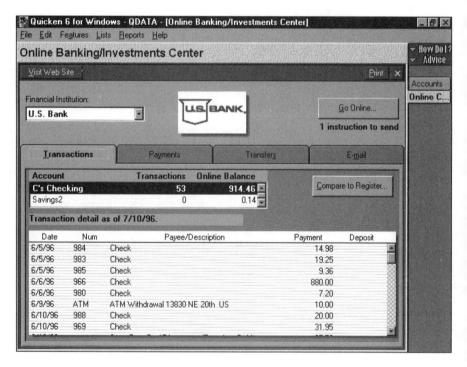

Figure 10.4.   The Transactions tab of the Online Banking/Investments Center window

If you have more than one account at the financial institution, you can use the drop-down–list box at the top of the tab to see the status of each

The ABCs of Quicken

account. Click on the name of the account you want to examine, and Quicken displays the data in the window below the drop-down–list box.

> **NOTE** In Figure 10.4, you can see one disadvantage of online banking at my bank. Because banks don't keep track of the names on the checks, all checks look as though they're made out to Check. After you transfer the information to your register, you can go through and change the Payee name and assign the category. Online Banking *does* supply the Payee name for your credit card accounts. Different banks seem to handle the register details differently, though.

To compare the downloaded data with your register, click on the Compare to Register button. Quicken splits the window, with the register showing in the top half and the list of transactions underneath, as shown in Figure 10.5. Use the scroll bars in each section to move through the lists and compare transactions. To accept a single transaction and add it to your register, highlight the transaction by clicking on it and then clicking on the Accept button. To accept all of the transactions at once, click on Accept All. To remove a transaction without adding it to your register, click on the transaction and then click on Delete.

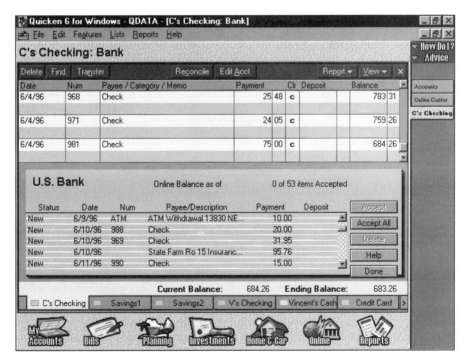

Figure 10.5. *You can compare the online transactions with the account register.*

Transferring Funds between Accounts

If you have two or more accounts at the same institution and you want to transfer money between accounts, open the Online Banking/Investments Center window by choosing Features ➤ Online ➤ Online Banking/Investments, then click on the Transfers tab. Quicken displays the dialog box shown in Figure 10.6.

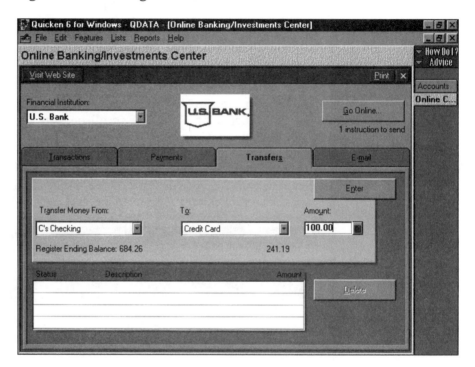

*Figure 10.6.   **The Transfers tab of the Online Banking/Investments Center window***

Use the Transfer Money From and To drop-down–list boxes to identify the accounts you're moving money between. Use the Amount text box to give the amount of the transfer. Click on the Record button to add the transfer to the list of transactions to be sent to the financial institution.

The text box at the bottom of the tab lists all of the transfers you have recorded. To remove a transfer, click on the transaction and click on Delete.

WARNING Some financial institutions do not process transfers electroni-cally; instead, they process the transfers manually at central clearinghouses. This procedure may cause a time lag between the time you send your trans-fer in and the time the bank actually processes it.

Corresponding with the Bank

If you have any questions, comments, or problems, you can corre-spond directly with your bank via Online Banking. Your messages are automatically transferred with your transactions.

To begin, click on the E-mail tab of the Online Banking/Investments Center window. Quicken displays a window that lists any messages you have received, as shown in Figure 10.7. To read a message, high-light it by clicking on it, then click on Read. Quicken opens a window containing your message. You can print the message by clicking on the Print button. After you're done, click on the Close button.

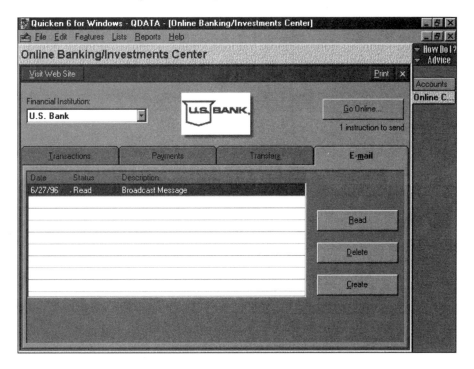

Figure 10.7. **The E-mail tab**

To send a message to your bank, click on the Create button in the E-mail tab. Quicken opens a dialog box. Click on Online Banking Message if you just want to send your bank a note. After you click on OK, Quicken opens the Message to [Your Financial Institution] dialog box, like the one shown in Figure 10.8. Fill in the text boxes to identify yourself, the subject of your message, and the account in question. Enter your message. To send your message, click on the OK button; Quicken adds your message to the list of transactions. Quicken does not actually send your message to the bank until the next time you click on Go Online and transfer transactions.

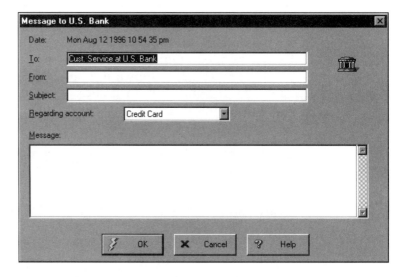

Figure 10.8.   *Use this window to send a message to your financial institution.*

CHAPTER 11

Exploring Quicken Deluxe

FEATURING

Using the Financial Address Book

Exploring the Mutual Fund Finder

Using the Home Inventory Program

Creating a debt reduction plan

Using the tax deduction finder

Checking your credit rating

THIS book focuses on how to use and benefit from the standard version of Quicken 6. As you might know, however, there is another version of Quicken 6, called Quicken Deluxe. I can't document all of Quicken Deluxe's features in detail, but this chapter reviews the most important ones. If you're new to Quicken Deluxe, this information may encourage you to explore some of Deluxe's special features. And even if you don't have Quicken Deluxe, this information may still be useful. It might, for example, lead you to upgrade your copy of Quicken 6!

Using the Financial Address Book

Quicken Deluxe comes with an address book you can use to maintain a database of names, addresses, and telephone numbers. To start the Address Book, choose Lists ➤ Track Important Addresses. Quicken starts the Address Book application (it's actually a separate program) and displays its application window on top of the Quicken application window, as shown in Figure 11.1.

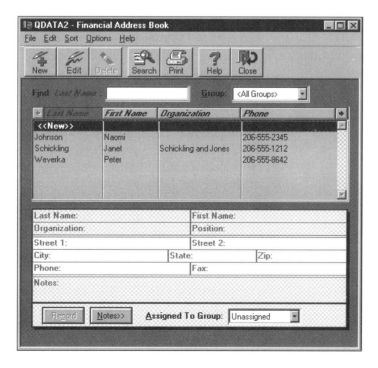

Figure 11.1.   The Financial Address Book application window

TIP   You can also start the Financial Address Book application by clicking on the Start button, and then choosing Programs ➤ Quicken ➤ Financial Address Book.

To add a person to your address book, you fill in the text boxes at the bottom of the window: Last Name, First Name, Organization, Position, Street (address), and so forth. To fill in the information, you click on the text box and then you start typing. When you're done describing someone, you click on Record. The Financial Address Book adds the name and address to the list box in the top half of the Address Book application window.

To see the names and addresses information you've collected on an individual, just click on his or her name in the list. If you've collected many names and addresses, of course, you may have to scroll through the list to get to a person's record.

 TIP   You can edit an existing name and address by selecting the person in the list box, clicking on Edit, and then using the text boxes at the bottom of the window to make your changes. After you've made your changes, click on Record. You can delete someone from the Financial Address book by selecting the person's name and clicking on Delete.

Boiled down to its essence, Quicken Deluxe's online address book is very similar to a handwritten address book. In effect, it's an electronic Rolodex.

Unlike a handwritten name and address list, however, a computerized name and address list provides several neat advantages. You can use the Sort menu's commands to arrange and rearrange the names and addresses in the Address Book. You can also group, or segregate, the people in your address book to make it easier to keep track of dozens or hundreds of names and addresses. For example, you can assign one person to the Family group, another to the Work group, and another to the Friends group. (Address Book supplies these three groups initially, but you can add others.)

Not surprisingly, you can also print the names and addresses in your list after you've sorted them or grouped them. To print names and addresses, you choose the File ➤ Print command or click on the Print command button.

Using the Mutual Fund Finder

Quicken Deluxe comes with an application called the Mutual Fund Finder. In essence, what Mutual Fund Finder does is help you select mutual funds based on your feelings about the risks you're willing to bear and the rewards you hope to achieve.

NOTE As of this writing, the Mutual Fund Finder in the beta version of Quicken 6 was not functional. I've included this section because the advice contained in the section is important, if you intend to use the Mutual Fund Finder. These instructions anticipate that, when finished, the Mutual Fund Finder will work in a manner similar to that in Quicken 5.

Selecting Mutual Funds with the Mutual Fund Finder

To start the Mutual Fund Finder, start Quicken and then choose the Features ➤ Investments ➤ Mutual Fund Finder command. The Mutual Fund Finder application starts and displays a dialog box with several tabs.

To use the Mutual Fund Finder, click on the Next button and answer the questions. Mutual Fund Finder solicits your opinions about mutual funds. It asks which asset classes you want to invest in, whether you want to pay a load (sales commission) or not, what expense ratio you expect, and so forth. Based on the answers to your questions and the Morningstar mutual fund rating system, the Mutual Fund Finder produces a list of mutual funds that meet your criteria.

If you want more information about a mutual fund that's listed in the Search Results window, select it and click on the Details button. Mutual Fund Finder displays another window that describes the fund's history, manager, and current expenses. This window also provides the fund's telephone number in case you want to call the fund manager and get a prospectus. If you click on the Graph tab of the Details window, Mutual Fund Finder displays a graphical history of the fund's returns.

TIP You can print the contents of the Search Results window or the Details window. Simply click on the Print button.

Practical Problems with the Mutual Fund Finder

Before you use the Mutual Fund Finder to help narrow your search for the perfect mutual fund, you should know about two practical problems of using it. The Mutual Fund Finder is probably a better tool than, say, throwing darts at the mutual fund page of the *Wall Street Journal*, but it bases its analyses on at least two suspect notions.

The most suspect notion, in my opinion, is the idea that a fund's past performance provides a clue about how it will do in the future. This implicit assumption is understandable, but almost all academic research supports the view that, in the securities markets, the past is no predictor of the future.

In fact, there is a strong tendency toward *regression to the mean*. If you're not familiar with this term, let me explain. Over long periods of time, a fund's average annual return averages out to the historical average of the stock market. If a fund has done 2 percent better on average than the market over the last ten years, for example, it probably will do about 2 percent worse on average over the next ten years. As a practical matter, chasing last year's winners more likely finds next year's losers, not next year's winners.

There are exceptions to the regression-to-the-mean truism, but they are few and far between. If you're reading this, you probably know the funds and the names of fund managers who have defied the trend: Peter Lynch and the Fidelity Magellan Fund. John Templeton and Templeton Growth Fund. John Neff and Vanguard Windsor Fund. But these are the exceptions to the rule. And knowing now that 25 years ago you should have invested with Lynch or Neff or Templeton isn't relevant. What you need to find is the next Lynch, the next Neff, or the next Templeton.

There's also another problem with the Mutual Fund Finder: The expense ratio data is misleading. One of the most important elements in picking a mutual fund is the fund's expense ratio. If you pick a mutual fund with a low expense ratio, you're likely to do better over the long haul, all other factors being equal.

 TIP To its credit, by the way, the Mutual Fund Finder suggests that you find no-load mutual funds with annual expense ratios of less than 1 percent.

Fortunately, the Mutual Fund Finder lets you sort the mutual funds it finds in order of increasing expense ratios. (To do this, you activate the Sort By drop-down–list box and select Expense Ratio.) But if you do this, you'll find that the first funds listed don't have expense ratios at all. They all show up as zero expense ratio funds.

Technically, this is right. Mutual funds don't have expense ratios. But the reason is that the funds will invest in other funds that do have expense ratios. For example, a fund from T. Rowe Price might charge no expense ratio because it invests in other T. Rowe Price funds that do charge expense ratios. The fund manager isn't trying to cheat you here—it's his or her way of being fair. You shouldn't, after all, have to pay the expense ratio twice. But the zero expense ratios of mutual funds that invest in other mutual funds make it more difficult to search for the lowest priced mutual funds.

 TIP If choosing a cheap mutual fund strikes you as being penny-wise and pound-foolish, remember that a big fund with a small expense ratio may still be able to pay its fund manager and research staff more money than a small fund with a big expense ratio. A 2 percent fee on a $1.5 billion dollar fund produces as much revenue to the mutual fund as a 2 percent fee on a $150 million dollar fund.

The Investor Insight for Researching Investments

Quicken Deluxe's Investor Insight lets investors use their computers to do online research on investments. Using Investor Insight, Quicken Deluxe users can retrieve recent price and volume information about selected securities. You can also retrieve recent *Wall Street Journal* articles and earning reports on different companies. To start Investor Insight, shown in Figure 2.2, choose Features ➤ Investments ➤ Investor Insight.

You select the securities you're interested in by placing them on a watch list. Then, whenever you want to get information about the securities on your watch list, you connect to Intuit's Investor Insight computer. You do this by clicking on the Call button.

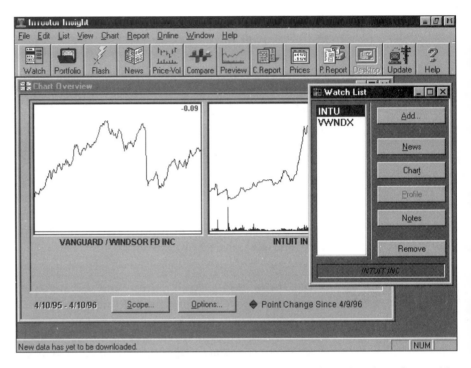

Figure 11.2.   Investor Insight collects price, volume and other information about the securities on your watch list, and it displays this information in windows on your screen.

 TIP You can tell Investor Insight to put the securities in your Quicken investment accounts on the watch list by choosing the File ➤ Get Quicken Investments command.

The Quicken Home Inventory

The Quicken Home Inventory program provides tools for making a complete personal inventory of all your property. Such an inventory might come in handy in any situation where you may have to prove ownership. For instance, if you were robbed and had to tell the police what had been taken, such an inventory could assure that you would not forget anything.

You begin Quicken Home Inventory by choosing Features ➤ Planning ➤ Quicken Home Inventory. Quicken opens a window which, after you add a few items, looks like Figure 11.3.

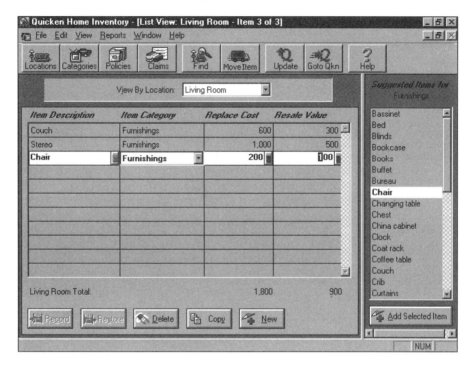

Figure 11.3.   **The Quicken Home Inventory helps you keep track of your belongings in case of an emergency.**

Here's how you compile your home inventory list:

1. Choose a room in the View By Location drop-down–list box.

2. Click on the first blank Item Description box and type the name of the item.

TIP If the Suggested Items For scroll box lists an item you own, you can double-click on it, and Quicken will add the item to your current list, along with its best guess as to the Replace Cost and Resale Value. If Quicken's guess is inaccurate, highlight the incorrect amount by double-clicking on it, then type the correct amount.

---

3. Use the Item Category drop-down–list box to categorize the item.

4. Click on the Replace Cost box and type in the amount which it would cost to buy an exact replacement of the same item.

5. The Resale Value is the amount you would get if you sold the item today. Quicken assumes that it would be half of the Replace Cost. If it isn't, highlight it, then type the correct amount.

6. Click on Record.

Repeat this process for each item of value.

> **TIP** You should also keep a list of any unique identifying marks with this information. For example, note the make and serial and model number of the item, if you have etched an ID number somewhere on the item, if you once scratched it when you dropped it, etc. If the item is stolen and recovered, this information may make the difference between getting the item back or not.

Quicken Home Inventory also allows you to track your insurance policies, including special riders. You can see Figure 11.4 by choosing View ➤ Policy List. Since it works in such a similar manner to other Quicken lists, I won't go into detail about how it works. Note, however, that it keeps a running tab of how much insurance you should carry to cover the value of the items you have listed.

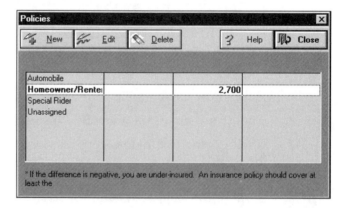

Figure 11.4.   The Policies List helps you keep your insurance current.

You can also keep a list of any insurance claims you have outstanding. You can see this list by choosing View ➤ Claims List. Again, this type of list is probably very familiar to you, so I won't go over the details.

Quicken Expert Advice

Quicken Deluxe includes advice from three personal finance experts. If your computer has multimedia capability, you may, by clicking on the Advice button, which appears above the Quick tabs, get a help window resembling Figure 11.5.

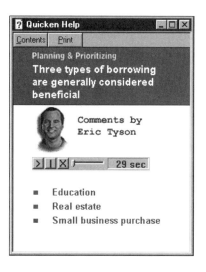

Figure 11.5. **An Expert Advice dialog box**

Clicking on the Right Arrow box plays a sound file of the expert's advice. Clicking on the box with the vertical line will pause the play-back, and clicking on it again will continue the playback from the point where you paused it. Clicking on the box with the X stops playback and rewinds the sound back to the beginning. If you click on the subject headings below the sound controls, a text box opens with further information on the subject.

The expert advice appears throughout the Help files and is generally worth examining and considering.

Creating a Debt-Reduction Plan

Quicken Deluxe includes a feature which helps you figure out the most painless way of and the profitability of reducing your present debts. To use the feature, you describe your debts in detail. With Quicken's help, you then develop a *practical* plan to repay your debts.

You open the Debt Reduction window by choosing Features ➤ Planning ➤ Create a Debt Reduction Plan. Quicken opens a window which resembles a file folder. When you click on Next, Quicken presents a window where you can choose to start a multimedia presentation about debt reduction. (The sound playback controls work just like the description in the previous section.) If you want to skip ahead, click on the Debts tab, and Figure 11.6 appears. Fill in the applicable information, then click on Next. Repeat until you complete the last tab. When you press Done, Quicken displays Figure 11.7. I've included some sample data, so that you can see the graph Quicken creates.

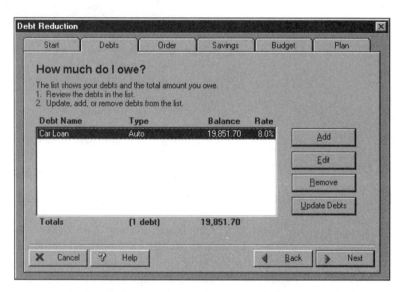

Figure 11.6. **List your debts here to create a debt reduction plan.**

The two lines represent the amount of money you would pay if you continued on your present path and the savings you would receive if you put your plan in action. It's usually pretty convincing.

If you want to adjust your plan, click on the New Plan button. From here you can edit the previous plan and see the revised results.

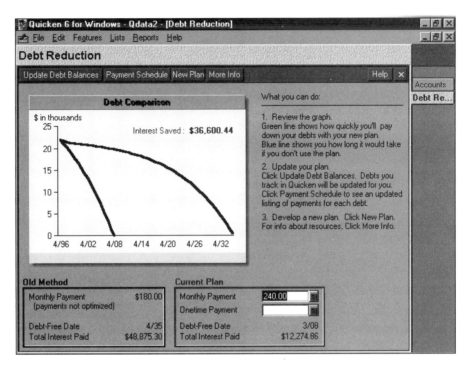

Figure 11.7. **The graph represents your debt reduction savings.**

Finding Tax Deductions

A new feature in Quicken Deluxe helps you to find tax deductions you may have missed in your planning, and also checks your eligibility for the deductions. Choose Features ➤ Planning ➤ Identify Possible Tax Deductions, and the Introduction to Deduction Finder appears. Click on OK and the window in Figure 11.8 appears.

You begin by choosing a Deduction Type in the drop-down–list box, then clicking on a possible deduction in the Choose A Deduction text box. Answer the Yes or No questions in the third section by clicking on the appropriate checkbox. When you answer all of the questions, the Deduction Finder tells you whether or not you may be eligible for that particular deduction.

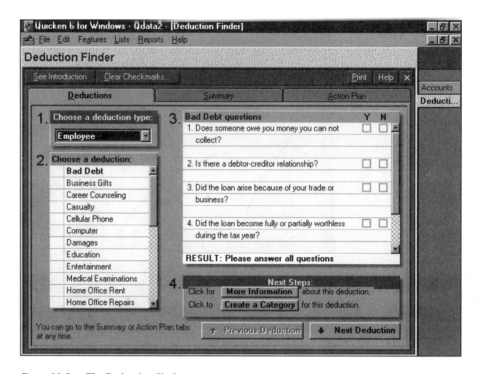

Figure 11.8.   The Deduction Finder

  TIP After you have consulted the Deduction Finder, be sure to talk over the information with your tax advisor before making any final decisions.

The Deduction Finder also keeps track of the deductions you have tried and develops an Action Plan for you, based on the results. Click on the Summary and Action Plan tabs to see the Deduction Finder's records.

Checking Your Credit

We've all heard horror stories about credit bureaus who, for some reason or another, have incorrect information, the use of which results in a temporary catastrophe. While credit bureaus are responsible for keeping a considerable amount of information about your financial well-being, it's a good idea to check periodically to make sure the information they have is accurate. (This is especially true if there is some impending event which will affect you financially, such as buying a house or changing your marital status.) At the very least, you should check your credit reports once a year.

You order a copy of your credit report from TRW, a major credit bureau. If you have a modem on your computer, Quicken gives you three options:

▶ *The U.S. Mail*: There is no charge for this service, but you won't receive your report for three to five weeks. Quicken will use the information you enter to produce a form letter, which you then send on to TRW.

▶ *Online though your modem*: There is a $6.00 service charge for this, and you receive your report within three to seven days. Quicken sends the information directly to TRW via the modem.

▶ *TRW's credit monitoring service*: Subscribing to this service allows you unlimited copies of your credit reports, notification if anyone asks for a copy of your report, and other services. At the time of this writing, the service costs about $50.00 per year, but there is a free three-month period, and you get your current request free.

To check your credit, choose Features ➤ Planning ➤ Check My Credit Online, and Quicken opens the Credit Check window. Unlike similar windows, you cannot skip steps by clicking on the tabs, so you must follow the entire process to get the results.

Quicken and Your Personal Finances

Quicken can be a major aid in achieving personal financial success. It can help you manage most aspects of your financial life, deal with your income taxes, plan for major financial objectives such as retirement, and make more-prudent insurance decisions. Use the information in the next five chapters to assure that Quicken helps in all these ways.

Chapter 12, *Cash or Charge?*, describes how to track credit-card and cash spending. In Chapter 13, *Loans and Mortgages*, you'll see how to use Quicken's loan calculator, set up amortizing loans, and track loan payments and balances. Chapter 14, *Estimating and Preparing Income Taxes*, tells you how to make sure you collect the information you need to prepare your federal and state income tax returns easily and accurately. Chapter 15, *Planning Your Personal Finances*, describes how to use the Quicken financial planners to make better decisions about things such as retirement planning and saving for children's college costs. Chapter 16, *Making Better Insurance Decisions*, demonstrates techniques for saving money on insurance, using the Investment Planner to estimate life-insurance needs, and keeping records on insured property.

CHAPTER 12
Cash or Charge?

FEATURING

You can use Quicken not only to track bank accounts but also to track just about any personal asset, most business assets, and just about any liability. This chapter describes how to use Quicken to track credit and debit cards as well as the cash you carry and spend (such as the money in your wallet or a business's petty cash fund). The chapter also describes how you can use the Quicken Loan Planner to calculate how long it will take you to pay off credit card balances.

Before You Begin

To begin using Quicken for credit-card tracking, you need to

► Know how the Quicken register works and how to record payments and deposits into it (see Chapter 2, *Using the Quicken Register*).

► Know your current credit or debit card balance and, ideally, your credit limit. (You should be able to get some of this information from your most recent credit card or debit card statement. If you've saved your transaction slips since the most recent credit-card or debit card statement, these will be useful too.)

► Have been approved for the Quicken Visa card, if you'll be using the optional IntelliCharge feature. You'll also need a modem if you want to retrieve your IntelliCharge credit-card statements by modem over the telephone line.

Paying Off a Credit Card

Credit cards can simplify and improve your financial life. You don't need to carry large sums of cash around, just a tiny rectangle of plastic. If you need a short-term loan—say a car breaks down or a child needs stitches—you have immediate funding at your fingertips.

Despite all the positive ways consumer credit influences our lives, it's easy for too much of a good thing to turn bad. To get into trouble, simply make that tempting minimum payment a few times on a credit card with a painfully high annual interest rate. Before you know it, you have hefty credit card balances, and you're paying hundreds or even thousands of dollars in annual interest charges.

If you find yourself in this predicament and want to get out of the credit card trap, you can use the Loan Planner to estimate what size payment pays off a credit card over a specified number of years. Just follow these steps:

1. Choose the Features ➤ Planning ➤ Financial Planners ➤ Loan command to display the Loan Planner dialog box, as shown in Figure 12.1.

2. Click on the Payment Per Period option button in the Calculate panel at the bottom of the dialog box, and use the Loan Amount text box to enter the amount you currently owe on a credit card.

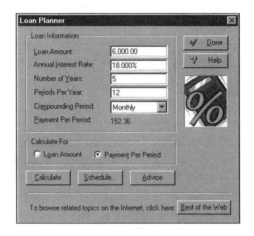

Figure 12.1. **The Loan Planner dialog box**

3. In the Annual Interest Rate text box, enter the annual interest rate charged on the card balance. If a card charges 18 percent annually, for example, type **18**.

4. In the Number of Years text box, enter the number of years over which you want to pay off the credit card balance. If you want to have the balance paid off in five years, for example, type **5**.

5. Verify that the Periods Per Year text box shows 12, which indicates that you'll be making monthly payments.

6. Click on the Calculate button.

   Quicken calculates the monthly payment that repays the credit card balance over the specified number of years and displays it at the bottom of the Loan Information panel. If you currently owe $6,000 on a credit card charging 18 percent annual interest, for example, paying off the $5,000 over five years will require monthly payments of $152.36.

   If you want to see a breakdown of payments to principal and interest, click on the Schedule command button to display a schedule of payments based on your figures. One is shown in Figure 12.2.

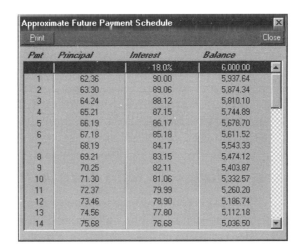

Figure 12.2. *The Approximate Future Payment Schedule dialog box shows how your regular monthly payment will repay the credit-card debt.*

 TIP If a credit-card issuer charges you interest from the date of the charge transaction, you also pay interest on charges you make over a month rather than on only the balance outstanding at the start of the month. It will take longer to repay the credit-card balance than the Loan Planner calculates if you continue to use the credit card.

Tracking Credit Cards

To track a credit-card in Quicken, you need to set up an account for the credit card, and then you need to record the charges and payments you make. If you've set up bank accounts before and worked with these accounts, you'll find credit card accounts easy to use.

When to Set Up a Credit-Card Account

Do you need to set up a credit-card account? Even if you use a credit card, you may not need to track it with Quicken. If you pay off your credit card in full every month, you can categorize your credit bill when you write the check to pay the credit company by using the Splits dialog box. And if you always charge nominal amounts that you don't need to keep careful track of, you probably don't need to set up a credit-card balance.

On the other hand, if you carry a substantial credit card balance, you'll want to set up a credit card account to categorize your credit card spending. You'll also want to set up a credit-card account if you want to track your spending by merchant—the businesses that accept your credit card charges—even if you always pay off the credit-card bill in full each month. Merchant information can't be recorded anywhere as part of writing a check to the credit-card company. Finally, you'll want to use a credit card account if you need or want to track your credit-card balance.

Setting Up Credit-Card Accounts

You set up a credit-card account in Quicken for each credit card you use. If you have both a Visa and an American Express card, you set up two credit-card accounts, one to track the Visa card and one to track the American Express card. To set up a credit-card account, follow these steps:

1. Click on the Accts icon or choose the Lists ➤ Account command to display the Account List window, as shown in Figure 12.3.

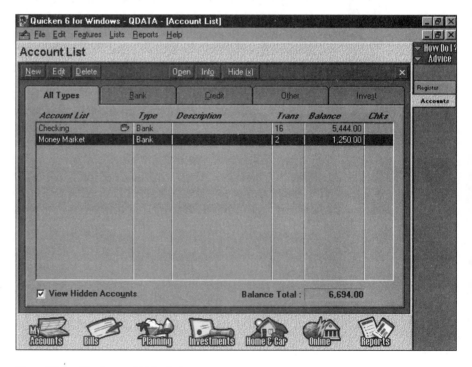

Figure 12.3.   *The Account List window*

2. Click on the New command button in the Account List window to display the dialog box you use to set up a new account, as shown in Figure 12.4.

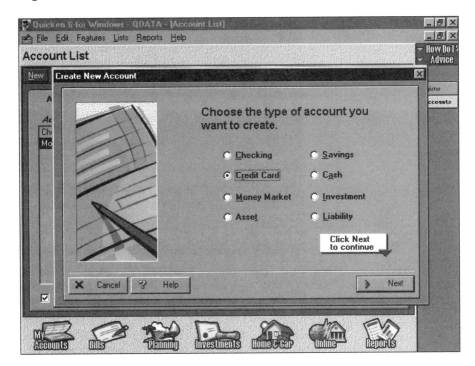

Figure 12.4. **Setting up a new account**

3. Click on the Credit Card button, and then click on Next.

4. When Quicken displays the Credit Card Account Setup dialog box, click on the Summary tab. (If you've been working with Quicken a bit, you won't need the extra hand-holding the other tab in the Credit Card Account Setup dialog box provides.) Figure 12.5 shows the Summary tab in the Credit Card Account Setup dialog box.

5. Enter an account name: Place the cursor in the Account Name text box and enter a short name for the credit-card account, such as **Visa** or **AMEX**.

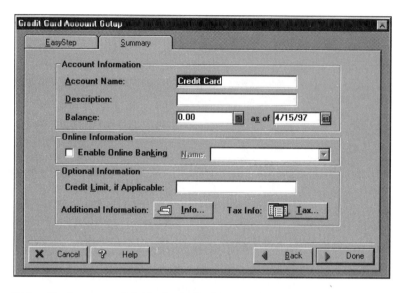

Figure 12.5. **The Summary tab in the Credit Card Account Setup dialog box**

TIP If you have more than one credit card of the same kind—such as two Visa cards—consider using the credit-card name and the issuer name to identify the credit card. For example, if you have Visa cards from Chase Manhattan and from Wells Fargo, you might name one credit card "Visa–Chase" and the other "Visa–Wells."

6. *If you want to provide an account description,* click in the Description text box. Enter a description of the credit-card account or additional account information, such as the account number or the credit card company. You can enter and display roughly 20 characters.

7. Enter the current credit-card account balance: Place the cursor in the Balance text box and enter the account balance on the day you'll start keeping records for the credit card.

TIP You can enter the credit-card balance as of the last statement date, but this figure won't include the payments you've made since the last statement or any charges you've incurred. Therefore, if you do enter the balance as of the last statement date, be sure to enter the transactions that have occurred since the last statement date when it is time to reconcile.

8. Enter the date on which you start keeping records for this account: Highlight the As of (date) text box and enter the date in ***MM/DD/YY*** fashion. For example, type July 4, 1997 as **7/4/97**.

9. *If you will retrieve your statements via modem,* mark the Enable Online Banking check box. Then, activate the Name drop-down–list box and select the bank that issued your credit card—that is, the bank to which you send the check to pay your credit-card charges.

> **NOTE** If you marked the Enable Online Banking check box, Quicken changes the name of the Done command button to the Next command button. When you click on Next, Quicken displays another set of text boxes for describing the bank issuing your credit card. You get the information you need to fill in these dialog boxes from the bank issuing the credit card.

10. *If you want to track the card limit,* enter the credit card's credit limit. To do that, click in the Credit Limit text box and enter the amount.

11. *If you want to collect and store more information about the credit-card account,* click on the Info command button. Then use the Additional Account Information dialog box, which Quicken displays, to enter this information. You might want use the Additional Account Information dialog box, for example, to store the credit card number and the telephone number you use to report a lost or stolen credit card. When you have completed this screen, click on OK.

12. Click on Done to tell Quicken the Create Credit Card Account dialog box is complete. If you indicated that you won't use Online Banking, you're done and can skip the rest of the steps described here. (If you've enabled Online Banking, click on Next instead of Done.)

    Quicken displays the Account List window (see Figure 12.3), and this time it includes your new credit card account.

13. *If you indicated you'll use Online Banking,* Quicken displays the Online Banking setup dialog box shown in Figure 12.6.

14. Enter the 9-digit routing number that is shown in the Routing Number text box of your Online Banking welcome letter.

15. Enter your credit-card number in the Credit Card Number text box. You can get it right off the face of your credit card.

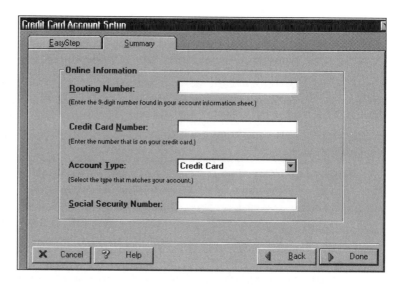

Figure 12.6.   **The setup information needed for an Online Banking credit card**

16. Verify that the Account Type drop-down–list box shows Credit Card as the account type. If it doesn't, activate the drop-down–list box and then select Credit Card.

17. Enter your Social Security number in the Social Security Number text box.

18. Click on Done.

Quicken displays the Account List window (see Figure 12.3), and this time it includes your new credit-card account with a lightning bolt next to the account type to indicate that it is an Online Banking account.

Telling Quicken Which Credit-Card Account You Want to Work With

As you may know, Quicken displays different registers for different accounts and different credit-card accounts. To record charges and payments related to a specific credit card, you'll need to be able to see a register's document window.

If you can see the Credit Card Register QuickTab in the Quicken application window, you can tell Quicken you want to work with the account simply by making its document window active. (You can make the document window active by clicking on its QuickTab.)

If you can't see a credit card's register in a document window, you display the Account List window (see Figure 12.3), select the account, and click on the Open button in the Account List window. (You can also double-click on the account name.)

Quicken then displays a register document window for the credit card account, and you're all set to begin entering credit-card charges and payments. Figure 12.7 shows a sample Credit Card register document window.

Part 2

Quicken and Your Personal Finances

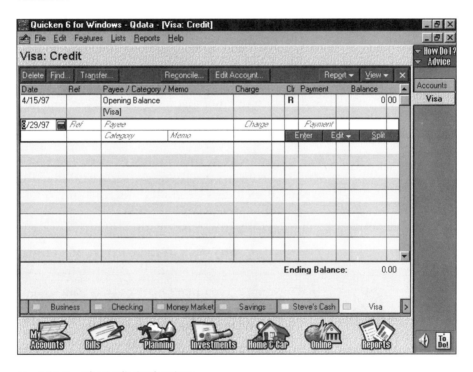

Figure 12.7. **The Credit Card register**

Recording Credit-Card Charges the Normal Way

As long as you're not working with an Online Banking account, you record credit cards the same way you record payments made from a bank account. (Because recording transactions into an Online Banking account is a little different, I'll describe that a little later in the chapter.)

To record a credit-card charge, use the arrow keys or the mouse or choose the Edit ➤ Transaction ➤ New command to move to the next empty row of the register. Then follow these steps:

1. Enter the credit-card charge date: Place the cursor in the Date text box. If the date shown isn't the correct transaction date, enter the date in *MM/DD/YY* format. You typically don't have to enter the year number; the one Quicken already shows is usually correct.

2. *If you want, you can enter a credit-card reference number* the same way you enter check numbers. (You might choose, for example, to enter a portion of the credit-card transaction number.) Enter the number in the Ref text box.

3. Name the merchant who accepted the credit-card charge: Place the cursor in the Payee combo box. If this is the first time you've recorded a charge with the merchant, type the payee's name. If you've recorded a charge before or written a check, though, activate the Payee drop-down list and select the merchant's name from it.

4. Enter the amount in the Charge or Payment text box. You don't have to enter currency punctuation—such as dollar signs or commas—but you should include a decimal to identify any cents.

5. *If you want to mark cleared transactions manually and the transaction you're entering into the register has already cleared or been recorded by the credit-card company,* click in the Clr text box to place an *R* there.

 NOTE Normally, you won't mark cleared transactions. Marking charges and payments as cleared is something you do as part of reconciling a credit-card account. If you're entering old transactions—say you're starting your record keeping as of the previous credit-card statement—you can mark cleared transactions to make your reconciliation easier.

6. *If you want to enter a short description,* click in the Memo text box and enter the description. You can enter anything you want in this field, but there's no reason to duplicate information you've entered or will enter someplace else.

7. To categorize the transaction, highlight the Category combo box and activate the Category drop-down list. Then select the category that

best describes the charge A charge at the office supplies store, for example, might fall into the Office Supplies category.

A payment will usually be recorded as a transfer from the bank account you'll use to write the check that pays the bill (see Chapter 2, *Using the Quicken Register*). If you can't find an expense category that describes the charge, you can enter a short category description directly into the Category combo box. (If you want to create a category named Office Supplies, for example, type **Office Supplies**.)

When you click on Enter and have not chosen a category, Quicken displays a dialog box asking if you want to select one from the list, as shown in Figure 12.8. If you want to select a category, click on the Yes button. Otherwise, click on the No button. If you don't want Quicken to continue to ask you about categories when you don't select one, check the Don't Show This Message Again check box.

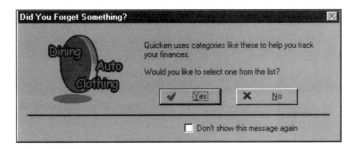

Figure 12.8. *A dialog box in which you can choose to select a category if you haven't already done so*

 TIP Chapter 14, *Estimating and Preparing Income Taxes,* provides help on setting up category lists that easily support your income tax planning and preparation.

8. Select Enter to record the credit-card charge or payment.

Quicken updates the credit-card balance and the remaining credit limit and then highlights the next empty row in the Account Register window. Figure 12.9 shows several credit-card charges and a single credit-card payment transaction.

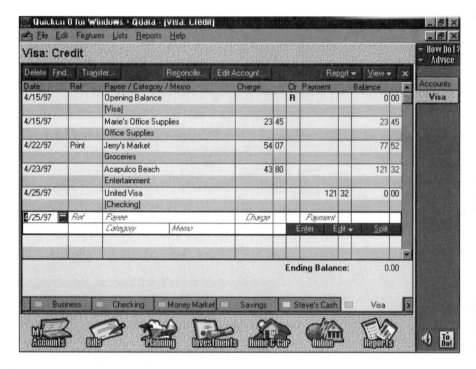

Figure 12.9.   *The Credit Card register with several charges and a single payment transaction*

Paying a Credit-Card Bill the Easy Way

The easiest way to pay a credit-card bill is just to record a payment transaction into the register. If you write a check, for example, the payment shows as a transfer from your bank account to the credit-card account, like the last transaction in the register in Figure 12.9. (Chapter 2 explains how transfer transactions work.)

Paying and Reconciling a Credit-Card Bill

You can also pay a credit-card bill as part of reconciling a credit-card statement. To do so, you go through the steps for analyzing the difference between your credit-card records and the credit-card company's records. (This process works just like a bank account reconciliation.) Then, at the end, you tell Quicken how much you want to pay.

To reconcile and pay a credit-card bill, be sure the Credit Card document window is active. Then follow these steps:

1. Choose the Features ➤ Banking ➤ Reconcile command or click on the Reconcile button to display the Credit Card Statement Information dialog box, as shown in Figure 12.10.

Part
2

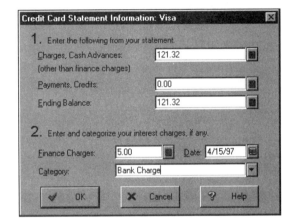

Quicken and Your
Personal Finances

Figure 12.10. **The Credit Card Statement Information dialog box**

2. Using the Charges, Cash Advances text box, enter the amount your credit-card statement shows as the total charges and cash advances.

3. Using the Payments, Credits text box, enter the amount your credit card statement shows as the total payments and credits.

4. Enter the ending credit-card–account balance from your statement in the Ending Balance text box.

5. Enter the monthly finance charge shown on the statement (if you haven't done so already) in the Finance Charges text box.

6. Tell Quicken when the finance charge occurred, using the Date text box.

7. Categorize the finance charge by using the Category text box. (If you don't remember which category you want to use, click on the down-arrow on the Category drop-down–list box to display a list of categories.)

8. Click on OK to display the Reconcile Credit Card Statement window, as shown in Figure 12.11.

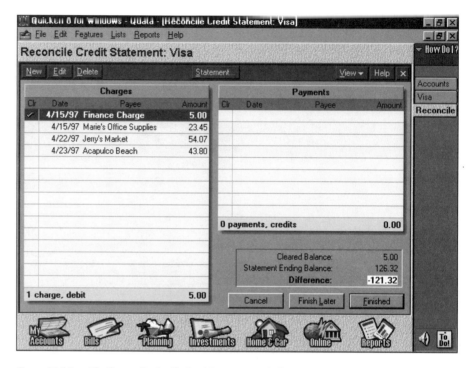

Figure 12.11.   *The Reconcile Credit Card Statement window*

 TIP If you have a question about a transaction shown in the Reconcile Credit Card Statement window, double-click on the transaction to display the credit-card account's register with the transaction highlighted. You can examine the transaction in more detail—for example, by reviewing the split transaction information. When you're ready to return to the Reconcile Credit Card Statement window, click on the Reconcile QuickTab.

9. Review the list of transactions shown in the Reconcile Credit Card Statement window, and highlight each of the transactions that has cleared: Quicken places a check mark by each transaction you highlight. If you accidentally mark a transaction as cleared when it should-n't be, click on it again or press the spacebar.

10. Select Finished when the difference between the cleared balance and the credit-card statement balance is 0.

As you indicate which transactions have cleared, Quicken continually recalculates a "cleared balance" figure. This figure is just your records' credit-card–account balance minus all the uncleared transactions. When the cleared balance equals the credit-card statement balance, your account balances, or reconciles. In other words, when the uncleared transactions total explains the difference between your records and the credit card company's records, you've reconciled the account.

Figure 12.12 shows the Reconcile Credit Card Statement window when this is the case. When you select Finished, Quicken updates the cleared status of the transactions you marked as cleared by changing the asterisks to *R*s. Then it displays a message box that asks if you want to make a payment on the credit-card bill.

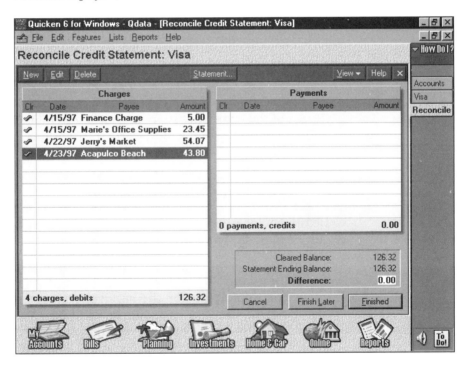

Figure 12.12. **The Reconcile Credit Card Statement window showing a cleared balance figure**

11. *If you do want to make a payment on the credit-card bill,* choose the bank account on which you'll write the check from the Bank Account drop-down–list box.

12. Use the Payment Method option buttons to indicate whether you will handwrite the check or use Quicken to print it:

- **Printed Check.** Click on this option button to display the Write Checks window for the account you selected in step 11 and fill out several of the text boxes in this window. When you finish describing the check, select Record Check.

- **Handwritten Check.** Click on this option button and click on Yes to display the bank account register for the account you selected in step 11 and begin recording a payment transaction. You complete the transaction and then select Enter.

Quicken also fills in the Category text box with the credit-card account name, but don't change this. When you pay off a portion of a credit-card balance, you actually are transferring money from your bank account to the credit-card company. Click on Enter when you finish describing the payment transaction.

Recording Credit-Card Charges with Online Banking

As long as you have either the Quicken credit card or a credit card issued by one of the banks that support Quicken's Online Bill Payment feature, you can retrieve your credit-card transactions from the credit-card company.

Setting Up Your Online Connection

Before you can begin to use any of Quicken's online financial services, you need to apply for online service.

To do so, click on the Online icon and then select Get Started with Online Banking. When you do, Quicken displays a series of dialog boxes for signing up for the service. I'm not going to show these dialog boxes here. They are simply text boxes for entering your name and address, the password you use to connect to the service, and some information Intuit uses to identify you if the need arises.

 NOTE Quicken automatically sets up your modem whenever you attempt to use any of its online services—including Online Banking. (If the automatic modem setup doesn't work correctly, use the Features ➤ Online ➤ Modem Setup command.)

Retrieving a Credit-Card Statement

Whenever you want to, you can retrieve your most recent credit-card transactions from Intuit Services Corporation, the company that runs the Online Banking and Bill Payments services.

To update your credit-card register, you click on the Reconcile command button. When Quicken displays the Reconcile Online Account dialog box, mark the Connect and Get Data check box. If this is the first time you've attempted to download data, Quicken displays a message box that tells you so and asks if you want to go to the Online Banking window.

When you click on Yes, Quicken displays the Online Banking window. Click on the Get Online Data command button. Quicken retrieves the data it needs from the Intuit Services Corporation computer.

What About Debit Cards?

You can track debit cards in Quicken too. The process varies from that used for tracking credit cards because a debit card isn't actually a liability. Rather, it's an asset, which makes it more analogous to a bank account; therefore, you treat a debit card like another bank account. You can record debit-card charges on the account the same way you record payments on a regular checking account. And you treat additions to the debit-card–account balance the same way as deposits into a regular checking account.

TIP A debit card attached to a regular bank account doesn't need a separate bank account. The debit-card transactions can be recorded directly into the bank account's register.

Tracking Cash

Most people won't need to track the cash they hold (like what's in a wallet) or the cash they spend and receive. It's usually easy enough to monitor cash balances by looking in your pocket. And it's often possible to record the income and expense categories associated with cash receipts and disbursements as part of cashing the check you use to get the cash or as part of withdrawing money from the bank. If you withdraw $100 from a bank account to spend on groceries, for example, you can categorize the $100 withdrawal as a Groceries expense.

Setting Up a Cash Account

To track your cash holdings, receipts, and expenditures more precisely than you can with an informal approach, you can set up a cash account the same way you set up other accounts: Display the Accounts List window and select the New command button. When Quicken displays the Account Setup window, indicate you want to set up a cash account and click on Next. Then, when Quicken displays the Cash Account Setup dialog box, click on the Summary tab, give the account a name or simply accept the default Cash, tell Quicken how much cash you're holding in the Balance text box and when you want to start tracking it in the As Of box. Then, click on Done.

To display a register that describes the cash account you've just set up, place the cursor in the cash account in the Accounts List and double-click on the name of the cash account or click on the Open command button. Quicken displays the cash version of the Account register, as shown in Figure 12.13.

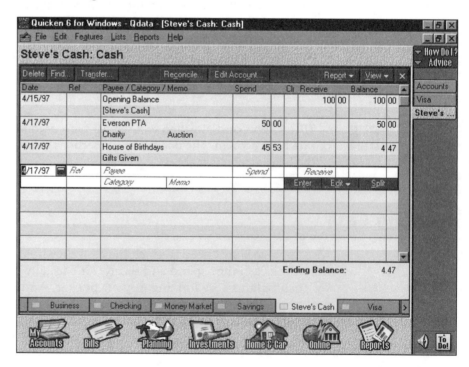

Figure 12.13. **A cash version of the Account register with example receipt and disbursement transactions**

Recording Receipts and Disbursements

Recording cash receipts and disbursements is similar to recording bank account withdrawals and deposits. You begin by placing the cursor in the next empty row of the register or by choosing Edit ➤ Transaction ➤ New. Then follow these steps:

1. Enter the cash receipt or disbursement date.

2. *If you want a more detailed record,* enter a cash receipt or disbursement reference number.

3. Name the person from whom you received or to whom you disbursed the cash.

4. Enter the receipt or disbursement amount. Use the Spend column for disbursements and the Receive column for receipts.

5. *If you want more details,* add a memo description.

6. Categorize the receipt or disbursement transaction. (Increases in cash because you cash a check should be recorded as a transfer from your bank account to your cash account.)

7. Select Enter to record the receipt or disbursement, and Quicken updates the cash balance and highlights the next empty row in the Account Register window.

NOTE When a cash account is displayed in the active document window, click on the Reconcile command button. Quicken displays the Update Account Balance dialog box. You can use it to enter a cash transaction that adjusts the current balance to whatever actual cash you hold. The Update Account Balance dialog box provides text boxes for entering the correct account balance, the category to use for the adjustment transaction, and the adjustment date. You just fill in the blanks and click on OK.

HOW TO CHOOSE AND USE CREDIT CARDS
··· *on the Road to Riches*

Credit cards are convenient, but they're also dangerous. A lot of people foul up their financial lives something terrible by turning the phrase "charge it" into a reflex. It's a real problem, and for that reason the rest of this chapter explains how to make good use of credit cards and how to choose a good credit card.

Selecting the Right Credit Card

Selecting a credit card is easy. If you don't carry charges forward from month to month, choose the card with the lowest annual fee. It doesn't matter to you if the credit-card company charges a painfully high interest rate, since you only pay that rate if you don't pay your monthly credit card bill in full and on time.

If you do carry a balance, it makes sense to choose the card with the lowest interest rate. Some credit-card issuers play interest rate calculation tricks that make it very difficult to make apples-to-apples comparisons of credit cards. But if you choose the credit card with the lowest annual percentage rate, you're doing about as well as you can.

The Right Way to Use a Credit Card

You shouldn't use a credit card as a way to borrow money. That means always repaying the charges within the grace period. You want to be what the bank calls "a revolver," which is a person who always pays his or her credit-card bills on time.

Credit-card–interest rates are way, way too expensive. One reason they are so expensive is that consumer interest, which is what credit-card interest is, is not tax deductible. You can't deduct it from your gross income for income-tax purposes the way you can a mortgage interest payment. And even if you ignore income taxes, credit-card–interest rates are usually way, way above the interest rate on a car loan or a mortgage. Because you can use amortizing debt (*amortizing debt* is a regular loan on which you make payments on both the interest and the principal over time), any time it makes sense to borrow money, it's a safe bet that you should probably never borrow money using your credit card.

WARNING If you carry a credit-card balance, you often pay interest on both the old and new charges. In other words, there is no grace period for your charges.

After a 401(k) or deductible IRA, the best investment you can make is to pay down credit cards that charge a high interest rate. Earning a tax-free interest rate of, say, 14 percent, which is what a 401(k) and deductible IRA pay, is too good to pass up.

Do Affinity Cards Make Sense?

In general, an affinity card—especially one that doesn't charge a fee—is a good deal as long as the interest rate is competitive. I have a General Motors credit card, for example, that includes a 5 percent rebate account. In other words, five cents of every dollar I charge on the card goes into a rebate account that I can use toward purchasing a new General Motors car. How big your rebate gets depends on the type of General Motors credit card you have. As of this writing, the regular General Motors credit card lets you accumulate up to $500 a year to a maximum of $3,500. The General Motors gold credit card lets you accumulate up to $1,000 a year to a maximum of $7,000.

NOTE An *affinity card* is a credit card that's issued by someone other than a bank—such as car manufacturer, an airline, a professional group, and so forth. Affinity cards typically combine the usual features of a credit card with some extra benefit connected to the issuer. In the case of a GM card, for example, you accumulate dollars in a rebate account by virtue of what you spend with the affinity card.

There are many different affinity cards. Ford has one. Most of the major airlines have them too. Airline affinity cards let you accumulate frequent flier miles based on the credit-card charges. In the plans I've seen, you usually get a mile a dollar.

The one sticky part of using affinity cards, however, is that getting even a 5 percent rebate isn't worth it if having the card makes you spend more money. Some studies show that you spend 23 percent more when you use a credit card. The same is very likely true of affinity cards.

If you're one of those people who spends more when you have a card in hand, you won't save any money by using an affinity card. Even if you get a new General Motors car for free or a handful of free airline tickets to Europe, you pay indirectly for your new car or airline tickets with all the extra charging you do. If you don't make use of the rebate, the situation is even worse. You've charged more, perhaps paid hefty annual fees, and you've received nothing in return.

How to Save Money on Credit Cards

Fortunately, you can use a bunch of different tactics to save money on credit cards. Following are the best ideas I know:

Leave Home without It

If you're like most people, you spend more money if you carry a credit card around. One study showed that credit-card holders spend 23 percent more on average even if they don't carry a balance on the credit cards. No investment pays an instantaneous 23 percent rate after taxes. Despite what American Express says, you're really better off if you leave home *without* it.

Cancel Unnecessary Credit Cards

If you don't carry credit-card balances, cancel credit cards that charge an annual maintenance fee. Lighten your wallet by canceling all the cards you don't use, for that matter. You'll only spend more if you use them, anyway.

Ask Your Bank to Waive Its Annual Fee

Call your bank and explain that, because of the annual fee, you might cancel your credit card. Tell the bank you think it should waive its annual fee. Your current credit card issuer will probably gulp and then waive the fee. For a two-minute telephone call, you'll be ahead by $20 or $30. (By the way, most credit-card issuers don't waive the fee on a gold card.)

Consider an Affinity Card

If you travel on business a lot, you can easily run up $10,000 or more on a credit card as you pay for airline tickets, hotels, and rental cars. In this case, it's well worth it to pay $50 for an affinity card. Once you have the card, charge all your purchases on it (your employer will likely reimburse you anyway). When you accumulate a whopping rebate, use it for a family vacation or a new car.

One caution here, however: Talk to your tax advisor, because there's a good chance your rebate will be considered taxable income if you go this route. On the other hand, if you only charge personal purchases on the affinity card, you can make a good case that the rebate isn't taxable income but is an adjustment in the price of the goods you bought.

Cancel Credit Insurance If You Have Any

Credit life insurance is usually a big waste of money. But read through the primer in Chapter 16, *Making Better Insurance Decisions*, first. You might need credit life insurance if you know your estate will collect and you can't get a better kind of insurance.

Credit disability insurance is usually another big waste of money. But you may need this insurance if you require disability insurance and you can't get better insurance.

Cancel Credit-Card Protection Insurance If You Have It

Credit-card protection insurance is another waste of money. If some nefarious type steals your credit card and runs up huge charges, you are only liable for the first $50 or so as long as you tell the credit card issuer that the credit card was stolen.

Never Make the Minimum Payment

Pay more than the minimum payment. Paying off high-interest-rate credit cards is one of the two best investments you can make. (The other is contributing money to a 401(k) plan in which the employer matches a portion of your contribution.) If you make minimum payments only, your credit-card debt quickly balloons. *Very* quickly balloons, I should say. Soon you are paying massive monthly finance charges.

Get Rid of Your Gold Card

You're paying for the privilege and prestige of that gold card. But you knew that, right? You can probably save yourself at least $40 or $50 just by having an old, boring, regular Visa or MasterCard.

CHAPTER 13

Loans and Mortgages

FEATURING

E ARLIER chapters described how you can use Quicken to track things such as bank accounts and credit cards and the ways you earn and spend your money. You can also use Quicken to track your debts and what they cost you. Performing this record keeping lets you more closely monitor your liabilities. And if you keep records of all your assets, it lets you track your net worth.

Before You Start

What you need to track loans and mortgages depends on what you want to do:

▶ To track any loan or mortgage, you need to know the current loan balance. (You can probably get this information from the most recent loan statement or by telephoning the lender.)

▶ To have Quicken break down loan payments into the interest and principal components, you need to know the loan's annual interest rate and the remaining number of payments. (You can get this information from the loan contract. And you may be able to get it with a telephone call.)

Using the Loan Planner

The Loan Planner introduced in Chapter 9 works well for experimenting with possible loan balances and payments. You can use this tool to see, for example, what the loan payment would be on that car you're eyeing or what size mortgage you can afford, given a specific payment amount.

To use the Loan Planner for these tasks, follow these steps:

1. Choose the Features ➤ Planning ➤ Financial Planners ➤ Loan command to display the Loan Planner dialog box, as shown in Figure 13.1.

2. Tell Quicken which loan variable you want to calculate: Click on the Loan Amount option button in the Calculate for panel to calculate a loan payment given the loan amount, or click on the Payment Per Period option button to calculate the loan amount given a loan payment.

3. *If you've indicated you want to calculate a loan payment,* enter the loan balance in the Loan Amount text box.

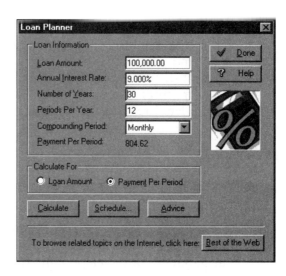

Figure 13.1. **The Loan Planner dialog box can calculate either the loan amount or the payment.**

4. Enter the loan's annual interest rate in the Annual Interest Rate text box. If a loan charges 9 percent annually, for example, type **9**.

5. Using the Number of Years text box, enter the number of years over which you will repay the loan. For a 30-year mortgage, for example, type **30**.

6. Enter the number of payments you'll make each year into the Periods Per Year text box. In Figure 13.1, this text box shows 12, which indicates you'll be making monthly payments.

7. *If you indicated in step 2 that you want to calculate a loan balance,* enter the loan payment you want to or will make in the Payment Per Period text box.

Once you complete these steps, click on the Calculate button, and Quicken calculates the variable you said you wanted to calculate. Figure 13.1, for example, shows that the monthly payment on a $100,000 30-year mortgage bearing 9 percent annual interest equals $804.62.

To create an amortization schedule that shows the periodic payments, the interest and principal portions of these payments, and the loan balance after each payment, click on the Schedule button. Quicken produces an amortization schedule report and displays it in its own dialog

boii. This dialog boii is shown in Figure 13.2. You can print the amor
tization schedule by clicking on the dialog box's Print command button (see Chapter 4, *Tracking Your Finances with Reports*).

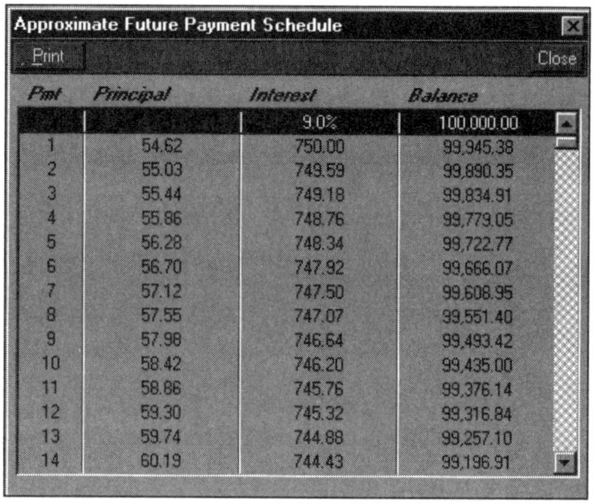

Approximate Future Payment Schedule

Pmt	Principal	Interest	Balance
		9.0%	100,000.00
1	54.62	750.00	99,945.38
2	55.03	749.59	99,890.35
3	55.44	749.18	99,834.91
4	55.86	748.76	99,779.05
5	56.28	748.34	99,722.77
6	56.70	747.92	99,666.07
7	57.12	747.50	99,608.95
8	57.55	747.07	99,551.40
9	57.98	746.64	99,493.42
10	58.42	746.20	99,435.00
11	58.86	745.76	99,376.14
12	59.30	745.32	99,316.84
13	59.74	744.88	99,257.10
14	60.19	744.43	99,196.91

Figure 13.2.   **The Approximate Future Payment Schedule dialog box**

Saving Money with Early Repayment

You can often save enormous sums by repaying a loan early. In the
preceding section, for example, I referred to a $100,000 30-year mort-
gage bearing 9 percent annual interest. Although such a mortgage loan
would call for monthly payments of $804.62, suppose a borrower
could afford to increase the payment amount by $20 to $824.62—and
the lender doesn't charge prepayment penalties. By making the larger
payment each month, the borrower would save $24,135.56. No, you
didn't misread the amount. An extra $20 a month results in roughly
$24,000 of interest savings!

You can calculate how much money you'll save by early repayment of
a loan such as a mortgage. To do this, you calculate the total regular-
sized payments you would have made according to the loan contract
and the total new-but-bigger payments you're now planning to make.
The difference between these two amounts equals the interest savings
from the new payment.

Making the Early Repayment Calculations

The calculations just described require several steps, so I've created a simple worksheet you can use to work through the numbers. It is shown in Table 13.1. The worksheet's left column of numbers shows how you would calculate the interest rate savings by adding an extra $20 to a monthly payment of $804.62 when you have a $100,000, 30-year mortgage bearing 9 percent interest. The worksheet's right column provides blank spaces you can use to calculate the actual interest rate savings you'd receive via early loan repayment.

Table 13.1. **The Early Loan Repayment Savings Worksheet**

Input Description	Example Loan	Your Loan
Line 1: Regular payment amount	$804.62	_____
Line 2: Number of remaining regular payments	360	_____
Line 3: Total regular payments (line 1 × line 2)	289,663.20	_____
Line 4: New payment amount	$823.12	_____
Line 5: Number of remaining new payments	324	_____
Line 6: Total new payments (line 4 × line 5)	266,690.88	_____
Line 7: Repayment savings (line 3 – line 6)	22,969.08	_____

To complete the worksheet, follow these steps:

1. Enter the regular payment amount on line 1.

2. Enter the remaining number of payments on line 2. If you've just closed on a 30-year mortgage with monthly payments, for example, you have 360 monthly payments remaining. If you're halfway through repaying the same loan, you have 180 monthly payments remaining.

3. Multiply line 1 by line 2 to calculate the total remaining payments (you can use the Quicken calculator) and enter the result on line 3. To calculate the total remaining payments when the regular monthly payment equals $804.62 and there are 360 months of payments left, for example, multiply $804.62 by 360 months for a result of $289,663.20.

4. To set up the Loan Planner so it's ready for calculating the number of new, larger payments you'll need to make, display the Loan Planner dialog box and click on the Payment Per Period radio button. Enter the remaining loan balance in the Loan Amount text box, the loan's interest rate in the Annual Interest Rate text box, and the number of payments per year—probably 12—in the Payments Per Year text box.

5. To estimate the number of years you'll make the new, larger payment, just keep entering new, smaller values in the Number of Years text box until you find the Number of Years value that results in a calculated loan payment that's close to your new payment; you probably won't be able to get a Number of Years value that produces a payment amount exactly equal to your new planned payment. In the example, setting the Number of Years to 27 produces a payment amount equal to $823.13 even though I've indicated that $824.62 is really the new payment planned. This means I have to calculate the early repayment savings stemming from a monthly payment of $823.13, not $824.62.

6. Enter the new payment in the Loan Planner dialog box on line 4 of the worksheet. In this case, this amount is $823.13. (Actually, you will probably make the $824.62 payment because that figure equals the extra $20 plus the regular payment of $804.62. Unfortunately, you can't calculate the early repayment savings that stem from an $824.62 payment, only from an $823.13 payment.)

7. Calculate the number of new, larger payments you'll need to make, and enter this value on line 5 of the worksheet. Do this by multiplying the value in the Number of Years text box by 12. If you'll make 27 years of monthly payments, for example, you calculate the number of payments as 324 (27×12).

8. Calculate the total new payments you'll make and enter this value on line 6 of the worksheet. To calculate the total remaining payments when the new monthly payment equals $823.13 and there are 324 months of payments left, for example, multiply the monthly payment of $823.13 by 324 months for a result of $266,694.12.

9. Calculate the difference between the total regular payments and the total new payments, and enter this value on line 7 of the worksheet.

In the example, this difference of $22,969.08 represents the interest savings stemming from early repayment of the loan using the payment amount shown on line 4. If a borrower actually paid an amount larger than the monthly payment shown on line 4, the early repayment savings would exceed those shown in the worksheet.

Should You Always Repay Early?

When you work through the numbers, the savings that stem from early repayment of a loan can seem almost too good to be true. Can a few dollars a month really add up to, for example, $25,000 of savings?

When you save money over long periods of time and let the interest compound, the amount of interest you ultimately earn becomes very large. In effect, when you pay an extra $20 a month on a 9 percent mortgage, you've saving $20 each month in a savings account that pays 9 percent. By "saving" this $20 over more than 25 years, you earn a lot of interest. In the earlier example, this monthly $20 really would add up to roughly $23,000.

But you can't look just at the interest savings. If you placed the same $20 a month into a money market fund, purchased savings bonds, or invested in a stock market mutual fund, you would also accumulate interest or investment income.

How can you know whether early repayment of a loan makes sense? Simply compare the interest rate on the loan with the interest rate (or investment rate of return) you would earn on alternative investments. If you can place money in a money market fund that earns 6 percent or repay a mortgage charging you 9 percent, you'll do better by repaying the mortgage. Its interest rate exceeds the interest rate of the money market account. But if you can stick money in a small company stock fund and earn 12 percent or repay a mortgage charging you 9 percent, you'll do better by sticking your money in the stock fund.

One complicating factor, however, relates to income taxes. Some interest expense, such as mortgage interest, is tax-deductible. What's more, some interest income is tax-exempt, and some interest income isn't tax-deferred. Income taxes make early repayment decisions a little bit complicated, but here are three rules of thumb:

▶ Usually, if you have extra money that you can tie up for a long time, you'll make the most money by saving your money in a way that provides you with an initial tax deduction, and where the interest compounds tax free, such as a 401(k) plan or an individual retirement account. (Opportunities in which an employer kicks in an extra amount by matching a portion of your contribution are usually too good to pass up—if you can afford them.)

▶ If you've taken advantage of investment options that give you tax breaks and you want to save additional money, your next best bet is usually to pay off any loans or credit cards that charge interest you can't deduct, such as credit-card debt. (Start with the loan or credit card charging the highest interest rate and then work your way down to the loan or credit card charging the lowest interest rate. For this to really work, of course, you can't go out and charge a credit card back up to its limit after you repay it.)

▶ If you repay loans with nondeductible interest and you still have additional money you want to save, you can begin repaying loans that charge tax-deductible interest. Again, you should start with the loan charging the highest interest rate first.

Understanding the Mechanics

Successful saving relies on a simple financial truth: You should save money in a way that results in the highest annual interest, including all the income tax effects.

It's tricky to include income taxes in the calculations, however. They affect your savings in two ways. One way is that they may reduce the interest income you receive or the interest expense you save. If interest income is taxed, for example, you need to multiply the pretax interest rate by the factor (1 – *marginal tax rate*) to calculate the after-income-taxes interest rate. And if interest expense is tax-deductible, you need to multiply the interest rate by the factor (1 – *marginal tax rate*) to calculate the after-income-taxes interest rate.

For example, suppose you have four savings options: a credit card charging 12 percent nondeductible interest, a mortgage charging 9 percent tax-deductible interest, a tax-exempt money market fund earning 6 percent; and a mutual fund earning 12 percent taxable interest income. To know which one of these savings opportunities is the best, you need to calculate the after-income-taxes interest rates. If your marginal income tax rate equals 33 percent—meaning you pay $.33 in income taxes on your last dollars of income—the after-income-taxes interest rates are as follows:

- ▶ 12 percent interest on the credit card

- ▶ 8 percent interest on the mutual fund

- ▶ 6 percent interest on the mortgage

- ▶ 6 percent interest on the tax-exempt money market fund

In this case, your best savings opportunity is the credit card; by repaying it you save 12 percent. Next best is the mutual fund because even after paying the income taxes you'll earn 8 percent. Finally, the mortgage and tax-exempt money market fund savings opportunities produce 6 percent.

TIP   The difference between, say, 12 percent and 6 percent may not seem all that large. Choosing the savings opportunity with the highest after-income-taxes rate delivers big benefits. If you invest $20 each month in something paying 6 percent after income taxes, you'll accumulate $5,107 over 25 years. But if you invest $20 each month in something paying 12 percent after income taxes, you'll accumulate $13,848 over 25 years.

The second complicating factor stems from the tax deduction you sometimes get for certain kinds of investments, such as individual retirement accounts and 401(k) plans. When you get an immediate tax deduction, you actually get to boost your savings amount by the tax deduction. This effectively boosts the interest rate.

For example, if you have an extra $1,000 to save and use it to repay a credit card charging 12 percent, you will save $120 of interest expense (12% × $1,000).

If you save the $1,000 in a way that results in a tax deduction—such as an individual retirement account—things can change quite a bit. Say your marginal income tax rate is 33 percent. In this case, you can actually contribute $1,500. ($1,000 / the factor [1 – *marginal tax rate*]).

The arithmetic might not make sense, but the result should. If you have $1,000 to save but you get a 33 percent tax deduction, you can actually save $1,500 because you'll get a $500 tax deduction ($1,500 × 33%).

What's more, by investing in a tax-deferred opportunity you don't have to pay income taxes while you're earning interest. (A tax-deferred investment just lets you postpone paying the income taxes.) If you invest in a stock mutual fund earning 10 percent, for example, you get to keep the whole 10 percent as long as you leave the money in the stock mutual fund. If you work out the interest income calculations, you would earn 10 percent on $1,500, or $150. So the tax deduction and the tax-deferred interest income mean you'll earn more annually on the stock mutual fund paying 10 percent than you will save on the credit card charging 12 percent.

Be aware that ultimately you pay income taxes on the money you take out of a tax-deferred investment opportunity, such as an individual retirement account. In the example, you would have to pay back the $500 income tax deduction, and you would also have to pay income taxes on the $150. (At 33 percent, you would pay $50 of taxes on the $150 of interest income too.)

In general, though, if you're saving for retirement, it usually still makes sense to go with a savings opportunity that produces a tax deduction and lets you postpone your income taxes. The reason is that the income taxes you postpone also boost your savings—and thereby boost your interest rate. (It's also possible that your marginal income tax rate will be lower when you withdraw money from a tax-deferred savings opportunity.)

Tracking Loans and Mortgages

You can keep detailed records of loan balances and the payments you make on the loan. First, however, you'll need to set up an account in Quicken. To create an account for a car loan, mortgage, or any other debt you owe, follow these steps:

1. Click on the Accts icon or choose the Lists ➤ Account command to display the Account List window, as shown in Figure 13.3.

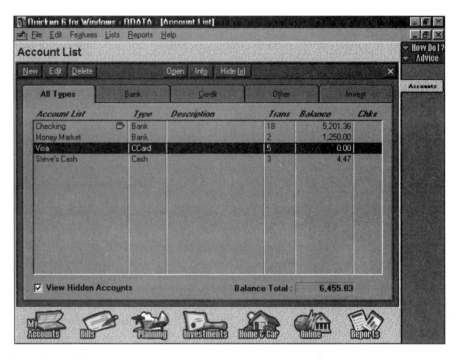

Figure 13.3.   The Account List window

2. Click on the New command button on the Account List document window to display the dialog box you use to select the type of account you want to create, as shown in Figure 13.4.

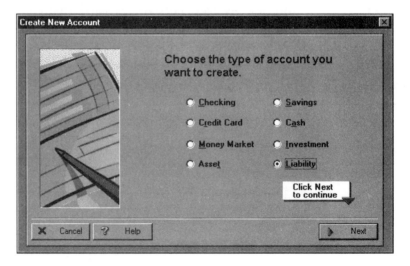

Figure 13.4.   The Account Setup window

3. Click on the Liability option button, click on Next, and then click on the Summary tab to display the Liability Account Setup dialog box, as shown in Figure 13.5.

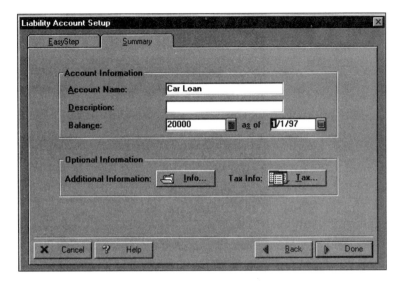

Figure 13.5. **The Liability Account Setup dialog box**

4. Enter an account name in the Account Name text box—such as **Mortgage** or **Car Loan**.

5. In the Description text box, enter a description of the loan or mortgage or additional information, such as the loan number or the lender's name.

6. In the Balance text box, enter the account balance on the day you'll start keeping records for the loan.

> **TIP** You can enter the loan balance as of the last statement date, but this figure won't include the payments made since the last statement. You will need to enter any transactions that have occurred since then.

7. Enter the date on which you start keeping records for the loan in *MM/DD/YY* fashion. For example, enter November 26, 1997, as **11/26/97**.

8. Click on Done to tell Quicken that the Liability Account Setup Information dialog box is complete.

9. When Quicken asks if you would like to set up an amortized loan, answer the question by clicking on either the Yes or No buttons. If you click on No, you're done with the liability account setup and can skip the rest of the steps listed here. If you answer Yes, be sure to click on the Summary button. Quicken displays the Loan Setup dialog box, as shown in Figure 13.6.

Figure 13.6.   **The Loan Setup dialog box**

10. Because I set up a Car Loan account, the Loan Type is Borrow Money, and the account is an existing car loan account. Since the account is new, no payments have been made; so click on the No radio button. Click on Next, and Quicken displays the next Loan Setup screen, as shown in Figure 13.7.

11. The Opening Date text box shows the date you entered in the Account Setup window. Confirm the original amount of the loan in the Original Balance text box. Note that you can display a pop-up calculator by clicking on the button at the right end of the Original Balance text box.

12. Use the Original Length boxes to specify how long you'll make payments on the loan. Enter the number of years or months in the first text box. Then, use the second box (a combo box) to specify whether you've entered the length in years or months.

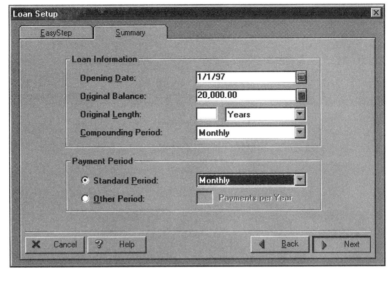

Figure 13.7. **Part 2 of the Loan Setup dialog box**

13. Use the Payment Period option buttons and boxes to indicate how often you'll make loan payments. The default payment period is a standard payment made monthly. You can select another payment period by selecting another period from the Standard Period drop-down–list box—Monthly, Bi-Monthly, Semi-Monthly, and so on. You can also use the Other Period button and box.

14. Click on Next when you finish providing Quicken with the Loan Information and Payment Period information. Quicken displays a new set of buttons and boxes, as shown in Figure 13.8.

15. If necessary, use the Balloon Information options to describe the loan's balloon payment. To do this, enter the number of months or years (or some other time period) that the lender used to amortize the loan balance and to calculate the regular payments. Then indicate how you've specified this amortization term: months, years, or some other time period. (If your loan includes a balloon payment and you don't know the amortization term but you do know the regular payment amount, you can mark the Calculate button in the Balloon Information options to have Quicken determine the balloon payment for you.)

16. Enter the loan's interest rate in the Interest Rate text box.

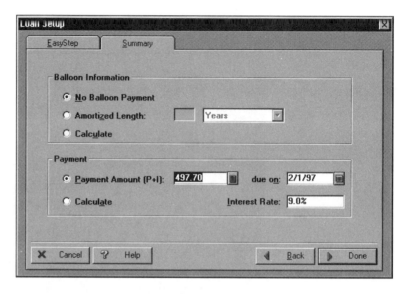

Figure 13.8. **Part 3 of the Loan Setup dialog box**

 NOTE Don't use the annual percentage rate figure as the annual interest rate, even though it is required by truth-in-lending laws in the United States and the United Kingdom (and maybe elsewhere). The annual percentage rate (APR) expresses all the costs of obtaining credit, including the loan interest, any fees, things like loan origination costs, and so on. APRs are an excellent way to compare the overall costs of one loan with another. But you can't use an APR to calculate loan payments because it's not the loan interest rate. To find the annual interest rate, look at your loan agreement.

17. What you do next depends on whether you will make a balloon payment:

- If you haven't specified that Quicken should calculate the balloon payment, mark the Payment option's Calculate button. Then click on Done to have Quicken calculate the loan payment. (Quicken presents a dialog box saying that it has estimated the amount of the payment and asking you to click on OK and then on Done to accept the estimate.)

- If you did tell Quicken to calculate the balloon payment, use the Payment Amount button and boxes to provide the regular principal and interest payment you'll make and the date the first payment is due. Then click on Done to have Quicken calculate the balloon payment.

18. Click on Done again. Quicken displays the Set Up Loan Payment dialog box shown in Figure 13.9.

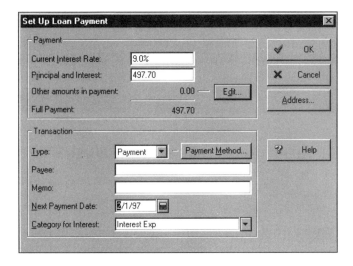

Figure 13.9.   **The Set Up Loan Payment dialog box**

19. If you'll pay other amounts with the loan payment, such as $25 a month for private mortgage insurance, click on the Edit command button to display a Splits dialog box. It is shown in Figure 13.10. This is the same dialog box you see whenever you split a transaction among multiple categories.

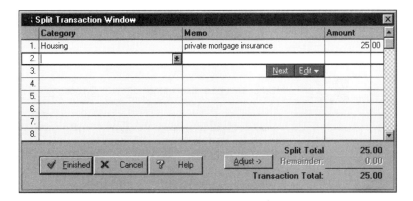

Figure 13.10.   **The Splits dialog box as it might be filled out for a loan payment transaction**

20. Enter the category and amount of any other expenses you'll pay with the loan payment. For example, $25 of private mortgage insurance might be categorized as a Housing expense. Click on Finished, and Quicken redisplays the Set Up Loan Payment dialog box.

21. In the Transaction area of the window, enter the information that will be used to complete the payment. In the Type drop-down list, choose Payment if you plan to write the payment from your checkbook, choose Print Check if you plan to use a Quicken memorized transaction to write the check, or select Online Pmt if you will use Quicken's Online Banking feature to make this payment.

22. Click on the Address command button (which is active only when you choose Print Check as the payment type) to open a dialog box you can use to enter the address to be printed on your check.

23. Click on OK. You're finished.

    You have done a lot of work, but you won't have to do anything further except to make an occasional "tweak" if some element of your loan changes. Ways to maintain and alter your loan are discussed in the following sections.

Making Payments

One of the final steps of setting up your new loan transaction was to use the Payment Method button in the Set Up Loan Payments window to specify whether your payment should be a scheduled, memorized, or repeating online payment transaction. Scheduled transactions are entered automatically on the date you specify. (Repeating online payment transactions are covered in Chapter 9, *Paying Bills Electronically*.)

 NOTE You can also use the Write Checks window in the steps that follow.

To use a memorized transaction, follow these steps:

1. Select the account you want to use and open its register.

2. Enter the date, check number, and the payee name. You will find that a memorized transaction was created when you set up the loan. When you click on Enter, Quicken opens a window:

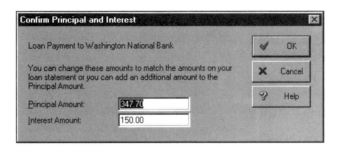

This window lets you confirm that the principal and interest amounts are correct. Confirm them or change them and click on OK to close the dialog box.

Maintaining Your Loan

Once you've set up a loan, you will want to track its progress and, if it is a variable-rate loan, change the interest rate from time to time. The View Loans window shown in Figure 13.11 is the key to these activities. To display the View Loans window, choose the Features ➤ Paying Bills ➤ Loans command. This window displays the details of the example loan set up for this chapter. You can choose the loan to view from the drop-down list that appears when you click on the Choose Loan command button at the top of the window. The Loan Summary tab of the View Loans window shows the specifications of the loan, such as payee, term, and interest rate. The Payment Schedule tab shows details of payments made, and the bottom center panel shows payments to come. The Payment Graph tab of the window shows a line graph that plots the loan balance.

Along the right edge of the View Loans window are four command buttons: Edit Loan, Edit Payment, Make Payment, and Rate Changes. Choosing the Edit Loan button opens the Edit Loan window containing the details of the active loan. You can edit the loan information, retracing the steps covered in the preceding section on setting up a loan.

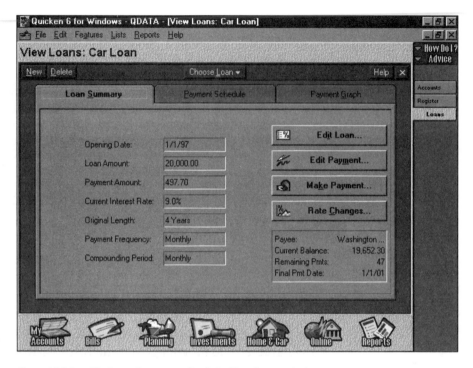

Figure 13.11. The Loan Summary tab of the View Loans window

If you choose the Edit Payment button, you open the Edit Payment window, in which you can edit the payment information. Choosing Rate Changes opens the Loan Rate Changes window shown in Figure 13.12. This window displays a history of rate changes involving the selected loan. Click on the Edit command button to change existing rates or click on New to enter new ones. Quicken will calculate the necessary change in payment based on the new rate.

When you change the interest rate or the payment in the Loan Rate Changes dialog box, click on OK, and then click on Close in the Loan Rate Changes dialog box. Quicken recalculates the payment or loan length and applies the changes to the payment history section in the View Loans window.

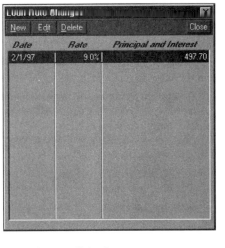

Figure 13.12. **The Loan Rate Changes dialog box**

Adjusting Interest Calculations

It's possible that the interest calculation Quicken makes won't agree with the interest calculation a lender makes. Such discrepancies are common when you're talking about things besides mortgages: car loans, business loans, and so on. If you make a payment a few days early or a few days late, for example, or if there's a delay in the mail, the number of days of interest you calculate will differ from the number of days of interest the lender calculates.

TIP Interest calculation discrepancies aren't as much a problem with mortgage interest calculations because your lender probably calculates a month's worth of interest even if you pay early or pay late. Of course, if you pay too late, the mortgage lender may also assess a late payment penalty.

To adjust the Quicken interest calculations so they agree with the lender's, you display the loan's register in the active document window. Then you click on the Reconcile command button. When Quicken displays the Update Account Balance dialog box, you enter the loan balance as of the date you're making the correction (often the loan statement date), the interest expense category you're using to summarize interest expense on this loan, and the date you're making the correction.

Figure 13.13 shows the Update Account Balance dialog box completed so as to adjust a loan balance to $19,504 on January 1, 1997. If the loan balance before this adjustment shows as $19,502.30, Quicken will add an adjustment transaction to the loan's register that reduces the loan balance by $1.70 and categorizes this change as interest expense. Figure 13.14 shows the adjustment transaction Quicken creates if you adjust the loan balance by $148.30.

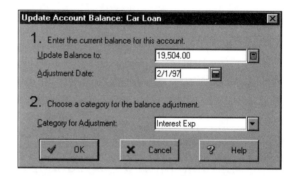

Figure 13.13. **The Update Account dialog box allows you to make adjustments to the account.**

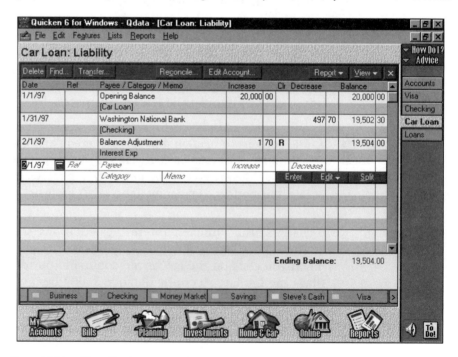

Figure 13.14. **The adjusting entry makes your balance match the lender's.**

If it's confusing to you that the adjustment transaction gets categorized as interest expense, remember this: When you set up an amortized transaction, Quicken splits all your loan payments between a principal category (which is actually a transfer to the liability account) and an interest category. If the liability account balance is wrong, it's because the split between principal and interest was wrong. And if the total principal splits are too low by, say, $1.70, it also means the total interest splits are too high by $1.70.

TIP If the interest expense you're recording in Quicken is tax deductible—probably because it's interest charged on a qualifying mortgage on a residence—you need to use the lender's total interest expense figure for your tax deduction, not the figure shown in your Quicken records. So, if you export Quicken's tax deduction information to a tax-preparation package, be sure to adjust your loan balance and interest category total to whatever the mortgage lender shows on the annual loan statement information.

Refinancing a Mortgage

There's one final loan transaction that's often tricky for people new to financial record keeping: recording a mortgage refinancing.

First, you set up a new liability account. The only difference is that you don't enter a balance for the new liability. You initially set the liability balance to zero by entering **0** into the Balance text box in the Liability Account Setup window.

To record the starting loan balance, you enter a transaction into the loan register. The amount of the transaction should be the loan amount. If the new loan equals the old loan, you enter the category as the old, now-refinanced loan. If the new loan doesn't equal the old loan amount—say you borrowed a little more money as part of refinancing—you need to use the Splits dialog box. One of the split transaction lines should show the old loan's account balance being transferred to the new loan's account balance. (This is really what you're doing—transferring a debt from one loan to another loan.) Any additional new loan amount you spend on items such as loan fees should be categorized using the appropriate expense. Finally, any cash you receive as part of the refinancing should be recorded as a transfer to the bank account into which you deposited the cash.

The rules of thumb people use regarding when and when not to refinance are often useless. Calculating whether it makes sense to refinance a loan actually requires very complicated analysis. Nevertheless, you can use some general rules in specific situations to determine easily when refinancing makes sense. First, you want to substitute lower interest rate debt for higher interest rate. You can tell whether a new loan truly costs less when you include all the costs of obtaining credit by comparing its annual percentage rate (APR) with your existing loan's interest rate. The APR is the cost of borrowing money as a percentage of the loan. It includes not only the loan interest, but most of the other costs as well, including loan origination charges, credit reports, escrow fees, and all the other ways the lender increases the cost of borrowing. If the new loan's APR is less than the old loan's interest rate, you will save interest—at least on a monthly basis—by substituting the new loan for the old loan.

You also want to make sure you don't pay a lot more in interest on the new loan because its term is longer. For example, it probably doesn't make sense to swap a 9 percent, 15-year mortgage for a 8⅞ percent, 30 year mortgage; even though with the new 30-year mortgage you'll pay a little less interest for the first 15 years, you'll make payments for an extra 15 years. To deal with this "years interest is charged" issue, ask the lender to calculate the APR on the new loan assuming you'll have the new loan paid off by the same time you would have had the old loan paid off. (This will make the APR higher, by the way.) You'll also want to make payments that are large enough to have the new loan paid off by the same time you would have had the old loan paid off.

 NOTE Chapter 15, *Planning Your Personal Finances*, describes the Quicken Refinance Planner.

HOW TO BORROW AND REPAY MONEY

Get smart about the way you borrow and repay money, and you can dramatically improve your finances. Smart borrowing, however, is tricky. Dozens of big-dollar traps are out there waiting to snare you, and you have only a handful of money-saving tricks at your disposal. The following two simple rules for handling debt will take you a long way toward staying in the black.

Rule 1: Choose the Cheapest Debt You Can Find

By choosing the cheapest debt you can find—in other words, by finding the least expensive loan—you save money. It's that simple. Surprisingly, even small differences in interest rates can add up to big savings over time.

In the case of a fixed–interest-rate loan, choosing cheap debt is pretty easy to do. All you need to do is look for the loan with the lowest APR.

Finding a cheap loan is also relatively easy to do in the case of adjustable–interest-rate debt. With this type of debt, the interest rate is readjusted periodically, usually every six months or every year. Again, you can focus on the APR, but there is a slight problem with doing that: You want to make sure that you can bear the added risk of borrowing money at an unknown interest rate. I tell you more about the risks of adjustable-rate loans later in this chapter.

Rule 2: Repay the Loan
Before the Thing You're Buying Wears Out

You should repay a loan before the thing you're buying wears out. By doing so, you pay off the loan you borrowed to buy the first thingamajig before you buy the second thingamajig. A side benefit of this "quick repayment" approach is that you save substantial amounts in interest payments because you're not paying interest for two things, only one.

A debt, or loan, is a way to spread out the cost of something over the years that you use it, and it should be treated as such. By taking out a loan, you can purchase a house, purchase a car, or go to college even though you don't have the cold, hard cash right now. For this privilege, you pay interest. But that doesn't have to be a bad situation as long as you're careful.

Thirty-year home mortgages are, for example, perfectly reasonable. You pay off a 30-year mortgage for most of your adult life, but that's okay, because you're using the loan to buy something that will hold its value and will benefit you for the entire 30 years. Homes built today, if they are well-maintained, can last for a 100 years or more. Student loans, although they can take ten or more years to pay off, are reasonable, because they provide long-term benefits such as preparation for a lifetime of employment.

To my mind, a 3-year car loan is pretty reasonable as long as the car lasts five or more years. Again, the car loan payments end long before the car wears out. An even better deal is saving the money first and then buying a car with cash, but often that can't be done.

Ways of Borrowing Money

Money is usually borrowed in one of two ways: with revolving credit debt or amortizing debt.

Revolving Credit

Revolving credit debt is the simpler approach. You probably have credit cards that fit into the revolving credit category. You borrow money on your credit card, interest is calculated on the amount you've borrowed, and at the end of the month you pay the entire balance, a portion of the balance, or the interest for the month.

As a borrower, revolving credit offers more flexibility—and for this reason it is the most popular way to borrow money. The bank or credit card company sets minimum payment amounts and maximum credit limits, but within those guidelines you borrow and repay as you please. Unfortunately, besides being the most flexible way to borrow money, revolving credit debt is also the most expensive.

Amortizing Debt

The other type of borrowing is *amortizing debt.* "Amortization" means paying off the balance on a loan in little increments over a period of time. Most home mortgages are of the amortizing variety: Each month you send the bank or mortgage company a check for the same amount. In the beginning, most of your payment goes toward reducing the balance of the loan. Over time, however, the little reductions in the loan balance begin to add up and thereby reduce the interest you're charged.

Assuming you make regular payments, over time this amortization of the loan's balance results in a larger and larger portion of each month's payment going to pay off the loan balance. Home mortgages aren't the only types of debt that are amortizing. Most car loans are amortizing, and so are student loans.

Which Type of Debt Is Better?

Which type of debt is better, revolving credit debt or amortizing debt? This is a good question. Certainly, revolving credit is more flexible. It's easy to borrow money the instant you need it. Putting aside the convenience angle, however, you can almost always do better by using amortizing debt. It provides three important advantages:

▶ Amortizing debt is much tougher to use for impulse purchases. When you get the urge for a new car or item of clothing, you can't simply pull out your wallet or purse and five minutes later be even deeper in debt. Impulse purchases are a problem for some people. If you're one of them, you should definitely stay away from revolving credit cards.

▶ The lender makes sure you pay off the debt before the thing you're buying wears out.

▶ Amortizing debts almost always have lower interest rates than revolving credit debts, and that is their chief advantage.

on the Road to Riches

Car Loans and Leases

A car is usually the second largest purchase that people have to finance (the largest purchase, of course, is a home). Not surprisingly, car loans and leases are an area where borrowing decisions dramatically affect financial progress.

Choosing a Car

The first decision to make concerning a car loan is which car to buy. Choosing a car is largely a personal decision, not a financial one, but two points are worth noting about buying a car:

▶ Check the insurance and, if applicable, state and city taxes. (These can end up being big, unhappy surprises if you're not careful.)

▶ Reforecast your budget once you've picked a car to make sure that you can afford to spend as much money as you're planning to spend. (Remember that you can calculate a loan payment, including a car loan payment, by using the Loan Planner described a bit later in the chapter.)

If you absolutely must have a luxury German or Italian import, consider getting a two-year-old car instead of a new one. Try to get a car that someone else owned for two years but discovered he or she couldn't afford. New cars take the biggest drop in value over the first two years of their lives, even though most of their lives are still left. (This advice, by the way, applies to just about any car. Buying a reasonably priced used car is usually an excellent way to purchase a car. Do have a mechanic you trust check the car first, however.)

Finally, be sure to "comparison-shop." Take notes. Don't go to just one dealer. And get whatever deal you're offered in writing. As a general rule, you can't rely on a promise made by a car salesman (or anyone else) unless the promise is made in writing.

 TIP If you can afford to wait, you can usually get a better deal by waiting until the start of the new model year and buying one of last year's models.

Picking a Car Loan or Lease

Car loans work just like other loans. For this reason, all you need to do is pick the loan with the lowest APR.

Call a couple of banks before you head on down to the car dealer's showroom. Most car dealers offer financing for the cars on their lots. To know whether or not you're getting a good offer, you need to be able to compare what the dealer offers with what the bank offers.

You probably shouldn't lease a car. Almost always, it's a better deal to purchase one. The reason is that when you get done making your car loan payments, you still have your car, but when you get done making car lease payments, you don't. It's that simple.

More About Car Leases

Why do people lease cars if it's such a bad deal? There are two big reasons: The inception fee you pay to get into a lease usually isn't as big as the down payment you're required to make on a regular car loan, and the monthly lease payment is usually less than the monthly loan payment. This makes sense, if you think about it for a minute. With a lease, you're really only renting the car for a couple years—maybe three. With a loan, you're buying the car.

Is there a good reason for leasing a car? You probably pay more money for automobile expenses if you do. Acquiring a car by means of a lease is inherently more expensive than getting a regular car loan. Another factor that makes leases more expensive—and this is just my intuition, since I haven't done a rigorous statistical study—is that people tend to get expensive cars when they lease.

These criticisms aside, however, I can think of several reasons why it makes sense to lease that shiny new car you've been eyeing. First, if you really, truly, absolutely must have a new car, leasing may be your only option if you're low on cash. If you have a job that requires having a better-than-average late model car, it probably does make sense to spend, say, an extra $5,000 on a lease so you can keep your $40,000 a

Part 2

Quicken and Your Personal Finances

year sales job. Unless you're independently wealthy, your biggest investment is your job. Doing things that help you keep a good job or that let you get a better job can be very worthwhile.

How Car Leases Work

Car leases, in essence, amount to long-term rental agreements. To get into a car lease, you need to pay an inception fee and probably a deposit. Then, over the course of the lease, you make monthly lease, or rental, payments.

When the lease expires, you usually give the car back to the leasing company. There are a couple of possible catches, however. Most lease agreements state that you can't run up 100,000 miles on the car. If you put, say, ten years' worth of mileage on a car that you've only leased for two or three years, you have to pay an extra charge for the extra miles you drove.

Another catch concerns damage done to the car: dings and dents, spilled milkshakes, and excess wear and tear. In all likelihood, you also have to pay extra for damages.

There's also usually one other complicating factor: Most car leases give you the option of either releasing the car or purchasing the car at the end of the lease. Sometimes this is a great deal and sometimes it isn't.

Picking a Mortgage

By making smart decisions about a mortgage, you can easily add tens of thousands of dollars to your net worth—and do it almost effortlessly. But to capture this easy source of wealth, you need to understand much more than most people do about choosing, refinancing, and ultimately repaying a mortgage.

NOTE *How to Choose a Home and Pick a Mortgage* at the end of Chapter 19 describes the general rules that most mortgage companies and banks use to determine mortgage affordability.

Perhaps the most important thing to do when you search for a mortgage is comparison shop. Borrowing money for a home is just like borrowing money for anything else. The main thing to do is find a mortgage lender that offers inexpensive loans. It's important to shop around and find the lowest APR.

Just for fun, I kept tabs on all the 30-year fixed mortgage interest rates that were available as I was writing this. The thing that struck me is how much the rates vary. From the lowest rate to the highest rate, there's a difference of roughly half a percent. On a $100,000 mortgage, that's equivalent to around $500 a year in payments for the first few years.

NOTE Fifteen-year and bi-weekly mortgages usually save you interest because you repay the mortgage earlier. (Usually, you save thousands of dollars.) But you shouldn't pay anything extra for these types of mortgages. In fact, because you've reduced the lender's risk by paying bi-weekly or paying off the mortgage in fifteen years, you should get a lower interest rate. You certainly don't need to pay some third party a special processing or handling fee, either, which is sometimes the case with a bi-weekly mortgage. If you want to get a 30-year mortgage paid off as quickly as you would pay off a bi-weekly mortgage, just add one-twelfth of your usual payment to your regular monthly payment. For example, if you're usually paying $1,200 a month in mortgage and interest, add another $100 a month to that payment. (Later in the chapter, I tell you how to use Quicken's Loan Planner to see how much money you save by repaying a loan early.)

Why You Should Consider an Adjustable-Rate Mortgage

With an adjustable-rate mortgage (ARM), the interest rate on the loan is adjusted every 6 months or every 12 months, and, as a result, the amount you pay is adjusted, too. The lender adjusts the rate by pegging, or tying, the mortgage interest rate to a well-known and respected interest rate *index*. For example, one such index is the six-month or one-year Treasury Bill rate. A typical adjustable-rate mortgage might adjust your mortgage interest rate to the six-month Treasury Bill rate plus two percentage points. In other words, if the six-month Treasury Bill rate is 5 percent, the interest rate on your loan is 7 percent.

The extra amount that gets added to the index (2 percent in this example) is called the *spread*. If interest rates rise or fall, the lender recalculates your payment by using the new interest rate plus the spread.

Tying the interest rate on a loan to an index sounds risky, but it's not quite as bad as it sounds, provided ARM interest rates are substantially lower than fixed-mortgage interest rates. In this situation, ARM payments are lower to begin with. The prospect of having your ARM payment bounce between $600 a month and $1000 a month sounds risky indeed, but it isn't actually as risky as it seems if the alternative is an $800-a-month payment on a fixed–interest-rate mortgage. What's more, there's usually a *cap*, or maximum amount, above which rates on an ARM can't rise. If interest rates drop, then your mortgage interest rate drops too. However, mortgage interest rates don't drop as often as you might think because of *teaser interest rates*.

Teaser interest rates are artificially low starting interest rates. Teasers aren't bad, really. They save you money. But with a teaser interest rate, your payment often rises at the next adjustment date. Be sure to recalculate your loan payment using the current index and spread. You can do this by using the Loan Planner. It is explained at the start of this chapter.

Do ARMs make sense? Despite the risk of interest rates and payments climbing and dropping, ARMs can be good deals for borrowers when interest rates are high. They usually save borrowers money because they charge a lower interest rate in the long run. What's more, if the index rate drops, your mortgage rate and monthly payment drop as well, and you don't have to go through the rigmarole and cost of refinancing your mortgage.

The only problem with an ARM is that you bear extra risk: When interest rates rise, your monthly payment is adjusted upward.

Common sense says that you shouldn't take an ARM unless you know you can make the maximum payment. To find out what a maximum payment is, calculate your monthly payment using the interest rate cap—the highest interest rate you are forced to pay—on your ARM. If the payment looks pretty ugly, it probably doesn't pay to pick an ARM.

Part 2

Quicken and Your Personal Finances

> **TIP** Here is a financial trick that an ARM borrower can use to reduce (and often reduce completely!) the risk of rising payments. Get an ARM but make the same payment you would make if you had a fixed-rate mortgage. In other words, if the ARM payment is $600-a-month and the fixed-rate mortgage payment would be $800-a-month, get the ARM and pay $800-a-month. The extra amount that you pay each month quickly reduces the mortgage balance. What's more, you get accustomed to making larger payments in case the ARM interest rate does go up. If you're lucky and interest rates don't jump up dramatically in the first few years, you may never see your payment increase. The reason is that if you pay, say, an extra $100 to $200 a month over a five or six year period, the effect of the extra principal payments may more than offset the effect of a rise in interest rates.

Tips for Picking an ARM

If I've convinced you that an ARM is something you should look into, here are some smart shopping tips for picking one:

▶ **Make sure the ARM has annual adjustment limit, or interest rate cap.** There should be a cap on how much the mortgage lender can adjust your payments upward in a year. If the cap is a percent a year or half a percent every six months (these are the figures I look for), you won't get caught in a budget crunch if interest rates rise quickly. Instead, your payment will be adjusted over several adjustment dates.

▶ **No negative amortization.** Make sure there's no possibility of negative amortization. *Negative amortization* means your loan balance increases because your payment doesn't cover all of the loan interest. You shouldn't have a problem with negative amortization on a fixed-rate loan as long as the lender doesn't calculate your payment incorrectly. But negative amortization is a possibility when interest rate adjustments are made to an ARM more frequently than payment adjustments are made. Don't sign up for an ARM if this is the case.

▶ **Compare spreads.** If two ARMs are tied to the same index, go with the one that has the lower spread. Remember that the spread is the percentage point amount added to the index to calculate the ARM interest rate.

➤ **Calculate the maximum payment.** I know this isn't any fun. I know it may cause a big argument with your spouse about whether or not buying a house is a good decision. But you need to consider the risk of rising interest rates before, and not after, you're locked into them.

➤ **Don't use an ARM to get a bigger house.** The reason that most people get an ARM, or so an honest mortgage lender will tell you, is so they can buy a bigger home. I think this is a mistake. If you need to stretch yourself by getting an ARM, you're setting yourself up for trouble when interest rates rise. And rates always rise at some point in the future.

➤ **Consider getting an ARM with annual adjustments.** To reduce the risk of rising payments, consider getting an ARM with annual rate adjustments. With annual adjustments, the chances of your getting a raise in salary or wages between adjustments is higher, and that raise could help with the increased payment. I should point out, however, that you usually pay a bit more in interest over the life of the loan if you go with annual adjustments. That's fair, however, since you're bearing less risk.

CHAPTER 14

Estimating and Preparing Income Taxes

FEATURING

Building category lists for tax purposes

Generating tax reports

Dealing with tax-preparation packages

Planning ahead for tax payments

BECAUSE Quicken largely (and perhaps completely) summarizes your financial affairs, much of the information you'll need to prepare your income tax return can and should be extracted from the Quicken accounts. What's more, Quicken provides an Income Tax Estimator that you can use to plan for your income tax expenses.

Building Appropriate Category Lists

There's only one real trick to using Quicken as a tool for income tax preparation: Use a category list that neatly ties to the tax form lines you need to fill in when you file your income tax return.

The problem with this trick, however, is that you won't actually know which tax form lines you're supposed to fill in until the year's almost over and you have performed most of the financial record keeping for the year. (Also, note that this year's tax forms may be different from last year's.) Use category lists that easily produce or combine to produce the tax form line inputs. Then, at the end of year, adjust the category total numbers provided by Quicken so the tax return's forms and schedules can be filled out correctly. All of this is explained in this chapter.

Determining Which Categories You Need for Income Tax Purposes

In case you don't have last year's forms handy, you can take a look at Figures 14.1 (1040), 14.2 (Schedule A), 14.3 (Schedule B), 14.4 (Schedule C), 14.5 (Schedule C-EZ), 14.6 (Schedule D), and 14.7 (Schedule E). Use these forms as guides for indicating which categories you need to complete in the 1995 and 1996 forms. Each input line on each form that you'll use should have its own category or set of categories.

Form **1040**
Department of the Treasury—Internal Revenue Service
U.S. Individual Income Tax Return   (99)   IRS Use Only—Do not write or staple in this space.

For the year Jan. 1–Dec. 31, 1995, or other tax year beginning   , 1995, ending   , 19   OMB No. 1545-0074

Label
(See instructions on page 11.)
Use the IRS label. Otherwise, please print or type.

Your first name and initial   Last name   Your social security number

If a joint return, spouse's first name and initial   Last name   Spouse's social security number

Home address (number and street). If you have a P.O. box, see page 11.   Apt. no.

City, town or post office, state, and ZIP code. If you have a foreign address, see page 11.

For Privacy Act and Paperwork Reduction Act Notice, see page 7.

Presidential Election Campaign
(See page 11.)

Do you want $3 to go to this fund? . . . .
If a joint return, does your spouse want $3 to go to this fund? . . . .

Yes   No   Note: Checking "Yes" will not change your tax or reduce your refund.

Filing Status
(See page 11.)

Check only one box.

1   Single
2   Married filing joint return (even if only one had income)
3   Married filing separate return. Enter spouse's social security no. above and full name here. ▶
4   Head of household (with qualifying person). (See page 12.) If the qualifying person is a child but not your dependent, enter this child's name here. ▶
5   Qualifying widow(er) with dependent child (year spouse died ▶ 19   ). (See page 12.)

Exemptions
(See page 12.)

6a   Yourself. If your parent (or someone else) can claim you as a dependent on his or her tax return, do not check box 6a. But be sure to check the box on line 33b on page 2

b   Spouse . . . .

c   Dependents:

(1) First name Last name	(2) Dependent's social security number. If born in 1995, see page 13.	(3) Dependent's relationship to you	(4) No. of months lived in your home in 1995

If more than six dependents, see page 13.

No. of boxes checked on 6a and 6b
No. of your children on 6c who:
• lived with you
• didn't live with you due to divorce or separation (see page 14)
Dependents on 6c not entered above
Add numbers entered on lines above ▶

d   If your child didn't live with you but is claimed as your dependent under a pre-1985 agreement, check here ▶
e   Total number of exemptions claimed

Income

Attach Copy B of your Forms W-2, W-2G, and 1099-R here.

If you did not get a W-2, see page 14.

Enclose, but do not attach, your payment and payment voucher. See page 33.

7   Wages, salaries, tips, etc. Attach Form(s) W-2   7
8a   Taxable interest income (see page 15). Attach Schedule B if over $400 . . . . .   8a
b   Tax-exempt interest (see page 15). DON'T include on line 8a   8b
9   Dividend income. Attach Schedule B if over $400   9
10   Taxable refunds, credits, or offsets of state and local income taxes (see page 15) . .   10
11   Alimony received   11
12   Business income or (loss). Attach Schedule C or C-EZ   12
13   Capital gain or (loss). If required, attach Schedule D (see page 16)   13
14   Other gains or (losses). Attach Form 4797   14
15a   Total IRA distributions .   15a   b Taxable amount (see page 16)   15b
16a   Total pensions and annuities   16a   b Taxable amount (see page 16)   16b
17   Rental real estate, royalties, partnerships, S corporations, trusts, etc. Attach Schedule E   17
18   Farm income or (loss). Attach Schedule F   18
19   Unemployment compensation (see page 17)   19
20a   Social security benefits   20a   b Taxable amount (see page 18)   20b
21   Other income. List type and amount—see page 18   21
22   Add the amounts in the far right column for lines 7 through 21. This is your total income ▶   22

Adjustments to Income

23a   Your IRA deduction (see page 19) 23a
b   Spouse's IRA deduction (see page 19) 23b
24   Moving expenses. Attach Form 3903 or 3903-F   24
25   One-half of self-employment tax   25
26   Self-employed health insurance deduction (see page 21) . .   26
27   Keogh & self-employed SEP plans. If SEP, check ▶   27
28   Penalty on early withdrawal of savings   28
29   Alimony paid. Recipient's SSN ▶   29
30   Add lines 23a through 29. These are your total adjustments . . . . ▶   30

Adjusted Gross Income

31   Subtract line 30 from line 22. This is your **adjusted gross income.** If less than $26,673 and a child lived with you (less than $9,230 if a child didn't live with you), see "Earned Income Credit" on page 27 ▶   31

Cat. No. 11320B   Form **1040** (1995)

Figure 14.1. The 1040 form

Form 1040 (1995)   Page 2

Tax Compu- tation (See page 23.)	32	Amount from line 31 (adjusted gross income)	32	
	33a	Check if: ☐ You were 65 or older, ☐ Blind; ☐ Spouse was 65 or older, ☐ Blind. Add the number of boxes checked above and enter the total here . . . . ▶ 33a		
	b	If your parent (or someone else) can claim you as a dependent, check here . ▶ 33b ☐		
	c	If you are married filing separately and your spouse itemizes deductions or you are a dual-status alien, see page 23 and check here . . . . ▶ 33c ☐		
	34	Enter the larger of your: { Itemized deductions from Schedule A, line 28, OR Standard deduction shown below for your filing status. But if you checked any box on line 33a or b, go to page 23 to find your standard deduction. If you checked box 33c, your standard deduction is zero. • Single—$3,900 • Married filing jointly or Qualifying widow(er)—$6,550 • Head of household—$5,750 • Married filing separately—$3,275 }	34	
	35	Subtract line 34 from line 32	35	
	36	If line 32 is $86,025 or less, multiply $2,500 by the total number of exemptions claimed on line 6e. If line 32 is over $86,025, see the worksheet on page 23 for the amount to enter .	36	
	37	Taxable income. Subtract line 36 from line 35. If line 36 is more than line 35, enter -0-	37	
If you want the IRS to figure your tax, see page 35.	38	Tax. Check if from a ☐ Tax Table, b ☐ Tax Rate Schedules, c ☐ Capital Gain Tax Worksheet, or d ☐ Form 8615 (see page 24). Amount from Form(s) 8814 ▶ e ____	38	
	39	Additional taxes. Check if from a ☐ Form 4970 b ☐ Form 4972	39	
	40	Add lines 38 and 39 . . . . ▶	40	
Credits (See page 24.)	41	Credit for child and dependent care expenses. Attach Form 2441	41	
	42	Credit for the elderly or the disabled. Attach Schedule R . .	42	
	43	Foreign tax credit. Attach Form 1116	43	
	44	Other credits (see page 25). Check if from a ☐ Form 3800 b ☐ Form 8396 c ☐ Form 8801 d ☐ Form (specify)____	44	
	45	Add lines 41 through 44	45	
	46	Subtract line 45 from line 40. If line 45 is more than line 40, enter -0- . . . . . . ▶	46	
Other Taxes (See page 25.)	47	Self-employment tax. Attach Schedule SE	47	
	48	Alternative minimum tax. Attach Form 6251	48	
	49	Recapture taxes. Check if from a ☐ Form 4255 b ☐ Form 8611 c ☐ Form 8828 . .	49	
	50	Social security and Medicare tax on tip income not reported to employer. Attach Form 4137	50	
	51	Tax on qualified retirement plans, including IRAs. If required, attach Form 5329	51	
	52	Advance earned income credit payments from Form W-2	52	
	53	Household employment taxes. Attach Schedule H	53	
	54	Add lines 46 through 53. This is your total tax . . . . ▶	54	
Payments Attach Forms W-2, W-2G, and 1099-R on the front.	55	Federal income tax withheld. If any is from Form(s) 1099, check ▶ ☐	55	
	56	1995 estimated tax payments and amount applied from 1994 return .	56	
	57	Earned income credit. Attach Schedule EIC if you have a qualifying child. Nontaxable earned income: amount ▶ ____ and type ▶ ____	57	
	58	Amount paid with Form 4868 (extension request)	58	
	59	Excess social security and RRTA tax withheld (see page 32)	59	
	60	Other payments. Check if from a ☐ Form 2439 b ☐ Form 4136	60	
	61	Add lines 55 through 60. These are your total payments . . . . ▶	61	
Refund or Amount You Owe	62	If line 61 is more than line 54, subtract line 54 from line 61. This is the amount you OVERPAID. .	62	
	63	Amount of line 62 you want REFUNDED TO YOU . . . . ▶	63	
	64	Amount of line 62 you want **APPLIED TO YOUR 1996 ESTIMATED TAX** ▶ 64		
	65	If line 54 is more than line 61, subtract line 61 from line 54. This is the AMOUNT YOU OWE. For details on how to pay and use Form 1040-V, Payment Voucher, see page 33 . . ▶	65	
	66	Estimated tax penalty (see page 33). Also include on line 65 66		

Sign Here
Keep a copy of this return for your records.

Under penalties of perjury, I declare that I have examined this return and accompanying schedules and statements, and to the best of my knowledge and belief, they are true, correct, and complete. Declaration of preparer (other than taxpayer) is based on all information of which preparer has any knowledge.

Your signature	Date	Your occupation
Spouse's signature. If a joint return, BOTH must sign.	Date	Spouse's occupation

Paid Preparer's Use Only

Preparer's signature ▶	Date	Check if self-employed ☐	Preparer's social security no.
Firm's name (or yours if self-employed) and address ▶		EIN	
		ZIP code	

♲ Printed on recycled paper

Part 2

Quicken and Your Personal Finances

*Figure 14.1.   **The 1040 form (continued)***

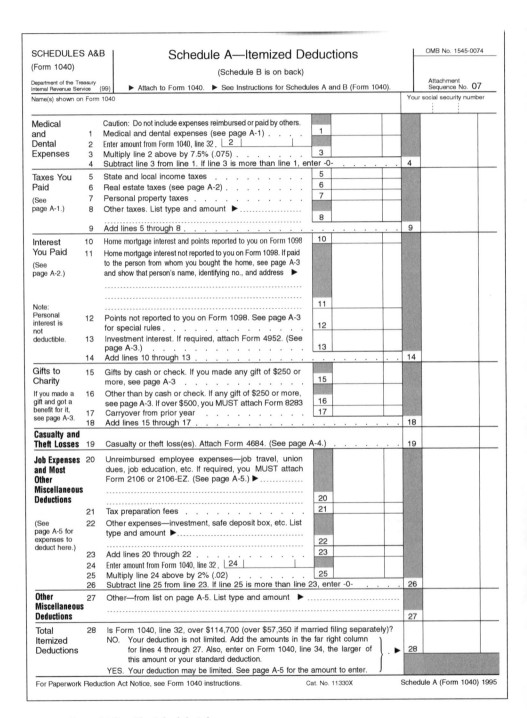

Figure 14.2. **The Schedule A form**

Schedules A&B (Form 1040) 1995   OMB No. 1545-0074   Page **2**

Name(s) shown on Form 1040. Do not enter name and social security number if shown on other side.	Your social security number

Schedule B—Interest and Dividend Income
Attachment Sequence No. **08**

			Amount
Part I **Interest** **Income** (See pages 15 and B-1.) Note: If you received a Form 1099-INT, Form 1099-OID, or substitute statement from a brokerage firm, list the firm's name as the payer and enter the total interest shown on that form.	Note: If you had over $400 in taxable interest income, you must also complete Part III.		
	1	List name of payer. If any interest is from a seller-financed mortgage and the buyer used the property as a personal residence, see page B-1 and list this interest first. Also, show that buyer's social security number and address ▶	
		....	**1**
	2	Add the amounts on line 1	**2**
	3	Excludable interest on series EE U.S. savings bonds issued after 1989 from Form 8815, line 14. You MUST attach Form 8815 to Form 1040	**3**
	4	Subtract line 3 from line 2. Enter the result here and on Form 1040, line 8a ▶	**4**

			Amount
Part II **Dividend** **Income** (See pages 15 and B-1.) Note: If you received a Form 1099-DIV or substitute statement from a brokerage firm, list the firm's name as the payer and enter the total dividends shown on that form.	Note: If you had over $400 in gross dividends and/or other distributions on stock, you must also complete Part III.		
	5	List name of payer. Include gross dividends and/or other distributions on stock here. Any capital gain distributions and nontaxable distributions will be deducted on lines 7 and 8 ▶	**5**
	6	Add the amounts on line 5	**6**
	7	Capital gain distributions. Enter here and on Schedule D* . **7**	
	8	Nontaxable distributions. (See the inst. for Form 1040, line 9.) **8**	
	9	Add lines 7 and 8	**9**
	10	Subtract line 9 from line 6. Enter the result here and on Form 1040, line 9 . ▶	**10**
		*If you do not need Schedule D to report any other gains or losses, see the instructions for Form 1040, line 13, on page 16.	

		Yes	No
Part III **Foreign Accounts and Trusts** (See page B-2.)	If you had over $400 of interest or dividends or had a foreign account or were a grantor of, or a transferor to, a foreign trust, you must complete this part.		
	11a At any time during 1995, did you have an interest in or a signature or other authority over a financial account in a foreign country, such as a bank account, securities account, or other financial account? See page B-2 for exceptions and filing requirements for Form TD F 90-22.1		
	b If "Yes," enter the name of the foreign country ▶		
	12 Were you the grantor of, or transferor to, a foreign trust that existed during 1995, whether or not you have any beneficial interest in it? If "Yes," you may have to file Form 3520, 3520-A, or 926 .		

For Paperwork Reduction Act Notice, see Form 1040 instructions.   ✪ Printed on recycled paper   Schedule B (Form 1040) 1995

Figure 14.3. **The Schedule B form**

| SCHEDULE C
(Form 1040)

Department of the Treasury
Internal Revenue Service   (99) | **Profit or Loss From Business**
(Sole Proprietorship)
▶ Partnerships, joint ventures, etc., must file Form 1065.
▶ Attach to Form 1040 or Form 1041.   ▶ See Instructions for Schedule C (Form 1040). | OMB No. 1545-0074
1995
Attachment
Sequence No. 09 |

Name of proprietor | Social security number (SSN)

A Principal business or profession, including product or service (see page C-1) | **B** Enter principal business code
(see page C-6) ▶

C Business name. If no separate business name, leave blank. | **D** Employer ID number (EIN), if any

E Business address (including suite or room no.) ▶ ....
City, town or post office, state, and ZIP code

F Accounting method: (1) ☐ Cash   (2) ☐ Accrual   (3) ☐ Other (specify) ▶ ....

G Method(s) used to value closing inventory: (1) ☐ Cost   (2) ☐ Lower of cost or market   (3) ☐ Other (attach explanation)   (4) ☐ Does not apply (if checked, skip line H) | Yes | No

H Was there any change in determining quantities, costs, or valuations between opening and closing inventory? If "Yes," attach explanation

I Did you "materially participate" in the operation of this business during 1995? If "No," see page C-2 for limit on losses

J If you started or acquired this business during 1995, check here ▶ ☐

Part I   Income

1	Gross receipts or sales. Caution: If this income was reported to you on Form W-2 and the "Statutory employee" box on that form was checked, see page C-2 and check here ▶ ☐	1	
2	Returns and allowances	2	
3	Subtract line 2 from line 1	3	
4	Cost of goods sold (from line 40 on page 2)	4	
5	Gross profit. Subtract line 4 from line 3	5	
6	Other income, including Federal and state gasoline or fuel tax credit or refund (see page C-2)	6	
7	Gross income. Add lines 5 and 6 ▶	7	

Part II   Expenses.   Enter expenses for business use of your home only on line 30.

8	Advertising	8		19	Pension and profit-sharing plans	19	
9	Bad debts from sales or services (see page C-3)	9		20	Rent or lease (see page C-4):		
10	Car and truck expenses (see page C-3)	10			a Vehicles, machinery, and equipment	20a	
11	Commissions and fees	11			b Other business property	20b	
12	Depletion	12		21	Repairs and maintenance	21	
13	Depreciation and section 179 expense deduction (not included in Part III) (see page C-3)	13		22	Supplies (not included in Part III)	22	
				23	Taxes and licenses	23	
14	Employee benefit programs (other than on line 19)	14		24	Travel, meals, and entertainment:		
15	Insurance (other than health)	15			a Travel	24a	
16	Interest:				b Meals and en- tertainment		
	a Mortgage (paid to banks, etc.)	16a			c Enter 50% of line 24b subject to limitations (see page C-4)		
	b Other	16b			d Subtract line 24c from line 24b	24d	
17	Legal and professional services	17		25	Utilities	25	
				26	Wages (less employment credits)	26	
18	Office expense	18		27	Other expenses (from line 46 on page 2)	27	

28	Total expenses before expenses for business use of home. Add lines 8 through 27 in columns ▶	28	
29	Tentative profit (loss). Subtract line 28 from line 7	29	
30	Expenses for business use of your home. Attach Form 8829	30	
31	Net profit or (loss). Subtract line 30 from line 29. • If a profit, enter on Form 1040, line 12, and ALSO on Schedule SE, line 2 (statutory employees, see page C-5). Estates and trusts, enter on Form 1041, line 3. • If a loss, you MUST go on to line 32.	31	
32	If you have a loss, check the box that describes your investment in this activity (see page C-5). • If you checked 32a, enter the loss on Form 1040, line 12, and ALSO on Schedule SE, line 2 (statutory employees, see page C-5). Estates and trusts, enter on Form 1041, line 3. • If you checked 32b, you MUST attach Form 6198.	32a ☐ All investment is at risk. 32b ☐ Some investment is not at risk.

For Paperwork Reduction Act Notice, see Form 1040 instructions.   Cat. No. 11334P   Schedule C (Form 1040) 1995

Figure 14.4.   **The Schedule C form**

Schedule C (Form 1040) 1995   Page 2

Part III   Cost of Goods Sold   (see page C-5)

33 Inventory at beginning of year. If different from last year's closing inventory, attach explanation . .	33	
34 Purchases less cost of items withdrawn for personal use	34	
35 Cost of labor. Do not include salary paid to yourself	35	
36 Materials and supplies	36	
37 Other costs	37	
38 Add lines 33 through 37	38	
39 Inventory at end of year	39	
40 Cost of goods sold. Subtract line 39 from line 38. Enter the result here and on page 1, line 4 . .	40	

Part IV   Information on Your Vehicle.   Complete this part ONLY if you are claiming car or truck expenses on line 10 and are not required to file Form 4562 for this business. See the instructions for line 13 on page C-3 to find out if you must file.

41   When did you place your vehicle in service for business purposes? (month, day, year) ▶ .... / ..../ ..... .

42   Of the total number of miles you drove your vehicle during 1995, enter the number of miles you used your vehicle for:

a   Business ....   b   Commuting   c   Other ....

43   Do you (or your spouse) have another vehicle available for personal use? . . . . ☐ Yes   ☐ No

44   Was your vehicle available for use during off-duty hours?   . . . . ☐ Yes   ☐ No

45a   Do you have evidence to support your deduction?   . . . . ☐ Yes   ☐ No
  b   If "Yes," is the evidence written? . . . . ☐ Yes   ☐ No

Part V   Other Expenses.   List below business expenses not included on lines 8–26 or line 30.

....		
....		
....		
....		
....		
....		
....		
....		
....		
46 Total other expenses. Enter here and on page 1, line 27	46	

✪   Printed on recycled paper

Figure 14.4.   **The Schedule C form (continued)**

SCHEDULE C-EZ
(Form 1040)

Department of the Treasury
Internal Revenue Service

Net Profit From Business
(Sole Proprietorship)

▶ Partnerships, joint ventures, etc., must file Form 1065.

▶ Attach to Form 1040 or Form 1041.   ▶ See instructions on back.

OMB No. 1545-0074

19 95

Attachment
Sequence No. 09A

Name of proprietor

Social security number (SSN)

Part I General Information

You May Use
This Schedule
Only If You:

- Had gross receipts from your business of $25,000 or less.
- Had business expenses of $2,000 or less.
- Use the cash method of accounting.
- Did not have an inventory at any time during the year.
- Did not have a net loss from your business.
- Had only one business as a sole proprietor.

And You:

- Had no employees during the year.
- Are not required to file Form 4562, Depreciation and Amortization, for this business. See the instructions for Schedule C, line 13, on page C-3 to find out if you must file.
- Do not deduct expenses for business use of your home.
- Do not have prior year unallowed passive activity losses from this business.

A Principal business or profession, including product or service

B Enter principal business code (see page C-6) ▶

C Business name. If no separate business name, leave blank.

D **Employer ID number (EIN), if any**

E Business address (including suite or room no.). Address not required if same as on Form 1040, page 1.

City, town or post office, state, and ZIP code

Part II Figure Your Net Profit

1 Gross receipts. If more than $25,000, you must use Schedule C.
Caution: If this income was reported to you on Form W-2 and the "Statutory employee" box on that form was checked, see Statutory Employees in the instructions for Schedule C, line 1, on page C-2 and check here . . . . ▶ ☐ | 1

2 Total expenses. If more than $2,000, you must use Schedule C. See instructions . . . . . | 2

3 Net profit. Subtract line 2 from line 1. If less than zero, you must use Schedule C. Enter on Form 1040, line 12, and ALSO on Schedule SE, line 2. (Statutory employees do not report this amount on Schedule SE, line 2. Estates and trusts, enter on Form 1041, line 3.) . . . . . | 3

Part III Information on Your Vehicle.   Complete this part ONLY if you are claiming car or truck expenses on line 2.

4 When did you place your vehicle in service for business purposes? (month, day, year) ▶ ..... / ..... / .....

5 Of the total number of miles you drove your vehicle during 1995, enter the number of miles you used your vehicle for:

a Business .... b Commuting .... c Other ....

6 Do you (or your spouse) have another vehicle available for personal use? . . . . ☐ Yes ☐ No

7 Was your vehicle available for use during off-duty hours? . . . . ☐ Yes ☐ No

8a Do you have evidence to support your deduction? . . . . ☐ Yes ☐ No

  b If "Yes," is the evidence written? . . . . ☐ Yes ☐ No

For Paperwork Reduction Act Notice, see Form 1040 instructions.   Cat. No. 14374D   Schedule C-EZ (Form 1040) 1995

*Figure 14.5. **The Schedule C-EZ form***

SCHEDULE D
(Form 1040)

Department of the Treasury
Internal Revenue Service   (99)

Capital Gains and Losses

▶ Attach to Form 1040.   ▶ See Instructions for Schedule D (Form 1040).

▶ Use lines 20 and 22 for more space to list transactions for lines 1 and 9.

OMB No. 1545-0074

1995

Attachment
Sequence No. 12

Name(s) shown on Form 1040

Your social security number

Part I Short-Term Capital Gains and Losses—Assets Held One Year or Less

(a) Description of property (Example: 100 sh. XYZ Co.)	(b) Date acquired (Mo., day, yr.)	(c) Date sold (Mo., day, yr.)	(d) Sales price (see page D-3)	(e) Cost or other basis (see page D-3)	(f) LOSS If (e) is more than (d), subtract (d) from (e)	(g) GAIN If (d) is more than (e), subtract (e) from (d)
1						

2 Enter your short-term totals, if any, from line 21	**2**		
3 Total short-term sales price amounts. Add column (d) of lines 1 and 2 . . .	**3**		
4 Short-term gain from Forms 2119 and 6252, and short-term gain or loss from Forms 4684, 6781, and 8824		**4**	
5 Net short-term gain or loss from partnerships, S corporations, estates, and trusts from Schedule(s) K-1		**5**	
6 Short-term capital loss carryover. Enter the amount, if any, from line 9 of your 1994 Capital Loss Carryover Worksheet		**6**	
7 Add lines 1 through 6 in columns (f) and (g)		**7** (	)
8 Net short-term capital gain or (loss). Combine columns (f) and (g) of line 7 . . . . . ▶		**8**	

Part II Long-Term Capital Gains and Losses—Assets Held More Than One Year

(a)	(b)	(c)	(d)	(e)	(f)	(g)
9						

10 Enter your long-term totals, if any, from line 23	**10**		
11 Total long-term sales price amounts. Add column (d) of lines 9 and 10 . .	**11**		
12 Gain from Form 4797; long-term gain from Forms 2119, 2439, and 6252; and long-term gain or loss from Forms 4684, 6781, and 8824		**12**	
13 Net long-term gain or loss from partnerships, S corporations, estates, and trusts from Schedule(s) K-1		**13**	
14 Capital gain distributions		**14**	
15 Long-term capital loss carryover. Enter the amount, if any, from line 14 of your 1994 Capital Loss Carryover Worksheet		**15**	
16 Add lines 9 through 15 in columns (f) and (g)		**16** (	)
17 Net long-term capital gain or (loss). Combine columns (f) and (g) of line 16 . . . . . ▶		**17**	

Part III Summary of Parts I and II

18 Combine lines 8 and 17. If a loss, go to line 19. If a gain, enter the gain on Form 1040, line 13. Note: If both lines 17 and 18 are gains, see the Capital Gain Tax Worksheet on page 24 . .	**18**	
19 If line 18 is a loss, enter here and as a (loss) on Form 1040, line 13, the smaller of these losses:		
a The loss on line 18; or		
b ($3,000) or, if married filing separately, ($1,500)	**19** (	)
Note: See the Capital Loss Carryover Worksheet on page D-3 if the loss on line 18 exceeds the loss on line 19 or if Form 1040, line 35, is a loss.		

For Paperwork Reduction Act Notice, see Form 1040 instructions.   Cat. No. 11338H   Schedule D (Form 1040) 1995

Figure 14.6.   **The Schedule D form**

Part
2

Quicken and Your
Personal Finances

Schedule D (Form 1040) 1998　　　　　　　　　　　　Attachment Sequence No. 12　　　Page 2

| Name(s) shown on Form 1040. Do not enter name and social security number if shown on other side. | | | | | | Your social security number |

Part IV　Short-Term Capital Gains and Losses—Assets Held One Year or Less　　(Continuation of Part I)

(a) Description of property (Example: 100 sh. XYZ Co.)	(b) Date acquired (Mo., day, yr.)	(c) Date sold (Mo., day, yr.)	(d) Sales price (see page D-3)	(e) Cost or other basis (see page D-3)	(f) LOSS If (e) is more than (d), subtract (d) from (e)	(g) GAIN If (d) is more than (e), subtract (e) from (d)
20						
21 Short-term totals. Add columns (d), (f), and (g) of line 20. Enter here and on line 2 . **21**						

Part V　Long-Term Capital Gains and Losses—Assets Held More Than One Year　　(Continuation of Part II)

22						
23 Long-term totals. Add columns (d), (f), and (g) of line 22. Enter here and on line 10 . **23**						

Printed on recycled paper

*Figure 14.6.　**The Schedule D form (continued)***

SCHEDULE E (Form 1040) Department of the Treasury Internal Revenue Service (99)	**Supplemental Income and Loss** (From rental real estate, royalties, partnerships, S corporations, estates, trusts, REMICs, etc.) ▶ Attach to Form 1040 or Form 1041. ▶ See Instructions for Schedule E (Form 1040).	OMB No. 1545-0074 Attachment Sequence No. 13

Name(s) shown on return | Your social security number

Part I   Income or Loss From Rental Real Estate and Royalties   Note: Report income and expenses from your business of renting personal property on Schedule C or C-EZ (see page E-1). Report farm rental income or loss from Form 4835 on page 2, line 39.

1   Show the kind and location of each rental real estate property:

A   ....

B   ....

C   ....

2   For each rental real estate property listed on line 1, did you or your family use it for personal purposes for more than the greater of 14 days or 10% of the total days rented at fair rental value during the tax year? (See page E-1.)

	Yes	No
A		
B		
C		

Income:

		Properties			Totals (Add columns A, B, and C.)
		A	B	C	
3 Rents received	3				3
4 Royalties received	4				4

Expenses:

5 Advertising	5				
6 Auto and travel (see page E-2)	6				
7 Cleaning and maintenance	7				
8 Commissions	8				
9 Insurance	9				
10 Legal and other professional fees	10				
11 Management fees	11				
12 Mortgage interest paid to banks, etc. (see page E-2)	12				12
13 Other interest	13				
14 Repairs	14				
15 Supplies	15				
16 Taxes	16				
17 Utilities	17				
18 Other (list) ▶	18				
19 Add lines 5 through 18	19				19
20 Depreciation expense or depletion (see page E-2)	20				20
21 Total expenses. Add lines 19 and 20	21				
22 Income or (loss) from rental real estate or royalty properties. Subtract line 21 from line 3 (rents) or line 4 (royalties). If the result is a (loss), see page E-2 to find out if you must file Form 6198	22				
23 Deductible rental real estate loss. Caution: Your rental real estate loss on line 22 may be limited. See page E-3 to find out if you must file Form 8582. Real estate professionals must complete line 42 on page 2	23	( )(	)(	)(	)

24   Income. Add positive amounts shown on line 22. Do not include any losses . . . . | 24 |
25   Losses. Add royalty losses from line 22 and rental real estate losses from line 23. Enter the total losses here . | 25 | ( ) |
26   Total rental real estate and royalty income or (loss). Combine lines 24 and 25. Enter the result here. If Parts II, III, IV, and line 39 on page 2 do not apply to you, also enter this amount on Form 1040, line 17. Otherwise, include this amount in the total on line 40 on page 2 . . . . | 26 |

For Paperwork Reduction Act Notice, see Form 1040 instructions.   Cat. No. 11344L   Schedule E (Form 1040) 1995

Figure 14.7.   The Schedule E form

Schedule E (Form 1040) 1988   Attachment Sequence No. 13   Page 2

Name(s) shown on return. Do not enter name and social security number if shown on other side.   Your social security number

Note: If you report amounts from farming or fishing on Schedule E, you must enter your gross income from those activities on line 41 below. Real estate professionals must complete line 42 below.

Part II   Income or Loss From Partnerships and S Corporations   **Note:** If you report a loss from an at-risk activity, you MUST check either column (e) or (f) of line 27 to describe your investment in the activity. See page E-4. If you check column (f), you must attach Form 6198.

27	(a) Name	(b) Enter P for partnership; S for S corporation	(c) Check if foreign partnership	(d) Employer identification number	**Investment At Risk?** (e) All is at risk	(f) Some is not at risk
A						
B						
C						
D						
E						

	Passive Income and Loss		Nonpassive Income and Loss		
	(g) Passive loss allowed (attach Form 8582 if required)	(h) Passive income from Schedule K–1	(i) Nonpassive loss from Schedule K–1	(j) Section 179 expense deduction from Form 4562	(k) Nonpassive income from Schedule K–1
A					
B					
C					
D					
E					
28a Totals					
b Totals					

29   Add columns (h) and (k) of line 28a . . . . | 29 |

30   Add columns (g), (i), and (j) of line 28b . . . . | 30 | (   ) |

31   Total partnership and S corporation income or (loss). Combine lines 29 and 30. Enter the result here and include in the total on line 40 below . . . . | 31 |

Part III   Income or Loss From Estates and Trusts

32	(a) Name	(b) Employer identification number
A		
B		

	Passive Income and Loss		Nonpassive Income and Loss	
	(c) Passive deduction or loss allowed (attach Form 8582 if required)	(d) Passive income from Schedule K–1	(e) Deduction or loss from Schedule K–1	(f) Other income from Schedule K–1
A				
B				
33a Totals				
b Totals				

34   Add columns (d) and (f) of line 33a . . . . | 34 |

35   Add columns (c) and (e) of line 33b . . . . | 35 | (   ) |

36   Total estate and trust income or (loss). Combine lines 34 and 35. Enter the result here and include in the total on line 40 below . . . . | 36 |

Part IV   Income or Loss From Real Estate Mortgage Investment Conduits (REMICs)—Residual Holder

37	(a) Name	(b) Employer identification number	(c) Excess inclusion from Schedules Q, line 2c (see page E-4)	(d) Taxable income (net loss) from Schedules Q, line 1b	(e) Income from Schedules Q, line 3b

38   Combine columns (d) and (e) only. Enter the result here and include in the total on line 40 below | 38 |

Part V   Summary

39   Net farm rental income or (loss) from Form 4835. Also, complete line 41 below . . . . . | 39 |

40   TOTAL income or (loss). Combine lines 26, 31, 36, 38, and 39. Enter the result here and on Form 1040, line 17 ▶ | 40 |

41   **Reconciliation of Farming and Fishing Income.**   Enter your gross farming and fishing income reported on Form 4835, line 7; Schedule K-1 (Form 1065), line 15b; Schedule K-1 (Form 1120S), line 23; and Schedule K-1 (Form 1041), line 13 (see page E-4) . . . . . . | 41 |

42   **Reconciliation for Real Estate Professionals.**   If you were a real estate professional (see page E-3), enter the net income or (loss) you reported anywhere on Form 1040 from all rental real estate activities in which you materially participated under the passive activity loss rules . . . | 42 |

✪ Printed on recycled paper

*Figure 14.7. **The Schedule E form (continued)***

GRAY AREAS IN THE TAX LAWS?

Despite what some people say, the business income tax laws don't actually have very many "gray areas." You need to know two basic rules. First, all business income is taxed—unless it's specifically excluded. Second, any business expense that's ordinary and necessary is deductible. The bottom line is that it's pretty clear if a particular amount flowing into the business should be be counted as income (it almost always does). And it's pretty clear if a particular expenditure is deductible (ask yourself, "Is this expense ordinary and necessary for the business?").

Telling Quicken If You Want Tax-Schedule–Specific Information

Quicken lets you tag categories, designating them to be imported to specific lines of specific tax forms. This feature makes it possible to export information from Quicken to another income tax-preparation program (such as TurboTax or TaxCut).

If you want to tag categories this way, choose the Edit ➤ Options ➤ Quicken Program command to display the General Options dialog box. Then click on the General tab and mark the selection Use Tax Schedules with Categories, as shown in Figure 14.8. Click on OK when you're done.

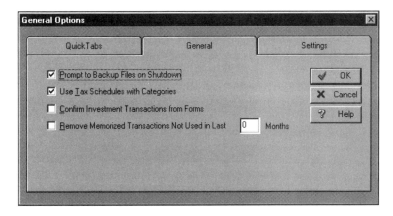

Figure 14.8. **The General tab of the General Options dialog box**

Modifying the Category List

If you accepted Quicken's suggestion to start with the default Home or Home and Business category list, you may need to make changes to the category list in order to better support your income tax preparation.

To make changes to the category list, click on the Cat List icon on the Iconbar or choose the Lists ➤ Category/Transfer command to display the Category & Transfer List window, as shown in Figure 14.9.

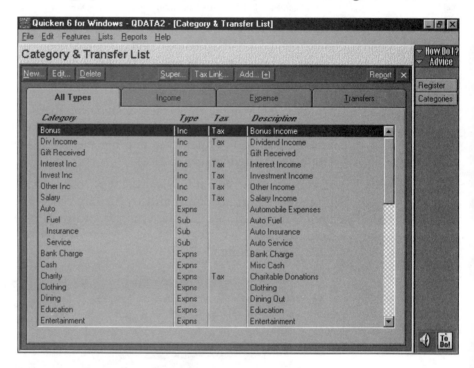

Figure 14.9. **The Category & Transfer List window**

 TIP Quicken sets up special categories for tracking investments when you create your first investment account. To identify these categories, Quicken starts each category name with an underline. You shouldn't change any of the investment categories.

Adding a Category for Income Taxes

To add a new category to the category list, follow these steps:

1. Click on the New command button in the Category & Transfer List window to display the Set Up Category dialog box, as shown in Figure 14.10.

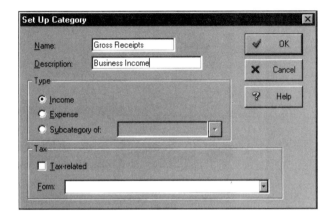

Figure 14.10. **The Set Up Category dialog box**

2. Enter a name for the category in the Name text box.

3. Enter a description of the category. (Quicken uses the description along with the category name on its reports to identify the category's total. If the description is left blank, only the name is used.)

4. Use the Type option buttons to indicate whether the new category tracks income or expense or is a subcategory of a category that tracks income or expense.

5. *If you clicked on the Subcategory of option button*, activate the drop-down–list box and select a category.

6. Mark the Tax-related check box to indicate that you'll use this category for tracking taxable income or tax-deductible expense items. (This tells Quicken the category total should appear on a Tax Summary report.)

7. Indicate on which tax form and tax form line the category total gets reported: Activate the Form drop-down–list box and select the list entry that names the correct form (or schedule) and the form (or schedule) line. Suppose, for example, that you want to set up a category for tracking the gross sales figure that will ultimately be entered on Line 1 of the Schedule C form. To do this, select the Schedule C: Gross Receipts entry.

> **NOTE** Until you mark the Use Tax Schedules with Categories check box in the General Preferences dialog box, Quicken doesn't display the Form drop-down–list box in the Set Up Category dialog box.

8. Click on OK when the Set Up Category dialog box is complete, and Quicken adds the category you described to the Category & Transfer list and closes the dialog box.

9. Repeat steps 1 through 8 for each tax category you want to add.

Editing a Category for Income Taxes

To edit an existing category so it works (or works better) for tracking taxable income and tax-deductible expenses, follow these steps:

1. Select the category in the Category & Transfer List window and click on the Edit command button to display the Edit Category dialog box, as shown in Figure 14.11.

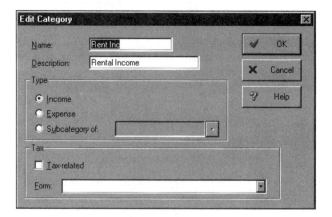

Figure 14.11.   Alter existing categories in the Edit Category dialog box.

2. If you need to, change the category name. (Quicken updates the transactions that used the old category name so they show the new category name.)

3. If you need to, edit the category description.

4. Use the Type option buttons to indicate whether the category tracks income or expense or is a subcategory of one that does.

TIP You can change a category into a subcategory and a subcategory into a category using the Type option buttons. If you demote a category, you must also complete step 5.

Part
2

Quicken and Your
Personal Finances

5. *If you mark the Subcategory option button,* select the suitable category from the drop-down–list box.

TIP You can have subcategories that roll up into subcategories. To do this, select the subcategory as a primary category from the drop-down list.

6. Mark the Tax-related check box to indicate that you'll use this category for tracking taxable income or tax-deductible expense items, or deselect the check box if the category is currently being treated as taxable or tax-deductible but shouldn't be.

7. *If the category is tax-related,* indicate on which tax form and tax form line the category total gets reported: From the Form drop-down–list box, select the list entry that names the correct form (or schedule) and the form (or schedule) line.

8. Click on OK when the Edit Category dialog box is complete. Quicken makes the changes and closes the dialog box.

9. Repeat steps 1 through 8 for each category you want to modify.

Deleting Extraneous Categories

You can remove categories you don't want on the Category & Transfer list. (This is a good idea, if you want to eliminate the chance of someone—perhaps you—accidentally using an incorrect category to summarize taxable income or a tax-deductible expense.)

To remove unneeded categories, select the category in the Category & Transfer List window and click on the Delete command button. Quicken removes the category from the Category & Transfer list and erases the Category text box for existing transactions that use the category.

TIP If you want to delete a category but want transactions that use the old category to use another category—I'll call this the new category—make the old category you want to delete a subcategory of the new category. Then delete the old category. This works because when you delete a subcategory, Quicken uses just the parent category to summarize the transaction.

Using Quicken's Tax Reports

Quicken provides two reports for helping you prepare your income tax returns: the Tax Summary report and the Tax Schedule report (see Chapter 4, *Tracking Your Finances with Reports*).

If you haven't connected taxable income categories and tax-deductible expense categories to tax schedule lines, you use the Tax Summary report. After you print the report, you enter the taxable income and tax-deductible expense category totals into the appropriate tax form or schedule input lines. You would, for example, enter the Total Charity figure shown in Figure 14.12 on the "Contributions by cash or check" line (line 13) of the Schedule A form (see Figure 14.2).

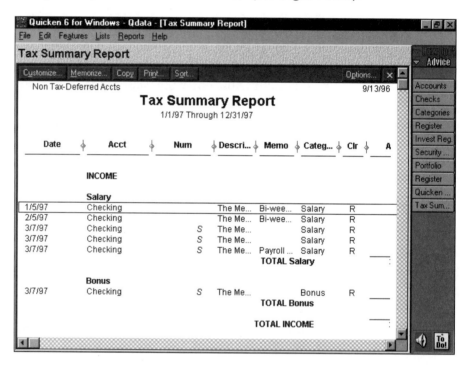

Figure 14.12.   The Tax Summary report lists all taxable income categories and tax-deductible expense categories—as long as you've correctly set up your category list.

If you have connected taxable income categories and tax-deductible expense categories to tax schedule lines, you use the Tax Schedule report. After you print the report, you enter the report's tax schedule line totals on the corresponding tax schedule lines. Figure 14.13 shows a portion of the Tax Schedule Report. It gives you the Total Salary and, at the top, it identifies the form as the W-2.

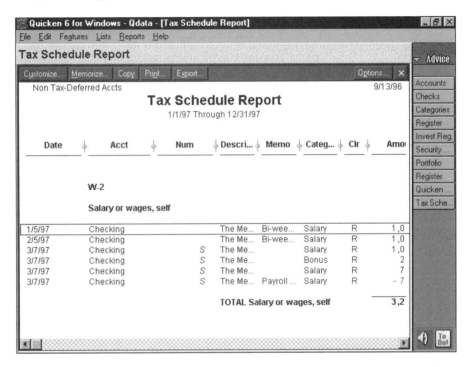

Figure 14.13.   **The Tax Schedule Report lists all taxable income categories and tax-deductible**
expense categories summarized by input lines on a tax schedule form.

Exporting to a Tax-Preparation Package

Quicken lets you easily export taxable income and tax-deductible expense information to a tax-preparation program such as TurboTax or TaxCut. If you've collected accurate taxable income and tax-deductible expense information in Quicken and have decided to use a tax-preparation program, you'll want to consider doing this.

Exporting to TurboTax

The TurboTax for Windows program is so clever about the way it uses your Quicken data that all you need to do is start TurboTax and tell it you want to import data from Quicken (if you've installed TurboTax, you can start it by choosing the Features ➤ Taxes ➤ TurboTax command). Turbo-Tax then starts Quicken, tells it to create a Tax Schedule report for the appropriate year, and uses the Tax Schedule report information to fill in the open tax return.

There are only two tricks to exporting Quicken data to TurboTax. First, the Quicken file with the tax information you want to use needs to be active so when TurboTax starts Quicken, it also gets the right file.

If you're using only one Quicken file—and you probably are—this isn't a problem. But if it is a problem, TurboTax gives you an out. It will display the name of the active Quicken file and ask you if it's correct, using a message box, before it imports the data. You can indicate that the active file isn't correct and then tell TurboTax which Quicken file it should have Quicken open. This may seem confusing, but Turbo-Tax can look at the Q3.DIR file in the Quicken directory to determine which Quicken data file was last used and, therefore, is active. It's also possible to include a command-line parameter that names the active file when starting Quicken. If you indicate that your tax information is in another Quicken file, TurboTax tells Quicken to make that file active when TurboTax starts Quicken.

A second trick to having TurboTax automatically import Quicken data is to make sure you use the correct version of TurboTax. If you use the 1996 version of TurboTax, for example, the Tax Schedule report that TurboTax has Quicken produce includes the transaction date range January 1, 1996, through December 31, 1996. Presumably, if you use the 1997 version of TurboTax, the Tax Schedule report that TurboTax has Quicken produce includes the transaction date range January 1, 1997, through December 31, 1997 (I say "presumably" because the 1997 version of TurboTax isn't available as I'm writing this).

This rigid transaction date range feature makes perfect sense, of course. Because the tax laws and tax tables change, you can't use the 1996 version of TurboTax to do your 1995 or your 1997 taxes. (you can't, for example, use this automatic importing feature to "guesstimate" what your 1997 income taxes will be using 1997 data and the 1996 version of TurboTax). Do be aware it exists, though.

Exporting to Other Tax-Preparation Programs

You can export the information shown in a Tax Schedule report to a Tax Exchange Format, or TXF, file. Almost any tax-preparation program you work with, including TurboTax, will import the data contained in this file and use it to fill in the lines of a tax return. (You don't need to first export your Quicken data to a TXF file if you're working with TurboTax, however. TurboTax will retrieve Quicken data automatically.)

To export the information shown in a Tax Schedule report, you first produce the report: You choose the Reports ➤ Home ➤ Tax Schedule command, complete the Create Report dialog box, and click on Create (see Chapter 4). Figure 14.13 shows a Tax Schedule Report.

Once you've created the Tax Schedule report and it appears in a document window, take these steps to export the tax schedule information to a TXF file:

1. Click on the Export command button on the button bar of the report to display the Create Tax Export File window, as shown in Figure 14.14.

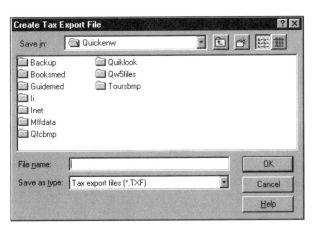

Figure 14.14. Name the export file in the Create Tax Export File dialog box.

Part 2

Quicken and Your Personal Finances

2. Use the File text box to name the TXF file. You don't have to specify TXF as the file extension; Quicken adds it for you. If you don't specify a path, Quicken puts the file in the current directory—which is probably the Quicken data directory.

3. *If you want to put the file in some other directory*—such as the TurboTax directory—precede the file name with the path name of the directory you want or use the Directories window in the dialog box to navigate to the destination directory. Then click on OK, and Quicken creates the TXF file.

To use the TXF file, you import it into the tax-preparation package you'll use to complete your return. Refer to the documentation or user's guide that goes with that product for information on how you do this. If you're working with Tax Cut, for example, you choose the File ➤ Import command in Tax Cut. Then you complete the dialog boxes supplied by the tax-preparation program to answer questions about where the TXF file is located.

QUICKEN AND TAX-PREPARATION PROGRAMS

You need to be careful when you export Quicken data to a tax-preparation program for a couple of reasons. First, the numbers you input on your tax form need to match what your informational returns—W-2, 1099s, 1098s, and so on—show, even if your Quicken reports show different numbers (if an informational return is wrong, you need to have the issuer of the information correct the return). Second, to determine which taxable income or tax-deduction transactions should be counted for a particular year, Quicken and the tax-preparation program can only look at the transaction date. If the transaction date shows the income or deduction amount falling in the tax year, it gets counted for that year. This sounds correct, but it often isn't. Usually, some transactions you enter at the very beginning of the calendar year really relate to the previous year's tax return.

Using the Tax Planner

Quicken 6 comes with a handy income tax expense estimator, built by the same people who create TurboTax. This tool is called the Tax Planner. Based either on direct worksheet entries or on Quicken data, the Tax Planner gives you a very accurate estimate of what you'll pay in income taxes for a particular year.

You may want to print out a copy of the Tax Schedule report before you estimate your income taxes. To do this, choose the Reports ➤ Home ➤ Tax Schedule command.

Estimating Your Income Taxes

To use the Tax Planner, follow these steps:

1. Choose the Features ➤ Taxes ➤ Tax Planner command. Quicken displays the Tax Planner dialog box, shown in Figure 14.15.

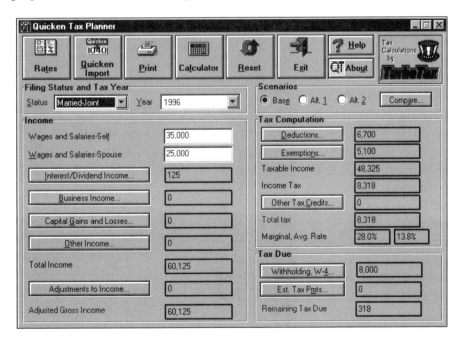

Figure 14.15. **The Tax Planner dialog box**

2. Activate the Filing Status drop down list box and select the appropriate filing status: Separate, Married Filing Joint, Married Filing Separate, Head of Household, and so on. If you have questions about your filing status, refer to the IRS instructions that came with last year's return.

3. Activate the Year drop-down list and select the year for which you're estimating your income tax expenses. Picking the right year is important because the tax rate schedules are annually adjusted for things like tax law changes and inflation.

4. Enter your total wages in the Wages and Salaries-Self text box.

5. Enter your spouse's total wages in the Wages and Salaries-Spouse text box.

6. *If you have interest or dividend income,* click on the Interest/Dividend Income button. Quicken displays a worksheet dialog box that contains labeled text boxes you use to describe your interest and dividends. Fill in the text boxes and select OK.

7. *If you have business income,* click on the Business Income button. Quicken displays a worksheet dialog box that contains labeled text boxes you use to describe any business income—such as income from a sole proprietorship. Fill in the text boxes and select OK.

8. *If you have capital gains or losses,* click on the Capital Gains and Losses button. Quicken displays a worksheet dialog box that contains labeled text boxes you use to describe any investment capital gains or losses you've realized. Fill in the text boxes and select OK.

9. *If you have other income that you haven't recorded elsewhere,* click on the Other Income button. Quicken displays a worksheet dialog box. Use it to describe this other income.

10. *If you have any adjustments to income,* click on the Adjustments to Income button. Quicken displays a dialog box that contains labeled text boxes you use to describe any adjustments, such as IRA or Keogh contributions, alimony payments, self-employment deductions, and early withdrawal penalties. Fill in the text boxes and select OK.

11. Click on the Deductions button. Quicken displays a worksheet dialog box you use to estimate your itemized deductions. Fill in the text boxes and select OK. Quicken uses the larger of your total itemized deductions or the standard deduction.

12. Click on the Exemptions button. Quicken displays a worksheet dialog box you use to specify the number of exemptions you're entitled to claim. Fill in the single text box provided and select OK.

13. *If you pay other federal taxes or are entitled to claim any income tax credits,* click on the Other Tax Credits button. Quicken displays a worksheet dialog box you use to specify any other taxes you pay—such as self-employment income—or any income tax credits. Fill in the text boxes and select OK.

With the information you provide in steps 2 through 13, the Tax Planner estimates your total federal tax bill and also calculates both your marginal income tax rate and your average income tax rate.

**Part
2**

**Quicken and Your
Personal Finances**

TIP   Your marginal income tax rate is a useful piece of information. It allows you to convert pretax investment yields and interest rates to after-tax investment yields and interest rates. All you do is multiply the pretax rate by 1 minus the marginal income rate. For example, to convert a 10 percent pretax rate to an after-tax rate if the marginal tax rate is 28 percent, you make the following calculation: 10%*(1–28%). This formula returns 7.2 percent.

14. Click on the Withholding W-4 button. Quicken displays a worksheet dialog box you use to describe the federal income taxes you (and your spouse if you're married) have already had withheld and how much you'll probably have withheld over the remaining payroll periods in the year. Fill in the text boxes and select OK.

15. Click on the Est Tax Pmts button. Quicken displays a worksheet dialog box you use to describe any estimated taxes you (and your spouse if you're married) have made and will make. Fill in the text boxes and select OK.

With the completion of steps 14 and 15, the Tax Planner calculates the remaining federal taxes you'll still owe at the end of the year after all your estimated withholding and any estimated income taxes.

To print a summary of the tax planning calculations, click on the Print button. Quicken displays a Print dialog box which mirrors the Print dialog boxes you use to print reports. If you've printed a report or two—presumably you have by this point—you'll have no trouble completing the Tax Planner's version.

To remove the Tax Planner dialog box and at the same time save your inputs, click on the Close button. To erase your inputs before removing the Tax Planner dialog box, click on the Reset button.

> **NOTE** Click on the Calculator button to display Quicken's calculator. You can use this to make quick calculations needed in your income tax estimating. You can also use the calculator's Paste button to paste the value showing on the calculator's display into a Tax Planner text box.

Using Tax Data from Account Registers

In general, I think the best approach for describing the inputs to the tax planning process is entering values directly into the Tax Planner's text boxes and worksheets. You have another choice, however. If you are using categories that tie, or connect, to specific lines in your tax return, as described earlier in the chapter, you can tell Quicken it should instead use the data from your account registers. To do this, click on the Quicken Data button in the Tax Planner. Quicken then looks through your registers, collects and tallies any transactions that should go into one of the Tax Planner text boxes or into the worksheet, and displays a window listing these transactions.

> **WARNING** If there are Tax Planner text boxes and worksheets that don't get filled in—perhaps you haven't yet entered the taxable income or tax-deduction information in a register—you'll need to fill them in manually, as described in the preceding discussion, of income tax estimation.

Updating the Tax Rate Schedules

Every year, the tax rate schedules change. This happens for a couple of reasons. One is that the income brackets are indexed for inflation, so that income brackets get bumped up every year by the most recent year's inflation rate. Another reason is that Congress is continually fiddling with the tax rates and the number of income brackets. To deal with this constant change, Quicken lets you update the tax rates by clicking on the Rates button. When you do, Quicken displays a dialog box you can use to change the tax rates for any of the filing statutes for 1995 and 1996. The basic mechanics are pretty straightforward.

You click on an option button to indicate the year, and select a filing status from a drop-down–list box. Then you fill out a set of text boxes that describe the income brackets and the tax rates. This isn't all that difficult. You simply transfer bracket and rate information from a tax-rate schedule provided by the Internal Revenue Service to the screen.

Comparing Different Income Tax Scenarios

You can store up to three sets, or scenarios, of inputs to the Tax Planner: Base, Alt 1, and Alt 2. Typically, you first create the Base scenario. You can create a second and third alternative scenario by marking the Alt 1 and Alt 2 option buttons in the Scenarios area in the upper-right corner of the Tax Planner dialog box. When you mark Alt 1 or Alt 2, Quicken asks if you want to copy the Base scenario inputs as a starting point for the new scenario. If you want to do this—and you probably do—click on Yes.

You can compare the inputs and the income tax calculations for two scenarios by clicking on the Compare button. Quicken displays a dialog box that summarizes the filing status, tax year, adjusted gross income, deductions and exemptions, taxable income, total tax, and tax rates for each scenario.

Using TurboTax to Prepare Your Taxes

TurboTax, as mentioned earlier in the chapter, is an income tax-preparation program. Because TurboTax is another Intuit program and because many Quicken users will be interested in knowing just a bit more about this program, let me make a few comments about it.

TurboTax is relatively easy to use (although not as easy as Quicken). You can use it a couple of different ways. If you're familiar with what forms you need to fill out to complete your federal and state income tax return, you can display on-screen forms that mirror the actual forms you file. Using this approach, you just fill in the blanks.

If you're not as sure of yourself when it comes to income tax laws and accounting, you can tell TurboTax you want to be "interviewed." The program will ask you a series of questions that you answer by filling in text boxes and clicking on buttons. Based on your answers, TurboTax

Part 2

Quicken and Your Personal Finances

then fills out your tax return. You can print a copy of your tax return directly from TurboTax.

The Benefits of Using TurboTax

Is TurboTax a good product? Yes, it is. In fact, I do my own tax returns with TurboTax, and I really like the program. You benefit in a couple of big ways from using a tax-preparation package. First, being able to print an entire return with TurboTax means never having to worry about whether you have all the right tax forms and schedules. If you need to file a particular form or schedule, TurboTax can print it. (Before TurboTax, I always found myself running over to the local public library or calling the Internal Revenue Service to get some obscure form or schedule I needed.)

A second benefit of TurboTax and programs like it is that you can easily make changes to your return. For example, when I used to prepare my return manually, I would invariably complete the entire return, think I was done, and then find a missing deduction or income amount I had to report. Because of this, I would have to input the new figure and then redo recalculations. With TurboTax, however, redoing your return for last-minute input is a breeze. You just start up TurboTax, input the new figure, and then tell the program to recalculate the return.

Who Should Use TurboTax

Does all of this mean everyone should go out and buy a tax-preparation program? No, I don't think so. First of all, if you pay a tax preparer to do your taxes now, I don't think you can use TurboTax as a substitute for a paid tax preparer. TurboTax automates and expedites the tax-preparation process, but it still requires you to answer a series of questions having to do with your income taxes.

If you file a really simple return, you probably don't need TurboTax. For example, if you're a single taxpayer with no itemized deductions whose only income is from a job, your taxes are pretty simple in the first place. It wouldn't make sense in your situation to get TurboTax only to have it make a few calculations automatically. Any tax-return-preparation time you save will be eaten up by having to install the program and learn the ropes.

You need to buy a new copy of tax-preparation programs such as TurboTax every year because the tax rates and sometimes the tax laws change. Unfortunately, tax rate changes and tax law changes don't occur until the very end of the year. For this reason, there are always two versions of tax-preparation programs: an early-bird version that's available late in the year and useful only for making estimates, and a final version that you need to actually prepare and print your return. Early-bird purchasers always get to upgrade for free to the final version, but you still need to be aware of the difference between the two versions. You don't, for example, want to purchase an early-bird version on April 15, thinking you'll have time to install the software and then prepare the return.

If you want to purchase a new copy of TurboTax, choose the Features ➤ Taxes ➤ TurboTax command. Quicken mentions that it is not installed on your system. Click on the Order Now button to get information on ordering it directly from Intuit. Once you install TurboTax, by the way, choosing the Features ➤ Taxes ➤ TurboTax command starts TurboTax.

HOW TURBOTAX COMPARES TO SIMILAR PROGRAMS

You might be curious as to how TurboTax compares with other tax-preparation programs. I can give you some helpful information in this area. For several years now, I've been reviewing income tax-preparation packages for *Home Office Computing* magazine. (The reviews usually run in the April issue, which is available sometime in March.) TurboTax always ranks near the top.

Common Tax-Preparation Problems and Solutions

There are some potential pitfalls to using your Quicken data as the one and only source of all your taxable income and tax-deductible expense information. This doesn't mean you shouldn't use Quicken, but you need to be careful—you can't blindly automate the process.

Discrepancies between Your Records and Informational Returns

When the IRS processes your return, one of the things they'll do is verify that any informational returns they've received match up with your return. They will compare the W-2 information provided by your employer (or employers) with what you enter as the "Wages, Sales, Tips, etc." line, and they will compare the 1099-Int and 1099-OID statements provided by almost anyone who's paid you interest with what you enter on your 1040 or Schedule B (Schedule B summarizes your dividend and interest income when you have more substantial amounts of either).

Any difference between what one of these informational returns shows and what you enter on a line of a tax schedule of your income tax return will almost certainly trigger a review of your return. In this case, the IRS will write you a letter asking for an explanation of the discrepancy. You'll then need to review your records to determine whether your return's number was the correct one or—and this is probably more likely—the informational return's number was the correct one. Then you'll need to fix the mistake.

This sequence of events points out a potential trouble spot. You can use Quicken to collect your taxable income and—in some cases—your tax-deductible expense information. But it may just be that there's another, more accurate source of the taxable income or tax-deductible expense numbers you need to enter on your tax return. When this is the case, it makes the most sense to use this other source for preparing your tax return. And even if you do record the information provided by this other source into Quicken, you may make an error entering the data.

For this reason, I think it's easiest and most accurate to get your salaries and wages information from employer-provided W-2s and to get interest and dividend information from the 1099 informational returns your broker or bank prepares.

Timing Differences

Another opportunity for error concerns timing differences. You may be required to report some item of income or deduct some expense in one year but not record the information into a Quicken register until a subsequent year. For example, if you're a partner in some partnership, you may be required to include in your taxable income a share of partnership profits earned in one year but paid in the following year. Or if you've invested in a long-term certificate of deposit (CD), you may be required to report any accrued interest for the year as income (the CD issuer may send you a 1099 OID statement of your interest earnings).

To use Quicken to keep records of taxable income and tax-deductible expenses like this, you need to use a transaction date that places the transaction into the year the transaction affects taxable income or tax-deductible expenses—which won't necessarily be the same year you make a deposit or write a check.

What to Do If You Use Quicken and Get Audited

Although your chances of being audited are probably remote, some of the people who read this chapter will be audited. Here are some things Quicken users should do when they get audited—and some things they shouldn't do.

Quicken Tasks You Should Complete

The Quicken Tax Summary report lists and tallies each of the taxable and tax-deductible transactions included on your return. Since the audit will probably consist of the agent reviewing these transactions and deductions, you'll want to have a listing of the transactions. A Tax Summary report gives this information.

If you know beforehand that a specific tax deduction is being questioned, be sure to bring all of the source documents that evidence transactions. For example, if the IRS is questioning your charitable contributions deduction, bring any canceled checks you used to make your contributions.

TIP   Don't bring Quicken on a laptop computer to the audit. The IRS agent may appreciate your enthusiasm, but remember that your Quicken file largely summarizes your financial life. And Quicken's reports make it easy for the agent to quickly review every nook and cranny, searching for income you may have missed or deductions you shouldn't have taken.

Other Audit Preparation Tasks

There are a couple of other things you should be sure you do before you attend the audit. First, make sure you understand all the numbers on your return, and remember that you signed it under penalty of perjury.

A second thing you may want to consider is asking your tax preparer to represent you at the audit. There are a variety of reasons for doing this. If you don't understand your return but your preparer does, it makes sense to have the preparer at the audit. Sometimes it also makes more sense to have a tax preparer represent you because he or she knows (or should know) quite a lot about the income tax laws but relatively little about your financial life. I know a tax attorney who follows this approach because the tax preparer can honestly answer many IRS questions by saying, "I don't know." The tax attorney feels like this response tends to terminate many spontaneous inquiries.

Things to Do during the Audit

An audit doesn't have to be a bad experience. All that really happens is that the IRS agent will ask you to explain and document items the IRS doesn't understand.

Nevertheless, let me provide you with two final suggestions. First, if the agent identifies himself or herself as a special agent, ask to terminate the interview so you can reschedule it. A special agent investigates criminal tax code violations, so you'll probably want a tax attorney present at any meetings.

Another thing I'd suggest is that you be very reserved in your comments. Don't lie, of course, but don't volunteer extra information. If you have questions about a deduction or how to treat an income item, ask a tax preparer or telephone the IRS's taxpayer assistance line, but don't expect the IRS agent auditing your return to answer tax-preparation questions. My feeling is that there's a very strong tendency for the auditor to look only for things that increase your income tax bill, not for things that decrease it.

HOW TO PLAN FOR AND SAVE ON TAXES

Understanding the conceptual framework of the federal income tax codes can help when you plan for and prepare your taxes. Also, understanding the significance of marginal income tax rates is important when you're working on personal finance planning issues. So let's look at each of these topics in turn.

Federal Income Taxes

Essentially, the federal income tax forms take you through the following formula when you calculate your taxable income:

adjusted gross income = total income – adjustments

taxable income = adjusted gross income – the standard deduction amount or *itemized deductions – personal exemptions*

Total Income

Your *total income* includes wages, sales, interest and dividend income, capital gains, and gambling winnings. In other words, it includes just about anything you receive that has value. Exceptions include tax-exempt interest income on state and local government obligations, insurance proceeds, and gifts from others.

The IRS allows certain adjustments to total income. One of the most popular is the individual retirement account (IRA) deduction. IRAs let you save money for retirement and not count the money you've saved as part of your total income. Other examples of adjustments (all of which are shown on the 1040 form) include penalties on early withdrawal of savings and alimony.

Adjusted Gross Income

Finding your *adjusted gross income* is an intermediate but important step in calculating your income taxes. Several itemized deductions for personal expenses, such as medical expenses, are allowed, but only to the extent that they exceed a certain percentage of your adjusted gross income. You either take the standard deduction or subtract the total of your itemized deductions from your adjusted gross income.

Most people don't itemize. It's easier to simply take the standard deduction because itemizing requires you to add up several categories of personal expenses, including home mort.gage interest, state and local property taxes, state income tax, charitable contributions, and other expenses. The income tax forms are relatively straightforward in explaining what to enter on each line, but you need to read the instructions carefully because the rules for itemized deductions have become more complex in the past few years. What's more, if you have an adjusted gross income that's above around $100,000, you may not be able to make all the deductions you want to make.

Personal Exemptions

To arrive at your taxable income, you subtract what are called *personal exemptions* from your adjusted gross income. You get one roughly $2,500 personal exemption for each person in your family during the tax year, as long as your adjusted gross income doesn't exceed $150,000 (this $2,500 personal-exemption figure is adjusted annually for inflation). If your adjusted gross income does exceed $150,000, you lose some portion of your standard deductions.

Calculating What You Owe

To calculate the taxes on your taxable income, you multiply the taxable income by the tax rates. It's a little tricky because different rates apply to different parts of your income. For example, you might pay a 15 percent tax on one part of your income, a 28 percent tax on another, and 31 percent tax on still another part. For example, a married couple with $50,000 of taxable income would pay a 15 percent income tax on the first roughly $40,000 of income and a 28 percent tax on the remaining income.

To calculate the actual income taxes you are required to pay on your taxable income and the amount of the additional payment you'll make or the refund you'll get, use the following formula:

Part 2

Quicken and Your
Personal Finances

tax before credits = taxable income × the tax rates

The tax before credits minus the tax credits equals your total income tax bill. From your total bill, you subtract withholding and estimated tax payments to arrive at a refund if the result is negative or a payment if the result is positive.

Currently, five income tax rates are in effect—15, 28, 31, 36, and 39.6 percent. In recent years, however, Congress has continued to add more and more rates, and this trend might continue. One other tricky point is that the parts of your income to which the rates apply aren't the same for everybody. Any of five breakdowns might apply to your situation, depending on whether:

▶ You're a widow or widower

▶ You have dependents

▶ You're married or single

▶ If you're married, you and your spouse file a combined, or joint, return or you file separate returns

Five different tax rate schedules show which dollars are taxed at which rates; each schedule corresponds to a filing status. The filing status is determined by your marital status, by whether you have dependents, and, if you're married, by whether you and your spouse file together or separately.

Tax Credits

After you calculate the taxes you owe by using the tax rates, you calculate your tax credits. *Tax credits* are reductions in the amount of your income taxes. Tax credits include the earned income credit and the child-care and dependent-care credit.

NOTE Don't confuse tax credits with tax deductions. Both reduce the taxes you pay, but credits are more powerful. Deductions reduce only your taxable income; tax credits reduce the amount of taxes you pay.

After subtracting any tax credits from the taxes on your taxable income, you arrive at the actual income taxes you owe. If this amount is more than you paid or withheld over the year, you pay the government additional money. If the amount is less than you paid or withheld, you get a refund. (Generally, income taxes are paid throughout the year, either when your employer withholds an amount and passes it along to the Internal Revenue Service, or you make quarterly estimated income tax payments.)

That, in a nutshell, is how the personal federal income tax calculations and laws work. Actually, the mathematics aren't very difficult. But a lot of little nuances and subtleties exist.

Alternative Minimum Tax

As you plan for and prepare your federal income tax return, you need to be aware of the alternative minimum tax. This tax is reached by yet another set of rules and methods for income calculation. If you have what the tax laws describe as "tax-preference items," such as accelerated depreciation deductions on rental property or tax-exempt interest on private-purpose municipal bonds, you need to calculate the alternative minimum taxes you owe. You pay whichever is more: the taxes you owe using the regular income tax rules or the taxes you owe using the alternative minimum tax rules. If you think you might be subject to alternative minimum taxes, confer with a tax accountant or a tax attorney.

Marginal Income Tax Rates

Personal financial planning professionals and investment advisors talk a lot about marginal income tax rates. These rates are very important, so you'll benefit by understanding what marginal income tax rates are.

Marginal income tax rates let you calculate the income that you either pay or save as a result of changes in your income or changes in your income tax deductions. For example, suppose you're considering buying a home and the mortgage interest you will pay will increase your itemized deductions by $10,000. To calculate the effect of this additional income tax deduction, you need to know the difference the

Part 2

Quicken and Your Personal Finances

deduction will make in your taxable income and, therefore, in your income taxes. Before you start thinking that marginal income tax rates are too messy to worry about, let's look at a quick example. After you see an example, the logic and arithmetic of marginal tax rates should be clearer to you.

If you were single in 1995, you paid income taxes of 15 percent on the first $23,350 of your taxable income, 28 percent on income over $23,350 but not over $56,550, 31 percent on income over $56,550 but not over $117,950, 36 percent on the income over $117,950 but not over $256,500, and 39.6 percent on income over $256,500. (Different tax rates and brackets apply to different people, but the basic logic is the same for each filing status. That is why I talk about single taxpayers here.)

What happens if you're single and your taxable income is $50,000? Suppose you're considering a mortgage that will add $10,000 to your itemized deductions. In this case, taking on the mortgage will reduce your taxable income from $50,000 to $40,000. Because all of those dollars are taxed at a marginal rate of 15 percent (everything between $23,350 and $56,550 is taxed at 28 percent), you can calculate the tax savings you'll enjoy by multiplying the marginal tax rate of 28 percent by the change in your taxable income of $10,000. The result is $2,800, so $2,800 is the income tax amount you will save.

Let's look at another quick example: Suppose you're single, your taxable income is $150,000, and you're considering putting $10,000 in a tax-deductible retirement plan such as a SEP/IRA. (A *SEP/IRA* is a special type of individual retirement account for employees of small businesses.) By identifying the marginal income tax rate—36 percent in this example—you can tell what amount of income taxes you'll save by making this contribution. In this example, the tax savings can be calculated as 36 percent times $10,000 (.36 × 10,000), which equals $3,600 of savings.

CHAPTER 15

Planning Your Personal Finances

FEATURING

Setting savings goals

Monitoring finances with supercategories

Setting up a budget

Using Quicken for strategic planning

Achieving financial independence

Quicken's record-keeping abilities are fabulous. In fact, that's probably the reason Quicken is so popular. But personal financial success requires more than just good record keeping. You need to intelligently monitor and plan your personal finances. This chapter describes the tools Quicken provides to help you plan.

NOTE There are no prerequisites for using Quicken to plan for achieving financial goals such as a financially secure retirement or paying for a child's college expenses. You do need to collect information about your actual income and spending if you want to compare this information to a budget.

Setting Savings Goals

Quicken lets you set savings goal amounts, calculate the periodic saving required to reach the goal, and track your progress toward the goal. While you don't need to use Quicken to achieve your savings goals, it can make the whole process much easier (by quantifying exactly what you need to do), and it can increase your chances of success (by focusing attention on your progress).

Creating a Savings Goal

To create a savings goal, choose the Features ➤ Planning ➤ Savings Goals command. Quicken displays the Savings Goals window. The window won't yet list any savings goals because you won't have described any. Click on the New command button. Quicken displays the Create New Savings Goal dialog box, as shown in Figure 15.1.

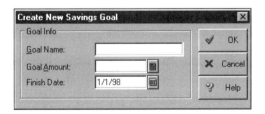

Figure 15.1. *The Create New Savings Goal dialog box*

Describe your savings goal by filling in the text boxes shown on the Create New Savings Goal dialog box. Enter a name for the goal (perhaps the item you're saving for) in the Goal Name text box. In the Goal Amount text box, enter the amount you want to accumulate. Using the Finish Date combo box, give the date by which you want to reach your goal. Click on OK. Quicken returns you to the Savings Goals window, which now lists the goal you described. Figure 15.2 shows an example.

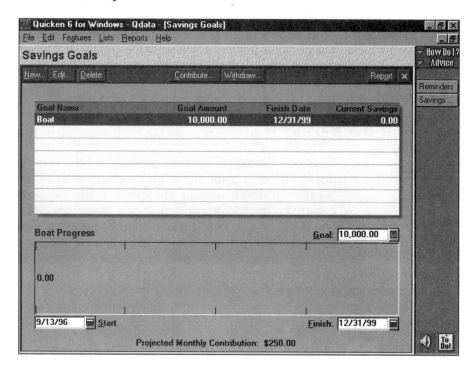

Figure 15.2.   The Savings Goals window

In the box in the top half of the Savings Goals window, Quicken lists each of the savings goals you've described. (In Figure 15.2, the list shows only one goal, Boat.) In the box in the bottom half of the Savings Goals window, Quicken draws a bar chart that depicts your progress toward the goal. (In Figure 15.2, the bar doesn't appear because zero progress has been made toward the goal.)

In the bottom-right corner of the Savings Goals dialog box, a number appears. This is the monthly amount you need to save in order to reach your goal by the finish date. Quicken calculates this figure by dividing the savings goal amount by the number of payments. (Quicken assumes that you won't earn any interest on your savings.)

TIP   You can print a list of your savings goals by displaying the Savings Goals window and clicking on Print. By clicking on Report, you can get a printable report which shows you your progress towards your goals. You can change a savings goal's description by selecting the goal, clicking on Edit, and then using the Edit Savings Goals dialog box to change the goal amount or finish date.

Saving Money toward a Goal

Using a savings goal is easy. When you set up a savings goal, what Quicken actually does is create a special type of account called a savings-goal account. This account works like a separate compartment you use to earmark funds you've stored in, say, your regular checking account. In other words, you might have $500 in your checking account, but $200 of this money may be earmarked for a savings goal. To set aside money for a savings goal, open the Savings Goals window and click on Contribute. (Quicken assumes that all contributions will be monthly.) The trans-action will appear as a transfer in the register of whatever account you have chosen. The money will remain in the account but will not be shown in your balance figure. The final transaction in Figure 15.3 is a transfer to the Boat account.

NOTE   Savings-goal transactions don't have any effect on bank-account reconciliations. When you reconcile a bank account with savings-goals transactions, Quicken hides all the savings-goal transactions.

You can delete a savings goal. To do this, you first display the Savings Goals window by choosing the Features ➤ Planning ➤ Savings Goals command. Then you select the goal and click on Delete. When you do this, Quicken returns the money to the source account and asks what to do with the account it created for the savings goal. You can tell Quicken to delete the account or to save the account. (You might want to save the account, for example, if you really did purchase the item you were saving for and now you want to keep the account for tracking that item.)

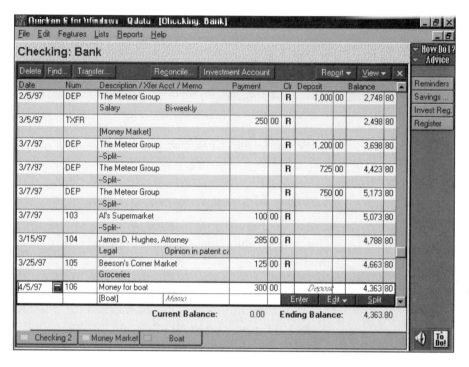

Figure 15.3. A transfer to a savings-goal account

Tracking Your Progress

You can track your progress toward a savings goal in a couple of ways. You can display the Savings Goals window by choosing the Features ➤ Planning ➤ Savings Goals command. (Figure 15.2, which appears earlier in the chapter, shows the Savings Goals window.) Or you can add a progress bar to the bottom of the Quicken application window.

You can also add a progress bar to the bank account in which you're saving money by choosing the Features ➤ Planning ➤ Progress Bars command. If you create a savings goal, go ahead and try this. If you don't like the way it looks, you can easily remove it by clicking on its Close button.

To change the savings goal shown on the progress bar—in case you're saving for more than one item—click on the Cust button. Then use the Customize Progress Bar dialog box that Quicken displays to pick the savings goal you want to see. (The Customize Progress Bar dialog box also lets you monitor a supercategory—something I'll talk about in the next section.) Be sure that the Gauge Type is Savings Goal and then use the Choose Goal button just below that text box to select the goal you'd like to appear on the progress bar.

Supercategories for Closely Monitoring Finances

Supercategories are just groups of categories you want to monitor especially closely. A family that's closely monitoring its finances and cash flow might want to track discretionary spending. A business with several sources of income might want to track its monthly revenue. You can perform this kind of monitoring by using supercategories.

Creating a Supercategory

To create a supercategory, display the Category & Transfer List window by choosing the Lists ➤ Category/Transfer command. Then click on the Super button at the top of the Category & Transfer List window. Quicken displays the Manage Supercategories dialog box, shown in Figure 15.4.

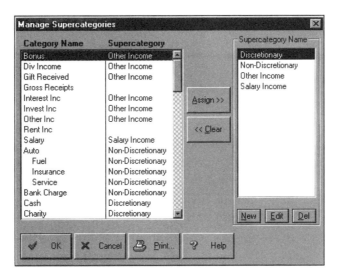

Figure 15.4. **The Manage Supercategories dialog box**

To create a supercategory, follow these steps:

1. Click on the categories you want to place into a supercategory. To select more than one at a time, hold down the Ctrl key as you click on the categories.

2. Select the supercategory you want to use to tally and track these categories. If you want, you can use one of the predefined supercategory names. Or you can click on the New button to display a dialog box that lets you create and name a new supercategory.

3. Click on the Assign button.

4. Click on the OK button.

Monitoring a Supercategory

The easiest way to monitor a supercategory is to add it to the progress bar. Follow these steps:

1. Display the progress bar by choosing Features ➤ Planning ➤ Progress Bar. (You only need to do this if the progress bar isn't displayed.)

2. Click on the progress bar's Cust button to display the Customize Progress Bar dialog box:

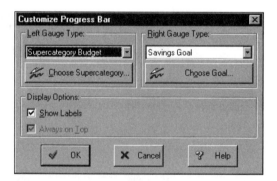

3. Activate one of the Gauge Type drop-down–list boxes and select Supercategory.

4. Click on the Choose Supercategory button. Quicken displays a list of supercategories.

5. Select a supercategory from the list that Quicken provides.

Setting Up a Budget

There's a lot written about budgeting, and most of the advice isn't all that bad—although it may not be too insightful. Mostly, the process is mechanical. You sit down, look at what you'll make, and then come up with a plan for spending the money you'll make.

Two Tricks for Successful Budgeting

You could read an entire book about budgeting. In the meantime, I'm going to give you some quick tips on how to use budgets and budgeting to make it easier to manage your personal financial affairs.

NOTE Much of the information discussed in the section at the end of this chapter relates directly to personal budgeting.

Start with a Categorized Report

You need to start someplace, and the best place is with an itemized list of what you've already been making and spending. In fact, it's probably most accurate to start by planning to spend in the future what you've been spending in the past.

If you've already been tracking your income and spending with Quicken, you can print out an itemized category report to get the information you need.

TIP If you can, look at an entire year's income and spending. It's too easy for an individual month's category total to be significantly higher or lower than average—for example, if you've been paid for a lot of overtime or if you pay more for heating costs in the winter.

Plan Not to Spend Every Dollar You Make

One of the bigger mistakes you can make in your budgeting is to plan how you'll spend every dollar you'll make. Two problems exist with this approach. One is that you will have some unexpected expenses during the year—the water pump on your car may need to be replaced, or you may have some unexpected medical expenses not covered by insurance.

Another problem with the spend-everything approach is that you will find some new ways you want to spend money during the year. You might see something six months from now that you need or want: chairs for summer nights in the backyard or perhaps even a book about Quicken.

If you leave yourself some extra money to pay for these things, they don't have to be financial emergencies. To do this, you might want to set up an Unbudgeted Expenses or Miscellaneous Emergencies category to track and tally just these sorts of expenditures. Then you'll be able to take the extra $150 needed for the car repair out of the Unbudgeted Expenses category.

How the Quicken Mechanics Work

Once you've figured out or estimated what you'll make and what you'll want to spend, you can record this information in Quicken in a budgeting spreadsheet. In fact, as Quicken will do a lot of the math for you, you may want to use this budgeting spreadsheet as a tool for building your budget.

Getting to the Quicken Budgeting Spreadsheet

To get to the Quicken budgeting spreadsheet so you can begin entering your budget, choose the Features ➤ Planning ➤ Budgets command. Quicken displays the Budget window, as shown in Figure 15.5. You'll use this window to describe by category the income and expense you plan.

Entering Income and Expense Budget Data

As you can see from Figure 15.5, the budget spreadsheet presents each month's data in a separate column. It uses a separate row for each income category and each expense category. The budget spreadsheet also includes subtotals for income and expenses and the difference between the total income and expenses.

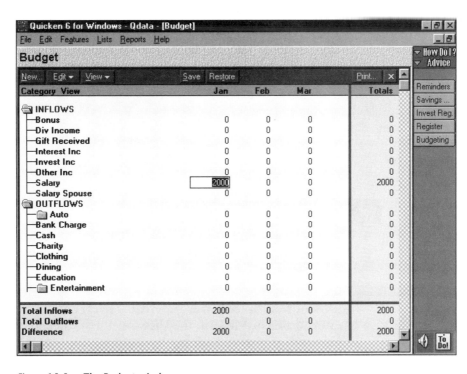

Figure 15.5. **The Budget window**

 TIP Use the vertical and horizontal scroll bars to move left and right or up and down in the spreadsheet if you can't see all the columns or rows.

The simplest way to enter a monthly income or expense budget amount is to highlight the area where you want to place the amount and type the number. To budget the January salary income as $2,000, for example, highlight the January Salary amount and type **2000**. When you move to the next field, Quicken updates the January Total Inflows amount, the Budgeted Inflows amount, and the Difference amount.

If you want to budget by income and expense subcategories, click on either the category name or the button that appears in front of the category name. Quicken displays any subcategories in the clicked-on category. You can click on the category name or button again to indicate that you don't want to budget these subcategories.

For a more sophisticated budget presentation, use the features that become available when you click on the View button on the Budget button bar. (It's the third button on the left.) Choosing the command opens the following menu:

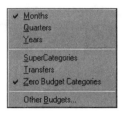

TIP Remembering which budget window button does what can be difficult, but Quicken provides a helpful aid for remembering, *fly-over help*. By moving the mouse pointer so it points (roughly) to the button, you can see the button's function in a small box. Use this technique if you're unsure about what a particular button does.

If you want to see your supercategories, choose SuperCategories. The next time you click on the View button, Quicken places a check next to it to tell you that the View SuperCategories option is on.

If you want to budget account transfers flowing into and out of an account, choose Transfers. Quicken then lists all the account names in both the Inflows and Outflows sections of the budget spreadsheet. Choose Transfers again to indicate you don't want to budget account transfers.

You can hide any unused budget categories or other categories with zero balances by choosing the Zero Budget Categories box. This will improve the clarity of your reports and produce more easily-viewed screens.

Budgeting by the Quarter or by the Year

Normally you'll want to budget on a monthly basis, but you can also budget by the quarter or by the year. To indicate which time period you want to budget, click on the Edit button and choose Month, Quarter, or Year. Quicken reconfigures the columns for the new budgeting time periods and also converts the existing budget data. If you switch from monthly budgeting to quarterly budgeting, for example, Quicken creates quarterly budget amounts from the monthly data you've already entered. January, February, and March, for example, get rolled together into the first-quarter budget amount.

Budgeting Biweekly Expenses

If an income or expense item doesn't fit neatly into monthly, quarterly, or annual time periods, you can budget the item by two-week intervals. You tell Quicken the biweekly amount, and Quicken calculates how much of the income or expense item goes into each budgeting period.

For example, if you get paid biweekly, you can budget your payroll checks as coming every two weeks. Quicken then calculates how many payroll checks you receive each month. In months with more than 28 days, you'll sometimes receive three paychecks.

To budget biweekly expenses, select the Income or Expense category and click on the Edit command button. (It's the second button from the left.) From the menu that opens, choose the 2-Week command. Quicken displays the Set Up Two-Week Budget dialog box:

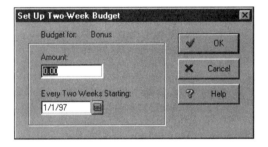

Enter the biweekly amount in the Amount text box. Then enter the first day you receive the biweekly income item or you pay the biweekly expense item and click on OK.

Data-Entry Tricks

You can reach several helpful data-entry commands from the menu that opens when you select the Edit command button. These commands let you copy, fill, and clear entries rapidly.

You can copy the budgeted amount for one budgeting period's income or expense category into future periods using the Fill Row Right command. To use this command, select the budgeted income or expense amount you want to use for the budgeting periods that follow. Then click on Edit and select Fill Row Right. To copy the January Salary Income budget into each of the months that follow, for example, select the January Salary Income amount, click on Edit, and select Fill Row Right.

You can copy an entire period's budgeted Income or Expense category amounts into future periods using the Fill Columns command. To do so, select a budgeted income or expense amount in the budgeting period column you want to copy, click on Edit, and select Fill Columns. To copy the July budget into each of the months that follow, for example, select a budget amount in the July column, click on Edit, and select Fill Columns.

The Copy All command lets you copy material you have highlighted to the Windows 95 Clipboard. From there, you can paste the material into another program, such as a spreadsheet.

The Clear Row command removes all entries from the row containing the highlight. Clear All removes every entry from the entire Budget window, leaving you with a clean slate.

The Supercategories command displays the Manage Supercategories dialog box described earlier in the chapter.

Building a Budget with Last Year's Data

It's often a good idea to use last year's actual income and expense information as a budget or as the starting point for a budget.

To use the previous year's Income and Expense category information to build your budget, you click on the Edit command button and then choose the AutoCreate command to display the Automatically Create Budget dialog box, as shown in Figure 15.6.

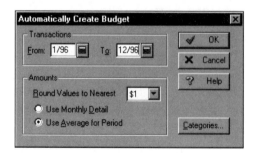

Figure 15.6. **The Automatically Create Budget dialog box**

Use the From and To text boxes to indicate the months in the previous year from which data should be retrieved. To get the entire previous year's income and expense data if it's now 1997, type **1/96** in the From text box and **12/96** in the To text box.

Use the Round Values to Nearest box to tell Quicken how to round the budgeted amounts created using the actual data: to the nearest dollar, to the nearest ten dollars, or to the nearest hundred dollars. You can use this approach, for example, to copy last year's actual category information for July and use it as this year's July budget.

The Use Monthly Detail option button will tell Quicken to copy the indicated budget month by month, category by category. If your budgeted amounts changed on a monthly basis (say, allowing for higher heating costs during the winter months), you might use this option. However, if you click on the Use Average for Period option button, Quicken fills each of the budgeting periods for the year with the previous year's average amounts for the periods you specified in the From and To text boxes. For example, if you base the budget on 1996, the budget entry for Groceries will be the average of grocery expenses for all 12 months in 1996.

Saving Your Budget

Clicking on the Save button records budget entries to a file on your computer's hard disk. The Close button (marked with an *X* in the upper-right corner of the window) does the same thing, but it also closes the Budgets window. When you click on this button, Quicken asks if you want to save the budget shown in the Budgets window. If you do, select Yes. If you don't, select No.

NOTE You need to save a budget before you can use it in a Budget report.

Working with More Than One Budget

In Quicken, you can work with more than one budget. You might do this, for example, if you're performing a what-if analysis and having two separate budgets helps you explore the ramifications of your decisions. You might also use more than one budget to assess the effect of a major change in your financial affairs. For example, if you are moving to a new home, if your spouse is going back to work, or if you are temporarily unemployed, you might create two budgets.

To create multiple budgets, click on View and choose Other Budgets. Quicken displays the Manage Budgets dialog box, as shown in Figure 15.7. This dialog box lists the budgets you've created. Once you've created more than one budget, you use this dialog box to choose which budget you want to work with.

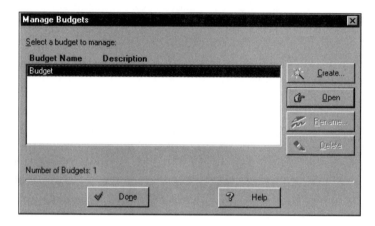

Figure 15.7.   The Manage Budgets dialog box

To create a new budget, click on the Create command button. Quicken displays the Create Budget dialog box:

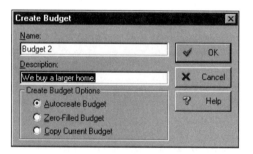

You can name and describe the budget with the Name and Description text boxes. You use the Create Budget Options option buttons to tell Quicken how it should create the new budget:

▶ **AutoCreate Budget.** Automatically creates the budget based on a prior year's actual income and spending. If you select this option and then click on OK, Quicken displays the Automatically Create Budget dialog box, which works as described earlier in this section of the chapter.

▶ **Zero-Filled Budget.** Tells Quicken you want to start with a blank slate. In other words, every income and spending budget line item equals zero.

▶ **Copy Current Budget.** Tells Quicken to copy the numbers in the current option budget

Using the Manage Budgets dialog box (see Figure 15.7), you can rename or delete a budget, as long as it isn't the currently open budget.

TIP To rename a budget, select it, click on the Rename command button, and then use the dialog box that Quicken displays to provide a new name or description. To delete a budget, select it and then click on the Delete command button.

What If You Make a Mistake in Your Budgeting?

If you make a mistake in your budgeting, you can retrieve the budget you previously saved by clicking on the Restore command button. Quicken retrieves the budget you previously saved and replaces whatever shows in the Budgets window with this previously-saved budget.

Monitoring Your Success in Achieving a Budget

The information you enter into the budget spreadsheet is valuable in its own right. You can use it to plan your income and spending in a way that makes the most sense for you and your family.

But this budget information can be even more valuable. You can use it to compare your actual income and spending with the budget. To do this, you produce a Budget report using the Reports ➤ Home ➤ Monthly Budget command (see Chapter 4).

Quicken's Tools for Strategic Planning

Savings goals, supercategories, and budgeting are important elements of successful personal financial planning. But while such budgeting improves your financial affairs on a short-term basis, it doesn't address your long-term, or strategic, objectives.

Presumably, there are financial objectives you want to achieve. Some day, for example, you may wish to quit working—or at least quit working for a paycheck. You may also want to send your children or your grandchildren to college.

Quicken provides several tools for addressing just these types of strategic-planning issues, including a Retirement Planner, a College Savings Planner, and a generalized Savings Planner.

Planning for Retirement

For most workers, early financial planning for retirement delivers enormous benefits. And for today's younger workers—people who are middle-aged and younger—it's probably imperative to do at least some financial planning for retirement. Early in the next century, the social security system will be under enormous pressure as the ratio of workers paying social security to retirees receiving social security drops to two-to-one. (Currently the ratio is more than three-to-one.) And the growth in federal entitlement programs like social security almost dictates that in the future upper–middle-class recipients will lose benefits.

What's more, with a shift from defined benefit plans to defined contribution plans, thoughtful workers will benefit by making forecasts of future total retirement savings and the investment income generated by those savings. Quicken's Retirement Planner lets you do this.

NOTE A defined *benefit* retirement plan pays a specified benefit—for example, 50 percent of your last year's salary. A defined *contribution* plan contributes specified amounts to a retirement account—such as $2,000 a year.

Using the Retirement Planner to Forecast Your Retirement Income

To use Quicken's Retirement Planner to estimate the retirement income you'll have, given your current savings plans, follow these steps:

1. Choose the Features ➤ Planning ➤ Financial Planners ➤ Retirement command to display the Retirement Planner dialog box, as shown in Figure 15.8.

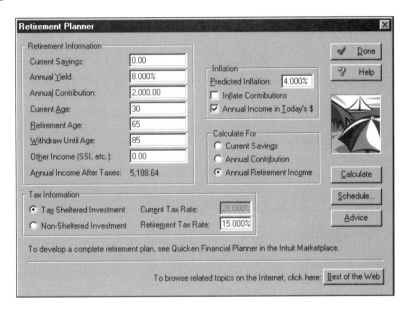

Figure 15.8.   The Retirement Planner dialog box

2. Make sure the Annual Retirement Income option button is marked in the Calculate For area of the dialog box.

3. Enter the amount you've already saved for retirement in the Current Savings text box. This would include amounts saved in employer-defined contribution retirement plans, such as deferred compensation programs and 401(k) plans, as well as amounts you've saved in things such as Individual Retirement Accounts (IRAs) and Keogh plans.

4. Enter the average annual yield you expect your investment portfolio to generate over your working years.

TIP   As a frame of reference, the stock market's annual return over the last 60 years or so has been about 10 percent, the average annual return on long-term corporate bonds over roughly the same period of time is just shy of 6 percent, and the average annual return on long-term government bonds is about 5 percent. These are gross return numbers, so if you invest in a way that results in investment expenses—such as a mutual fund that charges fees—you may want to adjust the historical return.

5. Enter the annual amount you'll contribute in the Annual Contribution text box. For example, if you plan to contribute $2,000 a year to an employer's 401(k) plan, type **2000**. If someone else, such as your employer, will contribute to your retirement savings, include this extra amount. Some employers, for example, match 401(k) contributions as a way to encourage employee retirement saving. If your employer will add 50 percent to your $2,000-a-year contribution, the total annual contribution you enter should be $3,000.

6. Enter your age in the Current Age text box, the age you want to retire in the Retirement Age text box, and the age through which you want to withdraw money in the Withdraw Until Age text box.

TIP   A reasonable way to build in a financial cushion for retirement is to assign a Withdraw Until Age value that's several years beyond when you expect to live. I do my retirement-planning calculations assuming I will withdraw money through age 95, even though I may well run out of steam long before this.

7. Use the Other Income text box to indicate how much other retirement income you'll have available. For example, you may be eligible for social-security benefits, or you may have invested in a defined-benefit retirement plan that promises to pay you some monthly amount.

TIP   You can get an estimate of your future social-security benefits by filling out a simple form (called an SS-4) and sending the form to the Social Security Administration. To get the form you need, just call the local social-security office. You may be surprised by the social-security benefit you're slated to receive. Social security benefits are paid according to a complicated formula that allows people with modest incomes (or only a few years of earnings) to get a benefit that's a much larger percentage of their current earnings than people who make a lot of money.

8. Use the Tax Information settings and Current Tax Rate text box to describe the income taxes you'll pay on your retirement savings. If you will use investment options like IRAs and 401(k)s that allow for deferral of income taxes, click on the Tax Sheltered Investment option button. If you will use investment options that result in your paying taxes on the investment income earned by your savings, click on the Non-Sheltered Investment option button. Then enter the marginal tax rate you'll pay on the investment income in the Current Tax Rate text box.

9. *If you want to estimate your after–income-taxes retirement savings account withdrawals,* you can estimate the income-tax rate in effect over the years you're retired and enter the figure in the Retirement Tax Rate text box. Alternatively, enter the Retirement Tax Rate as **0**. With this input, the Planner calculates the pretax withdrawal you'll make.

10. Enter the inflation rate you expect over the years you'll work and be retired. As a frame of reference, the inflation rate over the past 60 years or so has averaged slightly over 3 percent.

11. *If you will make annual contributions and will adjust these amounts for inflation over the years you work,* mark the Inflate Contributions check box. With 3-percent inflation and $1,000-a-year contributions, for example, Quicken assumes you contribute $1,000 the first year, $1,030 the second year ($1030 is 103 percent of $1,000), $1,060.90 the third year ($1060.90 is 103 percent of $1,030), and so on.

12. Make sure the Annual Income in Today's $ check box is marked to tell Quicken to estimate an annual retirement income figure that uses the same size dollars you make and spend today. (If you don't mark this check box, Quicken estimates an annual retirement-income figure using the inflated dollars you'll actually receive, in, say 30 years.)

13. Click on the Calculate button.

14. Click on the Schedule command button to see a scrollable list of the annual amounts you'll contribute or withdraw, the annual interest earnings, and the retirement savings balance.

   Figure 15.9 shows a Deposit Schedule, depicting retirement savings activity in a schedule.

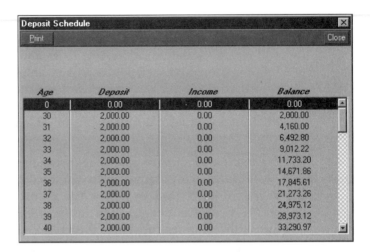

Figure 15.9.   **The Deposit Schedule details the progress of your plan.**

15. Once you've entered all the needed information and told Quicken how it should make the calculations, you can scroll down and look at the Income column for your indicated retirement age. It shows the estimated annual retirement income you'll receive based on your forecasting assumptions.

To close the Deposit Schedule box, click on the Close button. To remove the Retirement Planner dialog box when you're finished with it, select Done.

Figuring Out How Much You Should Save

The preceding discussion calculates how much you'll have in the way of retirement income, given your current savings and your plans about how you'll save in the future. If instead you want to provide for a specific level of retirement income, you can calculate the current savings you must already have accumulated in order to reach your retirement income goal. Or you can calculate how much you need to be saving on a regular basis in order to reach that income goal.

To calculate how much you need to have already saved, given all the other retirement information, go back to the Retirement Planner and click on the Current Savings option button. To calculate how much you need to save on an annual basis, given all the other retirement information, click on the Annual Contribution option button. Once you've indicated what savings figure you want to reach, enter the annual retirement income you want in the Annual Income After Taxes text box. Then fill each of the remaining text boxes and mark the appropriate option buttons and check boxes.

Finding the Money You Need to Save for Retirement

It can be more than a little discouraging to start making retirement calculations. You'll usually find that to achieve the annual retirement income you want, you have to be saving a lot more than is practical.

Suppose, for example, that the Retirement Planner calculates an annual savings amount equal to $5,200 a year—which is the same as $450 a month. (This savings amount will produce roughly $15,000 a year of retirement income if you start with $0 savings, increase your annual contributions 3 percent each year because of inflation, and earn 9 percent over 20 years of contributions.)

While $450 a month seems like a lot of money, you may be able to come up with this figure more readily than you might think. Say, for example, that you work for an employer who's generous enough to match your 401(k) contributions by 50 percent. In other words, for every dollar you contribute, your employer contributes $.50. Also suppose that you pay federal and state income taxes of 33 percent and that you can deduct your 401(k) contributions from your income. In this case, the actual monthly out-of-pocket amount you need to come up with equals $200, not $450.

Here's how the arithmetic works. You need to come up with $300 a month to have $450 a month added to your retirement savings because of your employer's 50 percent matching, as shown here:

Amount you contribute	$300
Employer's matching amount	$150
Total 401(k) contribution	$450

However, if your last dollars of income are taxed at 33 percent, the $300 tax deduction you'll receive because of your $300 401(k) contribution will save you $100 in income taxes. So the actual amount you need to come up with on a monthly basis equals $200, as shown here:

Amount contributed by you	$300
Income taxes saved	(100)
After-tax contribution	$200

Admittedly, $200 a month is still a lot of money. But it's also a lot less than the $450-a-month savings figure the Retirement Planner calculations suggest.

These calculations also suggest a couple of tactics to consider using when you save for retirement. If an employer offers to match your contributions to something like a 401(k) plan, it will almost always make sense to accept the offer—unless your employer is trying to force you to make an investment that is not appropriate for you.

> **TIP** If you do want to contribute $300 a month to a 401(k) plan and need to reduce your income taxes withheld by $100 a month to do so, talk to your employer's payroll department for instructions. You may need to file a new W-4 statement and increase the number of personal exemptions claimed.

What's more, any time you get a tax deduction for contributing money to your retirement savings, it's almost certainly too good a deal to pass up. As described in the preceding example, you can use the income-tax savings because of the deduction to boost your savings so they provide for the desired level of retirement income.

While people often have an emotional aversion to locking money away in tax-sheltered investments, there are only three situations in which it may be a poor idea to use tax-sheltered investments:

▶ You need (or may need) the money before retirement. In this case it may not be a good idea to lock away money you may need before retirement because there is usually a 10 percent early-withdrawal penalty paid on money retrieved from a retirement account before age 59½. But you will also need money after you retire, so the "What if I need the money?" argument is more than a little weak. Yes, you may need the money before you retire, but you will absolutely need money after you retire.

▶ You've already saved enough money for retirement. Using retirement planning vehicles, such as IRAs, may be a reasonable way to accumulate wealth. And the deferred taxes on your investment income do make your savings grow much more quickly. Nevertheless, if you've already saved enough money for retirement, it's just possible that you should consider other investment options as well as estate planning issues. This special case is beyond the scope of this book, but if it applies to you, I encourage you to consult a good personal financial planner—preferably one who charges you an hourly fee, not one who earns a commission by selling you financial products you may not need.

▶ You'll pay more income taxes when you're retired than you do now. The calculations get tricky, but if you're only a few years away from retirement and you believe income-tax rates will be going up (perhaps to deal with the huge federal budget deficit or because you'll be paying a new state income tax), it may not make sense for you to save, say, 15 percent now but pay 45 percent later.

Read This If You Can't Possibly Save Enough for Retirement

It's relatively easy to save for retirement when you're still young. Five thousand dollars set aside for a new baby grows to an amount that generates over $100,000 a year in current-day dollars if the money earns 12 percent annually and inflation runs 3 percent. (The data is a little sketchy, but small-company stocks probably deliver average returns of around 12 to 13 percent over long periods of time. Small-company stocks are, however, very risky over shorter periods of time.)

The flip side of this is that it becomes difficult to save for retirement if you start thinking (and saving) late in your working years. If you're 60, haven't started saving, and want $25,000 a year in income from your retirement savings at age 65, you probably need to contribute annually more than you make.

Say you're in your 50s—or even a bit older. What with the kids' college expenses, or perhaps a divorce, you don't have any money saved for retirement. What should you do? What can you do? This situation, though unfortunate, doesn't have to be disastrous. There are some things you can do.

One tactic is not to retire—or at least, not yet. After all, you save for retirement so the earnings from those savings can replace your salary and wages. If you don't stop working, you don't need retirement savings producing investment income.

Note, too, that "not retiring" doesn't mean you need to keep your same job. If you've been selling computers your whole life and you're sick of it, do something else. Get a job teaching at the community college. (Maybe you'll get summers off.) Join the Peace Corps and go to South America. Get a job in a daycare center and help shape the future.

A second tactic is to postpone retirement a few extra years, which, of course, also reduces the number of years you're retired. Rather than working to age 62 or 65, for example, working until age 67 or 69—a few more years of contributions and compound interest income—will make a surprising difference, and you'll boost substantially the money you receive from defined-benefit retirement plans. If you're paying on a mortgage, maybe that'll get paid off in those few extra years too.

A third and more unconventional tactic is to decide that less is more and tune into the art and philosophy of frugality. A good book on this subject is *Your Money or Your Life* by Joe Dominquez and Vicki Robin (Viking Penguin, 1992). And if you decide to live on less while you're still working, you'll end up saving a lot more over the remaining years you work.

Planning for a Child's College Expenses

Quicken provides another financial planner, similar to the Retirement Planner, that helps you prepare for the expenses of a child attending college.

Calculating the Amount You Need to Save

To use the College Financial Planner, follow these steps:

1. Choose the Features ➤ Planning ➤ Financial Planners ➤ College command to display the College Planner dialog box, as shown in Figure 15.10.

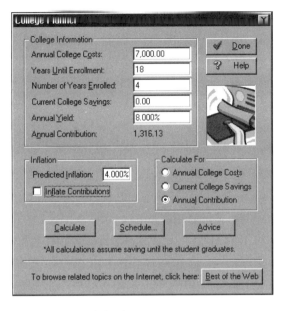

Figure 15.10. **The College Planner dialog box**

2. Make sure the Annual Contribution option button is marked in the Calculate For area at the lower-right corner of the dialog box.

3. Enter the current annual costs of college in the Annual College Costs text box. (If you don't know for sure which college your child will attend, enter an annual–college-costs figure that's representative.)

4. Enter the number of years until the child enrolls in college in the Years Until Enrollment text box.

5. Indicate how many years the child will attend college. If you assume the child will enroll in a regular four-year undergraduate program, type **4**.

6. Enter the amount you've already saved for college in the Current College Savings text box.

7. Enter the average annual yield you expect the college savings money to generate and the inflation rate you expect.

As noted earlier, the inflation rate over the last 60 years or so has averaged slightly over 3 percent. College tuition, however, has risen much faster than inflation. (Some recent studies show average tuition hikes in the 7 percent neighborhood!) It seems unlikely that college costs will continue to outpace inflation because few people will be able to afford college if the percentage increases continue to be more than double the inflation rate. For this reason, I use a 3 percent inflation rate in my calculations—and cross I my fingers.

8. *If you will adjust your college-savings contributions for inflation,* mark the Inflate Contributions check box. For example, with 3 percent inflation and $1,000-a-year contributions, Quicken assumes you contribute $1,000 the first year, $1,030 the second year, $1060.90 the third year, and so on.

9. Click on the Calculate button.

10. Click on the Schedule command button to see a summary of the annual amounts you'll contribute or withdraw, the annual interest earnings, and the college-savings balance.

Once you've entered all the needed information and told Quicken how it should make the calculations, you can look at the Annual Contribution field. It shows the estimated annual contribution you'll need to make each year until your child finishes college, based on your forecasting assumption.

The preceding discussion calculates how much you need to save annually to be able to pay for college. You can also calculate the current savings you must already have accumulated in order to pay for college. And you can calculate the college costs you can afford given your current and planned savings.

To calculate how much you need to have already saved, click on the Current College Savings option button, then click on Calculate. To calculate what college costs you can afford, click on the Annual College Costs option button. Indicate what figure you want to calculate, fill in the dialog box's remaining text boxes, and mark the appropriate option buttons and check boxes. Then click on Calculate. (For help with a text box entry or in deciding whether to mark an option button or check box, see the discussion earlier in this chapter about using the Retirement Planner.)

What You Should Know
About Income Taxes and College Savings

There's a minor flaw in the way the college-savings calculations work: The College Planner doesn't make any allowance for income taxes, but the interest income the college savings earn will be subject to income taxes.

To deal with this deficiency, you can just increase your annual contributions to pay the income taxes (or assume the child pays the income taxes). For example, if you have $10,000 of college savings earning a respectable 9 percent, you'll be taxed on $900 of investment income. If the marginal income tax rate is 33 percent, you'll need to come up with an extra $300 for income taxes (33 percent of $900 is $300), so you would need to contribute an extra $25 a month.

You can also consider giving the money to the child in the form of a trust account so the child is taxed, not you. The benefit is that much and perhaps all of the investment income earned probably won't be taxed because of the standard deduction the child gets. In 1997, for example, a minor less than 14 years of age who's claimed as a dependent on someone else's return gets a standard deduction of about $600, which allows the child to escape taxes on at least the first $600 of investment income. What's more, in 1997 roughly the next $600 of investment income gets taxed at the low 15 percent marginal income-tax rate. After that, the child's investment income gets taxed at the parent's marginal tax rate.

After a child reaches age 14, the 1997 standard deduction amount jumps to roughly $4,000, which means the child can earn up to $4,000 in either wages or investment income without paying any taxes or much taxes. In other words, taxing the child allows you to avoid much of the income taxes you'd otherwise have to pay.

There is a drawback to having the child rather than the parent pay the income taxes: the savings need to be given to the child for the investment income earned by the savings to be taxed to the child. This means, for example, that the $8,000 you've scrimped and saved for and put into an account for college will ultimately get spent on what the child decides—which might be a sports car instead of a college education. By putting the money in a trust, you, as the custodian of the trust, retain control of the trust as long as the child is a minor. But when the child reaches the age of majority, the child can decide how to spend the money.

Planning for Other Savings Goals

Quicken provides another financial-planning tool you'll sometimes find helpful—the Savings Planner. The Quicken savings calculator works like a regular financial calculator. It calculates future value, present value, and payment amounts.

Calculating a Future Value

One of the most common financial calculations you make when you plan savings is the *future value*, the amount your savings or investment will be worth at some point in the future—including any profits you've reinvested or left invested. For example, if you plan to save $2,000 a year in a mutual fund for 25 years and expect to earn 9 percent annually, you can forecast the future value of the mutual fund investment.

To perform a future value calculation, follow these steps:

1. Choose the Features ➤ Planning ➤ Financial Planners ➤ Savings command to display the Investment Savings Planner dialog box, as shown in Figure 15.11.

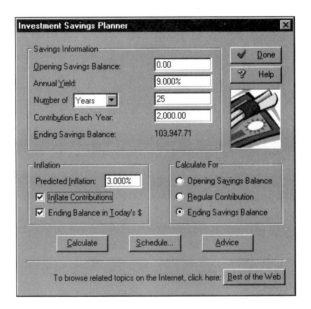

Figure 15.11. **The Investment Savings Planner dialog box**

2. Click on the Ending Savings Balance option button in the Calculate For area in the lower-right corner of the dialog box.

3. Enter the starting savings balance in the Opening Savings Balance text box. If you haven't yet saved anything because you're just starting, type **0**.

4. Enter the annual yield you expect your savings to earn. If you've invested in a mutual fund you expect will earn 9 percent, type **9**.

5. Use the Number of drop-down–list box to indicate the time period you'll use to describe the length, or term, of the investment—weeks, months, quarters, or years—and use the Number of text box to indicate the number of terms you'll make contributions and let interest compound. For example, if you'll contribute $2,000 to an IRA for 25 years, select Years from the Number of drop-down–list box and type **25** in the Number of text box.

6. Use the Number of drop-down–list box to indicate how often you'll add to the investment—each week, each month, each quarter, or each year and use the Contribution Each text box to indicate how much you'll contribute. For example, if you'll contribute $2,000 to an IRA for 25 years, select Years from the Contribution Each drop-down–list box and type **2000** in the Contribution Each text box.

7. Enter the annual inflation rate you expect over the years you will save in the Predicted Inflation text box.

8. *If you will increase your contributions for inflation over the years you save,* mark the Inflate Contributions check box. With 3 percent annual inflation, for example, and $100-a-month contributions, Quicken assumes you contribute $100 the first month, $100.25 the second month, $100.50 the third month, and so on. (Quicken calculates the monthly inflation by dividing the annual inflation by 12.)

9. Make sure the Ending Savings Balance check box is marked to tell Quicken to estimate an ending balance figure that uses the same-size dollars you make and spend today. (If you don't mark this check box, Quicken estimates a future-value figure using inflated dollars you'll actually accumulate, in, say 25 years.)

10. Click on Calculate.

11. Click on the Schedule command button to see a scrollable list of the annual amounts you'll save, the annual interest earnings, and the ending savings balance. When you're finished viewing the schedule, select Close.

Part 2

Quicken and Your Personal Finances

Once you've collected all the necessary information, Quicken calculates the ending balance. Figure 15.11, for example, shows that in today's dollars, you accumulate slightly more than $100,000 by contributing $2,000 annually.

> **NOTE** The Savings Planner calculations assume you make your contributions at the end of the year, quarter, month, or week. (This is called an *ordinary annuity*.) If you make your contributions at the beginning of the period, you earn an extra period of interest. (This is called an *annuity due*.)

Calculating a Contribution

If you don't know the regular savings, or contribution, amount, you can calculate it by setting the ending savings balance. To do this, you follow the same basic steps you use for calculating a future value, with just a couple of exceptions. In this case, you click on the Regular Contribution option button rather than the Ending Savings Balance option button, and you enter the ending savings balance, not the regular contribution amount. When you click on Calculate, Quicken calculates the regular contribution amount.

When do you calculate the regular contribution? You calculate the contribution when you want to accumulate a specific future-value amount—say $1,000,000—and you want to know how much you need to be contributing in order to achieve your future-value goal.

> **NOTE** If you don't know the opening savings balance but you know everything else, you can calculate the opening savings balance too, as described in Chapter 15, *Planning Your Personal Finances*.

Planning a Mortgage Refinancing

Favorable mortgage rates in recent years have prompted a rush of mortgage refinancing. If you find yourself in a position to refinance, Quicken's Refinance Planner, shown in Figure 15.12, can rapidly compute the potential savings and time to recover the refinancing costs. When you fill in the text boxes, Quicken calculates the costs and savings automatically. To use this feature, select Features ➤ Planning ➤ Financial Planners ➤ Refinance.

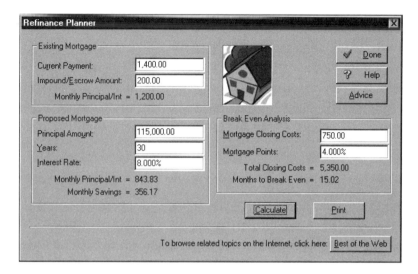

Figure 15.12. **The Refinance Planner dialog box**

Part
2

Quicken and Your
Personal Finances

To use the Refinance Planner, follow these steps:

1. Enter your current monthly principal and interest payment in the Current payment text box.

2. Enter any additional amounts you pay into an escrow or impound account each month in the Impound/escrow amount text box. (These amounts might include property taxes and insurance, for example.)

3. Enter the new, refinanced mortgage amount in the Principal amount text box. For example, if the new mortgage balance will equal $115,000, enter this figure into the Principal amount text box.

4. Enter the number of years you'll be making the mortgage payments in the Years text box. For a 30-year mortgage, for example, you need to enter **30**.

5. Enter the annual interest rate in the Interest rate text box. Note that the annual interest rate isn't the same thing as the annual percentage rate. The annual interest rate is what the lender uses to calculate your monthly payments. The annual percentage rate is a rate that lets you compare the total costs of borrowing among lenders. An annual percentage rate includes the interest costs of borrowing as well as all the other costs of borrowing such as loan fees and discount points.

6. Enter the closing costs—appraisals, loan processing fees, and the like—into the Mortgage closing costs text box.

7. Enter the total loan fee and discount points in the Mortgage points text box. If the loan fee is 2 percent and you'll pay 2 percent in discount points, for example, enter **4** in the Mortgage points text box.

8. Click on Calculate.

Once you enter all the Refinance Planner inputs, you use the monthly savings output, the total closing costs output, and the months to break even output to assist you in your decision. In Figure 15.12, for example, the calculations show monthly savings of about $350 and a pay-back period of slightly less than nine months.

A MINOR PROBLEM WITH THE REFINANCE PLANNER

There is one minor problem with the way the Refinance planner works: it tells you whether your monthly payment will go down and how many months it will take to recoup your closing costs, but that information doesn't really let you determine whether or not you're saving monthly over the life of the mortgage.

To understand this point, consider the case of a person who has only one year left on a $20,000 30-year mortgage and is considering refinancing over the next 30 years. On the face of it, this refinancing makes sense because the monthly mortgage payment will go way down and it will only take a month or two to recoup the closing costs. But by refinancing, the homeowner has 29 extra years of payments! That means, over the long haul, the homeowner pays much more interest by refinancing. In this case, the imprudence of refinancing is clear, but the reasonableness of refinancing gets rather murky if you're considering whether to refinance a mortgage for which you have 24 years of payments.

Fortunately, you can apply a couple of rules to make sure you save money by refinancing. You need to make sure that

▶ The APR on the new loan is lower than the interest rate on the old loan.

▶ You get the new loan paid off just as quickly.

HOW TO ACHIEVE FINANCIAL INDEPENDENCE

For most people, wealth doesn't have to be an impossible dream. With the right strategies and the appropriate tools, you can achieve financial independence. In fact, I truly believe that many and maybe most of the people who buy this book can become millionaires if they want to.

Building a fortune, however, is very similar to building a house. You need time. You need the right tools. You also need a plan. In most cases, people have the time. And if you have Quicken, you have all the tools you need. All you need after that to enjoy financial independence is a plan.

The Three Routes to Riches

Let me talk for a minute about the various ways you can achieve financial independence. In a nutshell, there are really only three routes to riches: instant wealth, entrepreneurial wealth, and investment wealth.

Instant wealth is the wealth one acquires by winning a lottery, receiving a monstrous inheritance, or making an overnight killing on some wildly speculative investment. Everyone has heard stories about people who have become rich this way: the factory worker who wins a twenty million dollar state lottery, the janitor who receives an unexpected inheritance from an uncle she never knew she had, or the neighbor who repeatedly tells how he made an overnight killing on a shady real-estate deal.

Unfortunately, there aren't any guaranteed "get-rich-quick schemes." You know that. Very few people actually get rich playing the lottery. Even if you have a rich uncle or aunt, you can't be sure your name is in the will. And wildly speculative investments produce losses more often than they produce profits.

NOTE People spend more on postage to enter the Publishers' Clearing House sweepstakes than the sweepstakes sponsor gives away in prizes.

Part
2

Quicken and Your
Personal Finances

on the Road to Riches

Despite what some would-be entrepreneurs think, entrepreneurial wealth amounts to a "get-rich-slow" scheme. Sometimes, of course, it can work out very well. A couple of bright kids start, say, a software company. They get a couple of lucky breaks and plow the profits back into their company. They work terribly hard. Fifteen or twenty years go by, the business prospers, and bang! The world has a couple of newly-minted billionaires. It happens. The preceding is, in a nutshell, the story of Bill Gates and Paul Allen, the founders of the Microsoft Corporation.

I don't want to discourage you from pursuing the entrepreneurial-wealth route. If you have the temperament and the skills, entrepreneurial wealth represents a way to accumulate a monstrous amount of money. However, entrepreneurial wealth isn't the best route to riches for most people. There's a much simpler, much safer way to achieve financial independence if your financial aspirations are more modest.

This simpler, safer way is to invest prudently and wisely. You need to become a disciplined saver and a smart investor. If you do these things, you will become rich by taking the third path to financial independence—the investment-wealth route.

No doubt, at this point, you're thinking one of two things. If you're a bit of a cynic, you're thinking, "If it's so easy, how come everybody isn't doing it?" Well, my response is that many, many people are— some of them without realizing it. What's more, a surprising number of people have already become millionaires.

 TIP The best figures available estimate that there are more than one million millionaires in the United States. The same figures also estimate that there are more than 80,000 *decamillionaires*, persons worth $10 million or more.

Another point is that it's a lot easier to say, "Oh, you just need to save religiously and invest smart," than it is to actually do it. I want to be candid with you: You need to be a disciplined saver. And the older you are, the more serious you need to be about saving.

TIP If a "pack-a-day" 20-year-old quits smoking and stashes the cigarette money in a savings account, he or she can accumulate roughly $150,000 by age 65.

What's more, to earn really impressive investment profits, you need to become a savvy, street-smart investor. You need to learn about taxes, inflation, and the right way to measure investment profits. You need to learn about stocks and bonds and real estate. And you need to make sure that once you start making money you don't start losing it.

TIP If the same pack-a-day smoker invests the cigarette money in an employer-sponsored 401(k) plan, he or she can accumulate as much as one million in uninflated dollars.

No, it isn't easy to accumulate a personal fortune. But it isn't all that difficult, either. The trick is to take the necessary time, have a plan, and use the right tools.

Obstacles to Attaining Wealth

I should point out that there are some major obstacles to achieving financial independence. The biggest obstacle, at least in my opinion, is the looking-rich trap. The very first thing you need to realize if you do choose the investment route to riches is that looking rich is far different from becoming or actually being rich. Looking rich requires you to live in a fancy neighborhood. Looking rich requires you to drive an expensive car. Looking rich requires you to wear designer clothes. But looking rich isn't the same as being rich. Most millionaires drive American cars and live in middle-class neighborhoods.

Television and the movies show the rich jetting to places like Paris to shop, slurp champagne, and gorge themselves on caviar. Here's the problem with these patently false images: This sort of consumption invariably prevents you from ever becoming rich. You end up spending all your money trying to look rich and there isn't any leftover money for saving and investing.

False affluence isn't the only obstacle to becoming rich. Another is the "I may die tomorrow" syndrome. People who fall into this trap generally don't think it's worthwhile to postpone enjoying the finer things in life. "Don't put off until tomorrow what you can enjoy today," is their motto and philosophy. I'll be the first to admit that you can't always live for the future. But there is a problem with this business of focusing on just today: Chances are, you won't die tomorrow, and that means that you need to prepare for the future. If you have children, you probably want them to attend college. Some day, presumably, you will retire. To do these sorts of things, you need to prepare financially by accumulating wealth.

Most of the obstacles to acquiring riches are illusory, but one obstacle is almost insurmountable: you may not have enough time. The problem is that the engine that powers wealth creation is something called compound interest. (I explain compound interest at the end of Chapter 17, *Mutual-Fund Investments*.) You need time for the compound-interest engine to work its magic. You can't use the compound-interest engine to become rich in a year or two.

This doesn't mean that you can't enjoy the benefits of financial success in the coming weeks and months, though. Rather, it means that years must pass before your wealth gives you complete independence from a job. In the meantime, you have to settle for things like financial peace of mind, financial progress, and a worry-free financial future.

How Much Is Enough: Picking a Wealth Target

All this talk leads quite naturally to a discussion about how much is enough. People always throw around the figure of one million dollars. But do you really need a million dollars? It depends. Usually, you don't need that much money. Let's take a hypothetical case to illustrate why. Say you're 40 years old and you're making $40,000 a year. Further, suppose that you want to achieve financial independence by age 65. Do you need enough investment wealth to generate $40,000 of income? Probably not. You may currently be spending money on a mortgage that will be paid off by the time you retire. Presumably, you'll receive some money in social-security or pension benefits. If that is the case, you won't need $40,000 a year when you retire.

Here is another example to make the whole thing clearer: Say you are making $40,000 a year, you currently pay $7,500 a year in mortgage payments, your mortgage will be paid off by the time you retire, and you will receive $7,500 a year in social-security and pension benefits. Once your mortgage is paid and you're eligible for pension benefits, you can live as well on $25,000 of investment income as you currently live on $40,000 in wages. What you need is enough wealth to produce an investment income of $25,000, because the $25,000 of investment income will make you financially independent.

> **TIP** As I noted earlier in the chapter, you can find out exactly how much social security you'll receive by calling your local social security office, asking them to send you an SS-4 form, and then filling out and returning the form.

Your next step is to determine how much wealth you need to produce $25,000 a year of investment income. In general, you need $20 of investment wealth to produce $1 of investment income. To generate $25,000 of income, therefore, you need $500,000 of investment wealth, because 20 times $25,000 equals $500,000. But you can and should make a more precise determination with the Retirement Planner. (I describe the Retirement Planner earlier in this chapter.)

Looking at the Big Picture

I want to conclude this discussion about financial independence with what will seem a funny digression but is really the most important point of all. I honestly believe you will be happier if you prepare for and eventually achieve financial independence, but I also don't believe wealth should be an end-all, be-all goal. I respectfully suggest that you consider financial independence as one of your minor life objectives. It certainly shouldn't be your only objective.

This may seem like funny advice coming from someone who makes his living by writing, thinking, and advising people about money. But my activities give me a rather unique vantage point. Because of the work I do, I get to meet a number of very wealthy individuals. I'll let you in on a little secret: having gobs of money doesn't make the difference you might think. All that will happen, if you do accumulate great sums of money, is that you'll acquire more expensive habits, hobbies, and friends. You'll still argue with your spouse or children about how you should spend money. You'll still encounter rude neighbors, dangerous drivers, and incompetent sales clerks. And you'll still have to answer all the big questions about life and love and death.

I don't think this perspective conflicts with the idea that you should accumulate a certain amount of wealth. Having $1,000,000 in wealth isn't essential to your happiness. I don't think it's bad, either. If you want to make financial independence your goal in life, great. My point is that, when you get right down to the specifics of your situation, $200,000 may be as good a target as one or two million. In any case, $200,000 is a lot easier to achieve.

CHAPTER 16

Making Better Insurance Decisions

FEATURING

Estimating how much life insurance you need

Constructing a property insurance list

Shopping for an insurance policy

Buying health insurance

QUICKEN supplies two useful tools for insurance purposes. The Savings Planner lets you make a sophisticated estimate of how much life insurance you should have in place. And the asset-account type of register helps you to build useful lists of the items you've insured.

NOTE There are no prerequisites to using Quicken to make better insurance decisions.

Determining How Much Life Insurance You Need

When considering life insurance, you're planning and preparing for an event most of us would rather not think about. But life insurance represents a critical step in managing your personal finances and ensuring your family's well-being.

The Two Approaches to Life Insurance

You can use one of two approaches to estimate how much life insurance you should buy: the *needs* approach or the *replacement-income* approach. Using the needs approach, you calculate the amount of life insurance necessary to cover your family's financial needs if you die. Using the replacement-income approach, you calculate the amount of life insurance you need to equal the income your family will lose. Let's look briefly at each approach.

NOTE The end of this chapter explains in detail how to make decisions about obtaining life insurance.

Using the needs approach, you add up the amounts that represent all the needs your family will have after your death, including funeral and burial costs, uninsured medical expenses, and estate taxes. However, your family depends on you to pay for other needs too—such as your child's college tuition, business or personal debts, and food and housing expenses over time.

The needs approach is somewhat limiting. Identifying and tallying family needs is difficult, and separating the true needs of your family from what you want for them often is impossible.

Using the replacement-income approach for estimating life insurance requirements, you calculate the life insurance proceeds that would replace your earnings over a specified number of years after your death. Life insurance companies sometimes approximate your replacement income at four or five times your annual income. A more precise estimation considers the actual amount your family needs annually, the number of years they will need this amount, and the interest rate your family will earn on the life insurance proceeds, as well as inflation over the years during which your family draws on the life insurance proceeds.

Using the Quicken Savings Planner, you can calculate what life insurance you need to replace earnings over a specified number of years. You can then add to this figure any additional needs-based insurance. The total insurance would be the amount calculated by Quicken as necessary to replace earnings plus the amount calculated by you as necessary to pay for any additional needs.

Be careful not to count items twice. For example, if you consider paying off your mortgage on the family home to be a final expense, your estimate of the annual living expenses should reflect this. Similarly, if you include the costs of a spouse's returning to and finishing law school as a prerequisite for supporting the family, reduce the number of years your family will need replacement income.

Using the Savings Planner to Estimate Life Insurance Needs

To use the Quicken Savings Planner to estimate the life insurance necessary to replace earnings over a specified number of years, follow these steps:

1. Choose the Features ➤ Planning ➤ Financial Planners ➤ Savings command to display the Investment Savings Planner dialog box, as shown in Figure 16.1.

2. Click on the Opening Savings Balance option button in the Calculate For box.

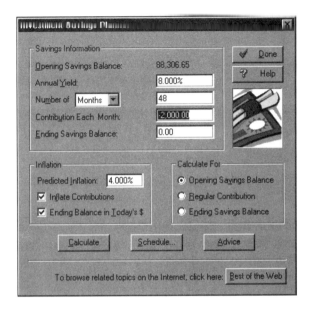

Figure 16.1. **You can use the Investment Savings Planner dialog box to estimate insurance needs.**

3. In the Annual Yield text box, enter your estimate of the annual interest rate you expect your savings, investments, and life insurance proceeds to earn when they are invested. Because this money might have to provide basic living expenses for your family, you might want to assume that this money is invested in conservative, lower-risk investments, which means you should expect lower interest rates.

4. In the Number Of drop-down–list box, select Months.

5. In the Number Of text box, enter the number of months you will use the life insurance proceeds and the interest earned on those proceeds to replace earnings of the insured. You might need replacement income only until a child completes an education or until your spouse returns to work.

6. In the Contribution Each drop-down–list box, select Month. (The selection in the Number of and Contribution Each drop-down lists must be the same.)

7. In the Contribution Each text box, enter the monthly amount your family will withdraw from the life insurance savings money at the end of each month to supplement their living expenses. For example, if you want your family to be able to withdraw $2,000 at the end of each

month, enter **−2000**. (You enter the amount as a negative number because your family will be withdrawing this amount from your savings, not adding it.)

> **TIP** If you have children and pay social security taxes, there's a good chance that social security survivors benefits will provide several hundred dollars a month. Call your local social security office for more information.

8. Enter the Ending Savings Balance as **0**.

9. In the Predicted Inflation text box, specify the annual inflation rate you expect over the years your income needs to be replaced.

10. Mark the Inflate Contributions check box to tell the Savings Planner that you want the monthly amounts withdrawn from the life insurance savings money to grow each month by the monthly inflation rate.

As you enter the values, Quicken calculates an opening savings balance, which equals the amount of life insurance needed to produce enough money to support or supplement the support of your family over the number of months you specified. The assumption is that your family will place the life insurance in a savings account or investment that will produce the annual return you forecasted and, at the end of each month, withdraw a monthly amount to replace your income.

To see a schedule that shows the monthly withdrawals and the end-of-month life insurance proceeds balance, click on the Schedule command button. Quicken displays the Deposit Schedule dialog box, as shown in Figure 16.2. The Number column identifies the months. The Deposit column actually shows the withdrawals. (This is confusing, but remember you're using the Savings Planner to do something the folks at Intuit never intended.) The Total column shows the balance after the monthly withdrawal.

> **NOTE** The monthly withdrawal amounts increase every month by the monthly inflation rate. Allowing for increasing withdrawal amounts is important if you want to replace earnings over a long period of time.

If you use the approach described here to plan life insurance needs, remember that you must add any additional special needs (such as final expenses or extraordinary debts) to the opening savings balance amount in order to come up with a life insurance amount that both replaces earnings and provides for special needs.

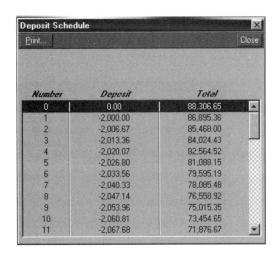

Figure 16.2. **The Deposit Schedule dialog box shows potential monthly withdrawals.**

Using Quicken to Build Property Insurance Lists

There's one other insurance-related task you can do with Quicken: You can build lists of the items you have insured or will insure with property insurance. You simply use an asset account to build a list of items and values. (It might even be that your insurance agent or property insurer will want to see this list.)

One benefit of this kind of list is that you'll get an idea of how much property insurance you should really have. You can compare the total value of the items on such a list with the personal property limit on your homeowner's or renter's policy. Another benefit is that, should something destroy your personal property, you'll have a record of what you've lost.

 TIP Keep a backup record of any property records away from your property. If something happens, you don't want whatever destroys your property to also destroy your records.

Figure 16.3 shows an asset property list. To create such a list, create an asset account and open the register. Then simply enter a transaction for each item you've insured. The dollar amount is the insured replacement value. You don't categorize the transactions. You may want to use the

Memo text box to cross-reference some other piece of information (such as the model number of the insured item or the merchant from whom you purchased the item).

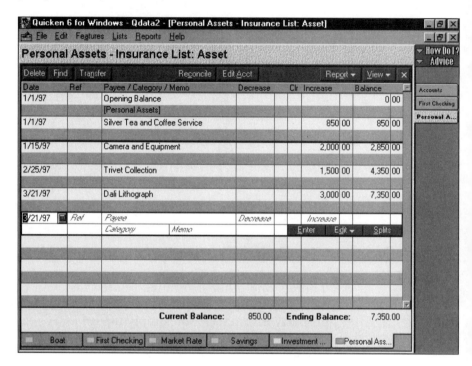

Figure 16.3. **An Asset register that lists property you've insured**

TIP Consider putting the asset account that lists the property in a separate file, especially if you've listed items such as clothing that have a substantial replacement value or cost (which is why you've insured them) but don't have much market value. This way, the value of things you've insured won't get included in your net worth. To create a separate file, choose the File ➤ New command to display the Creating New File dialog box. Click on the New Quicken File option button and then OK. When Quicken displays the Create Quicken File dialog box, use the File Name text box to give the file a name and then click on OK. Quicken creates the new file in the Quicken directory. It is to this file that you'll add the asset-list account. To switch between your two Quicken files, choose the File ➤ Open command. When Quicken displays the Open Quicken File dialog box, select the file you want to work with from the File Name list box.

To create an asset list account for property insurance records, follow these steps:

1. Click on the Accts icon. Quicken displays the Account List document window.

2. Click on the New command button. Quicken displays the dialog box, shown in Figure 16.4.

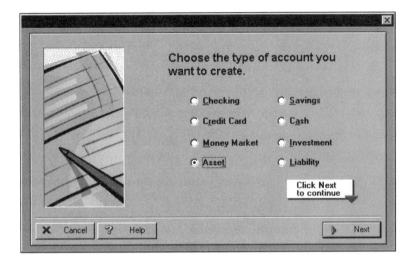

Choose the type of account you want to create.

- Checking
- Savings
- Credit Card
- Cash
- Money Market
- Investment
- Asset
- Liability

Click Next to continue

✕ Cancel   ？ Help   ▶ Next

Figure 16.4. **You can choose the type of new account you want.**

3. Click on the Asset command button on the dialog box, then click on Next. Quicken displays the Asset Account Setup dialog box. It is shown in Figure 16.5.

4. Click on the Summary Tab.

5. Complete the Asset Account Setup dialog boxes by entering a name for the account, a description, a 0 balance, and a starting date.

6. Click on Next and then click on Done.

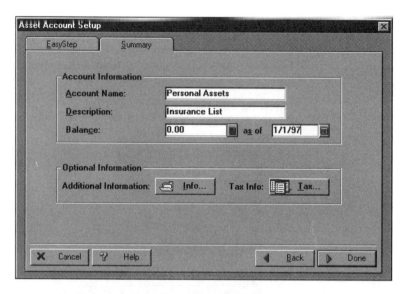

Figure 16.5.   **The Summary tab of the Asset Account Setup dialog box collects the information you need to create an account for listing insured property.**

From the account list, locate and open the new asset account that you just created. Quicken displays the Asset register in a document window. Enter a transaction for the item you want included on the list. Figure 16.3 shows an example of how the register looks after you enter several items.

TIP   If you can, make a video of things you've stored in all the rooms of your house, including closets, the garage, and the attic. And if the video camera records sound, add comments about the items you're filming, their prices, and where you got them.

HOW TO GET THE RIGHT INSURANCE POLICY
on the Road to Riches

A lot can be said about making smart decisions when it comes to getting insurance. Rather than write a lengthy and encyclopedic description of how insurance policies work, I want to focus on eight general rules for buying insurance of any kind. Then I'll explain how to buy the two kinds of insurance that most everyone needs, life insurance and health insurance.

Eight Rules for Buying Insurance of Any Kind

By following the eight rules explained here, you can save money, and just as importantly, you can save yourself from making serious mistakes when you shop for and acquire insurance policies.

Rule 1: Only Buy Insurance for Financial Risks You Can't Afford to Bear on Your Own

The purpose of insurance is to cover catastrophes that would devastate you or your family. Don't treat insurance as a chance to cover all your losses no matter how small or insignificant, because if you do you'll fritter away money on insurance you really don't need. For example, if your house caught fire and burned down, you would be glad you had homeowners insurance. Homeowners insurance is worth having, because you likely can't cover and you certainly don't want to cover the cost of rebuilding a house. On the other hand, insuring an old clunker is a waste of money if the car is only worth $800. You'd be throwing away money for something you could cover yourself if you had to.

Rule 2: Buy from Insurers Rated A or Better by A.M. Best

Insurance companies go bust, they are bought and sold, and they suffer the same economic travails that all companies do. Between 1989 and 1993, 143 insurance companies declared bankruptcy. You want to pick a reliable company with a good track record.

A.M. Best is an insurance company monitoring service that rates insurance companies on reliability. Look for insurers rated A or better by

A.M. Best, and periodically check to see whether your insurer is maintaining its high rating. If your insurer goes down a notch, consider finding a new insurance company. You can probably get A.M. Best's directory of insurance companies at your local public library.

Rule 3: Shop Around

There are many, many, many kinds of insurance policies, and insurers don't advertise by price. You have to do some legwork to match your needs with the cheapest possible policy. Talk to at least two brokers to start with. Look for *no-load* insurance companies—companies that sell policies directly to the public without a broker taking a commission—since they usually offer cheaper prices.

Rule 4: Never Lie on a Policy Application

If you fib and get caught, the company can cancel your policy. If you lie on an application for life insurance and die during the first three years you hold the policy, the company will cancel your policy, and your beneficiaries will receive nothing. Health, life, and disability insurers run background checks on applicants through the Medical Information Bureau, so you can get caught lying. The medical examination you take for life insurance can also turn up a lie. For example, if you smoked tobacco in the previous year, it will come up in the test.

Rule 5: Don't Buy Specific-Risk Policies—Buy General Policies Instead

When it comes to insurance, you want the broadest coverage you can get. Buying insurance against cancer or an uninsured motorist defeats the purpose of having an insurance policy. If you have ulcers, your cancer insurance will not help you. Get comprehensive medical coverage instead.

Uninsured motorist insurance is supposed to protect you if you get hit by someone who doesn't have car insurance or doesn't have adequate car insurance. But, in my opinion, you don't need it if you have adequate car insurance yourself, as well as health, disability, and life insurance. I should point out that some attorneys advise you to carry uninsured motorist insurance because, by doing so, you may be able to recover damages for "pain and suffering.")

Rule 6: Never Cancel One Policy until You Have a Replacement Policy in Place

If you cancel a policy without getting a replacement, you will be uninsured for however long it takes to get a new policy. And if disaster strikes during this period, you could be financially devastated. This rule goes for everyone, but especially for people getting on in years, since older folks sometimes have trouble getting health and life insurance.

Rule 7: Get a High Deductible

You save money by having insurance policies with high deductibles. The premium for high-deductible policies is always lower. Not only that, but you save yourself all the trouble of filing a claim and having to haggle with insurance company representatives if you have a high deductible and you don't have to make as many claims.

People who buy low-deductible policies usually do so because they want to be covered under all circumstances. But the cost, for example, of a $400 fenderbender is usually worth paying out of your own pocket when compared to the overall cost of being insured for $400 accidents. Statistics show that most people have a fender-bender once every ten years. The $400 hurts to pay, but the cost of insuring yourself for such accidents over a ten-year period comes to far more than $400.

One other thing: If you have a low deductible you will have to make more claims. That means you become an expensive headache for the insurance company. That means your rates go up, and you don't want that.

Rule 8: Use the Money You Save on Insurance Payments to Beef Up Your Rainy Day Account

While you can save money on your insurance premiums by following the rules mentioned earlier, it's probably a big mistake to use that money for, say, a trip to Hawaii. Instead, use any savings to build a nice-sized rainy day fund that you can draw on to pay deductibles. A big enough rainy day fund can cover both periods of unemployment and your insurance deductibles.

Buying Life Insurance

Not everyone needs life insurance. The first thing to do is make sure you need it. Life insurance is really meant for your family members or other dependents who rely on your earnings. You buy life insurance so that, if you die, your dependents can live the same kind of life they live now. Strictly speaking, then, life insurance is only a means of replacing your earnings in your absence. If you don't have dependents (say, because you're single) or you don't have earnings (say, because you're retired), you don't need life insurance. Note that children would rarely need life insurance because they almost never have dependents and other people don't rely on their earnings.

If you do need life insurance, you should know that it comes in two basic flavors: *term insurance* and *cash-value* insurance (also called "whole life" insurance). Ninety-nine times out of 100, what you want is term insurance.

Term life insurance is simple, straightforward life insurance. You pay an annual premium, and if you die, a lump sum is paid to your beneficiaries. Term life insurance gets its name because you buy the insurance for a specific term, such as 5, 10, or 15 years (and sometimes longer). At the end of the term, you can renew your policy or get a different one. The big benefits of term insurance are that it's cheap and it's simple.

The other flavor of life insurance is cash-value insurance. Many people are attracted to cash-value insurance because it supposedly lets them keep some of the premiums they pay over the years. After all, the reasoning goes, you pay for life insurance for 20, 30, or 40 years, so you might

Part 2

Quicken and Your Personal Finances

as well get some of the money back. With cash-value insurance, some of the premium money is kept in an account that is yours to keep or borrow against. This sounds great. The only problem is, cash-value insurance usually isn't a very good investment even if you hold the policy for years and years. And it's a terrible investment if you only keep the policy for a year or two. What's more, to really analyze a cash-value insurance policy, you need to perform a very sophisticated financial analysis. And this is, in fact, the major problem with cash-value life insurance.

While perhaps a handful of good cash-value insurance policies are available, many—perhaps most—are terrible investments. And to tell the good from the bad, you need a computer and the financial skills to perform something called discounted cash-flow analysis. (If you do think you need cash-value insurance, it probably makes sense to have a financial planner perform this analysis for you. Obviously, this financial planner should be a different person than the insurance agent selling you the policy.)

The bottom line? Cash-value insurance is way too complex a financial product for most people to deal with. Note, too, that any investment option that's tax-deductible—such as a 401(k), a 401(b), a deductible IRA, a SEP/IRA, or a Keoghs—are always a better investment than the investment portion of a cash-value policy. For these two reasons, I strongly encourage you to simplify your financial affairs and increase your net worth by sticking with tax-deductible investments.

If you do decide to follow my advice and choose a term life insurance policy, be sure that your policy is non-cancelable and renewable. You want a policy that cannot be canceled under any circumstances, including poor health. (You have no way of knowing what your health will be like ten years from now.) And you want to be able to renew the policy even if your health deteriorates. (You don't want to go through a medical review each time a term is up and you have to renew.)

Buying Health Insurance

Everybody needs health insurance. With medical costs skyrocketing, you simply can't pay for this stuff on your own. Too many families get wiped out by a stroke, a car accident, or some other major medical emergency because they didn't have medical coverage and had to pay for the surgeries and hospital visits themselves. Even worse, if you don't have health insurance, you may not be able to get the treatment you need to save your life.

The problem, however, is that heath insurance is very expensive. Fortunately, there are some good ways to save money on health insurance.

Buy Major Medical Coverage and Self-Insure the Minor Stuff

How much your deductible and co-payments are is the biggest determining factor in how much you pay in premiums. If you have a large deductible, your premiums will fall accordingly. If you co-pay the first $2,000 to $5,000 in medical bills—that is, if you pay a certain percentage of these bills, usually 20 to 50 percent—your premiums drop dramatically.

The surest way to save money on health insurance is to get a high deductible and a large co-payment. Under this plan, you pay for check-ups and minor cuts and scrapes. The insurance company only starts paying when your bills soar due to a major medical emergency. Follow this plan only if you're healthy and you have enough tucked away in a rainy day account to pay the deductible and make the co-payments. You don't want to be stuck in a hospital bed wondering how you can make co-payments or pay a deductible.

Don't Get One-Disease Insurance

Some insurers prey on people's fears by offering them cancer or other types of one-disease insurance. The problem with cancer insurance is it won't do you any good if you get ulcers, the gout, athlete's foot, or any other disease except cancer. Buy broad health insurance that covers all the illnesses you might get. One-disease insurance is too expensive and it can too easily leave holes in your coverage.

Make a Living Will

This is awkward for me to write about. It's awkward for you to read about. A *living will* tells the doctor and your family that, if you're dying, you don't want your life extended by aggressive life-support measures. Although a living will seems like a funny topic for anyone who's healthy, drawing up a living will is a really smart thing for you to take care of now. For a set of blank living-will documents you can fill in, write to Society for the Right to Die, 250 West 57th St., New York, NY 10107. Include a self-addressed, stamped envelope. Include a small donation to pay for the forms and the shipping.

Don't Get Coverage for Prescription Drugs

Unless you have a chronic illness that requires buying lots of expensive prescription drugs, don't pay an extra premium for prescriptions. Usually, it isn't worth it.

Skip Maternity Coverage—As Long As Your Policy Covers Complications from Pregnancy and Newborn Care

Having a baby is expensive. But even so, maternity coverage usually isn't a good deal. If you work out the numbers, you need to have a baby about every year or every other year just to break even on the extra cost (the premiums, in other words) of having this benefit.

You do need to be very careful about skipping maternity coverage if there's even the slightest chance that you or your spouse will have a baby in the near future. If there are any complications from the pregnancy or if your newborn needs special care, the costs of having the baby can increase astronomically. Ideally, then, you either want a policy that doesn't cover maternity benefits or one that does cover them, as well as covering complications from pregnancy and newborn care.

Compare Doctor and Hospital Prices

It would be great if doctors wore prices on their foreheads the way used cars have prices on their windshields. Comparing doctor and hospital prices is not easy, but it can be done simply by asking.

on the Road to Riches

Look for a Doctor Who Accepts Assignment If You're on Medicare

Accepting assignment means that the doctor charges no more than what Medicare deems appropriate. You still pay the deductible and the co-payment, but you can rest assured that the bill will not go above that.

Ask for Generic Drugs

Once you take the tiny little words off the capsules or pills, they're exactly the same as their generic counterparts. Did you know that generic drugs and name brand drugs are often made in the same laboratories? Always opt for generic drugs, and use the money you save to see a good movie.

Use 24-Hour Emergency Clinics instead of Hospital Emergency Rooms

Clinics are much cheaper than hospital emergency rooms. Cheaper still is seeing your own doctor. If you can manage to wait until your doctor is in, hold off and avoid emergency clinics as well as emergency rooms.

Get a Guaranteed Renewable Policy

You should be able to renew your policy without having to pass a medical exam. A nonrenewable policy defeats the purpose of having health insurance. You buy health insurance in case you get sick. You don't buy it for when you're healthy.

Quicken for Investors

Do you invest in mutual funds, stocks, bonds, or real estate? Quicken includes some of the most powerful investment-management tools available anywhere. To make sure you use these tools correctly and get the most from them, read the next three chapters, which describe Quicken's investment record-keeping capabilities in detail.

Chapter 17, *Mutual-Fund Investments*, explains the basics of Quicken's investment record-keeping tools and guides you through tracking mutual-fund investments. (This is a good place to start even if you don't invest in mutual funds.) Chapter 18, *Stocks, Bonds, and Other Equity and Debt Securities*, builds on the discussion in Chapter 17 by explaining how to use Quicken to track common stock investments as well as other equity investments, such as put and call options. You also learn how to track debt security investments such as corporate bonds, negotiable certificates of deposit, and zero-coupon bonds. Chapter 19, *Tracking Real-Estate Investments*, explains how to use Quicken to track your investment in a home or rental property.

CHAPTER 17

Mutual-Fund Investments

FEATURING

Tracking IRA and 401(k)
mutual-fund investments

Describing mutual-fund
purchases and distributions

Handling account fees and stock splits

Recording mutual funds in Quicken

MUTUAL funds are an excellent way to invest. Even with relatively small amounts of money, you get tremendous diversification. And if you want, you can have some of the best investment advisors in the world managing your money for you.

Unfortunately, mutual fund record keeping can be tricky. When the profits you earn from a mutual fund investment are taxable, the profit calculations—in particular, the capital gain or loss calculations—quickly become cumbersome. Fortunately, in this case Quicken comes to your rescue.

 TIP Even if you don't invest using mutual funds but instead invest directly in stocks and bonds, this chapter is a good place to start learning. Quicken's stock and bond record-keeping features represent an extension of its mutual fund record-keeping features.

Some Prerequisites

To track a mutual-fund investment in Quicken, you need to:

▶ Keep records that document the mutual fund shares you've purchased and sold. (Quicken is, after all, a record-keeping tool. If you don't have the raw data you want to record in Quicken, you can't use Quicken.)

▶ Know the mechanics of using the Quicken register. (To keep records of investments, you use many of the same windows and commands you do to keep records of bank accounts, credit cards, and other assets and liabilities.)

What to Do About IRA and 401(k) Mutual-Fund Investments

This chapter begins with a brief discussion of whether or not you should use Quicken to track a mutual fund investment.

It probably doesn't make sense to track tax-deferred mutual-fund investments in Quicken. There's no harm in doing so, but you don't get anything extra for your effort. Here's the reason. If your mutual-fund investing is through tax-deferred accounts such as employer-sponsored 401(k) accounts, IRAs, and self-employed pension plans such as SEPs and Keoghs, your investment profits aren't taxed—dividends and interest aren't taxed, capital gains aren't taxed, and capital losses aren't tax-deductible.

Instead, money you withdraw from the account is taxed. Restated in terms of Quicken mechanics, when you deposit money that's been withdrawn from, say, your IRA account into a bank account, you just categorize the bank account deposit as income. (The income category could be named something like IRA Distribution.)

Because you don't need to keep records for the purpose of tracking your mutual-fund profits, there's little reason to go to the extra work of keeping mutual-fund–investment records in Quicken. If you want to know the current value of your mutual-fund investment, you can just look at your last statement from the mutual-fund investment management company or telephone company. The big mutual fund management companies all have 800 numbers that give fund price and account value information. If you want to see what taxable income you have because of the mutual fund, you can look at your bank accounts and summarize the deposits you've made into these accounts. Also, you can get the annual return on the investment by looking at the annual report the mutual-fund management company sends you at the end of the year.

WHEN YOU SHOULDN'T USE QUICKEN TO TRACK MUTUAL FUNDS

There are other situations—similar to the case of the IRA and 401(k) mutual-fund investment angle—in which it doesn't make sense to track a mutual-fund investment with Quicken because you don't get any new information or added value from your record-keeping effort.

Suppose you have retirement money in a mutual fund, you don't buy and sell shares, and you don't reinvest your mutual-fund profits (because you live on these profits). In this case it doesn't make sense to track your mutual fund investments in Quicken. You can actually keep a record of the mutual fund profits by using appropriate income categories when you deposit the dividend, interest, or capital gains distributions check into your bank account.

What's more, you can get investment activity and current market value information by looking at a recent statement or by telephoning the mutual fund investment company.

Setting Up a Mutual-Fund Account

If you do decide to track a mutual-fund investment in Quicken, you need to set up an investment account. It will be into this account that the mutual-fund investment transactions get recorded. You'll set up one investment account for each mutual fund in which you own shares.

To set up a mutual fund account, follow these steps:

1. Click on the Accts button on the Menu bar or choose the Lists ➤ Account command to display the Account List document window.

2. Click on the New command button in the Account List document window or choose Edit ➤ Account ➤ New to display the dialog box used to create a new account.

3. Click on the Investment option button, click on Next, and then click on the Summary tab to display the Investment Account Setup dialog box, as shown in Figure 17.1.

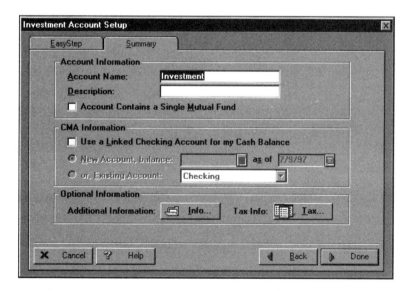

*Figure 17.1.   **The Investment Account Setup dialog box, showing the Summary tab.***

4. Enter an account name in the Account Name text box. You can use the mutual fund's name as your account name. (If you have shares of the Vanguard Index 500 Trust fund, for example, you might choose to name the account Vanguard or Index 500.)

5. *If you want to further describe or collect additional information about an account*, use the Description text box. You can enter up to 21 characters.

6. Mark the Account Contains a Single Mutual Fund check box to tell Quicken that you'll use the account for a single mutual-fund investment.

7. Leave the Include a Linked Cash Account for Cash Management check box blank. This feature doesn't apply to mutual-fund accounts, or at least doesn't apply to mutual-fund accounts as I'm suggesting you use and set them up here.

8. *If you want to store additional information about an account*, click on the Info button to display the Additional Account Information dialog box. You can use it to further describe the mutual-fund management company in the Bank Name text box, the mutual fund account number in the Account Number text box, and so forth. (Some of these fields don't make sense for an investment account because Quicken uses the same Additional Account Information dialog box for all account types.) Click on OK to close this information dialog box.

9. Click on the Tax Info command to display the Tax Schedule Information dialog box, as shown in Figure 17.2.

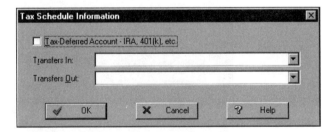

Figure 17.2. **The Tax Schedule Information dialog box**

10. *If the mutual-fund account won't produce taxable income or tax-deductible capital losses*, mark the Tax-Deferred Account check box. This tells

Quicken that it should not count this account's income and expense amounts as taxable or tax-deductible.

11. *If the transfers into and out of the investment account should be reported on your income tax return,* use the Transfers In and Transfers Out drop-down–list boxes to identify on which tax return form or schedule (and on which line on the form or schedule) these transfers should be reported. (In the case of a mutual-fund investment that's part of your Individual Retirement Account, for example, transfers to the account are reported as IRA contributions.)

12. Click on OK to close the Tax Schedule Information dialog box.

 NOTE If you own shares in more than one mutual fund and want to track all of your investments in a single account, follow the approach for setting up accounts described in the next chapter, but don't mark the Account Contains a Single Mutual Fund check box.

13. Click on Done to tell Quicken the Create Investment Account dialog box is complete. Quicken next displays the Set Up Mutual Fund Security dialog box, as shown in Figure 17.3.

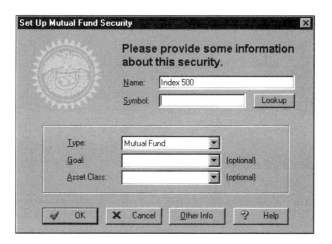

Figure 17.3.   **The Set Up Mutual Fund Security dialog box**

14. If you will update the mutual fund's share prices by using the Quicken Quotes service and your modem, enter the security symbol for the mutual fund in the Symbol text box.

15. Activate the Type drop-down–list box and select the Mutual Fund entry.

16. If you want to segregate your investments by investment goal, activate the Goal drop-down–list box and select one of the goals listed.

17. If you want to monitor your mutual fund investments by the type of investments made, activate the Asset Class drop-down–list box and select the asset class that most closely matches the mutual fund's principal investments.

18. Click on OK. Quicken adds the mutual fund account to the account list and redisplays the Account List window.

19. Select the investment account from the Account List window and click on the Open command button to display the Create Opening Share Balance dialog box, as shown in Figure 17.4. Usually, you don't want to use it because you don't get to enter the actual cost data that is useful for tax calculations.

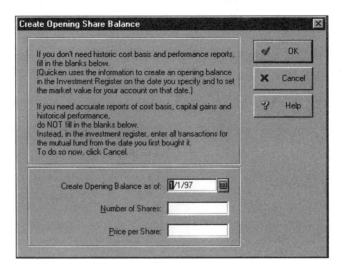

Figure 17.4. **The Create Opening Share Balance dialog box**

20. Click on Cancel to display the investment account version of the Register window, as shown in Figure 17.5. Don't enter anything into the Number of Shares and Price Per Price text boxes. You don't enter the opening shares balance and price information here. You enter that information later.

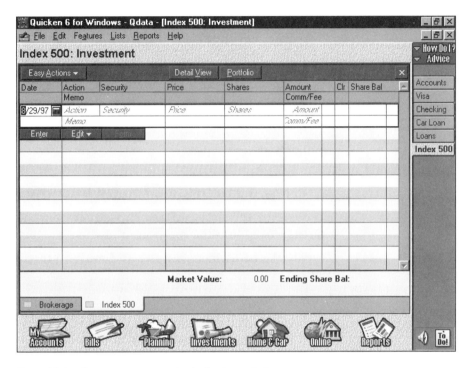

Figure 17.5.   Investment account in the Register window

 NOTE The dialog box says you can enter date, number-of-shares, and price-per-share information in the Create Opening Share Balance dialog box if you won't use the data for calculating the tax basis and, as a result, for calculating taxable profits or tax-deductible losses. But if you don't need to calculate taxable investment profits or tax-deductible losses, you also don't need to use Quicken for your investment record keeping.

Describing the Mutual-Fund Shares You Buy

The first mutual-fund transaction you record is the purchase of shares. This is easy as long as you have your monthly statement or confirmation slip. You'll need information, however, on the number of shares purchased, the price per share (or the transaction total), and the commission paid (if any).

Quicken provides two methods for recording transactions such as share purchases. You can enter a purchase transaction directly into the register, or you can use an Investment Form dialog box to collect the share purchase transaction and then have Quicken enter the purchase transaction into the register. Each has its unique strengths, and if you become active in your investment record keeping, you'll probably employ both methods.

Entering a Purchase Directly into the Register

To describe the first and any subsequent purchases of mutual-fund shares directly into the register, follow these steps:

1. Display the Investment register and move to the first empty row of the register.

2. Enter the purchase date in the Date text box.

> **TIP** Be sure to enter the actual purchase date and not the date you mailed the check to the mutual-fund management company or the broker or the date you recorded the purchase. Quicken categorizes any capital gain or loss as short-term or long-term based on the difference between the purchase and sales dates shown in the register.

3. *If you made this purchase sometime in the past,* enter the action as ShrsIn, and if this is a purchase you're currently making, enter the action as BuyX: Either place the cursor in the Action combo box and type either **ShrsIn** or **BuyX** or select the ShrsIn or BuyX entry from the Action list box.

4. Tab past the Security text box.

   Quicken fills in the Security text box with whatever you named the mutual-fund account. (You specified this name using the Set Up Mutual Fund Security dialog box as part of setting up the mutual fund.)

5. Enter the price per share you paid in the Average Cost or Price text box. You can enter the share price in dollars and cents, such as 10.25, or in dollars and eighths, such as 10 1/8. (Quicken changes the name of the box that holds the share price data from Price to Average Cost if you record a ShrsIn transaction.)

6. Enter the shares you purchased in the Number of Shares text box or the total amount you paid in the Basis text box.

    Quicken calculates whatever piece of data you don't enter. For example, if you enter the price as $10.00 and the number of shares as 100, Quicken calculates the total as $1,000.00.

7. If you want to record some additional piece of information, such as the order number, use the Memo box.

8. If you're recording a BuyX action, use the XFer Acct combo box to show which account you wrote the check on to pay for the purchase.

> **NOTE** If you enter an account name in the XFer Account field, Quicken records a payment transaction in the account equal to the value you enter in the XFer Amt text box.

9. *If you entered the action as BuyX*, either enter the amount you paid for the mutual fund shares and any commission in the XFer Amt text box or enter the commission you paid in the Comm Fee text box. (If you purchased shares of a no-load mutual fund, the commission equals 0.)

    Quicken calculates whatever piece of data you don't enter. For example, if you enter the total paid for the mutual fund shares as $1,000.00 and the commission as $50.00, Quicken calculates the XFer Amt as $1,050.00.

> **NOTE** You don't have to pay commissions, or *loads*, when you purchase mutual fund shares. To purchase shares of a mutual fund without paying a commission, you simply purchase shares of a no-load mutual fund. Flip through the pages of the *Wall Street Journal* to see advertisements from mutual fund management companies that sell their shares directly to their investors rather than through stockbrokers.

10   Select Enter.

Quicken records the transaction into the Investment register and moves to the next empty row of the register so you can enter another transaction. If you entered the Action as BuyX, Quicken also records a payment transaction in the XFer Acct. Figure 17.6 shows the Investment register with two transactions: a ShrsIn transaction for $2,000 and a BuyX purchase for $5,000.

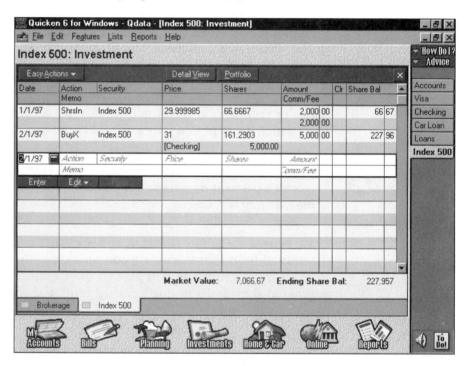

Figure 17.6.   Investment register with example share purchases

Using the Buy/Add Shares Form to Record a Current or Earlier Purchase

You can use the Buy/Add Shares Form dialog box to record the current purchase or an earlier purchase of mutual-fund shares. A current purchase is one for which you not only want to record the purchase of the mutual-fund shares, but also need to record the corresponding payment transaction—probably the check you wrote to purchase the shares. An earlier purchase is one for which you only want to record the purchase of the mutual-fund shares but not the corresponding payment transaction. Here's how both transactions work:

1. Display the Investment account in a register, move the cursor to the next empty row of the Investment register, click on the Easy Actions button to display the Action menu, and then choose the Buy/Add Shares command to display the Buy/Add Shares dialog box.

2. Click on the Summary tab of the Buy/Add Shares dialog box. Figure 17.7 shows the Summary tab of this dialog box.

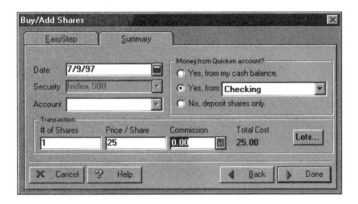

Figure 17.7.   **The Buy/Add Shares dialog box**

3. Enter the purchase date in the Date text box.

4. Tab past the Account text box and Security text box.

   Quicken fills in the Security text box and the Account text box with whatever you named the mutual-fund account. (You specified this name using the Set Up Mutual Fund Security dialog box as part of setting up the mutual fund.)

5. Enter the shares you purchased in the Number of Shares text box, the price per share you paid in the Price/Share text box (in dollars and cents or dollars and eighths), and the commission you paid, if any, in the Commission text box.

6. If you're recording a current purchase, mark the Yes From button (which appears in the Money from Quicken Account settings) and then use the Yes From drop-down–list box to identify the account from which the payment was made. If you're recording an earlier purchase,

mark the No button (which appears in the Money from Quicken Account settings).

7. Click on Done.

Quicken uses the information you've entered in the Buy/Add Shares dialog box to record a current purchase or an earlier purchase for the investment account.

Describing Mutual-Fund Profit Distributions

Periodically, a mutual fund distributes profits to the shareholders. On a monthly basis, for example, a money-market or bond-mutual fund may distribute interest income. On a quarterly basis a stock-mutual fund probably distributes dividend income. And on an annual basis most mutual funds make distributions of capital gains or losses.

 NOTE A capital gain occurs when the fund sells a stock, bond, or other security held by the fund for more than the security originally cost. A capital loss occurs when the fund sells a security held by the fund for less than the security originally cost.

What to Do When You Receive a Check from the Mutual-Fund Manager

With Quicken, you can record mutual-fund distributions you receive either directly into the register or using an investment form. The advantage to using the investment form approach is that it lets you describe the distribution just once. The directly-into-the-register approach makes you sequentially describe each type of distribution separately: the dividend distribution, the short-term capital gain distribution, the long-term capital distribution, and so forth.

To record a mutual-fund distribution you receive by check using the Income form, follow these steps:

1. Display the investment account's register, move the cursor to the next empty row of the register, click on the Easy Actions button, and then choose the Record an Income Event command. You see the Record Income dialog box, as shown in Figure 17.8.

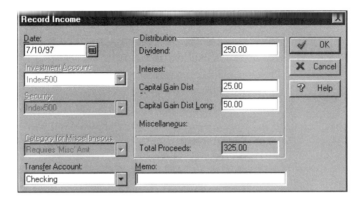

Figure 17.8.   The Record Income dialog box

2.   Enter the distribution date in the Date text box.

> **TIP**   Be sure to enter the actual distribution date, not the date you received the distribution or the date you recorded it. The reason is that the date you enter determines in which year's income the distribution is counted. For example, if you receive a distribution of 1996 capital gains in 1997, you need to enter the distribution date as 1996 so the capital gains are counted in 1996's taxable income and not in 1997's taxable income.

3.   Tab past the Account text box and Security text box to accept the mutual-fund security name.

4.   Enter the dividend income amount in the Dividend text box.

> **NOTE**   The mutual-fund statement will give the amount of each type of distribution.

5.   Enter the short-term capital gain amount in the Capital Gain Dist Short text box and the long-term capital gain amount in the Capital Gain Dist Long box.

6.   Enter the name of the account into which you'll deposit the distribution check in the Transfer Account combo box.

7.   *If you need to collect any additional information,* use the Memo text box.

8. Click on OK.

Quicken takes the information entered in the Income dialog box and records transactions into the Investment register. Quicken records one transaction for each type of distribution. Figure 17.9 shows the Investment register with a $250 dividend distribution. (This is the selected transaction and the third transaction showing.) The figure also shows a $25 short-term capital gain distribution and a $50 long-term capital gain distribution.

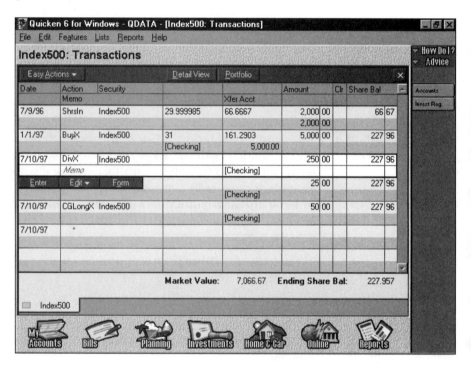

Figure 17.9.   **How Quicken records an income distribution into the register.**

As noted earlier, you don't have to use the Income command and dialog box to enter income distribution transactions into an Investment register, but it makes things easier.

What to Do When You Reinvest a Mutual-Fund Distribution

When you reinvest a mutual-fund distribution by buying additional shares, you essentially combine two of the transactions I've already talked about: receiving a distribution and buying shares. You can record this sort of transaction directly into the register, but as with income distributions you don't reinvest, the easiest approach is to use an investment form. To record a reinvested mutual-fund distribution using the investment form, follow these steps:

1. Display the investment account's register, move the cursor to the next empty row of the register, and click on the Easy Actions button. Then choose the Reinvest Income command to display the Reinvest Income dialog box, as shown in Figure 17.10.

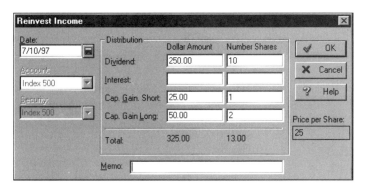

Figure 17.10. **The Reinvest Income dialog box**

2. Enter the distribution and reinvestment date in the Date text box.

3. Tab past the Account text and the Security text box to accept the mutual fund security name.

4. Enter the dividend income amount in the Dividend Dollar Amount text box.

5. Enter the number of shares purchased with the reinvested dividend in the Dividend Number Shares text box.

 NOTE The mutual-fund statement will give the amount of each type of distribution.

(right margin) **Part 3**
Quicken for Investors

6. Enter the interest income amount in the Interest Dollar Amount text box.

7. Enter the number of shares purchased with the reinvested interest in the Interest Number of Shares text box, the short-term capital gain amount in the Cap Gain Short Dollar Amount text box, the number of shares purchased with the reinvested short-term capital gains in the Cap Gain Short Number Shares text box, the long-term capital gain amount in the Cap Gain Long Dollar Amount text box, and the number of shares purchased with the reinvested long-term capital gains in the Cap Gain Long Number Shares text box.

NOTE Quicken calculates the total dollar amount of the reinvested distribution, the total number of shares purchased, and the average price per share based on the information you enter in steps 4 through 7. These totals and the average price values will agree with what your mutual-fund statement shows if you've correctly completed these steps.

8. If you need to collect any additional information, use the Memo text box.

9. Click on OK.

Quicken takes the information entered in the Reinvest Income dialog box and records transactions into the Investment register.

As with an income distribution that isn't reinvested, Quicken records one transaction for each type of distribution. Figure 17.11 shows an Investment register with a $250 reinvested dividend distribution, as well as a $25 reinvested short-term capital gain distribution and a $50 reinvested long-term capital gain distribution. (These are the last three transactions shown in Figure 17.11.)

Again, you don't have to use an investment form—in this case, the Reinvest Income command and dialog box—to enter the reinvested distribution transactions. You can enter the transactions shown in Figure 17.11 directly into the register, one transaction at a time, but be sure to specify the correct action for each transaction.

TIP As with distributions you don't invest, the mutual-fund statement will indicate what kind of distribution you've reinvested.

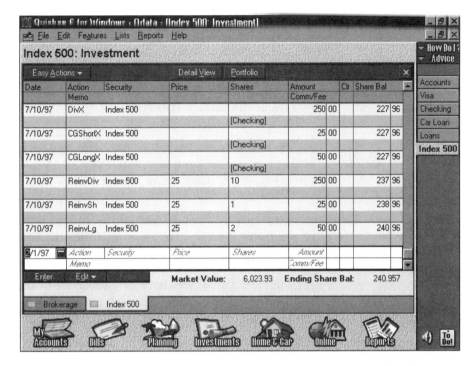

Figure 17.11. **How Quicken records an income distribution into the register when the money is reinvested**

Describing the Mutual-Fund Shares You Sell

At some point you'll probably sell the mutual-fund shares you originally purchased with a check or that you acquired by reinvesting the dividends or capital gains. As with the other types of mutual-fund transactions you record, this is easy as long as you have the necessary information: the number of shares sold, price per share (or the transaction total), and commission paid (if any).

Again, you have two ways to record the sale of mutual-fund shares: directly into the register or using an investment form. Because both record-keeping approaches are fast and convenient, I'll describe both.

Part
3

Quicken for Investors

Recording the Sale Directly into the Register

To record the sale of mutual-fund shares directly into the register, follow these steps:

1. Place the cursor in the next empty row of the register and enter the sales date in the Date text box.

> **TIP** Be sure to enter the actual sales date. Quicken categorizes any capital gain or loss as short-term or long-term based on the difference between the purchase and sale dates shown in the register.

2. If this is a sale you made sometime in the past, enter the Action as ShrsOut. If this is a sale you're currently making, enter the Action as SellX.

3. Tab past the Security text box to accept the mutual-fund-security name.

4. Enter the sales price per share you received in the Price text box, and enter the shares you sold in the Shares text box or the total amount you sold in the Amount text box.

    Quicken calculates whatever piece of data you don't enter. For example, if you enter the price as $10.00 and the number of shares as 100, Quicken calculates the total as $1,000.00.

5. *If you want to record some additional piece of information,* such as the sales order number, use the Memo text box.

6. *If you're recording a SellX action,* use the XFer Acct combo box to show the account into which you will deposit the check you receive from the sale of the shares.

> **NOTE** If you enter an account name in the XFer Account text box, Quicken records a deposit transaction in the account equal to the value you enter in the XFer Amt text box.

7. *If you entered the Action as SellX,* either enter the amount you received for the sale of the mutual-fund shares less any commission you paid in the XFer Amt text box, or enter the commission you paid in the Comm Fee text box. Again, Quicken calculates whichever piece of data you don't enter.

8. Select Enter to display a message box that asks if you want to specifically identify the shares you're selling.

TIP Specific identification of the shares you sell gives you control over the capital gain or loss stemming from the sale. People often use this control to minimize or postpone capital-gains taxes and accelerate or maximize deductible capital losses. For example, by selling the most expensive shares first, you minimize the capital gain or maximize the capital loss on the sale of these shares. If you don't use specific identification, Quicken assumes that the first shares you purchased are the first shares you sell. You may have heard this costing assumption referred to by its acronym, FIFO (First In First Out).

9. *If you want to use specific identification,* select Yes, and Quicken displays a dialog box similar to the one in Figure 17.12.

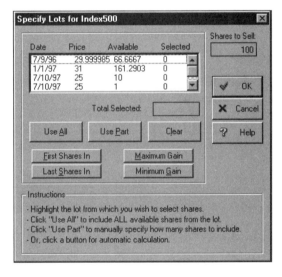

Figure 17.12. **This dialog box lets you tell Quicken which shares you're selling, thereby exercising control over the capital gain or loss calculation.**

10. Indicate which lot you're selling (a *lot* is just a set of shares you purchase at the same time) by clicking on it or by highlighting it and choosing Use All. You can select a portion of a lot by highlighting it and choosing Use Part. If you choose Use Part, Quicken displays a message box that asks for the number of shares from the lot you want to sell. You can enter some number of shares or accept Quicken's suggestion. (Quicken suggests you sell as many shares as you need to complete the specific identification.)

LOTS THAT MINIMIZE OR MAXIMIZE YOUR CAPITAL GAINS

You can tell Quicken to pick lots that minimize your capital gain (and therefore your capital-gains taxes) by clicking on the Minimum Gain button. You can tell Quicken to pick lots that maximize your capital gain (and therefore your capital-gains taxes) by clicking on the Maximum Gain button. You can tell Quicken to sell the oldest lots first by clicking on the First Shares In button or the newest lots first by clicking on the Last Shares In button.

If you make a mistake in your specific identification and want to start over, choose Clear. Quicken shows you how many shares you've said you'll sell and how many you've identified. When you've specifically identified as many as you've said you'll sell, click on OK.

Quicken records the transaction into the Investment register and selects the next empty row so you can enter another transaction. If you entered the action as SellX, Quicken also records a deposit transaction in the XFer Acct. Figure 17.13 shows 100 shares of the Vanguard Index 500 Trust being sold on July 10 at $28 a share.

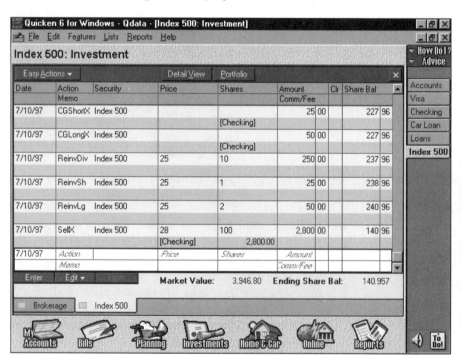

Figure 17.13. **Investment register with an example sale transaction**

Using the Sell Form to Record a Current or Earlier Sale

To record the sale of shares using an investment form, follow these steps:

1. Display the investment account's register and place the cursor in the next empty row of the register.

2. Click on the Easy Actions button and choose the Sell/Remove Shares command to display the Sell/Remove Shares dialog box and then click on the Summary tab:

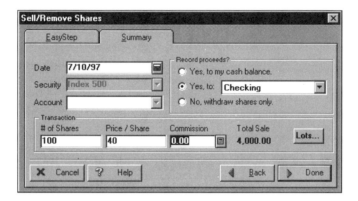

3. Enter the sale date in the Date text box.

4. Tab past the Security name text box and the Account name text box to accept the mutual-fund security name.

5. Use the Number of Shares text box to indicate how many shares you are selling.

6. *If you want to specifically identify the shares*, click on the Lots command button.

    Quicken displays the Specific Identification of Shares dialog box (see Figure 17.12). This works as described earlier.

7. When you've specifically identified as many shares as you've said you'll sell, click on OK to close the dialog box and return to the Sell/Remove Shares dialog box.

NOTE If you don't use the Lots command button to specifically identify the shares you're selling, Quicken uses a first-in, first-out costing assumption to calculate the capital gain or loss on the sale. In other words, it assumes the shares you sell are always those you've held the longest.

---

8. Enter the share's sale price in the Price/Share text box and the sale commission you are paying, if any, in the Commission text box, and Quicken calculates the total amount of the sale.

> **TIP** You need to enter only three of the following four inputs: number of shares, price, commission, and total. Quicken can use any three of these inputs to calculate the fourth input.

9. If you're recording a current sale, indicate the account into which you'll deposit the sales proceeds by marking the Yes To button and then selecting the account from the Yes To drop-down–list box. (The Yes To button and drop-down–list box appear in the Record Proceeds settings.) If you're recording an earlier sale and don't want to adjust a bank-account balance for the sale, mark the No button.

10. Click on Done, and Quicken records the sale and enters a transaction describing the sale into the register.

Account Fees, Stock Splits, and Reminders

In the preceding sections, I talked about the various record-keeping actions allowed for a mutual-fund account. There are, however, three additional mutual-fund transactions you may need to record. Probably the most common is an account fee transaction (such as a mutual fund management company might charge for an IRA). In addition, there are two remaining actions: StkSplit (which you use to record mutual-fund share splits) and Reminder (which you use to put reminder notes in the Investment register).

Recording Account Fees

Some mutual funds periodically levy account fees. For example, I used to have an IRA in a T. Rowe Price mutual fund. T. Rowe Price charged me an annual IRA custodian fee of $10. To pay the custodian fee at the end of every year, either I had write a $10 check to T. Rowe Price Company or T. Rowe Price sold $10 worth of the mutual-fund shares.

If You Write a Check to Pay the Account Fee

If you write a check to pay an account fee, you don't need to do anything special in the Investment register. You just write the check in the usual way.

Categorize the check that pays an account fee as investment expense or a similar expense category. Things like IRA account and custodial fees are miscellaneous deductions. At the time I'm writing this, miscellaneous deductions in excess of 2 percent of your adjusted gross income may be used as an itemized deduction.

If You Sell Shares to Pay an Account Fee

If you sell shares—or, more likely, the mutual-fund manager sells shares—to pay an account fee, you need to do a little more work to record the account fee: You need to record a SellX transaction in the Investment Account register, as described in the section "Describing the Mutual Fund Shares You Sell" earlier in this chapter.

There's a slight trick to recording this type of SellX transaction. Your commission or fee text box entry equals the total sales amount. If you record directly into the register the sale of $10 of mutual-fund shares to pay for, say, a $10 account fee, both the Total Amount and Comm Fee text boxes show 10. The XFer Amt text box, as a result, shows as 0. (When you record this transaction, Quicken sets the Price text box value back to 0, so both the Price and XFer Amt text boxes show 0.)

If you use the Sell/Remove Shares command from the Easy Actions menu and its subsequent dialog box to record an account fee transaction, you enter the number of shares you need to sell to pay the account fee, the sales price per share, and the commission. If you've correctly entered these inputs, the total sale shows as 0 because the commission—really the account fee—entirely eats up the sales proceeds.

Part 3

Quicken for Investors

CONCERNING INVESTMENT EXPENSES...

Check with your tax advisor concerning investment expenses such as account maintenance fees paid for by selling shares. While the approach described here is the only one you can easily do in Quicken, it causes your account maintenance fees to show up as capital losses equal to whatever you originally paid for the shares. Unfortunately, this overstates your capital loss by the amount of the account fee and understates your investment expenses by the amount of the account fee. On your tax return, therefore, you need to adjust your capital losses or gains and your investment expenses (a possible miscellaneous deduction) for this discrepancy.

Recording a Mutual-Fund Share Split

A share split occurs when the mutual fund company gives each current shareholder new shares. In a two-for-one split, for example, a shareholder receives one new share for each share already held. Someone who holds 100 shares prior to the split, for example, holds 200 shares after the split. You can record share splits directly into the register or with an investment form.

To record a mutual-fund share split directly into the register, follow these steps:

1. Place the cursor in the next empty row of the register and enter the split date in the Date text box.

2. In the Action combo box, enter StkSplit as the action.

3. Tab past the Security text box to accept the suggested security, the mutual fund name.

4. *If you want to update your mutual-fund price per share data,* enter what the price per share will be after the split by using the Price text box.

5. Enter the number of new shares you'll receive for a specified number of old shares in the New Shares text box. (When you indicate the action as StkSplit, Quicken replaces the Number of Shares text box with the New Shares text box.)

6. *If you want to record some additional piece of information about the split*—perhaps to cross-reference the mutual-fund statement that explains or reports the split—use the Memo text box.

 NOTE The New Shares and Old Shares text boxes let you specify the stock split ratio. If the stock split results in your getting two new shares for every old share you own, for example, you enter ❷ in the New Shares text box and ❶ in the Old Shares text box.

---

7. Enter the number of old shares you'll give up to receive a specified number of new shares using the Old Shares text box. (When you indicate the action as StkSplit, Quicken replaces the XFer Account combo box with the Old Shares text box.)

8. Select Enter.

    Quicken records the transaction into the Investment register and adjusts the number of mutual-fund shares you're holding according to the new-shares-to-old-shares ratio. Then it selects the next empty row of the Investment register so you can enter another transaction. Figure 17.14 shows the investment register with a stock split transaction. (The stock split transaction appears last.)

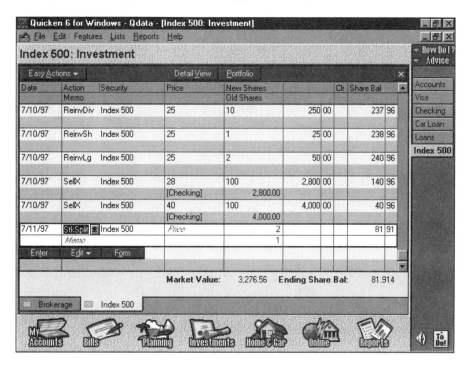

*Figure 17.14.   **The Investment register with a stock split transaction***

To record a stock split transaction using an investment form, follow these steps:

1. Display the investment account in a register and move the cursor to the next empty row of the investment register.

2. Click on the Easy Actions button to display the Action menu.

3. Choose the Stock Split command to display the Stock Split dialog box:

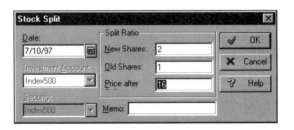

4. Enter the split date in the Date text box.

5. Tab past the Investment Account text box and Security text box to accept the mutual-fund security name.

6. Enter the number of new shares equal to one old share in the New Shares text box.

7. Enter the number of old shares equal to one new share in the Old Shares text box.

8. *If you want to update the share price information*, enter the price per share after the split in the Price after Split text box.

9. *If you want to describe some additional piece of information about the stock split*, use the Memo text box.

10. Click on OK, and Quicken uses the information you've entered to record a stock split transaction for the investment account.

Using the Quicken Investment Register to Store Reminder Messages

Reminder messages aren't really transactions. But because your investment activity may require you to do things by certain dates—cash a certificate of deposit by June 3, for example—you can use the Investment register to store these sorts of reminder messages. Reminder messages work because if you have the Billminder utility turned on, Billminder will alert you to any reminder messages you should read just as it alerts you to checks that need to be written and electronic payments that need to be transmitted (see Chapter 6).

To enter a reminder message into an Investment register, just enter the date by which you want to be reminded in the Date text box, enter the action as Reminder, and then type your message in the Security or Memo text box. If you wanted to remind yourself about a certificate of deposit that needs to be either cashed or rolled over by June 3, 1998, for example, you set the date as 6/3/1998 and the action as Reminder. You might also enter the text **Cash Big National CD?** in the Memo text box.

The Billminder message box will include a note that says you have an investment reminder due when June 3, 1998, is right around the corner.

To enter a reminder message with an investment form, you follow the same basic process, but you click on the Easy Actions button and then select Advanced ➤ Reminder Transaction. Quicken then displays a dialog box that collects the date and the reminder message.

To stop Quicken from reminding you, you can delete the reminder message transaction or place an asterisk in the Clr text box to mark the reminder message as cleared.

Editing Mutual-Fund Transactions

Just as with the transactions that appear in any other account, you can edit investment account transactions. There are two ways to do this. The first—and most obvious—is to highlight the incorrect transaction in the register and then fix the incorrect pieces of the entry. Be sure to click on the Enter button when the edit is complete.

Another way you can fix a transaction is by using an investment form. To take this approach, you also select the transaction that needs to be fixed. Then you choose the Form button. Quicken displays an investment form like the one you might have used originally to record the transaction—but the dialog box is already filled out with the transaction's information. You just make your changes and click on OK.

Success Strategies for Mutual-Fund Record Keeping

Once you're familiar with the mechanics, you'll find it very easy to use Quicken to keep records of your mutual-fund investments. Before you make the jump, however, and start using Quicken for all your mutual-fund record keeping, here are some strategies to consider.

ShrsIn and ShrsOut versus BuyX and SellX

It can be confusing to choose between the ShrsIn and BuyX actions and between the ShrsOut and SellX actions. Follow this basic rule: Use the ShrsIn and ShrsOut transactions when the cash effect of an investment purchase or sale has already been recorded, and use the BuyX and SellX transactions when the cash effect of an investment purchase or sale hasn't yet been recorded.

In general, then, you use the ShrsOut and ShrsIn actions when you're entering old investment transactions so you have a historical record. And this raises an important question: Is it worth it to go back and enter historical records? I think it is if you're dealing with a taxable mutual fund—a mutual fund that's not being used as an IRA or a 401(k) plan account.

One of the biggest benefits of using Quicken for your mutual fund record keeping is that it lets you more easily track the tax basis, or cost, of the mutual-fund shares you've acquired through the years. When you sell the mutual-fund shares, you need to report the capital gain or loss stemming from the sale on a Schedule D tax form. And to do this, you'll need to know not only the sales proceeds, but also the cost of the shares you sell.

Reviewing the Investment Reports and Charts

Quicken's reports and charts provide a handy means of summarizing and organizing the investment information stored in the investment account registers. (Chapter 4 describes how you produce all of Quicken's reports—including its investment reports.)

Tracking Market Values

You can store current share price information about investments. By doing so you'll be able to track the market value of your mutual-fund investments over time. You'll also be able to calculate the performance of your mutual-fund investment over any time period. Your mutual fund probably provides the quarterly and annual returns of the fund in its quarterly and annual reports. If you invested sometime other than at the start of the year or the start of the quarter, however, these performance figures don't actually give the performance of your shares.

Entering Market Price Information

To provide the current price-per-share information to Quicken, follow these steps:

1. In the Investment Account register, display the Portfolio View window of the investment account, shown in Figure 17.15, by clicking on the Portfolio button at the top of the register or by choosing the Features ➤ Investments ➤ Portfolio View command.

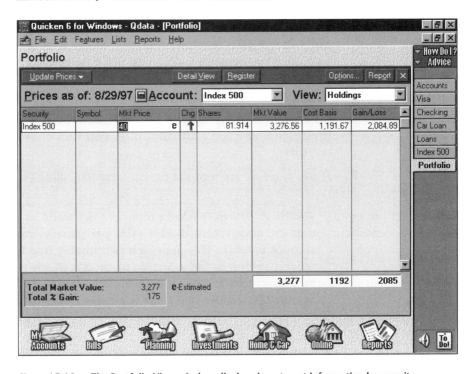

Figure 17.15.   The Portfolio View window displays investment information by security.

The Portfolio View window lists each of the securities you hold. (In the case of a mutual fund account with only one security, the list contains a single entry.) An *e* shows next to the prices of those security prices that are only estimates.

 NOTE Quicken uses an asterisk (*) to identify security prices that are estimates on investment portfolio value reports.

2. *If the date shown beneath the Portfolio View's button bar isn't the current date*, use the Calendar button located just to the right of the date display to select the current date.

3. *If you've set up more than one investment account*, make sure the Account list box to the right of the Date field shows *All Accounts* so you can update the market prices of all your securities, not just a single mutual fund.

4. Select the security for which you want to record the current market price.

5. Enter the current market price in the Mkt Price column. Typically, you can enter mutual-fund prices in dollars and cents, such as 13.87, but you can also use fractional prices, such as 8 7/8. (Use the + and − keys to incrementally adjust the price by one-eighth.) If the estimated price is correct, you can just press the asterisk key.

6. Repeat steps 4 and 5 to enter the current market price for each of the other mutual funds shown in the Portfolio View window. You will see the results of each adjustment as you move your cursor to the next security.

7. *If you want to return to the Register window*, click on the Register button.

 WARNING When Quicken produces a net worth or balance sheet report, it uses the most recent market price per share to calculate the value of an account balance. This approach is probably fine for personal net worth reports as long as the valuation method is clearly disclosed, but reporting securities at their fair market value on a business's balance sheet isn't the accepted convention unless the fair market value is less than the original cost.

Changing the Portfolio View

The View drop-down–list box lets you change the information shown in the Portfolio View window. If you activate this box, Quicken displays a list of seven views: Holdings (the default, or suggested, view), Performance, Valuation, Price Update, Quotes, Custom1, and Custom2. Each of these views shows the securities in the account, the security symbol, the market price per share, and the number of shares. Beyond this basic information, however, the views emphasize different aspects of your investments.

▶ The Holdings view emphasizes the security values by showing the number of shares held, the total market value of a security, the cost basis, and the unrealized capital gain or loss.

▶ The Performance view emphasizes the profitability of an investment by showing your original investment, the dollar return, and the percentage return.

▶ The Valuation view combines aspects of the Holdings and Performance view by showing by security the dollars invested, the return in dollars, and the total market value.

▶ The Price Update view emphasizes price-per-share information showing both the current price or estimated current price and the last recorded price.

▶ The Quotes view emphasizes share price and volume information, including the last price, the change from the opening price, the daily high, the daily low, and the daily shares volume. (Quicken gets the share price and volume information from Quicken Quotes.)

▶ The Custom1 and Custom2 views initially show the price per share, the number of shares, the market value, and the unrealized capital gain or loss, but you can change this.

> **NOTE** In general, a mutual fund will have only one security. You can, however, put more than one mutual-fund security in an account—for example, if you invest in a mutual-fund family.

Creating Custom Portfolio Views

You can create customized views of the Portfolio, as alluded to in the preceding sections. To do this, click on the Options button and then click on the Custom Views tab. Quicken displays the Custom Views tab of the Portfolio View Options dialog box, as shown in Figure 17.16. It provides a set of option buttons and drop-down–list boxes for specifying which investment information and which calculation results a custom view should display. (You can't hurt your Investment register data by experimenting with Portfolio view customization, so it's safe to learn about it by experimenting with the different options.)

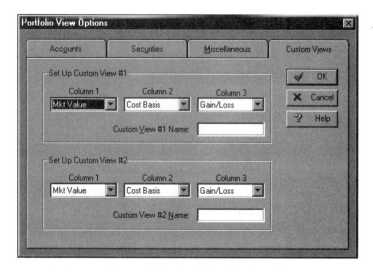

Figure 17.16.   **The Custom Views tab of the Portfolio View options dialog box**

Charting Market Price and Value Information

You can plot the total value of the selected security in the Portfolio View window as well as the price per share. Just click on the Detail View button. Quicken displays a window like the one shown in Figure 17.17. The Security Detail View window shows the price-per-share values and share volumes using charts. (If security has been split, you can mark the Adjust for Splits check box to tell Quicken to plot shares as if they were split from the very beginning.) The window also lists all transactions for a security using a scrollable list box. And it summarizes your holdings of a particular security (using the My Holdings box).

You can record investment activity when the Security Detail View window is displayed. This approach doesn't make as much sense for mutual funds as it does for brokerage investment accounts, but you should know the capability exists. To record investment transactions when the Security Detail View window is displayed, click on the Easy Actions button to display the Easy Actions menu and use its menu commands to display the appropriate investment form dialog box. Then fill

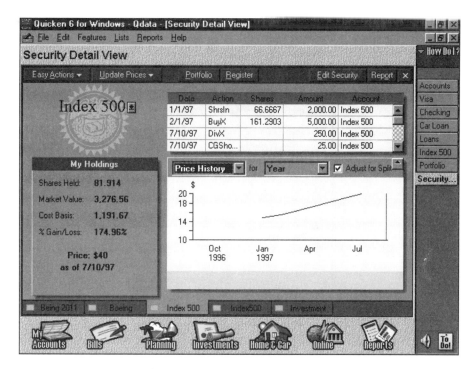

Figure 17.17.   *The Security Detail View window plots share prices and volumes in charts and provides other security-specific information.*

in the dialog box's text and combo boxes. For example, to record the purchase of mutual-fund shares, click on the Easy Actions button, choose the Buy/Add Shares command and use the Buy/Add Shares dialog box to describe the purchase.

You can expand the size of the share price and share volume charts by clicking on the small, upward-pointing arrowhead that appears above the top right corner of the chart. Figure 17.18 shows the expanded chart.

You can print the price history charts by clicking on the Print button that appears in the upper-right corner of the window, or by choosing the File ➤ Print Graph command. You can close the Graph Price History dialog box by clicking on its Close button.

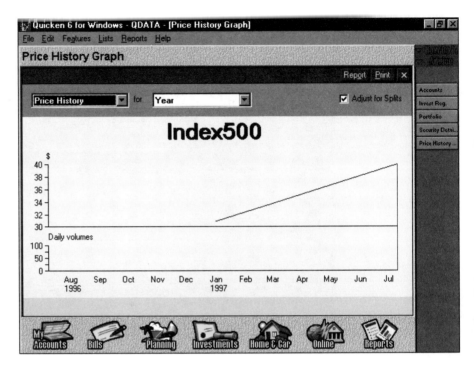

Figure 17.18.   *The Price History window shows an expanded version of the same charts shown by the Security Detail View window.*

Importing Prices

You can retrieve security price information from a delimited text file that contains the stock symbol for a security, its price, and optionally the date. Prodigy's Quote Track feature, for example, will create a delimited text file with security price information. And you may be able to download security prices from other online services too. Quicken Quotes, for example, lets you retrieve share price and volume information for each of the securities in your portfolio simply by clicking on the Update Prices command button and then choosing the Get Online Quotes command. (Refer to Chapter 18, *Stocks, Bonds, and Other Equity and Debt Securities*, for more information about Quicken Quotes and other online services as well.)

About the Prices Text File

Each security's pricing information needs to appear on a separate line of the text file, with the stock symbol first, then the price, and then the date, if this is included. The security price information can be enclosed in quotation marks, but it doesn't have to be. The three pieces of information need to be separated with commas. (In other words, the security pricing information needs to be a *comma-delimited* text file.) The file needs to use csv as its file extension. For example, to import pricing information for Allstate, Boeing, and Campbell Soup as of April 8, 1997, your text file would look like this:

```
ALL,28 3/8,4/8/1997

BA,38 3/4,4/8/1997

CPB,39 4/8/1997
```

As you can probably guess, the first line of the text file provides the security price for Allstate. (ALL is the Allstate symbol.) Its price on April 8, 1997, is 28³/₈. The second and third lines provide the security prices for Boeing (symbol BA) and Campbell Soup (symbol CPB).

Retrieving the Prices Information

To retrieve the prices information in the text file, display the Portfolio View window and choose the File ➤ File Operations ➤ Import Prices command. (This command shows only when the Portfolio View window is active.) Quicken displays the Import Price Data dialog box. Enter the full path and file name of the prices text file in the File text box. If the prices file doesn't contain dates—remember that the date is optional—verify that the security price date is shown in the Date text box and click on OK. Quicken imports the price data from the text file and uses this to update the securities prices shown in the Portfolio View window.

Entering and Correcting Old Price-per-Share Information

If you want to, you can go back and enter historical price data for a security. Once you've displayed the Portfolio View window, select the security and then choose the Update Prices command button and select Edit Price History . Quicken displays the Price History for dialog box, as shown in Figure 17.19.

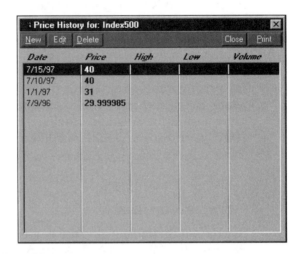

Figure 17.19.   **Price History dialog box**

To enter a new price, click on the New command button. Quicken displays the New Price for dialog box:

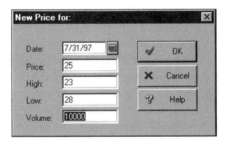

This dialog box provides five text boxes: Date, Price, High (Price), Low (Price), and Volume. To add a new price to the history, enter the date and price and click on OK. Optionally, enter the daily high price, daily low price, and the trading volume for that day. When you click on OK, Quicken adds the price to the price history.

To correct a price that already shows on the price history, select the price and then click on the Edit command button. Quicken displays the Edit Price dialog box, which asks what the correct share prices and volume should be for the selected date. To correct the prices or volume shown, enter this data and click on OK. Quicken updates the price history.

You can also delete a price from the price history. To do this, select the price and then select Delete.

If you want to print the Price History—perhaps to compare a hard copy list of the prices to an annual or quarterly mutual fund report—click on the Print command button, complete the Print dialog box that Quicken displays, and press Enter or click on OK.

To close the Price History dialog box and return to the Portfolio View window, click on Close.

HOW TO BE A SMART INVESTOR
on the Road to Riches

At the end of Chapter 14, in a section called *How to Achieve Financial Independence*, I suggest that creating wealth requires two very simple tactics: disciplined saving and smart investing. A lot of people, unfortunately, think smart investing means complicated investing. That's not true. Smart investing is usually simple investing. In fact, the most important things you can do relate to the way you go about investing, not the specific investments you pick.

The First Secret: Compound Interest

Compound interest represents the first secret. Does that seem strange? True, compound interest doesn't seem very powerful at first blush. You put, say, $1,000 into an investment that returns a 10 percent profit. The first year, the $1,000 earns $100. Let's say you leave the $100 in the savings account and add another $1,000 to boot. The second year, you earn $210. If you continue saving this way, you earn $330 in the third year.

Compound interest produces a very interesting result. Your interest earnings grow because you continue to add to your investment. Some of the addition comes from additional savings. But more and more of the interest earnings come from the interest you're earning on the interest—what's called compound interest.

By year seven, for example, you typically earn more in interest than the regular amount you annually save. And the interest earnings continue to grow and grow. After 25 years, you earn around $10,000 a year in interest. After 35 years, you earn around $27,000 a year in interest. After 45 years, you earn around $72,000 a year in interest. And all of this from a $1,000-a-year savings plan.

Nothing is tricky about compound interest. You need to be able to save some money and then reinvest the interest. And you need to be able to earn a decent interest rate, or investment rate of return (which is basically the same thing). By meeting these simple requirements, you can grow rich.

How quickly you grow rich depends on the interest rate and your savings. The higher the interest rate and the bigger the savings, the faster and more impressive the compounding.

The Second Secret: Opt for Tax-Deductible, Tax-Deferred Investment Choices

You need to use tax-deductible, tax-deferred investment vehicles such as individual retirement accounts (IRAs) or, even better, an employer's 401(k) or 403(b) plan. Let me show you how powerful these two tools are.

To provide a backdrop against which to discuss your future investing, let's suppose that your personal wealth target requires you to save $6,000 a year. This figure may be much more or much less than what your savings goal is, but we'll use $6,000 a year as an example. And just to make things fun, let's also pretend that $6,000 is an absolute impossibility. Let's say that you're currently spending every dollar you make and you couldn't come up with an extra $500 a month even if your life depended on it.

Here's the secret of meeting the $6,000-a-year goal: Tax-deductible investments let you borrow a huge chunk of the money from the federal and state government. Suppose, for example, that you're working with an employer who provides a 401(k) plan but doesn't contribute any matching money. You want to save $6,000 a year because that amount will ultimately allow you to become financially independent. By using a tax-deductible investment such as a 401(k), you would, in effect, be able to borrow roughly $2,000 a year. Here's why: If you stick $6,000 in your 401(k) plan, you will save about $2,000 in income taxes. Of the $6,000 in annual savings, then, $4,000 would come from your pocket and $2,000 would come from the federal and state government.

Notice what you've already accomplished by using the powerful concept of tax-deductible investing: you've cut your out-of-pocket cash by around a third.

Things get even better if you happen to work for an employer who matches a portion of your 401(k) contribution. Let's say, for example, that your employer matches your contributions by contributing $.50 to your savings for every $1.00 you contribute. The math gets a little tricky in this case. If you contribute $4,000, you get another $2,000 from your employer. You also get roughly $1,500 in government contributions in the form of tax savings. The bottom line is, you only need to come up with about $2,500 of your own money to reach your $6,000-a-year savings goal.

If you work for an employer who generously matches a portion of your 401(k) contributions, most of the money you need to achieve financial independence will come from your employer and the government. That's right—*most of the money comes from your employer and the government.*

In a tax-deferred investment vehicle like a 401(k) or IRA, income taxes on your interest or investment profits are deferred. For this reason, you effectively earn a much higher rate of interest inside a tax-deferred account. The reason is that the federal and state income taxes you pay on interest and investment income wipes out anywhere from 15 to 40 percent of your profit, with most people paying about a 30 percent tax on their profits. But inside a tax-deferred investment vehicle like a 401(k) or IRA, you might get to earn compound interest at the annual rate of 10 percent. Outside a tax-deferred investment vehicle, on the other hand, you might instead earn around 7 percent.

Those differences may not seem very big, but over time they have a cumulative impact on compound interest calculations. For example, suppose you are a 20-year-old adult just entering the work force and you're trying to decide how to invest $2,000 a year for retirement at age 65. If you compound interest using a 7 percent annual rate, you end up with around $570,000 by the time you retire. If you instead compound interest using a 10 percent annual rate, you end with around $1,400,000—roughly $800,000 more.

To sum things up, tax-deductible, tax-deferred investment vehicles are the best and most effective method of accumulating wealth. There is no better method for moving toward financial independence. None.

TIP You can save up to roughly $10,000 a year by using a 401(k) or 403(b) plan.

What if You're Unlucky?

The financial power of tax-deductible, tax-deferred investment choices such as 401(k)s begs an important but awkward question. Let's say your employer doesn't offer a 401(k) plan, 403(b) plan, or an equivalent tax-deductible, tax-deferred savings program. Is this whole tax-deductible, tax-deferred investing business such a big deal that you should consider switching employers?

First, if you're serious about achieving financial independence, I recommend moving to a new employer with a 401(k) or equivalent, tax-deductible, tax-deferred investment plan. The wealth creation benefits are just too enormous to pass up. Likewise, if your employer does offer a matching plan, well, free money is free money. I'm not saying that you should keep a job you hate, but I would think long and hard about leaving an employer who has put you on a fast track toward financial independence.

What if you're working where there isn't a 401(k)? If I were you, I would start by talking to other employees and gauging their interest. Then, assuming you're not alone in your feelings, I'd approach management. A simple 401(k) plan for a small company costs a few thousand bucks a year. As you know now, such a plan delivers enormous benefits. If it were me, I would rather have a 401(k) plan than a fancy holiday party or a summer picnic. If the truth be told, I'd even forgo part of my next raise.

I should note here, too, that you may be eligible to contribute up to $2,000 a year in a tax-deductible individual retirement account. If you're married and your spouse works, you may both be able to contribute $2,000 a year. Even if your employer doesn't provide a 401(k) plan, it may be worthwhile to save several thousand dollars a year by using tax-deductible investment choices. They may be all you need to progress toward your wealth target.

TIP Individual retirement account earnings on allowable contributions are always tax-deferred.

The Third Secret: Work Your Money Hard

Most people don't make their money work very hard. Not surprisingly, their profits reflect this. They earn returns of 3 or 5 percent. By working their money harder, they could have doubled or tripled their returns and earned 9 percent, 10 percent, or more.

You make your money work harder by investing in riskier investments. If the idea of investing in, say, the stock market, scares the living daylights out of you, you've made way too big a deal out of stock market risks.

Let's start by discussing the concept of risk. What you mean by risk, I'll venture, is really two things, volatility and the fear of losing your investment.

As for the volatility of the stock market, some days the market is up and some days the market is down. Up and down, up and down. It's enough to make some people sick. However, people make way too big a deal over day-to-day fluctuations in the weather. Stock prices are like the weather. Some days it's warmer and some days it's colder. Some days the market is up and some days the market is down. This up and down business gives the nightly news anchor something to talk about, but it's only so much blather. It's pseudo-news.

You don't let day-to-day temperature fluctuations bother you. The fact that it was two degrees colder last Thursday doesn't matter. Neither should you let day-to-day stock market fluctuations bother you. It's just plain silly. The only thing that really matters is the change in price between the time you buy a stock and the time you sell it.

The other feeling about risk, based on the fear of volatility, is that what you buy today for, say, $1,000, won't be worth $1,000 when you sell it. You have only to look at day-to-day fluctuations in the market to realize that. However, if you take the long view, you will see that the general trend in the stock market is always up. You can't buy a handful of stocks today and be certain that they will increase in value over the coming weeks, but you can be certain that they will grow in value over a decade or, even better, over two or three decades.

> **NOTE** Since 1926, common stocks have delivered an average 10 percent return.

"Well, even so," you're thinking, "I'll still stick with something a little safer. All that bouncing about makes me nauseous." Unfortunately, there is a simple problem with so-called safe investments: they appear to safe because their values don't jump around, but they aren't profitable. Your money doesn't earn anything or much of anything.

> **TIP** Since 1926, long-term corporate bonds have delivered an average 5 percent return. U.S. Treasury Bills over the same time period have delivered an average 3.5 percent return.

If you adjust the historical long-term bond return for inflation and income taxes, you just break even. If you adjust the historical U.S. Treasury Bill return for inflation and income taxes, you lose about a percent a year. These two options, remember, are so-called safe investments.

History teaches investors two lessons. One is that you profit by sticking your money in riskier investments such as stocks and real-estate—ownership investments. The other is that that you don't make any real profit by loaning your savings to the government, a corporation, or a local bank. To profit from your investments, you need to be an owner, not a loaner.

"Now, wait a minute," you're thinking. "That may be true over recent history. But the world is a far more dangerous place today. We can't be sure things will run so smoothly in the future."

Actually, I agree with you. But I would say that the last 70 or so years haven't been smooth. The stock market collapsed. The world suffered a global recession. A demoniac madman named Adolf Hitler almost succeeded in turning the entire world into a place of darkness. We saw the first use of nuclear weapons. We had a 50-year cold war that, for peace, relied upon the threat of thermonuclear exchange.

The world *is* a dangerous place, but it's been a dangerous place for a long time. And yet, in spite of all the terrible things that have happened, ownership investments have been profitable. For that reason, I firmly believe that the only way to achieve financial independence—the only way to accumulate any significant amount of wealth—is by investing money in ownership investments such as stocks or real estate.

The Fourth Secret: Broadly Diversify

There is one other point of which you need to be aware, and it's a very quick point but crucially important: You need to be well-diversified. Ideally, in fact, you should have a couple of dozen, equal-sized investments in different areas.

You should also make sure that you're not heavily dependent on a single industry or tied to a particular geographical location. You don't, for example, want to own twenty rental houses in the same town. And you wouldn't want to own twenty bank stocks.

This business about broadly diversifying is a statistical truth. Unfortunately, the statistics are too daunting—and too darn unpleasant—to explain here. Suffice it to say, the only way you can hope to achieve the average returns I've talked about in the preceding secret is by having enough individual investments so that they "average out" to the historical average.

Diversification has a really interesting ramification, by the way. Even with several thousand dollars of savings a year, you need, as a practical matter, to invest in mutual funds. To own a portfolio of, say, 20 or 25 common stocks and to keep your commissions cost reasonable, you would probably need to be able to invest $40,000 or $50,000 at a time. That way, you can purchase round, 100-share-lots of stocks, thereby lowering your expenses. To own a portfolio of 20 or 25 rental houses, you probably need to invest several times that much. You also have the challenge of geographically diversifying yourself. It is much harder, obviously, to own houses in many different parts of the country than it is to own stocks in many different places. So picking a mutual fund is the way to go.

Picking a stock mutual fund isn't tough. But rather than try to give you a bird's-eye view of this subject, I encourage you to read a wonderful book on the subject by Richard D. Irwin, called *Bogle on Mutual Funds* (Richard D. Irwin, Inc., 1994). John C. Bogle was chairman of The Vanguard Group of Investment Companies. This easy-to-read book provides hundreds of pages of worthwhile and honest advice on picking mutual funds.

The Fifth Secret: You Don't Have to Be a Rocket Scientist

None of this investment business requires as much know-how as is needed to be a rocket scientist. That's maybe the most important thing for you to know. All you need to know is the following, which I explained in the preceding pages:

▶ Compound interest is a mathematical truth that says you should regularly save and reinvest your profits.

▶ Use tax-deductible and tax-deferred investment choices such as 401(k)s and individual retirement accounts. These investment vehicles boost your savings and the interest rate you earn on your investments.

▶ The case for investing in ownership investments is simple: It's the only real way to make money over time.

▶ Diversification is important because it increases the probability that investment profits closely match the stock market's historical returns. However, for diversification to work, you must invest for long enough periods of time.

CHAPTER 18

Stocks, Bonds, and Other Equity and Debt Securities

FEATURING

F you invest in common stocks through a brokerage account, you can set up a special investment account that tracks all the securities you hold in the brokerage account. In addition, this special investment account keeps a record of the brokerage account's cash balance if the account includes an associated cash or money-market account.

Tracking stocks and other equity securities with Quicken works very much like tracking mutual funds, as described in Chapter 17. In fact, the only basic difference is that Quicken provides a lengthier list of investment actions since the cash effect of these transactions can affect the cash account associated with a brokerage account or your regular bank account.

Before You Begin

To track a stock investment in Quicken, you need:

▶ Records that document the stock you've purchased and sold (the raw data you want to record in Quicken).

▶ To know the mechanics of using the Quicken Investment register. (To keep records of stock investments, you use many of the same windows, dialog boxes, and commands you do to keep records of mutual funds.)

Setting Up a Brokerage Account

You'll need to set up a separate investment account for each brokerage account you have. If you have one brokerage account with a full-service broker and another with a discount broker, you need two investment accounts. If you also hold stocks (and other securities) outside of a brokerage account, you can set up another investment account for these.

TIP   A good general rule is to set up an investment account for each brokerage statement you receive.

Setting Up the Quicken Investment Account

To set up an investment account for tracking stocks and other securities, follow these steps:

1. Click on the Accounts Quicktab or choose the Lists ➤ Account command to display the Account List document window.

2. Click on the New button in the Accounts List document window or choose the Edit ➤ Account ➤ New to display the dialog box you use to create a new account.

3. Click on the Investment button and then Next to display the Investment Account Setup dialog box.

4. Click on the Summary tab. Quicken displays the Summary tab of the Investment Account Setup dialog box, as shown in Figure 18.1.

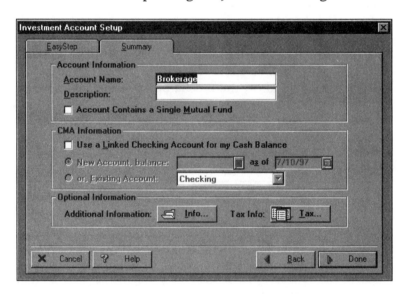

Figure 18.1.   The Summary tab of the Investment Account Setup dialog box

5. Enter an account name in the Account Name text box.

6. *If you want to enter a description of the brokerage account or additional account information, such as the account number,* use the Description text box.

7. Make sure the Account Contains a Single Mutual Fund check box is not marked. This tells Quicken that you'll use the account for tracking a brokerage account.

8. *If your brokerage account includes a cash account or cash-management account (it probably does),* mark the Use a Linked Checking Account for my Cash Balance check box. If your investment account uses a linked cash account, Quicken assumes that any time an investment action affects cash, the cash goes into or comes out of the linked cash account.

9. *If you need to set up a new account for the Linked Account,* mark the New Account button. Specify the account balance using the Balance text box and the transaction date Quicken should use for the opening balance transaction using the As of box.

10. *If you will use an existing checking account,* mark Or Existing Account option button and then select the account from the Or Existing Account drop-down–list box.

11. Click on Tax. Quicken displays the Tax Schedule Information dialog box, as shown in Figure 18.2.

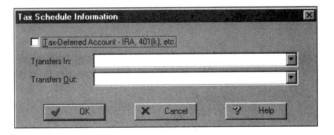

Figure 18.2. **The Tax Schedule Information dialog box**

12. *If the investments in the brokerage account won't produce taxable income or tax-deductible capital losses,* mark the Tax-Deferred Account check box. This tells Quicken that it should not count this account's income and expense amounts as taxable or tax-deductible.

13. *If the transfers into and out of the investment account should be reported on your income tax return,* use the Transfers In and Transfers Out drop-down–list boxes to identify on which tax-return form or schedule (and on which line on the form or schedule) these transfers should be reported. (In the case of a mutual-fund investment that's part of your

Individual Retirement Account. For example, transfers to the account are reported as IRA contributions.) Click on OK when you finish entering this information.

 NOTE *If you want to store additional information about an account,* **click on the Info button to display the Additional Account Information dialog box. You can use it to further describe the brokerage firm in the Bank Name text box, the brokerage account number in the Account Number text box, and so forth. (Some of these fields don't make sense for an investment account because Quicken uses the same Additional Account Information dialog boxes for all account types.) Be sure to click on OK on the information screen when you have completed the entries.**

---

14. Click on Done to tell Quicken the Investment Account Setup Information dialog box is complete. Quicken displays the Investment Setup dialog box, which you can use to describe the securities (individual stocks and bonds) you'll track with the account. However, I recommend you not use the Investment Setup dialog box and instead individually set up securities on your own, as described in the next section of this chapter. If you want to follow my suggestion, click on Cancel to close the Investment Setup dialog box. Alternatively, to use the Investment Setup dialog box, just follow the on-screen instructions.

Describing the Stocks You Already Hold

Once you've set up the brokerage account, you're ready to describe the stocks you hold in the account. To do this, you describe the individual stocks or securities and provide the number of shares and original purchase-price information.

Naming the Stocks or Securities You Hold

To name the stocks or securities you hold once you've provided the starting cash balance, display the brokerage account's register. Then follow these steps:

1. Choose the Lists ➤ Investment ➤ Security command to display the Security List window, as shown in Figure 18.3.

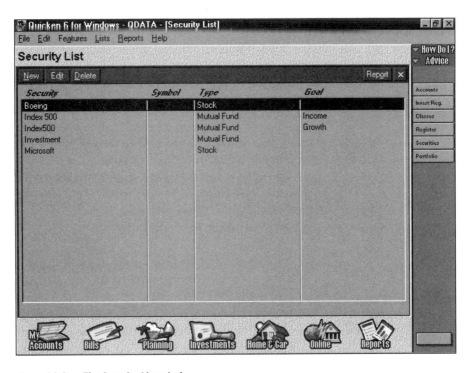

Figure 18.3. **The Security List window**

2. Click on the New button in the Security List window to display the Set Up Security dialog box, as shown in Figure 18.4.

Figure 18.4. **The Set Up Security dialog box**

3. Enter the name of the security in the Name text box.

4. *If you want to import security prices from a text file or use Quicken Quotes to download security prices with your modem,* enter the symbol used to identify the stock in the Symbol text box.

5. From the Type drop-down–list box, select Stock.

> **NOTE** You can create your own security type by choosing the Lists ➤ Investment ➤ Security Type command. Quicken displays the Security Type List dialog box. Select New to display the Set Up Security Type dialog box. Then enter a name for the new security type into the Type text box and use the Price Display option buttons to indicate whether you want to use cents or fractional dollars for the security's price.

6. *If you've earmarked this investment as funds for a specific purpose,* select the appropriate investment goal from the Goal drop-down–list box.

> **NOTE** You can create your own goal by choosing the Lists ➤ Investment ➤ Investment Goal command. Quicken displays the Investment Goal List dialog box. Select New to display the Set Up Investment Goal dialog box. Then enter a goal in the Investment Goal dialog box.

7. If you want to collect additional information about the security, click on the Other Info button. Then when Quicken displays the Additional Security Information dialog box, use its boxes and buttons to further describe the security. And mark the Tax-Free check box if you don't pay taxes on the income produced by the security. And if you want to track estimated income for a security, use the Est. Annual Income ($) per Share text box. When you finish entering any additional information, click on OK. Quicken closes the dialog box and redisplays the Set Up Security dialog box.

8. Click on OK when the Set Up Security dialog box is complete. Quicken adds the stock to the security list and redisplays the Security List window.

9. Repeat steps 2 through 8 for each stock or each stock lot you want to add. When you finish, close the Security List window.

> **TIP** You can track shares of mutual funds that invest in stocks and shares of publicly-traded real-estate investment trusts the same way you track stocks. You may want to set-up securities for these other equity investments now, too.

Describing the Shares of Stock You Hold

To describe each of the shares you hold, you need to know the number of shares of each stock or lot, the price per share (or the stock or lot total), and the commission paid (if any).

You can describe the shares you hold either by entering them directly in the register or by using an investment form. I described the "directly into the register" approach in Chapter 15. Because the investment form approach makes most sense for brokerage accounts, I'll describe that method here.

To describe each of the stocks or lots you hold using an investment form, first display the investment account register window (as described earlier) or display the Detail View window (by clicking on the Detail View button on the investment register or portfolio view window). Then follow these steps:

Part 3

Quicken for Investors

1. Choose the Easy Actions button to display the Action menu and then choose the Buy/Add Shares command to display the Add Shares to Account dialog box, as shown in Figure 18.5. Click on the Summary tab to display the buttons and boxes you'll use to describe your holding.

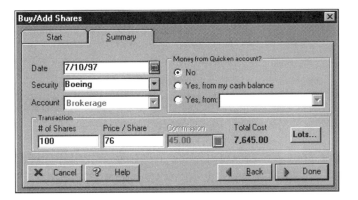

Figure 18.5.   **Summary tab of the Buy/Add Shares dialog box**

NOTE You don't have to position the cursor on a blank register row to enter a transaction using the Easy Actions menu command. Quicken automatically enters your investment transaction into the next empty row of the register.

2. Enter the stock or lot purchase date in the Date text box.

> **TIP** Be sure to enter the actual purchase date. Quicken categorizes any capital gain or loss as short-term or long-term based on the difference between the purchase and sales dates shown in the register.

3. Enter the stock name in the Security text box or use the Security dropdown list to select it. (You specified this name using the Set Up Security dialog box as part of naming the stocks you hold.)

4. Enter the shares you purchased in the Number of Shares text box.

5. Enter the price per share you paid using the Price/Share text box.

> **NOTE** You can enter stock prices either as dollars and cents (7.50) or as fractional amounts (7 1/8.) If the Price text box is highlighted, you can incrementally adjust the price by eighths using the + and − keys.

6. Enter the brokerage commission you paid using the Commission text box.

7. Click on Done, and Quicken records the transaction into the Investment register.

8. Repeat steps 1 through 7 to record each of the stocks or lots you hold.

> **NOTE** If you hold mutual funds in a brokerage account, you can treat these as stocks for purposes of your investment record keeping.

Keeping Records of Your Stock Purchases, Sales, and Profits

Once you've set up the brokerage account records, you're ready to begin recording stock purchases, sales, and any profits. If you've used Quicken for mutual fund record keeping, by the way, you'll notice many similarities in the way stock investment record-keeping works.

Describing the Shares You Buy

Whenever you buy additional shares of a stock, you'll need to record the purchase. To do this, you name the security as described earlier in the chapter and record the purchase of shares. You can record the purchase of new shares either directly into the register or using the Action menu's Buy command. To record the purchase of shares using the Buy command, follow these steps:

1. Click on the Easy Actions menu and choose the Buy/Add Shares button to display the Buy/Add Shares dialog box. Click on its Summary tab (see Figure 18.5).

2. Enter the purchase date, stock name, number of shares purchased, and the price per share you paid in the appropriate boxes.

3. Enter the sales commission or transaction fee paid using the Commission text box.

4. *If you need to record some additional piece of information*, perhaps to record the confirmation order number or to indicate whether you decided to buy this stock on the basis of the broker's recommendation or your own analysis, use the Memo text box.

5. *If you are using cash from an account besides the brokerage account*, mark the Yes From button and then use the Yes From combo box to show which account you wrote the check from to pay for the purchase.

NOTE If you enter an account name in the Yes From combo box, Quicken records a payment transaction in the account. If you don't enter an account name, Quicken reduces the cash held in your brokerage account.

6. Click on Done, and Quicken records the transaction into the Investment register.

Describing Dividend Interest and Capital-Gains Distributions

Many companies disburse a quarterly dividend to their shareholders, and sometimes they even disburse special dividends—as the result of a particularly good year, perhaps. And mutual funds, which you can also track in a brokerage account, may pay interest or capital gains.

You can record these sorts of investment profits either directly into the register (as described in the last chapter) or by using an investment form. The investment form approach, by far the easiest, is described here.

TIP You don't need to worry about which kind of distribution is which. The 1099 statement (and probably the brokerage statement, too) will tell you what kind of distribution you've received.

To record a dividend, interest, or capital gains distribution using the Income command and dialog box, follow these steps:

1. Click on the Easy Actions button and then choose the Record An Income Event command to display the Record Income dialog box:

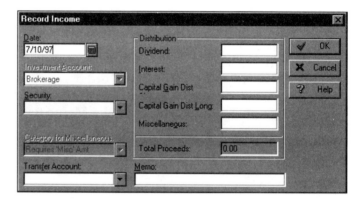

2. Enter the distribution date, stock name, amount of the dividend, interest payment, short-term capital gain payment, and long-term capital gain payment in the appropriate text boxes.

3. Enter the amount of any other payment in the Miscellaneous text box. Use the Miscellaneous combo box to show how the miscellaneous payment should be categorized. (Quicken doesn't show this combo box until you enter an amount in the Miscellaneous text box.)

4. *If you will deposit the distribution in another account*—in other words, not the brokerage account—use the Transfer Account combo box to identify the other account. Note, however, that this combo box isn't available unless you're using an account that doesn't have a linked cash account.

5. *If you need to record some additional piece of information*—for example, to cross-reference the source that documents the distribution—use the Memo text box.

6. Click on OK.

Recording Reinvestment Transactions

Sometimes you reinvest investment profits by purchasing additional shares of a stock or mutual fund. Some companies even have formal reinvestment programs called DRIPs (Dividend Reinvestment Programs). With a DRIP, you get to buy additional shares of a company—using your dividends—and often without having to pay any commissions or transaction fees.

To record reinvested investment profits, you can use either the register or an investment form, but the investment form approach is the easiest and most efficient. (To learn how to record reinvestment transactions directly into the register, see Chapter 15.)

1. Choose the Reinvest Income command from the Easy Actions menu to display the Reinvest Income dialog box:

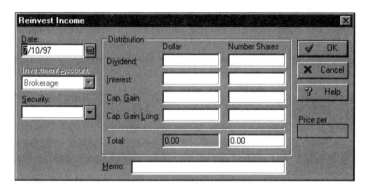

2. Enter the reinvestment date and stock name in the appropriate text boxes.

3. Use the Dividend Dollar Amount and Number Shares text boxes to describe the dividends you reinvested and the number of shares acquired with the dividends.

4. Use the Interest Dollar Amount and Number Shares text boxes to describe the number of shares acquired with the interest.

5. Use the Capital Gain Short Dollar Amount and Number Shares text boxes to describe the short-term capital gains you reinvested and the number of shares acquired with the capital gains money.

6. Use the Capital Gain Long Dollar Amount and Number Shares text boxes to describe the long-term capital gains you reinvested and the number of shares acquired with the capital gains money.

Part 3

Quicken for Investors

NOTE Using the values you enter in the Dollar Amount and Number Shares text boxes, Quicken calculates the total dollar amount reinvested and the total number of shares purchased by reinvesting, as well as the average price per share you're paying.

7. *If you need to record additional information about the reinvestment,* use the Memo text box.

8. Click on OK, and Quicken records the distribution and the purchase of new shares.

Describing the Shares You Sell

As with the other types of stock transactions you record, describing the shares you sell is easy as long as you have the necessary information: the number of shares sold, the price per share (or the transaction total), and the commission paid (if any).

NOTE You can record a short-sale transaction. Quicken asks you to confirm your action, however, since it knows you don't hold the stock you're selling.

You can record stock sales either directly into the register or by using an investment form, but the investment form approach is easiest. Just follow these steps:

1. Click on the Easy Actions button and choose the Sell/Remove Shares command to display the Sell/Remove Shares dialog box. Click on the Summary tab.

2. Enter the sales date in the Date text box.

TIP Be sure to enter the actual sales date. Quicken categorizes any capital gain or loss as short-term or long-term based on the difference between the purchase and sale dates shown in the register.

3. Name the stock you're selling using the Security combo box.

4. Enter the number of shares you sold using the Number of Shares text box.

5. Enter the sales price per share you received using the Price/Share text box.

6. Enter the sales commission or transaction fee using the Commission text box.

7. *If you want to use specific identification,* click on the Lots command button on the far right side of the Transaction section. In the Specify Lots for dialog box, identify the lots you want to sell. (For more information about specific identification of shares, see the section "Describing the Mutual Fund Shares You Sell" in Chapter 17.)

8. *If you will deposit the sales proceeds in some account other than the brokerage one,* click on the Yes To button and use the Yes To combo box to show the account. Alternatively, mark the No button if you don't want to record the proceeds. (Note: By default, Quicken assumes you will deposit proceeds into a cash, or linked, account.)

9. Click on Done, and Quicken records the transaction.

Stock Splits, Stock Dividends, and Reminders

Chapter 17 explained how you record stock split transactions and investment reminder transactions in mutual-fund accounts. These two transactions work the same way for brokerage accounts.

One point I should make here, however, concerns stock dividends. With a stock dividend a company might increase the number of shares held by each shareholder by a set percentage. A company, for example, might give current shareholders a 20 percent stock dividend. In this case, the company increases the number of shares held by each shareholder by 10 percent.

Stock dividends are really just stock splits, and to record them you enter the old-shares-to-new-shares ratio. If a company issued a 10 percent dividend, for example, the ratio is 1 to 1 to 1. In other words, for every old share, a stockholder receives 1.1 new shares.

 TIP Quicken also provides a special advanced action for stock dividends. To use this action, click on the Easy Actions button, choose Advanced, and then choose Stock Dividend. Quicken displays a dialog box that collects the information it needs to record a stock split transaction that shows the effect of the stock dividend.

Recording Brokerage Account Fees

Many brokerage accounts levy annual fees. Some also charge exit fees when you close the account. Recording these account fees isn't difficult, but how you record them depends on the type of investment account you've set up.

If you've set up an investment account that has a linked cash account, you record these fees directly into the linked cash account's register as an account withdrawal. When you record the withdrawal, you categorize the expense as falling into an investment expense category. This process, by the way, works the same way as recording bank service charges for a regular bank account.

If you've set up an investment account that doesn't have a linked cash account, you can use either the investment register or an investment form. Using an investment form is easiest. To record one of these fees using an investment form, follow these steps:

1. Click on the Easy Actions button and choose the Miscellaneous Expense command to display the Miscellaneous Expense dialog box.

2. Enter the date the fee is charged in the Date text box.

3. *If the fee is tied to a specific stock or if you have only one stock in the account,* enter the stock's name in the Security text box.

4. Enter the amount of the fee in the Amount text box.

5. In the Category drop-down list, select the expense category you use to track and tally investment expenses. (Investment expenses may be deductible as miscellaneous deductions.)

6. *If you need to further describe the fee—for example, to note that a fee is charged annually for account maintenance*—use the Memo text box.

7. Click on OK, and Quicken records the account fee and adjusts the brokerage account's cash balance accordingly.

 NOTE If you write a check to pay an account fee, you don't need to do anything special in the Investment register. You just write the check in the usual way—probably by using the Write Checks window or the Register window. Be sure, however, to categorize the check that pays an account fee as investment expense since it may qualify as a miscellaneous deduction.

Recording Cash Balance Interest and Miscellaneous Brokerage-Account Income

It's likely that you'll earn interest or other income on the cash balances you hold in your brokerage account. To record this, you choose the Record an Income Event command from the Easy Actions menu and fill out the Record Income dialog box. I described how you use this command to record income from stocks earlier in the chapter. The only thing different about recording cash-balance interest and miscellaneous brokerage account income is that you don't identify a specific security.

TIP The 1099 or brokerage account statement will indicate what kind of distribution the check is for.

NOTE You can reconcile mutual-fund investment accounts and brokerage investment accounts. In a mutual fund you reconcile just the shares, and in a brokerage account you reconcile shares and the cash balance. Mechanically, though, reconciling an investment account works like reconciling a bank account (see Chapter 5). Once you do this, you'll have no trouble reconciling investment accounts.

Handling Tricky Stock Investment Transactions

The earlier portions of this chapter described the most common investment transactions you need to record for common stocks you hold in a brokerage account. There are, however, several additional transactions you may need to record—particularly if you're an aggressive investor (one who's willing to bear increased risk in the pursuit of greater returns). I'll briefly describe how you record these other transactions here.

Short Sales

A *short sale* occurs when you sell stock you don't actually hold. The logic of a short sale is that rather than buying low and later selling high, you first buy high and then sell low. (To effect the transaction, you actually borrow the stock from your broker.)

To record a short sale transaction in Quicken, you just sell a stock you don't own. To show that these are shares you actually owe your broker, Quicken displays the number of shares and the current market value as negative amounts in the Portfolio View window.

To record the transaction in which you close out your short position by buying the stock you've previously sold, you record a stock purchase in the usual way.

Margin Loans and Margin Interest

If you purchase a security and the total purchase cost exceeds the cash balance in a brokerage account, Quicken assumes you've borrowed the needed cash on margin from your broker. To show the margin loan, it displays the cash balance as a negative value.

▶ To record margin-loan interest in cases where you have a linked cash account, you record the margin loan interest as an expense when you record the withdrawal from the linked cash account that pays the margin interest.

▶ To record margin loan interest in cases where you don't have a linked cash account, you choose Easy Actions ➤ Advanced ➤ Margin Interest Expense. When Quicken displays the Margin Interest Expense dialog box, use it to describe the margin interest.

Writing Calls and Puts

A *call* is an option to buy a share of stock. A *put* is an option to sell a share of stock. When you write a call or put, what you really do is collect money from someone in return for promising the person the option, to buy or sell a share of stock at a specified, or strike, price by some future date.

When a call or put expires without being exercised—and this is the usual case—recording the transaction is simple. If you're the one writing the call or put, you just record the transaction as miscellaneous income.

Buying Calls and Puts

If you're the one buying the call or put, you just record the option purchase the way you do any other stock purchase. If the call or put expires and becomes worthless, you just record the sale as a stock pur-chase with the amount set to 0. (This is the most common case.)

If, on the other hand, you sell the call or put before the expiration date because the call or put can be profitably exercised, you record the sale as a stock sale with the amount set to whatever you sell the option for.

Exercising Calls and Puts

You probably won't actually exercise a call or put. You'll probably sell it, as described above. If you do exercise a call or buy option, however, you need to record two transactions.

▶ To record the exercise of a call option, first record a transaction that sells the call option for 0. Then record a transaction that purchases the optioned number of shares at the option price.

▶ To record the exercise of a put option, first record a transaction that sells the put option for 0. Then record a transaction that sells the optioned number of shares at the option price.

TIP   For income tax purposes, what you pay for a call needs to be counted as part of the purchase price if you exercise the call option and purchase shares. What you receive for a put needs to be counted as part of the sales price if you exercise the put and sell shares. This can get a little complicated, so you may want to consult your tax advisor.

Employee Stock Options

You can track the value of employee stock options like you track shares of stock. (The purchase price in this case is 0 if you don't pay anything for the option.) The value of the option, of course, is the difference between the exercise price and the fair market value of the vested shares.

The income tax accounting for stock options can get a little tricky, depending on whether the options are part of a qualified incentive stock option plan or a nonqualified stock option plan. You may have a taxable gain when you are granted or when you exercise the option, or you may have a taxable gain only later when you sell the shares. If you have questions about the income tax treatment, consult your tax advi-sor. You'll need to show him or her the stock option plan document, so be sure to bring that with you.

Dealing with Corporate Reorganizations, Mergers, and Spin-Offs

If you look closely at the Easy Actions menu that Quicken displays when you click on the Easy Actions button, you will notice that the last command, Advanced, actually displays another submenu of investment actions. Most people won't need to use these options, but those I haven't already described earlier are briefly described here:

Action	Description
Transfer Shares Between Accounts	Lets you move securities between investment accounts.
Corporate Name Change	Lets you change the name of a security without losing any of your financial records for the security.
Corporate Securities Spin-Off	Lets you describe new securities you're adding to an account as coming from existing securities you already own. In this way, your rate of return calculations don't ignore "spun-off" securities in their calculations of investment profits.
Corporate Acquisition (Stock for Stock)	Lets you record stock-for-stock corporate mergers.
Stock Dividend (non-stock dividend)	Lets you record a stock dividend, which is essentially a type of a stock split.

Bonds and Other Debt Securities

To keep records for bonds and other debt securities, you use the same brokerage account described earlier in the chapter. Tracking them works very much like tracking stocks.

Getting Ready for Bond Record Keeping

You'll need to set up a separate investment account for each brokerage account you have. If you have one brokerage account with a full-service broker and another with a discount broker, you need to set up two investment accounts. If you also hold stocks and bonds outside of a brokerage account, you can set up another investment account for these.

Once you've set up the brokerage account, you're ready to describe the bonds and any other debt securities you hold in the account. This process works the same way for bonds and debt securities as it does for stocks and mutual funds.

> **WARNING** Bond prices are quoted as a percentage of their face, or par, value. A $1,000 par value bond that sells for $950, for example, has a price of 95. Because Quicken calculates the total security amount as the price times the quantity, however, you can't enter the bond price as a percentage. Instead, you need to enter the actual dollar price. To describe a bond you've purchased for $950, for example, you enter the price as $950.

Keeping Records of Your Bond Purchases, Sales, and Profits

Once you've set up the brokerage account records, you're ready to begin recording bond purchases, sales, and any profits. If you've used Quicken for stock investment record keeping, you'll find that bond record keeping works pretty much the same way.

Describing the Bonds You Buy

Whenever you buy additional bonds, you need to record the purchase and any accrued interest, so you actually record two transactions. As with stocks and mutual funds, you can record bond purchases directly into the register or by using an investment form. Because the investment form approach is easiest, it's the one I'll describe here. (To learn how to record transactions directly into the register, see Chapter 17. It describes how you record mutual fund transactions directly into the register, but the same basic approach works for stocks and bonds.)

To record a bond purchase, follow these steps:

1. Choose the Buy/Add Shares command from the Easy Actions menu and then click on the Summary tab to display the Buy/Add Shares dialog box, as shown in Figure 18.6.

Figure 18.6. **The Buy/Add Shares dialog box**

2. Enter the purchase date in the Date text box, the bond name in the Security combo box, and the quantity of bonds you purchased in the Number of Shares text box.

3. Enter the dollar price per bond you paid in the Price/Share text box. (Remember that Quicken expects you to enter the actual dollar price you paid, not the price as a percentage of the bond's face, or par, value.)

> **WARNING** You don't include the accrued interest in the bond price in step 3. You record that bit of information later.

4. Enter the brokerage commission you paid in the Commission text box.

> **NOTE** You can enter any three of the following four inputs: Number of Shares, Price, Commission/Fee, or Total of Sale. Using the three values you do enter, Quicken calculates the fourth value.

5. *If you will use cash from some other account for the purchase instead of cash from the brokerage account,* mark the Yes From button and use the Yes From combo box to add the account. You only do this, however, when you're not using a linked cash account.

6. Click on Done, and Quicken records the transaction.

After you record the bond purchase, you usually need to record accrued interest paid to the previous holder. In effect, what you're really doing by paying accrued interest is giving the previous bond holder his or her share of the next interest payment. To record this accrued interest, follow these steps:

1. Click on the Easy Actions button and then choose the Return of Capital command to display the Return of Capital dialog box, as shown in Figure 18.7.

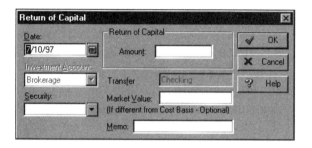

Figure 18.7.   The Return of Capital dialog box

2. Enter the purchase date in the Date text box and the bond or lot name in the Security text box.

3. In the Amount text box, enter the accrued interest you paid as a negative number.

4. *If you want to identify the transaction as an accrued interest adjustment,* use the Memo text box.

5. Click on OK, and Quicken records the accrued interest transaction.

Describing Bond Interest and Return of Capital Distributions

Most bonds pay monthly or semi-annual interest. In addition, some bonds—for example, mortgage-backed securities such as GNMA bonds—return a portion of the bond principal with each interest payment.

TIP   Don't worry about which kind of distribution is which. The 1099 statement (and probably the brokerage statement, too) tells you what kind of distribution you've received.

As with other investment transactions, you have a choice as to how you record bond interest and return of capital transactions. You can enter these transactions directly into the register, as discussed in

Part
3

Quicken for Investors

Chapter 17, or you can use an investment form. An investment form is the easier method, so it's the one I'll review here.

To return an interest payment, click on the Easy Actions button and select Record an Income Event. In the Record Income dialog box, identify the interest payment date, the security paying the interest, and the amount. You fill in the Record Income dialog box's text and combo boxes as described in Chapter 17 and earlier in this chapter. The steps for recording bond income largely parallel those for recording stock or mutual fund income.

To record a return of capital distribution—including the payment of interest you previously accrued—you click on the Easy Actions button and choose the Return of Capital command. When Quicken displays the Return of Capital dialog box, give the interest payment date, name the security paying the interest, and indicate the amount of previously accrued interest you're now receiving.

Recording Accrued Interest Shown on a 1099-OID

You aren't always paid the interest you've earned. If you purchase a negotiable certificate of deposit, for example, the bank issuing the CD may accrue the interest you've earned through the end of the year and then add this amount to the CD's value. If you purchase a zero-coupon bond, you don't receive periodic interest payments at all. Rather, the bond issuer accrues interest each year and then repays the bond and the total accrued interest at maturity. Even though you aren't paid interest, you need to record the interest you've earned because you need to report the accrued interest as taxable income. Fortunately, in most cases the bond issuer sends a 1099-OID form that reports on the amount of accrued but not paid interest.

NOTE Bond issuers also report the amortization of original-issue discounts on 1099-OID forms. In fact, OID is an acronym for Original Issue Discount. Because original-issue discounts effectively increase the annual interest earnings, you also need to record these.

To record accrued interest, you actually record two transactions, as described in Chapter 17 and earlier in this chapter. You click on the Easy Actions button, choose the Record an Income Event command button and then complete the Record Income dialog box. Then you click on the Easy Actions button, choose the Return of Capital command, and fill in the Return of Capital dialog box so it describes the accrued but unpaid interest as a negative return of capital. (This is the same technique used earlier in the chapter to deal with accrued interest paid with the bond purchase.) By entering the return of capital as a negative number, Quicken increases the bond cost, or carrying value, by the accrued interest amount.

ACCRUED INTEREST AND THE 1099-OID FORM

Accrued interest income can get messy when, for income tax purposes, you need to record accrued interest that isn't reported on a 1099-OID form. The reason is that you're required to report the accrued interest—even though you won't get a 1099-OID amount. Later on, when you ultimately do get a 1099-INT or 1099-OID that includes the previously recorded accrued interest, you need to adjust this figure so it doesn't double-count the accrued interest. Many people don't report accrued interest income until it's reported on a 1099-OID form or actually paid and reported on a 1099-INT form. With this simplified approach, you don't evade income taxes on the interest income, but you do delay paying the income taxes. Once the interest is accrued, the IRS does insist that you pay income taxes. If this applies to your situation, talk to your tax advisor.

Describing the Bonds You Sell

Describing the bonds you sell is easy as long as you have the necessary information: the number of bonds sold, the price per share (or the transaction total), and the commission paid (if any). You also need to know the amount of accrued interest you will be paid.

As with other investment transactions, you can record bond sales either directly into the register or by using an investment form. Still, using an investment form is easiest. To record a bond sale, you click on the Easy Actions button, choose the Sell/Remove Shares button and, in the Sell/Remove Shares dialog box, you give the sales date, name the bond being sold, give the sales amount and sales commission, and indicate where you'll deposit the money. (Chapters 17 and 18 describe how investment sale transactions work.)

After you record the bond sale, you need to record the amount of accrued interest you're being paid. (In effect, the bond purchaser pays you your share of the next interest payment.) To do this, you click on the Easy Actions button, choose the Record an Income Event command, and fill out the Record Income dialog box so it describes the accrued interest being paid. From your perspective, it's irrelevant that the bond purchaser rather than the bond issuer pays the interest, so recording this accrued interest payment works just like recording a regular interest coupon payment, as described earlier in this chapter.

Recording Early Withdrawal Penalty Transactions

Early withdrawal penalties on certificates of deposit are a special type of tax-deductible expense. Like IRA contributions, alimony, and a few other items, they are deductions from your total income and are used to calculate your adjusted gross income. Therefore, be sure to record any early withdrawal penalties you pay with a separate transaction. If you're using an investment account with a linked cash account, record the early withdrawal penalty as if it's paid from the cash account. If you're not using an investment with a linked cash account, use the Easy Actions menu's Miscellaneous Expense command. In either case, when you do record the early withdrawal penalty, categorize the early withdrawal penalty expense in a way that lets you easily report this penalty on your income tax return. (You might want to set up a new expense category called Early Withdrawal Penalty.)

Quick Tips for Tracking Other Debt Securities

You can use Quicken to keep records of most other debt securities. Here's a list of some of the other common debt securities, along with suggestions as to how you can treat them in Quicken:

Debt Security	How To Handle It
Certificates of deposit	Treat negotiable certificates of deposit like bonds. (Mechanically, jumbo negotiable CDs are almost identical to corporate and government bonds.) Consider treating non-negotiable certificates like bank accounts.
U.S. savings bonds	Treat these as you do a regular bond. You won't record interest payments, but you will need to accrue interest.
Zero-coupon bonds	Treat these the same way you would U.S. Savings Bonds. You won't need to record interest payments (the bond won't pay these) but you will need to accrue interest.

Understanding Quicken's Annual Return Calculations

The Investment Performance Report calculates an internal rate of return for each security, as described in Chapter 4. Here I'll describe why you use the internal rate of return (IRR) tool and how it compares with the other standard performance measurement tools.

What Is an IRR?

The IRR tool calculates the annual profit an investment delivers as a percentage of the investment's value at the start of the year. For example, in a simple case, if you buy an investment for $100 and the investment pays $10 in dividends at the end of the year and then is sold for $95, your IRR is 5 percent.

There are actually two steps to making this calculation. First, you need to calculate the annual profit. You can do this by combining the $10 of dividends with the $5 capital loss (calculated as $95–$100) for a result of $5 of annual profit. Second, you divide the $5 of annual profit by the $100 investment value at the start of the year. $5/$100 equals 5 percent, and that's the IRR.

By calculating an IRR you get to quantify the performance of a stock you've purchased and of your investment portfolio as a whole. This is particularly true with individual stocks and brokerage accounts because you often don't really know how your stock picks, your broker's picks, and your portfolio have done and are doing relative to the market as a whole and relative to other investments.

NOTE In comparison, you usually have a pretty good idea as to how well a mutual fund does on a quarterly or at least an annual basis. The fund manager will report to you on the quarterly and annual returns.

Some Mechanical Problems with the IRR

Now that you understand the basic logic of the IRR tool, you should know that the IRR, for all of its usefulness, isn't flawless. Quicken (and every other investment record-keeper's computer program) calculates a daily IRR and then multiplies this percentage by the number of days in a year to get an equivalent annual IRR.

This sounds right, but it presents problems in the case of publicly traded securities because a short-term percentage change in a security's market value—even if modest—can annualize to a very large positive or negative number. If you buy a stock for $10 1/8 and the next day the stock drops to $10, the annual return using these two pieces of information is a whopping –98.9 percent! If you buy a stock for $10 1/8 and the next day the stock rises to $10 1/4, the annual return using these two pieces of information is an astronomical 8,711 percent.

To minimize the problems of annualizing short-term percentage changes, you probably want to refrain from measuring IRRs for only short periods of time. An annualized daily return can be very misleading.

One other thing to note is that the IRR calculation becomes more difficult when you try to calculate the average annual profit percentage, or IRR, for a series of years when the starting value is changing from year to year. The basic problem is that the IRR formula is what's called an nth root polynomial. (n is the number of days in the IRR calculation.) A one-year IRR calculation is a 365th root polynomial. (Remember that Quicken calculates daily IRRs and then annualizes these daily percentages.)

The problem with an nth root polynomial is that, by definition, it can have up to n real and imaginary solutions. An annual IRR calculation could theoretically have 365 correct IRRs. You would not normally have this many solutions, but you could still have several correct solutions. So you can see that by using IRR-based return calculations, there's an opportunity for real confusion. Quicken, recognizing these problems, doesn't attempt to calculate IRRs for investments that look like they may have more than one IRR. You'll know, therefore, for which investments you can't calculate an IRR, but you won't know how those investments did.

Online Investment Services

The newest version of Quicken provides several on-line services to make it easier for you to use Quicken and to expand the work you can do with Quicken. One of these services, Quicken Quotes, helps with your investment record-keeping by providing you with recent securities prices for investments such as stocks and mutual funds.

Using Quicken Quotes is very easy. You display the Portfolio View window. (You can do this by clicking on the Portfolio command button that appears at the top of any investment account register.) Then you click on the Update Prices command button and choose the Get Online Quotes command.

NOTE If you haven't used any of Quicken's online services before, Quicken has you sign up for an Intuit Membership. It also tests your modem.

As long as you've provided symbols for each of your securities (you do this as you describe the securities), Quicken connects you to the Quicken Quotes online service and retrieves share price and trading volume data. (This is the same information you get from the stock page of your local newspaper or from the *Wall Street Journal.*)

Part 3

Quicken for Investors

HOW TO AVOID INVESTMENT MISTAKES

Smart people sometimes make dumb mistakes when it comes to investing. One reason for this, I guess, is that most people don't have the time to learn what they need to know to make good decisions. Another reason is that oftentimes when you make a dumb mistake, somebody else—an investment salesperson, for example—makes money. Fortunately, you can save yourself lots of imoney and a bunch of headaches by not making bad investment decisions.

Don't Forget to Diversify

At the end of the previous chapter, I mentioned that the average stock market return is 10 percent or so, but to earn 10 percent you need to own a broad range of stocks. In other words, you need to diversify.

Everybody who thinks about this for more than a few minutes realizes that it is true, but it's amazing how many people don't diversify. For example, some people hold huge chunks of their employer's stock but little else. Or they own a handful of stocks in the same industry.

To make money on the stock market, you need around 15 to 20 stocks in a variety of industries. (15 to 20 isn't a range that I made up, by the way. I came up with that range by performing a statistical calculation that many upper-division and graduate finance textbooks explain.) With fewer than 10 to 20 stocks, your portfolio's returns will very likely be something greater or lesser than the stock market average. Of course, you don't care if your portfolio's return is greater than the stock market average, but you do care if your portfolio's return is less than the stock market average.

By the way, to be fair I should tell you that some very bright people disagree with me on this business of holding 15 to 20 stocks. For example, Peter Lynch, the outrageously successful manager of the Fidelity Magellan mutual fund, suggests that individual investors hold four to six stocks that they understand well. His feeling, which he shares in his books, is that by following this strategy an individual investor can beat the stock market average. Mr. Lynch knows more about picking stocks than I ever will, but I nonetheless respectfully disagree with him for two reasons. First, I think that Peter Lynch is one of those modest geniuses who underestimate their intellectual prowess. I wonder if he underestimates the powerful analytical skills he brings to his stock picking. Second, I think that most individual investors do lack the accounting knowledge to accurately make use of the quarterly and annual financial statements that publicly-held companies provide in the ways that Mr. Lynch suggests.

Have Patience

The stock market and other securities markets bounce around on a daily, weekly, and even yearly basis, but the general trend over extended periods of time has always been up. Since World War II, the worst one-year return, for example, was –26.5 percent. The worst ten-year return in recent history was 1.2 percent. Those numbers are pretty scary, but things look much better if you look longer term. The worst 25-year return was 7.9 percent annually.

It's important for investors to have patience. There will be many bad years. Many times, one bad year is followed by another bad year. But over time, the good years outnumber the bad. They compensate for the bad years. Patient investors who stay in the market in both the good and bad years almost always do better than people who try to follow every fad or buy last year's hot stock.

Invest Regularly

You may already know about *dollar-average investing*. Instead of purchasing a set number of shares at regular intervals, you purchase a regular dollar amount, such as $100. If the share price is $10, you purchase 10 shares. If the share price is $20, you purchase five shares. If the share price is $5, you purchase 20 shares.

Dollar-average investing offers two advantages. The biggest is that you regularly invest—in both good markets and bad markets. If you buy $100 of stock at the beginning of every month, for example, you don't stop buying stock when the market is way down and every financial journalist in the world is working to fan the fires of fear.

The other advantage of dollar-average investing is that you buy more shares when the price is low and fewer shares when the price is high. As a result, you don't get carried away on a tide of optimism and end up buying most of stock when the market or the stock is up. In the same way, you also don't get scared away and stop buying a stock when the market or the stock is down.

One of the easiest ways to implement a dollar-average investing program, by the way, is by participating in something like an employer-sponsored 401(k) plan or deferred compensation plan. With these plans, you effectively invest each time money is withheld from your paycheck.

NOTE To make dollar-average investing work with individual stocks, you need to dollar-average each stock. In other words, if you're buying stock in IBM, you need to buy a set dollar amount of IBM stock each month, each quarter, or whatever.

Don't Ignore Investment Expenses

Investment expenses can add up quickly. Small differences in expense ratios, costly investment newsletter subscriptions, online financial services (including Quicken Quotes!), and income taxes can easily subtract hundreds of thousands of dollars from your net worth over a lifetime of investing.

To show you what I mean, here are a couple of quick examples. Let's say that you're saving $7,000-a-year of 401(k) money in a couple of mutual funds that track the Standard & Poors 500 index. One fund charges a .25 percent annual expense ratio and the other fund charges a 1 percent annual expense ratio. In 35 years, you'll have about $900,000 in the fund with the .25 percent expense ratio and about $750,000 in the fund with the 1 percent ratio.

Here's another example: Let's say that you don't spend $500 a year on a special investment newsletter, but you instead stick the money in a tax-deductible investment such as an individual retirement account. Let's say you also stick your tax savings in the tax-deductible investment. After 35 years, you'll accumulate roughly $200,000.

Investment expenses can add up to really big numbers when you realize that you could have invested the money and earned interest and dividends for years.

Don't Get Greedy

I wish there were some risk-free way to earn 15 or 20 percent annually. I really, really do. But, alas, there isn't. The stock market's average return is somewhere between 9 and 10 percent, depending on how many decades you go back. The significantly more risky small company stocks have done slightly better. On average, they return annual profits of 12 to 13 percent. Fortunately, you can get rich earning 9 percent returns. You just have to take your time. But no risk-free investments consistently return annual profits significantly above the stock market's long-run averages.

I mention this for a simple reason: People make all sorts of foolish investment decisions when they get greedy and pursue returns that are out of line with the average annual returns of the stock market. If someone tells you that he has a sure-thing investment or investment strategy that pays, say, 15 percent, don't believe it. And, for Pete's sake, don't buy investments or investment advice from that person.

If someone really did have a sure-thing method of producing annual returns of, say, 18 percent, that person would soon be the richest person in the world. With solid year-in, year-out returns like that, the person could run a $20 billion investment fund and earn $500 million a year. The moral is: There is no such thing as a sure thing in investing.

Don't Get Fancy

For years now I've made the better part of my living by analyzing complex investments. Nevertheless, I think that it makes most sense for investors to stick with simple investments—mutual funds, individual stocks, government and corporate bonds, and so on.

As a practical matter, it's very difficult for people who haven't been trained in financial analysis to analyze complex investments such as real-estate partnership units, derivatives, and cash-value life insurance. You need to understand how to construct accurate cash-flow forecasts. You need to know how to calculate things like internal rates of return and net present values with the data from cash-flow forecasts.

CHAPTER 19

Tracking Real-Estate Investments

FEATURING

Monitoring your investment in a home

Monitoring your investment in rental property

Buying a home and choosing a mortgage

Deciding whether to buy or rent

QUICKEN isn't really set up specifically for tracking real-estate investments. Yet, because Quicken is probably where you'll keep all your other financial records—and because real estate often amounts to one of your most valuable assets—you may want to use it for real-estate record keeping. In this chapter, I describe how you can use Quicken to keep tax records for your home and for income property investments.

Tracking Your Home as an Investment

Tracking the value and cost of a home delivers one of two benefits. You can track your home in a way that lets you include your home's value in your net worth report, or you can track it in a way that lets you minimize the capital gains tax you may ultimately pay when you sell your home. This chapter will help you decide whether it's worth more to you to focus on and track your home's market value or to save capital gains taxes at some point in the future.

Focusing on Your Home's Market Value

To track your home's market value and, as a result, the home equity you've accumulated, all you do is set up an asset account for your house and a liability account for your mortgage (see Chapter 13, *Loans and Mortgages*).

Setting Up the House Account

To set up an asset account for tracking your home's value, follow these steps:

1. Display the Account List window and click on the New button.

2. Select the Asset button to indicate you want to set up an asset account; then click on Next to display the Asset Account Set Up dialog box.

3. Click on the Summary tab.

4. *If you want to provide an additional description,* such as the street address, use the Description text box.

5. Enter a name for the new account—such as **House**—in the Account Name text box, the current market value of the house in the Balance text box, and the date as of which the current market value is correct in the As Of text box.

6. Click on Done, and Quicken adds the new account, then redisplays the Account List window.

Updating Your Records for Changes in the Market Value

To update your records for changes in your home's market value, follow these steps:

1. In the Account List window, select the House account and click on Open to display the House account information in its own Register document window, as shown in Figure 19.1.

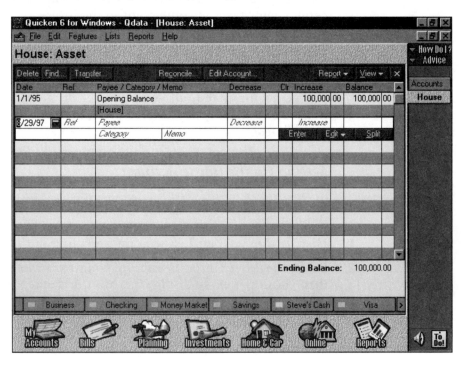

Figure 19.1. **The House Asset in its own register**

2. Click on the Reconcile button to display the Update Account Balance dialog box, as shown in Figure 19.2.

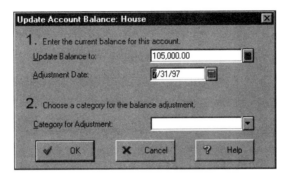

Update Account Balance: House

1. Enter the current balance for this account.

Update Balance to: 105,000.00

Adjustment Date: 6/31/97

2. Choose a category for the balance adjustment.

Category for Adjustment:

✔ OK   ✗ Cancel   ❓ Help

Figure 19.2.   **The Update Account Balance dialog box**

3. Enter the current market value in the Update Balance to text box.

4. Enter the date as of which the current market value is correct in the Adjustment Date text box and click on OK.

5. Make sure the Category for Adjustment text box is blank. (By convention, you don't include changes in a home's market value in your income and expense summaries.)

Quicken adds an adjustment transaction to the register that changes the House Account balance to whatever you specified in step 3. Figure 19.3 shows an House Asset account register with a single adjustment transaction.

Focusing on Saving Capital Gains Taxes

A second approach for keeping financial records of your investment in a home is to track the home's *adjusted cost basis,* which is the initial home purchase price plus the cost of any home improvements you've made: new cabinetry, landscaping, an addition, and so on.

By tracking a home's adjusted cost basis, you may be able to save capital gains taxes when you someday sell the home.

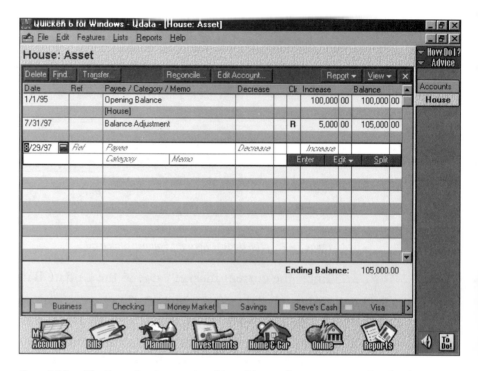

Figure 19.3.   The House Asset account register with an adjustment transaction that increases a home's value to $105,000

WHAT'S WRONG WITH THE CURRENT MARKET VALUE APPROACH

The current market value approach presents a problem: It's difficult to pick the correct current market value. You could periodically have your home appraised, of course, but appraisals are expensive and imprecise. You might be able to get a reasonable estimate of your home's value from your annual property tax assessment if it's based on estimated market value, but again, this number is only an estimate.

If you do use the assessed value as your current market value, one advantage is that you'll have a piece of paper that documents and triggers the current market value adjustment. Every year when you get the assessment notice, you'll know it's time to adjust the market value.

As it turns out, though, the only way to truly ascertain your home's market value is to find someone who's interested in buying your home.

Mechanics of the
Saving Capital Gains Taxes Approach

To keep financial records that will minimize the capital gain you ultimately pay when you sell a home, you set up an asset account as described earlier in this chapter, but you set the starting balance to the home's initial purchase price. (Be sure also to include any of the related costs you incurred to purchase the home—escrow and closing fees, appraisals, and so on.)

Then, whenever you make an improvement to the home, record the improvement as an increase in the house account's balance. Usually it's easiest to just categorize the check you write to pay for the improvement as a transfer to the house account.

As long as the home improvements are considered capital improvements, they increase the home's tax basis. Since the capital gain on which you'll ultimately be taxed when you sell the home is based on the difference between the home's sale price and the home's tax basis, the larger the home's tax basis, the smaller the capital gains tax.

> **TIP** If you sell your home, be sure to show a copy of the House Account register to your tax advisor, who can review each of your increase transactions and make sure they can be counted as capital improvements.

The Weakness of the
Saving Capital Gains Taxes Approach

I used to recommend that everybody use the "saving capital gains taxes" approach, and I still think it's a pretty good idea, but the approach isn't perfect.

Here's the problem: While the approach does require you to do extra record-keeping, it doesn't necessarily save you any capital gains taxes. Why? Because you may be able to avoid capital gains taxes on the sale of your home by taking advantage of any one of several loopholes.

You may never have to pay income taxes on a home sale—even if you've made a lot of money—because the federal income tax laws include three interesting provisions related to the capital gains taxes owed on the sale of your principal residence (the place you live most of the time).

One provision says that if you buy a home of equal or greater value within two years of selling your old home, you can defer any gains on the sale of your old home in your calculations of taxable income.

If in the future you sell your home and decide not to purchase another home or a less expensive home, you'll have to include as taxable income all the gains you've been deferring over the years. But that's when a second provision takes effect. If you're 55 years old or older, you can take a one-time exemption of up to $125,000 for any gain on the sale of your principal residence. By combining the first and second provisions mentioned here, you stand a good chance of never having to pay income taxes on gains from home ownership.

A third provision further reduces the potential capital gains taxes. For purposes of calculating the capital gain on an asset held in your future estate—including your home—the estate's trustee will probably subtract the asset's value at the date of your death from the sales price. This means that if you never sell your home and just leave it in your estate for your heirs, your estate won't have to pay capital gains taxes (although the estate may have to pay federal and state estate taxes).

> **TIP** If you have specific questions about deferring or avoiding capital gains on the sale of a home, confer with a tax advisor. Your advisor will be aware of nuances in the law that apply to your specific situation. In addition, it's always possible that Congress will change the income tax laws relating to calculation of capital gains on sales of a principal residence.

Because of these factors, it may just be that you won't get anything for tracking the cost of your home plus any improvements. In fact, for the "saving capital gains taxes" approach to actually save you money, you'll need to be someone who can't defer a capital gain on the sale of a home (perhaps because the home isn't a principal residence or because you'll be buying a smaller home rather than a larger home) and who can't avoid the capital gains tax by using the $125,000 exemption (for example, because you're not yet 55 years old or because you or your spouse has already used the exemption).

Tracking Rental Property

Quicken's account registers and categories provide a handy format for tracking real-estate investments such as income property. Quicken will help you prepare summaries of income and expenses for each property so you can monitor your individual real-estate investments. You can also easily complete the Schedule E income tax form.

Moreover, if you set up asset accounts for each of the individual real-estate properties you hold and then use these to record both capital improvements and any depreciation, you can easily calculate any capital gains or capital losses stemming from the sale of a piece of real estate.

Describing Your Real-Estate Holdings

To track income and expenses by individual real-estate property, you need to do two things. First, you need to set up the necessary income and expense categories. As noted in Chapter 14, make sure that whatever income and expense categories you set up support completion of the Schedule E tax form.

Second, you need to set up a class for each individual real-estate property and then, whenever you categorize an income or expense item for a particular property, you'll need to identify the property by providing the class.

> **TIP**   If you have only a single real-estate investment and you know for certain that you'll never add another real-estate investment to your portfolio, you don't need to set up classes.

To set up classes for your real-estate investments, follow these steps:

1.   Choose the Lists ➤ Class command to display the Class List window, as shown in Figure 19.4.

Part 3

Quicken for Investors

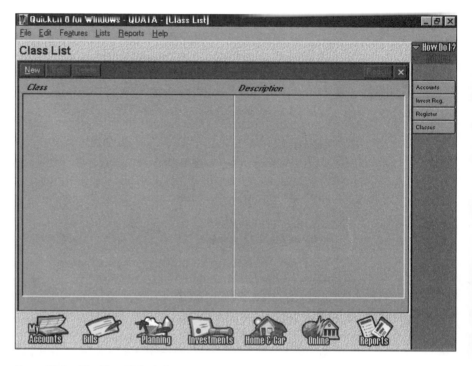

*Figure 19.4.   **The Class List window***

2. Click on the New button to display the Set Up Class dialog box:

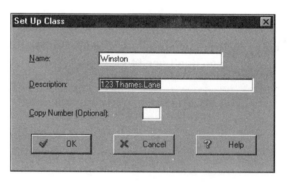

3. Use the Name text box to provide a brief name for the real-estate property. (If you're setting up a class for a rental property and the property
   has a name such as The Winston Apartments, you might use the property name or a part of its name—Winston, for example.)

4. *If you need to describe the property in more detail*—such as the street address—use the Description text box.

5. Click on OK, and Quicken adds the new class to the list shown in the Class List window.

6. Repeat steps 2 through 5 for each real estate property you want to track with Quicken.

SUBCLASSES FOR REAL-ESTATE INVESTMENTS

You can set up subclasses, which are simply classes used to classify the components of a class. For example, if you set up a class for the Winston apartments but wanted to separately track income and expenses related to a certain type of tenant—such as low-income tenants—you could create two subclasses: Qualified, for tenants who qualify as low-income tenants, and Nonqualified, for tenants who don't qualify. (You might need to do this, for example, if you're claiming federal low-income housing credits for a property and therefore need to track tenants by class too.) To set up a subclass, you take the same steps you use to set up a class. Keep in mind, however, that you can use only 31 characters to enter categories, subcategories, classes, and subclasses, and all of this information goes into the Category combo box, so use short names. Note, too, that Quicken lets you use subclasses and classes interchangeably: You can use a class as a subclass and a subclass as a class. Therefore, if you do choose to use subclasses, you need to be more careful in your data entry.

Tracking Income and Expenses by Property

Once you've set up classes for each of your individual properties, you're ready to begin tracking income and expenses by property. To do this, you simply enter both the income or expense category and the class name in the Category text box, separating the category from the class with a slash.

To record a rent check from one of your Winston Apartments tenants when Rental Income is the income category and Winston is the class name, type **Rental Income/Winston** in the Category combo box.

If you've used subclasses, such as "Qual" and "Nonq" for Qualified and Nonqualified to identify tenants as qualified and nonqualified low-income tenants, follow the class name with a colon and the subclass name. To record a rent check from one of your Winston Apartment "qualified" tenants when Rental Income is the income category and Winston is the class name, type **Rental Income/Winston:Qual** in the Category combo box.

> **NOTE** Classes can be a little tricky for a couple of reasons. You can flip-flop the classes and subclasses because Quicken doesn't track each of them separately. From its perspective, they're both the same. And you can't tell Quicken to always remind you to enter a class. So always be careful to use classes and subclasses. If you find that a report shows unclassified amounts, you need to use QuickZoom to locate the unclassified transactions you need to fix.

When you want to print an income and expense report by property, produce the Job/Project report by choosing the Reports ➤ Business ➤ Job/Project command and then clicking on the Create button. (For more information about how to produce and print reports, refer to Chapter 4.)

Figure 19.5 shows a Job/Project report that uses classes for column headings. The two classes (Chelsea and Winston) represent two fictitious properties: Chelsea Hall and Winston Apartments. Because each class represents an individual property, each column shows income and expense data for a specific real-estate investment.

Setting Up Real-Estate Investment Accounts

You can use Quicken accounts to track the adjusted cost basis of individual real-estate investments. You calculate the gain or loss upon sale by subtracting the adjusted cost basis of a property from the net sales price.

To do this, set up an asset account for individual real-estate properties the same way you would for your home if you've been keeping records to minimize any future capital gains taxes, as described earlier in this chapter.

As with a home, whenever you make an improvement to the property, record the improvement as an increase in the property's balance. Usually the easiest way to do this is to just categorize the check you write to pay for the improvement as a transfer to the House account.

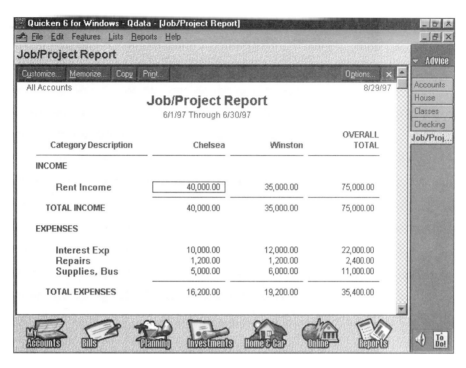

Figure 19.5. Job/Project Report showing income and expense data by specific real-estate investments

TIP As with a home capital gain calculation, be sure to show a copy of the Property Account register to your tax advisor, who can review each of your increase transactions and make sure they can be counted as capital improvements.

You can also record the periodic depreciation you'll use for calculations of the taxable profit or loss on the real-estate investment. To do this, first set up a depreciation expense category, such as Depreciation. Then record an annual depreciation expense transaction that decreases the property's account balance.

To record a depreciation on Winston Apartment when Depreciation is the expense category and Winston is the class name, for example, type **Depreciation/Winston** in the Category text box.

You can't see the complete Category text box entries because only part of the class name shows, but Figure 19.6 shows an Asset Account register for the fictitious real-estate investment, Winston Apartments. Note that I've recorded more than a single year's depreciation. For income tax purposes, the adjusted cost basis is the account balance at the date of sale.

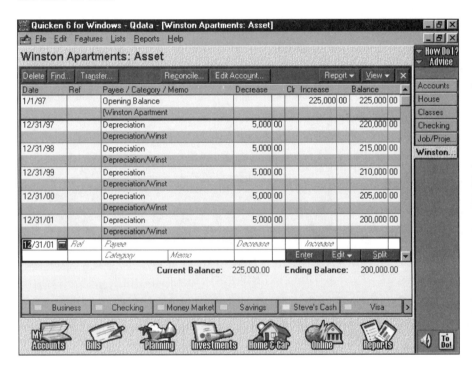

Figure 19.6.   **The Winston Apartments register**

TIP You can learn what depreciation expense is allowable on a property for tax purposes by consulting your tax advisor or telephoning the IRS.

HOW TO CHOOSE A HOME AND A MORTGAGE

Home ownership is usually considered the most important part of the so-called American Dream. Many consider home ownership a national birthright. It's often called the average American's best investment. And, usually, it results in the single, largest debt a person takes on: the 30-year mortgage. Given these major financial characteristics, it makes sense to talk about home ownership. This part of the chapter discusses deciding to purchase a home, affording a home, and choosing a mortgage.

Deciding Whether to Buy or to Rent

The first decision you need to make, of course, is whether to buy a home or rent one. This decision isn't an easy one to make, at least if you look at the impact of a home in purely economic terms.

Since World War II, a single family home has been, on the average, a very reasonable investment. Calculating the profits of home ownership is quite complicated, but I can sum things up quite nicely by stating that home ownership produces two benefits: rent savings and appreciation. Home ownership has been profitable for people because these benefits have more than paid the average homeowner's property ownership expenses and mortgage interest. When you boil down home ownership to its financial essence, it's really that simple.

A few years ago, an economist at the Mortgage Banking Association did a national survey of the investment returns of home ownership. He found that, on average, home ownership produced returns of around 10 to 12 percent. This figure is very respectable in light of the stock market's 50 year average of 10 percent and the 12 to 13 percent average of small company stocks.

Before you trot off and use this bit of real-estate trivia in your decision-making, however, it's important to understand the fundamental reason why home ownership has been a good investment. Suppose a person is considering two options, renting a three-bedroom house for, say, $600 a month or purchasing the same house for $100,000 with a $95,000, 9.25 percent mortgage. Initially, the renter pays just $600 a month, while the homeowner pays a mortgage payment equal to $780 plus another $220 in property taxes and maintenance. So, renting costs $600 a month and owning costs $1,000 a month.

With gradual inflation, however, things change. Assume that there's 3 percent inflation rate, for example (3 percent is the historical average of this century). After 10 years of 3 percent inflation, the renter pays around $800 a month in rent; after 20 years, the renter pays around $1,080 in rent; after thirty years, when the home owner's mortgage is presumably paid off, the renter pays around $1,460 a month in rent. Even when the home owner has paid off the mortgage in thirty years, he or she would still pay about $530 a month in property taxes and maintenance, but this figure is still roughly $900 a month less than what the renter pays.

The graph in Figure 19.7 shows this financial reality by comparing monthly housing costs when you purchase versus monthly housing costs when you rent. At first, purchasing is more expensive. Gradually, over time, however, the costs of renting and purchasing converge and then flip-flop. The big change, however, comes when the homeowner finally pays off his or her mortgage. In Figure 19.7, this is when the homeowner line drops. At that point, the homeowner pays only property taxes and maintenance costs. The renter, meanwhile, is still writing a monthly check to a landlord.

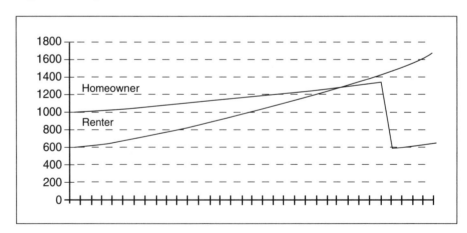

Figure 19.7.   ***Housing costs—renting versus buying***

If you understand the graph in Figure 19.7, you understand why home ownership can be a good investment. In recent history, rents and real-estate values have inflated at annual rates in excess of the 3 percent average. People who purchased their own homes locked in, or froze, the major portion of their housing expenses. With higher inflation, of course, the two lines cross much earlier. In the 1970s, when the nation suffered double-digit inflation, it didn't take long at all for buying to be cheaper than renting.

However, as you might know, one of the very best ways to boost your investment profits is to take advantage of investment vehicles that either increase your investment (such as the matching that employers sometimes provide to their employees with 401(k) plans) or that produce immediate tax savings (such as tax-deductible individual retirement accounts). Home ownership produces neither of these benefits. Employers don't pay more to homeowners. And you can't claim your down payment as a tax deduction. A home ownership investment is probably a respectable investment, but it doesn't hold a candle to a 401(k) plan (especially if there's employer matching!) or tax-deductible individual retirement plans.

About the Tax Benefits of Home Ownership

Many people claim that mortgage interest deductions are a tax benefit, but this isn't always true. For most people, the interest on a mortgage is an itemized deduction that reduces taxable income and therefore income taxes. But the same thing is usually true of interest on a loan used to purchase an investment. Deductible mortgage interest really isn't a tax benefit when you're talking about the investment qualities of buying a home versus, say, the investment qualities of putting money into a mutual fund.

One loophole by which homeowners may benefit, however, concerns the gain on the sale of a principal residence (the place where you live most of the time). As I mentioned earlier in the chapter, you might be able to use two income tax rules to postpone indefinitely paying income taxes on any appreciation in the value your house. If you buy a home of equal or greater value within two years of selling your old home, for example, you can defer any gains on the sale of your old home in your calculations of taxable income. Or, if you sell your home and decide not to purchase another home (or to purchase a less expensive home) and you're 55 years old or older, you can take a one-time exemption of up to $125,000 for any gain on the sale of your principal residence.

The Problems of Home Ownership as an Investment

As an investment, however, home ownership isn't flawless. Financially, you must consider several things if you're trying to decide whether or not to buy or rent. Perhaps the first thing to consider is this: Home ownership is very illiquid. In other words, it's very difficult to turn an investment in a home into cash. The value of liquidity is debatable. Suppose that you need money for an unexpected expense, perhaps because you've lost your job. An investment in a publicly traded stock or a stock mutual fund takes only minutes to convert to cash. Equity in a home takes weeks or months to reach. (This illiquidity business, by the way, is the reason why it's not really a good financial idea to repay debts such as mortgages, despite what some of the popular financial writers say.)

Another problem with real estate as an investment is that the transaction costs are extremely high. To buy a home, for example, you must pay for things like loan fees and appraisal expenses. To sell a home, you have to pay a real-estate broker a commission that can reach as high as 7 percent of the home's value. Due to high transaction costs, home ownership loses its investment shine if you frequently buy and sell homes, perhaps because you want to trade up to a larger home, buy a smaller home, or you have to move to a new state. In fact, if a home appreciates, say, 3 percent a year and your transaction costs amount to 9 percent, as they easily can, it takes three years of steady 3 percent inflation just to pay for the 9 percent transaction costs of trading homes.

One final problem that's more important than most people realize is the financial principle of diversification. When you store a large chunk of your financial wealth in one place—your home—it's much easier for a single event to damage or destroy your financial situation. It's easy to think of these sorts of "single events" as hurricanes, tornadoes, or fires. But when you're thinking about a home as an investment, the real danger (if you want to call it that) is that your home won't appreciate in value or, even worse, that its value will depreciate. Take another quick look at the line chart shown in Figure 19.7. If you look closely at the date, you'll see that it takes more than twenty years of steady 3 percent inflation before home ownership becomes less expensive on a monthly basis than renting. If home values fall or they just don't rise in value for a few years, home ownership isn't a good investment. In fact, it becomes a very poor investment.

One final problem of home ownership as an investment is that it's a leveraged purchase. "Leverage" simply means you borrow much of the money you use to make the purchase. I'm not going to get into a lengthy discussion here about the goodness or badness of financial leverage. In my mind, financial leverage is a tool that, like any tool, can be used and misused. Nevertheless, it's important to point out that financial leverage can dramatically impact the goodness or badness of an investment, including a home.

The problem of financial leverage is a simple one. You owe the mortgage company the money you borrowed plus any accrued interest regardless of whether the home you purchased with the borrowed money increases in value or decreases in value. Suppose, for the sake of illustration, that you borrow $95,000 to purchase a $100,000 home. If the home increases in value a mere 10 percent to $110,000, you still only owe $95,000, so your $5,000 investment grows to $15,000—a 200 percent return. On the other hand, if the home decreases in value a mere 10 percent to $90,000, you still owe $95,000, and you've actually lost your entire investment—the down payment. You need to come up with an additional $5,000 if you sell the home.

What's the Bottom Line?

Focusing entirely on the financial issues, one can draw several conclusions. First, be sure to take advantage first of superior investment options like employer-sponsored 401(k) plans and deductible individual retirement accounts before you invest in a home. You probably need a certain amount of money for things like retirement. A home isn't the best way to accumulate the financial wealth you need when you no longer work.

If you have exhausted the superior investment opportunities available— like 401(k) plans and deductible individual retirement accounts—home ownership is a very prudent investment. It is prudent if you will be able to live in the home for at least five years and preferably ten to twenty years. As a diversification measure, a real-estate investment in home ownership nicely balances retirement savings invested in the stock market. Real estate often represents a reasonable hedge against inflation. What's more, most of the problems of real estate—such as illiquidity and leverage—aren't really problems if you're willing to live someplace for a long time and you have other savings.

Don't, however, assume that the bigger a house is, the better the investment is. People often and erroneously justify a larger, more expensive home because "it's a good investment." Admittedly, I haven't seen a lot of good data that conclusively disproves this particular theory. There is evidence, however, that suggests modest and middle-class housing is the better investment. What's more, luxury housing is often much more illiquid.

Maybe the most important thing to say, after all of this, is that if you can't afford a home, don't worry about it. Really. There are better investments. Not owning a home means being far more mobile than you would be if you owned one. Remember, too, that it takes renters years and years before they spend more for housing than their home-owning friends. Finally, even when your home-owning friends have repaid their mortgages, you'll be in very good shape if you've been salting money away in things like 401(k)s or individual retirement accounts.

Can You Afford It?

A home costs more than you probably have in your checking account, so to buy one you need to borrow money from either the seller or a lender. It's impossible to generalize about what an individual seller might do. In fact, most of the creative financing schemes available today, including most of the "nothing down" schemes, rely on a seller doing what a regular lender won't do—take a down payment in a form other than cash, trade properties, loan money at below-market interest rates, and so on.

Regular lenders such as banks and mortgage companies usually follow three rules to determine how much money to lend and how much house you can afford: the housing expenses rule, the long-term debt payments rule, and the down-payment rule.

The Housing Expenses Rule The first loan qualification rule is the housing expenses rule. Typically, a lender suggests that your total monthly housing expenses should not exceed 25 to 28 percent of your gross monthly income. Monthly housing expenses include mortgage payments and insurance, property taxes, maintenance, and utilities. Your gross monthly income might include your wages (before taxes), investment income, and miscellaneous income items such as pension benefits or alimony. (In some areas of the country, higher standards apply because housing expenses in general are very high.)

Because the loan calculations are complicated without a financial calculator, I created a table (Table 19.1) that rates how many "dollars" of 30-year mortgage a "dollar" of income supports at various interest rates. The figures all suppose that you can spend 25 percent of your monthly gross income on a mortgage payment. This really means that a lender will be applying the 28 percent rule and that the extra 3 percent will go for the non-mortgage-payment part of your housing expenses.

Using the numbers in this table, if interest rates are 8 percent, for example, someone making $25,000 a year would be able to qualify for a mortgage of $2.84 times $25,000, or $71,000.

Long-Term Debt Payments Rule The second loan-qualification rule, the long-term debt payments rule, sets a limit on the amount of long-term debt you can have. The general rule is that long-term debt payments shouldn't exceed 33 to 36 percent of your monthly gross income. Lenders want to be sure that you can comfortably bear the total debt burden you'll have after you get the mortgage. Long-term debt includes mortgage payments and any other debt borrowers still have in 10 to 12 months.

As long as your long-term debts don't exceed about 10 percent of your income, the long-term debt rule usually isn't the limiting factor that determines how large a mortgage you can afford. If you have a lot of long-term debt—car payments, student loans, and so on—you will be very limited as far as the mortgages you can afford are concerned.

•• *on the Road to Riches*

Table 19.1.   *Dollars of Mortgage One Can Afford Per Dollar of Income*

Mortgage Interest Rates (%)	Mortgage Dollar Per Income dollar
7.00	$3.13
7.25	$3.05
7.50	$2.98
7.75	$2.91
8.00	$2.84
8.25	$2.77
8.50	$2.71
8.75	$2.65
9.00	$2.59
9.25	$2.53
9.50	$2.48
9.75	$2.42
10.00	$2.37
10.25	$2.32
10.50	$2.28
10.75	$2.23
11.00	$2.19

The Down Payment Rule   In addition to the rules that have to do with the size of the mortgage, there's another rule for determining affordability. Lenders typically do not lend the full purchase price of homes. Most lenders want the borrower to put up 10 to 20 percent of the purchase price, although they might require as little as 5 percent down. Federal Housing Administration and Veterans Administration loans allow even smaller down payments, from 0 to 5 percent. However, if you put down less than 20 percent, you have to pay private mortgage insurance. This type of insurance protects the lender against loss if you default on your mortgage payments.

Another way to look at the down payment business is by expressing the mortgage you can have as a percentage of the price of the house. With a 20 percent down payment, for example, a lender puts up 80 percent of the purchase price in the form of a mortgage; with a 10 percent down payment, a lender puts up 90 percent; and with a 5 percent down payment, a lender puts up 95 percent.

To take our earlier example, if interest rates are 8 percent and your family gross income is $25,000, you can't go out and buy a house for $71,000, because the lender doesn't want to put up 100 percent of the purchase price. You need to put up a part of the purchase price—at least 5 percent in most cases—in the form of a down payment

By the way, lenders aren't concerned only with the percentage of the purchase price that you can supply. Usually, the lender is also interested in how you come up with the down payment. From a lender's perspective, some sources are acceptable and some are not. Acceptable sources include savings, investments, and gifts from parents and relatives. Unacceptable sources include draws on credit cards and loans (not gifts) from parents and relatives.

A Final Word About Affordability

The rise in home values in many parts of the country has made it very difficult for many people to afford a home. If you've spent time working through the numbers and found yourself thinking that owning a home is more like the impossible dream than the American dream, don't give up for a couple of reasons.

First, don't depend too much on what I've said here. Lender guidelines often vary, so you should place a telephone call to your local bank.

Second, interest rates have a dramatic impact on home affordability. They bounce up and down. Although you can't afford a home today, a lower interest rate next month or next year might mean you can afford a home then.

Choosing a Mortgage

Choosing a mortgage is easier than you might think, thanks to federal truth-in-lending laws. You basically have two choices: a fixed-interest rate loan or an adjustable-interest rate loan. The first question to ask yourself is whether you should go with a fixed-interest rate or an adjustable-interest rate mortgage.

> **NOTE** See *Ways of Borrowing Money* in Chapter 13 if you need to know precisely how adjustable-rate mortgages and fixed-rate mortgages work.

Fixed-Rate versus Adjustable-Rate Mortgages

Some financial writers and perhaps most of your neighbors think adjustable-rate mortgages are worse than bad. To be quite blunt, their advice is influenced more by fear and emotion than by the hard facts. Several studies have shown that, for the most part, adjustable-rate mortgages cost homeowners with mortgages less money. This cost-savings feature is particularly true of adjustable-rate mortgages with capped, or increase-limited, interest rates in which the rate of interest cannot rise above a certain rate.

The cost-savings can add up quickly. As you may know, in the early years of a mortgage, very little of the mortgage payments are actually applied to reducing the principle. This fact suggests an interesting money-saving and risk-reduction technique. Suppose a homeowner chooses an adjustable-rate mortgage and then uses the interest rate savings (as compared to a fixed-rate mortgage) to reduce the cost of the mortgage. In other words, the borrower gets an adjustable-rate mortgage but makes the larger fixed-interest rate payment. If interest rates don't jump up for at least a few years, the homeowner is very unlikely to loose money because the mortgage balance ends up getting reduced so quickly.

As part of writing this chapter, in fact, I constructed a little computer-based model that did just this. My model calculates what happens if a person looking for a $90,000 mortgage chooses an adjustable-rate 7 percent mortgage with a $598-a-month payment but then makes the

$724.16-a-month payment that would be required on the alternative 9 percent fixed-rate mortgage. In this case, the extra payment amount—roughly $125 dollars—is applied directly to principal.

Here's the interesting thing about all this: It turns out that even if interest rates rise by a full percent each year, you would pay less with an adjustable-rate mortgage than you do with a fixed-rate mortgage until the fourth straight year of rising interest rates. At this point, the adjustable-rate mortgage borrower ends up paying about an extra $50 a month.

However, if interest rates don't immediately rise but stay level for even a few years, the person with the adjustable rate mortgage saves a bundle of money. And even if interest rates skyrocket later on, this person will never pay more than the person with the fixed-rate mortgage because the extra monthly principal payments made early on so quickly reduce the mortgage balance.

Another thing to consider about all this is that if interest rates are rising rapidly, as you would assume if you're seeing back-to-back interest rate increases, it probably means that inflation has kicked up again. With strong inflation, it's very possible that your wages or salary will be adjusted annually for inflation and that your house will be inflating in value as well.

Given these characteristics, many people really should consider adjustable-rate rather than fixed-rate mortgages when adjustable-rate mortgage interest rates are significantly below fixed-rate mortgage interest rates. Sure, there's a little more risk, as there always is in any financial investment. But with a limit on the year-to-year increases a lender can make (such as 1 percent) and on the total increases a lender can make (such as 5 percent), you are more likely to save money by going with an adjustable-rate mortgage.

If fixed-interest mortgage rates are low, fixed-interest mortgages certainly are worth considering. What's more, to truly reduce the financial risk of an adjustable-rate mortgage, you need to be the sort of person (or the sort of family) who has the discipline to always add that extra amount to the payment.

It's not a good idea to use an adjustable-rate mortgage because it's the only mortgage you can afford. The reason for this—and, admittedly,

I'm pretty conservative—is that if an adjustable-rate mortgage is the only mortgage you can afford, it likely means that you can't afford your mortgage payments to increase, and that is what will happen the next time interest rates jump up. By picking an adjustable-rate mortgage when that is the only kind of mortgage you can afford, you're almost certain to have the unpleasant task of someday trying to figure out how to pay for something you can't really afford.

Note, too, that many adjustable-rate mortgage lenders use what are called teaser rates. *Teaser rates* amount to a marketing ploy where a lender offers a special, temporary, lower-than-normal interest rate. The problem with a teaser rate is that even if the underlying interest rate index doesn't change, your payment still increases the next time it's recalculated because the lender used a special rate to entice you. Teasers aren't bad, by the way. They do save you money. It's just that you need to be ready for the payment bump that occurs when the teaser interest rate gets adjusted.

Comparing Mortgages

Once you make the fixed-rate versus adjustable-rate decision, the rest is easy. To compare fixed-interest rate mortgages, all you need to do is compare the annual percentage rates, or APRs. Then, you pick the one that's lowest. That's it.

APRs measure the total cost of a mortgage, including the periodic mortgage interest you need to pay and all other costs of obtaining credit, such as the loan origination fee and processing costs. By comparing APRs, for example, you don't need to get bogged down wondering whether, for example, an 8.5 percent mortgage with a 2 percent fee is a better deal than a 9 percent mortgage with no fee. The APR combines all the costs into one, easy-to-understand number that, in effect, expresses all the loan costs as an effective interest rate.

Adjustable-rate mortgages also can be compared by using APRs. Unfortunately, it's often more difficult to get the lender to provide an APR because the calculation is more involved. Nevertheless, you should still be able to get an APR if you press the lender for it.

Quicken in a Small Business

The next three chapters describe how you can use Quicken for common business accounting and financial-management tasks. Here you'll learn how to prepare payroll (Chapter 20), track accounts receivable and accounts payable (Chapter 21), and monitor cash flow and business profits (Chapter 22).

CHAPTER 20
Payroll

FEATURING

Setting up categories for businesses

Preparing a payroll check

Memorizing and scheduling
transactions for businesses

Understanding payroll
tax returns and payroll taxes

You can use Quicken to prepare payroll checks, calculate payroll taxes, and expedite the preparation of federal and state payroll and payroll tax returns. In this chapter, you'll learn how.

 NOTE At the end of this chapter I describe what you need to do before you hire your first employee to address federal and state payroll tax collection and reporting requirements. If you haven't already hired your first employee, read the end of this chapter to make sure that you're ready to start processing a payroll with Quicken.

Setting Up the Categories and Accounts You Need

Once you've taken care of the federal and statement payroll and employment prerequisites—and you do need to take care of these items first—you're ready to set up Quicken to prepare payroll checks and tax returns. To do this, you set up categories (or subcategories) for each payroll expense you, the employer, pay. For example, you set up a Payroll Expense category to track wages, social security, Medicare, and federal unemployment taxes, as well as any state payroll taxes you pay (such as state unemployment and workers' compensation).

You also need liability accounts for every payroll tax liability (amount you owe someone) you incur, such as the amounts you owe the IRS for the federal income, social security, and Medicare taxes you withhold from the employee's payroll check as well as the federal payroll taxes, social security, and Medicare taxes you pay as an employer. (Social security and Medicare taxes are paid by both the employer and the employee.)

The easiest method is to set up a Payroll Expense category and then set payroll expense subcategories for each of the types of payroll expense you actually pay: wages, social security, Medicare, federal unemployment, state unemployment, and so forth.

Setting Up Payroll Categories

To set up an expense category for payroll, follow these steps:

1. Choose Lists ➤ Category/Transfer to open the Category & Transfer List window. Click on the New button to display the Set Up Category dialog box, as shown in Figure 20.1.

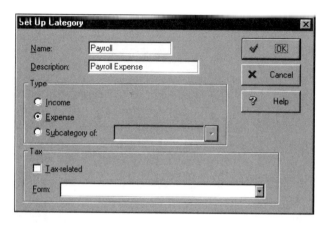

Figure 20.1.   **The Set Up Category dialog box**

2.   Enter **Payroll** in the Name text box. (You'll use this as the main expense category for payroll.)

3.   *If you want to describe the payroll expense category in more detail,* use the Description text box.

4.   Make sure the Expense option button is marked.

5.   *If you're going to be processing payroll that is or may be a tax-deductible expense,* mark the Tax-related check box and choose the appropriate entry from the Form drop-down–list box.

Here are some suggestions:

Type of Employer	Entry You'll Select
Sole proprietors who use Schedule C	Schedule C: Wages Paid Entry
Real estate investors who use Schedule E	Schedule E: Wages Paid
Farmers who use Schedule F	Schedule F: Labor Hired
Parent preparing to process payroll for an employee providing child care	2441: Childcare

6. Click on OK, and Quicken adds the Payroll expense to the Category & Transfer list.

> **TIP** If you don't see the Form drop-down–list box, go ahead and click on OK to set up your account. Then choose the Edit ➤ Options ➤ Quicken Program command. When Quicken displays the General Options dialog box, click on the General tab and then mark the Use Tax Schedules With Categories checkbox. Next, close the dialog box and click on the Tax Link button. Use the Tax Link Assistant dialog box to assign a tax form to the category you just created.

To set up the subcategories you use to track the various types of payroll expenses—wages, social security, Medicare, federal unemployment, state unemployment, and so forth—take these steps:

1. In the Category & Transfer List window, click on the New button to display the Set Up Category dialog box (see Figure 20.1).

2. Enter the name for the payroll expense subcategory in the Name text box. (You can use an abbreviation such as Wages, SS, Med, or FUTA.) Do not use the same names you will use for your Liability accounts. Quicken does not allow duplication of names in accounts and categories.

3. *If you want to further describe the payroll expense subcategory,* use the Description text box. Wages might be described as "Gross Wages," SS as "Social Security," MCARE as "Medicare," FUTA as "Federal Unemployment Tax," and so on.

4. Click on the Subcategory of option button and enter the name of the Payroll expense category into the text box. (If you've followed the instructions so far, the expense category name will be Payroll.)

5. *If you're going to process payroll that is or may be a tax-deductible expense,* mark the Tax-related check box.

6. Click on OK, and Quicken adds the payroll expense subcategory to the Category & Transfer list.

7. Repeat steps 2 through 6 for each of the payroll expense subcategories.

Part 4

Quicken in a Small Business

THE THREE PAYROLL CATEGORIES YOU DEFINITELY NEED

You need at least three payroll subcategories to handle the payroll:

▶ gross wages subcategory to track what an employee really earns

▶ social-security subcategory to track the social-security taxes that you owe as an employer

▶ Medicare subcategory to track the Medicare payroll taxes that you owe as an employer

If your employees are subject to federal unemployment tax, you also need a subcategory to track that expense. Finally, you need subcategories to track any state payroll taxes that you are required to pay as an employer. Note that you don't need any subcategories to track amounts that an employee pays through payroll deductions.

Setting Up Payroll Liability Accounts

The next task is to set up liability accounts to track the amounts you owe the federal and state governments, such as unemployment taxes and employee taxes you've withheld.

To set up the payroll liability accounts you need, follow these steps:

1. Display the Account List window by choosing Lists ➤ Account.

2. Click on the New button so Quicken displays the dialog box for creating new accounts.

3. Click on the Liability button.

4. When Quicken displays the Liability Account Setup dialog box, shown in Figure 20.2, click on the Summary tab.

5. In the Account Name text box, enter an account name for the payroll liability. Make *Payroll* the first word in the account name. To track the federal withholding amounts, for example, you might use the name Payroll-FWH, and to track the social security taxes owed, you might use Payroll-SS. To track the Medicare taxes owed, you might use Payroll-MCARE.

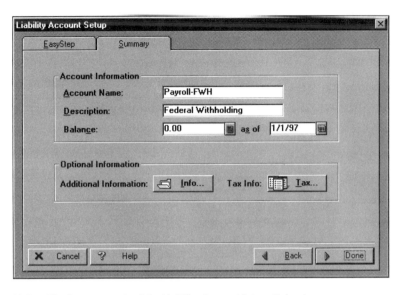

Figure 20.2. The Summary tab of the Liability Account Setup dialog box

 TIP You start each payroll liability with the word *Payroll* so you can easily prepare a report of payroll transactions and account balances. The Payroll report on the Business Reports menu does just this; it summarizes transactions that use categories and accounts starting with the word *Payroll*.

6. *If you want to describe the payroll liability account in more detail,* use the Description text box. For example, if you abbreviated the liability name for the account name, you might enter the full payroll liability name.

7. In the Balance text box, enter the amount you currently owe on the payroll liability.

8. In the As Of text box, enter the date for which you owe the amount entered in step 7.

9. Click on Done. When Quicken asks if you want to set up an amortized loan for the account, select No. Quicken adds the new payroll liability account.

10. Repeat steps 2 through 9 for each of the other payroll-tax liability accounts you want to add.

Part 4

Quicken in a Small Business

TIP   Set up payroll-tax liability accounts for federal income taxes withheld, state income taxes withheld, social security owed, and Medicare taxes owed. If there are other significant payroll-tax liabilities, set up payroll-tax liability accounts for these, too. If a payroll-tax liability is very small—federal unemployment taxes, for example, can equal .08 percent—you may want to skip tracking the liability. In this case, just categorize the check that pays the tax using a payroll-tax category.

Preparing a Payroll Check

Once you've set up the needed categories and accounts, you're ready to use Quicken to prepare employee payroll checks. To do this, you first calculate the employee's wages and the payroll taxes you and the employee pay based on those wages. Second, you record a transaction in the Quicken register that summarizes the payroll check and the related payroll taxes.

Calculating an Employee's Wages and Payroll Taxes

There are really two parts to figuring out what a payroll transaction is supposed to look like. You need to calculate the employee's gross wages and the payroll taxes you, the employer, owe. (This is usually the easiest part.) And you need to describe the payroll deductions you withhold from the check.

Calculating Gross Wages and Employer's Payroll Taxes

Calculating an employee's wages and payroll taxes starts with the actual gross-wages calculation. For example, if an employee works 40 hours and you pay $7.50 an hour, you owe the employee $300, calculated as 40 times $7.50. If an employee works for a month and you've agreed to pay $1,000 a month, you owe the employee $1,000.

NOTE In the following payroll-tax examples, I use round numbers to keep things simple. The wages you pay as an employer might be much more or less than the example numbers.

Once you know the employee's gross wages, you can calculate the payroll taxes you owe as a result of wages. Just multiply the payroll-tax rate by the gross wages amount. Suppose, for example, you owe an employee $1,000 for a month of work. To calculate the social-security taxes you owe because of the $1,000, multiply the $1,000 by the social security taxes percent—which is currently 6.2 percent. (*Employer's Tax Guide* usually prints this information right on the front of the guide, but you can also consult a table in the *Guide* to find out what number is 6.2 percent of $1,000.)

To calculate the Medicare taxes you owe because of the $1,000, either multiply the $1,000 by the Medicare-taxes percent, which is currently 1.45 percent, or consult the table in the *Guide* to find out what number is 1.45 percent of $1,000.

 TIP You can start the Quicken calculator accessory by selecting the Edit ➤ Use Calculator command.

If you owe an employee $1,000 in gross wages but need to pay 6.2 percent in social-security taxes and 1.45 percent in Medicare taxes, the total payroll expenses you incur are equal to those shown in Table 20.1.

Table 20.1. **Payroll Expenses**

Description	Amount
Gross wages	$1,000.00
Social security	$62.00
Medicare	$14.50
Total payroll expenses	$1,076.50

If you owe other federal and state payroll taxes, such as a 1 percent state unemployment tax paid by the employer, you calculate them the same way, obtaining the data you need from your state equivalent of the *Employer's Tax Guide*.

 TIP Each of the payroll expenses in Table 20.1 would be recorded using a separate payroll expense subcategory.

Calculating the Payroll Deductions

An employee doesn't get paid the gross-wages amount. You, the employer, are required to deduct from the employee's gross wages amounts for federal income taxes, social security, and Medicare. You may also be required or allowed to deduct amounts for other payroll taxes.

The amount an employee pays for social-security and Medicare taxes through a payroll deduction is calculated the same way as the amount an employee pays for social-security and Medicare taxes: You just multiply the appropriate tax rate by the gross-wages amount. In the case of a $1,000 monthly paycheck, social-security taxes equal $62.00 (calculated as 6.2 percent of $1,000), and Medicare taxes equal $14.50 (calculated as 1.45 percent of $1,000). If there were other payroll taxes paid by the employee, you would calculate these the same way.

The amount of federal income taxes you withhold is dictated by the IRS. You look at the employee's W-4 to obtain the filing status and the number of personal exemptions claimed. Then you look up (in the *Employer's Tax Guide*) the employee's gross-wages amount in the appropriate pay-period table for the employee's filing status. For example, to determine what federal income taxes to withhold for an employee who makes $1,000 a month and files a tax return using the Married Filing Jointly status, you use the Married Persons—Monthly Payroll Period table. Figure 20.3 shows this page from *Employer's Tax Guide*.

WARNING Don't use the information shown in Figure 20.3! You need to get your own *Employer's Tax Guide* to make sure you're using the most up-to-date income tax rates.

Look down the first column of the table until you find the gross-wages row for monthly wages equal to $1,000. Then look across that row until you get to the withholding amount specified for the claimed number of withholding allowances. For example, if the employee claimed two exemptions on the W-4, the table in Figure 20.3 says you should withhold $9 in federal income taxes. Table 20.2 summarizes the calculation.

MARRIED Persons—MONTHLY Payroll Period
(For Wages Paid in 1996)

If the wages are—		And the number of withholding allowances claimed is—										
At least	But less than	0	1	2	3	4	5	6	7	8	9	10
		The amount of income tax to be withheld is—										
$0	$540	0	0	0	0	0	0	0	0	0	0	0
540	560	2	0	0	0	0	0	0	0	0	0	0
560	580	5	0	0	0	0	0	0	0	0	0	0
580	600	8	0	0	0	0	0	0	0	0	0	0
600	640	13	0	0	0	0	0	0	0	0	0	0
640	680	19	0	0	0	0	0	0	0	0	0	0
680	720	25	0	0	0	0	0	0	0	0	0	0
720	760	31	0	0	0	0	0	0	0	0	0	0
760	800	37	5	0	0	0	0	0	0	0	0	0
800	840	43	11	0	0	0	0	0	0	0	0	0
840	880	49	17	0	0	0	0	0	0	0	0	0
880	920	55	23	0	0	0	0	0	0	0	0	0
920	960	61	29	0	0	0	0	0	0	0	0	0
960	1,000	67	35	3	0	0	0	0	0	0	0	0
1,000	1,040	73	41	9	0	0	0	0	0	0	0	0
1,040	1,080	79	47	15	0	0	0	0	0	0	0	0
1,080	1,120	85	53	21	0	0	0	0	0	0	0	0
1,120	1,160	91	59	27	0	0	0	0	0	0	0	0
1,160	1,200	97	65	33	1	0	0	0	0	0	0	0
1,200	1,240	103	71	39	7	0	0	0	0	0	0	0
1,240	1,280	109	77	45	13	0	0	0	0	0	0	0
1,280	1,320	115	83	51	19	0	0	0	0	0	0	0
1,320	1,360	121	89	57	25	0	0	0	0	0	0	0
1,360	1,400	127	95	63	31	0	0	0	0	0	0	0
1,400	1,440	133	101	69	37	5	0	0	0	0	0	0
1,440	1,480	139	107	75	43	11	0	0	0	0	0	0
1,480	1,520	145	113	81	49	17	0	0	0	0	0	0
1,520	1,560	151	119	87	55	23	0	0	0	0	0	0
1,560	1,600	157	125	93	61	29	0	0	0	0	0	0
1,600	1,640	163	131	99	67	35	3	0	0	0	0	0
1,640	1,680	169	137	105	73	41	9	0	0	0	0	0
1,680	1,720	175	143	111	79	47	15	0	0	0	0	0
1,720	1,760	181	149	117	85	53	21	0	0	0	0	0
1,760	1,800	187	155	123	91	59	27	0	0	0	0	0
1,800	1,840	193	161	129	97	65	33	1	0	0	0	0
1,840	1,880	199	167	135	103	71	39	7	0	0	0	0
1,880	1,920	205	173	141	109	77	45	13	0	0	0	0
1,920	1,960	211	179	147	115	83	51	19	0	0	0	0
1,960	2,000	217	185	153	121	89	57	25	0	0	0	0
2,000	2,040	223	191	159	127	95	63	31	0	0	0	0
2,040	2,080	229	197	165	133	101	69	37	6	0	0	0
2,080	2,120	235	203	171	139	107	75	43	12	0	0	0
2,120	2,160	241	209	177	145	113	81	49	18	0	0	0
2,160	2,200	247	215	183	151	119	87	55	24	0	0	0
2,200	2,240	253	221	189	157	125	93	61	30	0	0	0
2,240	2,280	259	227	195	163	131	99	67	36	4	0	0
2,280	2,320	265	233	201	169	137	105	73	42	10	0	0
2,320	2,360	271	239	207	175	143	111	79	48	16	0	0
2,360	2,400	277	245	213	181	149	117	85	54	22	0	0
2,400	2,440	283	251	219	187	155	123	91	60	28	0	0
2,440	2,480	289	257	225	193	161	129	97	66	34	2	0
2,480	2,520	295	263	231	199	167	135	103	72	40	8	0
2,520	2,560	301	269	237	205	173	141	109	78	46	14	0
2,560	2,600	307	275	243	211	179	147	115	84	52	20	0
2,600	2,640	313	281	249	217	185	153	121	90	58	26	0
2,640	2,680	319	287	255	223	191	159	127	96	64	32	0
2,680	2,720	325	293	261	229	197	165	133	102	70	38	6
2,720	2,760	331	299	267	235	203	171	139	108	76	44	12
2,760	2,800	337	305	273	241	209	177	145	114	82	50	18
2,800	2,840	343	311	279	247	215	183	151	120	88	56	24
2,840	2,880	349	317	285	253	221	189	157	126	94	62	30
2,880	2,920	355	323	291	259	227	195	163	132	100	68	36
2,920	2,960	361	329	297	265	233	201	169	138	106	74	42
2,960	3,000	367	335	303	271	239	207	175	144	112	80	48
3,000	3,040	373	341	309	277	245	213	181	150	118	86	54
3,040	3,080	379	347	315	283	251	219	187	156	124	92	60
3,080	3,120	385	353	321	289	257	225	193	162	130	98	66
3,120	3,160	391	359	327	295	263	231	199	168	136	104	72
3,160	3,200	397	365	333	301	269	237	205	174	142	110	78

Figure 20.3. Page from **Employer's Tax Guide** *showing the table used for an employee using the Married Filing Jointly status*

Part 4

Quicken in a Small Business

Table 20.2   New Wages Calculation

Description	Amount
Gross wages	$1,000.00
Social security	$(62.00)
Medicare	$(14.50)
Federal income taxes	$(9.00)
Net wages	$914.50

Preparing the Payroll Check

Now you're ready to prepare the payroll check and record it.

NOTE I'm assuming you'll print the check in Quicken by using the Write Checks window to record it. If you don't want to print the check but only to record it, you can use the Register window.

Recording Gross Wages, Deductions, and Net Wages

To record gross wages, deductions, and net wages, follow these steps:

1. In the Write Checks window, enter the payroll date in the Date text box, the employee's name in the Pay to the Order Of text box, and the net wages amount in the $ text box.

2. *If you'll mail the check in a windowed envelope,* type the employee's address in the address block of text boxes.

3. *If it will help you or the employee identify the payroll period,* enter additional information in the Memo text box.

4. Click on the Split button to display the Split Transaction window.

5. Enter the gross wages amount on the first split transaction line: In the Category field, type **Payroll**, a colon (:), and the name of the gross wages subcategory. (If you used Gross wages as the gross wages subcategory, for example, you would type **Payroll:Wages**.) Then type the gross wages amount in the Amount field.

6. Enter the social-security tax deduction on the second split transaction line: In the Category field, type the name of the payroll liability account you set up to track what you owe for social security. Then, in the Amount field, enter the social-security taxes paid by the employee as a negative number.

> **NOTE** Be sure that you use payroll liability accounts in steps 6, 7, and 8. You don't want to use payroll subcategories. By using the payroll liability accounts, you show that it's the employee who is paying these amounts. If you incorrectly use payroll subcategories, you show that it's you, not the employee, who is paying these amounts.

7. Enter the Medicare tax deduction on the third split transaction line. To do this, put the cursor in the Category field and type the name of the payroll liability account you set up to track what you owe for Medicare. Then highlight the Amount field and enter the Medicare taxes paid by the employee as a negative number.

8. Enter the federal income taxes withheld from the employee's payroll check on the fourth split transaction line: In the Category field, type the name of the payroll-liability account you set up to track what you owe for federal income taxes withheld. Then enter the federal income taxes withheld as a negative number in the Amount field. Figure 20.4 shows the Split Transaction window after you enter the gross wages and the social-security, Medicare, and federal income taxes withholding information.

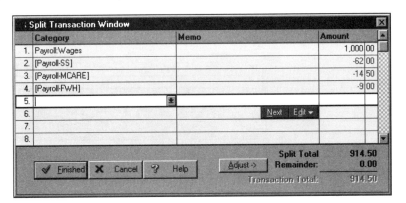

Figure 20.4.   **The Split Transaction window**

Part 4

Quicken in a Small Business

TIP If the employee pays other payroll taxes through deductions, you record these the same way you record federal income taxes.

 NOTE In steps 9 through 12, you record the social security and Medicare payroll taxes that you as the employer must pay. This is the information shown in Table 20.1.

9. Move to the seventeenth line of the Split Transaction window. (Since only the first 16 lines of the split transaction detail appear on check stubs, the employer's payroll taxes won't appear there.) Enter the employer's social-security–taxes expense on the seventeenth split transaction line: In the Category field, type **Payroll**, a colon (:), and the name of the social-security–taxes subcategory. (If you used SS as the social-security subcategory, you would type **Payroll:SS**.) Then enter the social-security–taxes amount in the Amount field.

10. Enter the employer's social-security–taxes liability (because of the social-security–taxes expense) on the eighteenth split-transaction line, as shown below. Click in the Category box then click on the down arrow. Scroll down the list until you find Transfer funds to [the social security liability account] and double-click on it. Then enter the social security taxes amount in the Amount field. (This will be a negative number.)

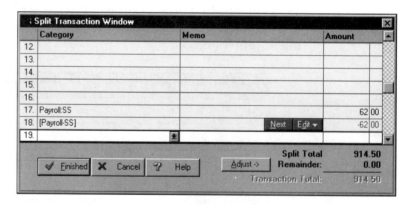

 TIP You use the same liability account to track both the amounts you owe for social security because you withheld money from an employee's check and the amounts you owe for social security because of the social-security payroll tax.

11. Enter the employer's Medicare-taxes expense on the nineteenth split transaction line. For example, if you used MCare as the Medicare sub-category, type **Payroll:MCare** in the Category field. Then enter the Medicare-taxes amount in the Amount field.

12. Enter the employer's Medicare taxes liability (because of the Medicare-taxes expense) on the 20th split transaction line. Click in the Category box, then click the down arrow. Scroll down the list until you find Transfer funds to [the Medicare liability account] and double-click on it. Then enter the Medicare taxes amount in the Amount field. (This will be a negative number.) Click on Finished to close the Split Transaction window, and press Record Check.

Figure 20.5 shows the social security and Medicare taxes owed by the employer but doesn't include the $1,000 of payroll expense shown in Figure 20.4. That expense was recorded earlier, in step 5.

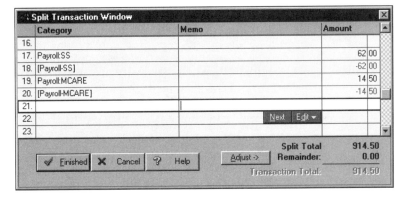

Figure 20.5. **The Split Transaction window with employer's payroll-tax information from Table 20.2**

 TIP You use the same liability account to track both the amounts you owe for Medicare because you withheld money from an employee's check and the amounts you owe for Medicare because of the Medicare payroll tax.

Quicken records the payroll check and any related payroll taxes into the Quicken register. Then it scrolls the just-completed check off your screen so you can write another one.

What to Do About Other Payroll Deductions

Other amounts may be deducted from an employee's check, for items like state income taxes, a 401(k) plan, and other employee-paid amounts. You can record these payroll deductions too. Just treat them as you treat the federal income taxes the employee pays: Set up a payroll liability for the deduction and transfer an amount to this account whenever you subtract the deduction from the gross wages. (When you later pay the amount for the employee, you categorize the check as a transfer to the liability account—just as when you pay the IRS amounts you've withheld for federal income taxes.)

SOME FACTORS THAT COMPLICATE PAYROLL

The payroll net wages and payroll-tax calculations described in the preceding section work well for most small businesses and for household employees. But be aware of a potential problem: Some payroll taxes and payroll deductions—social security is the best example—apply to salaries and wages only up to a specified limit. Social-security taxes, for example, are levied on roughly only the first $60,000 of income. This rule means that for more highly-paid employees, you need to first verify that the employee still owes or that you the employer still owe the tax.

You can do this manually (with a pencil and a scratch pad), but if you need to track things like the net wages subject to social security, get a real payroll program or go to an outside service bureau. (See the discussion of the QuickPay utility and outside service bureaus later in this chapter.)

Using Memorized and Scheduled Transactions

You can memorize the payroll transactions you regularly record. Then, the next time you want to record the same or almost the same transaction, you can recall the transaction from the Memorized Transactions list. Quicken uses the memorized transaction's information to fill in the text boxes of the transaction.

Memorizing a Transaction

To memorize a transaction, follow these steps:

1. In the Write Checks window, display the payroll check you want to memorize or, in the Register window, select the payroll check or any other transaction.

2. Choose the Edit ➤ Transaction ➤ Memorize command to display a message box asking if you want to memorize the split amounts as actual dollars-and-cents figures or as percentages of the transaction total shown in the Write Checks window. Since you want to memorize the split amounts and not the split percentages, select No. When the This transaction is about to be memorized message appears, click on OK. Quicken adds the selected payroll transaction to its memorized-transactions list.

TIP One handy technique is to enter percentages on the split transaction lines. Just type a percentage—like 75%—rather than an amount. Quicken then calculates the split amount by multiplying the percentage by the transaction amount shown in the Write Checks window or Register window.

It's likely that Quicken is automatically memorizing transactions as you create them. To check on this, click on the Options button in the Write Checks window to display the Check Options dialog box and then click on the QuickFill tab to display the QuickFill Preferences settings. If the Auto MemorizeNew Transactions check box is marked, Quicken is automatically memorizing all your transactions as you record them.

Reusing a Memorized Transaction

To reuse a memorized transaction, follow these steps:

1. Display an empty check in the Write Checks window or select the new empty row in the Register window.

2. Choose the Lists ➤ Memorized Transaction command to display the Memorized Transaction List window, as shown in Figure 20.6.

3. Select the memorized transaction you want to reuse and click on the Use command button. Quicken uses the memorized transaction to fill in the text boxes in the Write Checks window or in the selected row of the Register window.

TIP Quicken automatically reuses a memorized transaction if you haven't turned off that option in QuickFill. To check this, display the QuickFill Options dialog box. If the Recall Memorized Transactions check box is marked, Quicken is automatically recalling transactions. All you do is enter the payee name and press Tab.

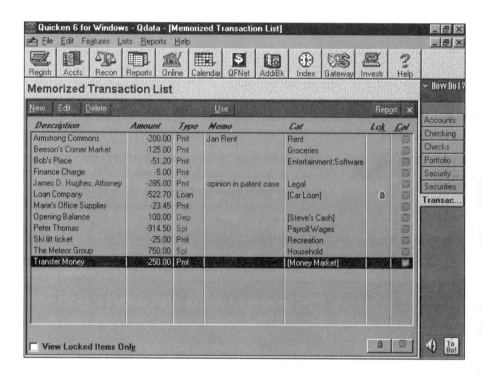

Figure 20.6.   The Memorized Transaction List window

Using Scheduled Transactions to Speed Payroll

If you have employees whom you pay, without fail, every week, Quicken's scheduled-transactions feature can help you. Tell Quicken it should automatically record a memorized transaction. To do this, you *schedule* the transaction in one of two ways: You can use the Lists ► Scheduled Transaction command or you can use the Financial Calendar.

TIP Scheduled transactions also make sense for automatic payments—such as those the bank may deduct from your account for your mortgage. Since these payments occur automatically, it makes sense to have Quicken record them automatically.

Getting to the Financial Calendar

To display the Financial Calendar window, as shown in Figure 20.7, choose the Features ➤ Paying Bills ➤ Financial Calendar command or click on the Calendar icon. The main part of the Financial Calendar window shows the current month's calendar. You can move backward and forward a month at a time by clicking on the Prev Month and Next Month buttons. The list box on the right half of the window shows the memorized transactions.

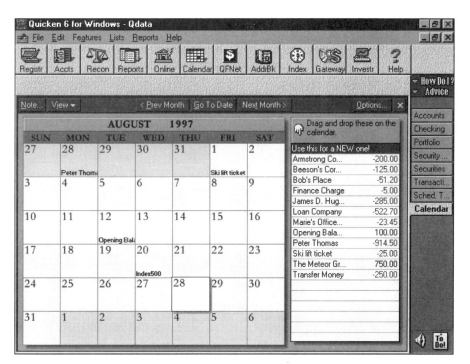

*Figure 20.7.   **The Financial Calendar***

NOTE If you want to display balances from only a selected group of accounts, first choose Show Account Graph from the View button, then click on the Options button to display the Calendar Options dialog box. Click on its Accounts tab, and then mark and unmark the accounts you want to see by clicking on them.

Scheduling a Transaction

To schedule one of the memorized transactions shown in the Financial Calendar window, follow these steps:

1. Display the first month you want to schedule the transaction using the Previous month and Next month buttons.

2. Select the memorized transaction by clicking on it; then drag the transaction to the first day it should be scheduled.

3. Quicken next displays the New Transaction dialog box, as shown in Figure 20.8. The information displayed on the dialog box describes the transaction you've just dragged.

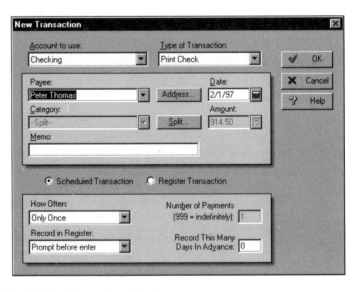

Figure 20.8.   The New Transaction dialog box

4. Activate the Account drop-down–list box, choose the account into which the transaction should be recorded, and click on OK.

5. Activate the Type of Transaction drop-down–list box to indicate whether you want Quicken to record a check, a deposit, or other type of transaction.

6. Use the next section's drop-down lists and text boxes to change any part of the recurring transaction.

7. Check either Scheduled Transaction or Register Transaction.

8. Activate the How Often drop-down–list box to display a list of payment frequencies: Only Once, Week, Two Week, Half Month, and so on. Then select the frequency with which the transaction should be scheduled.

9. *If you want to schedule more than one occurrence of this payment,* use the Number of Payments text box to enter the number of payments you want Quicken to enter.

10. Use the Record in Register drop-down–list box to specify whether you want Quicken automatically to enter the transaction or prompt you to enter the transaction.

11. *If you're using Quicken's Billminder feature* to remind you of unprinted checks, investment reminder notices, and scheduled transactions, use the Record This Many Days In Advance text box to specify the number of days of advance warning you want for this scheduled transaction.

12. Click on OK.

TIP Quicken automatically displays the Reminder window when you start Quicken if there's something it wants to remind you about. You can also display this window by choosing the Features ➤ Paying Bills ➤ Reminders command.

Quicken schedules the transaction. To show the scheduled transaction, Quicken puts the payee name on the calendar for each day the transaction will be recorded.

Changing the Scheduled Transactions

If you want to delete or edit a scheduled transaction, choose the Lists ➤ Scheduled Transaction command. Quicken then displays the Scheduled Transaction List window, which simply lists the scheduled transactions. To delete a scheduled transaction, select it, choose Delete, and choose OK. To edit a transaction scheduled , select it, choose Edit, and make your changes using the dialog box that Quicken displays. You can also add new scheduled transactions using the dialog box's New button.

 WARNING Do not delete a transaction scheduled prior to today's date from the Calendar because Quicken deletes both the scheduled transaction and the register entry.

Using the Financial Calendar's Reminder Notes

The Financial Calendar provides one other useful feature for managing and monitoring your payroll activities. You can post notes on calendar days—such a note might say, "Payroll tax deposit due." Quicken then uses the note text to remind you that, for example, the payroll tax deposit is due.

To post a note, follow these steps:

1. In the Financial Calendar window, select the day you want to be reminded.

2. Click on the Note button to display the Note dialog box.

3. Type your note and select Save.

 TIP Yellow is the traditional color for reminder notes, but you can change the color Quicken uses with the Note Color drop-down–list box.

Quicken saves your note and adds a yellow square to the calendar day to show you there's a calendar note for the date. (To later see the note, click on the yellow square.)

Customizing the Financial Calendar

The Options button in the upper-right corner of the Financial Calendar window displays a dialog box with two pages: Accounts and QuickFill. You can use these option settings to specify which accounts, scheduled transactions, and regular transactions appear on the calendar (an Account page setting), and to specify how QuickFill works (a QuickFill page setting).

NOTE To display scheduled transactions, recorded transactions, or both types of transactions on the calendar, click on the View button and select Show Recorded Transactions in Calendar, select Show Scheduled Transactions in Calendar, or select both. If you click on the View button and choose its Show Account Graph command, Quicken displays a chart beneath the calendar. This chart uses bars to depict the daily account balances.

Preparing Payroll-Tax Returns and Paying Payroll Taxes

There are two other payroll tasks to complete on a regular basis: You need to pay the IRS both the amounts you've withheld from employee checks and the amounts you owe for payroll taxes. And you need to prepare payroll-tax returns—usually on both a quarterly and an annual basis.

What to Do When You Write the Check

The rules for remitting federal tax deposits change frequently, so I'm not going to attempt a description here, but note that one useful piece of information concerns how much you owe. For example, as I'm writing this, if you owe less than $500, you don't have to pay a tax deposit until the end of the quarter. (If you owe more than $500, your best bet is just to immediately pay what you owe.)

But how do you know how much you owe the IRS? It's simple: you know by looking at the payroll liability accounts. The account balances in these accounts are the amounts you owe for various employer payroll taxes and employee payroll deductions.

WARNING Read through the section in the *Employer's Tax Guide* that describes the rules for depositing taxes. It describes how quickly you'll need to make deposits—including information such as a reminder that you should allow time for the check to clear. It also describes the penalty you must pay if you're delinquent.

Along with your check, you need to send a Federal Tax Deposit (Form 8109) coupon. This coupon gives your Federal Tax Identification number. The IRS should send you a booklet of these forms a few weeks after you apply for your employer identification number. The booklet of Federal Tax Deposit coupons has instructions about how you fill out the form and where you mail it.

Here's how to record the check you use to make the deposit. Let's say you currently owe the amounts shown in Table 20.3.

NOTE The payroll-tax–liability account balances shown in Table 20.3 equal the amounts you would owe if you have prepared one payroll check for $1,000 of gross wages, as described earlier in the chapter. The $9 in federal taxes is the amount withheld from the employee's check. The $124 is the total social security owed, including both the $62 paid by the employee as a payroll deduction and the $62 social-security payroll tax paid by the employer. The $29 is the total Medicare tax owed, including both the $14.50 paid by the employee as a payroll deduction and the $14.50 Medicare payroll tax paid by the employer.

Table 20.3.   *Payroll Liability Account Balances*

Description	Amount
Social security	$124.00
Medicare	$29.00
Federal income taxes	$9.00
Total taxes owed	$162.00

To record a check that makes the federal tax deposit for the payroll tax liabilities shown in Table 20.3, you write a $162 check. To show that your payment reduces the payroll tax liability account balances, you use the Split Transaction window to record transfers to the liability accounts in the amount shown in Table 20.3. Figure 20.9 shows the Write Checks window and the Split Transaction window that records this federal tax deposit.

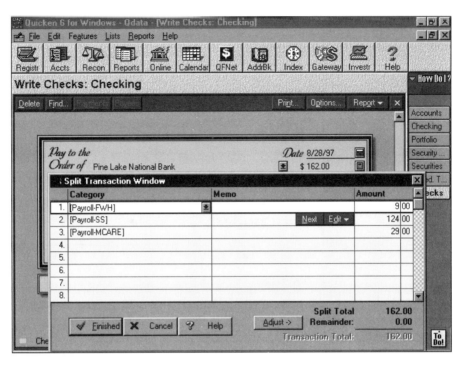

Figure 20.9. *The Write Checks window and the Splits dialog box that records a federal tax deposit*

TIP When you make a federal tax deposit, you use the depository's name for the payee.

Preparing Payroll-Tax Returns

To get the payroll information you need to fill out a payroll-tax return, you simply print the Business Payroll report using the Reports ➤ Business ➤ Payroll command. Figure 20.10 shows an example of the Payroll report. (For more information about how to produce and customize Quicken's reports, see Chapter 4, *Tracking Your Finances with Reports*.)

Payroll Report
7/1/97 Through 8/23/97

Category Description	Opening Balance	Peter Thomas	Pine Lake Nati...	OVERALL TOTAL
EXPENSES				
Payroll:				
Wages	0.00	1,000.00	0.00	1,000.00
SS	0.00	62.00	0.00	62.00
MCare	0.00	14.50	0.00	14.50
TOTAL Payroll	0.00	1,076.50	0.00	1,076.50
TOTAL EXPENSES	0.00	1,076.50	0.00	1,076.50
TOTAL INCOME LESS EX...	0.00	-1,076.50	0.00	-1,076.50
TRANSFERS				
TO Payroll-FWH	0.00	0.00	-9.00	-9.00
TO Payroll-MCARE	0.00	0.00	-29.00	-29.00
TO Payroll-SS	0.00	0.00	-124.00	-124.00
FROM Payroll-FWH	0.00	9.00	0.00	9.00
FROM Payroll-MCARE	0.00	29.00	0.00	29.00
FROM Payroll-SS	0.00	124.00	0.00	124.00
TOTAL TRANSFERS	0.00	162.00	-162.00	0.00
Balance Forward				
Payroll-SS	0.00	0.00	0.00	0.00
TOTAL Balance Forward	0.00	0.00	0.00	0.00
OVERALL TOTAL	0.00	-914.50	-162.00	-1,076.50

Figure 20.10. **First page of the Payroll Report**

Quarterly and Federal Payroll Tax Returns

Most and maybe all of the quarterly and federal payroll-tax returns you file will simply ask for the total gross wages you've paid for the quarter or for the year. In Figure 20.10, you get this number from the Gross Wages row in the Overall Total column. (This is $1,000 in Figure 20.10, and it includes only the $1,000 paid to one employee.)

The trick to getting a quarterly or annual gross wages total, of course, is that you need to use the appropriate Report From and Through Date ranges.

You can tell the total federal income taxes you've withheld by looking at the TRANSFERS FROM Payroll-FWH row in the Overall Total column. (It is $9 in Figure 20.10.)

Most of the other numbers you fill in on a quarterly or an annual report for things like social-security taxes, Medicare, and unemployment taxes are calculated by multiplying the tax rate by the gross wages total. If you fill out the quarterly 942 form (which you use to show social security and Medicare taxes for household employees like a nanny), you multiply the gross wages total by 12.4 percent to calculate the total social-security taxes owed, and you multiply the gross wages total by 2.9 percent to calculate the total Medicare-taxes owed.

You'll probably get a rounding error of a few pennies, but you can double-check your calculations—at least roughly. Whatever you calculate as the social-security tax and Medicare tax for the quarter or year should be within a few pennies of the TRANSFERS FROM amounts shown for the payroll liability accounts you've set up to track social security ($124 in Figure 20.10) and Medicare ($29 in Figure 20.10).

Employer Wage Statements such as W-2s and W-3s

You also use the Payroll report for filling out employee wage statements for state unemployment tax returns (where you often need to provide gross wages information by employee) and for things like the annual W-2 wage statements and the W-3, which just summarizes your W-2s. To do this, you just use the column of information shown for a specific employee. The Gross Wages amount shown in the column summarizing an employee's wages and payroll taxes is the amount you report as the total wages. The line that shows the federal–income tax withholding amount (TRANSFERS FROM Payroll-FWH in Figure 20.10) shows the amount you withheld for the employee's federal income taxes. And one half of the amounts on the lines that show the social security taxes and Medicare taxes transfer amounts (TRANSFERS FROM Payroll-FICA and TRANSFERS FROM Payroll-MCARE in Figure 20.10) provide the raw data you need to figure out how much in social security and Medicare taxes to withhold from an employee's gross wages.

> **NOTE** Both the employer and employee pay equal amounts for social security and Medicare taxes, so one half of the total social security taxes and one half of the Medicare taxes equal the amount withheld from the employee's payroll check.

Saving Payroll-Tax Deposit Money

You may want to set aside the payroll-tax money you owe and the amounts you deduct from employee wages. You can easily do this using another bank account or a Savings Goal account. Which you use depends on the way you actually save, or set aside, the money.

If you will save the money in another bank account, such as a savings account, you just set up another bank account in Quicken. Then, when you deposit money into this other account, you record an account-transfer transaction (see Chapter 2).

If you won't save money in another bank account but want to show that some of the money you have in, say, your checking account is really payroll tax deposit money, you set up a savings goal account. (You do so as described in Chapter 15.) Then, whenever you want to set aside money for the payroll tax deposits, you transfer the money to this Savings Goal account the same way you record any transfer. Quicken then records both the decrease in your bank account and the increase in your Savings Goal account, so your account records show the bank-account balance minus the payroll-tax deposit money, and the Savings Goal account will show the payroll-tax deposit money you've accumulated. Here's what's different about a Savings Goal account, though: Account transfers to and from a Savings Goal account don't show up as real transactions during a reconciliation, nor do they show up as account transfers on Quicken reports. In effect, then, for purposes of reconciling and reporting, Quicken just ignores any transfers to a Savings Goal account.

Using QuickPay or Using a Service Bureau

Let's say you've used (or tried to use) the payroll-preparation procedures described in this chapter and that they haven't worked well. In this case, you should either get the QuickPay add-in, which makes it easier to prepare payroll checks and helps with calculating the payroll taxes and net wages amounts, or you should use a payroll service bureau. But which choice is for you?

NOTE QuickPay is discussed in Appendix B.

The QuickPay payroll utility performs much of the work associated with calculating an employee's gross pay, looking up the appropriate federal income tax withholding amounts, and calculating social-security and Medicare taxes. If you find the payroll-preparation process too tedious and time-consuming, even though you understand the mechanics, QuickPay is an ideal solution. (If you have several employees or you pay hourly employees, QuickPay will make the gross-wage calculations much easier, for example.)

But perhaps your payroll problems stem from confusion about the mechanics of preparing payroll or you aren't comfortable doing all the arithmetic required when you do payroll. In this case, your best bet is to pay a service bureau to do the work for you.

NOTE Even many medium-sized businesses use payroll services because they're convenient and relatively cheap and because they improve confidentiality.

If you want to purchase a new copy of QuickPay and you have a modem, choose the Features ➤ Online ➤ Intuit Marketplace command. This gives you access to the latest prices and information available from Intuit. You do not need a web browser to use Intuit Marketplace.

**Part
4**

**Quicken in a Small
Business**

HOW TO HANDLE FEDERAL AND STATE PAYROLL PAPERWORK

Few things are as exciting—or as scary—as hiring your first employee. Whether you're a small business that is doubling its work force (from one employee to two employees!) or a busy professional hiring your first household employee, it's a big step to suddenly assume the responsibility of regularly meeting a payroll.

Unfortunately, in addition to all the other issues that you now have to address—whether you can afford new employees, picking the best person for a job, and so forth—you also have mounds of new paperwork to deal with.

I can't describe all of this new paperwork, but I can give you an overview of what you need to collect and prepare for the federal and state governments. If you have questions about all this, I suggest you confer with an accountant or bookkeeper who specializes in helping small businesses prepare their payroll and payroll-tax returns.

When You Become an Employer

As an employer, you need to do the following:

▶ Request and receive a Federal Tax Identification number from the Internal Revenue Service. To do this, fill out IRS form SS-4 (call the IRS to request one) and return it to the IRS. The IRS will send you a Federal Tax Identification number.

> **TIP** You can also receive a Federal Tax Identification number over the telephone. You tell the IRS how you filled out the SS-4 form, and they enter it into their computer and give you the number. You still need to send or fax in the SS-4 form, however.

▶ Obtain a copy of the *Employer's Tax Guide*, commonly referred to as a Circular E, from the IRS. This pamphlet tells you how much federal income tax you need to withhold from a person's check and what social security and Medicare taxes you and the employee pay.

▶ If your state requires it, get an employer identification number from your state for filing state payroll tax returns like unemployment taxes, workers' compensation, and so on.

▶ If you intend to withhold state income taxes, obtain your state's equivalent of Circular E. It tells how much state income tax to withhold from an employee's payroll check.

▶ Obtain federal and perhaps state tax-deposit coupons so you can remit federal and state tax deposits to the IRS and the equivalent state revenue agency. (Ask for these if you don't get them automatically.)

▶ At the end of the first quarter during which you employ people, obtain the appropriate federal and state quarterly payroll-tax return forms. For federal payroll taxes, businesses should use the 941 form, and household employers (if you've hired a nanny, say) should use the 942 form. You also probably file equivalent state quarterly payroll-tax returns.

▶ At the end of the year, obtain the appropriate federal and state annual payroll-tax returns. For federal unemployment-tax returns, for example, you need the 940 or the 940EZ form, and again, you probably need the equivalent state form for annual payroll-tax returns.

When You Hire a New Employee

Whenever you hire a new employee, the employee must fill out a W-4 form. This form provides you with the employee's social-security number, filing status, and personal exemptions. You need both the filing status and the personal exemptions to determine how much federal income taxes to withhold, and you need the employee's social-security number so you can prepare a year-end W-2 statement.

WARNING You will very likely have other, non-income tax, requirements to meet. For example, you probably have to verify to the Immigration and Naturalization Service (INS) that the person you're employing either is a U.S. citizen or has a valid work permit. Be sure to check for this type of requirement. (The IRS's *Employer's Tax Guide* and the equivalent state information guide can supply most of the information you need.)

Part 4

Quicken in a Small Business

CHAPTER 21

Accounts Payable and Accounts Receivable

FEATURING

Tracking accounts payable

Tracking accounts receivable

Improving your bookkeeping skills

ACCOUNTS receivable are simply the amounts your customers or clients owe you. Accounts payable are the amounts you owe your vendors. Quicken, because it's basically a checkbook-on-a-computer program, doesn't provide the same tools for managing accounts receivable and accounts payable that a full-blown accounting package provides. But you can still use Quicken to track the amounts customers owe and the amounts you owe vendors. To use Quicken for tracking receivables or payables, you simply need to know how to work with the Quicken register.

Accounts Payable

It is easy to track accounts payable with Quicken. You simply enter payment transactions for the amounts you owe using the Write Checks window. You enter the check date as the date the payment is due. Then, whenever you want to see what you owe your vendors, you print an A/P by Vendor report, using the Reports ➤ Business ➤ A/P by Vendor command. (See Chapter 3, *Printing Checks*, and 4, *Tracking Your Finances with Reports*, if you need help using the Write Checks window or printing a report.)

Looking at Figures 21.1 and 21.2, you can clearly see how accounts-payable tracking works. Figure 21.1 shows a Register window with several unprinted checks. (Notice that Quicken identifies the unprinted check transactions as checks by putting Print in the Num field. Quicken assigns a number when you print the checks.) Figure 21.2 shows an A/P by Vendor report that summarizes the unprinted-check information from Figure 21.1.

If you use unprinted checks for tracking accounts payable, be sure to use the same name for every transaction with a particular vendor because the A/P by Vendor report summarizes unprinted transactions by payee names.

You can easily keep payee names consistent by using the QuickFill feature. QuickFill automatically completes the entry of a payee name it recognizes. Another good approach is to select the payee name from the Payee drop-down–list box.

TIP   To display information about the unprinted checks that need to be paid, choose Features ➤ Paying Bills ➤ Reminders. Click on the Print Checks command button in the dialog box that appears.

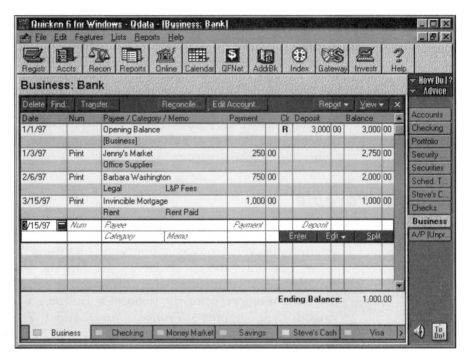

Figure 21.1. **The Quicken register with unprinted check transactions**

Selected Accounts   8/20/97

                                                                                          Page 1

A/P (Unprinted Chks) by Vendor
1/1/97 Through 3/20/97

Payee	1/1/97	2/1/97	3/1/97	OVERALL TOTAL
Barbara Washington	0.00	-750.00	0.00	-750.00
Invincible Mortgage	0.00	0.00	-1,000.00	-1,000.00
Jenny's Market	-250.00	0.00	0.00	-250.00
OVERALL TOTAL	-250.00	-750.00	-1,000.00	-2,000.00

Figure 21.2. **An A/P by Vendor report summarizing the unprinted-check information from Figure 21.1**

EARLY-PAYMENT DISCOUNTS

Early-payment discounts, which many vendors offer, are often too good to pass up. Suppose a vendor bills you $100 but offers you a 2 percent discount if you'll pay within 10 days instead of the usual 30 days. So, you can pay $98 on, say, the 10th, or $100 if you wait until the 30th. In effect, the 2 percent (or $2) early-payment discount is interest. And while this may not sound like much, charging a 2 percent interest rate for 20 days works out to an annual rate of more than 36 percent (because there are roughly eighteen 20-day periods in a year). As there are usually cheaper ways to borrow money, it almost never makes sense to borrow money from your vendors by foregoing early-payment discounts.

Here are the precise equivalent annual interest rates for early-payment discounts allowed by paying a vendor 20 days early:

Early-Payment Discount (%)	Equivalent Annual Interest Rate
1	18.43%
2	37.24%
3	56.44%
4	76.04%
5	96.05%

Accounts Receivable

To use Quicken to keep accounts-receivable records, you need to first set up a separate asset account. You then use this account to keep a list of the amounts customers or clients owe. (As your customers or clients pay their bills, you need to update the list with their payments.) For your efforts, you get the ability to produce a list of the accounts receivable by customer, organized by due date.

Setting Up a Receivables Register

To set up an Accounts Receivable register, set up an asset account by following these steps:

1. In the Account List window, click on the New command button to display the Create New Account dialog box.

2. Click on the Asset radio button and then click on Next.

3. In the Asset Account Setup dialog box, click on the Summary tab Quicken displays the Asset Account Setup dialog box, shown in Figure 21.3.

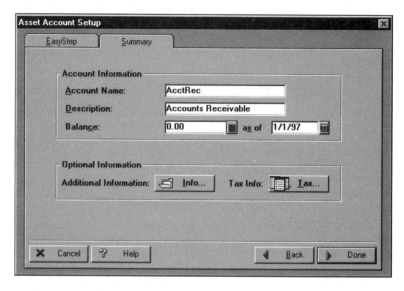

Figure 21.3.   **The Asset Account Setup dialog box**

4. Enter a name for the accounts-receivable account—such as AcctRec—in the Account Name text box.

5. Enter **0** in the Balance text box. (You calculate the accounts-receivable balance by entering the individual customer invoice amounts.)

6. Leave the as of text box entry (probably the current system date) as is. You don't need to enter anything.

7. Enter a brief description of the new account.

8. Click on Done. Quicken adds the new account and redisplays the Account List window.

Building a List of Accounts Receivable

To build a list of the accounts receivable your customers or clients owe, follow these steps every time you invoice:

1. Display the Accounts Receivable account register, as shown in Figure 21.4.

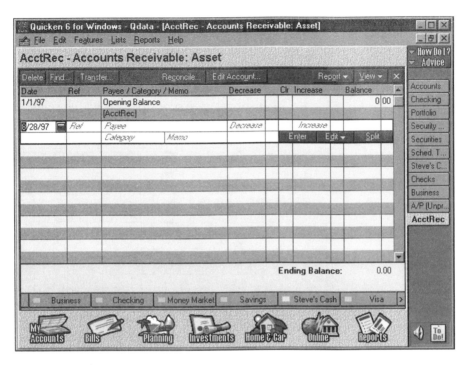

Figure 21.4.   The Asset Account version of the register, which you use for tracking accounts receivable

2. Delete the Opening Balance transaction since it shows as 0. Quicken removes the transactions and selects the first and now empty row in the register.

3. Enter the invoice date and invoice number in the appropriate text boxes.

4. Enter the name of the customer or client in the Payee combo box. If this is the first time you've recorded an invoice to this person or business, type the name. If you've previously recorded an invoice to this person or business, select the person's or business's name from the Payee drop-down list.

5. Enter the invoice amount in the Increase text box.

6. *If you want to add a memo description*—for example, to cross-reference a customer's or client's purchase order number—use the Memo text box.

7. Select Enter. If Quicken asks, confirm that you don't want to use a category. (In a cash-basis accounting system, you don't categorize accounts-receivable transactions as income; you categorize as income the customer

deposit that pays an account receivable.) Quicken updates the account balance and moves the cursor to the next empty row in the Account Register window.

8. Repeat steps 3 through 7 for each invoice your customers owe.

Figure 21.5 shows an Accounts Receivable register with several unpaid customer invoices.

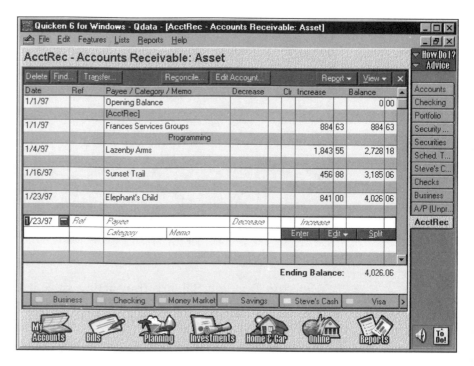

Figure 21.5. *An Accounts Receivable register showing unpaid invoices*

Printing an Accounts Receivable Report

To see a report that summarizes accounts receivable by customer and ages accounts receivable by invoice date, follow these steps:

1. Choose the Reports ➤ Business ➤ A/R by Customer command to display the Create Report dialog box shown in Figure 21.6.

2. Select a reporting period and click on Create to display the A/R by Customer report.

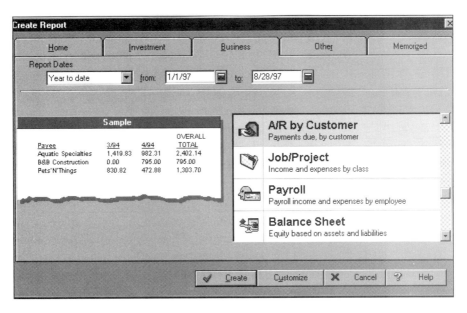

Figure 21.6. **The Create Report dialog box listing the business reports**

3. Click on Customize so that Quicken displays the Customize A/R by Customer dialog box. Then click on the Accounts tab so that Quicken displays the Accounts tab settings, as shown in Figure 21.7.

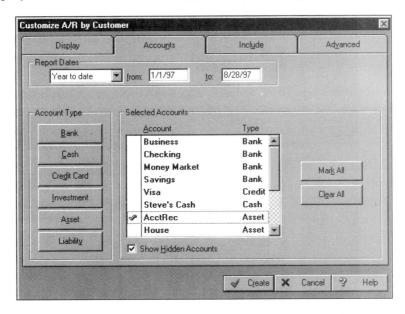

Figure 21.7. **The Customize A/R by Customer dialog box with the Accounts tab settings showing**

4. Quicken initially selects each of the asset accounts for inclusion in the A/R by Customer report. (If you have only one asset account—the accounts receivable account—it is the only one selected.)

5. Select accounts to add or delete from the report by clicking on them or by pressing the spacebar. When the proper accounts are selected, click on Create to return to the Report window. (See Chapter 4 for a discussion of customization options.)

6. Choose File ➤ Print Report or click on the Print command button in the Report window to print the Accounts Receivable report as it is displayed. Figure 21.8 shows an A/R by Customer report.

Checking 2   8/20/97

A/R by Customer
1/1/97 Through 1/31/97

Page 1

Payee	1/1/97
Elephant's Child	841.00
Frances Services Groups	884.63
Lazenby Arms	1,843.55
Sunset Trail	456.88
OVERALL TOTAL	4,026.06

Figure 21.8. **An A/R by Customer report**

USING AN A/R BY CUSTOMER REPORT FOR COLLECTION ACTIVITIES

You can—and probably should—use the A/R by Customer report as a guide to your collection activities. When a customer owes amounts from a previous month, for example, you might want to verify that the customer received the invoice and that payment is forthcoming. When a customer owes amounts that are from the months before the previous month—meaning at least one invoice is one or more months past due—you might want to consider more aggressive collection measures such as a letter from you, your attorney, or even a collection agency.

Keeping Your Accounts-Receivable List Current

The A/R by Customer report prints a list of all the uncleared transactions in the selected account, summarized by payee name. For this reason, the Quicken documentation suggests that an easy way to keep track of which customer invoices have and haven't been paid is to mark those that have been paid as cleared.

Unfortunately, there's a problem with this approach: All the transactions in a Quicken register—including both the uncleared and the cleared transactions—get counted to compute the account balance; so if you use the "just mark paid invoices as cleared" approach, your accounts-receivable account balance won't be right. (In other words, it won't equal the total accounts receivable your customers owe.)

If your accounts-receivable account balance isn't correct, your balance-sheet report won't fairly present your financial condition because it will overstate your accounts receivable, your total assets, and your net worth by the total paid customer invoices.

A better approach is to use the Split Transaction Window to keep a record of the original invoice amount and the payments a customer or client makes. The original invoice amount should show as the first split-transaction detail line, and payments should show as negative values on the subsequent lines, as shown in Figure 21.9. One tricky aspect of using the Split Transaction window is that after you enter a customer-payment amount, you need to select Adjust so that the transaction amount shown in the Accounts Receivable register equals the balance still owed on the invoice.

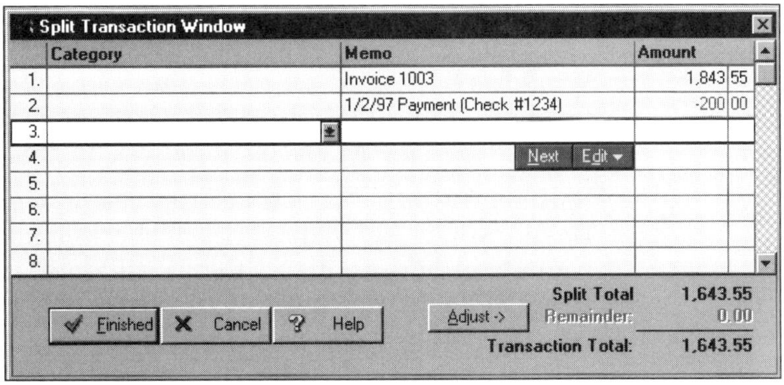

	Category	Memo	Amount
1.		Invoice 1003	1,843 55
2.		1/2/97 Payment (Check #1234)	-200 00
3.			
4.		Next Edit ▼	
5.			
6.			
7.			
8.			

Split Total 1,643.55
Remainder: 0.00
Transaction Total: 1,643.55

✓ Finished   ✗ Cancel   ? Help   Adjust ->

Figure 21.9. **The Split Transaction Window filled out to record customer payments on an invoice**

Part 4

Quicken in a Small Business

HOW TO BE
A GOOD BOOKKEEPER WITH QUICKEN

If you're a bookkeeper for a small business—or you do the bookkeeping for a small business even though you're not really a bookkeeper—this part of the chapter is for you. It describes what you need to know about your computer to be a bookkeeper, what you need to know about Windows 95, and what you need to know about Quicken. It also explains how to perform financial record keeping in a small business and where to get additional help if you need it.

What You Need to Know
About Quicken and Windows 95

Remember that accounting systems do three things: They let you calculate profits, they generate business forms, and they let you keep records of assets and liabilities. Quicken lets you calculate profits by tagging bank account deposits as income and bank account withdrawals as expense. If this approach doesn't work for the small business you're keeping the books for, you need to use another program. Quicken lets you generate only one business form, a check. If you need other business forms such as invoices, you need to use another program. Also, Quicken keeps detailed records of bank accounts only; if you need to keep detailed records of other business assets also, such as inventory, you need to use another program.

You need to know how to work within the Microsoft Windows 95 operating environment to use Quicken; the more you know about Windows 95, the easier you'll find using Quicken. You can read the first part of this book and get most of the useful information, and you can also read the Microsoft Windows documentation.

Spend a few days—maybe even a week or two—working with Quicken. Be sure you've entered a series of checks and deposits, and experiment with Quicken's reports. If things still don't click for you, you may be trying to do too much with Quicken.

•• *on the Road to Riches*

What You Don't Need to Know

As a bookkeeper, you need to know how to keep financial records that let your employer assess profitability and cash flow; how to keep records for a bank account and reconcile the account; and, in some cases, how to prepare payroll checks and returns. But there is also a list of things you don't need to know—information that goes beyond the scope of your job:

▶ You don't need to be an expert on federal or state income taxes. It's helpful if you know a few things, but, for example, your boss shouldn't expect you to understand the income tax rules for employee fringe benefits, asset depreciation, or partnership taxation. Your boss can get this type of information and analysis from a CPA or from an attorney who specializes in income tax planning.

▶ You don't need to be a computer genius. Yes, you need to know how to work with Windows 95 and Quicken, but you don't need to know how to drop an Ethernet card into a computer or reformat the hard disk. A local computer retail or repair shop can take care of these things.

▶ You also don't need to—and shouldn't—provide legal advice to your employer. An employer who wants to incorporate, deal with an employee's legal threats, or determine whether a contract is fair should talk to an attorney.

A Weekly Bookkeeping Checklist

Use the following list of tasks as a checklist at the end of each week:

▶ Enter all the payment and deposit transactions for the week (see Chapter 1, *Getting Started*, and 2, *Using the Quicken Register*).

▶ Back up the Quicken file to a floppy disk so that you won't lose the data if there's a computer problem or a human error (see Chapter 7, *Protecting Your Financial Records*).

▶ Check to see if you should remit any payroll tax deposit money by looking at the payroll tax liability account balances (see Chapter 20, *Payroll*).

▶ Print out a copy of the check register for the week and store it as a permanent financial record (see Chapter 2).

A Monthly and Quarterly Bookkeeping Checklist

Here is a checklist of tasks you should usually complete at the end of each month:

▶ Reconcile all your bank accounts (see Chapter 5, *Balancing Bank Accounts*).

▶ Print monthly Cash Flow and Profit & Loss Statement reports. Give a copy to the owner for assessing the month's profitability and cash flow, and put another copy in a permanent financial reports file (see Chapter 4).

▶ Prepare any monthly or quarterly payroll tax reports. Most businesses prepare the quarterly 941 payroll tax statement (see Chapter 20).

▶ Make quarterly estimated tax payments for the owner—or remind the owner to make the estimated tax payments. A small business owner is typically required to make quarterly payments of estimated taxes owed on April 15, June 15, September 15, and January 15.

An Annual Checklist

Here are the things you should do at the end of each year:

▶ Print annual Cash Flow and Profit & Loss Statement reports. Give one copy to the owner for assessing the year's profitability and cash flow, and put another copy in a permanent financial reports file (see Chapters 4 and 22, *Measuring Cash Flow and Profits*).

▶ Prepare a tax summary and tax schedule (see Chapter 11, *Exploring Quicken Deluxe*).

▶ Consider creating a disk version of the Tax Schedule report so that the Quicken data can be exported to a tax-preparation package (see Chapter 11).

▶ Prepare any annual payroll-tax reports. Most businesses prepare the annual 940 payroll tax statement and W-2 employee wage statements (see Chapter 18, *Stocks, Bonds, and Other Equity and Debt Securities*).

▶ Archive a copy of the previous year's financial records (see Chapter 7).

Two Things Bookkeepers Should Never Do

There are a couple of things you should never do. If you're not careful, they can, quite literally, lead to financial ruin.

Don't Borrow Payroll-Tax Deposit Money

Don't ever borrow the payroll-tax deposit money and don't ever help the business owner borrow the payroll-tax deposit money. This issue was discussed in Chapter 20, and the important thing is that the IRS takes a very dim view of this practice. If you're the bookkeeper and you've actively participated in borrowing the payroll-tax deposit money, the IRS can collect the money from you. (The IRS assumes that this borrowing amounts to stealing and that, as an accomplice to the theft, you may as well be the one to pay.)

If you've already been doing this, my advice is that you stop immediately. If the small business you keep the books for owes payroll-tax money it can't repay, I suggest you confer with a tax attorney.

Don't Participate in Misrepresentation

Financial misrepresentation occurs when you (or the business owner with your help) juggle a few of the financial figures to make the business look a little more profitable or a little healthier. Although the practice may seem innocent enough, it's a serious crime. Never participate in misrepresentation.

A business owner might juggle the figures to get a bank or a vendor to lend money or to get an investor to contribute money. When this happens, the bank, vendor, or investor contributes money because of a lie. If the bank, vendor, or investor loses money or discovers you've lied, both you and the business owner can end up in serious trouble. People do go to jail for this.

If you've been participating in financial misrepresentation or are being asked to participate, I suggest that you try to find a new job and that you talk with an attorney to see if there is some way you can extricate yourself from the mess.

NOTE Income tax evasion is basically just another form of financial misrepresentation. In this case, however, it's the IRS that's being lied to rather than a bank or investor.

Part 4

Quicken in a Small Business

CHAPTER 22

Measuring Cash Flows and Profits

FEATURING

Measuring a business's profitability

Forecasting profits and cash flows

Calculating the break-even point

Managing a business better

By collecting bank account payment and deposit information in Quicken registers, you can easily track the cash flows of a business. All of your business cash flows move into and out of your bank accounts. While Quicken's registers provide a wonderful structure for monitoring your cash flows, there is more work to do if you want to accurately measure your profits with these same registers.

Before You Begin

To measure cash flows, you need to set up Quicken bank accounts for each of the actual bank accounts you have. You should also know how to use income and expense categories to summarize payments and deposits (see Chapter 1, *Getting Started*, and Chapter 2, *Using the Quicken Register*).

To measure profits, you need to know how to set up asset and liability accounts (see Chapter 13, *Loans and Mortgages*, and Chapter 21, *Accounts Payable and Accounts Receivable*), as well as how to record account transfers (see Chapter 2).

Measuring Cash Flows

To monitor a business's actual cash flows in Quicken, choose the Reports ➤ Business ➤ Cash Flow command. When Quicken displays the Create Report dialog box shown in Figure 22.1, select Cash Flow and click on Create. Quicken produces a Cash Flow report like the one shown in Figure 22.2. (If you have questions about how to print reports, see Chapter 4, *Tracking Your Finances with Reports*.)

As Figure 22.2 shows, a Cash Flow report summarizes by income and expense category the money flowing into and out of bank accounts and cash accounts. A checkbook program like Quicken does a better job of describing and summarizing cash flows than any of the full-featured, double-entry bookkeeping systems because it uses the cash-basis method of accounting.

TIP Because Quicken summarizes income and expense cash flows, you budget by cash flows too. This means that the Budget window really amounts to a cash-flow budgeting spreadsheet.

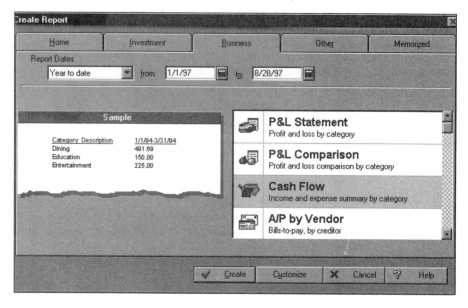

Figure 22.1. **The Create Report dialog box**

Cash Flow Report

1/1/97 Through 8/20/97

Category Description	1/1/97- 8/20/97
INFLOWS	
Salary	3,000.00
Bonus	200.00
Gift Received	-25.00
Uncategorized Inflows	1,000.00
TOTAL INFLOWS	4,175.00
OUTFLOWS	
Entertainment:	
Software	51.20
TOTAL Entertainment	51.20
Housing	200.00
Groceries	325.00
Recreation	25.00
Household	-1,500.00
Legal	285.00
TOTAL OUTFLOWS	-613.80
OVERALL TOTAL	4,788.80

Figure 22.2. **A Cash Flow Report**

Measuring Profits

Cash flow is important, but it doesn't always indicate whether a business is profitable. Cash flows into a business, for example, when a bank loans you money, a customer makes a deposit, or an investor contributes cash—yet none of these actions has anything to do with profit.

And often, a cash outflow can't be included in a single month's or single year's profit calculations. A shareholder draw, for example, isn't really an expense. Neither is a deposit you make with a vendor. And if you're in the trucking business, for example, the purchase of a new, $50,000 truck doesn't actually mean you should include the $50,000 as an expense for the month you purchase the truck. (It probably makes more sense to apportion the $50,000 of truck cost as expense over the months or years it will be used.)

To measure your profits precisely, you need to enter transactions that adjust cash flows. And to adjust the cash flows data, you need to know how to:

▶ Postpone cash inflows so that they are counted as future income

▶ Postpone cash outflows so that they count as future expense

▶ Count future cash inflows as current income

▶ Count future cash outflows as current expense

Postponing Cash Inflows So They're Counted as Future Income

Suppose you receive a $10,000 deposit from a customer and that deposit is a down payment for work the customer wants performed next year. If you record this deposit in the usual way—by categorizing it as income—you end up counting the deposit as income in the current year, but it really makes more sense to record the $10,000 as income in the following year.

To postpone cash flows so that they're counted as future income, you need to set up a liability account. Name the liability account something like "Def. Rev." and give the account a description such as Deferred Revenue.

When you record a deposit that really represents income for a future year, record the deposit as a transfer to the Deferred Revenue account. In effect, by doing this you record the increase in the bank account that stems from depositing the $10,000, and you record the fact that you actually owe the customer $10,000 because you've taken a deposit but haven't yet performed the work. (Think about it this way: If you take a $10,000 deposit from a customer, you may not owe the customer $10,000 in cash, but you do owe the customer $10,000 of products or services.)

When you earn the income you've previously deferred, record a transaction that reduces the Deferred Revenue account balance by the amount of revenue earned. Categorize this transaction using the appropriate income category.

Figure 22.3 shows a liability account with two transactions: a $10,000 increase in the liability account, such as would occur if you deferred $10,000 of revenue, and a $10,000 decrease in the liability account, with the decrease categorized as income.

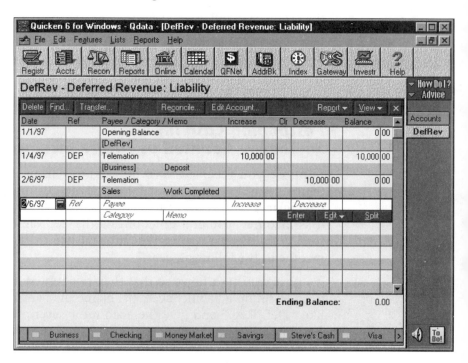

Figure 22.3. *A deferred-revenue liability account might look like this.*

Postponing Cash Outflows So They're Counted as Future Expense

Sometimes you want to postpone counting all or part of a cash outflow as an expense. Say you purchase a $50,000 truck. If you will use the truck for five years, it probably makes sense to allocate, or depreciate, the truck's cost over those five years. (In this case, you might want to record $10,000 of truck expense in each of the five years.)

To postpone cash outflows so they're counted as future expenses, you need to set up an asset account. In the case of a truck, for example, you would set up an account for the truck.

When you record the payment that really represents expenses for a future year or for future years, record the payment as a transfer to the new asset account. (Think about it this way: The amounts you pay for future years' expenses amount to prepaid expenses.)

Then you enter decrease transactions for each of the years you want to record an expense. Categorize this transaction using the appropriate expense category.

Figure 22.4 shows a truck account with five transactions—a $50,000 increase in the truck account, which would occur if you purchased a $50,000 truck, and four $10,000 decreases in the truck asset account, with the decreases categorized as truck depreciation expense.

Counting Future Cash Inflows as Current Income

In Chapter 21, I described how you can use an asset account to build a list of accounts receivable. While the approach described there works if you're willing to record income whenever you deposit cash, you need to use a slightly more sophisticated approach if you want to record income when you earn it.

For example, if you perform $5,000 of consulting for a client, you might want to correctly count the $5,000 as income in the year you perform the consulting services rather than wait until you collect the cash.

To count future cash inflows as current income, you need to set up an accounts-receivable–asset account for each customer.

When you want to record income, you enter an increase transaction in the appropriate customer's or client's accounts-receivable account, and you categorize the increase by using an income category.

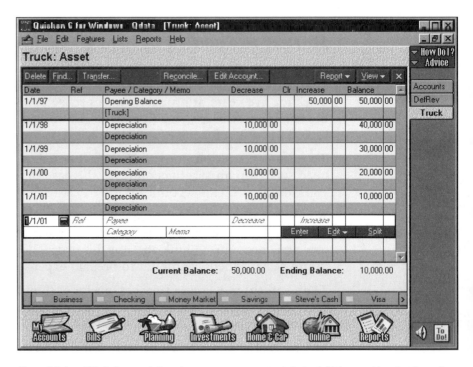

Figure 22.4. *This is how a deferred cost asset account might look if the asset is a truck you're depreciating.*

When you ultimately collect the income, you record a deposit in the appropriate bank account. But you categorize the deposit as a transfer from the customer's or client's accounts-receivable account using the Splits dialog box for the invoice transaction in the accounts receivable account.

Preparing a Profit & Loss Statement

To prepare a Profit & Loss Statement that includes the sorts of adjustment transactions I've described, you use the Reports ➤ Business ➤ P&L Statement command. Figure 22.5 shows a Profit & Loss Statement. It differs from the Cash Flow Report shown in Figure 22.2 in one important way: The Profit & Loss Statement category totals include transactions from all the accounts in the Quicken file. For example, if you had set up an asset account for recording depreciation expense, the Profit & Loss Statement would show that expense. (In comparison, a Cash Flow Report's category totals include only those transactions from bank and cash accounts.)

Profit & Loss Statement
1/1/97 Through 8/20/97

Category Description	1/1/97-8/20/97
INCOME	
Salary	3,000.00
Bonus	200.00
Gift Received	-25.00
Uncategorized Income	1,000.00
TOTAL INCOME	4,175.00
EXPENSES	
Entertainment:	
Software	51.20
TOTAL Entertainment	51.20
Housing	200.00
Groceries	325.00
Recreation	25.00
Household	-1,500.00
Legal	285.00
TOTAL EXPENSES	-613.80
TOTAL INCOME LESS EXPENSES	4,788.80

Figure 22.5. **A Profit & Loss Statement**

TIP Although the adjustment techniques described should let you better measure your profits, you may still want to prepare your income tax return using cash-based accounting. If this is the case, you need to prepare your income tax returns using the information shown in the Cash Flow Report, not the Profit & Loss Statement. (You may want to confer with your CPA about this.)

If Quicken Doesn't Work for Your Accrual-Based Accounting

Quicken isn't really set up to handle accrual-based accounting—which is what you're doing when you try to record income when you earn it and expenses when you incur them.

Part
4

Quicken in a Small
Business

If your business needs the increased precision of accrual accounting and you can't practically or successfully employ the techniques described, it may be time to consider one of the other, more powerful—but more complicated—accounting programs such as Intuit's QuickBooks, M.Y.O.B., or Peachtree Accounting for Windows.

Forecasting Profits and Cash Flows

The newest version of Quicken comes with a Forecasting tool. It lets you estimate your future cash flows and profits by extrapolating past information. Quicken looks at your register and scheduled transactions, assumes that these transactions will occur in the future, and then creates pro forma registers for producing cash-flow and income statement reports.

 NOTE This forecasting tool can also be used for personal financial management for someone whose personal finances are very complex. Using the forecasting tool in this way is probably overkill, however, for most individuals.

Creating a Forecast

The steps for creating a forecast are quite simple. You just need to do the following things:

1. Choose the Features ➤ Planning ➤ Forecasting command. Quicken displays the: Forecasting–Base Scenario dialog box. Click on Create to display the Automatically Create Forecast dialog box:

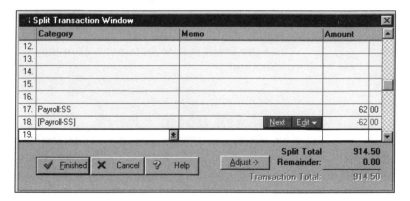

2. Use the Date Range to Read text boxes, From and To, to describe the period of time that should be used to create the forecast.

3. Click on the Advanced button to access the Forecast Items to Create option buttons, and then use these buttons to indicate the type of transactions Quicken should use as the basis for the forecast:

   - Known Items (from Scheduled Txns) tells Quicken to use scheduled transactions to create the forecast.

   - Estimated Items tells Quicken to forecast future income and expense amounts by using average income and expense amounts from either your register or your budget.

   - Create Both tells Quicken to use scheduled transactions and average income and expense amounts.

4. Use the From Register Data or From Budget Data option buttons to indicate whether Quicken should create estimates using the register transactions or your budget.

5. *If you want Quicken to forecast only certain income and expense categories,* click on the Categories command button. Quicken displays the Select Categories to Include dialog box. Indicate which categories you want to forecast by marking them—you can mark and unmark categories by clicking on them—and then selecting OK.

6. *If you want Quicken to forecast only certain account balances,* click on the accounts command button. Quicken displays the Select Accounts to Include dialog box. Indicate which accounts you want to forecast by marking them—you can mark and unmark categories by clicking on them—and then selecting OK.

7. Click on Done to save your advanced options.

8. When you select OK, Quicken displays the Forecasting–Base Scenario window, as shown in Figure 22.6.

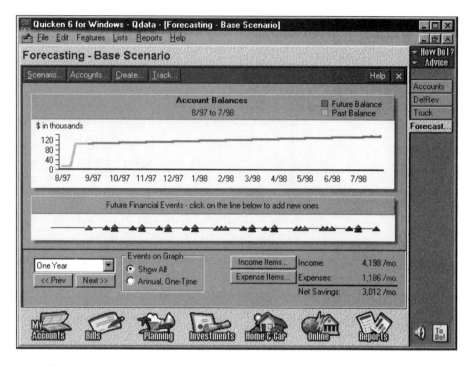

Figure 22.6. **The Forecasting – Base Scenario window**

Reading a Forecast

The line chart shows the forecasted account balance in either all or a selected group of accounts. You can select which accounts get included in the account balances line by clicking on the Accounts button and then, when Quicken displays the Select Accounts to Include dialog box, by marking the accounts you want to include. (You can mark and unmark accounts by clicking on them.)

You can change the forecasting interval—to month, half-year, full-year, and so forth—by activating the drop-down–list box in the lower-left corner of the window. You can change the forecasting period—such as from April to May if you've selected Months as the period—by clicking on the Prev and Next buttons. Clicking on the Prev button displays the account balances line chart for the previous period. Clicking on the Next button displays the account balances line chart for the next period.

If you click on the Track button, you can build a budget based on your forecast. (You may need to provide additional data to Quicken in order for it to build a budget in this manner.)

Updating a Forecast

To change the parameters used to create the forecast, click on the Create button. Quicken redisplays the Automatically Create Forecast dialog box. From here you can change any of the parameters you initially supplied to Quicken.

In the lower-right corner of the Forecasting window, Quicken summarizes the forecasted income and expense totals. If you want to see the income and expense details that Quicken uses to forecast the account balance, click on the Income Item and Expense Item buttons. Quicken displays a list of the forecasted income or expense categories and the forecasted amount. Quicken also shows the frequency and forecasting method. A monthly frequency, for example, means Quicken is forecasting one transaction a month. A Date column entry of average tells you Quicken is forecasting the category by looking at past averages.

You can change any of the forecasted amounts by clicking on the amount and then entering a new value. (You can flip-flop between the income and expense forecasts by clicking on the Income Items and Expense Items option buttons that are located on the right side of the Forecast Income or Expense Items dialog box.) If you want to add new forecasted events, click on the New button and then fill in the dialog box that Quicken displays. You can change existing forecasted events by clicking on the Edit button and then filling in the dialog box that Quicken displays. To remove a forecasted event, select it and click on Delete. To save your changes to these forecast items, click on Done.

NOTE The Events on Graph option buttons tell Quicken whether you want to see all the financial events for a forecasting interval or just those that occur on a one-time or annual basis.

Creating Multiple Forecast Scenarios

You can work with multiple forecasts, or scenarios, by clicking on the Scenario button in the Forecasting–Base Scenario dialog box. When you do, Quicken displays the Manage Forecast Scenarios dialog box, as shown in Figure 22.7. To name and save the current forecast, click on the New button and enter a name for the scenario when Quicken displays the Create New Scenario dialog box. (By default, when you create a new scenario, the Copy Current Scenario button is checked and Quicken actually makes a copy of the current scenario.) When you click on OK to save this scenario name, you go back to the Manage Forecast Scenarios dialog box. To later display a forecast, choose the Scenario button and simply select it from the Scenario Data drop-down list. You can also edit and delete scenarios by using the Edit and Delete command buttons.

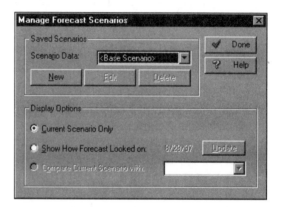

Figure 22.7.   *The Manage Forecast Scenarios dialog box lets you work with multiple forecasts.*

If you create a baseline scenario that you always want to show, create a comparison line. To do this, first make sure the scenario is the one currently shown. (You may need to use the Scenario Data drop-down–list box to activate the scenario.) Then click on New and enter a name in the dialog box that Quicken displays.

Calculating a Business's Break-Even Point

Break-even analysis allows you to determine the income necessary to pay all your expenses. Break even analysis is a simple and powerful financial-management technique related to business profits. At the break-even point, a business doesn't make any money, but it also doesn't lose any money. In general, you want to know a business's break-even point because it represents a sales level you must surpass to make money.

The Trick to Calculating Break-Even Points

To calculate a business's break-even point, you need to determine the total fixed costs of a business and its gross profit margin as a percentage.

A business's fixed costs are those expenses a business must pay regardless of the sales volume. In a retailing business, for example, fixed costs probably include rent, salaries of sales clerks, and other overhead expenses such as utilities and insurance. If a business's fixed costs include $2,000 in monthly rent (which also includes utilities and property insurance) and $4,000 in salaries, the business's fixed costs equal $6,000 a month.

A business's gross profit margin percentage is the difference between sales and its variable costs expressed as percentage of sales. You can calculate the gross margin percentage either on a per-unit basis or by using total sales and total variable costs. Suppose you want to calculate the gross profit margin on a per-unit basis. If you own a retailing business that sells T-shirts for $15 and the T-shirts cost you $3, your gross profit margin per unit is $12 or, restated as a percentage, your gross profit margin is 80 percent, calculated as $12/$15.

To calculate a break-even point, what you really do is figure out how much gross profit margin needs to be generated in order to pay for the business's fixed costs. In the case of the T-shirt retailing business with $6,000 of fixed costs and an 80 percent gross profit margin, the retailer must sell enough T-shirts so that the gross profit earned on the T-shirts pays the fixed costs.

Part 4

Quicken in a Small Business

To calculate the T-shirts that must be sold to break even, use the following formula:

Break-even point = (fixed costs/gross profit margin)

In the case of the T-shirt retailing business, you can calculate the number of T-shirts that must be sold to break even like this:

Break-even point in units = ($6,000 fixed costs/80 percent)

When you divide the $6,000 by 80 percent, you calculate the sales necessary to break even: $7,500. (At $15 a T-shirt, this works out to 500 T-shirts.) You can test this number by creating a worksheet that describes the income and expenses expected if the retailer sells 500 T-shirts, as shown here:

Income	$7,500	Calculated as 500 T-shirts @ $15 each
T-shirt expenses	$1,500	Calculated as 500 T-shirts @ $3 each
Fixed expenses	$6,000	
Profit (Loss)	0	

Using Quicken to Make Break-Even Calculations Easier

The preceding discussion described how you can determine your business's break-even point if you know your fixed costs and your gross profit margin. As a practical matter, however, you probably don't know these two figures—at least not right off. Does not knowing them mean you can't calculate your break-even point? No, you can easily use Quicken to develop the raw data you need.

To collect the raw data you need for your break-even analysis, you set up a couple of classes: one named Fixed, for tracking your fixed costs, and one named Variable, for tracking your variable costs (see Chapter 17, *Mutual Fund Investments*).

Setting Up the Fixed and Variable Cost Classes

To set up classes for segregating your fixed and variable costs, follow these steps:

1. Choose the Lists ► Class command to display the Class List window. It is shown in Figure 22.8.

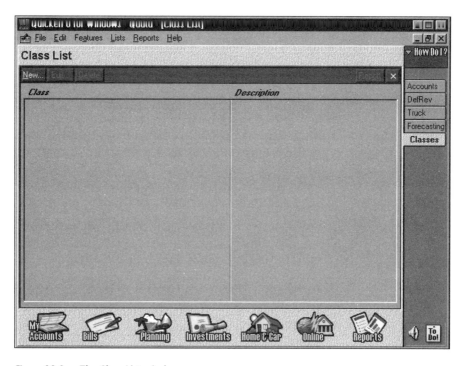

Figure 22.8. **The Class List window**

2. Click on the New command button to display the Set Up Class dialog box:

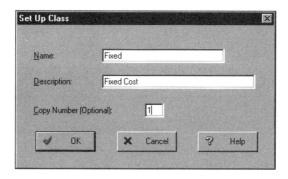

3. Use the Name text box to enter the class names, Fixed and Variable.

4. *If you want to further describe the cost classification,* use the Description text box.

5.   Click on OK, and Quicken adds the new class to the list shown in the
     Class List window.

You can set up subclasses the same way.

Collecting the Break-Even Raw Data

Once you set up the fixed and variable cost classes, classify each cost
you incur as either fixed or variable. Things such as rent, utilities,
insurance, and salaries are probably fixed, and things such as sales
commissions, costs of products or services you sell, and delivery or
freight charges are probably variable.

To classify an expense as either fixed or variable, follow the expense
category with a slash and the class name. Figure 22.9 shows a register
with the selected transaction illustrating this.

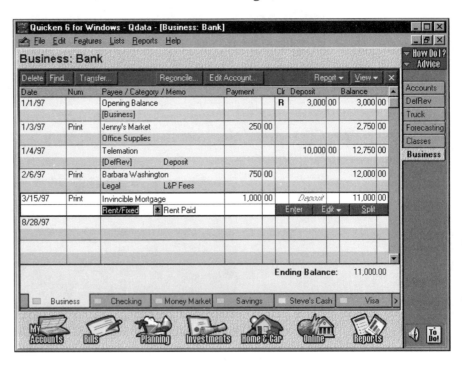

Figure 22.9.   A Transaction that is both categorized and classified

To see what fixed and variable costs you've incurred in a year or month, print a P&L statement that summarizes costs by both category and class. This will give you the total fixed costs—one of the pieces of data you need.

To calculate your gross profit margin, you can use the total sales and total variable costs figures and the following formula:

Gross profit margin = (sales – variable costs)/sales

If the data you collect shows sales of $20,000 and variable costs of $16,000, you calculate your gross profit margin percentage as 80 percent ($16,000/$20,000). Then you simply divide the fixed costs by the gross profit margin percentage to calculate the break-even point. If the fixed costs were $6,000, your break-even point is $7,500 ($6,000 divided by 80 percent equals $7,500).

HOW TO BE A BETTER BUSINESS OWNER

If you're a business owner, this part of the chapter is for you. The earlier chapters of this book provided information about using Quicken in a small business setting. This chapter takes a slightly different tack by discussing some issues that are specific to business owners who use Quicken.

Thinking About Security

You're going to use Quicken for an important and, possibly, confidential job: managing your financial affairs. Here are some things you can do to increase the security of the financial management system:

▶ Set up a password to restrict access to the Quicken system and your financial records if the PC running Quicken is used by employees who don't work with Quicken (see Chapter 7, *Protecting Your Financial Records*).

▶ Lock up the business forms you use, such as the Quicken checks. You don't want to allow anyone to steal check forms that can later be used in a forgery.

▶ Be sure you (or an employee) regularly enter payment and deposit transactions. You can't run a successful business without knowing how much cash you have and whether you're making money, and with Quicken, getting this information should take only a few minutes a day.

▶ Be sure you regularly back up your Quicken data files. This protects you from hard disk failures and human error.

▶ Be sure you reconcile your bank accounts on a monthly basis. This will help you catch the errors that people make.

The Problem of Embezzlement

Employee theft is extremely common. People steal office supplies in the fall (to use as school supplies for the children), deal with vendors who provide kickbacks (often in the form of expensive gifts and services), and sometimes even find clever ways to steal inventory and pilfer cash.

Most people don't steal, but it does happen; so it makes sense for you to consider what you can do to minimize your employees' opportunities to steal.

Sign Checks Yourself

It's a good idea to sign all checks—even small ones—yourself. This can be a lot of work (as a corporate controller, I used to sign about $100,000 of checks every week), but you can have an employee prepare the checks for your review and signature.

The benefit of signing all your checks is that your signature will be a requirement for money to leave the business. No cash will get deducted from the business bank account without your knowing about it.

If you sign all checks, an employee who wants to steal cash from you might try to convince you to write a check that the employee can cash. (You wouldn't write out, say, a $1,000 check to the employee without asking questions.) This means the employee would need to set up a fictitious vendor and then convince you to pay this vendor some amount. Or the employee might have you pay someone the employee needs to pay anyway. (I saw an employee have the employer write a check that paid the employee's Visa bill.) Carefully review the checks you sign to minimize the employees' opportunities for committing these crimes.

If you'll be on vacation for, say, a couple of weeks, the business will probably need to pay some bills while you're away. You can deal with this in a couple of ways. You can decide to trust an employee enough to leave behind a signed check or two—the employee can then use these signed checks to pay for things such as an unexpected C.O.D. shipment—or you can decide to simply require vendors to wait. If you leave signed checks, be sure to leave specific instructions as to what these checks should be used for, and review the checks when they come back from the bank to be sure your instructions were followed.

Part 4

Quicken in a Small Business

Review Canceled Checks

Be sure to intercept the bank statement when it comes and review the canceled checks. (An easy way to do this is to have the bank send the bank statement to your home.) This way you can make sure no one is forging your signature and writing a check or two for nonbusiness reasons. This might seem unlikely, but if your business writes a hundred checks a month totaling tens of thousands of dollars, would you really notice an extra check or two if the amounts were "only" a few hundred dollars?

Separate Mailroom Duty from Bank Deposit Duty

One of the most common ways to embezzle money from an employer is called *lapping*. To lap, an embezzler skims a little bit of the cash that comes in each month and then adjusts the books to hide the skimming. As long as the person skimming the cash also maintains the checkbook, it's easy for the theft to go unnoticed. The embezzler simply ignores or hides the fact that, for example, the $500 Customer A owes you has been paid.

You can minimize the opportunities for lapping if you have one employee open the mail and make a list of the incoming cash and another employee enter the bank deposit information into the checkbook. For this approach to work, you simply compare the list of incoming cash maintained by the mailroom person with the bank deposit information shown in the check, and you contact customers about past-due payments. This way you can discover, for example, that Customer A actually paid the $500 owed and that the check has cleared the bank.

Protect Other Valuable Assets

From an embezzler's perspective, cash is the most convenient item to steal. It's portable, easy to store, and easy to convert to other things an embezzler might want. Because cash is usually watched so closely, however, embezzlers often steal other items of value—such as office equipment, inventory, and supplies.

You can follow a couple of general rules to minimize losses such as these. You can keep a record of the things your business owns and periodically compare what your records show you have with what you actually hold. If you buy and sell inventory, for example, keep a record of what you buy and sell. Then, once a month or once a year, compare what your records show with what you have in your warehouse or storeroom.

WARNING   If, in your business, you buy and sell inventory, Quicken will not meet your needs. Consider upgrading from Quicken to a small business accounting system that tracks inventory, such as Intuit's QuickBooks Pro for Windows or Peachtree Accounting for Windows.

You can also restrict access to any valuable assets the business owns. Warehouses and storerooms should be locked. Access should be limited to people who really need what is being kept under lock and key. If you have items of high value in a storeroom, for example, and several employees have access, it's also a good idea to make it a rule that people go into the storeroom in pairs only. (A dishonest employee is less likely to steal if someone else who may see and report the theft is present.)

Require Vacations

There's a final embezzlement prevention tool that many big businesses use and which you should probably consider: Require regular vacations of a week or two. (Banks almost always do this.)

Here's the rationale: Some embezzlement schemes are so clever that they're almost impossible to catch. The one typical weakness of these super-clever schemes, however, is that they usually require ongoing maintenance on the part of the embezzling employee. By making the employee take a vacation, you get to see what happens if the employee's not around. Here are a couple of examples.

One embezzler who managed a concession stand had a simple but clever technique: He always pocketed a few hundred dollars of cash sales each week. This scheme worked for years. The owner assumed that cash sales were typically about $4,000 a week—even though they were really quite a bit more than that—and that he was losing about $200 a week of ice cream cones, soda pop, and popcorn because of spoilage and, perhaps, a little shoplifting. The concession stand manager never did take a vacation, but he did eventually have a heart attack. And a funny thing happened. Cash sales increased overnight (literally). Even more dramatic, profits jumped because sales increased but expenses stayed level. When the owner looked into the situation in the employee's absence, he figured out that sales and profits had increased because the employee was no longer pilfering cash from the till.

Another embezzler who got tripped up by a vacation requirement was a salesman selling profitable remodeling jobs for a company I'll call XYZ Construction. His scheme was to have every fourth or fifth job done by a company he'd set up, which I'll call XYZ Remodeling. He regularly used the resources and reputation of XYZ Construction to sell a remodeling job for XYZ Remodeling and thereby collect the 40 percent profit his employer (XYZ Construction) would have made rather than his usual 10 percent sales commission. As long as he stayed in town, his little ploy worked reasonably well. He could answer all his telephone calls—both those from XYZ Construction customers and those from XYZ Remodeling customers—and handle any problems that surfaced for either set of customers. When he went on vacation, however, the whole thing blew up as soon as an XYZ Remodeling customer called XYZ Construction to ask about a remodeling project in progress.

Finding Good Bookkeeping Help

In any business, it's a challenge to find and keep good people. It can be even more difficult to find good people to do something such as bookkeeping when you are not particularly knowledgeable about the subject, but there are some guidelines you can follow.

First, if you're hiring someone who is simply going to keep your checkbook, that person needs to know basic arithmetic, of course, but doesn't need to know how to use Quicken. If Quicken works well for you and you have no plans to upgrade to a more powerful program, the person can learn to use Quicken on the job. It will help if the employee already knows a thing or two about computers and has worked with Windows 95 or a program that runs under it, such as WordPerfect for Windows.

One other thing: You'll do well to find someone who knows how to do payroll net wages and payroll tax calculations. Mechanically, preparing payroll is one of the more complicated things you do in Quicken. An employee who understands these procedures will have an easier time using Quicken for payroll.

> **TIP** The IRS and many state revenue agencies sponsor free small-business taxpayer education programs (sometimes referred to as STEP workshops) that explain how things such as payroll taxes work. If a bookkeeper needs to learn how to do payroll, find out if there are any such workshops in your area.

How to Tell If You've Outgrown Quicken

Small business accounting systems—Quicken is one when you use it in a small business setting—are supposed to do three things:

▶ Measure your profits and cash flow so that you can prudently manage your business

▶ Track the assets and liabilities of the business so that you know what you own and what you owe

▶ Generate the business forms that you use to transact business

As long as you keep these three accounting system tasks in mind, you'll find it easy to tell when you've outgrown Quicken and should move up to a more full-featured small business accounting system.

Quicken measures income and expenses using cash-based accounting; so you generally record income when you deposit money into a bank account and record expenses when you write a check. In comparison, accrual-based accounting measures profits more precisely. They record income when you earn revenue and they record expense when you incur costs. If you want to do accrual-based accounting rather than cash-based accounting, you can't use Quicken. You'll need a more full-featured accounting system, such as QuickBooks from Intuit or Peachtree Accounting for Windows.

To keep detailed records of assets besides cash and your investments, you also need to use a small-business accounting system. For example, if you buy and sell inventory items and want to track these items, you need an accounting system that includes inventory management features. (Most small business accounting packages provide these features.) If you own a lot of depreciable assets and want to track them, you need an accounting system that includes a fixed-assets module. (This is a less common feature, by the way.) If you want job costing, point-of-sale accounting, or other special features, you also need to upgrade to a more powerful accounting system.

One other issue is business forms. Quicken produces check forms, but you probably need to produce other business forms too: invoices, customer statements, purchase orders, and so forth. If you want to automate production of these other forms with an accounting system rather than prepare them manually, you need to upgrade to a more powerful system.

Before you purchase a new accounting system to take care of the tasks I've just described, there are a couple of things to keep in mind. First, no accounting system is perfect. I've seen more than one business waste enormous amounts of time, energy, and money pursuing the perfect accounting system. If you have a system that works reasonably well, lets you gauge the performance of your business, and in general does most of the things you need it to do, you may create more problems than you solve by converting to a more complicated new system.

Also, the more powerful small-business accounting systems generally require you (or someone who works for you) to know a lot more about accounting than you need to know to operate Quicken. When you get right down to it, all you need to know to operate Quicken is how to use a checkbook and enter payments and deposits into a check register. In comparison, to use a full-featured small-business accounting system, you (or your employee) should know how to perform double-entry bookkeeping, understand the tricks and techniques used in accrual-based accounting (accruals, deferrals, reversing journal entries, and so on), and be able to read and use the financial information contained in a standard set of accrual-based financial statements (income statements, balance sheets, and cash-flow statements).

> NOTE The cash-flow statement produced by an accrual-based accounting system won't look anything like the cash-flow statement produced by Quicken.

Two Things Business Owners Should Never Do

There are a couple of final points I want to make about using Quicken in a small-business setting—two things you should never do.

Misrepresent Your Financial Affairs

You should never misrepresent your financial condition and your business's financial performance. You may think you would never do that, but let me tell you how it always seems to start. You go to the bank for a loan (perhaps a home mortgage). The bank loan officer looks at your Quicken Profit & Loss statement and then tells you you're not making quite enough money or that your debts seem a bit high.

It appears that a fair number of business owners go home, mull things over, and then think, "What if I made more money?" Asking and answering this question leads quite naturally to a careful review of the Quicken register, and suddenly the business owner has recategorized a series of business transactions as personal expenses. This has the nice effect of increasing the business profits. When the bank loan officer looks at your new Quicken Profit & Loss Statement, the loan is approved.

This may seem like a harmless solution, but misrepresenting your finances subjects you to two extremely serious risks. First, by misrepresenting your finances, you've committed a felony because you fraudulently obtained your loan. In a worst-case scenario, the bank can probably force you to repay the loan immediately. Many of the laws that normally protect you if you're a borrower don't protect you if you've fraudulently obtained a loan. (In a bankruptcy proceeding, for example, you probably can't escape repayment of fraudulently obtained loans.)

Another serious risk you run by misrepresenting your finances occurs if the IRS audits your return. If the IRS sees that expenses you claimed as business deductions on your tax return are later described as personal expenses on a Profit & Loss Statement, they can probably disallow the business deductions. If you assured the bank that $3,000 of travel expenses were for a personal vacation, you'll need to do a lot of backpedaling to convince the IRS that the $3,000 was really for business travel.

Borrow Payroll-Tax Deposit Money

Never borrow the money you've deducted from an employee's payroll check for taxes, and never spend the money you've set aside for the payroll taxes that you owe as the employer. If for any reason you can't repay the money, the IRS will pursue you with merciless vigor.

If you get to the point where you can't continue business without dipping into the payroll-tax deposit money, don't compound your problems by getting into trouble with the IRS. It doesn't matter what you want to use the money for. If you can't make payroll, can't get a supplier to deliver goods, or can't pay the rent without borrowing a bit of the payroll-tax deposit money, you simply can't make payroll, receive the goods, or pay the rent. If you did, you'd be stealing from the IRS. And when they find out, they may padlock your business some afternoon, thereby putting you out of business; seize any valuable personal assets you own, including your home; and garnish your wages if you get another job. In short, they will do anything they legally can to collect the money you should have paid them.

Because of all this, I can't imagine a situation in which it makes sense to "borrow" the payroll-tax deposit money. If things are so bad that you can't go on without taking the payroll-tax deposit money, it's time for you to consider drastic action—perhaps closing the business, filing for bankruptcy, laying off employees, or finding an investor.

Appendixes

APPENDIX A

Installing Quicken 6 and Setting Up Your First Accounts

This appendix describes how to do the two things necessary to start using the Quicken 6 for Windows application: install the actual application and set up your first bank account.

 NOTE See Chapter 1, *Getting Started*, for a detailed description of how to work with Quicken for Windows, including the various ways to accomplish different tasks, such as choosing menu commands and filling in dialog boxes.

Installing the Quicken Application under Windows 95 or Windows NT

To install Quicken in Windows 95 or Windows NT, first exit any programs you're running. Then follow these steps:

1. Choose Settings from the Start menu.

2. Choose Control Panel from the Settings menu.

3. In the Control Panel dialog box, double-click on Add/Remove Programs. Windows 95 or Windows NT displays the Add/Remove Programs Properties dialog box, shown in Figure A.1

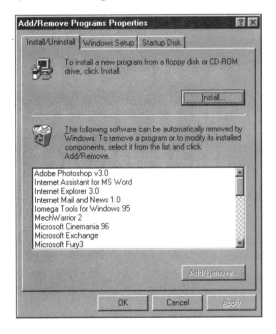

Figure A.1. **The Add/Remove Programs Properties dialog box**

4. Click on Install, and Windows 95 (or Windows NT) displays the dialog box shown in Figure A.2.

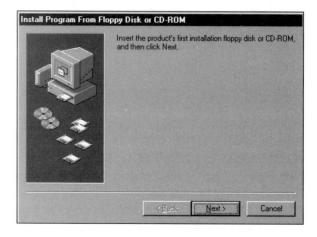

*Figure A.2.   **The Install Program From Floppy Disk or CD-ROM dialog box***

5. Insert Quicken floppy disk 1 into your floppy drive or the Quicken CD-ROM into your CD-ROM drive. (You may have more than one floppy drive.)

6. Click on Next and Windows 95 or Windows NT displays the Run Installation Program dialog box shown in Figure A.3. Windows will locate the setup program on your disk or CD-ROM and the program command line will appear in the text box.

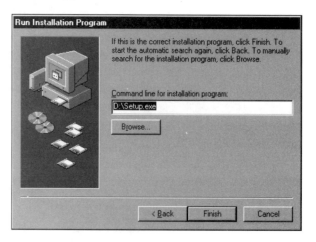

*Figure A.3.   **The Run Installation Program dialog box***

7. Click on Finish.

    Windows 95 or Windows NT starts the Quicken installation program, and it begins installing Quicken on your hard disk. (As you might know, this is mostly a matter of copying the files that Quicken needs from the floppy disks or CD-ROM to your hard disk.)

8. After the Quicken installation begins, the Quicken setup program asks if you want an Express Installation or a Custom Installation and if you want the U.S. or Canadian version installed. Use the dialog box's buttons to make these installation decisions (or just accept the default suggestions if you're unsure). Click Next twice. Quicken next asks if you want to accept the default program group and directory location. The Quicken setup program will continue the installation. If it asks you to insert the next floppy disk, do this and then click on OK to continue.

> **NOTE** If you choose a custom installation, Quicken displays dialog boxes that let you specify where the Quicken files are stored, the component you want to install, and where the Quicken program is stored.

When the Quicken installation program finishes, it displays a dialog box telling you that the installation is not complete until your computer has been rebooted and asks if you wish to reboot now or later. Click Finish if you want to use Quicken immediately.

9. When the Windows 95 desktop reappears, close the Control Panel by clicking on the close box in the upper-right corner of the window.

10. Double click on the Quicken 6 for Windows icon.

11. If you have a modem, Quicken asks if you want to register Quicken. To register—and it's not a bad idea—click on OK. Then, fill in the text boxes in the dialog boxes that the installation program displays to ask about your name, address, and use of Quicken.

> **NOTE** Intuit wants your name for its mailing list, of course. Even though you probably have an aversion to junk mail, it's a good idea to register. If you register you'll be notified of product updates and add-on products. (Sometimes existing users get special, discount prices on upgrades!) And in the unlikely event of a serious bug, you will be notified.

Setting Up Your First Accounts

Installing a record-keeping system like Quicken isn't just a matter of copying program files to your computer's hard disk. You also need to set up your first accounts.

> **NOTE** If you've been using an earlier version of Quicken and you've already set up an account, click on Cancel and go to File Open. Choose your data files from the folders and when asked if you wish to convert your files choose Yes. Even if you haven't backed up your files, Quicken will store a backup copy of your files just in case something goes wrong. You can move directly to the main chapters of this book. If you're just starting to use Quicken for Windows, after you finish this setup, you may want to turn to Chapter 1, *Getting Started*.

If you haven't used Quicken before, Quicken runs something called the New User Setup when you start Quicken for the first time. To complete the New User Setup, you follow these steps:

1. When Quicken displays the first Quicken New User Setup dialog box, click on Next.

2. Quicken asks you a few questions: if you are married, if you have children, if you own a house, and if you own a business. Answer these questions by clicking on the Yes or No buttons (see Figure A.4). Quicken uses your responses to determine which buying and spending categories it should create for you.

3. Click on Next to set up your first checking account.

4. Type in a name for the account (or accept the default Checking). Click on Next to continue.

5. Quicken asks you if you have your last statement for the account. If you click on Yes, the next dialog box asks for the statement date and balance. If you click on No, Quicken tells you it will create the account on January 1 with a balance of $0.00. It's okay if you don't have your last statement with you because you can change the opening balance and statement date later.

6. Click on Next. Quicken displays the new account name, statement date, and ending balance as shown in Figure A.5. Make any changes you need and click on Next.

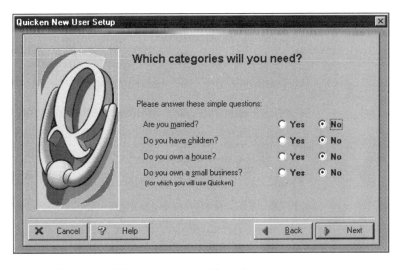

Figure A.4. Quicken asks which categories you will need.

Figure A.5. Quicken summarizes your new checking account.

7. When Quicken displays the next dialog box, you can click on the Overview button if you want to take a tour of Quicken, or just click on Done to begin using Quicken. (You can take the tour at any time by choosing Help ➤ Quicken Overview.)

8,   Quicken displays the checking account register window. The first transaction in the window is the opening balance you just created.

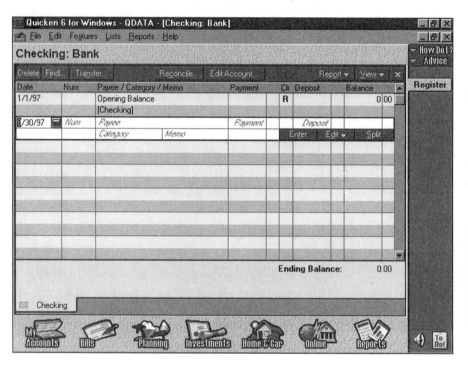

Figure A.6.   *The Quicken Register window*

APPENDIX B
Using QuickPay

QUICKPAY helps you prepare your payroll checks, reports, and tax returns. It works with Quicken to make it easy for small business owners to pay their employees by automatically calculating wages, deductions, and taxes. Once QuickPay calculates this information, it files payroll checks in the right accounts and in the correct categories.

 NOTE This appendix describes the steps for using the most current version of QuickPay (release 3). Please note, however, that the QuickPay program is usually revised on a different schedule than Quicken. Therefore, by the time you read this, it's quite possible that a newer version of QuickPay will have arrived. You should still find the information in this appendix useful, however, because the basic mechanics for setting up QuickPay and for preparing payroll checks should still be the same.

Installing QuickPay on Your Hard Disk

To install QuickPay, follow these steps:

1. Turn on your computer.

2. Click on the Start button on the taskbar.

3. Select Run from the Start Menu to display the Run dialog box.

4. Insert the QuickPay Install/Program disk in your floppy drive. (You may have more than one floppy drive.)

5. Type **a:install** if you inserted the disk in your A floppy drive or **b:install** if you inserted it in your B floppy drive.

Figure B.1 shows what the Run dialog box would look like after you type **a:install**.

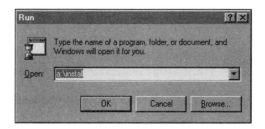

Figure B.1. **The Run dialog box**

6. Click on OK and Windows 95 begins installing QuickPay. Figure B.2 shows the first screen the QuickPay installation program displays, the QuickPay Install dialog box.

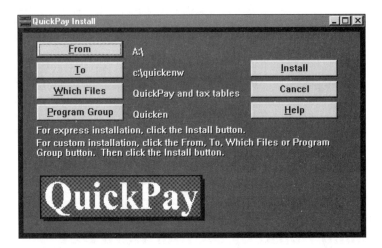

Figure B.2.   **The QuickPay Install dialog box**

    NOTE If you're not an experienced computer and Windows 95 user, skip steps 7, 8, 9, and 10.

7. *If you want to install QuickPay from a disk other than the disk you used to start the installation,* click on the From button or press Alt+F. QuickPay displays the Where are you installing from? dialog box. Either click on the button for drive A or B, or press Alt+A or Alt+B to tell the QuickPay installation program you want to install it from the A or B floppy disk. (In this case, you also need to give the name of the hard disk folder, or directory, in which the QuickPay installation program is stored.) Then click on OK. Note that there is usually no good reason to install from a different drive.

    WARNING If you're changing the QuickPay Install From setting, be sure you thoroughly understand the way Windows 95 organizes your disks and folders, and how to work in the Windows 95 operating environment.

8. *If you want to install the QuickPay program into a folder (directory) other than the quickenw folder, the one suggested by QuickPay,* click on the To button or press Alt+T to display the Destination dialog box. Use the drop-down–list box to select the disk where QuickPay and its files should be placed. Then either select the open folder in the text box (quickenw) or select the c:\ folder and double-click on it to display the list of all folders on the C drive. Scroll through the list and select the folder you want. (To place the QuickPay files in a new subfolder, you must first open the Windows 95 Explorer program and create a new subfolder with the File ➤ New ➤ Folder command. Name the new subfolder and drag-and-drop it where you want it to be. Then select it in the scroll box in the Destination dialog box.) Once you've specified where you want the QuickPay program installed, click on OK or press Enter to return to the QuickPay Install dialog box shown in Figure B.2.

9. *If you click on the Which Files button,* QuickPay displays a dialog box that asks: Would you like to install the QuickPay program, tax tables, or both? If you are installing QuickPay for the first time, you will probably want to install both the program and the tax tables. Since this is the default, click on OK to return to the QuickPay Install dialog box. If you are upgrading from an earlier version of QuickPay, you may choose to install only the tax tables, only the updated program, or both. Click on the option button for the files you want, and then click on OK to return to the QuickPay Install dialog box.

10. *If you want QuickPay to use a program group other than the default Quicken program group,* click on Program Group or press Alt+P. QuickPay displays the Which program group should the QuickPay program be added to? dialog box. You can enter a new program group into the combination text and list box the dialog box provides, or you can scroll through the list box and select an existing program group. When you've made your choice, click on OK to return to the QuickPay Install dialog box.

11. Click on the Install button, and the QuickPay installation program begins installing the QuickPay program into the folder you specified.

12. When the QuickPay installation program is finished, it displays a dialog box like the one shown in Figure B.3. Click on OK to close the dialog box, and Quicken displays the Quicken window, as shown in Figure B.4. To begin setting up your company payroll files, double-click on Quick-Pay 3 for Windows.

B

APPENDIX

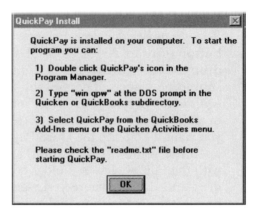

Figure B.3.   **The Installation Done dialog box**

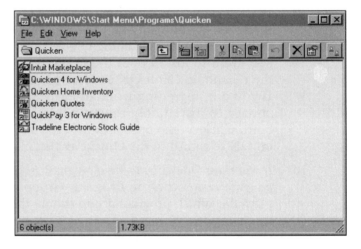

Figure B.4.   **The Quicken window**

Setting Up a Company

When you run it for the first time, QuickPay displays the Set Up Company dialog box, as shown in Figure B.5. Here you give QuickPay the information about your company that it needs to set up your payroll. (You can go back into the Set Up Company dialog box at any time to change any of the information. Just select Set Up Company from the File menu in the QuickPay main window.)

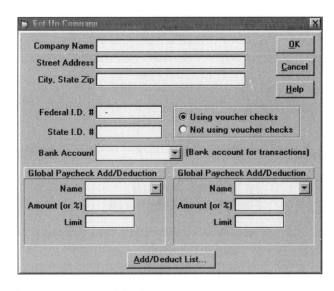

Figure B.5. **The Set Up Company dialog box**

Describing Your Company

The first thing you need to do is describe your company, including its name and address, Federal Employee Tax Identification Number, the State Employer Identification Number, and so on. To enter this data, follow these steps:

1. Enter the name of your company or business in the Company Name text box.

2. Enter your company's address in the Street Address, City, State and Zip text boxes. QuickPay uses the address information for printing checks and tax reports like W-2 forms.

3. Enter your Federal Employer Tax Identification Number in the Federal ID # text box. This is the nine-digit number the federal government issues to you when you start a business. You can find it on the notice the IRS sends when you file form SS-4 or on your form 941 quarterly payroll tax return.

4. *If your state requires you to have one,* enter your State Employer Identification Number in the text box marked State ID #. You can find this number on your state quarterly payroll tax return.

5. In the Bank Account drop-down–list box, select the name of the bank account from which you will pay your payroll checks. You should have already set up this account in Quicken. If you haven't, see Chapter 20, *Payroll*, in this book.

6. Tell QuickPay whether or not you are using voucher checks to pay your employees by choosing one of the two option buttons. Voucher checks have an extra stub attached on which QuickPay prints the employee's hours, earnings, taxes, and deductions.

Entering Global Paycheck Additions and Deductions

Once you've described the company, you should provide any standard, or "global," paycheck additions or deductions. For example, if you've set up a Simplified Employee Pension (SEP) retirement plan and you add a standard 15-percent SEP contribution to each employee's paycheck, you would want to describe that as a standard, or global, addition to each paycheck. To describe these global paycheck additions and deductions, follow these steps:

1. Enter the name of any global paycheck addition or deduction in the drop-down–list box marked Name. Global paycheck additions and deductions are those that apply to every employee on your payroll without exception; for example, a deduction for a mandatory employee retirement plan would be a global addition.

 NOTE Additions and deductions that apply only to certain employees are entered elsewhere, in the Add Employee dialog box. When you enter the name of a new global addition or deduction and then click on OK, QuickPay displays the error message "Addition/Deduction not setup."

2. Click on Add in the message window. QuickPay displays the Misc. Addition/Deduction dialog box, as shown in Figure B.6. You must set up each global addition and deduction separately by filling out the Misc. Addition/Deduction dialog box as many times as necessary.

3. Tell QuickPay whether each entry is a Paycheck Addition, Paycheck Deduction, or Company Contribution, by choosing the appropriate option button. Company contributions are amounts that your company

pays but that do not affect the amount of the paycheck. For example, your company may pay into a retirement account for each employee that is paid to the employee upon retirement.

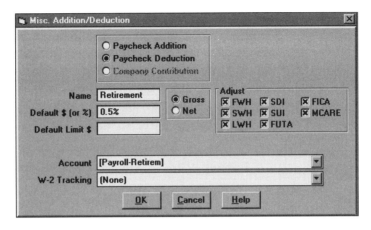

Figure B.6. **The Addition/Deduction dialog box**

4. Enter the name of the addition, deduction, or contribution in the Name text box.

5. Enter the amount of the addition, deduction, or contribution in the text box marked Default $ (or %).

   • If, for instance, the amount to be deducted is the same each pay-check, enter a number in the box. (Enter **10** for a $10 deduction.)

   • If the amount to be deducted is a percentage, enter a number followed by the percent sign: for example, **0.8%**.

   Depending upon whether the entry is for an addition, deduction, or company contribution, the amount of the entry is either added to or deducted from the employee's gross or net pay, or added to the company's liabilities.

6. *If there is an annual limit to the amount that can be added,* deducted, or contributed, enter this amount as a number (for example, **1000** for a $1,000 limit.) Once the limit has been reached, QuickPay no longer adds or deducts the amount.

7. *If you choose the Paycheck Addition or Paycheck Deduction option button,* QuickPay asks whether the amount is to be added to or deducted from

gross pay or net pay. Choose the Gross or Net option button accordingly. Amounts added to gross pay, such as bonuses, are taxable.

- Amounts added to net pay, such as reimbursements of employee cash outlays, are not taxable.

8. Enter the name of the Quicken expense category or liability account to which this addition, deduction, or contribution is to be charged. (You should already have set up these categories and accounts in Quicken. If you haven't, see Chapter 20.)

- If you selected an addition to gross pay, QuickPay suggests a default expense category, such as Payroll:Gross:Bonus.

- If you selected a deduction, QuickPay suggests a default payroll liability account, such as Payroll:Health.

- If you selected a company contribution, QuickPay suggests a default payroll liability account such as Payroll:Retirement:Company.

NOTE QuickPay does not allow you to use certain accounts for miscellaneous additions and deductions. For instance, you cannot assign a miscellaneous deduction to a payroll liability account that is set up for paying taxes. And you cannot assign an addition to gross pay to the gross wages account; you may, however, set up a subcategory such as Payroll:Bonus to include bonus pay.

9. *If the addition or deduction must be reported on form W-2*, the Wage and Tax Statement issued to employees at the end of each year, enter a tracking option in the drop-down–list box. A bonus, for example, is tracked as Compensation. Enter none if the addition or deduction need not be reported on form W-2.

TIP Check with an accountant to be certain which items are reportable and which aren't.

10. *If you choose the Paycheck Addition or Paycheck Deduction option button*, QuickPay displays the Adjust dialog box. The Adjust dialog box contains eight check boxes that correspond to taxes commonly withheld from paychecks. Mark a check box if the addition or deduction is subject to the tax specified. For example, a bonus is subject to federal withholding tax, so the FWH check box should be marked if the paycheck addition is a bonus. If the addition or deduction is not subject to

a particular tax, leave that check box blank. The acronyms stand for the following taxes:

Abbreviation	Description
FWH	Federal Withholding
SWH	State Withholding
LWH	Local Withholding
SDI	State Disability Insurance
SUI	State Unemployment Insurance
FUTA	Federal Unemployment Tax
FICA	Social Security Tax
MCARE	Medicare Tax

TIP If you have questions, consult your tax advisor to determine which taxes your employees' additions and deductions are subject to.

11. Click on OK to close the Misc. Addition/Deduction dialog box and return to the Set Up Company dialog box.

12. Add whatever miscellaneous global additions and deductions you are required to add. (To review the list of global additions and deductions, click on the Add/Deduct List button or press Alt+A.)

13. When you're done, click on OK in the Set Up Company dialog box. QuickPay displays the QuickPay main window.

    The next time you start QuickPay, it displays the main window. From there you can reach all of QuickPay's features or easily return to Quicken.

Editing the Addition/Deduction List

From time to time you may need to change some of the information on the Addition/Deduction List for your company's payroll. It's easy to reach the Addition/Deduction List from the QuickPay main menu. To make changes to the Addition/Deduction List, follow these steps:

1. Choose the Add/Deduct List on the Edit menu or press Ctrl+L. QuickPay displays the Addition/Deduction List dialog box, as shown in Figure B.7.

B

APPENDIX

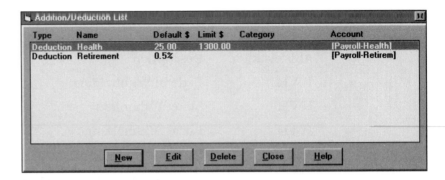

Figure B.7. **The Addition/Deduction List dialog box**

2. To add a new global addition, deduction, or company contribution to the list, click on the New button or press Alt+N. QuickPay displays the Misc. Addition/Deduction dialog box. Fill in the blanks as you did when you set up your company. When you have entered all the information, click on OK to return to the Addition/Deduction dialog box.

3. To change an existing entry on the list, select the entry you want and click on the Edit button or press Alt+E or Enter. QuickPay displays the Misc. Addition/Deduction dialog box you filled out before. Make any necessary changes in the dialog box and click on OK to return to the Addition/Deduction dialog box.

4. To cancel an addition or deduction altogether, select it and click on Delete or press Alt+D. QuickPay deletes the addition, deduction, or contribution from the list, and no longer pays that amount on your company's payroll. Click on Close or press Alt+C to return to the Quick-Pay main window.

Customizing Quicken Accounts and Categories

You can change the names of the Quicken expense categories and payroll liability accounts that QuickPay uses to keep track of your payroll expenditures. While this may seem frivolous, it can be very useful if, for instance, you are required or simply prefer to use account numbers rather than names. To change category and account names, follow these steps:

1. Choose Customize Account Names on the File menu, or press Alt+F and then Alt+A. QuickPay displays the Customize Accounts and Categories dialog box, as shown in Figure B.8.

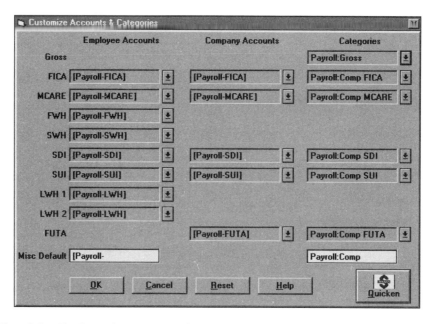

Figure B.8. **The Customize Accounts and Categories dialog box**

2. For each category or account name you wish to change, select the new name in the drop-down–list box for that category.

> **NOTE** You must already have set up the account and category names in Quicken. If you haven't, you can click on the Quicken button to set them up now.

3. To reset all accounts and categories back to their default names, click on the Reset button or press Alt+R. When QuickPay asks you for verification, click on Yes.

4. When you've made all the changes you want, click on OK to return to the QuickPay main window.

Protecting Your Payroll Files

You can prevent unauthorized people from examining your payroll files by protecting your files with a password. If you have more than one QuickPay payroll file, you can protect multiple files with the same password, or you can use a different password for each one.

Setting Up a Password

To set up a password, follow these steps:

1. Choose Set Up Password from the File menu. QuickPay displays the Set Up Password dialog box:

2. Enter a password of up to 16 letters in the Password text box. Quick-Pay doesn't differentiate between upper- and lowercase characters, so you only have to remember the letters in your password, not their case. As you type the password, QuickPay displays a series of asterisks in the text box, instead of the actual characters you type to prevent someone from looking over your shoulder and learning your password.

3. Click on OK. QuickPay displays the Confirm Password dialog box:

4. QuickPay asks you to confirm your password. In the text box, type the same password you just typed.

5. Click on OK. QuickPay compares what you entered in the Set Up Password dialog box with what you entered in the Confirm Password dialog box. As long as the two passwords are identical, QuickPay closes the Confirm Password dialog box and displays the Main window. You now have a password.

NOTE If the two password entries aren't identical, QuickPay redisplays the Confirm Password dialog box. You need to enter the identical password you entered in the Set Up Password dialog box to get QuickPay to assign your password. If you can't enter a match—perhaps because you made a mistake entering the password the first time—you can click on the Cancel button and start all over again.

You won't need to use your password to continue the current session, but the next time you start QuickPay and try to access your file, Quick-Pay will display the Set Up Password dialog box. You'll have to enter your password in order to access the file.

Changing Your Password

To change your password, choose the File ➤ Set Up Password command. When QuickPay displays the Change Password dialog box, type your current password into the Old Password text box and the new password you want to use in the New Password text box:

Click on OK when you are done.

If you've been using a password but don't want to do so or don't need to do so any longer, you can leave the New Password box blank. QuickPay will remove the old password and your files will no longer be password-protected.

WARNING Don't forget your password. Write it down and keep it in a safe place. If you forget your password and haven't kept a copy where you can find it, you will lose access to your files. You'll have to enter all your data all over again from scratch.

Setting Up Employee Files

Before you can issue a payroll, you must give QuickPay some information about your employees by setting up employee files. QuickPay needs specific data about each employee, such as his or her name, social security number, salary, and number of exemptions. You could use the Add Employee dialog box to give QuickPay the data it needs for each employee. However, if you have more than one employee, chances are good that two or more have data in common. For instance, it is more than likely that many or most of your employees pay taxes in the same state. You can save typing time by setting up an employee template and entering data that most or all employees have in common. Then you don't have to enter that data again on each individual employee record.

 NOTE If you have only one or two employees, skip to the section titled *Adding Employees*.

Setting Up an Employee Template

As mentioned in the preceding paragraph, you can create an employee template that provides employee information common to most or all employees: city, state, and possible zip code address information, pay period, W-4 status, and so forth.

Entering General Employee Information

The first set of information you need to collect is some general information not related to employee taxes, but information related to where your employees live and how you pay them. To enter this general employee information, follow these steps:

1. In the QuickPay main window, click on Edit Template or press Alt+T. QuickPay displays the Edit Employee Template dialog box, as shown in Figure B.9.

 NOTE Some of the text boxes seem to be missing. That's because this is a template; it is meant only to hold information common to more than one employee. It wouldn't make sense to be able to enter a social security number on a template, because every employee's social security number is different.

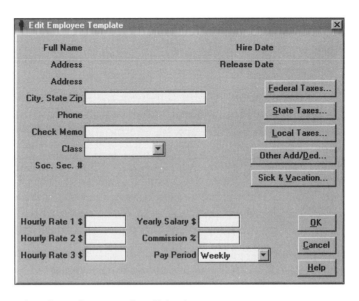

Figure B.9. **The Edit Employee Template dialog box**

2. Fill in any information that's the same for most or all of your employees. (You can change any incorrect information when you enter the data for each individual employee.)

3. In the City, State Zip text box, enter the address that is common to the largest number of your employees. For instance, let's say seven out of ten live in Seattle. Enter Seattle, WA 98 (the first two numbers in the zip code). You can fill in the rest of the zip code later for each employee, and you can change the entire line for any employee who lives elsewhere.

4. *If you would like to send the same message to all of your employees on every check,* enter anything you like in the Check Memo text box. For instance, if you write "Thanks!" in this box, it will show up on the memo line on all employee checks. (To make this work, however, you must also change QuickPay's default message, which is the employee's social security number. Open the Preferences dialog box by choosing Preferences on the Edit menu. Clear the check box called Print Social Security # in check message field.)

5. *If you classify your employees in Quicken by job level,* department, place of work, project, or any other parameter, you can use the Class drop-down–list box to assign your employees to classes. Doing this can help

you more easily keep track of certain costs. Set up the classes in Quicken first, and they will be displayed when you click on the arrow of the list box. On the Employee Template, enter the most common class, or leave the line blank.

6. *If many of your employees earn the same hourly wage*, enter this wage in the Hourly Rate 1 text box. If all of your employees are salaried, you can use this box for the most common overtime rate, if you wish.

7. *If many of your employees earn the same overtime and holiday wages*, enter these in the Hourly Rate 2 and Hourly Rate 3 text boxes.

8. *If many of your employees earn the same annual salary*, enter it in the Yearly Salary text box. You can enter both a salary and an hourly wage in the Employee Template, and then eliminate one or the other when you create each employee's file.

9. *If many of your employees earn the same commission*, enter the commission rate as a percentage in the Commission % text box. Enter the percentage as a number. (For an 8 percent commission rate, enter **8**.) Each payroll period you tell QuickPay the amount (based, for instance, on gross sales) that the commission is paid on, and QuickPay uses this rate to calculate the amount to be paid. You can enter a commission rate even if you've also entered hourly wage rates or a yearly salary.

10. *If many of your employees have the same pay period (for instance, if they are paid every two weeks)*, select that period in the Pay Period drop-down list.

11. *If many of your employees have a similar tax status*, as declared on the W-4 forms they file, you can put that information on your employee template.

Entering Federal Tax Information

Much of the federal income taxes information you need for preparing payroll will be the same for all your employees. For this reason, take the following steps to add federal income tax information to the employee template:

1. Click on the Federal Taxes button (or press Alt+F) to open the Federal Taxes dialog box, as shown in Figure B.10.

2. *If most of your employees must pay federal withholding tax*, check the FWH check box.

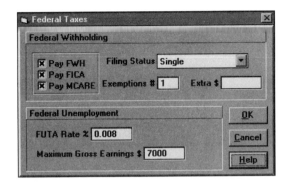

Figure B.10. **The Federal Taxes dialog box**

 TIP Refer to the Circular E, the *Employer's Tax Guide,* for information about how to determine an employee's tax status.

3. *If most of your employees must pay social security tax,* check the FICA check box.

4. *If most of your employees must pay Medicare tax,* check the MCARE check box.

5. *If many of your employees have the same tax filing status,* select that status on the drop-down list in the Filing Status box. The default is single. You can find the tax status of your employees on their form W-4, Employee's Withholding Allowance Certificate.

6. *If many of your employees have the same number of exemptions (as shown on their W-4 forms),* enter that number in the Exemptions text box.

7. *If many of your employees desire an extra amount withheld from their taxes,* enter that amount in the Extra text box. Most likely you will leave this box blank.

8. Enter the federal unemployment tax rate in the FUTA Rate text box. This is a tax paid by employers—you can't deduct it from your employees' pay. You can find the FUTA rate in IRS Circular E. (The 1996 rate is 6.2 percent.) Enter the rate as a number (e.g., **0.8**).

 TIP Generally, you are eligible for a FUTA tax credit based on the state unemployment taxes you pay. Check Circular E before you enter your rate.

B

APPENDIX

9   Enter the maximum wages that are subject to FUTA tax. (For 1996, the limit is $7,000.) Check Circular E to find the current limit.

10.   Click on OK to return to the Employee Template.

Entering State Tax Information

Most states tax the income of their residents. For this reason, you probably want to take the following steps to add state income tax information to the employee template:

1.   Click on the State Taxes button or press Alt+S to open the State Taxes dialog box, as shown in Figure B.11.

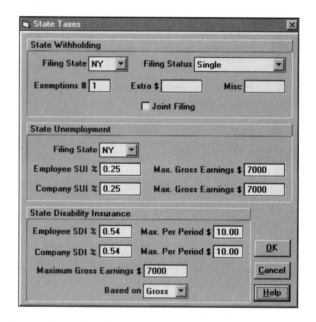

Figure B.11.   The State Taxes dialog box

2.   *If many of your employees live in the same state,* select the two-letter abbreviation for that state in the Filing State drop-down–list box. QuickPay will use the state tax table for that state to calculate state withholding tax.

3.   Leave the rest of the State Withholding box blank on the employee template. There are too many combinations of filing status, exemptions, and state tax considerations to make it likely that any one set will

do for all your employees. Fill in these boxes when you enter information for individual employees.

4. Keep the default (None) in the Filing State drop-down–list box. If your employees all work in the same state, QuickPay automatically calculates state unemployment tax for that state. If they work in different states, enter that information for individual employees.

5. *If your employees are required to make a contribution to state unemployment insurance in your state*, enter the appropriate rate in the Employee SUI text box. Check with your state authorities or with an accountant to make this determination. If an entry is required, enter the percentage as a number. (Enter **2.1** for 2.1 percent, for example.) Enter the maximum gross earnings subject to employee contributions in the Max. Gross Earnings text box on the same line.

6. Enter the rate of state unemployment insurance your company is required to pay in the Company SUI text box. Enter the percentage as a number. Enter the maximum gross earnings per employee that is subject to company contributions in the Max. Gross Earnings text box on the same line.

7. *If your employees are required to make a contribution to state disability insurance in your state*, enter the appropriate rate in the Employee SDI text box. Check with your state authorities or with an accountant to make this determination. If an entry is required, enter the percentage as a number. (Enter **2.1** for 2.1 percent, for example.) If there is a maximum an employee can contribute in one pay period, enter that amount in the Max. per period text box on the same line.

8. Enter the rate of state disability insurance your company is required to pay in the Company SDI text box. Enter the percentage as a number. Enter the maximum contribution per employee that the company must make in any pay period in the Max. Per Period text box on the same line.

9. *If there is an annual limit on the earnings per employee subject to contribution*, enter it in the Maximum Gross Earnings text box. It will apply both to employee and company contributions.

10. Check with your state authorities or with an accountant to determine whether state disability insurance in your state is based on gross earnings, hours worked, or days worked. Make the appropriate choice from the Based on drop-down list.

11. Click on OK to return to the Edit Employee Template dialog box.

Entering Local Tax Information

Some localities, including New York City, require employees to pay local taxes. If many of your employees are required to pay local taxes, take the following steps to add local income tax information to the employee template:

1. Click on the Local Taxes button or press Alt+L to open the Local Taxes dialog box, as shown in Figure B.12.

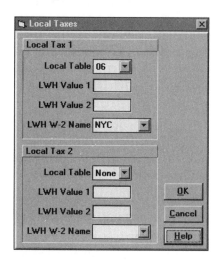

*Figure B.12.   **The Local Taxes dialog box***

2. QuickPay uses a two-digit code to identify different types of local tax. Check with your local authorities or with an accountant to determine how your local taxes are based. Then refer to the Local Tax table in the QuickPay manual to decide which code applies to your employees. Select that code from the drop-down list in the Local Table list box.

3. Look at the row of the Local Tax Table that applies to your employees. If there is a value in the LWH Value 1 column in that row, enter it in the LWH Value 1 text box.

4. Do the same for the LWH Value 2 text box, finding the appropriate value in the LWH Value 2 column.

5. Enter the name of the locality that collects the local tax in the drop-down–list box named LWH W-2 Name. QuickPay will enter this name in Box 19 on the employee's W-2 form.

6. *If your locality collects two local taxes*, fill out the text boxes in the Local Tax 2 box of the Local Tax dialog box, using the same procedures you used for Local Tax 1.

7. Click on OK to return to the Edit Employee Template dialog box.

8. If there are any other global additions, deductions, or company contributions that you didn't enter when you set up your company in Quick-Pay (remember, "global" means they affect every employee in your company), you can enter them now by clicking on the Other Add/Ded button or pressing Alt+D. QuickPay will open the Other Additions/Deductions dialog box. It will also prompt you to open the familiar Misc. Additions/Deductions dialog box that you saw during setup. Refer to the section on Setting up Your Company for detailed instructions on completing this dialog box.

Entering Sick Day and Vacation Information

If many of your employees accrue sick days and vacation time according to the same schedule, you can enter that information on your employee template:

1. Click on the Sick and Vacation button or press Alt+V to open the Sick & Vacation dialog box, as shown in Figure B.13.

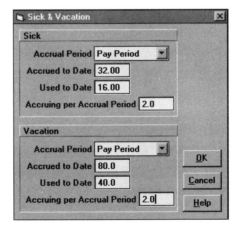

Figure B.13. **The Sick & Vacation dialog box**

2. In the Accrual Period drop-down–list box, select the period in which your employees accrue a unit of sick time. This could be one pay period (whether it's a week, two weeks, or a month) or it could be a year.

3. Enter the amount of sick time that accrues in that period in the Accruing per Accrual Period text box. If, for example, your employees accrue two hours of sick time every pay period, enter 2 in the text box.

4. In the same way, fill in the Accrual Period and Accruing per Accrual Period text boxes for Vacation time.

5. Click on OK to return to the Edit Employee Template dialog box.

6. Click on OK to return to the QuickPay main window.

Adding Employees

Once you have finished setting up your employee template, or if for any reason you don't need or want an employee template, you must set up records for each employee. Even if your employees have many things in common, they don't have all things in common. Some information is unique to each employee, and you must enter that information in the Add Employee dialog box. (Any information you entered in the Employee Template will show up for every employee.) Click on the Add Employee button or press Alt+A to display the Add Employee dialog box, as shown in Figure B.14.

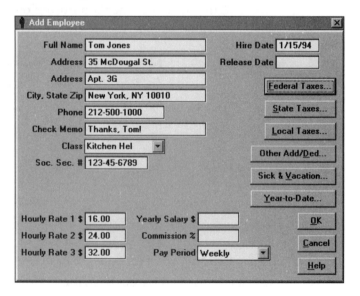

Figure B.14.   The Add Employee dialog box

The Add Employee dialog box is exactly the same as the Edit Employee Template dialog box, with two important exceptions. First, all of the text boxes are there—none of them are grayed out. Second, there is one additional button, the Year-to-Date button, which opens a dialog box that asks for information about year-to-date totals for your employees. This is important if you are starting to use QuickPay mid-year, because QuickPay has no other way of knowing that information. It will show up later on employee pay stubs and W-2 forms, as well as in your company records.

To fill out the Add Employee dialog box for each employee, follow these steps:

1. In the Full Name text box, enter the employee's name, as it should appear on paychecks and tax forms (W-2).

2. In the Address text boxes, enter the employee's full address. The address is required for the W-2 form.

 TIP It's a good idea to buy window envelopes if you mail paychecks to your employees. QuickPay prints the address right where it shows through the window.

---

3. *If the city, state, and zip information from the employee template is wrong for any employee*, change it.

4. Enter the employee's phone number in the Phone text box. The phone number isn't required, but it may be useful to have it here.

5. *If you would like to send the same message to an employee on every check*, enter anything you like in the Check Memo text box. For instance, if you write "Thanks!" in this box, it will show up on the memo line on this employee's checks. (To make this work, however, you must also change QuickPay's default message, which is the employee's social security number. Open the Preferences dialog box by choosing Preferences on the Edit menu. Clear the check box called Print Social Security # in check message field.)

6. *If you classify your employees in Quicken by job level, department, place of work, project, or any other parameter*, you can use the Class drop-down–list box to assign your employees to classes. Doing this can help you more easily keep track of certain costs. Set up the classes in Quicken first, and they will be displayed when you click on the arrow

of the list box. In the Class list box, select the class to which you want to assign this employee or leave the line blank. If the entry from the employee template is incorrect for any individual employee, change it.

7. In the Soc. Sec. text box, enter the employee's social security number. It will show up on the W-2 form for each employee automatically. To have the social security number show up on employee checks or check vouchers, make sure the appropriate boxes are checked on the Preferences dialog box. You can open this dialog box from the Edit menu of the QuickPay main window.

> **NOTE** If you check the Print Social Security # on Check Memo Line check box in the Preferences dialog box, any special check memo you enter in the Add Employee check memo text box won't print.

8. *If this employee is paid an hourly wage*, enter this wage in the Hourly Rate 1 text box. If this employee is salaried, you can use this box for an overtime rate if you wish. Change any incorrect information from the employee template.

9. *If this employee earns overtime and holiday wages*, enter these in the Hourly Rate 2 and Hourly Rate 3 text boxes. Change any incorrect information from the employee template.

10. *If this employee earns an annual salary*, enter it in the Yearly Salary text box. You can enter both a salary and an hourly wage if that is appropriate. Change any incorrect information from the employee template.

11. *If this employee is paid on commission*, enter the commission rate as a percentage in the Commission % text box. Enter the percentage as a number. (For an 8 percent commission rate, enter **8**, for example.) Each payroll period you tell QuickPay the amount (based, for instance, on gross sales) that the commission is paid on, and QuickPay uses this rate to calculate the amount to be paid. You can enter a commission rate even if you've also entered hourly wage rates or a yearly salary.

12. Select the pay period (for example, weekly, biweekly, or monthly) in the Pay Period drop-down list. Enter the pay period even for salaried employees. Change any incorrect information from the employee template.

13. In the Hire Date text box, enter the date this employee went on the payroll. QuickPay uses today's date as the default. Change it as necessary.

This information is merely for your records and is not used for any tax or payroll calculations.

14. In the Release Date text box, enter the last day the employee was (or will be) on your payroll. Use the same format as for the hire date (for instance, 11/08/96). QuickPay won't write checks for employees who have release dates, so you won't pay them accidentally.

15. Click on the Federal Taxes button (or press Alt+F) to open the Federal Taxes dialog box, as shown earlier in Figure B.10. Use this dialog box to describe which federal taxes the employee pays, the employee's filing status, and the number of withholding allowances the employee claims. If you have questions about how to complete this dialog box, refer to "Entering Federal Tax Information" earlier in this appendix.

 TIP Generally, you are eligible for a FUTA tax credit, based on the state unemployment taxes you pay. Check Circular E before you enter your rate.

16. Click on the State Taxes button or press Alt+S to open the State Taxes dialog box, as shown earlier in Figure B.11. Use this dialog box to describe which state taxes the employee pays. If you have questions about how to complete this dialog box, refer to "Entering State Tax Information" earlier in this appendix.

 NOTE The QuickPay user documentation provides an appendix that describes and discusses some of the state-specific employment tax rules.

17. Click on the Local Taxes button or press Alt+L to open the Local Taxes dialog box, as shown in Figure B.12. Use this dialog box to describe any local taxes an employee pays. If you have questions about how to complete this dialog box, see "Entering Local Tax Information" earlier in this appendix.

18. Click on the Sick and Vacation button or press Alt+V to open the Sick and Vacation dialog box, as shown in Figure B.13. Use this dialog box to describe the specific sick and vacation pay an employee has accumulated. If you have questions about how to complete this dialog box, refer to "Entering Sick Day and Vacation Information" earlier in this appendix.

19. Click on Year-to-Date to open the Year-to-Date dialog box. For each employee, enter the figures from your records for each of the categories and

accounts on the Year-to-Date dialog box in the appropriate text box. For example, in the YTD Gross text box, enter the gross pay you've paid this employee so far this year. Fill in the rest of the text boxes in the same way.

NOTE If you're starting a new business, adding a new employee, or if this is the beginning of a new year, you don't have to enter any year-to-date information. As you issue payrolls, QuickPay starts keeping this information for you automatically. If you've been using Quicken to keep your records, QuickPay transfers the information for you, as long as the Quicken account names match those in QuickPay. If, however, you have an existing business, you're starting to use QuickPay in mid-year, or you haven't been using Quicken to keep your records, you have to bring QuickPay up to date on your year-to-date expenses by using the records you kept before you started to use QuickPay.

Editing Employee Information

To view or change an employee's payroll information (if, for instance, the employee gets a raise), select the employee and click on the Edit Employee button in the QuickPay main window. QuickPay opens the Edit Employee dialog box for that employee. Find whatever information you need, make any necessary changes, and click on OK to return to the QuickPay main window.

To make changes in the employee template, click on the Edit Template button. QuickPay opens the Edit Employee Template dialog box. Make any necessary changes and click on OK to return to the QuickPay main window.

NOTE Remember that any changes you make in the employee template will affect all your employees.

Deleting an Employee

If you delete employees when they leave your company, you delete important payroll records for those employees. Instead of deleting an employee, it's a better idea simply to enter a release date in the Edit Employee dialog box. If you must delete an employee, select the employee on the employee list. Then choose Delete Employee from the Edit menu.

Preparing Payroll Checks

When you've set up your company and entered employee information for all your employees, you're ready to begin preparing payroll checks. Fortunately, preparing a payroll check is much easier than setting up the employee files.

Preparing a Payroll Check

Once QuickPay is set up, it's surprisingly easy to prepare individual payroll checks with QuickPay. To write payroll checks for your employees, follow these steps:

1. In the QuickPay main window, select an employee from the employee list.

2. Click on the Process Paycheck button. QuickPay opens the Process Paycheck dialog box for the selected employee, as shown in Figure B.15.

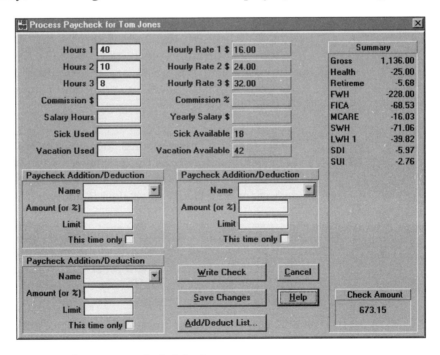

Figure B.15.   **The Process Paycheck dialog box**

3. In the Hours 1, Hours 2, and Hours 3 text boxes, enter in turn the employee's regular, overtime, and holiday hours for this pay period.

4. In the Commission text box, enter the amount of sales during this pay period upon which the commission is based. (QuickPay already knows what percentage of sales to use to calculate the commission.)

5. *If the employee is salaried*, you need not make an entry in the Salary Hours text box unless your state or locality needs to know the number of hours worked for purposes of figuring state disability insurance or local taxes. If you enter a figure in the Salary Hours box, it will appear on the employee's check voucher. Overtime hours for salaried workers should be entered in one of the Hours Worked boxes.

6. In the Sick Used text box, enter the number of sick units (days or hours) that the employee used this pay period.

7. In the Vacation Used text box, enter the number of vacation units (days or hours) that the employee used this pay period.

8. In the Name text box of the Paycheck Addition/Deduction Box, you can set up a new deduction from or addition to the paycheck of this employee. If this is an addition or deduction that you've entered before, it will be on the drop-down list. If not, enter it's name and QuickPay will prompt you to open the Misc. Addition/Deduction dialog box to fill in the necessary information about this addition or deduction. If this is a one-time addition or deduction, check the "This time only" check box.

 NOTE There's no need to enter the names of regular additions and deductions that are already on this employee's payroll record. QuickPay figures them in automatically. (If you enter the name of one of these additions or deductions now, QuickPay will figure it in twice.)

---

9. QuickPay displays a summary list of all payroll amounts for this employee, including pay, all additions and deductions, and the amount of the check the employee will receive. If you make any changes (if, for example, you discover you forgot to enter the employee's overtime), QuickPay adjusts the summary accordingly.

10. When you're satisfied the employee's payroll information is correct, you can either write the employee's check immediately or save the information and write the check later.

11. To save the payroll information and write the check later, click on the Save Changes button or press Alt+S.

12. To write the check immediately, click on the Write Check button or press Alt+W. QuickPay writes the check in Quicken.

> **NOTE** Writing the check is not the same as printing the check. Writing the check means that QuickPay adds the check to the register of the Quicken checking account you specified in the Set Up Company dialog box of QuickPay. Actually printing the check is a separate procedure that's also done in Quicken. See Chapter 3, *Printing Checks*, for more information.

13. In the QuickPay main window, select another employee and repeat the process until you've written checks for all your employees.

Correcting Mistakes in a Payroll

If, after you've written a check, you find you've made a mistake entering payroll information, you can cancel the check. You must also, however, delete the record of the transaction in Quicken.

To cancel the last check you wrote, follow these steps:

1. In the QuickPay main window, select the employee whose check is in error.

2. Choose Undo Last Paycheck form the Edit menu. QuickPay cancels the check and adjusts your records accordingly.

3. Click on the Quicken button to enter Quicken. Click on the Check button.

4. Page through the checks in the Write Checks window until the check you want to cancel is displayed.

5. Click on Delete or choose Delete Transaction from the Edit menu.

6. When Quicken asks, "OK to delete transaction?", click on Yes.

7. Go back into QuickPay, correct your mistake, and write a new check.

To cancel a check other than the last one you wrote, follow these steps:

1. In the QuickPay main window, select the employee to whom the check is written.

2. Click on the Edit Employee button. QuickPay displays the Edit Employee dialog box.

3. Click on Year-to-Date. QuickPay displays the Year-to-Date dialog box.

4. Click on Hour Transactions. QuickPay displays the Hour Transactions dialog box.

5. Select the transaction that describes the check you want to cancel.

6. Click on Delete to delete the check.

7. Click on the Quicken button and open the register of your payroll checking account.

8. Select the transaction you want to delete.

9. Choose the Edit ➤ Delete Transaction.

10. Return to QuickPay by choosing Add-ons ➤ QuickPay.

11. Click on the Edit Employee, then the Year-to-Date button.

12. Click on the Adjust button to ensure that the records in QuickPay match those in Quicken.

Processing Several Checks at Once

To process several checks at once, follow these steps:

1. In the employee list of the QuickPay main window, select all the employees for whom you wish to write checks.

2. Click on the Batch button. (If you click on the Batch button without selecting more than one employee, QuickPay prompts you to select another.)

3. QuickPay opens the Process Paycheck dialog box for each employee in succession. Fill in the required payroll information (hours, etc.) for each employee.

4. Write the check, or save the changes.

> **NOTE** If you have a group of employees whose pay is the same every pay period—salaried employees, for example—you can tell QuickPay to process their checks without opening the Process Paycheck dialog box. This speeds up the process considerably, but you have no opportunity to enter and review payroll data before QuickPay writes the check to the register in Quicken. You also can't enter sick and vacation time. If this option makes sense for your company, choose the Send all without review option button in the Edit/ Preferences dialog box.

Viewing Payroll Checks

To view payroll checks before you print them, follow these steps:

1. In the QuickPay main window, click on the Quicken button.

2. In Quicken, click on the Register button.

3. Click on the Check button at the top of the screen. Quicken displays a check.

4. Press Page Up or Page Down to view additional checks.

5. To see to which accounts various deductions are allocated, click on the Splits button. Quicken opens the Splits dialog box.

Printing Payroll Reports

QuickPay can print three reports that make it easier for you to see your company's financial picture and keep track of your employees. These reports include the payroll report, the employee roster, and the liability report. In addition, QuickPay can print W-2 statements for you to send to your employees and file with the various taxing authorities at the end of each year.

Printing the Payroll Report

The payroll report summarizes each payroll that you write. It lists all the information associated with the payroll for every employee and for the entire company, including gross and net wages, salaries and commission, additions, deductions, and company contributions, as well as taxes, hours worked, and sick and vacation days. To generate the payroll report, follow these steps:

1. In the QuickPay main window, choose Payroll Report from the Reports menu. QuickPay opens the Create Payroll Report dialog box:

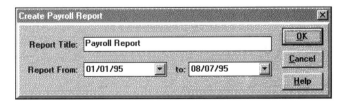

B

APPENDIX

2. Give the report whatever title you like.

3. Enter the dates you want the report to cover. QuickPay can generate a report on the current pay period, another pay period, or several pay periods going back to the beginning of the year.

4. Click on OK and QuickPay opens the Select Employee(s) to Use window, shown in Figure B.16.

Figure B.16.   **The Select Employee(s) to Use window**

5. Select the names of the employees you'd like to include on this report. Click on the Mark button to include or exclude a single employee. Click on the Mark All button to include or exclude all employees.

6. Click on OK and QuickPay generates the report on your monitor screen in the Reports window. You print a QuickPay report in the same manner as you print a Quicken report. (Refer to Chapter 4, *Tracking Your Finances with Reports*, for more information.)

Printing the Employee Roster

The employee roster lists your employees' names, addresses, phone numbers, and social security numbers. It's a handy way to generate a list of the most frequently needed information about your employees. To generate the employee roster, choose Employee Roster from the Reports menu. QuickPay opens the Reports window and displays the roster.

Printing a Liability Report

The liability report lists all your company's payroll-related debts. It lists the balance for each payroll liability account. To generate the liability report, choose Liability Report from the Reports menu and press Enter. QuickPay shows the Liability Report.

Printing W-2 Forms

At the end of every year, you are required to file form W-2 Wage and Tax Statements that list all the wages earned by each of your employees during the year, as well as the taxes you withheld. You send each employee three copies: one to file with each taxing authority (federal, and state or local) and one to keep. You keep a copy of each employee's form, and send copies of all of them to the federal and state governments, along with form W-3, Transmittal of Wage and Tax Statements. Filling all these forms out manually is tedious, time-consuming, and prone to error. Instead, QuickPay can do most of the work for you with just a few clicks of your mouse.

To generate W-2 and W-3 forms, choose the Reports ➤ W-2 Wage and Tax Statement command. When QuickPay opens the W-2 Wage and Tax Statement dialog box, select the name of an employee. Click on the View W-2 button to review the W-2 information for that employee, make any changes necessary, and then click on OK. (You want to repeat this process for each of your employees.) Once you've reviewed the W-2 information for your employees, mark the names of the employees whose forms you wish to print and click on either Print W-2 or Print W-3 to produce the printed forms.

APPENDIX C

Financial Information on the World Wide Web and the Internet

WHEN you first install Quicken 6 for Windows, the program asks if you want to install a Netscape Web browser to access Intuit's World Wide Web site. (Intuit is the maker of Quicken.) The Netscape browser and other tools included with Quicken allow you to connect only to Intuit's World Wide Web sites, including the Quicken Financial Network (QFN). For an additional monthly fee, you can use the QFN to access the entire Internet, including newsgroups and other World Wide Web sites.

If you're not all that familiar with the Internet, stepping into cyberspace is a little bit like parachuting into the great unknown. When you land, you may not know where you are, and you may not have any familiar landmarks. This appendix is a primer for people who don't know that much about the Internet but would like a little background before they jump.

What Is the World Wide Web?

The simple definition of the World Wide Web—also known as the Web, WWW, and W3—is a group of documents, accessible from almost any Internet connection in the world, that are linked together. Each document contains *links* (sometimes called *hot links*) to other documents by way of a format called *hypertext*. When you are looking at a Web document about Shakespeare, for example, the words, "Globe Theatre" may be highlighted. By clicking on those words, you are sent to another document relating to the Globe Theater. It may have pictures, or historical information, or just about anything else you can imagine. That document, in turn, may have links to other topics.

As a result, the World Wide Web is structured a bit like a spider web. To get to any point on a web, there are many paths. One point links to another, which links to another, and so on. By traveling through these links, you can go to many different points on the way to your final destination. And, in theory, you can get from any point in the entire system to any other point by just following these links.

Each document is described by a *uniform resource locator*, or URL. The URL not only provides your computer with the name of the document, but also tells your computer the document's location on the Internet. These documents are usually grouped together to form a *Web site*.

In this next section, I will introduce you to the Quicken Financial Network and to Intuit's Web site. After that, I will discuss a few other helpful sources of information on the Internet and the World Wide Web.

The Quicken Financial Network (QFN)

Over the past year, Intuit has vastly expanded the QFN. It now covers a much wider range of services, with information on everything from personal banking to small-business finances and investments. Because part of the fun is poking around and finding out what is available, I'll just hit some of the highlights of the QFN.

There are two ways that you can get to the QFN:

▶ Some people have access to the Internet only through Quicken. If this is the case with you, start Quicken, then choose Features ➤ Online ➤ Quicken Live (Internet) ➤ QFN Preview. Then click on one of the hyperlinks. Quicken automatically starts Netscape and opens the URL of the Quicken Financial Network, as shown in Figure C.1.

▶ If you do not use Quicken to access the Internet and you have your own Internet service provider, point your Web-browsing software to http://www.qfn.com, which is the URL for the Quicken Financial Network. (A URL gives the Internet address of something such as a web site or web page. You enter the URL into the Location box, as shown in Figure C.1.)

In Figure C.1, you can see the buttons labeled with the names of QFN's six centers to the right of the QFN logo. You can click on any of these buttons and go to the corresponding part of the Web site. The following is a short description of QFN's six sections:

Investments covers stocks and mutual funds. There are two major services available here: NETworth, which provides stock quotes and company information, and Investor Insight, which allows investors to keep track of their personal portfolios.

TIP The information in many stock quote services, such as NETworth, has a time delay. (NETworth's, for example, is 15 minutes.) If you like to track your stocks' progress closely, this delay may pose a problem.

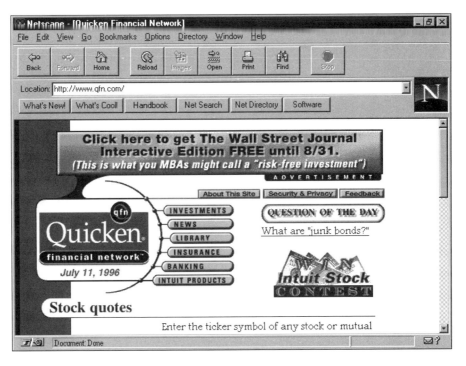

Figure C.1.   The opening screen of the Quicken Financial Network

News provides article titles and abstracts, divided into subject areas. In some cases, you can obtain the full text of articles, but there is currently a $3.95 monthly fee for unrestricted access.

Library has free information on business and finances. Access to other areas is available for $4.95 per month.

Insurance gives you access to a new Quicken service, InsureMarket, and basically serves as a clearinghouse for life, automobile, and home insurance information.

Banking provides information on online banking and online bill payment, along with links to banks who work with Intuit to make these services available.

Intuit Products will take you to an Intuit page in QFN. This page links to the Intuit Web site, which I describe in the following section.

The Intuit Web Site

The Intuit Web site provides product-specific information regarding all of Intuit's products, includes technical assistance, lists of frequently asked questions (or FAQs), and offers current product information. You can also ask questions about any Intuit software here.

Intuit is constantly updating the Web site, using it as a primary means of communicating with Quicken users around the world. In the past, for instance, a wide range of information has appeared on the site, such as technical solutions to problems posed by users, updates to Intuit software (which can be downloaded by any user with WWW access), and samples of Intuit products. Even if you don't consider yourself a first-class Webmaster, it's worth the effort to check out the site every once in a while.

There are two ways to get to the Intuit Web site:

▶ Pressing the Intuit Products button on the Quicken Financial Network Web page will take you to an Intuit page in QFN. This page contains links which can take you directly to any place in the Intuit Web site, including the Quicken page.

▶ If you point your Web browser to http://www.intuit.com, which is the URL for the Intuit Web site, you will see the Intuit home page shown in Figure C.2.

One other note: Although the information in Intuit's Web site is sorted by product, be sure to take a look at the other product sections, even if you are not interested in the products themselves. The QuickBooks section, for instance, contains information relating to small businesses, while the TurboTax section contains advice on personal taxes. You might pass up some useful information if you stick to just the Quicken section. Besides, you miss out on half of the fun of the World Wide Web if you don't let curiosity get the best of you every once in a while.

Clicking on the words, "Quicken and Personal Finance" will open the section devoted to Quicken, called *Quicken Online.* The Quicken On-line section is split into five different sections, as you can see from the header sections in Figure C.3. To go to each section, you just click on the name of the section you are interested in.

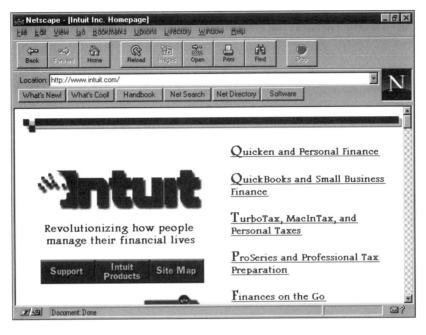

Figure C.2.   **The Intuit Web site**

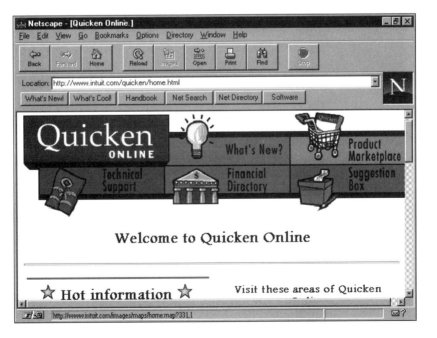

Figure C.3.   **The Quicken Online home page**

In my opinion, the sections that you should pay special attention to are What's New? and the Technical Support section. In these sections, you will get the most current information available on Quicken and its related services, product notes, answers to questions often posed by Quicken users, and so on.

In the next section, I will show you other services available on the Internet that may be handy. This appendix is not meant to be comprehensive by any means, but it will introduce you to some of the financial worlds which are available in cyberspace.

Other Information on the Internet

Of course, there is much more financial information on the Internet than that found on Intuit's Web site. The following sections assume that you have access to all Internet services, either through the Quicken Financial Network or through an outside Internet provider.

The World Wide Web

The most useful place to start on the World Wide Web, in my opinion, is the Alta Vista site, whose URL is `http://www.altavista.digital.com`. Besides being an index of many, many existing sites, it provides a means of searching for sites by way of keywords. If you are searching for information about investing in gold, for example, Alta Vista might come up with a list of sites that have pages about the subject.

 WARNING Keep in mind that marketing on the Web has become big business and the ratio of advertising to useful information can be overwhelming if you're not ready for it. Confirm important information from independent sources before taking action. And be prepared to look through a lot of dreck until you find sites you like or develop search techniques of your own.

Here are some sites that may be interesting to you, with their URLs:

▶ The Vanguard Group (`http://www.vanguard.com`) has one of the best sites for financial information. Vanguard is a no-load mutual-fund–management company; their Web site seems to be designed primarily to help investors, rather than to merely push Vanguard's products. Their Investor Education section contains entire "courses" on investor-related subjects, and their Retirement Savings Calculator and Portfolio Planner provide some useful tools.

▶ Financenter (`http://www.financenter.com`) provides information on purchasing or financing homes and automobiles. They also have some interesting credit-card information, including a calculator which can compare all those offers you get in the mail from competing credit-card companies.

▶ If you have a potential college student in your household, CollegeAssist (`http://www.edworks.com`) will not only help with choosing a school, but will provide tips and information on admissions criteria, costs, and another very important subject—financial aid.

TIP Many colleges have Web sites of their own, and a site frequently has enough information to help your son or daughter decide whether or not they want to write to that college for admission materials. (Since the sites often have pictures of the campus, the sites can also serve as mini-tours!) You can easily find a college's Web site by searching Alta Vista (`http://www.altavista.digital.com`) under the college's name.

▶ If you are looking for some basic articles on investing, Frank Armstrong has some information on GNN (`http://nearnet.gnn.com/gnn/meta/finance/feat/21sdt/index.html`). I don't agree with all of the information, but some of it is quite good.

▶ The Security and Exchange Commission has a Web site named Edgar (`http://www.sec.gov/edgarhp.htm`) which provides the quarterly and annual reports that all U.S. publicly-held companies must file.

Internet *newsgroups* provide information and a means of finding out about other Web pages. In the next section, I introduce Internet newsgroups to you and suggest a few that might be of interest.

APPENDIX

C

Internet Newsgroups

A newsgroup is the cyberspace equivalent of the office water cooler, a place where people gather and chat about common interests. There are newsgroups for just about anyone, from fans of Mystery Science Theater 3000, to amateur and professional astronomers, to people looking for fat-free recipes. Anyone can start a subject on a newsgroup by posting a message. And anyone can add their two cents to an existing topic by replying to someone else's message. Figure C.4 shows a typical newsgroup posting.

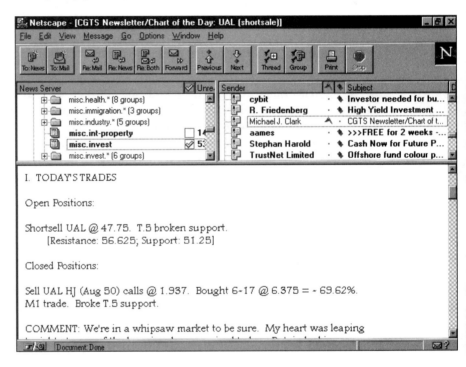

Figure C.4.   A typical newsgroup posting

To begin, choose the Window ➤ Netscape News command to open the newsgroup window. In Figure C.4, you can see that there are three parts of this screen.(Your screen may look slightly different until you download a newsgroup.) The News Server area, in the upper-left corner, lists the newsgroups available from your Internet service provider. (If no groups are shown, try choosing the Options ➤ Show All Newsgroups command.)

> **TIP** You can shorten your list of newsgroups by "subscribing" to the ones you prefer. Click in the box to the right of the newsgroup's name, and Netscape places a check in the box to indicate that you are now subscribed. (In Figure C.4, I have subscribed to misc.invest.) Repeat this with each group you are interested in, then choose Options ➤ Show Subscribed Newsgroups. Netscape will only display the newsgroups you have checked. To unsubscribe from a newsgroup, click in the check box again to clear the check mark.

In the News Server pane, the newspaper icon indicates a newsgroup. A folder indicates a number of newsgroups that begin with the same name as the folder. You can double-click on a folder icon to display all newsgroups in the folder.

When you click on a newsgroup, Netscape lists the available articles in the pane to the right. Scroll up and down the list to find an article that interests you. Once you see an interesting message, just click on it to highlight it, and Netscape displays the message in the bottom pane of the screen.

To reply to a message you are reading, make sure the message is highlighted, then click on the Re: News button. Netscape opens a window which you can use to write your reply, shown in Figure C.5.

The original message is automatically included in your reply, and is indicated with right arrows in the left margin. (By the way, it's considered common courtesy to delete any quoted sections that do not pertain directly to your reply.) The message is also automatically addressed to the newsgroup, and the subject line is filled in. After you have composed your reply, click on the Send button to post your message to the newsgroup.

To start a new subject, or *thread*, on a newsgroup, highlight the newsgroup in the News Server window and click on To: News. Netscape opens a window similar to the one in Figure C.5, but the Subject line is left blank for you to fill in. Click on Send when you are ready to post your message.

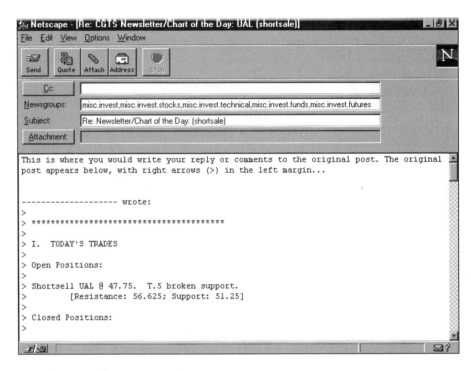

*Figure C.5.   **A reply to a news posting***

The Internet provides more than 10,000 newsgroups, many of which touch on financial matters. The list below gives the names of those that are probably most germane to individuals interested in personal finance:

    alt.invest.penny-stocks

    clari.biz.currencies.misc

    clari.biz.currencies.us_dollar

    clari.usa.gov.policy.financial

    misc.invest

    misc.invest.canada

    misc.invest.funds

    misc.invest.futures

    misc.invest.real-estate

    misc.invest.stocks

    misc.invest.technical

New newsgroups are created daily, so there likely will be other groups by the time you read this. When a new one is created, an announcement of some kind is usually made in all newsgroups of related interest.

WARNING It is impossible to know anything about the people who post messages in a newsgroup, so treat whatever information you get with a grain of salt. Be sure to spend some time reading the group's messages before you post any messages yourself. (On the Net, this is referred to as *lurking*.) Not only is lurking considered good etiquette, but it can also save you embarrassment.

WARNING Also, consider the fact that any message you post is probably going out to an audience of thousands. It's a heady experience, when you think about it, and with that power comes a certain amount of responsibility. Treat people the same way you would if you were face-to-face with them, with respect and graciousness.

Internet Mailing Lists

A *mailing list* is similar to a newsgroup, except the messages are sent by e-mail. Anyone with an e-mail account can take part in a discussion on a mailing list. Moreover, every message sent to the mailing list ends up in your mailbox, so if your Internet provider charges you according to the number of messages you receive, being on a mailing list can be costly. You subscribe to a mailing list by sending an e-mail message to a list server with pertinent information.

NOTE The first message you usually get when you sign on a mailing list is an acknowledgment of your subscription and instructions on how to use the list and unsubscribe if you need to. Print out these documents and keep them in a file folder somewhere. It's frustrating both to you and to the other subscribers when people can't figure out how to unsubscribe and end up sending messages to everyone on the list for instructions.

Here are three mailing lists that might prove useful information. In the instructions, substitute *your name* with your real name and *your e-mail address* with your e-mail address. For example, where the text says *your name*, I would substitute Stephen L. Nelson, and where it says *your e-mail address*, I would substitute stphnlnlsn@msn.com.

The Futures list discusses futures and commodities trading:

Mail to: `sub.futures@stoicbbs.com`

Message: `Subscribe Futures` *your e-mail address your name*

The Personal Finances list discusses personal finances:

Mail to: `majordomo@shore.net`

Message: `subscribe persfin-digest`

Advice for getting investment information on the Net can be found here:

Mail to: `listproc@gmn.com`

Message: `subscribe pfc-update` *your name*

Your mailbox will soon be filled with messages! You may need to spend some time sifting through information to find exactly what you need, but you'll be surprised at how quickly you can find information. You may even develop friendships with people who have similar interests.

APPENDIX D

Using Quicken in Canada

I r you live in Canada or conduct business there and want to use Quicken to track your finances, you can do so, but you have to take a few extra steps. Once you are finished customizing Quicken for use in Canada, you can track your finances with the techniques in this book.

Reconfiguring Windows 95 and Quicken

The first thing for you to do is reconfigure Windows 95 for use in Canada. This is quite easy to do by following these steps:

1. Click on the Start button and choose Settings.

2. Choose Control Panel.

3. When the Control Panel window opens, double-click on the Regional Settings icon. The Regional Settings Properties window appears, as in Figure D.1.

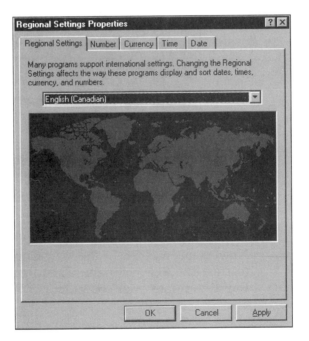

Figure D.1. *The Regional Settings Properties window*

4. Under the Regional Settings tab, use the drop-down–list box to choose English (Canadian). Now Canadian English is the default for your system, as is the Canadian date style of DD/MM/YY.

5. Click on OK.

    Having told Windows 95 that English (Canadian) is your regional setting, you need to reinstall Quicken and tell it that you want the Canadian setting. Do this even if Quicken is already installed on your computer.

    Begin installing Quicken according to the instructions in Appendix A of this book. When you get to the Type of Installation window, click on the Canadian Version radio button, as shown in Figure D.2.

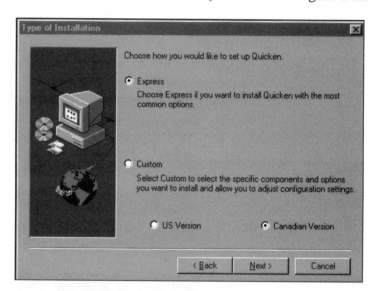

*Figure D.2.   **The Type of Installation window***

Now, click on Next. In the Start Copying Files window, click on Next to start the Setup for the Canadian version. When asked, click on Finish to restart your computer.

Using Canadian Categories

Before you start processing transactions, you need to be aware of the ways in which the Canadian version differs from the America one.

Categories & Transfers

When you create a new file for keeping financial records, you are given the opportunity to choose which kinds of categories you want—Home categories, Business categories, or both. When you tell Quicken to configure the program for use in Canada, Quicken adds several categories to the Category & Transfer List.

Two expense business categories are added: Goods and Services Tax (GST) and Provincial Sales Tax (PST). For the default Home categories, Quicken adds the previous two expense categories as well as Registered Retirement Savings Plan (RRSP) and Unemployment Insurance Commission (UIC). In addition, there are two new income categories: Canada Pension Plan (CPP) and Canada Pension Plan (CPP/QPP). These become important when you start processing transactions.

Tracking the GST and PST Categories

Basically, the trick to tracking the GST and PST categories of your personal finances is to use split transactions, as explained in Chapter 2 *Using the Quicken Register*. When you are entering a transaction, enter the total as you normally would, but when you get to the category box, click on the Splits button. (As you probably remember, you split a transaction to break a total into different categories.) Enter the actual amount of the purchase, and use the next two lines for the GST and PST categories and the appropriate amounts.

If you are not working from a receipt and need to calculate the amounts, either use the pop-up calculator or create a memorized transaction that calculates the amounts for you.

Tracking Business Finances

Tracking GST and PST becomes a necessity when you use Quicken to track business finances. Accurate records are extremely important when dealing with taxes, and this is where Quicken can really show its stuff.

Rather than using the GST and PST categories in your banking transactions, create separate liability accounts for them. This way, you can get up-to-the-minute reports on the status of those accounts and separate any GST you collect from the amounts that are reported as your net worth in reports.

First, create a GST (and, if necessary, a PST) liability account as described in Chapter 10, *Banking Online*. Be sure to name the account or accounts appropriately. Figure D.3 shows the Summary tab of the Liability Account Setup dialog box filled out to create a GST window. After you click on Done, answer No when Quicken asks whether you want to set up an amortized loan to go with the account.

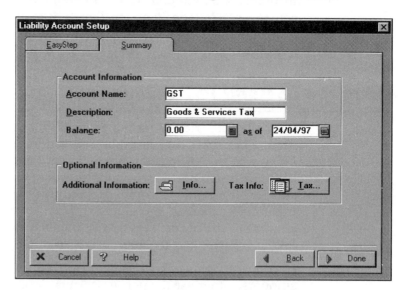

Figure D.3.   The Summary tab of the Liability Account Setup dialog box

After you create these accounts, you're ready to enter information.

Recording Business Transactions

Suppose you sold 1,000 widgets to Bob's Widget Warehouse. To record this sale, you put the information in your business account as you would normally. The amount you charge for the widgets, in this case, is $600, which you can write in the Amount box of the register. You then split the categories and include lines that transfer the GST, PST or QST amounts to the appropriate liability accounts (*not* the categories), as shown in Figure D.4.

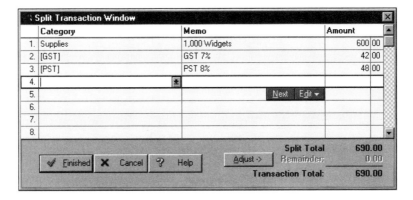

Figure D.4.   **You can transfer GST and PST amounts using the Split Transaction window.**

 TIP You can use the pop-up calculator to calculate the appropriate amounts or create a memorized transaction. A memorized transaction, however, would only work with simple transactions and may not be worth your time.

When you are recording a business *purchase* you have made, however, the PST you pay should *not* be credited to you, although the GST (and, if you live in Quebec, QST) should be credited to you. Because the amount of the PST should not appear as a credit in your liability account, when you record a business purchase, process the transaction by using the PST *category* and not as a transfer to the PST *liability account* in the Splits window.

APPENDIX D

Obtaining Business Tax Reports

For a simple report, open the register of the tax liability account you want to examine and click on the Report command button. Keep in mind that reports automatically include all transactions in the register. If you want to narrow the report to particular transactions or a particular time period, press the Customize button and select those transactions, and enter the correct dates in the appropriate dialog boxes.

Here is the meaning of each report total:

Total	What It Means
Total Inflows	The total tax credit you receive for the GST or QST you have paid out to others.
Total Outflows	The total taxes you have received from your customers that you are liable for.
Net Total	The total outflows minus the total inflows—in other words, the amount that you will pay to your tax authority.

In some cases, you may need (or want) more detail. In this case, open the account you use for your regular business transactions (not the tax liability account) and follow these steps:

1. Choose Reports ➤ Other ➤ Transaction and click on Create.

2. When the report appears, click on the Customize button.

3. Click on the Display tab and select Split Transaction detail. This gives you all the tax amounts for each transaction.

4. Click on the Accounts tab and make sure all your business accounts are selected.

5. Click on the Advanced tab. In the Transaction Types drop-down–list box, make one of the following choices:

   • Payments: Choose this to display only purchases.

   • Deposits: Choose this to display only sales.

6. After you are done, click on the Close button.

Paying Your Taxes

After running reports and examining the balances of the tax liability accounts for the appropriate period, you likely owe money to the tax authority. If you do, write a check to the appropriate agency. Be sure to use the appropriate tax liability account in the Category field too. If you are to receive a refund, record the amount as a deposit in your checking account, and use the appropriate tax liability account in the Category field.

Glossary

Glossary of Accounting and Financial Terms

401(k) plan   a retirement plan, sponsored by an employer, that allows employees to set aside some of their wages or salary for retirement. The set-aside money is not taxed. Some employers match 401(k) contributions.

AAA   the highest rating that can be given to a municipal bond. Bonds with this rating are considered a safe investment by banks and other financial institutions.

ABA transit number   the number that identifies which bank a check is drawn against. Every check has an ABA (American Bankers Association) transit number, usually in the upper-right corner. The number—actually two numbers separated by a hyphen—identifies the bank's location and the bank's name.

abusive tax shelter   a tax shelter is considered abusive when its organizers knowingly misrepresent its tax benefits or value. The IRS imposes special penalties on abusive tax shelters.

access code   the password or number you punch in at an automatic teller machine to make deposits and withdrawals. Also called personal identification number (PIN).

account   the record of transactions in a checking, savings, securities, trust, or charge account, including the account's up-to-date balance.

account number   the number that identifies the holder of an account. All accounts must have an account number.

accountant's opinion   the results of an audit of a company's records and books.

accrual basis   in accounting, income and expenses can be recorded on an accrual or a cash basis. With the accrual method, income and expenses are recorded as they occur, not when they are completed. For example, a check you write on March 1 is subtracted from your balance on that day, not the day the check is cashed. With the cash-basis method, transactions are recorded when money actually changes hands.

accrued interest   interest earned on a bond or certificate of deposit, but paid at some future date—such as when the bond or certificate of deposit is sold.

actuary   the person who determines what your annual insurance payments are.

ad valorem   Latin for *to the value.* Sales and property taxes are calculated ad valorem, as a percentage of the property value or the thing being sold.

adjustable-rate mortgage (ARM)   a mortgage whose interest rate is adjusted periodically, usually every six months. ARMs are usually tied to some sort of money index, like the prime lending rate or the cost of Treasury bills. When the index goes up or down, so does the monthly mortgage payment.

adjusted gross income   your annual income after you've subtracted retirement contributions, alimony, and other deductions allowed by the IRS.

adjuster   the insurance-company representative who decides how much insurance settlements should be.

affidavit   a signed statement promising you will fulfill an obligation. Affidavit means *has pledged his faith* in Latin.

affinity card   a credit card issued by a bank and an organization such as a charity. Usually, the charity gives its membership list to the bank. In return, the bank gives part of the interest income from the card to the charity or club.

aggregate demand   a measure of how well the economy is doing. The aggregate demand is the monthly total spent by consumers, governments, and investors for goods and services.

allonge   when there isn't enough room to write endorsements, a piece of paper attached to a check, draft, bill, or promissory note for writing endorsements.

altered check   a check whose signature, date, payee name, or amount has been changed or erased. Banks can refuse to honor altered checks.

alternative minimum tax   a flat-rate tax that trusts, corporations, and wealthy individuals must pay, regardless of how much or how little tax they owe. The alternative minimum tax ensures that wealthy people and companies pay at least some tax.

American Bankers Association (ABA)   the professional association of U.S. banks. The ABA sponsors conferences and lobbies before Congress, among other activities.

American depository receipt (ADR)   a security issued by a U.S. bank on behalf of a foreign corporation.

American Stock Exchange (AMEX)   America's second-largest stock exchange, where the stocks of medium- to small-sized companies are traded.

amortization   the gradual paying off of a debt or loan.

amortization schedule   a schedule for making payments on a mortgage. The schedule shows the number of payments, when payments are due, how much of each payment goes toward the principal and how much goes toward paying interest, and the declining amount of money owed on the loan as payments are made.

annual cap   adjustable rate mortgages usually have an annual cap—a percent rate above which mortgage payments cannot rise, no matter how much interest rates rise.

annual percentage rate (APR)   the cost of a loan, expressed as a percentage of the amount of the loan.

annual percentage yield (APY)   the amount of interest income that an account will earn in a year, expressed as a percentage rate.

annual report   a report showing the financial status of a corporation. Public corporations are required to issue annual reports to their shareholders.

annuity   a sum of money paid to policyholders or shareholders either annually or at regular intervals.

appraisal   an estimate of the current market value of an asset.

appreciation   the amount that an asset has increased in value over its value in an earlier period. Appreciation is expressed as a percentage or as a monetary value. For example, a house that cost $200,000 five years ago, if it increases in value to $220,000, has appreciated by $20,000, or 10 percent, in five years.

arbitrage   buying the same items in one market and selling them in another in order to profit from the difference between the two market prices. For example, if the U.S. dollar cost 1.5 Deutsche mark (DM) in New York but only 1.45 DM in London, a trader could simultaneously buy deutschmarks in London and sell them in New York, thereby earning a profit.

arbitration   submitting a dispute to a third party for settlement instead of to a court of law. If the arbitration is binding, the parties involved are required to agree to the settlement.

arm's-length transaction a transaction made between a buyer and seller who have no relationship to one another. Transactions made between subsidiary companies are not arm's-length transactions because the companies may not be acting in their own self-interest but in the interest of a parent company.

arrears being behind in payments. You are in arrears if you have one or more unpaid debts.

asked price the price at which a seller offers an item. The asked price is often different from the bid price—the most anyone will pay for the item being offered.

assessed valuation for tax purposes, the value of a property. Usually, property taxes are paid as a percent of the assessed valuation of the property.

assessment the amount charged, such as for property taxes.

asset any property that has value. Real estate, personal items, and even trademarks are examples of assets. The value of all your assets is called your total assets.

asset-based lending in this lending method, a company's accounts receivable and inventory are used as collateral for the loan and as the basis for determining whether the company is worthy of receiving a loan.

asset dividend a dividend paid as property instead of cash. For example, in lieu of cash, a corporation might pay dividends in the form of stock certificates to it stockholders.

assumable mortgage a mortgage in which the borrower, if he or she subsequently sells the property, has the right to pass on the unpaid portion of the mortgage to the new buyer. With an assumable mortgage, if one person buys a house and sells it 10 years later, the subsequent buyer assumes payments for the remaining 20 years of the mortgage.

attorney-in-fact a person hired to act in the name of another person. Also called power of attorney.

audit a formal examination of the accounts, assets, liabilities, and transactions of a company or individual.

auditor's opinion the results of an audit of a company's records and books.

automated teller machine (ATM)   a machine that allows bank patrons to make withdrawals and deposits without entering a bank. Know your password before you reach the front of the line and push those buttons fast so the people behind you don't get irritated and start cursing.

available balance   the amount of money in a bank account after all deposits are cleared. You can make withdrawals and write checks up to the amount of your available balance. When you deposit a check, it is entered on your balance, but you cannot make use of the money until the check has cleared and become part of your available balance.

average annual yield   the interest income you can earn on a certificate of deposit or bank account, expressed as a percentage.

back-end load   a sales commission that the investor pays to the broker only if the investor sells or disposes of mutual funds. With a front-end load, the investor pays the sales commission when purchasing the funds from an investment house.

bad check   a check that a bank refuses to honor. A check is considered "bad" if it is not filled out completely, if it does not have the proper endorsement signatures, or if there are not sufficient funds to cover the check.

balance of payments   the total payments of the businesses, people, and government of one country, less the total payments made by all other countries. A country with a favorable balance of payments receives more money than it pays out to other countries.

balance of trade   the difference between the amount of goods a country imports and exports. If a country imports more than it exports, it has a negative balance of trade. If it exports more, it has a favorable balance.

balloon maturity   a bank loan in which the last payment is a large lump-sum payment.

balloon mortgage   a mortgage in which the last payment is much larger than the other payments. Typically, a balloon mortgage is given to home buyers who anticipate a large appreciation of their property and who intend to sell before the mortgage matures. Balloon mortgages are also given to borrowers whose incomes are likely to rise.

balloon payment   a large lump-sum payment made as the last payment on a loan.

bank a somewhat stodgy institution that loans money, takes deposits, and performs other financial services. Banks figure prominently in western movies, where they are often robbed. The old ones have marble floors and brass hand rails.

bank discount rate the rate that banks charge customers for the use of banker's acceptances and other financial instruments.

bank draft a check written by a bank that draws on funds the bank holds in another bank. For example, if a customer in Las Vegas needed funds right away, a bank in Boston might issue a bank draft on its account in Las Vegas so the customer could get the money quicker. Banks charge for this service.

bank holiday a day on which banks are closed, whether to observe a holiday or by order of the federal government.

bank reserves the funds a bank has to cover requires cash. "Reserves" refers to actual cash on hand and assets that can be turned into cash quickly.

bank run when many depositors try to withdraw their money from a bank at short notice. When depositors fear that a bank is failing or lose confidence in a bank, a bank run can result.

banker's acceptance a short-term credit instrument used by importers and exporters to speed international trade. The exporter sends a bill of exchange to a bank in the U.S., which accepts the bill of exchange and agrees to pay it if the importer cannot pay.

bankruptcy the legal procedure for deciding how to handle the debts of a business or individual who can't meet credit obligations. If the debtor is declared insolvent, the property is put under the control of a trustee or receiver so that the property can be distributed to creditors.

base rate for indexing purposes, the interest rate used to establish the price of bank loans. For example, many banks use the prime rate—the rate banks charge their most trustworthy customers for commercial loans—as the base rate for determining mortgage rates.

basis the original cost of an asset, used to calculate capital gains and capital-gains taxes.

basis point .01 percent, the smallest percentage point for quoting bond yields. If a bond yield changes from 6.00 to 6.85 percent, it has moved 85 basis points in yield.

bear   a securities or stock market investor who believes that the market will decline. The opposite of a bear is a bull.

bear bond   a bond expected to rise in value with rising interest rates.

bear market   a market, usually a stock market, in which the price of shares is declining. The opposite of a bull market.

bearer bond   a bond that belongs to the person who has it in hand. Bearer bonds are not registered to individuals or institutions. To receive payment, the bearer must present the bond. By contrast, owners of registered bonds are sent payments automatically when they fall due.

bearer instrument   a financial instrument, such as a bearer bond, payable to the person who possesses it. Bearer instruments are not registered to any party and do not have to be endorsed before payment is made.

beneficiaries   the people who benefit, or receive annuities, from a life-insurance policy when the policyholder dies.

bequest   a gift of money or personal items made in a will.

beta   a measure of how volatile the price of an investment or stock is, as compared to the entire market. If the price changes dramatically, the investment has a high beta. If the price is stable, it has a low beta.

bid   the highest price that prospective buyers will pay for an item. The bid is often different from the asking price—the price at which a seller offers an item.

bid and asked   in the over-the-counter market, refers to the price range of quotes for a security, the bid price being the highest price a prospective buyer will pay, and the asked price being the owner's offering price.

Big Board   the New York Stock Exchange.

bill of exchange   a financial instrument by which one party instructs another party to pay a third party. Also called a draft.

biweekly mortgage   a mortgage payment schedule requiring payments every two weeks instead of once a month. Biweekly mortgages can be paid off in about 17 years, nearly half the 30 years required for a typical mortgage.

blank endorsement   a check or bill of exchange in which the Pay to the order of line is left blank.

blanket mortgage   a mortgage that covers more than one piece of property.

blanket policy   an insurance policy that covers more than one piece of property, or that offers insurance of more than one type for a single piece of property.

blue-chip stock   stock in a well-established company noted for its stability and reliable earnings

blue-sky laws   state laws governing how securities are issued and traded. Blue sky laws are meant to prevent fraudulent transactions.

board of directors   advisors elected by stockholders to manage a public company. The board of directors' job is to represent stockholder interests. The board makes recommendations to the company's CEO.

boiler room   a term to describe an out-of-the-way place in which shady salespeople sell fraudulent securities over the telephone.

bond   an interest-bearing certificate of public or private indebtedness. Bonds pay a fixed interest rate and are redeemable after a certain time period. Also the last name of a famous fictional secret agent.

bond, bull   a type of bond that does well when interest rates are falling. Bull bonds are mortgage-backed, principal-only bonds. When mortgage rates fall, people refinance their homes, making mortgage-backed bonds more attractive.

bond, discount a bond is said to be selling at a discount if the price it is sold for is less than the value its issuer promises to pay when the bond reaches maturity.

bond, fidelity or surety   fidelity and surety bonds are binding promises that principal(s) will perform certain acts to obligee(s), with the obligee(s) being paid sums of money if the principal(s) do not fulfill their obligations. Fidelity bonds pay employers in case their bonded employees prove to be dishonest. Surety bonds guarantee that the principal, often an employer, will fulfill certain duties.

bond issue   bonds of the same type of class offered at the same time.

bond, premium   a bond is said to be selling at a premium if the price it is sold for is more than the value its issuer promises to pay when the bond reaches maturity.

bond prices   bond prices are quoted as percentages of their principle amount. For example, a $500 bond quoted at 95 would sell for $475. One quoted at 105 would sell for $525.

bond rating   a ranking system for assessing the financial solvency of bonds. AAA is the highest ranking. Bonds are ranked by Standard & Poor's and Moody's Investor's Service, among others.

book value   the original value of an asset less the cumulative depreciation. The book value is the value of an asset on the balance sheet. The book value is different from the market value.

borrowed stock   stock borrowed from a broker in order to complete a short sale. See also *short sale.*

bridge loan   refers to short-term loans provided while long-term financing is being finalized. A homeowner who has purchased a new home but has yet to sell the old one can get a bridge loan to tide him- or herself over until the old home is sold and the proceeds from the old home arrive.

broker   someone who negotiates the buying and selling of stocks, securities, commodities, insurance, or real estate for a fee or a commission.

brokerage firm   a business that negotiates the buying and selling of stocks, securities, commodities, insurance, or real estate for its customers—for a fee or a commission, of course.

bull   a stock broker who is very optimistic about the future success of a market, stock, or commodity. Not to be confused with a bear.

bull market   a market where prices are on the rise and brokers are confident of its future success. The opposite of a bear market.

bullet loan   a loan for which the interest and principal are paid in one payment, in one lump sum.

bullion   uncoined gold or other precious metals in bars or ingots.

business plan   a plan explaining to loan officers how a new business or a business that is restructuring will use the loan money. New and restricting business are required to submit a business plan.

cable   a bank draft sent from one bank to another by cable.

call   a demand for payment of a loan. A lender can make a call if the borrower has failed to make timely payments or has breached a contractual agreement regarding the loan.

call option   an option to purchase shares of a stock at a specific price in a certain time period. Brokers exercise a call option if the price of the stock rises above the option price during the option period.

callable bonds   bonds that issuers can pay off before the maturity date is reached.

callable preferred stock   stock that the can be called in by the issuer and redeemed for cash at any time. Stockholders of callable preferred stock are required to give back their shares when the issuer asks them to do so. Also called redeemable preferred stock.

calls and puts   options to sell or buy stock shares at a certain price within a certain time. The holder of a put can require a buyer to buy an option, within the agreed upon time period, at the specified price. The holder of a call can demand that a seller sell an option, within the agreed upon time period, at the agreed upon price. Investors buy put and call options as a hedge against large declines or rises in stock prices.

canceled check   a check that has been endorsed by a payee and paid by the bank from which it was drawn.

capital   all items of value owned by an individual or corporation, including cash, inventory, and property.

capital gain (or loss)   the difference between the purchase price of an asset and the resale price. If the resale price is higher than the purchase price, a capital gain results. If the resale price is lower than the purchase price, a capital loss results. Capital gains are subject to taxation, but how much taxation is a subject that politicians constantly wrangle about. Capital losses are tax deductible.

capital lease   for accounting purposes, a lease that is treated as an owned asset. Equipment is often leased to companies on a capital basis. The company leasing the asset enjoys the tax benefits of ownership, including deductions for maintenance expenses. When the lease expires, the company leasing the asset is usually allowed to purchase it.

capital market   a general term referring to stock markets and bond markets where governments and corporations can sell securities, stocks, and bonds in order to raise capital.

cash   money that can be used for financial transactions, including funds held in checking accounts.

cash basis   in accounting, income and expenses can be recorded on a cash or an accrual basis. With the cash method, income and expenses are recorded when money actually changes hands. For example, a check you write on March 1 is not subtracted from your balance until the day the check is cashed. With the accrual method, the check is subtracted on the day you write it, regardless of when it is cashed.

cash dividend   stock dividends paid in cash, not in shares of stock.

cashier's check   a check written by a bank against its own funds. Cashier's checks are guaranteed to be redeemable, since they are drawn on banks.

cash surrender value   the amount of money that a life-insurance policy pays out if the holder gives up the policy or cancels it. The cash surrender value of a life-insurance policy can be used as collateral on a loan.

caveat emptor   Latin for *let the buyer beware.* This saying means that buyers should not rely on sellers to present goods in their true light, but should investigate goods themselves before buying.

caveat venditor   Latin for *let the seller beware.* Refers to the obligation on the part of the seller to deliver goods as described in the sales contract.

central bank   a bank, usually operated by a government, that controls a nation's banking system and acts as the fiscal agent of the government.

certificate of deposit (CD)   a bank deposit that pays a fixed rate of interest over a stated period of time. Most CDs cannot be redeemed until a maturity date is reached.

certified check   a check that has been guaranteed by a bank and can be considered as good as cash. Before giving its acceptance, the bank makes sure enough money is in the account to cover the check and that the signature is valid.

charitable contribution   a contribution to a charity that can be deducted for income-tax purposes.

charitable gift annuity   an annuity purchased from a charitable organization for more than the annuity's market value. The amount paid over and above the market value is considered a charitable donation.

chartist   a securities broker who bases purchasing decisions on graphs and charts of past sales activity.

chattel mortgage a lien on personal property as a security against a loan. Chattel refers to personal property such as jewelry or equipment. In a chattel mortgage, the collateral is in the form of personal property, not real estate.

cheap money low-interest credit made available because interest rates are low.

check a written order instructing a bank to pay a sum to a third party. With a capital C, a Check is a citizen of the Check Republic.

check kiting an illegal scheme for fraudulently inflating the account balance of checking accounts. For example, a man with two checking accounts, one in Bank A and one in Bank B, writes a check on account A for $5,000 to his Bank B account. He deposits the check in Bank B. Until the check clears, he has $5,000 in both Bank B and Bank A. Next, he writes a check on account B for $5,000 to his Bank A account. He deposits this check too. Until the checks clear, he has $10,000 in his Bank A account and $5,000 in his Bank B account. On paper he has $15,000, when really he has only $5,000.

Chinese Wall the name for the division between a bank's trust department and its credit department. The departments are not supposed to talk to one another, since one is engaged in extending credit and the other in making investments and communication between the two might be a conflict of interest.

churning unnecessarily trading on a customer's account for the purpose of acquiring broker's commissions.

claim a demand for money from an insurance company. You file a claim when believe you are entitled to compensation from an insurer.

class action a lawsuit filed on behalf of a group of people who have been wronged in the same way.

clear to settle or discharge an account. Checks are cleared when they are redeemed for cash.

clearing house a convenient place where banks in a given area exchange checks written against one another. Clearing houses make it easier for banks to clear and settle checks, since bank representatives can meet in a central place without having to visit one anothers' banks.

Clifford trust a trust established for ten or more years whereby assets are transferred from one individual to another and then back again when the ten or more year period is over. Before laws governing Clifford trusts were changed in 1986, they were often used to transfer assets, such as college funds, to children, who are taxed at a lower tax rate than adults. After the ten or more year period, the adult could reclaim the trust.

closed-end fund   a fund that issues a fixed number of shares instead of continuously offering new shares to buyers.

closing price   the final price of a stock or commodity at the time the exchange closes for the day.

cloud on title   a title that cannot be transferred to someone else because liens, court judgments, or other impediments prevent the owner from selling it.

co-insurance   refers to a percentage amount that an insurance policyholder must be covered for. For example, if a fire insurance policy has a 70 percent co-insurance clause, the insured must be covered to at least 70 percent of the value of his or her home.

collar   a device that protects the lender and the borrower from fluctuations in interest rates. The collar consists of the floor, the lowest the interest rate on the loan can go, and the cap, the highest interest rate that the bank can charge the borrower.

collateral   as part of a loan agreement, the property or securities that the borrower pledges to the lender in case the borrower can't pay back the loan.

collateral loan   a loan given on the strength of the borrower's collateral, as opposed to the borrower's good standing in the community or good character.

collateral trust bond   bonds backed by the issuer's collateral. With this type of bond, the issuer pledges assets in the event that the bond cannot be paid when it falls due.

collateralized mortgage obligation (CMO)   a bond that is backed, or collateralized, by one or more real estate mortgages.

collateral value   the value of the properties and securities that a prospective borrower has pledged when applying for a loan.

collection agency   an organization whose job is to collect outstanding debts from individuals on behalf of companies and businesses.

collection letter a letter, always very polite but vaguely threatening, asking you to please pay an overdue bill.

collusive bidding when bidders agree among themselves to offer one (usually low) bid. Collusive bidding always results in a lower bid than competitive bidding, in which the bidders do not know one another's bids.

commercial bank a full-service bank owned by stockholders that makes loans, accepts deposits, and offers other commercial financial services.

commercial paper promissory notes, such as checks, drafts, and IOUs, that constitute a debt of some kind. Commercial paper is negotiable and can be traded.

commission the fee that brokers and agents charge for their services. A commission is often a percentage of the total value of a sale.

commodity exchange a marketplace where dealers and traders can meet to buy and sell goods.

common law the body of law developed in England, based on precedents and custom, that forms the basis for the legal system in all states except Louisiana, where Napoleonic law is practiced.

common stock securities that represent ownership in a corporation. By law, holders of common stock can receive dividends only after claims by preferred stockholders, creditors, and bondholder have been satisfied. Common stockholders are the last to be paid if a corporation goes bankrupt.

compensating balance a minimum balance that borrowers who wish to secure a loan from a bank must keep on deposit with the bank.

compound interest interest compounded on the original principal of a deposit plus all accrued interest.

condominium an individual unit in an apartment house or other multi-unit building. Condominiums are different from apartments or flats in that they can be owned. Usually, condominium owners belong to a tenants association that is responsible for upkeep and maintenance.

conglomerate a large, unwieldy corporation with subsidiaries all over the place that engage badly in various sorts of business all unrelated to each other.

consent decree a judicial decree in which the parties settle their dif ferences by agreeing to change their practices rather than by litigation.

conservator a person appointed by a court to manage the affairs of an estate or the affairs of a person deemed incompetent.

consignment sold on consignment means that the manufacturer or person who made the goods is paid only after the goods are sold. Normally, the retailer buys the goods outright from whoever made them.

construction loan a loan covering construction costs, paid out at intervals as the construction project is completed. Also called a construction mortgage.

constructive notice a notice published in a newspaper announcing some action, such as a lien or the confiscation of property by the state. By law, some actions must be given constructive notice so that anyone objecting can presumably take action.

consumer credit credit given to individuals so they can buy personal things.

consumer-credit protection act an act passed by Congress in 1969 requiring lenders to be truthful about how they compute finance charges. Under the consumer protection act, finance charges must be expressed as an annual percentage rate of the loan amount. Also called truth in lending.

consumer durables items that consumers purchase infrequently and use over a period of years, such as TVs and washing machines. Also called durable goods.

consumer lease the lease of a consumer item, such as a car or mink stole, with a value under $25,000.

consumer price index an index that measures cost of living in the United States. The U.S. Labor Department is responsible for monitoring the consumer price index.

contract a legally binding agreement between two or more parties, where the responsibilities of each are clearly outlined.

conventional mortgage a mortgage not backed by the Federal Housing Administration.

convertible an adjustable-rate mortgage that the holder can exchange for a fixed-rate mortgage. Usually the holder must make the conversion, if he or she opts to do so, in the first few years of the mortgage.

convertible currency   currency that is easy to exchange for the currency of another nation. Countries whose currency is not convertible set restrictions on how their currency can be traded.

co-payment   in a health insurance plan, a percentage of a medical bill that you pay (the insurer covers the rest). Typically, you co-pay bills until you reach a certain dollar limit. After that point, the insurer pays 100 percent of your medical bills.

corpus   Latin for *body*. The corpus is the principal of a fund or estate, as distinguished from the interest or other income it generates.

cosigner   a joint signer of a promissory note. Cosigners are jointly responsible for paying back loans.

cost-of-funds index (COFI)   an index that banks use to help determine the cost of adjustable-rate mortgages. If the index goes up, so do adjustable-rate mortgage payments.

cost-of-living increases   payment increases that pensioners and social-security recipients get to offset cost-of-living increases brought about by inflation.

counterfeit   money, bank cards, or checks that look real but aren't.

countersign   a signature that asserts the authenticity of a document already signed by another. In most companies, large checks require a countersign.

country risk   the risk that an economic or political upheaval in a country will deplete its foreign reserves and prevent the country from paying back international loans.

coupon   a certificate attached to a bond stating how much interest is due. When the coupon is presented, the interest payment is made.

coupon bonds   bonds with coupons attached that state when interest payments are due and how much the payments are.

covenant   a written agreement between parties that has been sealed from public disclosure.

credit   money placed at a person's disposal by a bank or other lending institution.

credit agency   an agency that obtains data about the credit history of individuals and companies and offers the data to creditors and others.

credit application   a request to obtain credit. Most lenders require applicants to provide information about their creditworthiness.

credit card   a plastic card you can use to pay for things. It seems magical until the monthly bill arrives, at which point you realize you're spending too much and you wish you didn't have a credit card.

credit clinic   slang term for an organization that claims to help consumers clear up unfavorable credit ratings. By law, creditors have 60 days to respond to credit challenges. If 60 days pass without a response, the challenger's creditworthiness is restored automatically. All a credit clinic does is advise people to contest all unfavorable ratings, the idea being that creditors will not respond within the 60-day period and will have to restore the challenger's favorable credit rating.

credit counseling   a service for companies or individuals who wish to get out of debt.

credit insurance   insurance purchased by banks as a defense against large credit losses.

credit limit   the most that a consumer or company can borrow at one time from a bank or other creditor.

credit line   the maximum amount of money that a creditor will extend to an individual or company.

credit rating   a lender's appraisal of a borrower's ability to pay back loans. Credit ratings are based primarily on the borrower's past history of paying back loans.

credit risk   the risk that a borrower will be able to pay back a loan.

credit slip   a notice removing a credit-card charge from a cardholder's bill. If you return something you've purchased with a credit card, you are issued a credit slip indicating that the payment no longer counts toward your credit-card balance.

creditor   a bank or other agency that extends credit to borrowers. A debtor is the opposite of a creditor.

creditworthiness   the ability of a person to pay back loans. Creditworthiness is judged according to your past history of loan payments, how long you have been employed, and other criteria.

cross-collateral   collateral that backs up several loans, not just one, as arranged by agreement with the lender.

currency　paper money in circulation. Also refers to the paper money issued by a nation. The dollar is the currency of the United States.

currency basket　currency unit comprising currency from different nations. International transactions are sometimes made in basket currency to protect against one currency being devalued. For example, a payment made in dollars as well as yen retains more of its value if the yen or dollar happens to fall in value.

currency swap　an agreement between companies to exchange equivalent amounts of one type of currency for another. Companies engage in currency swaps, for example, to diversify their portfolios. At the end of the agreement the currencies are swapped back.

currency translation　changing balance-sheet entries and totals from one currency to another. Multinational corporations perform currency translations on their balance sheets as a way of measuring financial performance. Some countries require corporations to do currency translations when reporting their income.

current account　the imports and exports, as well as transfer payments, between two countries. A country that has a surplus current account with another country has exported more goods and made more payments than it has received. A deficit current account means the country has imported more and received more payments than it has exported or paid out.

current assets　assets that can easily and readily be converted into cash.

current yield　the annual interest rate paid by a bond or other security, expressed as a percentage of the principal.

cushion　the time between the date a bond is issued and its first call date—that is, the day it can be redeemed either in whole or in part.

custodian　a institution or broker that oversees the management of a group of assets.

custody account　a bank account held in trust by a parent or guardian on behalf of a minor.

customs　taxes placed on goods being imported.

cycle billing　billing one set of customers from a customer list on specific days of the month. For example, customers whose last names begin with *A* would be billed on the first of the month, *B* on the second day, and so on. The idea is to spread out the paperwork over a month and keep bill payments coming in regularly.

daily interest   interest compounded daily on a bank deposit. Although the interest is compounded daily, it is deposited in accounts at weekly, bi-weekly, or monthly intervals.

dealer   a person who trades in securities on his or her own. Dealers trade with their own money and take the risks themselves, whereas brokers trade on behalf of others.

debentures   unsecured bonds backed by the general credit of the issuer, not by the issuer's assets.

debit   an entry, made on the left side of a balance sheet, that records an expense.

debit card   a bank card that draws directly on the holder's bank accounts, not on a credit line. Charges made on a debit card are subtracted immediately from the user's checking or savings account.

debt   money owed.

debt limit   the most that a government can legally borrow. State legislatures and constitutions decide the debt limits of state and local governments. The federal government can raise its debt limit as it pleases, since its limit is decided by Congress.

debtor nation   a nation that is behind in its interest or principal payments to banks.

debt service   interest or principal payments on a mortgage. "Debt service" usually describes either the monthly payments or the total annual payment.

decedent   legal term for a person who has died.

deductible the part of a bill that your pay out of your own pocket. The insurer pays the rest.

deed   a signed document describing a legal agreement or contract.

deed of trust   legal document giving the bearer title to a property. Banks usually hold the deed of trust until the borrower has paid the mortgage in full. After that, title is given over to the borrower.

default   to fail to pay back a loan or meet an obligation.

default risk   the risk that a bond issuer will not be able to pay either the interest or principal.

deferred annuity   an annuity whose payments, by agreement, will begin in the future.

deferred compensation   earnings to be received in the future, not when they are earned. Deferring compensation sometimes has tax advantages.

deferred gifts   gifts to a charity or nonprofit organization that are to be given at the time of the giver's death. Arrangements for giving deferred gifts are sometimes written into wills.

deferred payment   a privilege sometimes offered to renters, credit cardholders, and others to skip or postpone payments. Deferred payments are usually offered as a sign-on incentive.

deficiency   the amount by which a taxpayer fails to fulfill tax obligations. For example, if you underpay by $500, that is a $500 deficiency.

deficiency judgment   a court order giving a lender authority to collect part of the proceeds from a sale of property, when the seller of the property has defaulted on a mortgage or other financial obligation.

deficit   the amount that a business's total assets fall below its total liabilities.

deficit financing   the federal government's fiscal policy of borrowing to cover its deficit.

defined benefit plan   a retirement plan set up for a corporation's employees. These plans pay no taxes on their investments and must be managed according to federal standards.

defined contribution plan   blanket term for various plans by which employees can make tax-deferred contributions to retirement plans.

deflation   a decline in prices. Inflation, a rise in prices, is the opposite of deflation.

delinquency   failure to fulfill a financial obligation. Loans with two or more payments overdue are considered delinquent.

demand deposit   any deposit account that can be withdrawn at a moment's notice. A checking account is a demand deposit.

demand draft   a written request to a bank to pay a third party. (In other words, a check.)

demand loan a loan that can be paid back at any time and has no maturity date. Interest is paid until the principal has been paid off.

deposit money entered in a bank account.

deposit insurance insurance on bank deposits to protect depositors in the event of a bank failure. The Federal Deposit Insurance Corporation, a government agency, insures bank accounts to $50,000.

depository a bank where funds and securities are deposited.

depreciation the decline in value of an asset. Assets depreciate as they are used or as they become obsolete.

deregulation a loosening of government regulations concerning business activity. Deregulation is supposed to stimulate business competition and make for a more prosperous economy.

derivatives a security whose value is based, or derived from, a stock or bond. Options to buy and sell stocks are derivatives, for example.

derivative mortgage-backed securities a derivative whose value is based on securities, usually bonds, that are collateralized by real estate mortgages.

devaluation the decline in value of a currency relative to another currency or to the price of gold.

direct deposit depositing paychecks automatically in employees' banks accounts. Many companies now offer their employees direct deposits.

direct placement selling a security issue to one group of investors without the use of underwriters. Long-term securities are sometimes sold to institutions this way.

discharge of bankruptcy a court order giving a bankrupt debtor release from all debt obligations. The debtor is no longer responsible for the debts, but the record of bankruptcy remains on the debtor's credit record for ten years.

disclosure information about the annual percentage rate, method of computing interest, and minimum monthly payment that banks must give mortgage customers. Federal law requires banks to disclose such information.

discount a reduction in price. In the bond market, the discount is the difference in price between what a bond costs today and its face value—what it will cost at maturity.

discount brokerage   a brokerage house that executes buy and sell orders without giving investment advice.

discount point   One percent of the principal of a mortgage. Home buyers typically pay the lender 1 discount point when their loans close.

discount rate   rate used to measure the value of money over time. As a practical matter, a discount rate is the same thing as an interest rate.

discount yield   method for computing treasury bill yields, in which the par value is computed instead of the purchase price. The formula for computing discount yields is the discount, divided by the par value amount multiplied by 360, divided by the number of days to maturity.

discounted cash flow   a mathematical technique used by financial analysts in which future-day dollars are converted into present-day dollars by adjusting for inflation and compound interest. A company's overall value (its share price times the number of shares outstanding) is typically calculated using discounted cash flow calculations.

discounting   converting future-day dollars into present-day dollars by adjusting for inflation and compound interest. Because discount calculations are cumbersome, one typically uses a computer to perform the actual calculations.

disinflation   refers to Federal Reserve policies meant to prevent inflation. In order to do this, the Fed slows down the money supply, leaving less money for credit.

disintermediation   when investors pull their money out of interest-earning bank accounts and reinvest it in other places, such as stocks and money market funds.

disposable income   the money left over for buying things or investing after taxes are paid.

diversification   investing in many different areas—real estate, stocks, and bonds, for example—as a hedge against decline in one area. Diversification means not putting all your eggs in one basket.

divest   to sell off assets or businesses because they are unprofitable or because they don't fit in a company's plans for the future.

dividend   a profit share paid out to a stockholder.

dividend reinvestment plan   a plan allowing corporate stockholders to be paid in cash or in stock.

double taxation refers to federal taxes on corporate earnings, and how these earnings are taxed twice, once in the form of corporate taxes and again when earnings are distributed to shareholders.

dower the right of a widow to inherit all or part of her deceased husband's property.

Dow-Jones Industrial Average an index used to measure price changes in the stock market.

Dow theory a stock market analysis method that, like all such methods, tries to detect price trends in the market and sometimes even succeeds.

down payment part of the full price of an item, paid at the time of delivery, with the rest to be paid later.

draft a financial instrument by which one party instructs another party to pay a third party. Also called a bill of exchange.

drawee the bank on which a check is drawn.

drawer the person who writes, or draws, a check that is to be paid by the drawee. The drawee is the bank where the check writer keeps a checking account.

due diligence the responsibility of bank officers to evaluate loan applications in a prudent and forthright manner. Due diligence is a credo of the banking industry.

dumping selling large amounts of stock in order to make share prices drop or the market itself decline.

Dun & Bradstreet (D&B) a company that rates corporations' financial performance for the benefit of investors.

durable goods items that consumers purchase infrequently and use over a period of years, such as TVs and washing machines. Also called consumer durables.

duration for a fixed-income security, the average time it takes to collect all payments of interest and principal.

Dutch auction gradually lowering the price of a security until a buyer is found. The Dutch auction system is used in securities underwriting.

duties tax on imported or exported items.

E bond a U.S. government bond issued before 1980.

early-withdrawal penalty   a fee charged to depositors if they withdraw their certificates of deposit or saving deposits before they reach maturity.

earnest money   a sum of money paid for property to assure the seller that the buyer is sincere. When the sales transaction is completed, the earnest money is counted toward the purchase price of the property.

earning asset   any asset that generates interest income.

earnings per share   the amount that each stock share earns in dividends after both preferred stockholders and taxes have been paid.

EE bond   a U.S. government bond issued after 1980.

effective annual yield   what a depositor earns on a certificate of deposit or savings account on a yearly basis, provided the money is not withdrawn.

efficient market   refers to an economic theory which says that today's prices for securities and commodities are a measure of what investors think their prices will be in the future.

electronic funds transfer (EFT)   transferring money by electric wire instead of by traditional paper means, such as check writing.

embargo   keeping ships from entering port or leaving port by government decree.

embezzlement   fraudulently appropriating money for personal use.

eminent domain   the right of a government to take private property and use it for the public good.

Employee Retirement Income Security Act (ERISA)   federal act describing how managers of profit-sharing funds and private pension funds may invest those funds. ERISA sets guidelines for fund managers.

employee stock ownership plans (ESOP)   a plan allowing employees to buy stock in the company they work for.

encumbrance   a claim against property that keeps the property from being sold. A lien is an encumbrance, for example.

endorsement   a signature that allows for the transfer of a negotiable item. The signature on the back of a check, for example, is an endorsement.

endowment insurance   a type of life insurance policy in which the insurance money is paid when the policyholder dies or when the term of the policy is finished.

equity kicker   an amount, in addition to interest, that a lender receives from the borrower. Equity kickers are common in large commercial real estate mortgages.

escrow   an agreement whereby a deed, a bond, or property is held in trust by a third party until some obligation is fulfilled.

estate   a deceased's property at the time of death. An estate is passed to the deceased's heirs if he or she left a will. If not, the matter of how to divide the estate is decided by a probate court.

estate tax   tax levied by federal and state governments on the transfer of property from an estate to its beneficiaries. Estate taxes are paid by the estate. Inheritance taxes—taxes the heirs pay for the property they receive—are paid by heirs.

estoppel   a legal bar preventing a witness in court from denying a fact if he or she took actions contrary to that fact at an earlier date.

Eurobonds   bonds issued in a currency other than the currency of the country where the bonds are being issued. Eurobonds got their name when corporations and governments in Europe began issuing bonds in U.S. dollars.

Eurodollars   U.S. dollars held in banks outside the United States.

European Monetary System   a system of balanced exchange rates for the national currencies of Europe. The System was set up by the European Economic Community to help stabilize exchange rates.

exchange rate   the rate that the currency of one country is trading against the currency of another. For example, an exchange rate of 99.99 yen to the dollar means that one U.S. dollar purchases 99.99 Japanese yen.

Exchange Stabilization Fund   funds managed by the U.S. Federal Reserve Bank, set aside to be spent to help stabilize the dollar and other international currencies.

excise taxes   taxes on acts, not property. For example, sales of liquor are subject to excise taxes.

executor   the institution or person named in a will to manage the estate of the deceased. The executor pays taxes, distributes the estate's assets, and pays estate debts.

exempt securities   securities that are not subject to the reporting rules of the Securities and Exchange Commission.

Export-Import Bank   a federally run bank set up to help U.S. companies export their products. The Bank provides loans to U.S. companies who cannot otherwise find commercial loans.

exposure   the likelihood that market fluctuations will cause financial losses or ruin. Also refers to credit extended to a borrower.

external audit   an audit conducted by an outside auditor on a business to determine its financial soundness. An outside auditor has no stake in the business being audited and therefore can be considered a disinterested party.

face value   the principal of a stock, bond, or other security. Also the principal of an insurance policy. Face value is sometimes called par value.

fair market value   the reasonable price of an asset. Fair market value is the price that a willing seller and buyer would negotiate for an asset, given that both know all the facts and are not under compulsion to buy or sell.

Fannie Mae   nickname of the Federal National Mortgage Association (FNMA), a publicly owned organization that buys mortgages from banks and resells them to investors.

Farmer Mac   common name of the Federal Agricultural Mortgage Corporation, a government agency that guarantees farm loans.

Federal Deposit Insurance Corporation (FDIC)   federal agency that insures bank accounts against bank failures. The FDIC insures accounts to $100,000.

federal funds   money purchased by commercial banks from the Federal Reserve.

federal funds rate   interest rate charged to commercial banks for purchasing federal funds. The federal funds rate is the benchmark for many commercial credit rates, including short-term business loans.

Federal Government securities   U.S. government bonds, which represent the debt of the United States government.

Federal Home Loan Bank System   name for the eleven regional banks in charge of selling money to U.S. Savings & Loan institutions.

Federal Housing Administration (FHA)   federal housing agency set up to aid home financing. The FHA insures home mortgages made by commercial banks.

Federal Insurance Contributions Act   also known as social security, the federal program that gives retirees, the disabled, and surviving spouses benefit payments.

Federal Open Market Committee (FOMC)   committee responsible for setting the Fed's short-term monetary policies. The chief job of this committee is to take actions that control the supply of credit.

Federal Reserve Bank   one of twelve regional banks that serve as creditors to commercial banks.

Federal Reserve Board (FRB)   board of governors of the Federal Reserve System. Members are appointed by the President and must be confirmed by the Senate.

Federal Reserve note   U.S. paper money. It says so right at the top of the bills—"Federal Reserve Note." Check it out.

Federal Reserve Regulations   rules establishing how banks may operate in the United States. There are thirty regulations, named *A* through *DD*.

Federal Reserve System   the central bank of the United States, The Fed's job is to regulate and control the supply of credit to the nation's bank.

Federal Unemployment Tax   tax paid on wages and salaries to pay for federal and state unemployment programs.

fiat money   money not backed by gold.

fidelity bonds   bonds that bankers purchase from insurance companies to protect themselves against robbery, employee fraud, and other wrongdoings. In some states, banks are required to purchase fidelity bonds.

fiduciary   a person who manages someone else's investments.

GLOSSARY

finance charge the cost of interest payments, filing fees, and other costs apart from the actual cost of an item. The finance charge is what you pay when you finance a purchase. When you pay cash straight up, you pay no finance charges.

finance company a private company that issues loans.

Financial Accounting Standards Board (FASB) the board that establishes rules for certified public accountants. This board also determines what the generally-accepted accounting principles are.

financial institution an institution, public or private, that collects money from depositors and lends it out or invests it.

financial planning counseling by financial planners to help individuals get the highest returns for their investments.

fiscal policy the financial policies of the federal government, including its taxation policies and spending.

fiscal year a period of 12 months—the period can begin at any point in the year—for which a company plans its budget and reports on its financial activity. The fiscal year and the calendar year often do not coincide.

fixed asset a tangible asset, such as equipment, that a company cannot dispose of without interrupting normal business activities.

fixed-rate loan a loan whose rate of interest does not change.

fixture personal property that becomes part of real property because of the way in which it is used. Fixture is a legal term. If you build shelves into your rented apartment, they become a fixture—that is, a part of the rental property.

float to place a bond on the market.

floating exchange rate exchange rate between currencies that is allowed to change as the market dictates. In a fixed exchange rate, governments or banks decide what the exchange rates between currencies are.

flood insurance insurance against damage from floods. Flood insurance, like earthquake insurance, is often hard to get—except in areas where flooding rarely occurs.

floor the minimum interest rate that borrowers can pay on a variable rate loan. By placing a floor on the interest rate, lenders can be assured that interest rates do not fall below an unprofitable margin. The ceiling is the maximum rate borrowers can pay on a variable rate loan.

floor limit   the most a merchant can accept as a credit-card charge without seeking confirmation from the credit-card issuer.

floor trader   a trader on a stock-exchange floor who shouts a lot.

forbearance   not seeking penalties against a borrower in default, on the condition that the borrower will fulfill obligations in the future.

foreclosure   legal proceeding in which a lender attempts to obtain the collateral that was secured for a defaulted loan.

foreign exchange   converting the currency of one country into its equivalent in the currency of another country.

foreign trade   importing and exporting goods between nations.

foreign trade zone   a place where goods can be imported and exported without being subject to customs duties or taxes. Foreign trade zones are meant to encourage trade.

forged check   a check whose drawer signature or endorsement signature is not valid.

forgery   fraudulently altering a document, such as a check.

Form 10K   the form used to file an annual financial report with the Securities and Exchange Commission. Large corporations are required to file the form.

Form 1099   disclosure form filed with the IRS that lists all unearned income from stocks, bonds, interest, and the like.

forward exchange contract   a contract by which two parties agree to trade currencies at a date in the future. Forward exchange contracts allow banks to protect themselves against currency fluctuations since the money is paid for at the current exchange rate, not the future exchange rate.

forward market   a market in which traders agree to deliver stocks, bonds, commodities, or other tradable items at a future date. Forward markets allow traders to protect themselves against future price hikessince the items are paid for at the time of sale, not the time of delivery.

franchise   a business arrangement whereby one party is allowed to use another party's name for a fee. Fast-food eateries are good examples of franchises.

franchise tax a tax imposed by a state on a business headquarters outside the state that does business in the state.

fraud intentional deception undertaken to trick someone else into parting with something of value. No legal definition of fraud exists.

front-end load a sales charge paid to a broker when purchasing mutual funds.

frozen account an account whose funds cannot be withdrawn, pending a judicial ruling.

full faith and credit the commitment of a government to pay the interest and principal on a bond. Municipal bonds and U.S. Treasury Bills are backed by full faith and credit.

full-service broker a brokerage firm that offers investment advice as well as the usual services.

fundamentalist a securities analyst whose bases investment decisions on the bond issuer's financial position. By contrast, a chartist bases decisions on the trends in the bond market.

funds transfer moving funds between accounts held by the same party.

fungible a security of the same value as another that can be exchanged easily with the other.

future value the value that a stock, bond, or commodity will attain in the future.

futures commodities to be delivered and paid for at a future date at a price agreed upon by the buyer and seller.

garnishment court judgment ordering a lender to be given part of the wages or salary of a borrower who has defaulted on a loan.

generally-accepted accounting principles (GAAP) the rules and guidelines that certified public accounts use when preparing financial statements.

general-obligation bond bonds issued to pay for public works projects, issued by a state or municipal government. Also called G-O bonds.

general partner a co-owner of a business. General partners receive a share of the business's profit and are partly responsible for its debts and liabilities.

gift tax a tax on gifts of cash or property. Gift taxes are paid by the donor.

GI loan name for special mortgage loans available to veterans of the U.S. armed services.

gilt-edged name for low-risk AAA corporate bonds that have proven earnings.

Ginnie Mae nickname for Government National Mortgage Association (GNMA), the government corporation that backs securities associated with Department of Veterans Affairs and the Federal Housing Administration. Securities backed by Ginnie Mae are considered very safe investments.

going concern name to describe a business that is in operation and is expected to remain so in the future.

gold card a credit card with a credit line of at least $5,000.

gold certificates a certificate giving the bearer title to gold in the United States gold reserve.

gold standard a monetary system in which currencies are backed by gold and paper bills can be exchanged for gold at any time.

government bond U.S. Savings Bonds, which the government issues to pay its debts. The bonds have high ratings and are sold in small denominations.

grace period the period of time during which a loan payment is to be paid. If the payment is not made during the grace period, it is overdue.

graduated payment mortgage (GPM) a mortgage with lower payments in the early years and higher ones as time goes by. GPMs are sold to borrowers whose incomes are expected to rise, the idea being that these borrowers will be able to make the higher payments in years to come.

grantor a person who writes a deed passing property from one party to another.

gross estate the property in an estate before debts, taxes, and other expenses are paid. The net estate is what remains after these expenses are paid.

Group of Ten the ten leading industrial countries and members of the International Monetary Fund. They are France, Japan, Italy, Sweden, England, Belgium, Canada, Germany, Holland, and the United States.

growing-equity mortgage (GEM) a fixed-interest mortgage with monthly payments that rise instead of decline, the idea being to pay off the mortgage faster.

growth stock stock in a company that is expected to grow quickly. Investors like growth stock, since it is expected to increase in value faster than other stock.

guaranteed bonds bonds whose principal and interest is backed by a corporation other than the issuer.

guarantor a person or corporation that guarantees a debt will be paid if another party defaults. Guarantors are considered co-endorsers of a debt and are therefore liable for the debt.

guaranty a promise on the part of an individual or corporation that it will pay the debt of another party if the other party defaults on a debt.

H bond U.S. government bond, or savings bond.

hard currency the currency of a developed nation that is easy to convert to other currencies.

hedging buying and selling commodities in a futures market to protect against price fluctuations.

HH bond U.S. government bond, or savings bond. HH bonds are sold in denominations of $500 to $10,000.

high-grade bond a bond with AAA or AA rating, considered a secure investment.

home-equity loan a loan backed by the equity in the borrower's home.

humped yield curve when medium-terms rates are higher than both short- and long-term rates. If you drew this on paper, you would have a humped curve.

hyperinflation very high inflation. Hyperinflation is usually defined as inflation higher than 600 percent a year.

illiquid refers to assets that are not easy to liquidate—that is, convert into cash.

impaired credit a bank loan that is not likely to be repaid.

import taxes taxes levied on certain imported items. Most nations have import taxes to protect domestic markets from foreign competition.

income statement a report describing a corporation's activities, its profit, and its losses over a fixed period.

indemnity an obligation to pay all costs of damage, pain, or suffering.

indenture a document that states the terms under which a bond is issued. The indenture declares the maturity date, the interest, as well as other information.

independent agent an insurance agent who represents more than one company.

independent bank a commercial bank that draws depositors from and serves the residing area. Independent banks, which are scarce and are getting scarcer, are not branches of large commercial banks.

index a numerical measurement that compares past and present economic activity. The Dow Jones Industrial Average is an index of stock performance. The Consumer Price Index measures the price of consumer goods.

individual retirement account (IRA) retirement account to which individuals can deposit up to $2,000 (or $2,250, if their spouse is not working) of their annual earnings. IRAs provide two significant income-tax benefits: IRA contributions may reduce an individual's taxable income and IRA earnings are not taxed. Withdrawals from an IRA can be made after age 59½, at which time the withdrawals are taxed as normal income.

individual retirement account rollover rule allowing holders of individual retirement accounts (IRAs) to pass on the accumulated savings in one IRA to another IRA, provided they do so within the first 60 days of closing the first IRA.

industrials securities of mining, manufacturing, construction, and other companies whose work is producing commodities or services.

inflation rises in prices. Inflation is caused by excess purchasing power among the general populace and by increasing production costs, which producers pass on to consumers.

inheritance tax tax that heirs must pay in order to receive property from an estate. Not all states have inheritance taxes.

inside director a member of a corporation's board of directors who also works inside the corporation as a manager.

insider information information available to managers and others in a corporation that could be used by to make sweet stock deals. Insider information is not available to the general public. The Securities and Exchange Commission forbids corporation directors and principals from buying or selling stock based on insider information.

insider trading trading stock with insider information. Insider trading is forbidden by the Securities and Exchange Commission.

insiders corporate managers, directors, principals, and officers are considered "insiders."

insolvency being unable to pay debts.

installment contract agreement to pay for goods in fixed installments—for example, weekly or monthly.

installment credit a loan that is repaid in monthly payments of the same amount.

institutional investor a corporation that invests many of its assets, even though its chief purpose is not to make investments. For example, an insurance company's job is to provide insurance, but they also make many investments. Institutional investors make up a large portion of the securities investment market.

insufficient funds what you have if you try to write a check for $10 and you have only $7.50 in your checking account or if you try to withdraw $20 from a savings account that has only $18 in it.

insurance agent a representative of an insurance company.

insurance broker someone who sells insurance policies.

insurance contract a contract between an individual and an insurance company, in which the individual promises to pay premiums and the company promises to pay a certain amount of money if the individual loses life, limb, or property.

intangible assets the assets of a company that aren't property but are assets nonetheless. For example, an established clientele is an intangible asset.

interest amount of money paid to borrow capital. Typically, the interest is expressed as a percentage of the principal that was borrowed.

interest-only loan a loan that requires the borrower to pay only interest for the term of the loan. Loan payments on an interest-only loan don't reduce the loan balance. At the end of the loan, the borrower makes a balloon payment equal to the original (and ending) loan balance.

interest-rate the price of borrowing money. The interest rate is usually expressed as a percentage of the total principal borrowed, although sometimes the rate of interest on a loan is tied to an index of some kind.

interest-rate cap a fixed limit on the amount that a borrower has to pay in interest on a loan.

interest-sensitive assets assets whose value rises and falls with changes in interest rates. Treasury Bills and variable rate mortgages are examples of interest-sensitive assets.

interim report a report showing stockholders how a company is doing. An interim report appears before the company's annual report.

interim statement a statement regarding account balances that you can get from an automatic teller machine. Interim statements are not as detailed as monthly statements.

interlocking directorate when members of the board of directors of one corporation also sit on the board of another, competing organization.

internal rate of return (IRR) the profit that an investment earns expressed as a percentage. Typically IRRs are stated as annual profit percentages. On an investment that pays interest and for which there is no change in value, such as a bank savings account, the interest rate is the IRR.

interstate banking expansion of banks across state lines, as they acquire subsidiaries in other states.

interstate commerce commercial trading of goods across state lines.

intervention when central banks buy or sell currency in order to influence exchange rates. By selling currency, a central bank can flood the market and lower the value of the currency. By buying currency, a central bank can create a seller's market and increase the currency's value.

inter vivos trust Inter vivos is Latin for *between the living*. An inter vivos trust gives one person's property to another person.

intrinsic value the benefit to the holder of an option contract If he or she doesn't exercise the option. The intrinsic value is the exercise price less the option price.

inventory in a business, a list of a stock on hand, with the value of each item and the total value of all items by category.

investment advisor a person or agency paid to research investments and make investment recommendations for another person or institution. Investment advisors are required to disclose any conflict of interest recommendations to the Securities and Exchange Commission.

investment banker a person or corporation that buys and sells (or assists in buying and selling) stocks, bonds, other securities, and even whole companies.

investment club group of individuals that studies investment opportunities together. Sometimes the individuals pool their funds and make investments.

investment companies companies that buy securities from other companies and then sell shares in those securities to investors.

investment counselor a person who researches investments, makes recommendations, and invests on behalf of others. Investment counselors must register with the Securities and Exchange Commission.

involuntary bankruptcy a petition by creditors asking a bankruptcy court to declare a firm bankrupt, the firm having failed to pay its debts and meet its financial obligations. Also called a creditor's opinion.

involuntary lien a lien made by the judgment of a court without the consent of the property owner.

irrevocable trust a trust that cannot be revoked without the approval of the beneficiary. An irrevocable trust cannot be changed in any way without the beneficiary's approval.

joint account a savings or checking account in the name of two or more people.

joint annuity an annuity that is paid out to two or more people.

joint custody when authorization is required by two or more people to undertake an action. For example, the customer and bank have joint custody of a safe deposit box: opening a box requires authorization of the customer and a bank officer.

joint endorsement   a check requiring the endorsement of two or more signers.

joint tenancy   when two or more people inherit an estate and each has equal interests. When one dies, the estate passes automatically to the survivor or survivors.

joint tenants with right of survivorship   the usual arrangement among married couples, in which each has the right to shared property, and the property passes to the other in the event that one dies.

joint venture   a business initiative undertaken by two different businesses, each working toward a common goal. Companies engage in joint ventures to pool their resources and help overcome the high cost of entering new markets.

jointly and severally   a legal term meaning that, when two or more people take out a loan together, all are liable so that if they default, the lender can take legal action against all of them or specific individuals.

judgment   the official decision of a court of law.

judgment lien   a court order placing a lien on the property of a debtor.

judicial sale   a sale of property, as ordered by a court, to satisfy a debt. A foreclosure is an example of a judicial sale.

jumbo certificate of deposit   a certificate of deposit with a principal of $100,000 or more.

junior mortgage   a second or subsequent mortgage on a property. If the property is in default, junior mortgages are paid only after the first mortgage has been paid.

junk bond   a bond whose creditworthiness is very low. Junk bonds usually have a rating of BB or below. To attract investors, junk bonds pay a higher interest rate than do other bonds, since the bonds carry a high risk of default.

Keogh plan   Retirement plan that allows you to set aside some of your wages or salary for retirement. Keogh plans are more complex to set up and to administer than SEP/IRA plans. But they may allow larger contributions.

kicker   an extra condition imposed by a lender before the lender will approve a loan. Part ownership in the property, or a share of its proceeds, are example of kickers.

kiting   an illegal scheme for fraudulently inflating the account balance of checking accounts. For example, a man with two checking accounts, one in Bank *A* and one in Bank *B*, writes a check on account *A* for $5,000 to his Bank *B* account. He deposits the check in Bank *B*. Until the check clears, he has $5,000 in both Bank *B* and Bank *A*. Next, he writes a check on account *B* for $5,000 to his Bank *A* account. He deposits this check too. Until the checks clear, he has $10,000 in his Bank *A* account and $5,000 in his Bank *B* account. On paper he has $15,000, when really he has only $5,000.

kwacha   the national currency of Zambia.

kyat   the national currency of Burma.

lagging indicator   an economic indicator that usually reflects not where the economy is headed, but where it has been. For example, gross national product (GNP) is a lagging indicator, since increases or declines in GNP aren't registered till after the fact.

land flip   real-estate scam in which property is sold repeatedly, usually within a matter of months, with the value of the property increasing with each sale until the last sucker buys it at an over-valued price and is stuck with it.

late charge   charge for tardiness in paying a bill or a mortgage payment.

laundered money   large cash deposits, often acquired by illicit means, accepted by banks as normal deposits. To prevent money laundering, banks are required to report any cash deposit of more than $10,000.

leading indicators   economic indicators that usually reflect where the economy is headed. For example, when the number of new investments goes up, it usually means that the economy is healthy.

lease   a contract that gives an individual or business the right to use a property for an agreed-upon price and time period.

leasehold   the right of occupancy that tenants enjoy as part of a lease.

legal tender   money that is valid legally for the payment of debts. A dollar bill is legal tender, as noted just northwest of George Washington's head, where it says, "This note is legal tender for all debts, public and private."

lender of last resort   the bank from which all money flows initially, the Federal Reserve Bank

letter of credit (L/C or LOC)   a document from a bank giving authority for payments to be made to a third party from the bank on behalf of a bank's customer.

leverage   credit acquired in order to improve an individual's or company's ability to invest or speculate.

leveraged buyout   when one company takes over another and uses the acquired company's assets in order to pay back the loans that were taken out in order to take over the company in the first place.

liability   all debts and obligations of a business.

liability insurance   insurance protecting the policyholder against financial losses resulting from injury done to others.

lien   a charge against real or personal property to secure the repayment of a debt.

life estate   an estate that gives income to a beneficiary until the time of the beneficiary's death, at which time the estate passes to another party. The beneficiary cannot sell any property belonging to the estate.

limitations   the conditions under which an insurer will either make limited payments or make no payments at all on a policy claim.

limited partnership   a partnership in which profits and responsibility for liabilities and debts are shared according to how much of the business each partner owns.

line of credit   a commitment on the part of a bank to lend up to a certain amount of money to a borrower.

liquidity   turning assets such as property into cash. An asset with good liquidity can be sold or converted into cash easily.

liquidity preference   refers to people's innate preference for liquid assets, such as cash, over hard assets, such as property. Liquid assets are easier to spend.

litigation   contesting a dispute in a court of law.

living trust   trust giving one person's property to another person. Also called an inter vivos trust.

load the commission that an investor pays to a broker when purchasing mutual funds. In a back-end load, the commission is paid when the investors sells the funds. In a front-end load, it is paid when the investors purchases the funds from the investment house.

load fund a mutual fund whose purchase price includes a commission. No-load funds do not charge commissions.

loan money lent at interest, to be repaid by a specific date.

loan committee a bank committee that reviews applications for large loans above what a loan officer has the authority to review.

loan shark a lender who charges exorbitant fees for loans. With the exception of some credit-card issuer banks, which charge upwards of 15 percent annually in interest on their cards, most loan sharks do not work out of commercial banks.

lock-in period the 30 to 60 day time period in which a lender must keep mortgage rates to the figure quoted in the loan application. The lock-in period protects borrowers in case interest rates rise before the mortgage is approved.

London interbank bid rate the rate at which banks in the London Interbank Market borrow from one another.

London interbank offered rate (LIBOR) rate at which the biggest banks in London lend money to one another. LIBOR is used as an index by some banks for pegging the interest rate charged to borrowers.

long position broker's term for a security owned free and clear, including all interest, income, and dividends. For example, a commodities dealer who owned 500 units of pork bellies outright could say, "I am long in 500 pork bellies," and she'd be right.

long-term in financial terms, long-term refers to a security that matures in ten or more years.

lump-sum distribution single payment to the beneficiary of a retirement plan. For tax purposes, the lump-sum may be treated as if it had been received over ten years, depending on the beneficiary's age and other conditions.

M1, M2, M3 ways of measuring the money supply. M1, the narrowest measure, includes only money held in hand by the public. M2 encompasses M1's definition, but also includes money in savings accounts and CDs. M3, the widest measure, encompasses M2 but also includes money-market funds and other long-term holdings.

maker   the writer of a check.

management report   report prepared monthly for the officers of a corporation describing company performance.

margin   money given to a broker that serves as a pledge to pay for securities. Investors are required to put up 50 percent of the cost of their investments as a margin. (Some brokers require more.)

margin call   demand by a securities broker for a client to put up more cash or collateral to back up investments. If the call is not met, the broker can sell existing collateral.

margin trading   buying securities with credit provided by a broker.

market   in financial terms, a place where traders gather to exchange commodities, securities, or stocks.

market risk   the likelihood that the price of items will rise or fall as economic conditions change.

Massachusetts trust   a business association, owned by stockholders and managed by trustees. Many mutual funds are Massachusetts trusts.

maturity   the date when the borrower is obliged to pay back the loan.

maximum out-of-pocket   the most you can pay for insurance in a year. Usually the maximum out-of-pocket is the sum of the premium, the deductible, and all co-payments.

mechanic's lien   a lien on real property made by a contractor or builder for payment overdue. A builder can request a mechanic's lien if he or she has not been paid according to the contract to build or improve the property.

merger   when two or more corporations pool their common stock and become one corporation.

minimum balance   the least amount of money that can be kept in a savings or checking account. Letting the balance drop below the minimum sometimes incurs a service charge.

minimum payment   the smallest payment that can be made on a monthly credit-card bill without incurring a service charge.

minor   in most states, a person under age 18. Minors have neither all the legal rights of adults nor the legal responsibilities.

mint   where money is coined and printed. Mints are operated by the U.S. Treasury Department.

mobile-home certificate   a certificate representing ownership of an investment in mobile-home loans insured by the Federal Housing Administration.

monetarist   one who believes that controlling the supply of money is the best way to control inflation and make the economy grow at a stable rate.

monetary policy   refers to the Federal Reserve Board's policies to promote the economic health of the United States. The Fed sets monetary policies designed to control inflation, increase employment, and achieve other such goals.

money-center bank   a bank found in an important commercial city that does business both domestically and internationally.

money laundering   depositing large amounts of cash, often acquired illicitly, in banks as though they were normal deposits. To prevent money laundering, banks are required to report any cash deposit of more than $10,000.

money market   market where short-term investment funds are traded. The money market is not organized like a stock exchange, but is the loose-knit organization of buyers and sellers of money-market funds.

money-market certificate   certificate of deposit representing a debt security. Money-market certificates must have a denomination of at least $2,500. The individual institutions that issue them set the rate of interest and maturity date.

money-market deposit account (MMDA)   money-market funds managed through a commercial bank. Bank customers can make deposits directly into their MMDAs from their banks.

money-market fund (MMF)   mutual fund that invests in Treasury Bills, CDs, and other short-term debt instruments. Investors own shares in the fund and receive regular interest payments.

money-market rates   the rate of return paid by individual money-market funds.

money supply the total sum of money available in an economy for spending and investing. Money supply is usually defined in one of three ways called M1, M2, and M3. M1, the narrowest measure, includes only money held in hand by the public. M2 encompasses M1's definition, but also includes money in savings accounts and CDs. M3, the widest measure, encompasses M2 but also includes money-market funds and other long-term holdings.

monopoly when an individual or corporation has complete control over a market, either through ownership of source materials, ownership of distribution in a certain area, or ownership of the means by which the product is made.

moratorium when a borrower officially declares that he or she can't pay back a loan.

mortgage a deed giving ownership of a property to a borrower on the condition that the borrower makes all interest and principal payments to a lender. The lender owns the mortgage until the borrower pays in full, after which the borrower becomes sole owner of the property.

mortgage-backed securities securities backed by mortgages and deeds of trust.

mortgage banker a banker who sells mortgages or pools of mortgages to investors.

mortgage broker a broker who helps people who want to acquire mortgages find willing lenders. Brokers work on commission.

mortgage payable an account in a ledger recording mortgage payments for a company asset.

mortgage REIT REIT stands for real-estate investment trust. REITs are trusts that supply capital to real-estate developers who want to build new housing.

mortgagee name for the lender who supplies mortgages and collects mortgage payments.

mortgagor on a mortgage, the borrower who must pay the interest and principal.

municipal bond bonds issued on behalf of municipalities—cities, states, as well as government agencies—to cover their debts.

municipal-bond insurance Insurance against the failure of a municipal bond. Private companies provide the insurance and agree to buy the bonds in the event of a default.

mutual fund investment company that trades in bonds, stocks, Treasury Bills, securities, real estate, and other things as well, on behalf of its stockholders. Shares in a mutual fund are offered on a continual basis, and investors can always buy in.

mutual insurance company an insurance company that is owned by its policyholders. Company earnings are paid to policyholders as dividends.

mutual savings bank savings bank, similar to a cooperative, in which bank assets belong to depositors and dividends are paid to depositors.

mutual wills wills written by two people each naming the other as beneficiary.

national currency the official currency of a nation. The national currency of the United States is the dollar; of Greece, the drachma.

national income all earnings from production in a nation, including earnings from interest, rental income, and business profits. The U.S. Department of Commerce publishes a monthly report on national income.

natural guardian the mother or father of a child, who acts by law as the child's guardian. Children who do not have natural guardians are appointed guardians by a court.

negotiable capable of being transferred from one party to another. Checks, drafts, securities, and commercial paper are negotiable.

negotiable certificate of deposit a CD issued by a commercial bank. Negotiable CDs are large-denomination CDs of $100,000 or more. Typically, they are held by institutional investors.

negotiable instrument a written order promising to pay a certain amount to the bearer upon demand or at a certain date. Checks, promissory notes, and bills of exchange are examples of negotiable instruments.

negotiable order of withdrawal (NOW) account a combination checking and savings account. Like a savings account, a NOW pays interest, and checks can be written against it like a checking account.

nest egg money not needed for day-to-day spending, set aside in a savings account. Also savings for retirement.

net-asset value the total value of a share in a mutual fund. The net-asset value is what each share would be worth if all shares were suddenly paid out.

net worth the total value of the assets of a business less the liabilities.

netting when banks or corporations settle debts with each other by balancing out what they owe instead of paying each other in full. For example, if company *A* owed $20,000 to company *B*, and *B* owed $25,000 to *A*, *B* could pay *A* $5,000 straight up instead of each company paying its debt in full.

New York Stock Exchange (NYSE) the Big Daddy of stock exchanges, located on Wall Street in New York, New York; the oldest and biggest stock exchange between the Atlantic and Pacific Oceans.

next of kin nearest blood relative to another. The next of kin inherits a dead person's property if no will is left behind.

no-load fund a mutual fund that charges no sales commission.

no-load insurance insurance sold directly to consumers without the aid of a broker. No-load insurance is usually cheaper because the buyer does not have to pay a sales commission.

nolo contendere Latin for *I do not contend it.* By pleading nolo contendere, a defendant admits to the facts of the case but does not admit guilt and is thereby free to contest the charge at another time.

nonaccrual loan a loan for which interest is not being paid because the borrower cannot pay the interest.

noncallable a bond or stock that cannot be redeemed, or called in, before a pre-agreed date or the date of maturity.

nonprofit corporation an organization that does not distribute its profits, if there are any, to owners. Profits are plowed back into the nonprofit's capital fund.

nonrecourse refers to the lack of a legal claim against a party to a contract. In a nonrecourse arrangement, one or both parties are not liable if the contract is not fulfilled. The wronged party, therefore, has no recourse to the law.

nonrecourse indebtedness   indebtedness for which the borrower is not liable.

nonrecourse loan   a loan for which the lender will be repaid by proceeds generated by the loan. For example, a loan for a housing development would be a nonrecourse loan if the builder intended to pay back the loan with proceeds from the sale of the completed project. The loan is called nonrecourse because if the borrower defaults, the lender has no recourse except to foreclose on the borrower's collateral.

notary public   public officer who attests to the authenticity of deeds, affidavits, and depositions.

note   a written promise to pay a debt or sum of money.

notes payable   in a general ledger, an account showing the business's liability for promissory notes.

notes receivable   in a general ledger, an account showing the business's promissory notes received from customers.

not sufficient funds (NSF)   what you have if you try to write a check for $10 and you only have $7.50 in your checking account or if you try to withdraw $20 from a savings account with $18 in it.

novation   an agreement to remove one party from a contract and replace that party with another. All parties in the contract must agree to the novation.

odd lots   lots not being traded in the usual number. For example, stock is usually traded in lots of 100 on stock exchanges, so an odd lot would be 50 or 75 shares.

off-board   describes transactions of stock not listed in a stock exchange, but traded directly by brokers and dealers.

offer   the lowest price that a seller will accept for stock.

offering price   the per-share price of a new stock offering or securities offering.

open-end lease   a car lease requiring monthly payments, at the end of which the borrower can either make a large balloon payment to buy the car outright or return the car to the lender.

open market   a market where securities and commodities are traded freely by competitive bidding. In open markets, bidding is not limited to members.

open-market rates   the interest rates paid on negotiable CDs, Treasury Bills, commercial paper and other money-market negotiables in the secondary trading market.

operating lease   a lease covering a time period shorter than the economic life of the asset. Operating leases can be canceled at any time.

opportunity cost   income that could be saved or earned by investing in another, more attractive endeavor. For example, if you had $10,000 in mutual funds paying $500 in dividends annually, and you knew you could earn $750 in dividends from stock, the cost of staying with your original investment—your opportunity cost—would be $250 annually.

option   a contract giving a dealer or broker the right to buy or sell a security during a certain time period at a certain price.

original issue discount (OID)   the difference between what a bond costs when it was issued and what its price is at maturity.

original maturity   the time between the day a bond was issued and the day it reaches maturity. The current maturity is the time between today's date and the date the bond reaches maturity.

origination fee   the fee that lenders charge loan applicants to handle loan applications and to conduct credit investigations.

overdraft   the amount that a check exceeds what is in the checking account it was written on. If you write a check for $20 and you only have $15 in your checking account, you have a $5 overdraft.

overdraft protection   a service offered by banks to their customers in which the bank pays overdrawn checks up to a certain amount.

over-the-counter   securities not listed with a stock exchange are traded over-the-counter by dealers and brokers.

paper gain/loss   name for capital gains or losses in an investment portfolio that have yet to be realized.

participating bond   a bond that entitles the bearer to minimum interest payments and proceeds from the profits of the company, as stated by the terms of a contract.

partnership   a business with two or more owners, who share equally in the profits as well as the liability for debts.

passbook   a book for recording deposits and withdrawals in a savings account. Some banks require the passbook to be presented when money is deposited or withdrawn.

pataca the national currency of Macao.

patent   an exclusive right to sell, make, and use an invention. Patents are awarded by the U.S. Patent Office.

pay to bearer   refers to bonds and other negotiables that are paid to the person who has them in hand, not necessarily to the person named on the bond or negotiable.

pay to order   refers to bonds and other negotiables, such as checks, that are to be paid to the person named, not necessarily to the one who has them in hand.

payee   the person or party to whom a check is written.

payment shock   when payers of adjustable-rate mortgages make their first high payment after the introductory payment period, they are said to experience payment shock.

payroll taxes   taxes on a payroll, including social security taxes and employment insurance taxes.

pegging   indexing the price of mortgage rates and other lending rates with a rate charged by a major bank or important banking institution. For example, mortgage rates are often pegged to the prime rate, the rate banks charge their most reliable customers for credit.

penalty clause   clause in many banking contracts stating that customers must pay a penalty for late mortgage payments, early withdrawals of savings accounts, and the like.

penny stocks   stocks whose offering price is less than a dollar per share. Penny stock prices are sometimes extremely volatile.

pension fund   a fund set up by a corporation to provide for its employees in retirement. Typically, employees contribute a portion of their pay checks to the fund. The fund is used to make investments as part of the company's pension plan.

pension plan   a plan by which a company provides for its employees in retirement. Employees—sometimes with matching contributions from employers—contribute to a pension fund, which is used to make investments as part of the plan. Managers of pension plans must follow strict investment guidelines.

perfect title a title to a property that is free of debts, liens, prior claims, and other encumbrances.

perfected lien a lien that has not only been filed by the lien holder but is also in force.

periodic rate the price of credit, expressed as a percentage and charged at periodic intervals. For example, a credit card that charges a 12 percent annual rate for outstanding debt would charge a 1 percent periodic rate if it billed customers monthly (12 times a year). If it only billed customers 6 times a year, it would charge a 2 percent periodic rate.

permanent financing a long-term mortgage, typically used to finance construction projects, covering all requirements of the project from legal costs to building materials.

perpetual bonds bonds that have no maturity date. Owners of the bond collect income as long as they hold it. Also called an annuity bond.

personal banker employee of a bank who manages a customer's accounts and acts as a financial counselor.

personal identification number (PIN) better known as an access code, the password or number you punch in at an automatic teller machine to make deposits and withdrawals.

personal loan a loan, usually for under $5,000, for the personal use of the customer, not for business use.

personal property items and things, as opposed to real property, such as buildings and land. By definition, personal property is not immovable—in other words, it can be moved. A baseball card is personal property; a baseball field is real property.

personal-property tax tax on valuable personal property, such as jewelry, cars, and yachts. Also called a luxury tax.

personal residence for tax purposes, the home you live in most of the year. Each taxpayer has one personal residence. Capital gains stemming from sales of a personal residence often receive preferential treatment.

personal trust a trust created for individuals or families. Personal trusts are set up for a variety of reasons, for the tax benefits or to benefit grandchildren, for example.

pit the floor of a commodity or stock exchange, where brokers and dealers make hand gestures and scream at each other.

pledge   placing property of collateral with a lender in order to secure a loan. For example, a watch left with a pawnbroker in return for a loan is a pledge.

plus sign (+)   in a newspaper report, a plus sign next to stock or mutual fund price means it rose that day. In a bond or treasury note price, a plus sign means that the price is expressed in sixty-fourths of a percentage point. For example, a par value of 89.52 means 89 and 52/64 of par.

plus tick   when a security is resold at a higher value, it is called a plus tick, or an up tick.

point   in stock prices, a point equals one dollar; in bond prices, ten dollars.

Ponzi scheme   to swindle by paying early investors with money from later investors, not with earned income. Eventually, the incoming investment money cannot keep up with payments to investors, and the whole deal collapses. Named for Charles A. Ponzi, a well-known swindler.

pool   when securities of a similar type are combined and bought and sold as a group. Securities can also be pooled as collateral.

portfolio   term for the total assets and investments held by an individual, company, or institution. For reporting and tracking purposes, a portfolio can be divided into smaller portfolios—for example, the loan portfolio, land portfolio, etc.

positive yield curve   curve that demonstrates how securities held longer yield a higher rate of return. Because interest rates are higher for long-term securities than they are for short-term ones, rates of return rise the longer a security is held.

posting   recording accounting entries on a general ledger.

power of attorney   a legal document that lets someone you trust run your financial affairs if you become unable to do so.

preapproved credit   credit extended automatically to prospective credit-card holders. Preapproved credit is used as an incentive to get customers to apply for cards. By custom, the amount of preapproved credit being offered is printed in bold red letters on the envelope in which the credit-card application comes.

preemptive right   the right of the Federal Reserve Board to over-rule state laws concerning the regulation of banks. Also the right of stockholders to buy new stock offerings before they are put on the general market.

preexisting condition   a sickness or injury that a person has before applying for health insurance. Most insurers will not cover pre-existing conditions immediately upon the issuance of a new health insurance policy. Instead, pre-existing conditions are covered only after the expiration of a waiting period.

preference   the selling or transfer of property within 90 days of filing for bankruptcy.

preferred stock   dividend-paying stock in a corporation that gives its holders advantages over holders of common stock. Preferred stockholders are paid before common stockholders. If the corporation goes bankrupt, preferred stockholders are paid from the assets of the corporation before common stockholders are but after any creditors are.

premium   sum above the face value of a bond when the bond is purchased at an above-par price. In insurance, the amount you pay for insurance coverage.

present value   the current-day equivalent of some future amount, or future value. In converting future values to present values, one adjusts for compound interest and for inflation.

price/earnings ratio   ratio between the current price of a stock and the earnings it will make over a specific period of time. Investors use the price/earnings ratio to measure the value of stocks.

primary market   market where loans are awarded to borrowers. Once a loan is made, it can be sold on the secondary market, where pools of mortgages are bought and sold by investors.

prime rate   the rate banks charge their most trustworthy customers for commercial loans.

principal   the actual money borrowed in a loan, as distinguished from the interest, the price of buying the loan. Also a deposit as distinguished from the interest it earns.

private banking   banking services for rich customers, including investment counseling and lending services.

private placement   selling the entire issue of a security to one group of investors.

privity   in a property, the relationship between all parties with mutual interests, such as the donor and recipient, or a landlord and tenant. Privity is a legal concept and is used in court to determine where fault, negligence, and conflicting interests arise.

probate   when a court examines a will to determine if it is valid. During probate, the court also assigns an executor to the will.

problem bank   a bank with a large amount of loans in default.

profit-sharing plan   a plan by which employees share in the profits of a company, either by receiving bonuses or having their profit shares put in a trust. Profit-sharing plans encourage employees to be more productive and more loyal to the companies they work for.

profit-taking   in stock trading, when investors sell shares after several days of rises in the market. A rising stock market encourages investors to sell and take advantage of higher prices—in other words, it encourages them to profit take.

progressive tax   tax rate that rises along with the amount being taxed.

promissory note   written promise to pay a sum of money at a future date to a specific person or to the bearer of the written promise.

property taxes   taxes on property, including real estate and stocks.

proprietorship, sole   when a business is owned by one person. Sole proprietorship is one of three types of business organization, the other two being a partnership and a corporation.

prospectus   Latin for *prospect*. A statement designed to attract investors to a newly formed corporation. Prospecti usually include the corporation's goals, a plan for how it will turn a profit, and an explanation of how investments will be used.

protectionism   giving domestic industries protection against foreign competition by levying taxes on foreign goods, using quotas, and other means.

proxy   a person who has authority to vote on behalf of a stockholder.

prudent-man rule   name of the law requiring trustees to invest only in securities that a prudent man or woman would buy. Trustees, who are legally responsible for others' money, may be held responsible under this rule if they make unwise investments.

public offering   bond issue offering to the general public.

puts and calls   options to sell or buy stock shares at a certain price within a certain time. The holder of a put can require a buyer to buy an option, within the agreed upon time period, at the specified price. The holder of a call can demand that a seller sell an option, within the agreed upon time period, at the agreed upon price. Investors buy put and call options as a hedge against large declines or rises stock prices.

pyramiding   in real estate, pyramiding means to finance property purchases with property that is already mortgaged. In banking, pyramiding means to use loans to pay off interest debt.

qualified opinion   when omissions in bank records prevent auditors from doing a thorough review of a bank's books, auditors give a qualified opinion—an best-available assessment of the bank's financial health.

quiet title action   a legal action meant to resolve all claims against a property.

quorum   the minimum number of people who must be present at a corporate meeting to conduct business.

quote   the highest bid to buy and the lowest offer to sell a security or commodity. Also called a quotation.

rate of return   money made on invested capital.

real-estate investment trust (REIT)   a trust that owns real estate and sells shares from the profits of that ownership to investors.

real-estate owned   term to describe real estate that a lender has acquired through foreclosure.

real income   income measured in terms of what it can buy, rather than in dollars-and-cents terms. For example, the real income of a low wage earner might be higher than that of someone who earns high wages, if the low wage earner lives in a region where goods and housing are inexpensive.

real-interest rate   interest rate that takes into account how interest yields are eaten away by inflation. To get the real interest rate, you subtract the inflation rate in a given period from interest earnings in the same period.

real property   land and buildings, as opposed to personal property, which comprises moveable items such as jewelry and equipment.

real money   coins and actual currency you could walk into a country store and buy a six-pack with. Checks and bank drafts, by comparison, are not considered real money.

real rate of return   rate of return on an investment that takes into account how rates are affected by inflation. The real rate of return is the rate of return less the rate of inflation over the length of the investment.

realized profit/loss   cash profit or loss from the sale of a security.

rebate   a return of part of a payment, made after the payment is received. Rebates are offered as incentives for consumers to buy or use products.

receiver   a person assigned by a court to help a bankrupt business reorganize its finances, satisfy its creditors, and become profitable.

receivership   a bankrupt business to whom a receiver has been assigned is in receivership.

record date   for payment of dividends, the date fixed by a board of directors for determining who will receive dividends.

record owner of stock   according to the records of a corporation, the individual or institution that owns shares of its stock.

recourse   being able to compel a debtor to cover debts.

redeemable bonds   bonds that issuers can repurchase if they so choose.

redeemable preferred stock   stock that the can be called in by the issuer and redeemed for cash at any time. Stockholders of redeemable preferred stock are required to give back their shares when the issuer asks them to do so. Also called callable preferred stock.

redemption   exchanging bonds for cash when the bonds reach maturity.

redemption price   price a corporation pays to bondholders when they redeem its bonds. Corporations pay the principal if the bonds are redeemed on their maturity date; they pay the principal and a premium if the bonds are called in before they reach maturity.

red herring   on page one of a prospectus, a statement printed in red saying that the material inside is not an offer to sell but is instead a public disclosure of facts. Also a distraction from the true issue at hand, from the practice of placing a smoked red herring across a path to confuse hunting dogs.

redlining   discriminating against minority and poor neighborhoods by declining to consider offering mortgages there. The name comes from the former practice of drawing red lines around these neighborhoods on maps.

refinancing   exchanging one mortgage for another in order to take advantage of better interest rates, for example.

regional stock exchange   a stock exchange that chiefly trades the stocks of corporations in the surrounding region.

registered bond   a bond registered to an individual or institution at the time of sale. Owners of registered bonds are known to the issuer and are sent payments automatically when the bonds fall due. Owners of bearer bonds, on the other hand, are not known to the issuer and must present their bonds in order to receive payment.

registered check   check purchased at a bank and backed by the bank that can be presented as payment to a third party. Registered checks work like money orders.

Regulation 9   regulation allowing national banks to have trust departments and manage the investments of customers.

Regulation A   Federal Reserve regulation establishing how Federal Reserve Banks advance money to financial institutions.

Regulation AA   Federal Reserve regulation governing how banks should handle customer complaints.

Regulation B   Federal Reserve regulation establishing guidelines for processing credit applications.

Regulation BB   Federal Reserve regulation requiring banks to serve the communities they reside in.

Regulation C   Federal Reserve regulations requiring lending institutions to disclose the locations where they lend money.

Regulation CC   Federal Reserve regulation streamlining how banks handle the return of unpaid checks.

Regulation D   Federal Reserve regulation requiring banks to keep a certain amount of money in reserve.

Regulation DD   Federal Reserve regulation establishing truth in lending laws.

Regulation E   Federal Reserve regulation setting rules for electronic funds transfers.

Regulation F   Federal Reserve regulation limiting the risks banks can take in dealing with other banks.

Regulation G   Federal Reserve regulation requiring lenders to report large credit extensions to brokers and dealers.

Regulation H   Federal Reserve regulation establishing membership requirements for banks in the Federal Reserve System.

Regulation I   Federal Reserve regulation stating how much stock member banks must purchase in the Federal Reserve Bank.

Regulation J   Federal Reserve regulation establishing how checks are collected and accounted for.

Regulation K   Federal Reserve regulation governing international banking.

Regulation L   Federal Reserve regulation governing interlocking directorships.

Regulation M   Federal Reserve regulation governing leasing companies.

Regulation N   Federal Reserve regulation governing bank transactions.

Regulation O   Federal Reserve regulation establishing how much credit banks may extend to their executive officers.

Regulation P   Federal Reserve regulation that establishes security guidelines for banks.

Regulation Q   Federal Reserve regulation requiring banks to deal fairly with customers.

Regulation R   Federal Reserve regulation building a better Chinese Wall in banks.

Regulation S   Federal Reserve regulation establishing how government agencies may seek information about bank customers.

Regulation T   Federal Reserve regulation governing how dealers and brokers may extend credit to customers.

Regulation U   Federal Reserve regulation governing how banks may extend credit for margin securities.

Regulation V   Federal Reserve regulation governing how banks may deal with firms in the defense industry.

Regulation X   Federal Reserve regulation applying Regulation G, T, and U to foreigners applying for credit in the United States.

Regulation Y   Federal Reserve regulation governing how banks may establish holding companies.

Regulation Z   Federal Reserve regulation establishing protections for consumers seeking credit.

remittance slip   attached to a check, a list of all deductions, corrections, discounts, taxes, or other information, along with the net amount of the check.

reorganization   after a business has declared bankruptcy, the restructuring of its assets in order to make it profitable again.

repossession   seizing the collateral for a loan due to inability to pay the interest or principal. Repossession is usually the last recourse for failure to pay a debt.

reserve   funds put aside for anticipated future costs.

reserve requirements   reserves that banks are required to keep on hand for their basic operations. These reserves are deposited at the bank's district Federal Reserve Bank.

residual value   the value an asset has when the asset's user or owner is finished using it.

Resolution Trust Corporation (RTC)   government institution established after the 1980s Savings & Loan debacle to sell off the assets of failed Savings & Loans. The RTC is attempting to recover some of the 500 billion lost to U.S. taxpayers during the freewheeling 1980s.

restraint of trade   refers to the concept, ingrained in U.S. law and in the American tradition, that no restrictions should be placed on the free flow of commerce.

restrictive covenant   a clause in an agreement or contract prohibiting a party or parties from taking certain actions. The most common restrictive covenant in business is one that prohibits a seller of a business from engaging in the same business for a certain number of years.

retained earnings   business profits that are used for expansion, not paid in dividends to stockholders or added to capital funds.

return of investment   when the earnings derived from a piece of capital equipment equal the price paid for the piece of equipment, you have a perfect return on your investment.

return on assets   a company's profits as a percentage of its assets. Return on assets is one way to measure a company's profitability.

revenue   total income from a given endeavor. Also gross income from an investment.

revenue bond   municipal bond for which the principal and interest are paid for by the project the bond finances. For example, a municipal bond issue for a harbor would be paid for by berth fees.

reverse mortgage   mortgage in which a lender makes payments to a borrower, with the understanding that the lender will take possession of the borrower's property at some later date. Retired people who need more income sometimes have reverse mortgages on property for which they possess the equity. These type of mortgages are rare.

reverse split   when stockholders exchange stock such that each owns the same number of shares. Reverse splits are undertaken so that stockholders all own the same percentage of a corporation.

revocable trust   a trust giving property to heirs that can be changed or revoked at any time by the person who originates the trust. Under this arrangement, the property is transferred to the heirs on the death of the trust originator and the estate does not have to go through probate.

revolving credit   most credit card accounts are revolving credit accounts. The account holder is given a credit line, runs up a bill, and pays off the amount owed in monthly payments. If the amount owed is not paid off monthly, interest charges are made. A minimum monthly payment is usually required on outstanding credit loans.

rigging   manipulating the price of a security to give it a false value.

right of foreclosure   the right of a lender to foreclose on a mortgaged property if the borrower can't meet mortgage obligations.

right of redemption the right of a debtor to buy a property at a sale of foreclosure is he or she has the means to do so. To redeem the property this way, the debtor has to pay the interest and principal on the defaulted mortgage, as well as all foreclosure costs incurred by the lender.

right of survivorship the right of surviving spouses to inherit the property of deceased spouses.

risk in financial terms, the possibility that an investment will not be repaid and that the method of investment will be rendered unprofitable by market conditions.

rollover the automatic renewal of a certificate of deposit at present rates of interest. Also, the automatic reinvestment of money market funds.

round lot a basic unit of common stock, usually 100 shares, bundled together for trading purposes.

Rule of 72 way of determining how long it will take for a sum of money to double at a specific interest rate, by dividing 72 by the interest rate. For example, a savings account earning 6 percent interest will double in 12 years, since 72 divided by 6 equals 12.

run when many depositors try to withdraw their money from a bank at short notice. When depositors fear that a bank is failing or lose confidence in a bank, a bank run can result.

rupiah national currency of Indonesia.

safe deposit box small safe in a bank vault that can be rented for storing valuables and important papers.

salary-reduction plan retirement plan in which money is taken automatically from employees' salaries and put in a retirement fund, such as a 401(k).

sales tax tax levied by state and local governments, usually as a percentage of retail sales.

savings account deposit bank account that yields interest. Cash can be deposited or withdrawn at the discretion of the holder.

savings bank bank that accepts deposits from customers and invests it in mortgages and securities.

savings bond   U.S. government bond, issued to finance the debt of the United States government. Savings bonds earn variable interest and are sold in denominations from $50 to $10,000.

seasonal adjustment   adjusting data collected throughout the year to an annual rate for the purposes of analysis. For example, retail sales rise in December when people shop for the holidays. Retail sales figures for December, therefore, have to be adjusted downward.

seasonal credit   line of credit extended to businesses during peak manufacturing and sales cycles.

seasonal variations   term for differences in economic statistics that repeat themselves year to year. For example, manufacturing rates decline in the winter due to cold weather, but rise again in the spring in any given year.

seat   a seat on a stock exchange. Members of a stock exchange are said to have a seat on the exchange.

second mortgage   second mortgage on a property, usually taken out to provide capital for home improvements or to finance a business. The obligations due the lender of a second mortgage are subordinate to the obligations owed the lender of a first mortgage.

secondary-mortgage market   market where first mortgages, or residential mortgages, are pooled and sold to investors. The secondary mortgage market serves as a capital fund for the mortgage originators, who sell their mortgages for the secondary market.

secured credit card   a credit card that is backed by a savings account. Issuers of secured credit cards can draw on cardholders' savings accounts if cardholders are unable to pay their credit-card bills.

securities   stocks, bonds, and other financial instruments that can be traded in a securities market.

Securities and Exchange Commission (SEC)   the regulatory agency charged with overseeing laws regarding the buying and selling of securities. Companies selling securities, and brokers and dealers who trade in them, must register with the SEC.

securitization   the conversion of loans and other bank assets into securities that can be traded in the securities market. Securitization enables banks to obtain capital.

security agreement   document that gives a lender a claim to the assets that the borrower has put up as collateral for a loan. The security agreement must be signed by the borrower to be valid.

security interest   the claim of a lender to assets that the borrower has pledged as collateral to back up a loan.

self-directed IRA   an individual retirement account that allows its owner to decide how the funds should be invested.

self-insurance   a rainy-day fund set aside for emergencies, illness, and periods of unemployment.

self-liquidating loan   a loan whose purpose is to give the borrower capital to acquire or manufacture goods, the sale of which will help repay the loan. For example, a loan to a farmer for seed money could be a self-liquidating loan, since the farmer would pay back the loan with revenue from the sale of crops.

seller's market   raising demand and raising the price that sellers can offer goods in short supply.

selling against the box   selling a stock with the idea of making a profit by rebuying the stock later when the price goes down. Selling against the box works like this: The seller, believing the stock will fall in price, has his or her broker borrow shares of the stock from one of the broker's clients. At the same time, the seller buys shares of the stock for him- or herself. Now all the stock is sold and the buyer of the stock gets the shares. Meanwhile, with luck, the stock drops in value. The seller buys the stock at the reduced price and returns the shares through the broker to the person they were borrowed from. The seller keeps the profits from shares of the stock he or she borrowed through the broker. However, if the stock went up instead of down after it was borrowed, the seller does not make a profit. Fortunately, the seller did buy shares of stock for him- or herself, and these now serve their purpose as a hedge against the stock's rise.

senior lien   the first mortgage on a property. When two or more liens have been placed on a property, the senior lien takes precedence over other liens and must be satisfied first.

serial bonds   bonds from the same issue that mature at different times. This way, the bonds do not all fall due at once and strain the finances of the issuer.

service charge   bank charge, as when an account is overdrawn or a check bounces.

settlement date   the actual date of the transfer of a security from the buyer to the seller.

severally but not jointly   in a stock offering, when the people selling the stock are each responsible for selling their part, but not for selling the entire offering. In a jointly but severally arrangement, all are responsible for the sale of the offering.

shared appreciation mortgage (SAM)   short-term mortgage offered at a low fixed rate of interest. In exchange for providing such favorable terms, the lender gets to benefit from the appreciation of the property's value.

sheriff's sale   an auction of a borrower's property as part of a foreclosure. The proceeds go to help pay the borrower's debts.

short   said of a trader who sells securities in the hopes that their price will go down and they can be bought back later at a lower price. By buying them for less than the trader sold them for, the trader can turn a profit.

short sale   selling a stock one does not own with the idea of making a profit by rebuying the stock later when the price goes down. A short sale works like this: The short seller, believing the stock will fall in price, has his or her broker borrow the stock from one of the broker's clients. The stock is sold. The buyer of the stock gets the shares the broker borrowed. Meanwhile, with luck, the stock drops in value. The short seller buys the stock at the reduced price and returns the shares through the broker to the person they were borrowed from. The short seller keeps the profits, unless of course the stock went up instead of down after it was borrowed. If the stock went up, the short seller still has to buy the shares in order to return them to the person they were borrowed from, and the short seller has to buy the shares at the higher price.

short-term financing   a loan that falls due in less than one year.

short-term gain   for the purpose of determining capital gains and losses, a gain on an investment that was held for less than a year. Whether an investment gain is short-term or long-term is important because long-term capital gains sometimes receive preferential treatment.

signature card   card that depositors fill out when they open a bank account.

signature loan   loan given without collateral, with only the borrower's promise to pay and his or her signature on a promissory note. Such loans are given on the basis of the good standing of the borrower.

Simplified Employee Pension Plan (SEP)   retirement plan for small businesses. It allows small-business people to set aside up to 15 percent of their gross income for retirement.

sinking fund   essentially a savings fund that accumulates money to pay off bonds or purchase a large asset.

sinking fund bonds   bonds for which the bond issuer has provided a sinking fund. All other factors being equal, a sinking fund reduces the chance that bond purchasers won't be repaid.

skip payment privilege   incentive clause giving a borrower the right to skip one or more payments.

slump   a slowdown in business activity. Also called a lull, an adjustment period, a valley, a slight downturn, a leveling off, a slow time, an introspection, and a gut check.

Small Business Administration   agency of the federal government that helps provide credit to small businesses.

smurf   a money launderer.

Social Security   insurance benefits provided by the federal government for old age, disabilities, and unemployment.

sole proprietor   when a business is owned by one person. Sole proprietorship is one of three types of business organization, the other two being a partnership and a corporation.

sovereign risk   risk that a foreign government will default on its debt payments. Sovereign risks present special risks to banks, since collecting debt from a foreign government is virtually impossible.

special offering   a block of securities so large it cannot be offered on the trading floor without depressing prices. Instead of being traded on the floor, special offerings are traded through members of the exchange, who sell them on their own.

specialist   a broker or dealer who specializes in trading a single commodity or security.

specie coins, not paper money.

specific identification method in an inventory, when each item is identified and accounted for. In some inventorying methods, similar items are grouped together.

speculation trading at a greater risk in order to obtain a fast profit.

speculator a person who trades in commodities, stocks, or bonds with the idea of making a quick profit by taking many risks.

spin-off when a corporation sees an opportunity to branch into a new but related field, it might create a spin-off company, a semi-independent company headed by members of the original corporation and drawing on the capital and expertise of its parent company.

split the dividing of existing stock into more shares. Individual stocks lose value, but the total value of the stock stays the same. Stock splits are often undertaken to make the stock easier to trade when companies are bought and sold.

spot in trading lingo, refers to the immediate delivery of orders or goods.

spot commodity in a commodity exchange, a good offered for immediate delivery.

spot market market for goods that are delivered and paid for immediately, not at some future date.

spot price commodity prices in the here and now, as opposed to trading in future prices.

spread covering the spread means to buy and sell the same commodity in a futures market as a hedge against price rises or declines. With orders to buy and sell, the trader is insured against market fluctuations.

squeeze shortage of funds in the money market, which causes a demand for money and a hike in interest rates.

stabilization the selling or buying of currency by a central bank in order to stabilize rates of exchange. When its currency is overvalued, a central bank sells its currency to flood the market and lower prices. When its currency is undervalued, the bank buys currency to increase competitive bidding and raise the price.

stale check a check that is more than six months old.

stamp taxes   taxes in the form of stamps, which manufacturers must buy and stick on their products or securities before they can be sold. You can see tax stamps on some brands of whiskey.

Standard & Poor's   the advisory service that rates securities for their creditworthiness.

standard of living   the goods and services that a social group requires for its well-being. The standard of living is an abstract term and cannot be measured against an index.

statute of frauds   a legal statue which says a contract cannot be enforced unless it has the signature of the person whom it is being enforced against. In the case of a mortgage or other assumable debt, the signature of the borrower is required. The statute of frauds should never be confused with the statue of frogs.

statue of limitations   a limit on the time within which a legal action can be brought or a file claimed.

stock certificate   a written document giving title to a share or shares of stock.

stock exchange   a market where stocks are traded.

stock purchase option   a benefit offered to employees, giving them the option to buy stock in the companies they work for. Usually the stock is offered at a reduced price.

stock split   the dividing of existing stock into more shares. Individual stocks lose value, but the total value of the stock stays the same. Stock splits are often undertaken to make the stock easier to trade when companies are bought and sold.

stop order   an order to buy or sell a stock or commodity when it reaches a certain price.

stop payment   to inform a bank not to honor a check. Even after a check is written and delivered, a bank customer can stop payment on it if he or she thinks the check was written in error.

Straddle   to order a call and put option at the same time, at the same date with the same price. Such an order would be made to take advantage of severe fluctuations in the market.

street   the street could only be one street, Wall Street in New York, New York, the address of the New York Stock Exchange and the place where so many financial decisions are made by men in tasseled loafers.

street name　a security registered in the name of a bank or brokerage firm, not in the owner's name.

strike price　the price that the holder of a put option can sell a security, or the holder of a call option can buy one, as stated in the option contract.

subject order　an order requiring confirmation.

subsidiary corporation　a company that is owned wholly or partly by another company. The company that does the owning is the parent company. The parent company usually owns a majority of the stock in the subsidiary.

Super NOW account　a three-in-one checking account, savings account, and money-market fund account.

supply-side economics　economic theory which says that lowering the tax rates drastically will put more capital in the hands of businesses, which will in turn create more jobs and more business activity. As the economy is stimulated this way, revenues will increase, which will increase the tax base and compensate for revenue lost by tax cuts.

surcharge　an extra charge made on people who pay with credit cards instead of cash. The surcharge pays for the extra costs of processing credit-card payments.

surety　a guarantee that a debt will be repaid. Also a person who is legally responsible for a debt.

surety bond　an agreement that if a housing development cannot be completed, an insurance company will take charge of the project, settle all disputes, and finish the project if necessary. Municipal development projects require surety bonds.

surplus　the amount by which a company's assets exceed its liabilities and capital stock, as shown on the company's balance sheet.

surtax　an added tax on income that has already been taxed once.

syndicate　an association of investment bankers formed to distribute an issue of new securities.

tape　nickname for the ticker tape that shows price quotations in securities and commodities markets.

tariff　taxes on import goods, levied to protect domestic industries or to raise revenue.

tax-deferred savings   tax-free savings that can be put in an individual retirement account (IRA) or other retirement plan. Taxes are not imposed on the interest or principal until funds are withdrawn at age 59½ or later.

tax-exempt bond   municipal bond that is free of all taxes.

tax-free rollover   the automatic renewal of a certificate of deposit, tax-free at present rates of interest. Also, the automatic tax-free reinvestment of money market funds.

tax lien   a lien on property for failure to pay property taxes.

tax sale   an auction of property to raise money for the payment of delinquent taxes.

taxable estate   the part of an estate that is subject to taxes. The taxable estate is what is left after all debts, funeral expenses, and taxes are paid.

taxpayer identification number (TIN)   for taxation purposes, the number that identifies corporations, nonprofits, associations, and partnerships to the IRS. Sole proprietors and individuals are identified by their social-security numbers.

teaser rate   low mortgage rate offered to borrowers as an incentive. Typically, the rate is brought up to normal mortgage rates after a few months or years.

technical analysis   a method, like charting and fundamental analysis, of predicting trends in the stock, securities, and commodities markets. Technical analysts examine volume, supply and demand, and other factors.

teller's check   a check written by a bank against its own funds. Teller's checks are guaranteed to be redeemable since they are drawn on banks.

tenancy at will   a lease that the landlord or tenant can terminate at any time.

tenancy by the entirety   an estate held by a wife and husband that cannot be terminated without both people's consent.

tenancy in common   an estate held by two or more people. If a partner in the estate dies, his or her share of the estate goes to heirs.

term   the time it takes for a loan or deposit to mature. The term is usually expressed in months.

testator person who dies leaving a will.

thin market said of a sluggish market with few offers and bids.

third-party check check transferred by the endorser to another party. The endorser writes "pay to the order of" and then the third party's name on the check, making it redeemable by the third party.

tick $\frac{1}{32}$ of a percentage point, the unit for measuring price changes in securities, bonds, and Treasury Bills.

tight money when the Federal Reserve tightens credit in order to raise interest rates and prevent inflation.

time deposit a deposit in a bank that pays a fixed rate of interest and cannot be withdrawn without penalty until a certain maturity date is reached.

time-value of money a general rule that says a dollar today is worth more than a dollar a year from today because if you have a dollar today you can invest it and earn interest over the next year.

title having ownership of real property. A deed, bill of sale, or certificate is required to prove title.

title company a company that determines who has ownership of a property. Having conducted a title search, the company issues a certificate of title to the owner.

title defect a claim, obstruction, or other condition that makes it hard to determine who the owner of a property is.

total lease obligation as required by the Federal Reserve, an accounting of all costs associated with a lease, including rent and interest payments, as well as the value of the leased property at the end of the lease.

trade date the day an order is made to buy or sell securities.

trader someone who buys and sells stocks, securities, and commodities, on her or his own behalf or on the behalf of others.

trading range the price range between the lowest bid and the highest offer for a stock, commodity, or security in an exchange market during a specific time period.

treasurer a financial officer of a corporation whose job is, among other duties, to manage cash payments and deposits, procure and budget funds, handle the payroll, and discharge tax liabilities.

Treasury Bill short-term bills issued by the U.S. government to cover its debt. The bills are in $10,000 denominations. They mature in periods of 13, 26, or 52 weeks.

Treasury bond long-term bonds issued by the U.S. government to cover its debts, sold in denominations of $10,000 or more.

Treasury stock stock that has been repurchased by the issuer.

troubled bank a bank with a large amount of loans in default.

trust property held by one person or persons for the benefits of others.

trustee the person who administers a trust.

trustor the person who establishes a trust.

truth-in-lending law Federal Reserve regulation (Regulation Z) establishing what information lenders must disclose to borrowers, including how finance charges are imposed, when additional charges will be made, and when a borrower may acquire a security interest in a property.

underlying lien a lien to which other liens and property claims are subordinate. A first mortgage, for example, is an underlying lien.

underwriter the person at an insurance company who processes applications for insurance and decides who gets and who doesn't get insurance.

underwriting in securities, when brokers and dealers buy securities in order to resell them. In banking, examining a credit application to see if the prospective borrower is worthy of receiving a loan.

unearned income income earned from investments and interest.

unemployment insurance federal- and state-run program that provides an income to unemployed workers. Contributions to unemployment insurance are deducted from salaries and wages.

Uniform Commercial Code (UCC) standardized state laws that establish rules for contracts, including how to prepare negotiables and handle deeds of title.

Uniform Consumer Credit Code law applicable in some states outlining how lenders and borrows should treat consumer loans under $25,000. The Code sets guidelines for fair lending practices and describes how lenders can recoup defaulted loans.

Uniform Gift to Minors Act   law applicable in some states regarding how property is to be transferred to minors. The act makes the minor responsible for property taxes and stipulates that a guardian be appointed for the minor.

uninsured depositor   a depositor with a savings or checking account larger than $100,000. Accounts above that amount are not insured by the FDIC.

unlisted securities   securities not listed with a stock exchange and traded over-the-counter by dealers and brokers.

unrealized profit/loss   profits or losses for securities that have been recorded but have yet to be collected.

unsecured creditor   a creditor who is owed a debt by a borrower who has declared voluntary bankruptcy. To be an unsecured creditor, the creditor can't have a security interest in the borrower's assets.

unsecured loan   a loan given without the borrower posting collateral or providing any other security.

up tick   when a security is resold at a higher value, it is called an up tick, or a plus tick.

U.S. savings bonds   U.S. government bonds, issued to finance the debt of the United States government. Savings bonds earn variable interest and are sold in denominations from $50 to $10,000.

usury   the lending of money at an exorbitant rate of interest. By law, usury is defined as charging an interest rate above the legal limit.

variable annuity   an annuity paid out at a variable rate, depending on interest accrued on a principal.

variable-rate certificate   certificate of deposit yielding a variable rate of interest.

variable-rate loan   a loan whose rate of interest changes. The rate is determined by a standard index, such as the prime rate.

variable-rate mortgage   a mortgage whose interest rate is adjusted periodically. These mortgages are usually tied to some sort of money index, like the prime lending rate or the cost of Treasury Bills. When the index goes up or down, so does the monthly mortgage payment. Also called an adjustable rate mortgage.

venture capital　capital available for new enterprises and startup companies.

vested interest　in financial terms, a stake in something that will give you money in the future. For example, employees have a vested interest in the prosperity of their company pension plans.

veteran's loan　mortgage backed partially or wholly by the Department of Veterans Affairs. Veterans are eligible for these loans, which are easier to acquire and service than conventional mortgages.

void　null and no longer applicable, as a voided check.

volume of trading　the total number of shares traded on a stock market. Trading volume is a measure of market activity.

voluntary bankruptcy　when a debtor declares bankruptcy in order to gain relief from creditors.

voluntary trust　a living trust in which the beneficiary has title and possession of a property, but the legal title stays in the hands of the one who set up the trust.

voting stock　stock in a corporation that entitles the owner to vote on matters important to the running of the corporation.

wage earner plan　part of a bankruptcy agreement, where the debtor agrees to pay some of the debt to creditors in installments.

wage garnishment　court judgment ordering a lender to be given part of the wages of a borrower who has defaulted on a loan.

Wall Street　the famous street in New York, New York, the address of the New York Stock Exchange and the place where so many financial decisions are made by men in tasseled loafers.

ward　a minor whose financial affairs are managed by a guardian appointed by a court. People whom the court has declared incompetent can also be wards of a court.

warrant　a certificate allowing the bearer to purchase stock at a fixed price at some future date.

warranty　a guarantee that what is written in a contract is indeed true.

warranty deed　a deed by which the seller of a property guarantees that the property is free of liens and encumbrances.

wash sale   a stock manipulation scheme in which traders buy and sell shares repeatedly in a short period of time to give the impression that the stock is a hot item, when really it's not.

watch list   banks that bank examiners have to "watch" because they are earning poorly or are undercapitalized.

wholly-owned subsidiary   a subsidiary completely owned by its parent company.

will   a legal document stating how a person wants his or her property disposed of after death.

window dressing   changing how accounts are organized to give a more favorable impression of a business's financial position without actually changing that position.

wire transfer   transferring money electronically, as opposed to by check or by means of another type of paper transfer.

withholding   taking deductions from income to cover taxes or liabilities.

without recourse   refers to the fact that the buyer of a promissory note is the one who takes the risk that it will not be paid. The buyer has no recourse to make the seller make good on the note.

with right of survivorship   a right by which joint owners of an asset inherit the asset if one or the other dies. The asset does not go the heirs of the deceased.

working control   control of a corporation by right of owning at least 51 percent of its stock.

workmen's compensation insurance   by state law, insurance paid by employers in case of injury on the job.

write-off   removing an item from an account ledger, the item having been fully depreciated or deemed worthless.

wraparound mortgage   refinanced mortgage in which the new rate of interest reflects both the rate on the old mortgage and current market rates. In this way, the old mortgage is wrapped with the new one.

yield curve   graph comparing the yields at maturity of different securities.

yield to call   the annual return, expressed as a percentage, of a bond or note if it is redeemed at the first possible call.

yield to maturity   the annual return, expressed as a percentage, of a bond or note redeemed at maturity.

yuan   the national currency of the People's Republic of China.

zero coupon bond   a bond issued without coupons and without a statement of its rate of interest.

zero coupon security   a bond that pays no interest until maturity, when the interest is paid in a lump sum.

Index

Note to the Reader: Throughout this index **boldface** page numbers indicate primary discussions of a topic. *Italic* page numbers indicate illustrations.

C

calendar. *See also* Financial Calendar; scheduled transactions
  entering dates with, **29**
  selecting calendar year or fiscal year calendar, 131
calls and puts, 430–431, **619–620, 663**
Canada, **601–607**
  business taxes, 606–607
  categories for, 603–605, *604, 605*
  date styles, 601–602, *602*
  Goods and Services Tax (GST), 603–605, *604, 605*
  installing Quicken for, 602, *602*
  Provincial Sales Tax (PST), 603–605, *604, 605*
  reconfiguring Windows, 601–602, *601*
  recording business transactions, *605*, 606–607
canceling insurance, 361
capital gains. *See also* taxes
  on brokerage accounts
    entering, **423–424**, *424*, 427
    reinvesting, 425–426, *425*
  mutual funds and, 380, 386, 389
  on rental properties, **456–458**, *457*
  reports, 83
  saving capital gains taxes on your home, **449–452**
    limitations of, 450, 451–452
    overview of, 451–459
car insurance, 360–361
car loans and leases, 264–266
case-sensitivity in passwords, 147
cash accounts, **229–231**. *See also* accounts
  adjusting account balance, 231
  creating, 230
  displaying register, 230
  entering transactions, 231
  register window, 230, *230*
cash balance in brokerage accounts
  entering, 416
  interest on, 429
cash flow reports. *See also* profits
  for businesses, **517–524**
    budgets and, 517

  creating, 82, 517, *518*
  taxes and, 523
  and tracking profits, 519–524
  for personal finances, 80, 85, *85*
cash-value life insurance, **362**
categories. *See also* classes
  for adjustment transactions, 117
  in Canada, **603–605**, *604, 605*
  confirmation option for uncategorized transactions, **127**
  controlling Category drop-down lists in QuickFill, **126**
  creating, **30–31**, *31*
    payroll expense categories, **473–476**, *474*
    rental property categories, 453
  for credit card charges, 222–223, *223*
  for deposits, 34
  hiding in budgets, **320**
  for income taxes, **273–285**. *See also* taxes
    adding, 287–288, *287*
    changing to subcategories and vice versa, 289
    deleting, 289
    determining categories needed, 273–285, *274–284*
    editing, 288–289, *288*
    editing category lists, 286, *286*
    investment categories, 286
    linking to tax schedules, 285, *285*, 474
  itemized categories reports, 81
  for payments, 30–31, *31*
  printing on voucher checks, **124**
  for QuickPay, **562–563**, *563*
  selecting
    for graphs, 156–158, *157*
    for transactions, 222–223
  subcategories
    changing to categories and vice versa, 289
    creating, 31
  supercategories, **315–316**. *See also* planning
    in budgets, 319
    creating, 315–316
    monitoring with progress bars, 316

Document Retention Rules and Guidelines

Document or Form	Years Retained
Asset purchase records (including investment registers)	Seven years after the asset is sold
Backup files	One year
Checks, canceled	Permanently
Check registers	Permanently
Monthly home tax summaries	Three years
Yearly home tax summaries and reports	Seven years after filing tax return based on report
Other home reports (including investment reports)	One year
Monthly business P&L and tax reports	Three years
Yearly business P&L and tax reports	Seven years
Other business reports	One year